A HANDBOOK ON THE COMMUNITY COLLEGE IN AMERICA

Its History, Mission, and Management

Edited by GEORGE A. BAKER III

JUDY DUDZIAK *and* PEGGY TYLER,
Technical Editors

GREENWOOD PRESS
Westport, Connecticut • London

Library of Congress Cataloging-in-Publication Data

A Handbook on the community college in America : its history,
    mission, and management / edited by George A. Baker III ; Judy Dudziak and Peggy
    Tyler, technical editors.
        p.   cm.
    Includes bibliographical references and index.
    ISBN 0–313–28028–2 (alk. paper)
    1. Community colleges—United States—History.   2. Education,
Higher—United States—Aims and objectives.   3. Community colleges—
United States—Curricula.   4. Community colleges—United States—
Administration.   I. Baker, George A., 1932–   .   II. Dudziak,
Judy.   III. Tyler, Peggy.
LB2328.15.U6H36   1994
378′.052′0973—dc20   92–45081

British Library Cataloguing in Publication Data is available.

Library of Congress Catalog Card Number: 92–45081
ISBN: 0–313–28028–2

First published in 1994

Greenwood Press, 88 Post Road West, Westport, CT 06881
An imprint of Greenwood Publishing Group, Inc.

Printed in the United States of America

(∞)™

The paper used in this book complies with the
Permanent Paper Standard issued by the National
Information Standards Organization (Z39.48–1984).

10 9 8 7 6 5 4 3 2 1

Copyright Acknowledgments

The edited and publisher gratefully acknowledge permission to use excerpts from
the following:

Arthur M. Cohen and Florence B. Brawer. *The American Community College 1st
and 2d ed.* San Francisco, Ca.: Jossey-Bass. 1982, 1989. Used with permission
from Arthur M. Cohen, Florence B. Brawer, and Jossey-Bass.

Carnegie Foundation for the Advancement of Teaching 1990. *Campus Life: In
Search of Community*, Copyright © 1990 by The Carnegie Foundation for the
Advancement of Teaching. Reprinted by permission of Princeton University Press.

The Commission on the Future of Community Colleges. *Building Communities: A
Vision for a New Century*. Washington, D.C.: AACC.

A Handbook
on the
Community College
in America

Contents

Preface

How to tell the story of a uniquely American institution—that was the challenge of putting together *A Handbook on the Community College in America*. At about the hundredth year of their existence, these institutions of higher learning are due a thoughtful and thought-provoking account of their past, present, and future. The contributors chosen to write for this reference volume are acknowledged as expert practitioners and theoreticians in their fields. They responded to the topics through the format of a review of the literature; the resulting handbook is more than just a compendium of singular opinions or various facets of the subject. Further, the writers represent a cross-section of leadership in community colleges: They reflect the variety of regional, cultural, and ethnic viewpoints that have influenced the community college movement over the years.

This reference, produced at a unique time in history, has janus-like character: While reflecting on the role of two-year institutions in the past, it also looks toward a new century in their history. In an even broader context, the end of the twentieth century finds this simultaneous looking back and looking forward occurring in all sorts of endeavors, with the expectation that the people responsible for the future must be informed of the past. For those interested in the future of community colleges, this combination of evaluation and prediction is a valuable guide for discerning the path that holds the most promise for the future.

This volume is divided into ten broad sections that provide a comprehensive overview of the issues central to community colleges in America. The chapters in each section address more particular concerns and reflect the experience and expertise of the authors. The volume concludes with a bibliographic essay on the most important works in the field.

The following pages summarize the contents of this reference volume in greater detail.

PART 1: HISTORICAL DEVELOPMENT OF THE COMMUNITY COLLEGE

The community college is a social system because its internal functions and parts are affected by outside forces, and the institution in turn affects its external environment. As a social system, the community college has altered its mission from one of primarily providing a university transfer program to one of providing a comprehensive range of offerings in response to a changing societal context. Part 1 is designed to describe the transformation of the junior college of the 1900s to the present day comprehensive community college, which provides a variety of functions to fulfill student and community needs. Essays will discuss (1) the historical development of community colleges with emphasis on social and political influences, (2) the impact of changing demographics on the development of the two-year college, (3) the community college relationship with senior colleges during the last nine decades, (4) the community college relationship with federal and state governments over the years, and (5) the comprehensive role that the community college has assumed in recent years.

The role of the junior college of the 1900s to early 1950s was substantially changed over time as external forces, including the GI Bill, the "baby boom," and Sputnik, stimulated national and local leaders to begin thinking in terms of educating the masses, community needs and services, open access, and vocational/technical education. The social context of the 1960s through the 1980s acted as a trigger to induce two-year colleges to begin thinking in terms of lifelong learning, education for community and economic development, and institutional services. The changing role of the community college, which resulted from a multitude of environmental influences throughout the last nine decades, has had a profound impact on the institution's internal organization and structure including such concepts as student development, faculty development, human resource management, curriculum and instructional development, fiscal management, and shared governance. Part 1 provides the historical framework for the remainder of the chapters by explaining how social and political forces have influenced the development of the community college and its internal operations from its inception to the present time.

This first part provides the historical context for the topics that have been included in this handbook because they are considered to be of importance to individuals interested in the community college from a historical perspective. The impact of changing demographics, the relationships of the community college with senior colleges as well as with federal and state governments, and the development of a comprehensive role for two-year colleges are highlighted in the essays contained in Part 1.

PART 2: THE MISSION AND FUNCTIONS OF THE COMMUNITY COLLEGE

The mission of the community college has grown from a rather simplistic focus on preparing students for transfer to a senior college or university to a very complex concept of meeting the needs of a diverse student population. The increasing complexity of the community college mission has been translated into a variety of different functions, which in turn have influenced the evolution of an organizational structure designed to provide the programs to meet the comprehensive mission. Part 2 will seek to describe in detail how the mission of the two-year college has developed, how it has been translated into a number of functions, and how the organization has evolved to provide the needed programs. Essays included in this section will describe (1) the development of the comprehensive community college mission, (2) the transfer function, (3) technical/occupation/career education functions, (4) community services, (5) developmental education for underprepared students, (6) the demographic and economic challenges facing urban community colleges, and (7) the demographic and economic challenges facing rural community colleges. As described in Part 1, the role or mission of the community college has been profoundly influenced by social and political forces in the environment since the 1900s. As a result of external pressures, the two-year college has been forced to expand its mission in order to provide those functions needed to remain a viable institution in an environment characterized by student diversity, rapidly changing technologies, a growing interdependent world, and economic change.

The transfer function, the focal point for the establishment of the junior college in the first place, is the most traditional role for the community college. The programs that have been developed to fulfill the transfer function are designed to meet the needs of students who are planning to transfer to four-year colleges or universities. Therefore, while program offerings may vary, a traditional core curriculum—including courses in mathematics, English and communications, introductory sciences, social sciences, history, fine arts, foreign language, and physical education—is usually offered to transfer students. The transfer function is complicated because different educational institutions are involved in the shared responsibility to meet the requirements of a traditional bachelor's degree.

The technical/occupational or career education functions are designed to prepare students for new careers, a career change, or a career advancement. The programs designed to fulfill the technical and career functions must meet a diversity of student needs for learning new skills, updating skills, enhancing skills, retraining for a career change, or preparing for transfer to a four-year college. Technical/occupation/career programs provide different levels of training, are usually individualized to meet the objectives of the students, and use different instructional strategies. Typical offerings include degree programs, career ladders, contract training, apprenticeship programs, "two-plus-two" programs with high schools, and international training programs.

The adoption of the "open door" policy by the community college has led to the need to provide a developmental function for those students who do not possess the skills for college-level work. Students enrolled in developmental programs include returning adults, high school dropouts, illiterate adults, immigrants and students with limited English proficiency, and some recent high school graduates. Therefore, typical programs provide opportunities for precollege-level skills development, obtaining a General Equivalency Diploma, adult basic education, and learning English as a second language.

The community service or continuing education function has developed as a result of the community college's expanding its mission to meet the needs of its local community and its citizens over an entire life cycle. Programs designed to fulfill this function must meet the needs of educated adults, employees of local businesses, professionals requiring certification, and community organizations. Therefore, the community college offers general interest/noncredit courses, training and retraining courses, lectures, performances, special events, seminars, workshops, and consultation services.

Even though the community college mission has made it necessary for the institution to provide a variety of functions and programs to meet those functions, additional challenges can come from the immediate environment. The community college that is located in a rural area faces different demands than one that is located in a large city. Therefore, this part will show the effect of this expanding educational concept upon the mission, functions, and programs of the community college.

PART 3: CURRICULUM AND INSTRUCTIONAL DEVELOPMENT IN THE COMMUNITY COLLEGE

Just as the mission of the community college has been influenced by external and internal forces so has curriculum and instructional development. The general public, governmental agencies, the media, business and industry, professions, graduate and professional schools, accrediting agencies, courts, faculty, students, administrators, and unions are just some of the outside influences on curriculum and instruction. In addition, a changing student population made up of returning adults, disadvantaged persons, high school dropouts, educated persons, and illiterate adults has necessitated changes in teaching and learning strategies. Part 3 therefore seeks to describe the process of curriculum and instructional development to meet the needs of a diverse student population, which has resulted in competency-based approaches to education, curriculum integration, and the increased use of educational technology for individualized instruction. Essays in this section will discuss (1) the process of curriculum development, (2) the process of instructional development, (3) historical development of academic programs in community colleges, (4) curriculum integration, (5) use of educational technology in community colleges, and (6) the application of mastery learning, systematic instruction, and individualized instruction in the community college.

Part 3 will demonstrate that the process of curriculum or instructional development begins with a series of questions including (1) Why is this taught? (2) Why is it taught in this way? (3) How is the content organized? (4) What is the appropriate technology to be used? (5) What are the student competencies that need to be achieved? (6) How will effectiveness and success be measured?

Principles of curriculum construction such as student-centered education, periodic revision, meaningful objectives, a broadened concept of areas to include field or work experience, relevance, utility to the learner, comprehensiveness, and teachability must be kept in mind. Multisensory approaches, cross-disciplinary thrusts, and obstacles to change must also be considered when designing a curriculum. The aforementioned axioms can be used with a variety of curriculum models including general, prescriptive, and elective approaches.

Similarly, instructional development is based upon a set of learning principles that must be kept in mind in order to help adult students develop as fully as possible in a desired direction. Part 3 seeks to describe how time-tested and new rules for learning are being used in instructional development along with educational technology to provide a more effective approach to individualized instruction to meet the diversity of student needs. Part 3 also expands upon concepts such as competency-based or mastery approaches to teaching and holistic strategies that emphasize a particular competency across the curriculum and reports on how these concepts are applied in community colleges.

Part 3 will also emphasize the roles that change strategy and specific administrative strategies play in curriculum and instructional development. Administrative strategies include organizational context, staffing, and resource allocation. Change strategy addresses methods, planning stages, internal and external participants, and the elements of successful change.

PART 4: LEADING AND MANAGING THE COMMUNITY COLLEGE

Part 4 seeks to focus on governance in the community college during a societal shift from industrial age administration and management to information age leadership. The governance process therefore implies new roles, attitudes, and skills for administrators in key positions. The planning, organizing, directing, coordinating, and controlling functions associated with management must be replaced by leadership skills, including planning, organizing, leading, coordinating, and guiding. Employees, students, board members, and other persons who come into contact with a community college leader must be lead and guided rather than directed and controlled. Individuals in administrative positions must be concerned with (1) boundary spanning, not boundary defending, (2) empowering people, not controlling them, (3) working cooperatively, not competitively, (4) focusing on process, not product, (5) organizational flexibility, not rigidity,

(6) quality, not quantity, (7) sharing information, not guarding it, and (8) creativity or intuition, not primarily rationality. The changes in society thus call for participatory management and leadership. Involvement in decision making is needed at all levels of an organization along with a leader who can create the proper climate in which people can manage and be responsible for themselves. What is needed is the development of leaders who are able to empower followers and encourage collaboration in decision making and problem solving. Essays in this part will therefore focus on (1) shared governance and consultative or participatory decision making, (2) the relationship between a community college president and the board of trustees, (3) leadership skills needed in a participative governance structure, (4) the relationship between a community college president and his or her leadership team, (5) the community college and the legislative process at the state level, and (6) the impact of national agencies such as the American Association of Community Colleges on federal legislation affecting community colleges.

The section will convey how the leadership skills needed to govern and lead a community college in a new age can be utilized in decision making with the adoption of consultative processes as shown through the use of faculty and academic senates, task forces, committees, and management teams. The decisions that are made at the lowest level possible within the organization and are close to those being affected by the decisions have a higher degree of acceptance. Moreover, involving others at all levels of the organization in decision making helps create a sense of community and a positive organizational climate, which adds to institutional effectiveness.

Attributes associated with effective community college leaders such as vision, credibility, empowering others, sharing information, respecting individual differences, fostering teamwork, sensitivity, patience, and high ethical standards help to promote good working relationships with internal and external individuals who are important to the institution. Part 4 will describe strategies for establishing good relations between the community college president and board members, the legislature, and other members of the leadership team. If the institution is to function effectively, the entire leadership team must share the same philosophy and vision. If the president of the community college is to achieve his or her vision, there must be support from the board of trustees as well as staff, faculty, and students. From the external perspective, funding and regulatory controls exerted by the legislature have made the community college president's role a political one requiring skill in lobbying, persuasion, selecting and using appropriate data, and communicating the college mission.

PART 5: RESOURCE DEVELOPMENT IN THE COMMUNITY COLLEGE

Part 5 will demonstrate that resource development in the community college is subject to both internal and external pressures in the same manner as are the mission, governance, and curriculum development. This section is based upon the premise that the budget is the educational plan of the community college expressed in dollars and therefore should reflect the priorities of the institution. In addition, as a social system, the community college is impacted by federal, state, and local economic shifts so that fiscal management must take into consideration times of plenty and austerity. Essays contained in this section provide information on (1) traditional and nontraditional sources of funding for community colleges, (2) the historical development of funding formulas to support capital and operational aspects of the community college, (3) allocating resources to maintain institutional integrity, (4) the historical process of budget decision making as the educational plan expressed in dollars, (5) the development of an organizational structure to support the fiscal function in the community college, and (6) the historical development and functions of the institutional development concept as a means for increasing support for community colleges.

Traditional and nontraditional sources of funding will be synthesized in this section because both are critical to institutional effectiveness given the instability of the American economy. Traditional sources of money such as federal, state, and local funding as well as tuition and fees no longer are able to provide sufficient funds to enable the community college to fulfill its comprehensive mission. As a result, nontraditional sources of funds including grants, foundations, contracts, and partnerships are becoming more necessary in order for a two-year college to function effectively.

Part 5 will develop the concept that a variety of funding formulas exist that can be utilized by the community college to allocate resources obtained from traditional and nontraditional sources. Approaches to budgeting include incremental (focuses on yearly increases or decreases), planning-programming-budgeting systems, PPBS (focuses on substance of programs and activities to weight costs and benefits), zero-based (considers everything significant), formula (fair share distribution of resources among institutions or areas), and cost-centered (relative ability of a unit to be self-supporting is taken into consideration) methods.

Ultimately, if the budget is viewed as the educational plan expressed in dollars, the allocation of resources—no matter where they come from or what budgetary approach is used—must maintain institutional integrity by supporting the mission. Part 5 will relate how community colleges can maintain integrity through the reorganization and revitalization of its fiscal function. When based upon a foundation of needs assessment and widespread employee participation, a college's budget can relate to institutional goals and objectives. In addition, the budget process is dependent upon institutional characteristics (organizational climate, decision-making processes, centralization of authority, communication and sharing information, priorities), external as well as internal political factors (law, community, mission), and future factors (inflation, changing demographics, technology).

PART 6: HUMAN RESOURCE MANAGEMENT IN THE COMMUNITY COLLEGE

A community college is only as effective as its faculty and staff; therefore, human resource management in the community college is of critical importance to overall institutional effectiveness. Part 6 deals with some of the crucial issues with regard to college personnel including staffing in the community college—recruitment, retention, replacement, and rewards—and linking staff development and organizational development for strategic planning.

A large and potentially debilitating turnover in community college personnel is anticipated within the next five to ten years. Consequently, recruitment, selection, development, and retention of employees are becoming major issues on many campuses. Recruitment includes finding people with the appropriate qualifications while providing adequate representation for minorities and women. The selection process must be developed in such a way as to enable the search committee to choose or recommend not only the most qualified person but also one who supports the institution's mission. Once a person has begun working in the community college setting, he or she must have the opportunity to grow and develop both professionally and personally in order to remain vital and to respond to environmental changes effectively. In addition, if an employee is not adequately rewarded either formally or informally for excellence in job performance, contributions to the college, or professional growth, the institution runs the risk of initially not developing its human resources appropriately and subsequently dealing with unmotivated employees.

This section will demonstrate the importance of linking staff development to both organizational development and to strategic planning in order to promote institutional effectiveness. Organizational development is generally defined as those programs that create an effective organizational environment involving all aspects of the campus and that facilitate an improvement in the decision-making process for both faculty and administrators. A comprehensive staff development program that meets the needs of all employees and those of the organization therefore can help provide an environment in which quality decisions are made by providing in-house training as well as a variety of opportunities for professional and personal growth thus enhancing the competency of personnel. Staff development is also an important part of strategic or long-range planning for several reasons: (1) internal resources including personnel need to be assessed in order to determine what competencies must be developed by faculty and staff that would lead to achieving the strategic objectives and (2) activities or programs must be provided so that employees can gain the required skills or knowledge in order to perform the complex tasks required of modern educational institutions.

PART 7: THE COMMUNITY COLLEGE FACULTY

While students are the focal point for any community college, effective teachers constitute the mainstay of the institution. Part 7 is therefore devoted to essays that discuss historical patterns of faculty preparation, characteristics of effective teachers, the relationship between faculty and students in community colleges, and faculty attitudes and practices in both teaching and disciplinary scholarship. The section will emphasize the fact that institutional effectiveness and student success are due largely to a committed, motivated, flexible, student-centered, and knowledgeable faculty.

Community college faculty members are acquired in a variety of ways and arrive with diverse backgrounds. Some instructors have not been exposed to teacher training but are hired for their technical expertise. Other faculty move to community college teaching from secondary schools or four-year institutions and have had little experience in teaching the typical community college student. Part-time instructors are often business men and women or practicing professionals who wish to share their knowledge and experience with others. The variation in faculty preparation, which has resulted from the development of the comprehensive community college mission, contributes to special problems regarding institutional effectiveness. This is most often measured by an estimate of student success.

While the experience and background of faculty members in a community college may vary, certain characteristics are shared by effective teachers no matter what their preparation or experience has been. This section will support the idea that excellent teachers (1) believe that any student can learn given time and the right conditions, (2) act positively, (3) are committed to their profession, (4) know how to motivate students, and (5) are empathic but have high expectations. In addition, successful instructors are objective, listen to students, use a variety of instructional strategies to reach students with various learning styles, and participate in continuing professional education in order to remain up to date and vital.

Part 7 also will link teaching success to student success since an effective teacher generally has good relationships with his or her students and is able to motivate them to perform. Exemplary instructors establish rapport with their students, modify instruction to meet a variety of needs, exhibit a positive attitude toward learning, and are enthusiastic about their careers in teaching. Under these conditions enhanced learning can occur.

PART 8: STUDENT DEVELOPMENT IN THE COMMUNITY COLLEGE

The community college provides a large variety of services to its students. Classroom instruction enables individuals to obtain or advance in a job, to further their education, or to pursue an area of interest. Collectively, student services or student development specialists provide the opportunities for students to grow personally, socially, and intellectually outside the classroom. However, instructional services must be linked with student services if an institution is to promote optimal student development. Thus, Part 8 will focus on the need for a student development strategy that employs a variety of resources and approaches within the community college structure.

The essays in this section will deal with (1) the traditional functions of student services, (2) meeting the needs of a diverse student population, (3) marketing the institution and student recruitment, (4) student placement and advisement, and (5) student management toward student success. The essays will emphasize the need for integrating instruction, consultation, and milieu management for student success and student development.

The community college student population is a diverse one with individuals of all ages and from all walks of life. Some students juggle class attendance, careers, and family resulting in excellent but goal-oriented action with neither time nor money for frills. Some minority or disadvantaged students have special needs and deficiencies because of poor educational preparation and language problems. The community college now must provide academic and student development programs for underprepared and special needs students, childcare services, career help, effective counseling and advisement, and a variety of short-term and long-term programs to meet individual needs. In addition, some environments call for extended instructional as well as developmental services to students at military bases, in prisons, from other countries, and often at satellite campus facilities.

This section will describe how student diversity and a comprehensive mission have changed the concept of student services from a specialized department with standardized responsibilities such as dealing with discipline, extracurricular activities, and traditional counseling to a more complex matrix management model of student development. Student development requires (1) identifying the characteristics and needs of the student population, (2) translating student needs into goals and objectives through assessment of developmental levels and instructional consultation, (3) implementing courses and programs to enable students to achieve their goals and objectives through a collaborative effort on the part of faculty, counselors, staff, and administration, and (4) monitoring student progress in order to intervene if problems occur. Student development relies upon a holistic approach that aligns student services with instruction in order to benefit students through adequate placement as well as continual and relevant advisement based upon appraisals of student performance and progress toward fulfilling academic and personal goals.

This section will synthesize the literature on student development that begins with an active recruitment effort to encourage students from all social strata to further their education. Registration procedures should then be easy and convenient so that students will not be frustrated when seeking admission to the community college. Next, students should be assessed upon entry to the college so that they are placed in classes appropriate for their needs and for their educational capabilities thus promoting an increased chance for success. Student progress should be continually monitored so that each individual is warned if he or she is in academic trouble, is aware of what courses have been taken and still need to be taken, and if he or she is meeting the institution's academic standards. The student development model as described in this section emphasizes student outcomes; uses a developmental, holistic approach to education; and requires collaboration of all college personnel.

PART 9: EXTERNAL FORCES AND THE COMMUNITY COLLEGE

Part 1 synthesizes the research describing the community college as a social system that is influenced by, and in turn influences, the external environment. A variety of external forces exert varying amounts of pressure upon the functions and effectiveness of the two-year college. The essays contained in Part 9 will present the environmental forces impacting the milieu of community colleges. Topics covered in this section include (1) historical development of the community college and secondary school partnership, (2) increasing the effectiveness of the transfer function, (3) expanding partnerships with business and industry, (4) increasing federal and state support for community colleges, (5) enhancing the image of the college through public relations, and (6) the community college as a vehicle for local and national economic and social development.

Articulation between the community college and secondary schools includes two-plus-two programs for technical education, opportunities for high school students to complete course work in a community college setting, and helping at-risk students in junior or senior high schools. Community colleges are working with potential students while still in the K–12 system to encourage them to remain in school and better prepare themselves to further their education after graduation from high school. Programs allowing students to take courses that provide high school credit and later result in community college credit help forge links between secondary and postsecondary institutions while increasing community college service to the community. Additionally, helping at-risk students to stay in school by providing community college staff to work with K–12 professionals or by inviting junior high and high school students to participate in summer programs and campus visitations helps to promote future community college mission accomplishment as well as student and community success.

Beyond strengthening ties with the K–12 school system, the community college must provide an effective transfer program for those students who seek this option. Another focus of this section is to report efforts to increase the effectiveness of the transfer function by a closer collaboration between two–year and four-year institutions. Many community colleges have contracts with local and regional four-year educational institutions whereby once students are admitted to the community college they are automatically accepted at a designated university or college. Through this process, the curriculum is reviewed and validated by both the sending and receiving institutions.

In order to help meet technical preparation and vocational functions, the community college is faced with the challenge of developing partnerships with business and industry. Specialized training for specific companies is the subject of contracts with two-year institutions as well as on-site community college courses. In addition, because of rapidly changing and expensive technologies, colleges are arranging to provide the instructional expertise while businesses are supplying needed equipment.

Part 9 will also focus on the need for the community college of the future to articulate its mission to legislators, many of whom have never attended a two-year college, in order to receive adequate funding and support. In addition, the community college must improve its image in the local community through effective public relations in order to garner local support and exert additional pressure on the legislature. As described in Part 4, the community college presidency has become an increasingly external and political position by focusing on public relations, sharing the community college mission with external groups, and lobbying with legislators.

In addition, this section seeks to show how the community college is becoming involved with economic development particularly in rural areas that are encountering periods of recession. The two-year college is linked to economic development in several ways: (1) in times of financial austerity, community college enrollment generally increases as adults seek training for new careers or retraining to remain at their current workplace and (2) some community colleges have begun working with economic development committees and chambers of commerce to provide consultative services and workshops for small business development and to assist with strategic planning by providing information about training possibilities and services that could be provided to industries moving into the area.

Part 9 will emphasize the fact that the community college is part of the community that it serves and is therefore closely influenced by the K–12 school system, business and industry, legislators, and four-year institutions. Therefore, the community college must seek to be positively influenced by external forces through effective articulation with other schools, good public relations, and working closely with business and industry to foster economic prosperity.

PART 10: THE FUTURE OF THE COMMUNITY COLLEGE

Part 10 will conclude *A Handbook on the Community College in America* by providing a discussion of issues and obligations influencing the development and mission of the community college system in the years ahead. Essays contained in this section will deal with (1) understanding the community college culture—the concept of building community, (2) a paradigm shift toward true participatory governance, (3) team building within the community college, (4) the majority/minority reversal in demographics, (5) strategic management, and (6) the community college in the twenty-first century.

Culture is a basic set of assumptions that have proven successful and are adopted by a given group as it learns to deal with internal and external problems and are therefore taught to new employees. The culture can be described as open (high degree of trust, esprit de corps, little need for close supervision, genuine behavior) or closed (low trust, low morale, close supervision, aloofness on the part of the administrators). Community colleges are exploring ways to foster an open, positive climate or culture in which all individuals commit to a set of values and a vision for the institution. Part of the development of a positive culture involves the concept of building a community. An internal sense of community is based upon shared governance where (1) decisions are made at the lowest level possible, (2) the administrators form a leadership team to work with staff and faculty toward accomplishing institutional goals and a shared vision, (3) systems are put into place to ensure student success, (4) all employees are given opportunities for professional and personal growth, and (5) active learning and effective teaching are encouraged as well as rewarded. An external sense of community is developed through coalition building, public relations, formation of partnerships, and articulation of the community college mission. Teamwork and participatory governance are key elements for building community whether inside or outside the organization.

This section will also describe processes that demonstrate that to be successful in a rapidly changing context a community college not only must foster a positive climate and sense of community but also must utilize strategic management and leadership to position itself effectively in its environment. Challenges posed by evolving technologies, uncertain funding, an unstable economy, and majority/minority demographic reversal in many environments are forcing community colleges to develop change strategies and concentrate on organizational development along with staff development in order to remain viable. Strategic or long-range planning can equip community colleges with the means to meet environmental changes in a proactive manner thus diminishing a number of potential negative effects by (1) focusing on the external community and adapting to planned change, (2) allowing the institution to be competitive, (3) concentrating on decisions not forecasts, (4) blending rational examination, political finesse, and participatory decision making, (5) depending upon an analysis of internal and external needs and resources, and (6) placing the welfare of the college and its students above anything else. A systematic method of planning therefore will allow the community college to define the future direction of the institution, improve management, improve the connection between goals and resource allocation, increase purposeful behavior, increase effectiveness as well as accountability, and improve communication.

Part 10 will bring this handbook to a close by discussing the importance of planning, a positive climate, and a sense of community in meeting future challenges. The community colleges that positively position themselves in the environment through strategic management and shared governance can successfully meet the changes imposed upon them by changing demographics, evolving technology, an interdependent economy, and an evolving information society.

Acknowledgments

The editor and technical editors express our sincere appreciation to the University of Texas and North Carolina State University for their support in developing this handbook on American community colleges. In addition, the Department of Educational Administration at the University of Texas, James Yates, Chairman, and the Department of Adult and Community College Education at North Carolina State University, Conrad Glass, Interim Chairman, provided resources and assistance for the development of this handbook.

At the University of Texas, Ms. Anne Psencik, Ms. Michelle Perkins, and Ms. Myra Custard provided technical assistance and worked with the various authors. At North Carolina State University, Project ACCLAIM staff and faculty and its director Ed Boone provided support in the final production of the handbook. This book would not have been possible without the dedicated work of these individuals.

We also express our gratitude to the staff at the American Association of Community Colleges and especially to President David Pierce and Senior Editor Ms. Bonnie Gardner. They not only helped with the development of the handbook but also recommended its editor to the Greenwood Publishing Group. The name of their organization was changed to the American Association of Community Colleges on September 1, 1992, during the development of this handbook. We, with Ms. Gardner's approval, have left all references to AACC publications as they were at the time of publication. Thus, some references will reflect AACC and some will reflect the previous acronym, AACJC. Finally, the editors express our sincere appreciation to Ann V. Doty, a graduate assistant from North Carolina State University, who accepted and completed the challenge of developing an index to the *Handbook* in an extremely competent manner.

Part 1

Historical Development of the Community College

Seven Streams in the Historical Development of the Modern American Community College

James L. Ratcliff

Over the past century, the United States has grown increasingly complex socially, ethnically, economically, politically, and technologically. This complexity has been enabled by the evolution and development of a citizenry of many talents, interests, abilities, and backgrounds. The geographic enormity of the country has meant that in any given year or decade there have been regions of poverty and economic depression during times of general prosperity. Conversely, some states, regions, and localities have escaped general economic downturns. The opening two decades of this century, like the closing decades, have provided an enormous influx of new citizens, cultures, religions, nationalities, and ethnicities to the fabric of American society. The impact of these demographic changes has similarly not been uniform across the country.

The United States has been able to adapt to and capitalize on this diversity of peoples, regions, and economics in part due to the pragmatic and adaptive nature of its educational system. A hallmark has been the multiple avenues of public access to education at all levels. At the postsecondary level, the comprehensive community college has made a singular contribution to this adaptiveness and pragmatism. Unlike countries whose higher education has been neatly divided into a binary system of universities and technical colleges or institutes accessible primarily through prescribed precollege programs and entrance examinations, American postsecondary education has remained committed steadfastly to inventing courses of study, educational programs, or even those institutions dedicated to the needs and expectations of a particular sector of society.

As a distinctively American invention, the comprehensive community college stands between secondary and higher education, between adult and higher education, between industrial training and formal technical education. Community colleges have provided educational programs and services to people who otherwise would not have enrolled in a college or university (Cohen and Brawer 1989). Access to community colleges has not been bounded by the norms of admissions examinations or high school grades. Community colleges have stood for open admissions, geographic proximity, and relative financial affordability to the potential students of the community and region served. Within the structure of American higher education, the community colleges's contribution has been increased accessibility and pragmatic curricular diversity geared to local and regional needs.

The community college evolved from seven streams of educational innovation. Two come from the last half of the nineteenth century: (1) local community boosterism and (2) the rise of the research university. The next three trace to the educational reforms of the Progressive Era: (3) the restructuring and expansion of the public educational system, (4) the professionalization of teacher education, and (5) the vocational education movement. The final two streams, (6) the rise of adult, continuing, and community education and (7) open public access to higher education, can be found even in the earliest junior colleges. However, these last two streams became prominent after World War II. It is the purpose of this chapter to profile and exemplify these seven streams. To do more—that is to provide a full history of the development of community colleges—is beyond the scope of this chapter. Here, we seek to cast a social context in which the evolution of community colleges can best be understood.

Each community college today has its foundation in several of the above seven streams. That evolutionary mix contributes to confusion over institutional mission and nomenclature. Many things are meant by the terms ''community college,'' ''junior college,'' ''technical college,'' and ''technical institute.'' The lack of definition of these terms is attributable in part to the wide variation in mission, governance, finance, and structure of two-year colleges in the United States. In this chapter, I use the term ''two-year college'' to refer to all institutions where the highest degree awarded is a two-year degree (i.e., Associate of Arts, Associate of Science, Associate of Applied Arts, Associate of Applied Science, etc.). ''Community colleges'' are those institutions that provide general and liberal education, career and vocational education, and adult and continuing education. Adding to the confusion is that the term ''community college'' is now used generically to refer to all colleges awarding no higher than a two-year degree. Yet, many two-year colleges do not offer the comprehensive curriculum just outlined and therefore are not truly community colleges in this comprehensive use of the term. ''Junior college'' refers to an institution whose primary mission is to provide general and liberal education leading to transfer and completion of the baccalaureate degree. Junior colleges often provide applied science and adult and continuing education programs as well. ''Technical college'' and ''technical institute'' here refer only to those institutions awarding no higher than a two-year degree or diploma in a vocational, technical, or career field. Technical colleges often also offer degrees in applied sciences and in adult and continuing education.

The array of institutional types, missions, and structures falling within the category of two-year colleges contributes to confusion over purpose and social role. According to Thomas Deiner,

One reason the junior college in the United States has been difficult to understand is that it has taken on so many forms of sponsorship and control. Is the junior college a high school and a part of secondary education? Is it collegiate and a part of higher education? Is it a unique educational enterprise standing apart from both of these worlds, yet, at the same time, able to link them in new and constructive ways? . . . While debates over definition and organizational form have waxed and waned, . . . a core of functions began to emerge, a core which . . . helped determine the essence of the junior college. (1986, 7)

Failure to recognize this diversity of types, roles, and missions—public, private, junior, technical, community, local, regional, branch campus—also has contributed to the confusion. Only by fully understanding the social context in which these institutions emerged can one overcome this confusion.

Higher education in the United States frequently is described in terms of the five Carnegie classifications of institutions: research universities, doctoral-granting universities, comprehensive institutions, liberal arts colleges, and two-year colleges. Yet, nearly one half of all higher education institutions are two-year colleges. The very existence of such a variety of two-year institutions (community, junior, and technical colleges) attests to the difficulty of providing a generic definition of the institution or casting meaningful generalizations about its role in society. The very mix and blend of the seven streams of educational reform in the history of each two-year college ensures that an exception can be found to most, if not all, generalizations about two-year colleges as a whole.

Contemporary discussion regarding the mission, role, and function of the community college relies on historical notions of the evolution of the institution. If one chooses to emphasize the vocational education stream, one may reach the conclusion that community colleges are leaving higher education (Clowes and Levin 1989). If one examines the success of students who otherwise would not have attended college, then one may conclude that community colleges track students into certain social strata or advance their station in society (Brint and Karabel 1989; Karabel 1972; Pincus 1980; Zwerling 1976). Examining the adult education and community services function leads one to conclude that the institutions' roots are to be found in providing educational programming and services to the local communities (Cross 1971; Gleazer 1968, 1980; Harlacher 1969). Also, to fully appreciate the nature of community colleges' interconnectedness with other innovations in secondary and higher education, we need a full history of the institution, one that recognizes its early role in the preparation of teachers and its relationship to the restructuring of secondary education. As suggested elsewhere, community college development was not a socially or educationally isolated phenomenon. Original junior colleges came into being at the same time as, and were enabled by, the advent of kindergartens, middle schools, junior high schools, and compulsory secondary education (Ratcliff 1984, 1986, 1987b). To fully appreciate and analyze the role and scope of the community college in American higher education, it is necessary to take all seven streams into account.

COMMUNITY BOOSTERISM

Unlike higher education in many countries, the development of colleges and universities in the United States was not guided by national controls or policy. In colonial times, colleges could not officially operate without a charter from the king of England, but the founders of colonial colleges did not strictly abide by this rule, and the American revolution clearly set college founders free of such restraints (Trow 1984). The U.S. Constitution gave the authority for college charters to the various states. The *Dartmouth College Case* gave colleges the status of independent corporations; once chartered, they were bound by the terms of their incorporation and were not directly accountable to the state (Alexander and Solomon 1972).

Under such circumstances, colleges multiplied. Each state established one or more state colleges to advance its reputation for an educated citizenry. And many towns established colleges to provide evidence, along with the museum, library, opera house, and symphony band shell, of its cultural stature (Boorstin 1965; Ratcliff 1987b). The distinctions between public and private institutions of higher education were blurred in the nineteenth century (Thelin 1982). Communities banded together to build the local college; the citizens laid the bricks and mortar and raised funds through bake sales. If the community was predominantly Lutheran, then the college might well be affiliated with the Lutheran congregations of the area. If the community had no clear religious denomination, or if the local chamber of commerce had been primary in fund raising, the college might be pbulic. In advocating the establishment of a two-year college in Wichita Falls, Texas, to a local community group, Superintendent of Schools Clark noted, "This is the time for the junior college to be backed up by either denominational or state support" (Gray 1959, 14). Whether public or private, communities had a great deal more enthusiasm for founding colleges than for supporting them, and many colleges that came into existence in the nineteenth century also failed during that century. With no clear sources of students or finances, economic downturns were particularly difficult for the local booster colleges.

One of these economic downturns, the Panic of 1894, led to some of the first formal thinking about two-year colleges. Reverend J. M. Carroll, president of Baylor University, had convened a convention of Baptist colleges in Texas and Louisiana that year. The convention recognized that there were insufficient finances and students to support the numerous, small Baptist colleges in the two states. Carroll advanced a pragmatic suggestion. The smaller Baptist colleges would reduce their curriculum to the first two years of college, and Baylor would accept their students providing years three and four of the baccalaureate degree (Eby 1927; Roark 1926). Thus, the two-year college was born. How could communities retain and maintain their college when there clearly was not enough money or students to go around? By limiting the curriculum of these institutions to the first two years, the institutions would require a smaller faculty, fewer resources, and fewer students to operate.

THE JUNIOR COLLEGE AND THE RISE OF THE AMERICAN UNIVERSITY

Two years after Carroll had made his proposal to the convention of Baptist colleges in Texas and Louisiana, two northern Baptists gave further credence to the notion of the junior college. William Rainey Harper, president of the University of Chicago, announced that if denominational colleges in the area wished to reduce their curricula to two years and send their students on to the university, formal arrangements could be made wherein their college work would be accepted toward the baccalaureate degree. Harper also proposed that high schools might extend their curricula to incorporate the first two years of college. Two fellow members of Harper's Baptist congregation were superintendents of local high schools, but they elected to develop junior colleges that were upward extensions of their local high schools (Ratcliff 1986, 1987a).

The role that university leaders played in fostering the initial junior college movement is perhaps one of the most frequently recounted and overemphasized aspects of community college history (Goodwin 1971; Ratcliff 1986, 1987a). During the latter half of the nineteenth century, American university presidents educated in Germany sought to bring greater organization and uniformity to higher education. Leaders like Tappan and Frieze, presidents of the University of Michigan; Lange of the University of California; Jordan, president of Stanford University; Folwell, president of the University of Minnesota; and Harper, founding president of the University of Chicago, sought to differentiate university and collegiate grades of work. Collegiate work was to provide breadth of education in the arts and sciences as well as develop the student's abilities to study and inquire. University education was devoted principally to the advancement of knowledge and the development of new knowledge, theory, and understanding. These nineteenth- and early twentieth-century university presidents were interested in restructuring university education, directing universities to set research as their primary purpose. As a result, they suggested that the first two years of undergraduate studies were best performed as part of precollegiate or secondary education, a function that could be best performed by high schools or the small liberal arts colleges.

These university presidents did not put forward these ideas in a vacuum. Their ideas were abetted by the growth of high schools and of compulsory secondary education. Consider the example of California. In 1907, the year in which legislation was passed permitting high schools to offer the 13th and 14th grades, there was less than one high school per county in the state. In that year, President Jordan advocated that Stanford abandon teaching the freshman and sophomore years, suggesting that those grades were the proper concern of the liberal arts colleges. Jordan made no mention of the upward extension of the high school. It was only after legislation was passed permitting collegiate work to be offered by high schools and after such high school postgraduate work was established at Los Angeles Polytechnic High School that Jordan began to see the high school as a provider of the first two years of collegiate education. For Jordan, as for Harper and Lange, the municipal junior college movement fit the plans for the reform of the university. They more endorsed than initiated the idea of the upward extension of high school grades (Ratcliff 1987a, 1987b; Young 1966).

JUNIOR COLLEGES AND THE RESTRUCTURING OF SECONDARY EDUCATION

The first great growth period of junior colleges occurred from 1910 to 1920, coinciding with the growth of kindergartens and junior high schools. In many school districts, the construction of a new junior high school was necessary to relieve the overcrowding in the existing high schools and elementary schools. However, once the junior high was constructed, the four-year high schools became three-year high schools. There was physical space to permit the operation of a junior college (see Table 1).

At the beginning of the twentieth century, there was great diversity in the quality and availability of secondary education. The original junior college movement came about as part of the general restructuring of secondary education. The junior high school and the junior college were twin educational developments that captured the attention of such early researchers as L. V. Koos (1924). George Zook, U.S. Commissioner of Education and an early advocate of the junior college, wrote,

The dominant motive, however, behind the junior college movement appears to me to be economy in education. By casting the responsibility for a six-year program on our educational administration we shall secure again that high degree of correlation throughout the six-year course which, unfortunately, we so much lack at present. Moreover, there is an implication that with better organization of elementary education, we could reduce the elementary grades in number by at least one year. . . . Such a reduction in the total number of years devoted to elementary and secondary education, including the junior college, would be a great boon to professional students, who under our present educational organization, are from 23 to 25 years of age at the time they begin the practice of their profession. (Zook 1922, 34)

Table 1
Cumulative Growth in the Number of Junior Colleges

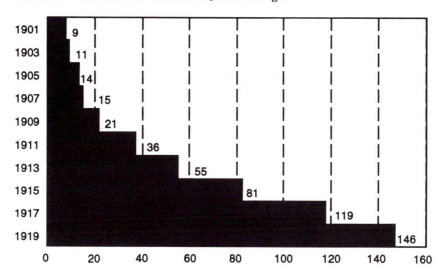

(Kees, 1924, p. 2)

Source: L. V. Koos. *The Junior College*. Minneapolis, MN: Research Publications of the University of Minnesota. Used with permission.

Throughout the educational literature of the 1920s, junior colleges were discussed as an element in various formulations of elementary, secondary, and higher education. The introduction of compulsory secondary education during the first two decades of the twentieth century permitted those reconsidering the organization and structure to think holistically of a system stemming from kindergarten and continuing through high school to "terminal" vocational and general education, the baccalaureate degree, or graduate and professional education conferred by the research universities.

During the 1980s, the quality of educational programs in the elementary and secondary schools reemerged as an issue. Although community colleges have yet to be central to the debates over strengthening elementary and secondary education, some educational leaders have seen a role for them in strengthening American secondary education. Dale Parnell, former president of the American Association of Community Colleges (AACC), has advocated that community colleges work with area high schools to develop new, intensive technical education programs. These programs consist of two years of science and technology preparatory work in the high school followed by specialized technical training in the community college. In a similar vein, the American Association for Higher Education has sponsored a number of two-year and four-year college partnerships with high schools to strengthen the articulation of curricula and students between the cultures of secondary and higher education. During the 1920s and, to a reduced degree, during the 1980s and 1990s, community colleges have advanced as an integral part of the rethinking and restructuring of elementary and secondary education.

JUNIOR COLLEGES AND THE NORMAL SCHOOL MOVEMENT

Many junior colleges first began as normal schools (Rowland 1949). Eells (1931) noted the connection between teacher preparation and the development of junior colleges in 1930, but since that time, little attention has been given in standard texts on junior colleges. The professional preparation of teachers began in the three normal schools of Massachusetts that were founded on the pedagogical principles of Horace Greeley. During the 1880s, normal schools were a form of alternative secondary education for those (largely women) who wished to teach as a profession. As the number of high schools grew, so too developed the belief that pedagogy should be a post–high school subject. As states adopted compulsory secondary education attendance laws and teacher certification standards, the demand for qualified teachers grew. There were fewer colleges offering normal school training than there was demand for graduates.

Local high schools developed normal school programs for their graduates, employing teachers with masters degrees as instructors of pedagogy. The Saint Joseph, Missouri, high school was such an institution. To meet the need for qualified teachers in the area in 1913, it added a normal school program. Local citizens' interest in college-level general and liberal education caused the local school superintendent to make inquiries of the University of Missouri to determine if the credits taken in the postgraduate high school program could be applied to the baccalaureate degree. President Hill had been among the leaders within the American Association of Universities in calling for the establishment of junior colleges to provide the first two years of college.

In January 1913 the Board of Education and the citizens of Saint Joseph, Missouri, began to lobby their state senators and representatives to pass a bill that would enable high schools to offer a postgraduate normal school course to prepare teachers to teach in area schools (Board of Education 1913, 234). Upon passage of the legislation, Saint Joseph School Superintendent Whiteford conferred with the Missouri state superintendent regarding the establishment of such a normal school attached to the Central High School of Saint Joseph. During that year, efforts were also mounted within the district to start a kindergarten program, to provide free textbooks to all students, and to introduce manual training and business courses into the secondary curriculum. Owing to a significant number of students attending Central High School from outside the school district and from neighboring Oklahoma towns, the school board also discussed the imposition of tuition for such students. Central High School was not only the provider of secondary education for the community but also to the region, owing to the paucity of secondary schools. Through the normal school program, Central High School also sought to fulfill the demand for qualified teachers as new schools sprang up in adjacent communities. The initial postgraduate normal school course was one year in duration. A graduate, upon passage of an examination, was authorized to teach in the elementary schools of the region.

In 1915 the school board authorized a bond election to raise financing to construct new buildings at Central High. Biology, botany, and agriculture were added to the curriculum, and new instructors were hired to teach them. In July of that year, the Saint Joseph Commerce Club requested that the school board consider establishing a junior college course at the high school (Board of Education 1915, 83). Through the advocacy of the Commerce Club and the First Ward Improvement Club, the school board unanimously approved the establishment of a junior college in the new buildings of Central High School. Materials and laboratory equipment for college-level science courses were ordered and purchased.

The Saint Joseph Junior College exemplified the mix of streams leading to the development of junior colleges. First, local boosterism and a shortage of qualified teachers led to the establishment of a normal school training course at the high school. Second, the restructuring of the local educational system made the addition of the junior college possible. The curriculum was augmented in the sciences, foreign language, business, and agriculture. The addition of kindergartens, the addition of buildings to Central High School, and the construction of a North End High School facility made it physically possible to add the 13th and 14th grades of instruction at Central High School. The passage of legislation permitting the high school to offer a two-year normal school course of study, together with the University of Missouri's interest in encouraging the development of a junior college course of study, all conspired to promote the development of Missouri's first junior college.

THE VOCATIONAL EDUCATION MOVEMENT

Frequently, the literature on the community college promotes the notion that vocational and technical education did not become functions of the community college until the Great Depression created the need for such curricula (Brint and Karabel 1989). However, many of the first two-year colleges were primarily or exclusively technical institutes. Lewis Institute in Chicago, founded in 1896, and the Bradley Polytechnic Institute (now Bradley University) in Peoria, Illinois, founded in 1897, were established under the guiding influence of William Rainey Harper (Eby 1927, 20). The first two-year college in Oklahoma was the University Preparatory School and Junior College of Tonkawa, which, founded in 1902, offered a junior college program beginning in 1904. To better adapt its curriculum to the interests and expectations of rural northern Oklahoma, the mission, curriculum, and name of the institution were changed in 1914 to the

Oklahoma Institute of Technology. Both two years of general and liberal education and a postsecondary industrial education program were offered thereafter (Ratcliff 1986, 15). Similarly, some of the earliest post–high school institutions in Michigan were technical institutes. Frederick Pratt converted the Pratt Institute, a vocational high school, into a two-year curriculum for adults "age thirty or so" (16). In 1891, the Detroit Young Men's Christian Association consolidated the evening and day classes it offered adults with the professional curriculum of the Detroit College of Pharmacy to form the Detroit Institute of Technology. Chartered in 1909, it provided collegiate instruction in mechanical, technical, industrial, professional and semiprofessional fields, and the literary and musical arts (Ratcliff 1986).

OPEN ACCESS TO HIGHER EDUCATION

Because colleges and universities were established usually before a system of secondary education developed, higher education has always had unique responsibility as the standard bearer within the American educational system. Harvard was founded long before there was any widespread college preparatory programs. Land grant colleges and universities were established long before universal secondary education was extended to the rural areas of this country. During their first years of operation, often more than half of the students at land grant colleges were in precollegiate studies. Women's colleges, historically Black colleges and universities, and colleges and institutes for Native Americans all were established before there were secondary educational programs to prepare these groups for collegiate level studies. This curious historical phenomenon consistently has placed higher education in the position of judging the qualifications of the students it admits, thereby articulating academic standards for college preparatory and secondary education in the process. It has also given higher education the responsibility for providing precollegiate instruction to remediate those students without adequate levels of academic preparation to succeed in college. From the outset, two-year colleges have provided developmental, remedial, and college preparatory courses in addition to collegiate level instruction (Ratcliff 1986; Zook 1922).

The rapid rise in immigrants in the first two decades of this century also fueled the demand for access to public higher education. With the increase in immigrants, the educational needs and the educational backgrounds of students diversified rapidly. The influence of the suffrage movement and the growing educational expectations of women encouraged coeducation and collegiate education for women and further contributed to the diversification of students applying for admission to college. At the outset of the decade, less than 4 percent of the American population (238,000) went to college. By the end of the 1920s, 12 percent of the high school graduates were attending college. Since 1980 there have been 6 million new immigrants to the United States. Once again, the United States is expanding and extending higher education to new segments of the population, some with little or no formal education or language skills, others with extensive education but few language skills, and yet a third group with English language skills but little formal education. Most of these new arrivals are outside the normal elementary to secondary to higher education scheme.

The diversity of cultures and educational backgrounds of college students once again is expanding rapidly. Community colleges have played a significant role in meeting immediate and short-cycle needs of the immigrant, the disabled, and the unemployed with a wide range of courses and programs that clearly expand the scope of higher education offerings to the practical and the pragmatic courses of study that meet the advanced educational needs of the society. The U.S. federal government has encouraged this expansion through incentives to colleges who serve such groups as displaced homemakers, students with disabilities, students needing adult basic education, and unemployed people seeking job retraining. Programs targeted for these students have broadened both the curriculum and the demographic profile of the students served by it. In the 1970s and at the outset of the 1980s, many higher educators predicted enrollment declines based on the decline in secondary school enrollments; instead, the demand for higher education rose as the value of a high school education declined. Much of this new enrollment did not come from the traditional eighteen-to-twenty-four-year-old college-going cohort. It was the newly arrived immigrant, the working adult, the mother reentering the work force, and the military veteran who swelled and diversified enrollments.

From as far back as 1914, the community college commitment to open admissions and access to higher education has been of paramount importance. According to the philosophy of the Oklahoma Institute of Technology, now Northern Oklahoma College, ''Democracy is no new ideal for this country. Quite true, but we are coming to a larger social vision and a larger interpretation of democracy. We have long proclaimed the equality of our citizens, but we are coming to see that equality must mean equal opportunity for self-realization, recognition of individual differences'' (Ratcliff 1986, 15).

THE RISE OF COMMUNITY SERVICES

Programs and services for adults—for the continuing education of workers in the skilled trades, technical occupations, and the allied professions—and courses and programs of general interest and value to personal and corporate development of the local community have always been distinguishing features of community and junior colleges. Still, it was after World War II and during the tenure of Edmund Gleazer as president of AACC that this function grew to prominence. Writing in 1969, Harlacher concluded that community services were the function that best fit the community college: ''for a unique role in future patterns of American education'' (1969, 107). Gleazer predicted in 1973 that the educational services rendered to the entire local community, not just to traditional college-age groups, would be the focus of community colleges in the coming decades

(230). The literature pertaining to the role of adult, continuing, and community education in the community college presents two conflicting views (Ratcliff 1976). One holds that they are adjunct to the principal functions of the college: general and liberal education and vocational and technical education. The second perspective suggests that adult, continuing, and community education, viewed as community services, is not so much a separate function of the college as it is an intrinsic quality that separates it from other forms of postsecondary education.

In the 1920s the junior college movement was beginning to emerge as a significant part of postsecondary education in the United States. By that time the land grant college and universities had developed quite extensive programs of adult and continuing education and community education and development through cooperative and general extension agencies. Bogue suggests that community services did not become a significant function of the community colleges until after 1930 (1950, 207). The Chautauqua movement, university extension, the public schools, and various state and occupationally related associations, organizations, and agencies offered community services. Still, during the 1960s and 1970s, the term "community services" increasingly was used in the community college literature to describe the unique contribution of the institution. Thornton, for example, held that two-year colleges did not reach their "full stature" until after World War II when the community services concept began to be widely adopted (1960, 66). Significant in this development was the President's Commission on Higher Education ("The Truman Commission") which gave primacy to the notion of service to the local communities:

Hence the President's Commission suggests the name "community college" to be applied to the institution designed to serve chiefly local community educational needs. It may have various forms of organization and may have curricula of various lengths. Its dominant feature is its intimate relations to the life of the community it serves (President's Commission 1947, Vol. 3, 5).

Increasingly, the very character of the two-year college was recast around the notion that community service was not just another function; it was intrinsic to the philosophy of the comprehensive community college. Community college leader and scholar, B. Lamar Johnson, wrote in 1955, "It is the considered judgment of this author that the most important development of the past twenty-five years has been the emergence of the concept of the public junior college as a community college" (482).

CONCLUSION

The community college, in all its various manifestations, is a truly unique component of American higher education. It provides higher education with a flexibility and adaptiveness to local social needs. It helps a complex industrialized society have a full range of education and training, so that one can find accountants with a high school diploma, with an associate's degree from a community college, with a bachelor's degree in accounting, or with a master's degree in business administration. It provides the legal aide and legal assistant with the general and the specialized knowledge and skills to work with the lawyer. Similarly, the community college educates numerous allied health professionals who work in support of physicians and surgeons. These educational programs are open largely to all. The community college provides the developmental and remedial course work necessary for individuals capable of postsecondary education to gain the necessary basic skills and abilities to succeed. The adaptive, flexible, and accessible characteristics of community, junior, and technical colleges have given them a singularly important role in American society.

REFERENCES

Alexander, K., and E. S. Solomon. 1972. *College and university law*. Charlottesville, Va.: The Michie Company.

Board of Education of St. Joseph, Missouri. 1913–1915. *Records of the board of education of the school district of St. Joseph*. Vol. 11. St. Joseph, Mo.

Bogue, J. P. 1950. *The community college*. New York: McGraw-Hill.

Boorstin, D. J. 1965. Culture with many capitals: The booster college. In *The Americans: The national experience*, 152–60. New York: Random House, Vintage Press.

Brint, S., and J. Karabel. 1989. *The diverted dream: Community colleges and the promise of educational opportunity in America, 1900–1985*. New York: Oxford University Press.

Clowes, D. A., and B. H. Levin. 1989. Community, junior and technical colleges—Are they leaving higher education? *Journal of Higher Education* 60: 349–55.

Cohen, A. M., and F. B. Brawer. 1989. *The American community college*. 2d ed. San Francisco: Jossey-Bass.

Cross, K. P. 1971. *Beyond the open door: New students to higher education*. San Francisco: Jossey-Bass.

Deiner, T. 1986. *Growth of an American invention: A documentary history of the junior and community college movement*. Westport, Conn.: Greenwood Press.

Eby, F. 1927. Shall we have a system of public junior colleges in Texas? *Texas Outlook* 20:22–24.

Eells, W. C. 1931. *The junior college*. Boston, Mass.: Houghton Mifflin.

Gleazer, E. J., Jr., 1968. *This is the community college*. New York: Houghton Mifflin.

———. 1973. *Project focus: A forecast study of community colleges*. New York: McGraw-Hill.

———. 1980. *The community college: Values, vision, and vitality*. Washington, D.C.: American Association of Community and Junior Colleges.

Goodwin, G. L. 1971. The historical development of the community-junior college ideology: An analysis and interpretation of the writings of selected community-junior college national leaders from 1890 to 1920. Ph.D. diss., University of Illinois-Champaign.

Gray, B. R. 1959. The growth and development of Midwestern University, 1922–1957. Master's thesis, University of Texas at Austin.

Harlacher, E. L. 1969. *The community dimension of the community college*. Englewood Cliffs, N.J.: Prentice-Hall.

Johnson, B. L. 1955. An emerging concept points to the future. *Junior College Journal* 25: 482–85.

Karabel, J. 1972. Community colleges and social stratification. *Harvard Educational Review* 42:521–62.

Koos, L. V. 1924. *The junior college*. Minneapolis, Minn.: Research Publications of the University of Minnesota (Education Series, Report no. 5).

Pincus, F. L. 1980. The false promises of community colleges: Class, conflict and vocational education. *Harvard Educational Review* 50: 332–61.

President's Commission on Higher Education. 1947. *Higher education for American democracy*. Volume III: Organizing higher education. New York: Harper & Brothers.

Ratcliff, J. L. 1976. An analysis of community-based policies for off-campus community services in selected nonmetropolitan two-year colleges of the northwest. Ph.D. diss., Washington State University.

———. 1984. A re-examination of the past: Some origins of the ''second best'' notion,. *Community/Junior College Quarterly of Research and Practice* 8(1): 273–84.

———. 1986. Should we forget William Rainey Harper? *Community College Review* 13(4): 12–19.

———. 1987a. Anthony Caminetti, university leaders, and the 1907 California Junior College Law. Paper presented at annual meeting of the Association for the Study of Higher Education, 23 November, Baltimore, Maryland.

———. 1987b. ''First'' public junior colleges in an age of reform. *Journal of Higher Education* 58(2):151–80.

Roark, D. B. 1926. The junior college movement in Texas. Master's thesis, Baylor University.

Rowland, E. 1949. Origin and development of Fresno State College. Ph.D. diss., University of California, Berkeley.

Thelin, J. R. 1982. *Higher education and its useful past*. Cambridge, Mass.: Schenkman Publishing.

Thornton, J. W. 1960. *The community junior college*. New York: Wiley and Sons.

Trow, M. A. 1984. The analysis of status. In *Perspectives on Higher Education*, ed. B. R. Clark, 132–62. Berkeley: University of California Press.

Young, M. E. 1966. Anthony Caminetti and his role in the development of a complete system of free public education in California. Ph.D. diss., University of Denver.

Zook, G. F. 1922. The junior college. *Texas Outlook* 6(1):33–38.

Zwerling, L. S. 1976. *Second best: The crisis of the community college*. New York: McGraw-Hill.

Evolution of Junior Colleges into Community Colleges

Edmund J. Gleazer, Jr.

In late 1991 public colleges in the United States reported that the economic recession required them to place limits on enrollments and to turn away thousands of students (*Chronicle of Higher Education* 1991, 38:12). Community colleges were not exempt. Budgetary constraints required community college leadership and those concerned with state educational policy to examine anew their admissions policies and, even more important, the breadth and the priorities of their institutional mission. Perplexing questions of financing and role which had surfaced some years earlier became acute. Breneman and Nelson (1981) had identified a tension between institutional mission and finance which they predicted would grow during the following two decades. They questioned whether the comprehensive mission could be maintained in a time of tight budgets. In their view, policy choices would be required. It is the aim of this chapter to contribute toward a context for those choices by tracing the development of the comprehensive community college from its more limited beginnings as a junior college.

At the second annual meeting of the American Association of Junior Colleges (AAJC) in 1922, the junior college was defined as "an institution offering two years of instruction of strictly collegiate grade" (Bogue 1950). However, just three years later, the definition was amplified:

The junior college is an institution offering two years of instruction of strictly collegiate grade. This curriculum may include those courses usually offered in the first two years of the four-year colleges; in which case these courses must be identical, in scope and thoroughness, with corresponding courses of the standard four-year college. The junior college may, and is likely to, develop a different type of curriculum suited to the larger and ever-changing civic, social, religious, and vocational needs of the entire community in which the college is located. It is understood that in this case, also, the work offered shall be on a level appropriate for high school graduates. (Bogue 1950, xviii)

One of the earliest uses of the term "community college" is found in an article written by the president of a junior college in Pennsylvania. In 1936 he emphasized that the junior college should be "meeting community needs . . . it should serve to promote a greater social and civic intelligence . . . provide opportunities for increased adult education . . . provide educational, recreational, and vocational opportunities for young people . . . and that the work of the community college should be closely integrated with the work of the high school and the work of other community institutions" (Hollinshead 1936). Hollinshead was among the early visionaries who perceived a mission beyond "two years of the four-year college." His emphasis upon "meeting community needs" anticipated the marketing approach of the present as did his view on close relationships with the high schools and other community institutions.

Another element of the community college, to extend educational opportunity, was encouraged by James Madison Wood, president of Stephens College. Wood chaired a junior college conference in 1920 at which the decision was made to organize a national association of junior colleges. Speaking at the annual meeting of the AAJC some twenty years later, Wood spoke of the great numbers of students who drop out of conventional high schools and colleges. He noted that junior colleges could play a major role in attacking this problem—with a caveat: "They need not allow themselves to become enmeshed in the interests and objectives of the traditional college" (Wood 1940).

It is interesting to note that both of these leaders in community college, though, were not from the public sector. They presided over independent or private institutions.

Relations with the community along with adult education were considered important features of the evolving junior college by Dr. George F. Zook, president of the American Council on Education and facilitator of the initial organizing meeting of the AAJC. To him it was unthinkable that "any junior college, whether publicly or privately controlled, can live in the throbbing life of our larger cities and towns without feeling a responsibility for educational leadership in the community" (Zook 1946).

In 1947 President Truman's Commission on Higher Education incorporated in its findings and recommendations a concept of community college mission that was expansive and included elements that had been sounded by junior college leadership.

The potential effects of the community college in keeping intellectual curiosity alive in out-of-school citizens, of stimulating their zest for learning, of improving the quality of their lives as individuals and citizens, are limited only by the vision, the energy, and ingenuity of the college staff and by the size of the college budget. But the people will take care of the budget if the staff provides them with vital and worthwhile educational services. (President's Commission 1947, vol. 1)

For an institution to achieve these ends, the commission postulated five characteristics:

First, the community college must make frequent surveys of its community so that it can adapt its program to the educational needs of its full time students. [The commission sees these needs as both vocational and general.]

Second, since the program is expected to serve a cross-section of the youth population, it is essential that consideration be given not only to apprentice training but also to cooperative procedures which provide for the older students alternative periods of attendance at college and remunerative work.

Third, the community college must prepare its students to live a rich and satisfying life, part of which involves earning a living. To this end the total educational effort, general and vocational, of any student must be a well-integrated single program, not two programs.

Fourth, the community college must meet the needs also of its students who will go on to a more extended general education or to specialized and professional study at some other college or university.

Fifth, the community college must be the center for the administration of a comprehensive adult education program. (President's Commission 1947, vol. 3)

Thus the name "community college" was given national recognition and a mission described which made the educational needs of the community the primary reference point. It is important to observe that the commission's recommendations for the community college were part of a broader call that public education be made available, tuition free, to all Americans able and willing to receive it, regardless of race, creed, color, sex, or economic and social status (President's Commission 1947, vol. 5).

Although a new name had been given to the junior college, community college leaders were concerned that the institution still did not have an identity of its own. In many respects, the universities and colleges to which the community college students were to transfer determined both the courses and methods of the community college, although it turned out that a majority of the students did not transfer. Therefore, it is not surprising to find in community college history a discernible search for institutional freedom to determine its program and to look to the community as the arbiter of the suitability of its programs rather than the universities. Bethel, Lindsay, and Bogue (1948) noted that "for the people of this community education is never ending, because the junior college is providing education and varying points of need in the life of each individual."

The first book with the term community college in its title was written by Bogue in 1950 when he was executive secretary of the AAJC and a former president of Green Mountain Junior College in Vermont. Finishing the manuscript while he taught the first summer school course on the community junior college offered by Harvard University, Bogue supported the view of the President's Commission that the curriculum of the college is derived from a continuing assessment of the educational needs of the people in the community. He further maintained that such needs are broader than those represented by an occupational focus. They include family life, civic and cultural interests, community service, and development of the whole person (Bogue 1950).

Writing some ten years later, Thornton, while recognizing the diversity that must exist among institutions serving a variety of communities, described what he considered "a common ideal" community junior college. Again, the emphasis was on "providing legitimate educational services, rather than on conforming to preconceived notions of what is or what is not collegiate subject matter, or who is or is not college material" (Thornton 1960).

Thornton's definition of the community junior college was commonly accepted as a goal in 1960 as these institutions moved into a decade of explosive growth. The American Association of Collegiate Registrars and Admissions Officers (1962) gave further credibility to the emerging identity of the evolving institution in its *Handbook of Data and Definitions in Higher Education*:

COMMUNITY COLLEGE. A two-year institution of higher education, generally public, offering instruction adapted in content, level, and schedule to the needs of the community in which it is located. Offerings usually include a transfer curriculum (credits transferable toward a bachelor's degree), occupational (or terminal) curriculums, general education, and adult education.

A substantial broadening of community college programs developed in the early 1960s as several states converted specialized vocational and technical schools into comprehensive community colleges. Actions taken in North Carolina were representative of this process: "We recommend that the State develop one system of public two-year post–high school institutions offering college parallel, technical-vocational-terminal, and adult education instruction tailored to area needs; and that the comprehensive community colleges be subjected to state level supervision by one agency" (Governor's Commission 1962).

Study of community college development leaves the impression that a major assignment of the evolving institution is to *extend* educational opportunity. One of the ways it does this is through *broadening* educational opportunity. In the early 1960s such an objective was viewed as an international need. In his foreword to the UNESCO publication *Access to Higher Education*, Zurayk encouraged such efforts by the educational community:

The present expansion in education is not only vastly increasing the number of students; it is also drawing them from many more diverse social origins. This trend should be encouraged further. We should cast our net wider and wider in order to identify, to catch and to bring within the scope of education all available talent, wherever it may be found. (Bowles 1963)

A similar theme was sounded by the president of the College Entrance Examination Board who saw implications for educational services in the kind of societal changes described by Zurayk. Pearson (1966) called for accommodation of the curriculum to the increasing diversity and individual needs of the community college student population.

Community colleges responded to the call for accommodating to a mounting diversity in the larger number of students enrolling. One factor that moved them toward "comprehensiveness" was the commonly practiced open-door admissions policy. The approach in the state of California was typical. All high school graduates could enter community colleges. In addition, the colleges could admit, and were encouraged to do so, all persons over eighteen years of age who could profit from instructional programs. Diversity of programs and extension of opportunity were held up as institutional goals (Coordinating Council for Higher Education 1965). In much the same way, the board of regents in New York State declared: "Comprehensive community colleges should be recognized and supported as the basic institutional approach to providing a broader public educational opportunity above the high school level in New York State" (New York State Board of Regents 1967). Similar provisions were incorporated into the statutes of other states such as Illinois, where the Public Junior College Act of 1965 promoted not only open admissions, but also counseling of students "according to their interests and abilities" (Anderson and Spencer 1967).

By 1970 the junior colleges, which in earlier years had offered primarily the first two years of the four-year degree, had become comprehensive community colleges. Soon, however, the environment in which they operated showed evidences of change, and the pace of enrollment growth slowed. At the same time, other kinds of institutions initiated programs that were often competitive. Commented one observer, "Developmental education, occupational education, and other services considered by the community colleges to be among their distinctive offerings are found in a growing number of institutions that have a new awareness of the educational market" (*Chronicle of Higher Education*, 25 November 1974).

An uneasiness developed in the educational community in anticipation of the enrollment projections that were made explicit just a few years later: "The age group conventionally known as 'college age' will continue to decline. . . . The group aged 25 through 44 will show a massive rate of growth, with around 25% projected. . . . The population served by traditional and conventional institutions known as schools, colleges, and universities will drop by 1985" (ERIC 1975).

Legislators and their staff members reacted to the charts and graphs that showed declining numbers of youth coming out of the schools in the years ahead by anticipating decline in college enrollments: "Hence the inevitable result: a winding down of the educational apparatus at all levels" (Gleazer 1980). While college and university leaders as well as legislators anticipated declining enrollments as a result of fewer high school graduates, Moses (1971) published a paper that initially was given little attention but later was acknowledged to be a blockbuster.

Moses rejected the notion that American education was carried out in a three-layered hierarchy, running from primary school through graduate school. This, he said, represented the "core," but it overlooked a "periphery" in which over

60 million adults pursued learning opportunities very important to their lives. Moses challenged the monopoly that the educational establishment had over public policy and public resources. His views suggested that, although declining numbers were projected in graduates from high schools and that enrollments of conventional students in colleges and universities would decline, the need and demand for educational services would continue to mount. Other authorities began to concur by noting that the desire for education could be described as "addictive." The more you get, the more you want.

But the question becomes "who will deliver the educational services?" According to Broschart (1976),

The Periphery, as a set of non-related but formal delivery systems, has always been designed to be related to new needs and to the fact of changing educational patterns and demands. It could well be in a position to respond with vigorous innovations to projected changes. However, it will find itself in an increased struggle, both internally among its many component parts and externally with the Core, for scarce dollar resources.

Marien (1972) raised another relevant question: "Is education to be organized around institutions, credits, and credentials, or is education to be organized around learners in an optimal system for distributing knowledge and encouraging its utilization?"

Attempts to "organize around the learners" had led to substantial changes in community colleges during the 1960s:

To provide an effective teaching-learning process, it was essential to know the communities in which the students lived, to understand their "rootage" system. People, students, and teachers alike, had to move out of the academic community, away from the college campus. A relationship grew involving health, housing, recreation, community action, family life, political movements, employment services, libraries, day care centers, museums, labor unions, and churches. . . . A basic element in their credo was that theirs was a mission to make educational opportunity available to people who had not had it before. (Gleazer 1973)

In a paper published by the American Association of Community and Junior Colleges (AACJC) in 1973, it was noted that, even though the community college was becoming "community-based," the services it offered to a remarkable diversity of students were still relatively conventional in form, with the accent "too often on the word 'college.' " Now it was proposed that this community-based institution organize itself around "the customers' needs," creating "value-satisfying goods and services" (AACJC 1973).

Among the needs identified were career development—career needs not confined to high school and college age students but needs persisting throughout life. Individual development was also cited—assistance from the college for the individual to establish personal goals throughout the developmental stages of a lifetime. Learning to be effective in family relationships was an obvious need. And a growing number of observers referred to the need for training and development of people in public agencies as well as in health fields and business and industrial organizations. The paper maintained that changes were occurring in the basic concept of postsecondary education and its clientele and that a service-oriented postsecondary enterprise would emerge. It was urged that the college become aggressive in searching out educational needs in the community.

That the clientele served by the community college had in fact changed the characteristics of the institution was evidenced in a study conducted by the California Postsecondary Education Commission in 1976. The report raised substantial questions as to whether conventional academic classifications and categories, such as attrition, dropout, transfer, and degree oriented, were of value any longer. It noted that "part-time students now comprise two-thirds of the headcount enrollment," and that, due to the characteristics, needs, and enrollment habits of this group, "continuing education for part-time, adult students has become the dominant function of Community Colleges, with no resultant neglect of the occupational, transfer and general education functions for more traditional students" (California Postsecondary 1976).

The community college, as described through Dorothy Knoell's research, bore characteristics much like those identified by the UNESCO Institute of Education (1976) as institutions functioning in a policy framework of lifelong education, defined as "a process of accomplishing personal, social, and professional development throughout the life-span of individuals in order to enhance the quality of life of both individuals and their collectives."

For most community college learners, education is concurrent with other responsibilities of adulthood. In many colleges, enrollees span the generations, another element in lifelong education. And community colleges relate to schools, places of work, culture and recreation, religious institutions, and mass media, a further mark of education that operates in the life space of the individual and for the entire life span (Gleazer 1980). By 1980 community colleges seemed to be in an advantageous position because of characteristics that they had developed to build on what appeared to be appropriate structures for a new era of education and community service and to be in the vanguard of change required in policies, institutional forms, and citizen attitudes.

Many examples demonstrated that the college focus was on people—people in the community. A cooperative effort in San Diego serves as just one illustration of the kind of institution that community colleges were becoming. In the heart of an economically depressed area, the community college district, in cooperation with city, county, and federal governments, built an Educational Cultural Complex to provide vocational training, basic and academic education, career counseling, child development programs, a community theater, a food service facility, and other community-oriented functions. It was designed as an adult community center. The city of San Diego built a branch of its public library in the complex.

According to the chancellor of the district, "[T]he complex serves as a 'one-stop' adult center for meeting the needs of the southeast San Diego community and its citizens in a creative innovative way" (Parnell 1978).

In describing the San Diego development, the chancellor, Dale Parnell, cited the need for "an urban extension act." In doing so he revealed a sizable obstacle in the path of community colleges as their mission continued to broaden. Although his appeal was to the federal level, it was evident that, at the state level as well, there was a need for change in the policy framework that guided the work and the financing of community colleges. Both mission statements and finance mechanisms appeared not only out of step with the times, but inappropriate for future plans (Gilder 1981).

The colleges found themselves navigating a tricky course between the "core" and the "periphery." As they moved toward the core, opportunities diminished. With greater movement toward the periphery, support patterns were left behind and resistance was encountered in the form of "tradition."

Nowhere have the dilemmas thus facing the comprehensive community college been more clearly delineated than in the studies conducted by Breneman and Nelson (1981) of Brookings Institution. They presented three general strategies for determining the direction of development in an institution. One possibility was commitment to a "comprehensive mission, giving equal priority to academic, vocational-technical, and community service programs." A second approach suggested was to "drop the strong community service orientation, placing renewed emphasis on the traditional collegiate functions—shifting the focus, in other words, from *community* to *college*." With this strategy, however, was the warning that tying the future of community colleges to this narrow program might limit its appeal. The other half of the dilemma, however, is that "the risk of moving farther *away* from traditional higher education is that adequate public support from programs of lifelong learning may fail to materialize" (emphasis added). The third approach Breneman and Nelson suggested, "advocated by Edmund Gleazer and others, is for the colleges to become community-based learning centers . . . with a diminished role for traditional college programs and students and an expanded role for part-time non-degree-seeking, adult learners."

The Brookings study found that in 1981 there was a general commitment to a comprehensive mission in the nation's community colleges. Since the major aim of this chapter has been to trace the evolution of the junior college to the comprehensive community college, the Brookings study could serve as a convenient terminal point. However, there is a current state of crisis that justifies further comment from one who has observed the development of these institutions.

The Brookings researchers were prescient in their assertion that the tightening of state budgets and "increased scrutiny of the value of all publicly supported activities" would require that decisions be made with respect to the college mission. Further, they forecast the present difficult times that would demand economic justification for the utilization of public funds. At this writing, community colleges *are* confronted by different choices. Policy decisions must be made with respect to program priorities. The quality of decisions is improved by good information. It is important to note, therefore, that while some elements of the community college mission have received a good deal of research attention, other elements have not. Research data concerning conventional university transfer and vocation-technical programs are more readily available and are useful for policymakers in the allocation of resources. Further, legislators generally understand and support these functions.

Another part of the comprehensive mission, often referred to as community services, on the other hand, can claim comparatively little research attention. This fact becomes important as one studies the evolution of the community college and finds a dominant persisting theme—''that the junior college should be a community college, meeting community needs'' (Hollinshead 1936).

Communities in the United States at the time of this writing were dealing with a multitude of problems: racial conflicts among Cuban-American, Caucasian, and Afro-American communities in Miami; economic conversion in the midwest and Texas due to layoffs in local defense industries; conflict between loggers and environmentalists in Oregon; rising disputes, claims, and counterclaims across ethnic, geographical, gender, political, and economic lines in much of America; and mounting numbers of homeless and hungry people in the cities. Moreover, there was a wave of immigration that matched that of the early years of the century, skyrocketing budgets, and a pervasive drug culture—and all of this in a democratic society where citizens argue that they had been ''pushed out'' of the political process and that their government and its public officials had failed them (Kettering Foundation 1991).

Do these ''community needs'' require a community college response? They appear urgent, complex, and even life threatening. In times of scarce resources, legislators and community college leaders cannot be faulted for questioning ''play writing for fun,'' as the 1947 President's Commission suggested as a curricular offering, but surely make a grievous error to neglect the contribution that community colleges can make to meet the critical learning needs of the communities that confront the most threatening problems of this century.

The Brookings study asserts that necessary financial support for such programs will not be forthcoming without economic justification as well as arguments that stress other than economic values. That seems to be a fair requirement. Measuring cost effectiveness, however, is sometimes a difficult task. It is especially troublesome in nontraditional areas. Nevertheless, impact studies are needed to provide a better basis for determinations of worth and, hence, suitable public investment.

Among the opportunities to examine the economic justification of programs and to consider ''other than economic values'' is one currently presented as a result of grants by a number of philanthropic foundations. The stated purpose of the grants is to assist community colleges to address issues of concern in their communities. Community leaders are to learn consensus building, as well as skills in negotiation and mediation. Citizens and community leaders will be brought together to discuss current problems in the community and to explore ways to solve them. Under the leadership of the college, projects will be initiated to develop the capacity of local citizens to address and respond to critical community issues (League for Innovation 1991a, b).

Useful information could be provided to those responsible for community college policy decisions if in these and similar efforts deliberate measures were taken to assess the value of the economic and social outcomes of such programs. Beyond this, it would then be possible to make sounder judgments about the nature and scope of an educational institution that is responsive to community needs.

REFERENCES

American Association of Collegiate Registrars and Admissions Officers. 1962. *Handbook of data and definitions in higher education.* Washington, D.C.

American Association of Community and Junior Colleges. 1973. After the boom: Now what for community colleges? *Community and Junior College Journal* 44(4).

Anderson, E. F., and J. S. Spencer. 1967. *Report of selected data and characteristics— Illinois public junior colleges, 1966–67.* Springfield: Illinois Junior College Board.

Bethel, L. L., F. B. Lindsay, and J. P. Bogue. 1948. *Junior college terminal education in your community.* New York: McGraw-Hill.

Bogue, J. P. 1950. *The community college.* New York: McGraw-Hill.

Bowles, F. 1963. *Access to higher education.* New York: Columbia University Press.

Breneman, D. W., and S. C. Nelson. 1981. *Financing community colleges: An economic perspective.* Washington, D.C.: Brookings Institution.

Broschart, J. R. 1976. *A synthesis of selected manuscripts about the education of adults in the United States.* Typescript. Available from Syracuse University, Adult Education Library.

California Postsecondary Education Commission. 1976. *Through the open door: A study of patterns of enrollment and performance in California's community colleges.* Report 76–1. Sacramento, Calif.

Chronicle of Higher Education. 1974. Two-year colleges: The boom slows. November 25.

———. 1991. 38: 12.

Coordinating Council for Higher Education. 1965. *A consideration of issues affecting California public junior colleges, a staff report.* Sacramento, Calif.

ERIC. 1975. *Some American demographic projections 1975–2000.* Syracuse, N.Y.: Syracuse University.

Gilder, J., ed. 1981. *Modernizing state policies: Community colleges and lifelong education.* Washington, D.C.: American Association of Community and Junior Colleges.

Gleazer, E. J., Jr. 1973. *Project focus: A forecast study of community colleges.* New York: McGraw-Hill.

————. 1980. *The community college: Values, vision, and vitality*. Washington, D.C.: American Association of Community and Junior Colleges.

Governor's Commission on Education beyond the High School. 1962. *Education beyond the high school*. Raleigh, N.C.

Hollinshead, B. S. 1936. The community junior college program. *Junior College Journal* 7:111–16.

Kettering Foundation. 1991. *Citizens and politics*. Dayton, Ohio.

League for Innovation. 1991a. *League funded by Hitachi to develop community college forums* (News release). Laguna Hills, Calif.

————. 1991b. Santa Fe Community College Lands $775,000 Kellogg Grant, *Community College Times*.

Marien, M. 1972. *Beyond the Carnegie Commission*. Syracuse, N.Y.: Educational Policy Research Center, Syracuse University.

Moses, S. 1971. *The learning force: A more comprehensive framework for educational policy*. Occasional Papers no. 25. Publications in Continuing Education. Syracuse, N.Y.: Syracuse University.

New York State Board of Regents. 1967. *The comprehensive community college: A policy statement*. Albany, N.Y.

Parnell, D. 1978. Needed: An urban extension act. *Community and Junior College Journal* 49 (October):10–13.

Pearson, R. 1966. *The Challenge of Curricular Change*. New York: College Entrance Examination Board.

President's Commission on Higher Education. 1947. *A report of the President's Commission on Higher Education*. Vols. 1, 3, and 5. Washington, D.C.: U.S. Government Printing Office.

Thornton, J. W. 1960. *The community junior college*. New York: Wiley and Sons.

UNESCO Institute of Education. 1976. *Foundations of lifelong education*. Paris.

Wood, J. M. 1940. Twenty years of progress. *Junior College Journal* (May): 518.

Zook, G. F. 1946. Changing patterns of junior college education. *Junior College Journal* 16(9):411–17.

The Fortunes of the Transfer Function: Community Colleges and Transfer 1900–1990

Judith S. Eaton

BACKGROUND: COMMUNITY COLLEGE TRANSFER UNTIL 1980

The First Fifty Years: How Important was the Transfer Function?

Transfer has been a primary aim of the community college since the earliest days of its precursor, the junior college, at the beginning of the twentieth century. All junior colleges, whether emerging from secondary schools or the restructuring of four-year institutions or established independently, made a commitment to ensuring that students had course work and programs available to transfer to a senior institution. In the main, the transfer experience was a liberal arts experience. Key leaders of the early junior college, including Eells (1931), Koos (1925), and Colvert (1939) as well as university presidents Tappan, Jordan, and Harper, stressed the transfer role (Diener 1986). One of the earliest statements of the American Association of Junior Colleges about the junior college mission, in 1922, included collegiate instruction as a major purpose of two-year institutions. College catalogs and surveys of course offerings during the first forty years of the junior college confirm that academic courses leading to transfer made up the majority of junior college work (Campbell 1930; Colvert 1947; McDowell 1919). Surveys of student enrollments—as distinct from course offerings—reflected transfer enrollments of from 60 to 70 percent between 1907 and 1940 (Lombardi 1979).

Transfer was not the sole purpose of the early junior college. As with the contemporary community college, the early junior college was a multipurpose institution. Its statement of mission included more than transfer education. From its inception, the junior college stressed "terminal education" as well as transfer education. The junior college's reason for being went beyond transfer to terminal education in the form of general education (not intended as preparation for a four-year institution) or education that should lead to immediate employment. While terminal general education and education leading to employment were debated over the years, they remained an important part of the junior college program.

The junior college emphasis on transfer was also accompanied by some doubts and concerns. The early junior college literature is replete with admonitions that these two-year institutions cannot exist merely to serve the senior institution (Monroe 1972; Taylor 1933; Weersing 1931). Concerns that junior colleges do not own their academic curricula were expressed over and over. Junior college leaders were challenged to develop the unique identity of the two-year school. Repeatedly, they were called upon to clarify the aims and purposes of the institution, especially in relation to the curriculum. With increasing frequency, efforts were made to build this unique identity by expanding the vocational role of the two-year institution.

The 1940s were a pivotal decade for the junior college. It was during these years that the transition to the community college took place. The GI Bill provided the financial means whereby enrollments could begin to grow dramatically. The Truman Commission's emphasis on vocational and community-based education provided the conceptual foundation for the community college. Throughout these years, attention continued to be paid to the transfer function as part of the comprehensive community college, but much of the creative energy of community college educators was shifting elsewhere—to the growing vocational and community-based functions.

The transfer function underwent a shift in status. Although transfer has never been the exclusive function of the junior college, it *was* the dominant function within the two-year institution. Transfer as the dominant function meant that emphasis was placed on traditional liberal arts curricula and that the relationships with senior institutions were important. It also meant that students staying in school to earn the baccalaureate was more important than immediate employment and that development of intellectual competencies described as "college-level" or "collegiate" was the desired goal. With an increasingly dominant vocational function, liberal arts curricula gave way to career curricula. Relationships with business and industry became more important than relationships with senior educational institutions. More attention was paid to preparation for immediate employment than the development of generic intellectual skills needed for further collegiate work and earning the baccalaureate.

Community Colleges 1950–1980: The Glorious Growth Years and the Transfer Function

Community college enrollments began to grow dramatically after 1945 and, based on the information available, vocational enrollments grew at the expense of liberal arts enrollments leading to transfer. In 1963, public and private two-year head-count enrollment stood at 850,361. By 1980, enrollment had grown to 4,526,287. This constitutes approximately a 230 percent increase in student attendance. During the same time period, four-year head-count enrollments grew by almost 100 percent, from 3,929,248 to 7,570,608 (NCES 1991).

Although data are limited, both liberal arts course enrollments and transfer activity declined in the 1960s and 1970s. Cohen and Brawer (1989) maintain that, in the 1960s and twenty years thereafter, vocational education enrollments grew at a faster rate than liberal arts enrollments. By 1975, vocational program enrollments were 35 percent of total enrollments. At the same time, the liberal arts or the collegiate curriculum experienced what Cohen and Brawer call an "extreme narrowing": Some of the humanities disciplines were abandoned and second-year courses became increasingly rare. Assignments such as the writing of term papers diminished in scope in humanities classes (Cohen and Brawer 1987). By the 1980s, the American Association of Community and Junior Colleges (AACJC) reported that the majority of students enrolled in community colleges were in vocational programs (AACJC 1986). Lombardi (1979) places the decline of the transfer function in the late 1960s with 43 percent of enrollments in transfer programs as compared to the earlier 60 to 70 percent. By the end of the 1980s, various surveys of transfer activity indicated that perhaps from 20 to 29 percent of community college students transferred to a four-year institution (Palmer and Eaton 1991).

Also known as career, occupational, and technical education, vocational education replaced the transfer function as the dominant community college function. Vocational education not only attracted growing numbers of enrollees, it also functioned as the defining value of the community college experience. The dominance of the vocational function did not mean, however, a total eclipse of transfer. It meant a diminishing of its importance in the institution. The vocational function itself could be used for transfer—although this is not its primary intent and is not strongly emphasized in vocational programs. Further, as others have pointed out, there is a difference between how students use vocational or liberal arts curricula and the labeling of these programs (Cohen and Brawer 1989; Eaton 1990b; Palmer 1990).

The dominance of the vocational function changed the curricular emphasis of the community college. It changed institutional expectations about the goals students would achieve, and it changed the relationships community colleges had with other organizations—educational and business—in the community. Since the 1960s, community colleges have placed primary emphasis upon degree programs in occupational areas, short- or long-term vocational training that may or may not be for credit, and special on-site technical education services to business and industry. Emphasis on the transfer function had meant emphasis on the liberal arts and traditional academic values that link the community college with the rest of the collegiate enterprise. Emphasis on the vocational function means attention to immediate employment. It links the community college to the workplace. Immediate employment is more important than long-range educational goals. Emphasis on the vocational function places vocational faculty in the ascendancy, and this is accompanied by reduced investment in the traditional liberal arts. There is a greater pressure for funding equipment and facilities, for example, and less attention is paid to concerns such as hiring faculty to teach upper level courses in the liberal arts.

THE TRANSFER FUNCTION AFTER THE 1980s: STATUS AND EXPECTATIONS

Implications of Transfer's Secondary Status

The shift in the importance of the transfer function diminished the scope of access in the community college and the country, and it weakened the perception of the community college as a collegiate institution within the family of higher education institutions. According to some critics, it also contributed to limiting the social and economic mobility of students.

The transfer function holding a secondary status has reduced the extent to which the community college is an effective access institution. If the value of access is in part determined by *how much* education can be obtained, the dominant status of the vocational function and the secondary status of transfer have meant access is less valuable—it is access to *less* education. With the vocational function as the dominant function of the community college, access means opportunity for at most the two-year degree. Students are likely to enroll in courses and programs designed for terminal education uses rather than baccalaureate uses. With transfer as the dominant function of the community college, access is broader: it is focused on the four-year degree. Access is more valuable because it is access to *more* education. More education is economically and socially rewarded to a greater extent in this society than less education.

The shift in importance of the transfer function distances the community college even farther from senior institutions. Rightly or wrongly, an emphasis on vocational education confirms the public perception of the community college as academically substandard. Skepticism concerning the quality of community college liberal arts offerings is affirmed. An emphasis on vocational education feeds the perception that two- and four-year institutions are significantly different from one another with the community college as the lesser partner. Fewer courses are likely to transfer. Fewer students are likely to transfer. This distancing occurs because vocational curricula at the community college are not available at the four-year institution and are therefore suspect. It occurs because vocational curricula are viewed as "less than collegiate." And it occurs because the goals of vocational education are different from the goals of liberal arts education and transfer.

A college culture that values the vocational over transfer can inhibit student mobility. According to some community college critics (Dougherty 1987; Karabel 1972; Zwerling 1976), community colleges function to sustain social inequality, and the combination of the vocational function as dominant and the transfer function as secondary contributes to this undesirable result. More students will be encouraged to establish vocational instead of transfer goals and will thereby remain at the same socioeconomic place from which they came. Those critical of supplanting the transfer function's dominance with that of vocational education also point to surveys of student intent over the years which consistently reflect a strong interest in transfer from the student population (Brint and Karabel 1989; Pincus 1980). They question making the vocational function dominant in the face of continuing student interest in transfer. They infer from this that dominance of the vocational function has not served students well. Those friendlier to the community college see the emphasis on the vocational function and its impact on students as a form of opportunity for students who would otherwise fail to have any collegiate experience at all.

Pascarella and Terenzini (1991), reviewing twenty years of research on how college affects students, point out that "there is consistent evidence that initial attendance at a two-year rather than a four-year college lowers the likelihood of one attaining a bachelor's degree" (372). They go on to say that this attendance may have an "indirect negative impact on occupational status and perhaps earnings" (590). Although they acknowledge that the community college does have a positive impact on educational opportunity and social mobility, the studies to date indicate that this is limited in relation to baccalaureate degree acquisition.

Transfer and the End of the Decade: Demands for Equity, Availability, and Accountability

In the latter part of the 1980s, transfer once again became a significant topic of discussion. Three factors in particular contributed to the reemergence of transfer as an important higher education issue. Concerns for educational mobility and especially the mobility of racial minority students triggered conversations about transfer. The changing attendance behavior of nontraditional students, especially their increasing tendency to attend more than one educational institution—two-year or four-year—during their undergraduate career called attention to the ease or difficulty of transfer. Finally, the state and federal emphasis on accountability in the latter 1980s was accompanied by the conviction that the extent to which students transferred and their success after transfer were important measures of institutional effectiveness. The new demands—equity, availability, and accountability—forced educators to pay additional attention to the transfer function and to begin to reconsider the role of the community college.

As civil rights efforts on behalf of racial minorities continued into the 1980s, concern that the opportunity and benefits that accompany especially baccalaureate education accrue to racial minorities intensified. This was in part the result of data indicating that the participation of Blacks and Hispanics in higher education had diminished since the 1970s (Wilson and Carter 1988). The community colleges, enrolling approximately one-half of all minorities during the 1980s, were urged to place additional emphasis on the transfer function especially in institutions housing large numbers of minority students. The AACJC, the Ford Foundation, the United States Department of Energy, the American Council on Education (ACE), and others sponsored various programmatic initiatives focused on strengthening transfer.

Nontraditional students, varyingly defined as older, part time, working, married, female, minority, or noncredit, had been part of the thinking of community colleges for many years. Some important accommodations to the attendance patterns of these students had been made over the years. These included evening and weekend colleges, special programs, on-site instruction, and credit for life experience. These accommodations, however, did not extend to the structure of the transfer relationship between two- and four-year institutions. Transfer, even throughout the 1980s, was traditionally structured on the twin assumptions that students were likely to be full time and degree seeking. Arrangements for students who did not seek an associate degree or students planning to attend either a two-year or four-year institution part time were few and far between.

Although data from systematic studies were not available, the perception that students made use of more than one educational institution to pursue the baccalaureate increased during the 1980s. This included not only transfer between community colleges and senior institutions but also transfer among four-year schools themselves. This perception led to increased scrutiny of how well the transfer function operated. This attention went beyond concern for the two-year/four-year relationship to the four-year/four-year transfer relationship and to "reverse transfer," moving from a four-year institution to a two-year school. Students moving about among higher education institutions increased the frequency of dealing with transfer-related issues such as course equivalency and distribution requirements.

School reform efforts in the 1980s, beginning with *A Nation at Risk* (National Commission on Excellence in Education 1983), generated a series of accountability efforts especially at the state level. By the end of the 1980s, the accountability effort had come to encompass higher education as well. State legislators, the National Governors' Association, and federal officials focused on the expected results of the collegiate experience. They sought to confirm that students completing a collegiate experience could function at a minimal level of competency and that entry to higher education resulted in degree completion. They were not satisfied with results in either sphere. Elected officials have always had difficulty understanding the educational role of the community college. They were especially concerned when students left the community college without a credential, did not transfer, or did not sustain employment. They viewed degree acquisition, transfer, and going to work as the three major indicators of community college effectiveness.

RESTORING THE DOMINANCE OF THE TRANSFER FUNCTION: WHAT NEEDS TO BE DONE

Transfer: The Need to Know More

The history of the study of the transfer function includes limited quantitative data and analysis. The record of transfer activity is composed mainly of a series of individual studies from which generalizations about the community college enterprise from a national perspective cannot be validly inferred. Lombardi (1979) cites Eells' California study in 1929 and his 1941 study of 190 public junior colleges. Medsker (1960) reports on transfer enrollments in Oregon, Wisconsin, New York, Pennsylvania, Iowa, and California. Other state studies were available throughout the 1970s. These studies affirmed that transfer activity was greater in the early years of the junior college and declined thereafter. They did not, however, provide a comprehensive national data base about changes in transfer and could not, with any confidence, speak knowledgeably about transfer.

In the 1980s, this trend continued. At the national level, information about transfer was still extremely limited. Relying mainly on the 1972 and 1980 longitudinal studies of students moving from high school to college generated by the United States Department of Education, at least six studies of transfer were completed during the 1980s (Palmer and Eaton 1991). These studies, as with earlier efforts, did not constitute a comprehensive picture of the transfer situation. The definitions of the transfer population and the general student population vary among studies. Some consider student intent; others do not. Some consider only full-time students: others include part-time students. Nonetheless, all the studies point to one in four or one in five students from community colleges transferring to four-year schools.

For example, Adelman (1988), using the longitudinal study of high school seniors in 1972, maintained that 20 percent of these students enrolled in a community college and then moved to a four-year institution. Lee and Frank (1990), scrutinizing high school seniors in 1980, determined that 24 percent of seniors who entered higher education within two years of high school graduation enrolled in a community college. Grubb (1991) identified transfer rates of 20 percent for 1980 high school seniors and 29 percent for 1972 seniors attending community colleges. The Transfer Assembly—a multiyear study that did not rely on the 1972 or 1980 longitudinal data—studied enrollments in fall 1989 and fall 1990 and identified an average transfer rate of from 23 to 24 percent among the 115 schools participating (Cohen 1991).

A comprehensive national data base is essential if community colleges are to determine their destiny as effective transfer institutions. Longitudinal studies of student flow must be undertaken on a routine basis to enable institutions to establish transfer goals and confirm whether they are achieving the expected results. These studies are required to establish a national transfer profile and to provide states and institutions with needed data by which to make public policy decisions for future transfer effectiveness.

Traditional Approaches to Transfer

There have been two traditional approaches to the management of the community college transfer function: reliance on documentation to oversee transfer and reliance on student support services to ensure transfer. Both approaches have their strengths and limitations. Neither is fully able to meet transfer needs of the future.

Managing transfer through documentation stresses the use of formal and informal arrangements, articulation agreements, between institutions as a critical means to manage the transfer function. This model is administrative and bureaucratic and responds to the question of what needs to be done institutionally to ensure transfer. Some thirty states have guidelines or policies concerning transfer (Kintzer 1989). There are numerous other bilateral agreements or agreements within systems (Bender 1990). Based on the limited scrutiny to date, there is little evidence that the document model has a significant positive impact on transfer (Banks 1992). There is no consistent positive correlation between institutions with high transfer rates and articulation agreements. At most, based on the evidence available, we can maintain that articulation agreements may help and do not harm transfer. On the other hand, when preoccupation with articulation agreements precludes other institutional actions that might strengthen transfer, they may be harmful.

Further, there is a considerable body of anecdotal evidence that articulation agreements fail to deal with the single greatest problem that students face upon transferring: receiving equivalent credit at the senior institution for course work undertaken at the community college. Articulation agreements are more likely to ensure that a certain *number* of credits will be accepted and not that *specific* course work will be accepted. This results in students having useless credits in some areas and being forced to retake courses. Ultimately, the benefit of an articulation agreement for a student rests upon faculty decision making about course acceptance. Many articulation agreements cannot deliver this.

The student support approach to transfer relies on two factors: information availability and personal assistance to students. Characteristically, student support transfer services include transfer counseling, orientation, course equivalency guides, electronic access to transfer information, college catalog rooms, and four-year college days. The information system tends to be essentially passive—relying on the students' willingness and ability to obtain needed facts about how, where, and when to transfer. The personal assistance tends to aid students in their transfer decision making, to help motivate them, and to assist in reducing some of the barriers that may confront them such as the need for additional financial aid. This model is valuable, but only to a limited extent. Most critically, it cannot ensure that students are armed with the two major skills they need for successful transfer: curricular experiences that prepare them for a four-year institution and experience with performance standards that are comparable to four-year expectations.

The Need to Augment Traditional Approaches: An Academic Model

An alternative—or complement—to either the document or the support service approach to transfer is an ''Academic Model'' (Eaton 1990a). This model focuses on the curricular and cognitive skills students need for successful transfer. At the heart of the transfer effort is an awareness that the relationship between a two- and four-year institution needs to change. This relationship needs a change in attitude, a change in modes of communication, and a change in approach to curriculum design and the setting of performance standards. The academic model addresses the faculty acceptance problem that is not adequately addressed through articulation agreements. It places emphasis on the intellectual competencies students need for successful transfer that cannot be addressed through student support services.

The academic model relies primarily on two- and four-year teaching faculty, their collaboration and their attention to curriculum and academic standards, and to the willingness of two- and four-year institutions to be held accountable for the results of their transfer efforts. The challenge is to overcome the mismatch between two- and four-year institutions in curriculum content and performance expectations for transfer. The model urges two- and four-year faculty to respond to the transfer challenge by developing a fit between courses that are nominally the same offered at each institution. With regard to standards, two- and four-year faculty need to ensure a fit between academic tasks—their extent and level of difficulty—in transfer courses.

Collaboration across institutions in the development of curricula and academic tasks is essential to strengthening transfer. Rather than devote unilateral faculty efforts within each institution to individually developing curricula and standards for transfer courses, faculty from both institutions need to be working together from the earliest stages of course and standards development. The academic model calls for a major investment in collaborative curriculum development across institutions to ensure that all students, independent of type of institution attended, obtain the needed academic skills and curricular background to achieve the baccalaureate.

For example, the National Center for Academic Achievement and Transfer, founded in 1989 and funded by the Ford Foundation and the American Council on Education, has financed approximately two dozen two-year/four-year partnerships in which faculty from each institution are coming together to develop or redesign discipline-based courses, develop new interdisciplinary courses, or develop new general education courses. Faculty working together across institutions is governed by an attitude of shared responsibility. This is in contrast to earlier experiences in which a senior institution that considered itself superior dictated curricular terms and conditions to a junior institution perceived to be less than adequate. Joint faculty development of lower-division course work is critical to reducing the likelihood of students being unprepared as they move from a community college to a four-year school.

Finally, the academic model calls for rigorous evaluation. Students who are provided this curricular experience must be tracked through the community college and the senior college to determine whether they transferred and their success after transfer. Determining student success will also enable two- and four-year institutions to evaluate their institutional effectiveness as transfer schools, to establish transfer goals, and to measure institutional success. This requires institutional commitment to defining the transfer population and tracking these students to the point of baccalaureate degree acquisition. The Transfer Assembly model provides the conceptual foundation needed for this purpose. Cohen (1991) defines the transfer population as all students with no prior college experience who take at least twelve college credits and, within four years, move on to a senior institution. This population can be compared to the general student population to determine an institutional transfer rate indicator and to evaluate transfer effectiveness.

COMMUNITY COLLEGE MISSION AND THE FUTURE

Is There a Place for Transfer?

Within the community college enterprise, the answer is an equivocal "yes." Educators maintain that there is a place for transfer *provided that* the comprehensive mission of the community college is sustained and that sustaining the transfer function does not move community colleges in the direction of the stereotype of the junior college—devoted *only* to the transfer. This is the response provided by the AACJC (1991) in its official literature.

For some community college educators, however, the commitment to the transfer function is limited. Parnell (1985) and Gleazer (1980), both past presidents of the AACJC, placed significantly less emphasis on the transfer function than other aspects of the community college mission. Parnell stressed vocational education above all, and Gleazer stressed a community-based model focused especially on meeting the needs of the adult population and community development. Neither Gleazer nor Parnell advocated elimination of the transfer function, but their emphasis on the alternative purposes of the community college and the lack of attention to transfer made their support of the function at best weak.

University-based researchers who are interested in the community college but are outside its framework also say "yes"—but under certain conditions. Those who point to the limited effectiveness of the community college urge that the community college undertake transfer work in a more serious and thoughtful manner thereby ensuring the transfer and success of many more students who start out in the community college. Or, they maintain that the limited effectiveness of the community college transfer function is reason to eliminate this aspect of the community college mission. Others seek to make transfer the primary purpose of the community college (Pincus and Archer 1989). Some argue that the community college has demonstrated that it is not an effective educational setting for lower-division collegiate work (Astin 1979) and that community colleges do not have a comparative edge in offering collegiate work (Breneman and Nelson 1981). Community colleges should devote themselves to their other purposes of vocational education, remedial education, and community service. Others urge placing lower-division collegiate work either in existing four-year schools, such as branch campuses of universities, or urge that community colleges become four-year institutions (Dougherty 1991).

The Need for Transfer as Dominant

Affirmation of the transfer function for the future can be neither equivocal nor conditional. If there is a future place for transfer in the community college, it must be more than only one aspect of the comprehensive community college mission. It must be first among equals—not precluding other functions but providing the value foundation for the campus environment. It cannot be secondary to the vocational function or community-based education. Transfer requires more attention, a focus on its effectiveness, and an expansion of its impact if students are to find the community college truly an entry to higher education. Transfer must once again be the dominant function of the community college.

In order that transfer dominate the community college agenda, three conditions need to be met. First, the values associated with transfer—the importance of the liberal arts, connections with senior institutions, generic intellectual skill development, and emphasis on long-range educational goals—need to be adopted as institutional values. Second, the values need to prevail even in vocational course work. This can take place if institutional general education or distribution requirements include college-level, discipline-based or interdisciplinary work. Given the growing body of evidence that transfer from career programs is at least as common as traditional transfer, opportunity for students to obtain college-level, discipline-based skills is essential. Third, this emphasis on transfer needs to manifest itself in increased enrollments in either the liberal arts or career-transfer programs. A critical mass of students needs to be engaged in education leading to transfer so that transfer is highly valued within the institution.

REFERENCES

Adelman, C. 1988. Transfer rates and the going mythologies: A look at community college patterns. *Change* 20(1):38–41.

American Association of Community and Junior Colleges. 1986. *Some telling facts about two-year colleges*. Washington, D.C.

————. 1991. *1991 public policy agenda*. Washington, D.C.

Astin, A. 1979. *Four critical years*. San Francisco: Jossey-Bass.

Banks, D. L. 1992. Environmental and organizational factors influencing the community college transfer function. Ph.D. diss., University of California, Los Angeles.

Bender, L. W., ed. 1990. *Spotlight on the transfer function: A national study of state policies and practices*. Washington, D.C.: American Association of Community and Junior Colleges.

Breneman, D. W., and S. C. Nelson. 1981. *Financing community colleges*. Washington, D.C.: Brookings Institution.

Brint, S., and J. Karabel. 1989. *The diverted dream: Community colleges and the promises of educational opportunity in America, 1900–1985*. New York: Oxford University Press.

Campbell, D. S. 1930. *A critical study of the stated purposes of the junior college*. Contribution to Education, 70. Nashville: George Peabody College for Teachers.

Cohen, A. M. 1991. The transfer indicator. *Working papers* 2(2). Washington, D.C.: American Council on Education/National Center for Academic Achievement and Transfer.

Cohen, A. M., and F. B. Brawer. 1987. *The collegiate function of community colleges*. San Francisco: Jossey-Bass.

————. 1989. *The American community college*. San Francisco: Jossey-Bass.

Colvert, C. C. 1939. *The public junior college*. Baton Rouge: Louisiana State University Press.

————. 1947. A half-century of junior colleges. *Junior College Journal* 17(6):244–47.

Diener, T. 1986. *Growth of an American institution*. Westport, Conn.: Greenwood Press.

Dougherty, K. 1987. The effects of community colleges: Aid or hindrance to socioeconomic attainment? *Sociology of Education* 60(April):86–103.

————. 1991. The community college at the crossroads: The need for structured reform. *Harvard Educational Review* 61(3):311–36.

Eaton, J. S. 1990a. An Academic Model of Transfer Education. *Working papers* 1(1). Washington, D.C.: American Council on Education/National Center for Academic Achievement and Transfer.

————. 1990b. Three myths of transfer education. *Community, Technical, and Junior College Journal* 60(6):18–20.

Eells, W. C. 1931. *The junior college*. Boston: Houghton Mifflin.

Gleazer, E. J., Jr. 1980. *The community college: Values, vision, and vitality*. Washington, D.C.: American Association of Community and Junior Colleges.

Grubb, W. H. 1991. The decline of community college transfer rates: Evidence from national longitudinal surveys. *Journal of Higher Education* 62(2):194–217.

Karabel, J. 1972. Community colleges and social stratification. *Harvard Educational Review* 42(4):521–62.

Kintzer, F. C. 1989. *Articulation and transfer: A review of current literature on statewide and interinstitutional program models and trends*. Prepared for the State of New Jersey Department of Higher Education. Los Angeles: University of California Press.

Koos, L. V. 1925. *The junior college movement*. Boston: Ginn.

Lee, V. E., and K. A. Frank. 1990. Student characteristics that facilitate transfer from two-year to four-year colleges. *Sociology of Education* 63:178–93.

Lombardi, J. 1979. *The decline of transfer education.* University of California, Los Angeles: ERIC Clearinghouse for Junior Colleges.

McDowell, F. M. 1919. *The junior college.* Department of the Interior, Bureau of Education Bulletin no. 35. Washington, D.C.: U.S. Government Printing Office.

Medsker, L. 1960. *The junior college: Progress and prospect.* New York: McGraw-Hill.

Monroe, C. R. 1972. *Profile of the community college.* San Francisco: Jossey-Bass.

National Center for Education Statistics. 1991. *Digest of education statistics 1991.* NCES 91–697. Washington, D.C.: U.S. Department of Education, Office of Research and Improvement.

Palmer, J. C. 1990. Is vocationalism to blame? *Community, Junior, and Technical College Journal* 60(6):21–25.

Palmer, J. C., and J. S. Eaton. 1991. Building the national agenda for transfer: A background paper. In *Setting the national agenda: Academic achievement and transfer, a policy statement and background paper about transfer education.* Washington, D.C.: American Council on Education/National Center for Academic Achievement and Transfer.

Parnell, D. 1985. *The neglected majority.* Washington, D.C.: American Association of Community and Junior Colleges.

Pascarella, E. T., and P. T. Terenzini. 1991. *How college affects students.* San Francisco: Jossey-Bass.

Pincus, F. 1980. The false promises of community colleges: Class conflict and vocational education. *Harvard Educational Review* 50(3):332–61.

Pincus, F. L., and E. Archer. 1989. *Bridges to opportunity: Are community colleges meeting the needs of minority students?* New York: Academy for Educational Development and the College Board.

Taylor, A. S. 1933. Curriculum research is urgently needed. *Junior College Journal* 3(5):246–48.

Weersing, F. J. 1931. Misconceptions regarding the junior college. *Junior College Journal* 1(6):363–69.

Wilson, R., and D. Carter. 1988. *Minorities in higher education: Seventh annual status report 1988.* Washington, D.C.: American Council on Education.

Zwerling, L. S. 1976. *Second best: The crisis of the community college.* San Francisco: Jossey-Bass.

The Shifting Focus in Determining the Legal Status of the American Community College

S. V. Martorana

What is the complete policy framework within which community colleges need to function? The answer to that question requires an understanding of the legal status of the institution, for it is from that broad threshold base of public policy that more particular policy requirements covering all aspects of community college operations flow. This chapter discusses the shifting focus of community college concern about the legal status of the institution and consequent relationships among governments (local, state, and federal) as reflected in the pertinent literature from the earliest writings recognizing the ''community college movement in America'' to the present day.

The legal status of the community college is defined as that statement of its purposes, scope, and modes of operations, protections, and obligations given to the institution by real law, that is, constitutions and statutes, as well as by case law, that is, the interpretation of law rendered by judgments of the courts, and administrative regulations which extend law as public policy to application in institutional operations. Since legal status is generated by actions of governments (local, state, federal) which also promulgate laws and applications of law for other aspects of public responsibility, such as health, welfare, transportation, and commerce, it is important to note that, conceptually, legal status is synonymous with public policy concerning the institution. In it, the general public through the machinery of government defines the place of the community college as a part, but only one part, of the total span of public responsibilities and concerns.

Several approaches were possible in the development of a presentation about community college legal status. One, for example, would emphasize the structural relationships created in the several states of the nation by the constitutions and statutes that establish public community colleges and define their realms of authority and responsibility as well as place them in some relationship with other units of government. These include administrative or regulatory boards of education or higher education and the executive departments typically found in a state's governmental structures. Another possible approach would emphasize attention to various aspects of institutional functioning, such as general administration, academic affairs, and student services, that are affected by governmental enactments. Neither of those two approaches is used here, however, for two reasons. First, they have been treated in other chapters of this handbook, albeit with less direct attention to definition and discussion of community college legal status. A secondary reason is that they have been extensively used and reported upon elsewhere. Examination of state-level structural relationships of state systems of higher education, including community colleges, dates back to the early 1960s (Glenny 1959; Martorana and Hollis 1960; Berdahl 1971), is a subject of recurrent reporting by the Education Commission of the States, and is covered comprehensively in a recent compilation cosponsored by the National Council of State Directors of Community Colleges and North Carolina State University (Fountain and Tollefson 1989). Examination of the impact of legislative actions upon particular aspects of community college operations is the objective of a long-standing series of monographs based on annual surveys of the states cosponsored by the National Council of State Directors of Community and Junior Colleges and the Center for the Study of Higher Education, Pennsylvania State University (Martorana et al., 1975–1991).

In this chapter, the approach to presentation centers upon the attention to concern evidenced by community colleges with respect to the locus of governmental authority at which the legal status of the community college is defined. Beyond this, it examines directions of change of the locus from one level of government to another, reactions in the field to those shifts, and the significance the reactions have to the present condition and the likely future of public community colleges.

DESCRIPTION AND BACKGROUND OF THE ISSUE

A reality surrounding community colleges, as in the case of all institutions serving a public purpose, is that they must function within a certain policy framework, that is, rules and regulations set by authorities outside of the institutions themselves. Most powerfully determining that framework are the actions of governments, particularly those taken by states. Given that reality, leaders and others interested in community colleges face an obligation and a choice. The obligation is to know, understand, and keep abreast of changes in the complete legal status of the institutions, for without that knowledge leadership in institutional development can encounter difficulties unnecessarily and institutional effectiveness can be impaired. The choice is whether to assume an active stance or a passive one in the shaping of public policy affecting community colleges. An active stance seeks a role in determining what the legal status of the community college is to be; a passive one leaves that determination to others and accepts the results that follow. Opportunity for leadership interests in the community college to influence and help shape the legal status of the institution exists even when the institution is largely associated in a legal structural sense with a single government as in the case of state-controlled and supported community colleges. The opportunity increases significantly when other governments at the local level and the federal government are seen as having a part in shaping community college legal status in a complete sense. How best to seize upon that opportunity and turn it to the advantage of the continued growth and development of the community college are persistent issues in the field.

Genesis

Evidence of concern about the legal status of community colleges appeared early in the literature on the American community college movement but attracted little attention at first. Two early general descriptions of the junior colleges in the United States (the precursor institutions to community colleges), both now considered classics in the literature, differed in the directions they saw the institutions developing. They, therefore, also differed with respect to the legal structure that their descriptions of the emerging institutions suggested would come to encompass them. One authority attached public junior colleges to the development of the American secondary school system (Koos 1924); the other put them more completely in the complex of college and university higher education (Eells 1931).

Neither Koos nor Eells, however, saw the legal status of junior colleges directly as a significant determinant in the case he was making. It is not until after more than 600 pages of detailed description of the status of junior colleges in the country in the early 1920s, during which the clear and consistent position is held that these institutions were to be established most commonly as extensions of public school systems, that Koos finally asked a question reflecting a concern about legal status. "Who will inspect the junior colleges?" he asked and then proceeded to reply that this duty should for a time remain as it was then "in the hands of the university of the state of location and the voluntary regional organization such as the North Central Association of Colleges and Secondary Schools" (641). In the next paragraph, however, he noted that, "there has been a rapid shift of responsibility in matters of inspection and supervision of high schools from the state university to state departments or state boards of education," and, later in the paragraph, he argued for "in time, an analogous shift of inspectional responsibility touching the junior college from state higher institutions to state departments of education" (641).

Eells dealt with the issue more directly, devoting a section headed "Legal Status" to the matter (Eells 1931, 37–40). In it he classified the kinds of statutory authorization given by the thirty states that, at the time of his reporting, had public junior colleges operating within their boundaries. He reported, "In twelve [states] they are authorized by general legislation, in seven others by special legislation, while in the remainder they seem to exist *without express legal sanction*" (40, emphasis added). Two observations about Eells' early writing are especially notable in the context of this chapter. The first is the important differentiation that Eells establishes between general and specific legislation. The former refers to state statutory authorization to any member of a certain class or type of local government such as school districts, cities, or counties, meeting general criteria specified in the law to establish a public junior college (or in more recent years to enter into a formal working arrangement with a community college); this type of legislation is also referred to as enabling legislation in works dealing with legal status. In contrast, special legislation is that which pertains specifically to a given subordinate authority identified in the law (a particular school district, a given municipality, a named four-year college or university) and defines for that authority a function connecting it with a junior or community college. Distinctions between general and special legislation are still applicable to enactments of the states and continue to be important in discussing legal status because they show a clearly different legislative intent. General legislation is more encompassing in its impact on community colleges in a state; special legislation has a more focused and limited application. Nevertheless, the latter type of enactment is often highly significant because of the ground-breaking or precedent setting effect (some may say the "camel's nose in the tent" effect) that it may have on community college developments, either positively or negatively, in a state.

The second notable observation in the matter quoted from Eells is the thought inherent in the claim that, in the eleven states having public junior colleges but operating under neither general nor special legislation, their presence was "without express legal sanction." That language clearly challenges the basic conclusion reached by Koos's earlier work and his relative inattention to the "legal status" of the junior college. Koos's position can be described as one that considered the legal status of the public junior college simply to be encompassed in the legal framework of the local public school district operating the college. Validity of such a view is apparent in the fact that there were, indeed, eleven states with public junior colleges but no evident authorizing legislation for their existence. Koos classified these junior colleges as "unified" (with secondary schools) and so properly to be seen as 13th and 14th grades. Although that view faded with time and community colleges now are clearly a part of higher education in America, the legal status of those institutions in many instances reflects their roots in the legal framework of the public schools as well as in that of public colleges and universities.

Finally, we should note the cogency of another generalization that Eells advances and its applicability to the present when approaches to defining the community college legal status are examined: "In too many cases, however, the laws passed represent the results of compromise, political manipulation, and guesswork rather than careful, scientific educational investigation and statesmanship. They represent what is, not necessarily what should be'' (556). That this generalization, because it is still quite valid, bears significant implications for community college leadership today is a major underlying theme of this chapter.

Persistence and Possibilities

In the sense of its fundamental legitimacy and a widespread acceptance of the community college in the society, questions about its legal status are now largely settled. Public institutions of the community college type are now found in all of the states except South Dakota. Early challenges to state constitutionality of their existence, including ones operating ''without express legal sanction,'' did not prevail (Simms 1948; McLeod 1983), and various forms of state opposition to their getting started proved to be ineffective (Pedersen 1987). Yet, in the sense of there being a clear-cut understanding of the complete legal status of the community college and the bearing that this has had on effective community college operations, confusion and ambiguity continue to be the case. When reporting on a restructuring and redirection of the American Association of Junior Colleges, Gleazer raised the question, ''Who calls the shots?'' and observed that ''[s]tate legislators are increasingly getting into the nitty-gritty of college operation, whether justified or not'' and tied the growing interest and involvements of the lawmakers to the issue of the need for increases in state financial support (Gleazer 1973, 127–28). Later, following an exhaustive survey of state structures and procedures for administering community colleges, Gleazer asked, ''Why should we be concerned to any great extent about legislative attitudes and the views of state-level officials if the community college destiny is so interwoven with the local scene?'' (Gleazer 1980, 92). Among the reasons that he offered were, again, the matter of needed financial support but also the need to keep the institution properly attuned to state interests, recognizing the strong hand of ''economic determinism'' and the fact that states like institutions change with the times. ''We miss something very important,'' he wrote, ''in our study of community colleges, however, if we assume that while these institutions are evolving state government remains unchanged. The fact is that state government has its own adaptive experiences to parallel those of the college'' (94). We will note the importance of a state's ''political culture'' in shaping community college legal status again later in this discussion.

We see in writings such as these the ambivalence of the community college with respect to a proper locus for determining the policy framework for its operations. Which government should have the strongest voice in determining the policy that guides community college development and, thereby, plays the predominant role in defining its legal status? Should it be the locality served, the state, the federal government, or, if all three, what kind of balance or proportion of power and influence should exist?

A quick answer to the question appears at hand when only structural and strictly constructed views are taken of provisions in constitutions and statutes. The ready answer is that the state has the clearest and strongest authority for setting public policy touching community colleges because the states derive authority for education in general from the residual powers clause of the 10th Amendment to the federal constitution. Any delegation of that authority requires action by the state, and determination of both the extent and nature of that delegation, therefore, is under control of state government. In that kind of legal context, a strict construction interpretation of locus of control would conclude that only the state and local governmental entities, when specifically delegated to do so by the state, would be able to shape the legal status of community colleges. There would remain, however, at least two major matters to resolve, both with high significance in development of a full understanding of community legal status. The first matter is which, from among the several subordinate components of a state's governmental structure, is to be given a part of the state's authority and so enter the picture of interorganizational involvements with the community college. Possibilities found in actual practice among the states include local boards of trustees with governing authority for community colleges, governing boards of four-year colleges or universities or systems of such institutions, state boards responsible for governance of or coordination of state systems of community colleges, boards of public schools, councils or commissions responsible for particular state governmental programs such as economic development or regional planning, and local general governmental jurisdictions such as townships, cities, and counties. Second is the matter of what should be scope, intensity, and the nature of the authority delegated. Possibilities, again drawn from actual state practices, range from full authority over all aspects of institutional operation to specific designation of a part or several parts. Examples are the sweeping authority of the institutional boards of the regional technical community colleges in Nebraska, on the one hand, and the specific restriction of involvement of local governments (counties, cities, school districts with local taxing authority) called upon to sponsor community colleges and to provide local tax support in Maryland, New Jersey, New York, and Pennsylvania.

The point to be noted here is that the states show a widely differing array of practices in discharging their authority and responsibility to provide education for their citizenry. Moreover, in developing those different approaches to determining a legal framework for community college operations, the states have put local governmental units (both those with primary duty for education and those with general governmental authority as well as ones with a quite narrow official purpose) in a position to shape community college legal status, but with varying points of concentration and power from state to state. Discussion of the reasons for this variation among the states is beyond the scope of this chapter, but they reflect differences in their economic and social evolution and the prevailing political culture (Garland and Martorana 1988).

Added to the reality that the local as well as state governments play significant roles in defining community college legal status is the fact that the federal government is also involved. While in the early years of the community college movement such a statement could not have been defended, it is clearly defensible today. How the federal government gets into the legal status picture and what behavior ought to be expressed in the community college field relative to the federal government's actions are unclear (Karabel et al. 1981; Cosand and Calais 1982). There can be no doubt, however, that the national interest is forcing a greater federal attention to education at all levels. Community college leadership for some years has shown a willingness to have the federal government be a significant partner in recognizing and facilitating the growth and development of their institutions. We will return to the way that the federal role is seen, sought, and reacted to later in this discussion.

Underlying Thesis

The main thesis underlying this chapter and the discussion to follow, then, must be seen in three parts parallel in their importance in examining the shifting focus of concern about the locus of control in determining the legal status of community colleges. One part of the thesis is that the lawmakers (local councils, boards, and executives; state legislatures and governors; members of Congress and the president) are the ones who formalize public policy and hence contribute to community college legal status when these institutions are involved. But when lawmakers do this, they proceed from the perspective of the public service that the institution is expected to provide; the lawmakers see community colleges as instruments for serving the special interests of the government of which they are a part. Another part of the thesis recognizes the contrasting view of leaders and others interested in community colleges who want to have legal status defined in such a way that the policy framework thus created will enable them to exercise a full degree of freedom in actions to enhance institutional conditions. The third part of the thesis is that the interplay generated by these differing perspectives between and among the several players involved develops into a political process, and the legal status of the community college is the result of that process. In sum, both the particular special interests of the different governments involved (several at the local level, the state, and the federal government), on the one hand, and the visions of institutional development held by the leadership of the community colleges, on the other, come to bear in understanding and developing a complete legal status for the community college.

Some might point out that there is a high congruity among the complex of these interests, much commonality in the sense of purpose to be served and direction of development to pursue, with respect to the interests of local, state, and federal government and the expectations of the institutions. From that conclusion, they might contend that the issue of a proper involvement of community college leaders in the formulation of the legal status of the community college and in promoting better understanding of it in a complete sense is not a significant issue or one of high interest in the movement. The literature on the movement and on the subject supports a different conclusion.

The longest and most continuous examination of the legal status of community colleges in the United States is available in various writings by Martorana (1950; 1952–1963). Reexamination of that fund of prior study and reflection upon its content viewed as a totality leads to four conclusions relative to the changing focus of attention to the governmental action that forms the legal status and public policy framework for community college operation. (1) The legislative intent of state statutory enactments is centered on community colleges as entities for serving primarily the state's best interests, not those of local communities or regions or that of a larger national or federal interest. This is so, even though at times state enactments are directed to enhance conditions at a local or regional level, because at the state level of government a statewide view prevails over a local one. Action initiated by a state can center in a locality and contribute to its welfare, but the larger outcome is expected to accrue benefit to the larger unit. (2) Areas of state legislative activity in which expressions of state interests are strongest are in the provisions of financial support as a steady and prevailing concern and in special enactments on individual topics of state interest which vary considerably from one period of time to another. (3) Three major factors contribute to the variation in topics attracting special legislative attention: changes in the state's and nation's economy and related concerns about economic development at all levels of government; enactments of the federal government taken in the national interest but structured for implementation at the state level; and a strong proclivity to deal with community colleges and to set policy to guide them as integral components of education in toto, all postsecondary or higher education, or even all state government as opposed to giving and holding for these institutions a clear and separate identity of mission, mode of operations, and needs. (4) Viewpoints of community college leaders as they deal with issues flowing from legal status and analysts of the challenges and opportunities put before the community colleges by virtue of shifts in public policy vary widely with respect to the response that the field should give to governmental actions both during the formative stages of legislation and after policy direction has become law.

In their quest for a response to governmental policy directives, community colleges shift the focus of their interest from one to another of the governments involved. The shift reflects an intent to ally with the governmental action or influence that appears most positively related to community college objectives and effective operations. The shift of community college attention among the governments involved is not a total one principally because of the state's predominant role. It is one, however, that has an impact on state government and community college relations and the legal status that results. We turn now to the direction of those shifts and their import to the movement.

FOCUS UPON LOCAL GOVERNMENTS

Discussion of community college legal status as a determination of local governmental action here is limited to three points. First, a definition of local governmental entities and their relationships to community colleges is advanced. Second, the drift away from the early focus on local governments and the resurgence of interest in them is explained. Third, the bearing of local governmental action on the perennial issue of financial support of community colleges being connected to policy direction and control is reviewed.

Definition of Local Governments

Jurisdictions of local government run a wide range: Some, such as towns, cities, and counties, have general governmental authority, and others, for example, public school districts and authorities caring for certain public utilities, transportation facilities, area land zoning, regional planning, and economic development, have a jurisdiction limited to particular functional areas.

Early literature on the legal status of the community college shows little concern about local governmental and public junior college relations except, as noted before, for the local public school districts. Questions about criteria for establishing junior colleges, their fiscal support, programming, and evaluation, were raised in a context either of public secondary education or as a part of college and university higher education and were deemed to lie in the province of authorities responsible for the schools or higher institutions. The issue of the balance of power between the state, on the one hand, and the local educational authority over the institution, on the other, however, soon became an intense issue and has been taken up in major general treatises on the community college (Bogue 1950; Medsker 1960; Cohen and Brawer 1982; Deegan and Tillery et al. 1985) and in many special examinations to the present day (Charles 1978; Stalcup 1978; Zoglin 1979).

Indications of concern and interest in authority exercised by types of local governments other than public school districts were virtually unknown. This was not universally true, however, for in some states, even in the early days of the movement, legal establishment of community colleges brought local governmental units other than those operating the schools into the picture. For example, the important role of the county governments in Mississippi in developing that state's system of junior colleges, one of the oldest in the country, is a major point in Bogue's overview of the movement (1950). Because the constitutions in several states restrict the number of authorities given a right to tax at the local level, and, further, because the general enabling laws for establishing community colleges in those states place them in the structure of higher education, these states devised another kind of relationship touching the community college. It requires that the local tax contribution to the formula for fiscal support of the institution be raised by authorities with the right to tax at that level, but it places general policy direction of the college in the hands of a local institutional board of trustees appointed in part by the governor and in part by the local authority or some form of joint action at the two levels. This structure is found in Maryland, New Jersey, New York, and Pennsylvania. It is interesting to note that, although in the realm of operations in these states the issue of the relationships best maintained by the community college with the local ''sponsor'' government that provides local tax support is a serious bone of contention, it has attracted little notice of scholar analysts in the field. An exception is a study of the case in New York State which found reasons for concern that sponsoring governments' oversight of community college budgets could complicate college operations (Phelon 1968).

Shift of Focus Away from and Back to Local Government

The shift from local to state government as the primary focus of concern in determining the legal status of the community college is well documented. It has been a matter of special attention in Millard's work and the spate of reports and publications he and others have produced under the auspices of the Education Commission of the States (Millard 1976) as well as in the series of reports on state legislation (Martorana 1975–1991) released by the Penn State Center for the Study of Higher Education and the series on community college financing at the University of Florida, Institute for Higher Education (Wattenbarger 1973–1990). The impact of the shift to focusing on state government and reactions of the field to it in terms of relationships with state government will be discussed more fully later in this chapter.

What has not yet caught a great deal of attention among analysts, however, is a new shift back from the state to local governments. It shows quite different objectives in legislative intent and brings community colleges into operating relationships with new forms of government at the local and regional levels. Legislative intent is economic development and is promoted by governmental interest at all three levels: local, state, and federal (Myran 1978). The result is that a still wider range of local entities with power to shape or influence the shape of community college programs and services is emerging. Community college literature in recent years discloses a growing interest in private business and industry councils, regional planning commissions, and similar governmental or quasigovernmental agencies. The widening scope of community college involvement with these new local and regional development agencies brings complications in community college programming and policy direction, opportunities for diversification of fiscal support, and openings for new forms of leadership operating at the local level in shaping the legal status of these institutions (Bard and Orlinsky 1974; California Association of Community and Junior Colleges 1978; Scott 1987; Jardine 1990). That this rediscovery of the need to connect the interests of local governments with those of a higher level is likely to attract more notice soon is evident in the heightening concern about the condition of American cities and public policies for their renewal (Parnell 1978).

Emergence and Persistence of Debate over Control of Policy and Fiscal Support

One of the most difficult problems facing community colleges is keeping separate the issues of the level of financial support provided by a government or other source and the level of control over the policy direction of the institution it is to exert. Indeed, the problem is a classic one that has confronted education in general for many years. The problem arises whenever action shaping the legal status of the community college is contemplated at any level of government. When local taxing authorities, for example, are required by state law to assume the role of "sponsors" of community colleges and are expected to provide local tax support, what roles de jure or de facto can they be expected to play? (Phelon 1968). They tend to get more involved when the federal government initiates nationwide programs for economic development and authorizes local or regional entities to work with community colleges, among other resources, to accomplish that purpose. The consequences for the community college can be a "two-edged sword" (Martorana and Garland 1984).

This issue beleaguers community colleges throughout the land. As they act to turn relationships with local governments to their advantage, they, once again, face the obligation to know what might be done and to choose active or passive involvement in the process.

THE BACK AND FORTH ON A STATE VERSUS A FEDERAL ALLIANCE

While the fact is that state government is most powerful in direct determination of the legal status of community colleges, an associated fact is becoming increasingly evident, namely, that a state's exercise of its power can be significantly influenced by actions of governments at other levels. This is particularly true of those actions taken by the federal government. Recognizing that their institutions serve the federal government in its promotion of the national interest, as well as state and local interests of concern to governments at those levels, community colleges seek affiliation with governments at all three levels with a different degree of emphasis and effort at different times.

Wooing Federal Identification

Following World War II and toward the close of the "boom" years of expansion of the community college movement that took place roughly between 1945 and 1970, community colleges sought strenuously to get a recognized status and identity in federal law. The reason for this was, in part, based on philosophic outlook and the argument that community colleges had a duty and a capability to serve the nation at large as well as the state and the federal government, making a case for having the federal government become a partner in recognizing and supporting the movement. In part, the thrust was based on the pragmatic perception that a stronger linkage with the federal government and its capacity to provide both programmatic and fiscal support was a useful alternative to preeminent dependence on state financing and state domination of policy control. The drive for a federal-level recognition was a coordinated effort of the American Association of Community and Junior Colleges, state, and local leadership which sought enactment of a comprehensive or "omnibus" bill on the community college (Martorana 1966). With the assistance of several key members of Congress, the effort culminated in the enactment of the Community College Act, Title X of the 1972 amendments to the Higher Education Act. This accomplishment led at first to a unit within the Office of Education and a strengthened staff attention to community college development in the nation, but in more recent years both the place of the community college within the structure of federal government and the level of direct attention it is getting in policy deliberations there have eroded. Nonetheless, there is clear involvement of federally determined public policy in legally structured operations of community colleges, and community college leadership, particularly that centered in the American Association of Community and Junior Colleges and the Association of Community College Trustees, devotes significant energy to keeping abreast and participating in the shaping of policy directions at the federal level.

Action toward increasing the federal government role in this respect, however, was not unanimously supported when it was first sought nor universally welcomed among community colleges when achieved. The impact of federal policy directions on community colleges became both a matter of debate (Howe 1979; Watson 1980) and one of study and analysis (Opacinch 1981; Cosand and Calais 1982; Bell 1988) with again a major concern expressed about the connection between control of policy and provision of fiscal support (Martin 1971; Orcutt 1974; Phillips 1985). It is worthy to note that this concern about relationships with the federal government was not confined to the public community colleges. Private, independent junior colleges felt it, too, and they launched similar efforts to understand the full impact of federal public policy on their institutions (Pelham and Fadil 1977).

WHERE IS THE GYROSCOPE? RETURN TO STATE-LEVEL FOCUS

An examination of the writings and research on the community college in recent years shows concern about the legal status of the institution in a continuing condition of flux. On the one hand, there is evidence of a fall back and acceptance of the dominant power of the state, on the other, there is evidence that the states are ready to permit a greater voice of the local and federal governments in shaping community college legal status particularly if in so doing there can be some relief to state obligation to provide fiscal support.

Resurgence of State Prominence and Field Reaction

Numerous publications at hand speak to the growing exercise of power by the state in setting community college policy directions. The discussion covered shows again the differing views of the lawmakers and community college leaders in the approach taken to policy direction. Some legislators state categorically a right to dominate the roles to be played (Gordon 1988). Field reaction to the trend toward more state governmental action brings calls for increased involvement and improved practices in lobbying in the state-level political process (Angel 1980; Phillips et al. 1980; Martorana and Broomall 1983) and suggestions that new conceptualization of leadership roles are needed (Terrey 1982; Martorana 1985, 1989).

Also emerging are a few thrusts to establish a more scientifically, empirically based determination of a proper approach to shaping the legal status of the community college. In my view, these instances do not match the degree that the subject merits attention in the field. As noted throughout this chapter, documentation and description of the structure by which governments and community colleges interact are well developed in available literature; so are the narration and analysis of the areas and topics of community college operations in which legislators are interested and tend to influence public policy. These are necessary steps toward development of a better theoretical approach to the subject, but more attention to the next steps is needed. A greater research and scholarly analytical effort, which builds on the established base of descriptive material, is badly needed.

Only a handful of doctoral dissertations pertinent to this subject can be found, and a similarly scant number of research-based reports are to be found in a review of scholarly journals. Several lines of inquiry are found in the research and scholarly materials review. One is a concern about organizational relationships involving governmental agencies and community colleges and modes of administrative practice within the various structures (Phelon 1968; McGovern 1984; Hobson and Glasman 1985; Theis 1986; Fain 1987; Knapp 1988; Fonte 1989). Another is concerned with the justification or explanation of the history, mission, or social purpose of community colleges with attention to perspectives of governmental as well as community college leaders (Glenn 1985; Dougherty 1988). Still another direction of research looks into the political process in which community colleges are caught when dealing with governments and the consequences generated by different factors entering into it (Bender 1976; Garland 1987; Haeser 1988; George 1990). Lach (1981) makes a good case for deepening and broadening the data bases pertinent to public policy concerns of community colleges and the research work related to them.

Another manifestation of community college effort to acquire more flexibility in dealing with state government, especially with respect to acquiring fiscal resources and support, is their relatively recent interest in attracting private sector support. The effort brings forth still another question in defining legal status: the place of community foundations and their working relationships with community colleges and the several levels of government. Community college foundations can be classified as quasi-public entities. They can be helpful mechanisms not only for acquisition of resources from private sources, but also for integrating local, state, and federal programs, all in the best interests of the institution.

Consequences of Reneging in State-Level Support

To some degree states, while continuing to assert primary governmental position in setting public policy over community colleges, are also yielding some way to voices of local and federal interests. Evidence of this is seen most clearly in the way in which fiscal support from local and federal sources, private sources, and tuition increases are making up shortfalls in state support (Wattenbarger and Mercer 1988). When state support declines significantly, community colleges within a legal structure that permits doing so go to other sources; those without such a permissive structure seek to acquire it. An example of the latter is found in the present efforts of some community colleges in Florida to hold citizen referendums to authorize temporary local tax support (Kelley 1992). Again, the result is a heightened involvement of community college leadership in the political process of intergovernmental action that shapes the community college legal status.

CONCLUSIONS AND IMPLICATIONS FOR THE FUTURE

Six conclusions are supported by the discussion in this chapter. (1) Given the nature of constitutions and statutory authority held in a strictly legal sense by the state, in contrast to local governments and the federal government, the strong likelihood is that the state will continue to be the primary focus for attention to matters of legal status. (2) Reaffirmation of the critical role played by community colleges in advancing the local and regional interests of local governments and the recognition of their growing importance in serving the larger national interest of the federal government will permit continuation and even enhancement of the current community college leadership practice of drawing upon all levels of government to help shape community college legal status. (3) Such a conclusion and the action to build upon it lead to the further conclusion that community college leaders will continue to be involved in a political process with representatives of all of the several governments having a voice in public policy direction. (4) Leadership among community colleges has yet to formulate a general plan and strategic line of action to follow at state and federal levels in the shaping of public policy directions. (5) Programs of clear purpose and substance designed to deepen the understanding of legal status and to improve the practice of community colleges in dealing with lawmakers and others in public policy formation and related political action in shaping or restructuring legal status, when that is deemed desirable for community college enhancement, are in the early stages of formation. (6) Research basic to the development of a sound foundation of knowledge and theory to undergird professional practice in the field is rudimentary and needs much more attention and a greater effort.

Confronting Issues

An axiom in social and political development is that change will occur and will affect institutions, particularly those that serve a public purpose, whether or not the personnel responsible for the institutions take part in the process of change. A large issue before community colleges today, therefore, is what decisions must be made about the strategy to be followed to keep abreast of the public policy that guides them and in what ways community college leadership should participate in the process. Wing (1982) advised a strategy of identifying consensual goals and concentrating on them.

Another issue related to that just stated is determination of the lines of action, that is, what is to be a constructive division of roles to be played by the several centers for community college leadership in the country in order to produce more concerted behavior toward shaping community college legal status constructively. Obvious among such centers are the national associations, especially the American Association of Community and Junior Colleges, the Association of Community College Trustees, and the National Council of State Directors of Community and Junior Colleges. Prominent also are the several universities that offer graduate school programs of leadership training for community colleges and the free-standing League for Innovation. Which among these and possibly other groups of community college workers should take the lead in developing strategies for community college involvement in the political process through which the legal status of these institutions is defined? A clear answer is yet to be seen.

Finally, among the issues community colleges must face in working toward a most advantageous public policy framework for the institution is that of finding its place in the total structure of education. The issue changes over time as already noted, but it will not go away. Forces, beyond the actions of the governments themselves, are encouraging creation of new structures involving community colleges along with a wide array of other educational and cultural factors, in effect a "communiversity," to engage in new forms of relationships with governments (Martorana and Kuhns 1985).

Implications for the Future

From their beginnings, community colleges have been viewed as instruments for serving the interests primarily of a local community or a closely defined region. That notion still dominates the definition of their educational mission. Increasingly, however, these institutions are taking on and delivering on a commitment to be of service to the public more broadly defined. The concept of its utility in public service and its obligation to respond has expanded from the locality and region to the state and, now by formal identification in federal law, to the nation. Some say that by virtue of their duty and capacity to engender in their students an awareness and appreciation of global conditions and concerns, community colleges are serving an international public interest and will do so more increasingly (Yarrington 1978).

If these observations are true with respect to these public interests, it follows that the governments responsible for upholding and promoting those interests will seek closer working relationships with community colleges. Prospects, therefore, are that the actions of governments at all levels in the future will likely touch upon community colleges more rather than less. Failure to recognize that tendency will isolate community colleges rather than involve them with other key participants in effecting social progress at local, regional, state, national, and international levels. The opportunity to build a common understanding and viewpoint among that complex of governments for which the community college is an agent and to translate that vision into a constructive interest in the institution is in the grasp of today's leadership of the movement. The shape of the future community college in America will be determined by how this opportunity is handled.

REFERENCES

American Association of Community and Junior Colleges. 1985–1990. AACJC public policy agenda. *Community, Junior, and Technical Journal*, vols. 55–59.

———. 1988. *Building communities: A vision for a new century*. Washington, D.C.

Angel, D. 1980. Legislative lobbying: It's 3-dimensional. *Community and Junior College Journal* 5(3):34–37.

Bard, H., and W. Orlinsky. 1974. Communicating with local governmental officials. *Community and Junior College Journal* 44(4):32–33.

Bell, T. H. 1988. The federal imprint. *New Directions for Community Colleges* 16(4):9–13.

Bender, L. W. 1976. Forces which damage constructive relationships from the two-year college system perspective. Paper presented at a seminar for state leaders in postsecondary education, January, Saint Petersburg, Florida.

Berdahl, R. 1971. *Statewide coordination of higher education*. Washington, D.C.: American Council on Education.

Bogue, J. P. 1950. *The community college*. New York: McGraw-Hill.

California Association of Community and Junior Colleges. 1978. *CETA comes to college*. Sacramento, Calif.

Charles, S. F., ed. 1978. *Balancing state and local control*. New Directions for Community Colleges 6(23). San Francisco: Jossey-Bass.

Cohen, A., M., and F. B. Brawer. 1982. *The American community college*. San Francisco: Jossey-Bass.

Cosand, J. P., and M. J. Calais. 1982. Shaping federal policy to maximize institutional impact. *New Directions for Community Colleges* 10(2):65–78.

Deegan, W. L., D. Tillery, and Associates. 1985. *Renewing the American community college*. San Francisco: Jossey-Bass.

Dougherty, K. J. 1988. The politics of community college expansion: Beyond the functionalist and class-reproduction explanations. *American Journal of Education* 96(3):351–93.

Education Commission of the States. 1973. *Coordination or chaos?* Report of the Task Force on Coordination, Governance, and Structure of Postsecondary Education. Denver, Colo.

———. 1989. *New issues new roles*. Denver, Colo.

Eells, W. C. 1931. *The junior college*. New York: Houghton-Mifflin.

Fain, A. 1987. Managerial role perceptions of chief executive officers of state community college systems. Ph.D. diss., University of North Carolina, Chapel Hill.

Fonte, R. 1989. Financial governance patterns among two-year colleges. Paper presented at the annual meeting of the Association for the Study of Higher Education, November 2–5, Atlanta, Georgia.

Fountain, B. E., and T. A. Tollefson. 1989. *Community colleges in the United States: Forty-nine state systems*. Washington, D.C.: American Association of Community and Junior Colleges.

Garland, P. H. 1987. The relationship between political culture and patterns of interaction within policy subsystems for community college education. Ph.D. diss., Pennsylvania State University.

Garland, P. G., and S. V. Martorana. 1988. The interplay of political culture and participant behavior in political action to enact significant state community college legislation. *Community College Review* 16(2):30–43.

George, O. J., Jr. 1990. Perceptions of Delaware Technical and Community College in budgetary and legislative process of the State of Delaware. Ph.D. diss., University of Delaware.

Gleazer, E. J., Jr. 1973. *Project focus: A forecast study of community colleges*. New York: McGraw-Hill.

———. 1980. *The community college: Values, vision, and vitality*. Washington, D.C.: American Association of Community and Junior Colleges.

Gleazer, E. J., Jr., and R. Yarrington, ed. 1974. *Coordinating state systems*. New Directions for Community Colleges, no. 6. San Francisco: Jossey-Bass.

Glenn, A. M. 1985. The influence of selected government legislation on the development of the community colleges in Manitoba. Ph.D. diss., University of North Dakota.

Glenny, L. A. 1959. *Autonomy of public colleges: The challenge of coordination*. New York: McGraw-Hill.

Gordon, J. D. 1988. The Gordon Rule: A state legislator fulfills his responsibility. *New Directions for Community Colleges* 16(4):23–30.

Haeser, P. N. 1988. Explaining state variations in community college policies. Ph.D. diss., University of Wisconsin, Milwaukee.

Hobson, A. R., and N. S. Glasman. 1985. The community college and statewide administration. *Community/Junior College Quarterly of Research and Practice* 9(4):303–16.

Howe, H. 1979. The view from the middle. *Community Services Catalyst* 9(1):4–7.

Jardine, D. K. 1990. Involving the community. Paper presented at the 1990 Summer

Academy of the Association of Washington Community College Administrators, August 7–9, Vancouver, British Columbia.

Karabel, J., et al. 1981. *The politics of federal higher education policy making: 1945–1980.* Washington, D.C.: National Institute of Education.

Kelley, J. T. 1992. Interview. Fort Lauderdale, Fla., Jan. 18. (Vice President, Miami-Dade Community College—North Campus).

Knapp, S. E. 1988. Formal organizational structure. Ph.D. diss., Temple University.

Koos, L. V. 1924. *The junior college.* Minneapolis: University of Minnesota Press.

Lach, I. J. 1981. Research for policy formation at the state level. *New Directions for Community Colleges* 9(3):5–15.

Martin, M. 1971. The federal government behind the open door. *Peabody Journal of Education* 48(4):282–85.

Martorana, S. V. 1950. Recent state legislation affecting junior colleges. *Junior College Journal* 20:241–52.

———. 1952, 1956, 1960, 1963. The legal status of American public junior colleges. *American Junior Colleges*, 3rd 4th, 5th, 6th eds. Washington, D.C.: American Council on Education.

———. 1966. A positive community junior college policy for lawmakers. Paper presented at the 46th annual convention of the American Association of Junior Colleges, February 27–March 3. Saint Louis, Missouri.

———. 1985. Why and how to develop a positive liaison with state lawmakers: A lesson from trends in state legislation affecting community, junior, and two-year technical colleges. In *Resource notebook: Academy on state legislation.* Washington, D.C.: Association of Community College Trustees.

———. 1989. Reflections on a movement. *Community, Technical, and Junior College Journal* 590(1):42–48.

Martorana, S. V., and J. Broomall. 1983. State, federal lawmakers must hear from college. *Community and Junior College Journal* 53(6):18–20.

Martorana, S. V., and P. H. Garland. 1984. Public policy for economic development: The two-edged sword. *Community and Junior College Journal* 55(3):16–19.

Martorana, S. V., and E. V. Hollis. 1960. *State boards responsible for higher education.* Washington, D.C.: U.S. Government Printing Office.

Martorana, S. V., and E. Kuhns. 1985. Designing new structures for state and local collaboration. In *Renewing the American community college*, ed. W. Deegan, D. Tillery, and Associates, 229–51. San Francisco: Jossey-Bass.

Martorana, S. V., et al. 1975–1991. *State legislation affecting community, junior, and two-year technical colleges.* University Park: Pennsylvania State University, Center for the Study of Higher Education.

McGovern, J. P. 1984. Who controls the community college? An analysis of the placement and appropriateness of effective authority in the governance of State University of New York community colleges. Ph.D. diss., Hofstra University.

McLeod, M. W. 1983. Constitutional provisions for community junior colleges. *Community/Junior College Quarterly of Research and Practice* 7:175–82.

Medsker, L. L. 1960. *The junior college: Progress and prospect.* New York: McGraw-Hill.

Millard, R. M. 1976. The new game. Paper presented at a seminar for state leaders in postsecondary education, December. Oklahoma City, Oklahoma.

Myran, G. A. 1978. Technology transfer: Emerging area of service. *Community and Junior College Journal* 49(1):10–12.

Opacinch, C. 1981. Federal postsecondary policy. *New Directions for Community Colleges* 9(3):17–23.

Orcutt, J. 1974. *Federal relations in community and junior colleges*. Washington, D.C.: National Council for Resource Development.

Parnell, D. 1978. Urban extension act: Needed federal support. *New Directions for Community Colleges* 6(1):65–69.

Pedersen, R. 1987. State government and the junior college, 1901–1946. *Community College Review* 14(4):48–52.

Pelham, P., and V. Fadil. 1977. *A survey of public policy priorities at independent two-year colleges*. Washington, D.C.: National Association of Independent Colleges and Universities.

Phelon, P. 1968. A study of the impact of local sponsors in the educational policy and operation of selected community colleges in New York state. Ph.D. diss., State University of New York at Albany.

Phillips, H. E., et al. 1980. Lobbying state legislators. Paper presented at annual conference of the American Association of Community and Junior Colleges, March 30–April 12. San Francisco, California.

Phillips, R. G. 1985. *Federal support for higher education: A positive perspective*. Miami: Miami-Dade Community College District.

Scott, R. 1987. Proven partners: Business, government, and education. *Community, Junior, and Technical College Journal* 57(3):16–19.

Simms, C. W. 1948. *The present legal status of the junior college*. Nashville: George Peabody College for Teachers.

Stalcup, R. 1978. Local control of community colleges: Myth and reality. *Community College Frontiers* 6(2):33–36.

Terrey, J. N. 1982. Toward effective state legislative relations. *New Directions for Institutional Advancement* 15:83–89.

Theis, A. S. 1986. Interorganizational coordination as a policy implementation strategy: Community colleges and service delivery areas in Maryland under the Job Training Partnership Act. Ph.D. diss., University of Maryland.

Watson, N. 1980. The community college in the 1980s: Promise and perils. Paper presented at the annual convention of the American Association of Community and Junior Colleges, March 30–April 2. San Francisco, California.

Wattenbarger, J. L. 1973–1990. *State financing of public community colleges*. Gainesville: University of Florida, Institute for Higher Education.

Wattenbarger, J. L., and S. L. Mercer. 1988. *Financing community colleges, 1988*. Washington, D.C.: American Association of Community and Junior Colleges.

Wing, P. 1982. Emerging relationships between community colleges and state and local agencies. *New Directions for Community Colleges* 10(2):51–64.

Yarrington, R., ed. 1969. *Junior colleges: 50 states/50 years*. Washington, D.C.: American Association of Junior Colleges.

———. 1978. *Internationalizing community colleges*. Report of the 1978 Assembly covered by the AACJC in cooperation with the Johnson Foundation, October 18–20, 1977. Wingspread, Wisconsin. Washington, D.C.: American Association of Community and Junior Colleges.

Zoglin, M. L. 1979. Thwarting the big bad wolf. *Community and Junior College Journal* 50(2):24–25.

The Community College Mission

Quentin J. Bogart

It is difficult, if not impossible, to describe an American higher education institution today without focusing on its *mission*. Defining and refining the mission has been a national, state, and local preoccupation among college and university leaders for the past decade—and this activity continues as communities and the social, political, and economic issues relating to and supporting them change.

The context for this chapter on "mission" is the institution we know today as the community college. Conceived and nurtured as the junior college in the late nineteenth and early twentieth centuries, it has changed over time. "During the 1950s and 1960s, the term junior college was applied more often to the lower-division branches of private universities and to two-year colleges supported by churches or organized independently" (Cohen and Brawer 1989). The 1960s through the early 1970s witnessed the community college's explosive development on the national educational scene with its community orientation, open-door admission, and comprehensive program.

MISSION DEFINED

The term, mission, according to the current edition of *Webster's Collegiate Dictionary*, means the specific task one is charged with—in the case of community colleges, the mission is what the institution purports to do. An expanded and somewhat more complex version is presented by Simerly and Associates in discussing the strategic planning process. They define mission as "what the institution will contribute to society, whom it will serve, how it will serve them, and (the) social benefits that will result" (Apps 1988). Gleazer (1980) believes the term mission is analogous to a process. Frequently such terms as role, function, and purpose are used interchangeably with mission in describing what the community colleges do.

STATUS AND BACKGROUND

According to *The Chronicle of Higher Education's Almanac* (1991), there were 1,408 two-year institutions in the fall of 1989. Of these, 968 were classified as public; the other 440 institutions were classified as private. Although many of these colleges and institutes appear to share similar missions, most have characteristics that set them apart from their peers.

Paul Elsner, chancellor of the huge Maricopa County Community College District serving the greater Phoenix, Arizona, area, echoes this notion. He indicates that defining the current mission of the American community college is an extremely difficult and complex task. "What makes it complex," he states, "is that we don't exactly have 50 versions in 50 states. One needs to take into account the fact that what may be a sound mission in one state, may only be part of a mission in another" (Elsner 1992). Thus, mission statements will vary to allow for the kaleidoscope of functions community colleges and the organizations representing them perform at the national, state, and local levels.

MISSION AND HISTORY

No discussion of the community college or its mission should be launched without briefly reviewing the history of the junior college and its role. Placed in a "time context," it covers what Deegan and Tillery (1985) term the first two generations (or developmental periods) of the two-year college's existence— Generation 1, extension of high school (1900–1930), and Generation 2, Junior College (1930–1950).

The American Association of Junior Colleges in 1922 reported the primary mission of the junior college as "offering two years of instruction of strictly collegiate grade" (Thornton 1972). Supporting this mission were the ideas that a system of junior colleges would relieve the pressure on universities that were growing rapidly, provide a nurturing atmosphere for youthful students during maturation, and enable struggling, small, church-related, and other private four-year colleges an opportunity to reorganize as stronger, more economical junior colleges offering only the freshman and sophomore years of university study. This mission was barely established before it was expanded to include "terminal" education—or occupational education as we now know it. Nevertheless, over the next forty years, the two-year college mission continued to focus primarily on the transfer function (Monroe 1972).

It is likely that the initial statement of the community college's mission evolved from the report of the President's (Truman) Commission on Higher Education in 1947:

Whatever form the community college takes, its purpose is educational service to the entire community, and this purpose requires of it a variety of functions and programs. It will provide college education for the youth of the community certainly, so as to remove geographic and economic barriers to educational opportunity and discover and develop individual talents at low cost and easy access. But in addition, the community college will serve as an active center of adult education. It will attempt to meet the total post–high school needs of its community. (Levine 1979)

This single statement, perhaps more than any other, set the tone for the mission—guiding the development of the community college and transforming it into the institution we see today.

THE IMPORTANCE OF MISSION

By definition and in practice, the mission of the American college community is the most important element of its being. Scores of writers including several of those noted earlier in this discourse have reviewed, researched, and redesigned its mission. It is a topic that is always timely and usually tepid.

Of all the words written about the mission of the community college, perhaps Gleazer's best describe its importance. Gleazer (1980) believes the community college mission is "to encourage and facilitate lifelong learning with community as process and product." Put another way, the community college should be so closely woven in the life of the community that it becomes difficult to determine where college programs end and community projects begin.

Triggering a recent and renewed interest in the mission of the American community college was *Building Communities: A Vision for a New Century* (1988), the report of the American Association of Community and Junior Colleges' (AACJC's) nineteen-member Commission on the Future of Community Colleges. In its opening chapter, the commission proposes that "*Building Communities* become the rallying point for the community college in America." According to the commission's report "Building communities is . . . an especially appropriate objective for the community college because it embraces the institution's comprehensive mission. . . . The building of community, in its broadest and best sense, encompasses a concern for the whole, for integration and collaboration, for openness and integrity, for inclusiveness and self-renewal." Given this national community college manifesto, states such as Arizona, California, North Carolina, and Virginia subsequently developed their own future reports focusing on system-wide missions.

The writings of Cross and Fideler (1989), Vaughan (1988), Clowes and Levin (1989), Martorana (1989), and Evans (1990) further supported this rekindling of interest in the community college mission. Given this emphasis and the current aggressive competition for public and private resources, the leadership of individual community colleges and other institutions of higher education have involved their faculties, administrators, staff, students, and other constituent groups in reexamining the institution's mission using a variety of strategic planning approaches (Apps 1988; Simmons 1991).

This writer, for more than twenty years, has had the privilege of teaching a graduate survey course on the community college. Frequently, changes and variations in the approach to the course are suggested and made; without exception, however, the initial and central topic covered by the class is the *mission* of the community college. Its open-door admission, its low cost, its comprehensive curriculum, its geographic accessibility, its focus on teaching, its concern for students, its community orientation, and its innovativeness and flexibility shape the mission in the most synergistic sense. Rest assured, the 2,500 to 3,500 course alumni know about and believe in this version of the community college mission! Many of them have had key roles in helping to fulfill it!

THE LITERATURE OF MISSION

The difficulty (and frustration) in trying to organize the literature describing the community college's mission covers a continuum from global to focused and from national to local with considerable overlap and confusion along the way. It has been organized by Cross into themes or foci labeled as "comprehensive, vertical, horizontal, integrated, and remedial" (Deegan et al. 1985); as "partnerships for learning, the curriculum to be taught, the community created by the classroom, the quality of campus life, the connections beyond the college, and the leadership required" by the Commission on the Future of Community Colleges (1988); and as "transfer, career preparation, basic skills and developmental education, continuing education and community service, and access" by Doucette and Hughes (1990).

For the purposes of this discourse, an attempt has been made to weave the literature on mission into six areas: (1) governance and leadership, (2) student development, (3) instruction and faculty, (4) curriculum/programs, (5) economic development, and (6) lifelong learning. Still there exists considerable overlap.

Mission as Related to Governance and Leadership

One could argue that every aspect of the community college's mission is tied to governance. Deegan and Tillery (1985) note "that governance and finance involve fundamental issues of social policy: equity, efficiency, and educational mission."

It would be difficult to dispute the fact that governance and the decision-making process not only impact institutional mission, but serve to shape it as well. Attesting to the importance of this relationship, John Losak, of the Miami-Dade Community College, a contributor to *Assessing Institutional Effectiveness in Community Colleges* (Doucette and Hughes 1990) wrote that "mission statements can be vital documents that reflect a college's explicit and focused purposes, which are examined and updated regularly by a consensual process involving all of its major constituents'' (4).

However, it can be claimed that the reverse is true also—that mission can influence governance and decision making. This view of the interrelationship of governance to mission is pointed out by Fryer and Lovas:

Whether stated formally in writing, articulated informally in conversations, or simply understood implicitly, the mission and philosophy of a community college shape the context for decision-making. When members of the organization share compatible philosophies and hold clear understandings of institutional mission, decisions are more readily arrived at than in places where fundamental differences about philosophy and conflicting understandings of mission exist among leaders and others in the organization. (1990, 28)

Obviously, then, the community college is mission, and the decision-making governance processes are inextricably linked. One of the basic themes found in *Shared Vision* (Roueche, Baker, and Rose 1989) is that community college leaders are ''visionaries'' when it comes to interpreting and communicating institutional mission and influencing changes in it. ''The function of leadership in governance,'' write Fryer and Lovas (1990, 33), ''is to create the conditions within which people want to decide and want to act in ways that maximize the institution's achievement of its purposes.'' Parnell, former AACJC president, expands on this position:

Nothing is more important for an effective leader than to clarify the mission of the organization. . . . Communicating vision is a fundamental task of leadership. Mission clarification and goal setting, therefore, are priority tasks for an effective leader. . . . A leader sets the tone, the motivation, and the positive attitudes about the future of an organization or the group that he or she is leading and articulates these clearly as part of the mission and goals of the organization. (1988, 1)

Those who govern and lead tend to present the community college mission in ''comprehensive'' terms, to use Cross's typology. According to Cross, ''Among community college educators, the comprehensive mission is far and away the favorite.'' She defines this *comprehensive mission* as including ''the five traditional programs of community colleges'' advanced by Cohen and Brawer in *The American Community College*: (1) career education, (2) compensatory education, (3) community education, (4) the collegiate function, and (5) general education (Deegan et al., 1985, 36).

Whether this leadership view of mission best represents the overall ''warp and weave'' of the American community college is subject to debate. Cross puts her mission typology in perspective when she states that the ''other [mission] foci are proposed . . . as priorities of or improvements needed 9in a given area within the comprehensive mission'' (Deegan et al., 1985, 36). To the casual student of the community college mission (or to its critics), this view may appear to be a paradox—and perhaps it is.

Alfred and Linder, in their study of the opinions of 2,410 trustees, executives, administrators, and faculty representing 130 community colleges in all fifty states, identified "eight important attributes of paradox." The first of these was "mission." "Effective community colleges," they write, "are simultaneously oriented toward a comprehensive mission that permits wide latitude in adapting to the environment and toward a specific mission which allow them to focus on the special needs of particular groups" (1990, 3–4).

Perhaps this effectively serves to point out that from a governance and leadership point of view the mission of the community college is both as comprehensive as its program and as narrow as the principal elements which compose it.

Mission as Related to Student Development

The mission of the community college from a student development perspective seems to focus on helping students succeed. Shaw, writing about student development reform and rebirth states, "The only new dimension . . . is the intricate web of support that helps students succeed" (1989, 83). The mission of student success tends to mandate that student development continue to embrace a variety of services including (1) assuring open-door admission; (2) providing educational, career, and personal counseling; (3) supplying financial and academic assistance; and (4) supporting a wide range of out-of-class college and community-based activities.

Most student development leaders see their professional endeavors as being "holistic" in nature—tied as closely to instruction and curriculum as they are to those services that directly support students. Perhaps this explains why much of the literature on student development links its mission with those related to instructional programs. An illustration of this interrelationship is found in O'Banion's essay, "Student Development Philosophy: A Perspective on the Past and Future" (1989). His section on the community college mission reviews the broad mission of the community college as expressed in terms of its open-door and its comprehensive program noting shifts in student demand away from the liberal arts toward the new technologies. "These challenges—the quality reformation, educational technology, finance, and the community college mission—are the major issues facing the community college in the coming decade. As such, they are also the major issues to be faced by the student personnel who will assume responsibility for defining the student development models of the future" (O'Banion 1989, 14).

A second aspect of mission related to student development is that of serving a diversity of students. The Commission on the Future of Community Colleges underscores the importance of student diversity: "The nation's community colleges should vigorously reaffirm equality of opportunity as an essential goal. Every college should declare . . . its determination to serve all ages and racial and ethnic groups" (1988, 10). The commission recommends some thoughtful steps for achieving both student diversity and success including (1) reaffirming equality of opportunity as an essential goal; (2) developing an aggressive outreach program for disadvantaged students; (3) expanding and improving outreach programs for adults—focusing particularly on displaced workers, single parents, and those leaving military careers; (4) concentrating greater attention on student retention; and (5) encouraging intellectual and social contacts among students by bringing together older and younger students and those from different ethnic and racial backgrounds to enrich learning. These recommendations obviously have ramifications for the community college mission in other areas such as instruction and program.

Mission as Related to Instruction and Faculty

Bauer, reporting on his twelve-institution sabbatical sojourn, describes how some community colleges link instruction to mission:

[T]wo colleges prepared a statement of student expectations for each course based on the college's mission statement. Each student was presented with a statement of expectations for each specific course and these goals were correlated with the college's requirements for graduation. Thus, each course could be viewed as a key part of the college's mission of providing knowledge and skills required for graduation. Thus, faculty could view their courses as major components in the college's mission. (1988, 37)

He is convinced that a strong local mission is dependent on the involvement and the vitality of the faculty.

Supporting this notion of the importance of the mission-faculty involvement relationship is Evans's description of Yakima Valley College's search for mission. There a "faculty group struggled with the questions, 'Who are we?' and 'What part can we play in the birth of a mission and goals statement?' " In responding to the latter question, she writes, "In order to define the faculty role . . . there was a need to describe the nature of the setting in which the teaching was done, the content of what was being taught, and most important the audience—the students" (1990, 8).

To accomplish this task, the group examined what was termed as four characteristics: student, faculty, setting, and content. "After considering the characteristics of these four areas, the faculty drafted a mission statement. The statement was derived from the imputed philosophical base and framed within the context of the information gathered about the students, faculty, setting and content characteristics. It provided a means for operationalization of the concepts identified and pointed the way toward college goals statements" (1990, 9).

Finally, the Commission on the Future of Community Colleges (1988) underscores the importance of faculty in fulfilling the community college mission by recommending that two-year institutions and their leaders commit themselves to (1) recruiting and retaining top-quality faculty, (2) identifying, employing, and nurturing faculty representing diverse groups, (3) providing for faculty renewal, and (4) establishing policies that address part-time faculty and their concerns and needs.

Because faculty stand at the confluence of the student and the curriculum directing the learning stream, they are vital to the fulfillment of the community college's mission.

Mission as Related to Curriculum/Programs

The importance of curriculum as related to mission is recognized by the Task Force for Guidelines and Issues on Institutional Effectiveness of the League for Innovation in the Community College. Its report, *Assessing Institutional Effectiveness in Community Colleges* (1990), focuses principally on five *missions* of the community college. Four of them—the transfer mission, the career preparation mission, the basic skills and developmental education mission, and the continuing education and community service mission—are programmatic. They speak to the ways in which a college "builds its community" and, thus, how the mission may be crafted to be unique or different. Each programmatic mission covered in the report contains a general discussion of its role and related issues, the clients it tends to serve, the various elements that constitute it, and a guide for assessing its effectiveness. The report was developed to be used as a tool in assessing the extent to which an institution is fulfilling its stated mission.

Building Communities: A Vision for a New Century (Commission on the Future of Community Colleges, 1988) also emphasizes curriculum as central to the development of the community college mission. Chapter 3 of this report, "Curriculum: From Literacy to Lifelong Learning," views the programmatic elements as providing literacy for all, a core of common learning, and the essentialness of work. Here mission is seen as relating to programs that enable students to (1) "become proficient in the written and spoken word," (2) "learn about the human heritage and the interdependent world in which they live," (3) experience "first-rate technical education and career-related programs," (4) enjoy "a rich array of short term and continuing education courses" as part of lifelong learning, and (5) "meet their social, civic, and career obligations."

U.S. News and World Report (Schrof 1991) recently featured Elsner's Maricopa County Community College District in a special issue on "America's Best Colleges." The article points to Maricopa's mission as having a strong social agenda, one pledged to addressing the economic needs of both its students and the businesses and industries located in the community, while at the same time providing excellent opportunities for those students interested in completing university degrees. Although Elsner believes that a strong social agenda is an essential part of the Maricopa mission, he maintains that academics as reflected in its program of general education is a dominant and central feature as well (Elsner 1992).

Clowes and Levin propose a "mission redefined" focusing not on the five programmatic functions or on the original transfer function, but, instead, on career education:

Several courageous and visionary writers have argued for a mission based on a redefinition of collegiate academic transfer education and have urged that the community college be restructured about this core function. Cohen has argued long and eloquently for this position, and Miami-Dade Community College under President McCabe's leadership has demonstrated that, in the appropriate environment, it can be done. However, there is little evidence that other institutions or leaders have followed that lead, instead, the data show a pronounced swing away from the collegiate transfer function. . . . We conclude that the only viable function for most community colleges is career education. This is a function the society needs and supports, it is a function the institution can and does provide, and it can serve as the essential element, the core function, the *Plan vital* about which community colleges may be restructured for a viable future. (1989, 352–53)

The career education element of the community college mission may have received as much emphasis as any other during the past decade. As a result of the AACJC-sponsored programs, Keeping America Working and Putting America Back to Work, career education, with its popular economic development component, has occupied a prominent place in the mission of the community college. According to Shearon and Tollefson, "This direction has been backed up by . . . the National Council for Occupational Education. In its 1986 study, the main conclusion was that . . . colleges are beginning to reexamine the impact they have on economic development." They further state, "Mission statements are being revised to include reference to economic development" (1989, 323).

Mission as Related to Economic Development

Economic development is so closely associated with career (or occupational or technical/vocation) education that it is sometimes difficult to separate the two. However, as a concept "economic development," with its linkages and partnerships with the community at large, tends to hold a position of greater relevance than career education. Economic development is a fairly recent thrust that the entire community college—not just one segment—must address. Although the program activities associated with economic development usually flow from career education, they are not bounded by it.

The importance of economic development and its corollary, human resource development, is the focus of "The Missing Link" in Parnell's volume: "One of the key emerging roles for colleges and universities to play in the decade ahead," he writes, "can be pictured in a new kind of economic development paradigm" (1990, 58).

Economic development has traditionally been defined as the process by which individuals or organizations are motivated to invest capital in a community, generating or expanding industrial, commercial, or service activities and, thereby, increasing or retaining jobs. Increasingly, this process has required the cooperation of three diverse groups: public-private employers and labor; public and private community, technical, and junior colleges; and research universities. Working together they form a new kind of economic development triangle. The success of this new paradigm hinges upon the commitment and cooperative efforts of the partners. (58–59)

Economic development is a community, region, and state-wide activity, and, as Parnell implies, it is a team effort. It is the eduation/training facet of economic development that links the community at large to the community college. Parnell supports this notion: "Many colleges and universities will reexamine their mission statements as related to community service, updating that mission to match the economic development needs of their service region or constituency" (62).

Viewed from the community perspective, the community college, as a total learning environment, possesses a "value added" dimension when it comes to economic development. Its mission should reflect this.

Mission as Related to Lifelong Learning

The skyrocketing birthrates of the post–World War II era of the 1950s became the college-age enrollment tidal wave of the mid-to-late 1960s. By the early 1970s significant changes were noted in American higher education enrollments and especially in community colleges—including student shifts from full to part time and from day to evening. Female registrants began to equal and then outnumber male registrants, and the average student age began to rise. About this time, the Congress and other federal agencies impacting education policy decided to embrace the concept of the "educational marketplace." Suddenly, legislation was enacted that effectively shifted federal dollars away from institutions and directed them, instead, to greater numbers of students through grants, work/study, and loans.

It was this loss in federal support, combined with a drop in the number of college-age students, that spawned the lifelong learning or recurrent education movement of the 1970s and 1980s. Groups like the American Association for Higher Education promoted the lifelong learning idea among their constituents. Adults were encouraged to use the community college (and other institutions of higher education) as educational cafeterias. "Take some courses, stop out, and come back for more" was the educational marketer's creed.

As a result, mission statements in two-year college catalogs and other related publications over the last two decades have acknowledged and reflected the community college's role in providing lifelong learning opportunities. An examination of the mission statements in recent catalogs of Miami-Dade (Florida), Central Piedmont (North Carolina), Monroe County (New York), Joliet (Illinois), and Spokane (Washington) community colleges revealed that "lifelong learning" is considered to be an important institutional role. Shearon and Tollefson support this lifelong learning aspect of the mission: "Community colleges have helped many adults prepare and retrain for meaningful work roles and experience a liberal education. These institutions have helped other adults prepare for life's transitions and experience life in a more meaningful way. Some have learned to read, to appreciate music and art, to speak a new language, or just to have fun. We hope and believe . . . community colleges will continue to help adults develop their abilities in liberal and practical ways for a better society'' (1989, 328–29).

COMMUNITY COLLEGE MISSION: A SEARCH FOR PERSPICACITY

Having devoured great chunks of printed commentary, observation, and analysis on the mission, role, and function of the American community college, one should be able to leave one's readers with an extremely perspicacious view of the community college mission. But, as this discourse reveals, mission, as found in the literature, is interpreted and seen in many different ways.

Even though the bad news is that the literature on mission can be clouded and unclear, the good news is that most community college leaders can and do communicate the mission clearly and effectively when it is made context specific. If the mission is tied to a specific setting, the job of describing it becomes much easier.

Martorana sees the challenge facing community college leaders as transforming ''the values inherent in its mission to the entire being of the institutions and organizations functioning to carry it out in today's social, economic, and political setting'' (1989, 43). Thus, the community college mission must not only be communicated to society in its context, it must be operationalized as well.

What will be the mission of the community college in the next decade and into the new century? Deegan and Tillery (1985) foresee dramatic changes. On the other hand, Vaughan (1988) indicates it may not change that much. He lists five constants in his discussion of mission. The community college (1) is an institution of higher education, (2) is a mirror of society, (3) is a teaching institution, (4) is committed to open access, and (5) offers a comprehensive program. Vaughan uses an interesting metaphor in describing the mission:

[T]hink of a large balloon with a rather thick but elastic skin, a skin that expands and contracts under various pressures. The mission . . . with its five constants, is encapsulated with the balloon. Any number of external and internal forces react with the mission, creating tensions, and as a result the shape of the balloon is changed. . . . No matter what shape the balloon takes, the mission never goes beyond the space contained within the balloon. . . . The successful college . . . will squeeze, push, and pull on the mission to make it conform to community needs. (1988, 25–26)

Taken in the spirit of Vaughan's metaphor, it is possible that the mission—except for a bit of bulging here and there—will remain relatively constant.

This author supports many of the ideas on the mission of the community college advanced by those colleagues cited here. A major concern related to the mission is—how will the current worldwide recession and the attendant economic downturn impact the community college and its mission? Will it, as "outside researchers and analysts" have predicted, according to Cross, cause the community college to set priorities?

The concept of *setting priorities* tends to fly in the face of the traditional community college mission statement. Yet, the economic realities of the time may well force our institutions and those who lead them to reexamine mission within the context of "given the available resources, what can and should be our role?"

Perhaps one idea that might hold promise as community colleges across America seek to conserve precious resources would be to encourage community colleges to act as community-wide educational clearinghouses. Assuming a brokering role, the community college could develop linkages and partnerships with public schools, universities, businesses, and other community sources. It could sanction, validate, and promote various programs and activities available through these external community agencies. This would allow the community college an opportunity to concentrate its resources in areas of its expertise as well as in those areas of need not otherwise covered.

What will the basic ingredients of the community college mission be as the world moves toward the year 2000? Certainly, *access* will continue to be the key word in most every institution's mission. Access implies opportunity—opportunity which encourages and supports *diversity*—not only in learners, but in those who lead them as well. Diversity is a key mission word too. The concept of diversity requires the availability of *comprehensive curricular and program options* to meet the needs of the community and all those who constitute it. It appears that a comprehensive program is another essential element in the mission of the community college. These three elements—access, diversity, and comprehensive programs—form the heart (and perhaps the soul) of the community college mission as it moves toward the twenty-first century.

By concentrating on these three basic elements in its mission and brokering those services provided by other community agencies, the community college could well be on its way to the continued realization of Gleazer's mission "to encourage and facilitate lifelong learning with the community as process and product!"

REFERENCES

Alfred, R. L., and V. P. Linder. 1990. Rhetoric to reality: Effectiveness in community colleges. Research report. Ann Arbor, Mich.: Community College Consortium.

Apps, J. W. 1988. *Higher education in a learning society: Meeting new demands for education and training.* San Francisco: Jossey-Bass.

Bauer, P. F. 1988. A sabbatical sojourn: Lessons from travels to some of America's best community colleges. *Community College Review* 16 (Winter): 34–37.

———. 1991. *The Chronicle of Higher Education Almanac* 38 (1):4.

Clowes, D. A., and B. Levin. 1989. Community, technical, and junior colleges: Are they leaving higher education? *Journal of Higher Education* 60 (May/June): 349–55.

Cohen, A. M., and F. Brawer. 1989. *The American community college.* 2d ed. San Francisco: Jossey-Bass, p. 4.

Commission on the Future of Community Colleges. 1988. *Building communities: A vision for a new century.* Washington, D.C.: American Association of Community and Junior Colleges.

Cross, K. P., and E. Fideler. 1989. Community college missions: Priorities in the mid–1980s. *Journal of Higher Education* 60 (March/April): 209–16.

Deegan, W. L., D. Tillery, and Associates. 1985. *Renewing the American community college.* San Francisco: Jossey-Bass, pp. 3–50.

Doucette, D., and B. Hughes, eds., 1990. *Assessing institutional effectiveness in community colleges.* Laguna Hills, Calif.: League for Innovation in the Community College, pp. 7–43.

Elsner, P. A. 1992. Recorded interview with author. Maricopa County Community College District office, Tempe, Arizona, January 6.

Evans, B. 1990. Community college mission and goals development: A process-oriented approach. *Community College Review* 18 (Winter): 7–11.

Fryer, T. W., Jr., and J. Lovas. 1990. *Creating conditions for successful decision making in the community college.* San Francisco: Jossey-Bass, pp. 28–155.

Gleazer, E. J., Jr. 1980. *Values, vision, and vitality.* Washington, D.C.: American Association of Community and Junior Colleges, pp. 1–16.

Levine, Arthur. 1979. *Handbook on undergraduate curriculum.* San Francisco: Jossey-Bass, p. 621.

Martorana, S. V. 1989. Reflections on a movement. *Community, Technical, and Junior College Journal* 60 (August/September): 42–48.

Monroe, C. R. 1972. *Profile of the community college.* San Francisco: Jossey-Bass, pp. 59–60.

O'Banion, T. 1989. Student development philosophy: A perspective on the past and future. In *Perspectives on student development,* ed. W. L. Deegan and T. O'Banion. New Directions for Community Colleges, no. 67. San Francisco: Jossey-Bass.

Parnell, D. 1988. Leadership is not tidy. *Leadership Abstracts* 1:4.

————. 1990. *Dateline 2000: The new higher education agenda.* Washington, D.C.: Community College Press, pp. 52–62.

Roueche, J. E., G. A. Baker, and R. R. Rose. 1989. *Shared vision: Transformational leadership in American community colleges.* Washington, D.C.: Community College Press, pp. 15–136.

Schrof, J. M. 1991. Community colleges. *U.S. News and World Report: America's Best Colleges* (special edition) 40–42.

Shaw, R. 1989. Telling the truth, warming the heart: The future of student development in the community college. In *Perspectives on student development,* eds. W. L. Deegan and T. O'Banion. New Directions for Community Colleges, no. 67. San Francisco: Jossey-Bass.

Shearon, R. W., and T. A. Tollefson. 1989. Community colleges. In *Handbook of adult and continuing education,* ed. S. B. Merriam and P. M. Cunningham. San Francisco: Jossey-Bass.

Simmons, H. 1991. Assessment! action! accreditation! *Community, Technical, and Junior College Journal* 61 (April/May): 26–30.

Thornton, J. W., Jr. 1972. *The community junior college.* 3d ed. New York: John Wiley and Sons.

Vaughan, G. B. 1988. The community college mission. *Community, Technical, and Junior College Journal* 58 (4):25–27.

The Evolution of State Systems of Community Colleges in the United States

Terrence A. Tollefson

STATE AUTHORITY AND AUTHORIZING LEGISLATION

The authority for state governments to regulate education has been traced to the 10th Amendment to the U.S. Constitution, which states, "The powers not delegated to the United States by the Constitution, nor prohibited by it to the States, are reserved to the States respectively, or to the people." Forty-nine state constitutions subsequently adopted provisions mandating that their respective state legislatures establish public school systems, and numerous court decisions have upheld the rights and duties of state legislatures to exercise their authority to regulate public elementary, secondary, and postsecondary education (Van Geel 1987, 66).

The various state legislatures, naturally enough, did not vigorously apply their constitutional authority to public education at the junior college level until there were sufficient numbers of such institutions and students to warrant their attention. The first enabling legislation authorizing public high schools to offer postgraduate courses was enacted by the California General Assembly in 1907 (Myers, in Fountain and Tollefson 1989, 15; Monroe 1972, 11; Fields 1962, 27). California also enacted the first legislation authorizing the provision of both state and local financial support for public junior colleges. That legislation, which was adopted in 1917, specified that such tax support would be on the same basis as was provided to the high schools, with the important restriction that only school districts with assessed valuations of at least $3 million could offer junior college instruction (Fields 1962, 29).

Other states soon followed California's lead in authorizing the upward extension of high schools and the establishment of separate public junior colleges. Kansas and Michigan, which enacted such legislation in 1917, were followed by Minnesota (1925); Arizona, Iowa, and Missouri (1927); Louisiana and Mississippi (1928); and Texas (1929). In the decade of the 1930s, many other states joined the public junior college movement by enacting enabling legislation, including Nebraska and North Dakota (1931); South Carolina (1935); Kentucky (1936); Colorado, Connecticut, and Illinois (1937); and Florida, Idaho, Montana, and Oklahoma (1939). There was a hiatus during World War II, but in the remainder of the 1940s, New Jersey (1946), Massachusetts (1947), New York (1948), and Oregon (1949) followed suit. Only three more states authorized public junior colleges in the 1950s decade: Alaska (1953) and North Carolina and New Mexico (1957). In the 1960s, Rhode Island (1960); Alabama, Maine, Maryland, New Hampshire, and Ohio (1961); Indiana (1962); and Pennsylvania (1963) adopted legislative authorizations (Blocker, Plummer, and Richardson 1965, 28–29). Hawaii authorized community colleges in 1964 (Tsunoda, in Tollefson and Fountain 1992b, 54); Delaware adopted such legislation in 1966 (Kotula and Kubala, in Tollefson and Fountain 1992b, 42); and Tennessee followed in 1972 (Doran, in Tollefson and Fountain 1992b, 205), bringing the total to forty-nine states that have adopted legislation to authorize the establishment of public community colleges. Only South Dakota to date has neither a state legislative authorization nor any public community colleges.

TRENDS IN SOURCES AND PROPORTIONS OF FUNDS

Because so many of the early public junior colleges began as extensions of the high schools, it seems logical that their funding patterns also would closely reflect those of the high schools, with considerable if not exclusive dependence upon local property taxes, in some cases augmented by tuition paid by the students or their parents. An early cogent case for increased state funding of public junior colleges was presented by Koos (1925, 407–18). Koos compared public high school and junior college costs and funding patterns in Minnesota and Michigan. He combined his "argument for generous state subsidy, rather than almost exclusive local support of junior colleges" (411) with a plea that public junior college students should not be required to pay tuition:

A state policy of generous subsidy for junior colleges is supported, moreover, with any admission that the movement is in accord with the inevitable forces of reorganization in secondary and higher education . . . [which] have disclosed the important fact that for most students enrolled the two junior college years may rightly be looked upon as the conclusive years of the period of general or secondary education. Universal practice in this country indicates that we have committed ourselves to a policy of providing the school patron with secondary education free of cost. It would therefore be difficult to show why, anticipating the evolution of the secondary school to include the junior college years, any policy should be followed which is likely to oblige the community maintaining the work to levy a tuition charge against those in attendance. Without generous subvention by the state, it would be difficult to avoid this charge, as is evident from any facts that illustrate the widely differing resources where junior colleges are otherwise feasible and from the imperativeness of safeguarding the interests of education on lower levels. (Koos 1925, 414–15)

No state aid was provided to institutions in a category labeled "local junior colleges only," according to studies conducted of the financing of public junior colleges in 1918 and 1930, but by 1942 state aid accounted for 28 percent of the income of public junior colleges in the United States. Tuition and fees accounted for 6 percent of public junior college income in 1918, rose to 14 percent in 1930, and declined to 11 percent in 1942. Local aid began at 94 percent of income in 1918, declined to 85 percent in 1930, and dropped precipitously to 57 percent by 1942. By 1986, tuition and fees had risen gradually to 16 percent of income, federal aid accounted for 10 percent, state aid had climbed sharply to 47 percent, and local support had plummeted to 17 percent of income (Cohen and Brawer 1989, 128).

TRENDS IN TYPES OF STATE-LEVEL COORDINATING/ GOVERNANCE STRUCTURES

The beginning of the period of the most rapid expansion of public two-year colleges in the United States, the decades of the 1960s and 1970s, also signified the onset of a major transition in the types of state-level coordination/governance structures for community colleges. In a 1963 study, Martorana discovered that public junior/community colleges were in operation in thirty-eight states (Blocker, Plummer, and Richardson 1965). Martorana found a complex pattern nationally, in which twenty-six states exercised control of community colleges through state agencies or offices that had been established to oversee public elementary and secondary education, thirteen states employed state boards of higher education or state university boards for that purpose, and only six states had state boards or commissions created exclusively for coordination or governance of public two-year colleges. The total of the foregoing numbers is greater than thirty eight because several states coordinated community colleges through more than one state agency.

A more recent study reveals that "[i]n the past quarter of a century, community colleges have emerged from the shadow of elementary and secondary education" (Tollefson and Fountain 1992a, 9), in the sense that many states have established separate state boards or commissions for community colleges or have assigned community college governance responsibilities to statewide university boards. By 1989, only six states still coordinated community colleges through state boards of education (Fountain and Tollefson 1989), contrasted with twenty-six in Martorana's 1963 study. Seven states in 1989 had assigned community college coordination responsibilities to statewide boards or commissions for higher education, and thirteen states utilized university boards of regents for community college coordination. The remaining twenty-two states had established separate state boards or commissions for community colleges and/or postsecondary vocational/technical institutions. The foregoing categorizations are somewhat over-simplified for several states with unusual combinations of types of institutions coordinated or governed by one board. Examples include Colorado, with a state board for community colleges and occupational education, and West Virginia, with a merged state board for community colleges and four-year state colleges (Tollefson and Fountain 1992b).

Although there is an established long-term trend toward shifting community college coordination from coordination of public schools to coordination by separate state boards for community college, state university boards of regents, or state boards of higher education, it is possible that a reversal of that trend may have begun. In 1991 the Minnesota state legislature enacted a law to con-solidate the state's community college, technical institute, and four-year state college systems into a single merged system by 1995. The governor and legis-lature of Oregon are considering the establishment of a single consolidated state board for all public education at elementary, secondary, and postsecondary levels (*Chronicle of Higher Education Almanac*, August 26, 1992:73, 93).

TRENDS REGARDING STATE-LEVEL COORDINATION VERSUS CONTROL

Berdahl's typology for all higher education is applied in simplified form to state-level structures for coordination of community colleges (1971, 18–21). He defined *coordinating boards* as having been "created by statute but not supersed-ing institutional . . . governing boards" (18) and single statewide *governing boards* "with no local . . . governing bodies" (19). "Coordination" is used here as the generic term for all state-level activities in relationship with local com-munity colleges, including "governance," which is interpreted to mean the authority and/or practice of a state-level board or agency to intervene in such internal matters of individual colleges as the hiring, evaluating, and, when deemed necessary, terminating of presidents, faculty, and staff members. A coordinating board may have limited or extensive regulatory powers to set state-wide academic and curricular standards, develop budget allocation formulas, adopt personnel policies, approve operational and capital budgets, and approve new educational programs, but still lack the authority of a governing board.

An important point to observe here is that state-level coordinating/governance authority over community colleges may be shared between the state-level board or an agency identified specifically with community colleges and numerous other state agencies, such as attorney generals' offices, state departments of admin-istration, labor and commerce, state licensing boards of nursing and other health fields, as well as governors and state legislatures.

State agency coordination of public junior colleges initially was minimal, but it increased as the numbers of colleges, students, and, perhaps more important, dollars requested increased in each state. Millard observed that the New York Board of Regents had been established in the American colonial period as the first statewide coordinating agency but that most states did not create similar agencies until at least the 1960s (Gleazer and Yarrington 1974). He stated that several states had not extended the oversight of community colleges to their statewide coordinating agencies for higher education. Millard also reported that the federal education amendments of 1972 required each state to create or designate a so-called 1202 commission for comprehensive postsecondary education planning, in order to be eligible to receive federal funds.

Glenny indicated the emergence of four conditions that rendered community colleges "so integral to the total scheme of postsecondary education that they can no longer escape state protection or control. These conditions are (1) new program developments, (2) shifts in student distribution among postsecondary schools and among the colleges themselves, (3) leveling of state funding for higher institutions, and (4) the commitment of states to stronger coordination encompassing all of postsecondary education" (Gleazer and Yarrington 1974, 54). Glenny supported his contention with data showing that the nationwide community college share of state appropriations for higher education had risen from 6.2 percent in 1963 to 15.5 percent in 1973 (63).

Enrollment growth in general and especially in occupational programs also was cited by Martorana as a factor leading to increased statewide coordination of community colleges (Gleazer and Yarrington 1974, 69–84). He described a very complex system of overlapping local and state agency jurisdictions, and he noted that a recent proposal in the state legislature to set state financial support at 60 percent of community college operational costs (after deducting tuition) and 60 percent of capital construction costs also had contributed to the need for more coordination at the state level.

Brossman similarly included the multipurpose mission of the California community colleges, especially their increased responsibilities for occupational and continuing education, as well as the reconstitution of a previous statewide higher education coordinating council into a new 1202 postsecondary education commission, as factors leading to what he hoped would result in a reversal of the previous degree of centralized state control over community colleges (Gleazer and Yarrington 1974, 87–96).

The "unusual balance of local control with state coordination and support" of the Florida community college system was described by Henderson as one that had received national recognition as a model system (Gleazer and Yarrington 1974, 97–106). He said that the state legislature in 1968 had transferred the authority for operating community colleges from local school boards to junior college boards of trustees, but the local school boards had continued to provide financial support to the community colleges until the state assumed community college funding responsibilities in 1970. He also noted that the state board of education had become responsible for community college coordination in 1969, further commenting that "the 1969 Reorganization Act has resulted in some centralization of decision making, because of the intent to establish accountability and to pinpoint responsibility" (103).

In the late 1970s, community colleges in many states were required to obtain state coordinating agency approval of new educational programs culminating in associate degrees, diplomas, or certificates before offering such programs to students. The majority of state community college coordinating agencies required detailed new program proposals that included program title, associate degree or certificate designation, program description including goals and objectives, projected numbers of students and graduates, and educational equipment needed to support the program. A majority of the states surveyed also had established associate degree standards that specified the types of associate degrees permitted (most commonly associate of arts, associate of science, and associate of applied science designations) and had set minimum numbers of semester credit hours (usually sixty or more) or quarter credit hours (generally at least ninety). A number of states also mandated minimum number of credit hours in such component areas as English, mathematics, natural science, social science, and humanities. In some states, associate degree programs were required to be approved by postsecondary education planning commissions as well as by the community college coordinating board or agency (Tollefson 1978, 1–11).

A national survey of funding and accountability for the years from 1976 to 1979 (Tollefson et al. 1980, 1–31) found that among twenty-nine responding states, most states employed formulas for calculating full-time-equivalent (FTE) students at each community college and that "[s]tudent enrollments, either past or projected, appear to represent the single-most important factor in determining the amount of state support" (10). All of the twenty-nine responding states indicated that fiscal audits of individual colleges were required; about half required fiscal audits every year and half required audits once per biennium. Eighteen states also required enrollment audits, and nine states reported at least some use of operational or program audits.

In a recent study based upon completed questionnaires from the chief state-level community college officials in forty-five of the forty-nine states with community colleges, Garrett reached the following findings and conclusions:

1. The percentage of state funding of total operational expenditures ranged from 23 percent in Massachusetts to 100 percent in Connecticut, Florida, Nevada, North Dakota, Oklahoma, and Utah (95).

2. The percentage of local funding of total operational expenditures varied from zero in nineteen states to 61 percent in Michigan (97).

3. The number of local public two-year colleges per state ranged from one in Delaware and Rhode Island to 107 in California (102).

4. The "index of state centralization" of control of community colleges (based upon a complex formula involving twenty-nine functions that could be controlled/performed at either state or local levels) was lowest at forty for Missouri and highest at 107 in Connecticut, with a midpoint for the forty-five responding states of 74, as compared with a midpoint of 73.5 on a scale ranging from 1 to 145 (104).

5. "[A]s the percentage of state funds increases, the centralization index increases. Based

upon the sample of this study, governance structure becomes more centralized as the proportion of state funds increases'' (105–106).

6. "State systems funded by more than 50 percent of state funds tend to have centralized governance structures. Also, state systems funded by local funds greater than 25 percent tend to have decentralized structures'' (106–107). (Tollefson and Fountain, 1992b)

THE ROLE OF STATE DIRECTORS OF COMMUNITY COLLEGES

Charles and Wattenbarger have chronicled the highlights of the first twenty years of the National Council of State Directors of Community and Junior Colleges and the contributions of a number of chief state-level community college officers variously titled state directors, chancellors, or presidents (1991, 11–21). The foregoing synthesis of the literature on state systems of community colleges has attempted to describe the influences of large-scale societal forces, history, and traditions, both nationally and in individual states. Nevertheless, it also is important to emphasize that individual leaders have profoundly influenced the evolution of state systems, and many state directors of community colleges are among those former and current leaders.

REFERENCES

Berdahl, R. O. 1971. *Statewide coordination of higher education*. Washington, D.C.: American Council on Education.

Blocker, C. E., R. H. Plummer, and R. C. Richardson, Jr. 1965. *The two-year college: A social synthesis*. Englewood Cliffs, N.J.: Prentice-Hall.

Brossman, S. W. 1974. Decentralization in California. In *Coordinating state systems*, ed. E. J. Gleazer, Jr., and R. Yarrington, 87–96. New Directions for Community Colleges, no. 6. San Francisco: Jossey-Bass.

Charles, S. F., and J. L. Wattenbarger. 1991. The National Council of State Directors of Community/Junior Colleges: The first 20 years. *Community College Review* 19(3):11–21.

Cohen, A. M., and F. B. Brawer. 1989. *The American community college*. 2d ed. San Francisco: Jossey-Bass.

Fields, R. 1962. *The community college movement*. New York: McGraw-Hill.

Fountain, B. E., and T. A. Tollefson. 1989. *Community colleges in the United States: Forty-nine state systems*. Washington, D.C.: American Association of Community and Junior Colleges.

Garrett, R. L. 1990. *Factors associated with the governance of state community college systems in the United States, 1990*. Ph.D. diss., North Carolina State University at Raleigh.

Gleazer, E. J., Jr., and R. Yarrington, eds., 1974. *Coordinating state systems*. New Directions for Community Colleges, no. 6. San Francisco: Jossey-Bass.

Henderson, L. G. 1974. Coordination: The Florida pattern. In *Coordinating state systems*, ed. E. J. Gleazer, Jr., and R. Yarrington. New Directions for Community Colleges, no. 6. San Francisco: Jossey-Bass.

Koos, L. V. 1925. *The junior college movement*. Boston: Atheneum.

Martorana, S. V. 1974. Critical issues in New York State. In *Coordinating state systems*, ed. E. J. Gleazer, Jr., and R. Yarrington. New Directions for Community Colleges, no. 6. San Francisco: Jossey-Bass. 69–85.

Medsker, L. L. 1960. *The junior college: Progress and prospect*. New York: McGraw-Hill.

Millard, R. M. 1974. Integrating the strengths of private, public, and proprietary institutions. In *Coordinating state systems*, ed. E. J. Gleazer, Jr., and R. Yarrington, New Directions for Community Colleges, no. 6. San Francisco: Jossey-Bass. 31–42.

Monroe, C. R. 1972. *Profile of the community college*. San Francisco: Jossey-Bass.

Palinchak, R. S. 1973. *The evolution of the community college*. Metuchen, N.J.: Scarecrow Press.

Thornton, J. W., Jr. 1960. *The community junior college* 2d ed. New York: Wiley and Sons.

Tollefson, T. A. 1978. *Final report on state associate degree/certificate standards and procedures for community college program approval*. Denver: Colorado State Board for Community Colleges and Occupational Education.

Tollefson, T. A., and B. E. Fountain. 1992a. A quarter century of change in state-level coordinating structures for community colleges. *Community/Junior College Quarterly of Research and Practice* 16(1):9–13.

Tollefson, T. A., and B. E. Fountain. 1992b. *Forty-nine state systems*. Washington, D.C.: American Association of Community Colleges.

Tollefson, T. A., G. D. Adkins, D. Gregory, and J. L. Buysse. 1980. *National Survey of Funding and Accountability of Public Community, Junior, and Technical Colleges, 1976–79: Final Report*. Denver: Colorado State Board for Community Colleges and Occupational Education.

Van Geel, T. 1987. *The courts and American educational law*. Buffalo, N.Y.: Prometheus.

Vaughan, G. B. 1982. *The community college in America: A short history*. Washington, D.C.: American Association of Community and Junior Colleges.

Hispanics and Community Colleges

Eduardo J. Padron

According to some students of American education, "the invention of the two-year community college is the great innovation of twentieth-century American education" (Brint and Karabel 1989, v). The institution was created and developed in the context of a rapidly expanding demand for higher education in the United States during most of this century (Cohen and Brawer 1989). As such, the community college has often been seen as the democratic educational institution par excellence, combining low cost, geographic and social accessibility, and nonselective admission (Fields 1962). Some critics of the community college have charged that, in the overall design of the U.S. educational system, community colleges have "faced two contradictory tasks: the democratic one of bringing new populations into higher education and the exclusionary one of channelling them away from the four year institutions they hoped to attend" (Brint and Karabel 1989, 208). Yet even the strongest critics concede that "in the absence of community colleges, many highly motivated and able individuals—among them, workers, immigrants, minorities, and women—would never have entered, much less graduated from, an institution of higher education" (Brint and Karabel 1989, 226).

Neither standard histories of the community college movement (Koos 1925; Fields 1962; Cohen and Brawer 1989) nor writings directly about Hispanics and community colleges (De los Santos 1980) identify any specific role played by Hispanics in the inception or development of the institution of the two-year college. The fact that until recently Hispanics have been nearly absent from leadership in American educational institutions as a result of a combination of disadvantage and exclusion is probably the major reason for this absence. One might also speculate that, as in the case of other areas of endeavor, those contributions that did occur have not been duly recorded in the history books.

Table 1
Growth of and Changes in Control of Two-Year Colleges, 1900–1987 (Selected Years)

Year	Number	Percent Public
1900–01	8	0
1921–22	207	34
1933–34	521	42
1947–48	650	50
1958–59	677	50
1970–71	1,091	78
1972–73	1,141	80
1974–75	1,203	82
1976–77	1,233	84
1978–79	1,234	85
1980–81	1,231	85
1982–83	1,219	87
1984–85	1,222	87
1986–87	1,224	87

Source: Adapted from Cohen and Brawer (1989), p. 11.

Since the birth of the two-year college about ninety years ago, the number of such institutions has multiplied rapidly, and student enrollment has soared. In addition, while in the early part of the century two-year colleges were predominantly private institutions, today the overwhelming majority are public. The focus and nomenclature also have changed from the era of the junior college to that of the community college, with a stronger emphasis on vocational and terminal programs in more recent decades (Brint and Karabel 1989). Increasingly, the racial and ethnic composition of students is also changing, as we shall see in detail below.

Table 1 demonstrates the explosive growth in the number of community colleges between 1900 and the 1970s and the still-growing percentages of such colleges that are publicly controlled. In the late 1970s, the total number of community colleges began to decline slightly, primarily as a result of the disappearance of some of the private institutions. Since the middle 1980s the number of public institutions has also shown a small decline. It appears that a saturation

Table 2
Total Enrollment in Two-Year Colleges, 1976–1988 (in thousands)

1976	1978	1980	1982	1984	1986	1988
3,879	4,028	4,521	4,740	4,527	4,680	4,868

Source: U.S. Department of Education (1991), p. 216.

point has been reached with regard to the number of community colleges in the United States.

However, as Table 2 shows, total student enrollment in two-year colleges has continued to increase. This indicates that enrollments have continued to grow within the existing institutions, despite the end of the period of explosive growth in the number of institutions documented in Table 1.

THE HISPANIC POPULATION OF THE UNITED STATES

The Hispanic population of the United States is currently increasing at a rate higher than either the Caucasian or the African-American population. Continued immigration from Latin America and the higher than average rate of natural increase among Hispanics in the United States virtually ensure the continuation of this trend for the foreseeable future. This means that Hispanics will make up an increasing percentage of community college students for some time to come.

The Hispanic population of the United States is growing not only in size but also in diversity. It is crucial to recognize and understand the existence and implications of major differences among the various Hispanic groups in geographical location and dispersion, socioeconomic background and status, immigration and citizenship status, naturalization rates, language proficiency and language dominance (Spanish vs. English), immigration and fertility rates, political attitudes, behavior and affiliation, and educational opportunity and achievement.

While Hispanics do have significant common characteristics and concerns, the differences among the various groups are such that one should be extremely cautious in generalizing across groups. Our experience at Miami-Dade Community College with Cuban-origin students can not necessarily be generalized to Puerto Rican students in New York, Chicano students in Los Angeles, or even Nicaraguan students at Miami-Dade.

HISPANIC EDUCATION

The education of this growing and diversifying population has become an issue of national concern. The Hispanic educational pipeline has been described as "narrow, leaking, and needing repair" (Fields 1988). The reasons are clear from a 1990 study of the subject published by the National Council of La Raza (De la Rosa and Maw 1990). The findings include (1) Hispanics are the most undereducated segment of the population; (2) Hispanics represent a growing segment of the school-age population; (3) Hispanic students face serious difficulties; (4) achievement test scores of Hispanics and African Americans remain lower than those of Caucasians, and in some cases the gap is widening; (5) Hispanic eighth graders have lower educational expectations than African Americans or Caucasians; (6) Hispanics are unlikely to have Hispanic teachers who can serve as mentors; (7) Hispanics continue to be at risk of academic failure and dropping out; (8) Hispanics continue to have the highest dropout rate of any group; (9) Hispanics continue to have the lowest high school completion rates of any group, and the gap between Hispanics and both African Americans and Caucasians is continuing to grow; (10) Hispanic enrollment in higher education is low, and Hispanic students tend to enroll in schools not offering advanced degrees; (11) compared to African Americans and Caucasians, Hispanics rely more heavily on student loans and less on grants to finance postsecondary education; and (12) Hispanic illiteracy rates are much higher than those of African Americans or Caucasians.

A more recent study commissioned by the National School Boards Association found that Hispanic students have become even more segregated than African Americans in American schools (Schmidt 1992).

While the condition of Hispanic education as a whole is critical, it should be noted that there are significant differences among Hispanic populations in educational outcome. In some cases, the differences among Hispanic populations are greater than the differences between some Hispanic subgroups and the Caucasian non-Hispanic population. For instance, among persons twenty-five years old and older, 9.9 percent of Hispanics have four years of college or more, compared with 11.8 percent of African Americans and 21.8 percent of whites (U.S. Bureau of the Census 1991). However, the percentage of Cubans (19.8 percent) and Central/South Americans (17.5 percent) with four or more years of college was closer to the Caucasian figure than to the figures for the two largest Hispanic populations, Mexicans (6.1 percent) and Puerto Ricans (9.8 percent). There are also differences between Mexicans and Puerto Ricans in some indicators. For example, for every year between 1975 and 1976 and 1988 and 1989, the average verbal and quantitative SAT scores for Mexican students exceeded the Puerto Rican average (U.S. Department of Education 1991).

TRENDS IN HISPANIC ENROLLMENT IN COMMUNITY COLLEGES

The student bodies of community colleges are becoming more diverse largely as a result of increases in the number of Hispanic and Asian students. Table 3

Table 3
Number and Percentage of Students Enrolled in Two-Year Institutions by Race and Ethnicity, 1976–1988 (in thousands)

	Total	Caucasian	African American	Hispanic	Asian	American Indian	Alien
1976	3,879	3,077	429	210	79	41	42
	100%	79.3%	11.1%	5.4%	2.0%	1.1%	1.1%
1978	4,028	3,167	443	227	97	43	52
	100%	78.6%	11.0%	5.6%	2.4%	1.1%	1.3%
1980	4,521	3,558	472	255	124	47	64
	100%	78.7%	10.4%	5.6%	2.8%	1.0%	1.4%
1982	4,740	3,692	489	291	158	49	61
	100%	77.9%	10.3%	6.1%	3.3%	1.0%	1.3%
1984	4,527	3,514	459	289	167	46	53
	100%	77.6%	10.1%	6.4%	3.7%	1.0%	1.2%
1986	4,680	3,584	467	340	186	51	53
	100%	76.6%	10.0%	7.3%	4.0%	1.1%	1.1%
1988	4,868	3,702	473	384	199	50	60
	100%	76.0%	9.7%	7.9%	4.1%	1.0%	1.2%

Source: U.S. Department of Education (1991), p. 216, p. 218.

shows changes in the distribution of community college students between 1976 and 1988.

Between 1976 and 1988, Hispanic enrollment grew by 174,000 students, or 82.9 percent. Asian enrollment grew by 120,00, or 152 percent. In contrast, Caucasian enrollment grew more absolutely (by 625,000) but much less proportionately (20.3 percent). African-American enrollment nearly stagnated, growing by only 44,000, or 10.3 percent. In 1976, African-American enrollment in community colleges (429,000) far exceeded Hispanic and Asian enrollments combined (289,000). By 1988, combined Hispanic and Asian enrollments (583,000) far exceeded African-American enrollment (473,000). The fact is that the community college student populations are slowly but surely becoming more Hispanic and Asian.

According to a report of a recent study, these trends will continue well into the 1990s. The study projects that "in most states the ranks of minority high-school graduates will expand and those of Caucasian graduates will shrink or remain stable over the next several years" (Evangelauf 1991). The study predicts that between 1986 and 1995 the highest growth rates will be among Asians (58 percent) and Hispanics (52 percent). The report also notes that "declines are expected in the ranks of African-American graduates and Caucasian, non-Hispanic graduates over the 10-year period covered by the study."

Therefore, while numbers of Hispanics enrolled in community colleges will undoubtedly continue to rise, this is not necessarily cause for celebration. An article by Orfield and Paul (1987–1988) on minority access to higher education in five metropolitan areas indicates that both African-American and Hispanic enrollment in both four-year and two-year institutions is actually decreasing as a proportion of these groups' 12th grade or high school graduate group enrollment. This suggests that rising community college enrollment reflect Hispanic demographic rather than educational gains. It also indicates that even in community colleges that have traditionally been the open door for minority students, budget problems and other factors are beginning to limit minority access to higher education.

A more recent study conducted by the American Council on Education (ACE) confirms this gloomy picture. The report found that between 1985 and 1990, the percentage of Hispanic students who finished high school actually fell. In addition, the percentage of Hispanic high school graduates aged eighteen to twenty-four who went on to college stagnated at 29 percent between 1985 and 1990. In contrast, Caucasian college attendance increased from 34.4 percent in 1985 to 39.4 percent in 1990, and African-American enrollment increased from 26.1 percent to 33 percent (*Miami Herald* 1992). According to Blandina Cardenas Ramirez, director of ACE's Office of Minorities in Higher Education, the major reason that Hispanics are faring badly is economic: Hispanic students attend the most segregated and least affluent schools in the country (Hendley 1992).

REVIEW OF THE LITERATURE

Hispanics and Community Colleges: A Special Relationship

For Hispanics, community colleges play an especially crucial educational role. Well over half of the Hispanics who attended a postsecondary institution attend two-year colleges. This is not the case for African Americans, Caucasians, or Asians, as shown in Table 4. Only Native Americans display such a predominant reliance on community colleges, although Hispanics exceed even that group in their reliance on two-year institutions. "Hispanic students have used open access community colleges as their primary passageway into higher education" (Rendón and Nora 1989). This means that community colleges will play a major role in determining the prospects for educational fulfillment and social and economic mobility for a very large and rapidly growing sector of the American population, a fact that places added responsibility on community colleges to serve this population.

Finally, not only are Hispanic students who go on to college extremely reliant on community colleges, they have become more reliant on them in recent years.

Table 4
Percentage of All Students Enrolled in Higher Education Who Are Enrolled in Two-Year Institutions by Race and Ethnic Group, 1988

Total	Caucasian	African American	Hispanic	Asian	American Indian	Alien
37.8	36.0	41.9	56.5	40.0	54.3	16.6

Source: Computed by the author from data in U.S. Department of Education (1991), p. 216.

Between 1976 and 1988, Hispanic student enrollment at two-year institutions increased substantially more (69.1 percent) than enrollment at four-year institutions (55.8 percent) (U.S. Department of Education 1991).

Hispanic Student Outcomes

Hispanics are attending community colleges in increasing numbers, and Hispanics rely on community colleges for much of their postsecondary education. But how well are Hispanic students doing in community colleges? Or, to put the responsibility where it must lie: How well are the community colleges doing in discharging their responsibility to educate Hispanic students?

The literature is devoid of authoritative studies to answer this question conclusively. Rendón and Nora summarized the situation: "While the persistence and progress of Hispanic students in community colleges have received limited research attention, a few studies provide both descriptive and inferential information that colleges may use to improve practice and policy" (1989, 17).

Obviously, there is much variation among community colleges in this regard as well as between different Hispanic subgroups. Miami-Dade Community College, for example, which has been selected by a panel of educators as the top community college in the United States (Roueche and Baker 1987), has a 52.7 percent Hispanic enrollment and more Hispanic students than any other school in the United States (Miami-Dade Community College 1990; Career Intelligencer 1991).

Though data are scarce and studies few, the consensus of the literature is that most community colleges are not fulfilling their promises to Hispanic students and that Hispanic students in community colleges are not doing as well as they should. Writing in 1980, De los Santos concluded that, while Hispanic students were flocking to community colleges, "all indications are that they are not receiving from the community colleges the quantity, much less the quality, of programs they need and deserve." More recently, Rendón and Nora have noted that "while transfer rates vary by institution, there is cause for concern that Hispanic transfer rates are often lower than 10 percent" (1987–88, 80). In general, their conclusion is that the experience of Hispanic students continues to be "marked by early departure" and that Hispanics "have attained only minimal success in moving from lower to upper division programs of study that lead to the baccalaureate" (Rendón and Nora, 1989, 17).

Cohen and Brawer (1989) state that the best estimates indicate that Hispanic students make up 6 percent of community college enrollments but obtain only 4 percent of the degrees; Caucasian students who make up 75 percent of the enrollment obtain 85 percent of the degrees. They argue, however, that the point is not whether most minority students transfer or not (they do not). The question is whether Hispanic students would do better in the absence of community colleges. In general, proponents of the community college argue that many Hispanic students would not attend *any* college were it not for the geographical accessibility, low tuition, and minimal entrance requirements provided by the community college. In addition, community colleges provide minority students with some critical services, such as remedial education, academic preparation, counseling, and other services that universities usually do not offer.

In addition to the point that graduation rates on average are lower for minorities who attend community college than for Caucasians in the same institutions, critics note that "minority students who begin their college education at a community college will do less well than those of equal ability who enroll at the senior institution and that this differential is greater for them than it is for the majority of students" (Cohen and Brawer 1989). For instance, Folger, Astin, and Bayer (1970) reported that, controlling separately for ability and socioeconomic status (SES), students who begin their education at community colleges are considerably less likely to obtain a college degree than those of similar ability and SES who begin their studies at four-year institutions.

While Cohen and Brawer indicate that community colleges in general tend to have a similar consequence for all their students, both minority and majority—most of both groups will not succeed in obtaining the baccalaureate—their overall conclusion reflects the unsatisfactory state of knowledge regarding the main issue:

The question whether community colleges are beneficial to minority students is thus unresolved. If sizable percentages of minority students would not attend any college unless there were a community college available, and if the act of attending college to take even a few classes is beneficial, then community colleges have certainly helped in the education of minority students. But if the presence of a convenient community college discourages minority students from attending senior institutions and reduces the probability of their completing the baccalaureate, then for those students who wanted degrees the college has been detrimental. (1989, 45)

On this question, what is clear is that Hispanics will continue to attend community colleges in large and increasing numbers and that the vast majority of Hispanic community college students want to attain a bachelors degree, but most of them do not make it (Rendón and Nora 1987–88). The most relevant issue, then, is how community colleges can serve students better and thus reduce the huge gap between aspirations and outcomes.

PROGRAMS AND POLICIES: WHAT IS TO BE DONE

The literature contains a wide variety of program case studies and policy recommendations intended to remedy the problems of Hispanic students in community colleges. De los Santos (1980) proposed a broader use of bilingual education, which has been employed successfully in many colleges, including Miami-Dade Community College.

More elaborate sets of recommendations are offered by Rendón and Nora (1987–88) who stress the need for early intervention at the high school level, including dropout prevention, financial aid and college awareness programs, and early exposure to fields in which Hispanics are underrepresented. At the community college level, they recommend Academic Partnership Programs, more faculty involvement in student retention, and honors transfer programs. They also recommend close cooperation between two-year and four-year college faculties and institutions, as well as increased institutional research. Rendón and Taylor's (1989–90) ten-point action plan for increasing access includes developing strong linkages with feeder schools, involving the Hispanic family in education, strengthening the quality of teaching and learning, improving counseling and advisement, and engaging students in the academic and social fabric of the college, among others.

While recommendations and models abound, a study by Nora (1990) identified the key variable in determining retention of Hispanic students in community college: financial resources. The main finding is that "while it was found that prior high-school grades had the largest impact on cumulative grade-point average, neither the students' high-school grades nor their academic performance at the community college had as large an effect on retention as did campus- and noncampus-based resources" (53). In other words, "Hispanic college students are not leaving higher education because of their academic performance but largely because of financial reasons" (54). Based on this finding, Nora concludes that "community college administrators need to develop a comprehensive financial aid and advisement program that reaches out to students and their parents not only after graduation but even before graduation from high school" (65).

This finding is particularly significant in light of the increasing budget crunch faced by community colleges and the contraction in student assistance. It makes clear that, if Hispanic students are to be successful in community colleges, then the community must mobilize to ensure that sufficient resources are devoted to afford them a decent chance of success.

The increasing activism and self-assertion of Hispanics within higher education organizations is a hopeful sign. The founding of a Hispanic Association of Colleges and Universities (HACU) in 1986 has served to increase awareness of the needs of Hispanic students (HACU 1989). It brings together "Hispanic

Serving Institutions (HSIs)," institutions of higher education with at least 25 percent Hispanic students, of which there were 112 in the United States and Puerto Rico in 1990 (HACU 1990). HACU, which receives its funding from foundations and corporations, has instituted a Hispanic Student Success Program to address low college attendance and high college attrition among Hispanic students and has lobbied for programs and resources for HSIs.

The establishment in 1990 of a Minority Education Initiative by the American Association of Community and Junior Colleges (AACJC) is another step in the right direction. The initiative is intended to "assist colleges with the adoption of aggressive policies and practices to improve the recruitment, retention, and success of students, helping to guide minority students through a successful college experience" (AACJC 1990). The initiative will also "include a special emphasis to encourage minorities to enter the education field as administrators and faculty." In 1991, the AACJC established an official commission to improve minority education, charging it with the responsibility of advising the organization on the progress of the Minority Education Initiative. Finally, the National Community College Hispanic Council, with a grant from the Ford Foundation, has established a leadership institute for Hispanic community college administrators.

HISPANIC FACULTY AND STAFF

If the data on Hispanic students is inadequate, data on Hispanic faculty and staff in community colleges is even more scarce. De los Santos states that "national data on full-time Hispanic faculty in the community colleges is not readily available" (1980, 23), a situation that continues to exist. For instance, the U.S. Department of Education's authoritative annual report, *The Condition of Education*, contains no data on Hispanic faculty in higher education. De los Santos (1980) reported that, in 1971, the ratio of full-time Mexican-American faculty members to Mexican-American students in the community colleges of five Southwestern states was 1 to 124; by 1976 the situation had gotten worse. Current available data is for all institutions of higher education. The percentage of full-time faculty at all institutions of higher education who are Hispanic increased only from 1.5 percent to 2.0 percent between 1979 and 1989 while Hispanic student enrollment increased from 3.9 percent to 5.5 percent during the same period (American Council on Education 1992, 24, 63). The higher the academic rank, the fewer the number of Hispanics. Among tenured faculty, only 1.4 percent are Hispanic; 1.3 percent of full professors are Hispanic. Moreover, as many as from 65 to 70 percent of these are concentrated in a few institutions with 25 percent or more Hispanic students (Brodie 1992). The extent to which community college faculties conform to this picture is not known, although I would suggest that Hispanic faculty are slightly but not dramatically better represented in community colleges.

Data on Hispanic community college administrators is also scarce. By 1992, there were thirty-six Hispanic community college presidents, or about 3 percent of all community college presidents (Solis 1992). There is an evident need to collect and disseminate current, comprehensive, and authoritative data specifically on Hispanic faculty in two-year institutions. Despite the inadequate data, it is nevertheless clear that Hispanics are extremely underrepresented on the faculty and at the higher levels of community college administration. With the continuing increase in Hispanic student enrollment, it is imperative that community colleges redouble their efforts to recruit Hispanic faculty and staff.

While the literature at this juncture fails to provide clear answers even to the most basic questions, the evidence is that a great deal more needs to be done in terms of resources, programs, provision of faculty role models, and financial aid if community colleges are to fulfill their democratic promise for Hispanics. The organization and mobilization of Hispanics themselves in such organizations as HACU has already begun to raise the awareness of foundations and corporations about the urgency of the problem.

In summary, it is clear that not only the community college, but Hispanic education as a whole, is in crisis and that government, business, and the community must mobilize if we are to prevent the development of a massive, permanent Hispanic underclass of the undereducated.

REFERENCES

American Association of Community and Junior Colleges. 1990. Mission statement, 1990. Washington, D.C.

American Council on Education. 1992. *Minorities in higher education*. Tenth Annual Report. Washington, D.C.

Brint, S., and J. Karabel. 1989. *The diverted dream: Community colleges and the promise of educational opportunity in America, 1900–1985*. New York: Oxford University Press.

Brodie, J. M. 1992. Minority enrollments show slight increase, says ACE study. *Community College Week* 4 (February 3):2.

Career Intelligencer. 1991. Hispanic-serving colleges listed. *Hispanic Business* December: 54.

Cohen, A., and F. Brawer. 1989. *The American community college*. San Francisco: Jossey-Bass.

De la Rosa, D., and C. E. Maw. 1990. *Hispanic education: A statistical portrait 1990*. Washington, D.C.: National Council of La Raza, Office of Research Advocacy and Legislation.

De los Santos, A. 1980. *Hispanics and community colleges*. College of Education Topical Paper no. 18. University of Arizona, Center for the Study of Higher Education.

Evangelauf, J. 1991. Study predicts dramatic shifts in enrollments. The *Chronicle of Higher Education* 38(September 18):A–40.

Fields, C. 1988. The Hispanic pipeline: Narrow, leaking and needing repair. *Change* 20:20–27.

Fields, R. 1962. *The community college movement*. New York: McGraw-Hill.

Folger, J., H. Astin, and E. Bayer. 1970. *Human resources and higher education*. New York: Russell Sage Foundation.

Hendley, V. 1992. Report shows more minorities attending college, but educators worry budget cuts threaten progress. *Community, Technical, and Junior College Times* 4 (January 28):1.

Hispanic Association of Colleges and Universities. 1989. *Hispanic association of colleges and universities: Triennial report*. San Antonio, Texas.

————. 1990. *HACU annual report*. San Antonio, Texas.

Koos, L. 1925. *The junior college movement*. Boston: Ginn.

Miami-Dade Community College. 1990. *Factbook September 1990*. Miami:

Miami Herald. 1992. January 20. 1a, 4a.

Nora, A. 1990. Campus-based programs as determinants of retention among Hispanic community college students. *Journal of Higher Education* 61:312–21.

Orfield, G., and F. Paul. 1987–1988. Declines in minority access: A tale of five cities. *Educational Record* 68:57–62.

Rendón, L., and A. Nora. 1987–1988. Hispanic students: Stopping the leaks in the pipeline. *Educational Record* 68:79–85.

————. 1989. A synthesis and application of research on Hispanic students in community colleges. *Community College Review* 17:17–24.

Rendón, L., and M. T. Taylor. 1989–1990. Hispanic students: Action for access. *Community, Technical, and Junior College Journal* 60:18–23.

Roueche, J., and G. A. Baker. 1987. *Access and excellence*. Washington, D.C.: Community College Press.

Schmidt, P. 1992. Study shows a rise in the segregation of Hispanic students. *Education Week* 11 (January 15):1, 19.

Solis, E. 1992. Telephone conversation with author.

U.S. Bureau of the Census. 1991. *Statistical abstract of the United States: 1991*. Washington, D.C.

U.S. Department of Education, National Center for Education Statistics. 1990. *The condition of education, 1991*, vol. 2, *Postsecondary education*. Washington, D.C.

————. 1991. *Digest of education statistics 1990*. Washington, D.C.

Women and Leadership

Rosemary Gillett-Karam

Solomon (1985) would suggest that the junior-community college idea was gen-erated explicitly for women; she cites as evidence William Rainey Harper's reaction to the unexpected success of women graduates at the University of Chicago. It seems that Harper believed that a "woman's place" in higher ed-ucation meant a separate institution for women. Thus, he proposed a "junior college," where women would not impede the progress of higher education. Obviously, there are others who would question this principle which guided Harper's founding of the junior college. It is reported here as a factor in the history of women in higher education in America. Researchers take note not only of the obstacles of women in higher education throughout American history as a condition of the limited numbers of women in positions of leadership. Women as leaders is a concept which is emerging. And while studies examine the role of women in positions of leadership (Kanter 1977; Loden 1985; Gillett-Karam 1988), a summary of these studies supports two major conclusions: (1) despite their ever-increasing numbers in the work force, very few women have risen to the top of the organization and (2) efforts to change this phenomenon should begin by examining societal and structural barriers that impede women in the selection to lead organizations. Two studies, one of which examined leadership effectiveness (Gillett-Karam 1988) and the other of which interpreted leaders' use of power (Gillett-Karam and Kishi forthcoming), focus on the role of the female leader in the American community college. Both studies demon-strate that gender is a critical factor in describing leadership.

Although the research cited in this chapter supports the conclusion that barriers limit the access of women to the level of chief executive officer (CEO), and that the current paradigm for leadership presupposes a male prototype, we are aware that by examining the behaviors of women who are currently recognized leaders of community colleges, we may begin to understand the practices and behaviors that make them distinctive leaders and thus begin to develop a new model for leadership that is dual-gender oriented. Women leaders can provide a new model for leadership in the American community college. Judith Eaton, former vice president of the American Council on Education and currently director of the National Center for Academic Achievement and Transfer, Washington, D.C., addressed the role of future leadership:

Community college education is being shaped by the forces of limited financing, economic change, shifts in life-style and life expectations, and the demographics of our population. At the same time, a call is emerging for new leaders with new ideas to adapt our institutions to changing external forces. Where are the new leaders to come from? What is the present status of untapped resources—women and minorities—in leadership positions in college? A focus on women may provide answers and insights for emerging leadership. (Alfred et al., 1984, 93–94)

Transformational leadership relates to influencing human behavior within the community college setting: It is the ability to influence, shape, and embed values, beliefs, and behaviors consistent with increasing faculty and staff commitment to both access and excellence. This definition focuses on the leader-follower relationship and emphasizes the behavioral characteristics of the relationship. Using this definition as a focus on leadership, a group of 256 participants (235 males, 21 females) was studied by Roueche, Baker, and Rose in 1989 to determine the behaviors of community college leaders.

Gillett-Karam (1988) chose to study these women separately to determine whether gender was a critical variable in leadership behavior. Several factors labeled "feminine factors of leadership" and "masculine factors of leadership" were determined and pointed out as different leadership behaviors on the basis of gender. The female respondents were asked a specific question about their conceptualization of gender as it related to the role of the presidency, and all the women in the study were interviewed. The primary framework for comparing female and male college presidents focused on leadership competencies and the comparative strengths exhibited in these behaviors. Another indicator of leadership competencies measured both the CEO and the CEO's leadership team. Demographic information was used to compare female and male CEOs. These three comparisons will be presented in order of perceived research value.

RESEARCH BASE

By synthesizing the ideas of many current researchers, the dynamics of the leader-follower relationship (Table 1) may be presented. From this alliance, it is noted that intended change results from the vision of the leader and from the abilities, behaviors, and characteristics that stem from her or his relationships with followers. The interactive nature of transforming leadership applies power

Table 1
Transformational Leadership Model

Dynamics of Change:	Intellectual Stimulation
	Conflict And Choice
	Motives And Values
	Revitalization And Renewal

Attributes of the Leader	Responses of the Follower
Arouses, Engages, and Satisfies Needs	Brings Commitment to the Leader
Has Vision and Sense of Future Direction	Identifies with Leader; Buys Dream
Inspires and Motivates	Has Imagination and New Insights
Creates Institutional Purpose, Mission, Culture	Commits to Purpose, Mission, Culture
Employs Power to Realize Human Potential	Conceptualizes and Solves Problems
Influences Followers Needs, Aspirations	Shares Goals with Leader
Has Heightened Awareness, Excitement, Energy	Becomes a More Productive Person
Values Ideas, Aligns Motives	Motives Are Satisfied
Values the Preeminence of People	Believes He/She Can Make a Difference
Has High Tolerance for Planned Change	Chooses to Follow Leader
Possesses Accurate Self-Esteem	Transcends Lower Needs and Wants
Models Moral Values	Embraces Moral Values
Seeks Intellectual Development	Is Empowered and Educated to Lead
Makes the Follower the Leader	Converts to Become Leader

positively; mutual influence empowers the follower so that the follower can lead in her or his respective domain. In addition, this unique way of conceptualizing leadership implies that transforming creations come from leader-follower interdependence.

In Table 1, the transformational leadership concept is explained. The theories of Bennis and Nanus (1985) among others are critical to the model. An interdependent relationship exists between leader and follower that builds on a dynamic framework that accounts for intellectual stimulation and development, allows for conflict and choices which grow out of conflict resolution, and builds on the specific needs, motives, and values of those who are served. This interdependent relationship ultimately allows the follower to learn leadership behavior so that he or she may become a future leader as the cycle of leadership begins anew. Geraldine Evans, the president of Rochester Community College in Minnesota, captured the essential nature of the transforming ability of presidents:

I inherited a junior college which had an egg-handling approach to students: they rolled in, they were sorted out, and they were sent out in a carton (with a diploma). We've undergone a total revolution after facing the fact that student enrollment had dropped 25 percent. We had to become a different college, with a different thrust based on changing demographics. Now we have outreach programs, we are involved in economic development, and we run classes early in the mornings, late in the evenings and on weekends. We've come a long way from the days in which we thought "there will always be students and our job is to grade and sort them (Interview 1988).

PRESIDENTIAL INFORMATION QUESTIONNAIRE

The most noteworthy data from the study of personal, demographic, experiential, and and time-use information focused on gender differences. Significant differences were found between women and men in the areas of age and career experience, educational background of parents, nature of entry level work experience, and time utilization.

Age and Career Experience

Women presidents assumed their first administrative career positions six years later than did the males of the study; women were thirty-four years old, and men were twenty-eight. Moreover, women assumed their first presidency at an average age of forty-three, which was seven years older than their male cohorts. (Women and men presidents shared a similar age of almost fifty. Moreover, they shared the career distinction of having been president at another institution just prior to accepting their present position.) Most of the literature suggests this is a normal time gap because women take time out to have and raise families, but it also suggests that the time lag relates more to the changing attitudes and values of a former androcentric society. Part of the time lag between women and men in career positions has to do with the fact that women have not long held executive positions in any field; for example, none of the women studied had been founding presidents of colleges.

Kanter (1977) found that only 2 percent of the 50,000 people she studied in executive positions in industry were women. She showed that neither gender nor individual characteristics had excluded women from leadership roles; rather, organizational structure had limited the opportunities of women—organizational structures shaped behavior in such a way that career paths confirm the prophecies of the institutional structure (158). Current data suggest that, although andro-centrism of organizational structure is better understood today and the attempt is being made to establish a more balanced view of culture as androgynous (Matlin 1987; Sargent 1983), barriers have not been completely eliminated for women assuming positions of leadership (Shakeshaft 1987). Conflicting reports suggest seven to eleven percent of public community colleges today have women presidents and ten percent of senior colleges and universities currently have women presidents. Some reports suggest these numbers have been decreasing since 1984 (*Chronicle of Higher Education* 1988; American Council on Edu-cation 1988). It comes as no surprise that women have held their present positions for much shorter periods than have their male counterparts. The average tenure for a woman in her present position is about five years; twelve years for a man. Vaughan (1986) found that the presidents he studied held presidential offices an average of only about five years, but his study was not limited to transformational leaders. It would appear that transformational leaders have greater staying power than do others. Phyllis Peterson, the president of Diablo Valley College in California, spoke to some effects of short tenure:

I've been in this job for only four years, so I always feel that I must stay abreast of the trends and note the future directions of our society. I need to know the needs of the working class, as well as the traditional student. I read a great deal and try to take a broader, longer look beyond the college to determine where the college fits in relationship to the "big picture." Then I listen and absorb as much as I can, as quickly as I can. (Interview 1988)

Parental and Personal Background

An unusual pattern appeared for the women community college presidents: The vast majority of their mothers were more highly educated than their fathers. Although the educational level of the male parent of the college presidents in this study is similar to that in Vaughan's study (where 51 percent of the fathers and 40 percent of the mothers had less than a high school education), the mother's educational level found here far exceeds that in Vaughan's (81 percent of the female college presidents' mothers had a high school education). Nellie Thor-ogood, the vice chancellor of North Harris Community College District in Texas, spoke of her mother and grandmother as exceptional mentors:

Although I was indeed fortunate to come to college in the 1960s when the women's movement was very strong, I was even more fortunate to have profited from the mentoring of my mother and my grandmother. My grandmother made me memorize the *Bible*, and I learned from her not only to develop my memory but also to defend what I knew. Every Sunday, she always announced, loudly and clearly, a correction to the minister's some-times bumbled *Bible* quotations. She was a powerful role model! (Interview 1988)

The presidents we studied had earned doctorates in almost all cases; although the women tended to earn the Ph.D. degree and the men the Ed.D., most of the doctorates were earned in higher education.

Female and male presidents had similar places of birth. The majority tended to be born in small towns of less than 25,000, but their mobility factor was high. Almost three-fourths of our presidents have left their home state; almost two-thirds had never left their birth states in Vaughan's study (however, Vaughan did not separate male and female presidents).

Entry Work Positions

About 40 percent of the women and men in this study began their administrative work experience as department heads or division chairpersons. Women were employed as public school administrators twice as often as men, and men were employed in student services positions twice as often as women. No one in this group began her or his career as president. Marjorie Blaha, the chancellor of Los Rios Community College District in California, spoke of her background and the value of her experiences:

I'm a very, very student-oriented person who comes out of years of teaching and years of instructional and services administration. I look for student-centered behavior from my faculty and staff. I think you have to model the behavior you want to see in other people . . . you can't run around in the world and be a pessimist and then expect your campus to have an optimistic environment. You can't be a hostile and adversarial person and expect your people to be positive and forward-looking, so I try to model the attitudes and values that I am hoping to help nurture in the institution. (Interview 1988)

Time Utilization Factors

Women in the study spent more hours at work per week, on the average, than did the men. Although all presidents worked long hours, the longer hours that women reported (as compared to the men presidents) were statistically significant. In brief, women spent more hours per week—worked more hours in the office, or at college-related activities, or at college work at home—than did men. This would seem to indicate that women work longer and harder at their jobs than do men, and some other researchers have shown this to be a significant factor in their studies, as well. Speaking of the time spent on college-related activities, Barbara Guthrie Morse, the president of West Virginia Northern in West Virginia, says:

I've been here for three years now; and although one has a honeymoon period, it doesn't last three years. Everyone has found out that the emperor has clothes, or that the empress has clothes. I think I have a good working relationship with my faculty and staff. We have a mutual attraction because we share the same values and attitudes, and we spend long hours working for what we want together—for example, we now have mandatory testing and placement and an assessment procedure in place. I find that all of us are motivated by setting high expectations. I tend to be an optimist; I have found very few problems in my life that couldn't be resolved if one focused enough time and energy on those problems. I tend to expect the people with whom I work also to have very high expectations of themselves. I can expect them to be as committed to the institution as I am. I can expect them to be as loyal to the institution and to their colleagues as I am. Then we exchange feedback, and we find that 90 to 98% of that feedback is positive. (Interview 1988)

Our study also found that women presidents spend significantly more time with their faculty than do men. They spend 25 percent more time consulting, conferring, and networking with faculty than do their male counterparts. Brunetta Wolfman, a past president of Roxbury Community College in Massachusetts, spoke to the sensitivity of women as college presidents:

I think there is a sensitivity that women have about gender and race. As women we need to recognize that sensitivity and the strength it gives us to act. Women are so much more fortunate to have been raised to be concerned about others, to be concerned about the environment, to be committed to helping others realize their potential. That is something that ought to be valued and not lost. (Interview 1988)

LEADERSHIP QUESTIONNAIRE

College presidents evaluated their leadership skills on the basis of a thirty-four-item questionnaire. In this analysis, no statistically significant differences were found on the basis of sex or gender, either by examining cluster variables or by conducting an item-by-item analysis. Moreover, approximately 85 percent of the administrative teams agreed with their presidents' self report and evaluations of their leadership behaviors. (This is not to say that the presidents or their followers responded to questions by indicating they were the best at what they did. In the Likert-type scale—in which the participants could rate their responses from highest to lowest, i.e., "frequently, if not always," "fairly often," "sometimes," "once in a while," and "not at all"—the presidents and their followers tended to respond with the answer "fairly often," indicating that they saw the dynamic of growth in the presidency and that they were still seeking and eliciting answers to questions concerning their institutions and their own development.)

The presidents gave themselves their highest scores for *vision*; the followers gave the presidents high scores in all clusters. Interestingly, both the leaders and the followers agreed about the poorest behaviors; both groups used the rating "sometimes" for the variables *rewards appropriately* (the CEO rewards the leadership team contingent on effort and performance) and *demonstrates sound judgment* (when acting with the administrative team, the CEO demonstrates consistent judgment). Finally, both the leaders and followers agreed that *values other* (seeks and values the opinions of others) was one of the best indicators of leader performance. (See Roueche, Baker, and Rose 1989 for further discussion.)

TRANSFORMATIONAL LEADERSHIP BEHAVIORS

From the perspective of the five cluster dimensions of transformational leadership—vision, people orientation, motivation orientation, empowerment, and values orientation, the concept of vision was most powerfully expressed by both female and male CEOs. The extent to which the concept of vision is present in the thinking of most leadership researchers today is overwhelming. "There is a need for vision and passion in leadership today. To inspire people to risk and create, leaders must be future oriented—focusing on new relationships between elements and people" (Connelly in Loden 1985, 243).

The concept of vision was the single most important concept of leadership mentioned by the leaders, regardless of gender. Moreover, followers cited the importance of visionary abilities in their leaders; an administrator at Central Piedmont Community College in North Carolina said this about her president, Ruth Shaw:

The college had a dispirited administration without a clear mission or unity of purpose. About a dozen vice-presidents ran uncoordinated programs on a decentralized basis. Our CEO reduced the number of vice-presidents, formed an executive cabinet, and held retreats to focus on a statement of purpose and mission. Then she empowered appropriately and instigated new designs of management. Slowly, the collective vision took place. Her correctives were handled with firmness, grace, and consideration for the individuals involved. As a result, I expect us to remain a "top five" community college. (Interview 1988)

Flora Mancuso-Edwards, the president of Middlesex County College in New Jersey, expressed the concept of vision most eloquently: "The hardest thing to pull off is to convince people to dream and not be afraid; then the next hardest thing is not letting them pull out of it."

The concept of *influence* was the other most statistically significant phenomenon assigned to transformational leadership. Richard Gilliland, the president of Metropolitan Community College, Nebraska, said:

I feel leadership is an egalitarian issue; the new generation of community college leaders need to maintain strength, courage, commitment, and a positive outlook. The founding fathers of the community college knew how important the challenge of leadership was to the community college. Joe Rushing and Bill Priest are the "forefathers" of the movement; today's presidents seem to be managers more than they are leaders. They are not risk-takers: what we need today is verve and enthusiasm; we need to be turned on and excited and committed. I believe that a good leader retains the "fire in the belly" that the early pioneers of the community college movement lit. (Interview 1988)

Table 2
Transformational Leadership Behaviors

Vision	Is a future orientated, has positive orientation toward change, takes risks, is commited to change, is mission oriented, shares vision, has commitment to student access and success.
People	Understands organizational ethos, rewards appropriately, demonstrates caring and respect, considers individual needs, is student centered, values others.
Motivation	Is flexible and creative, develops others, clarifies expectations, inspires.
Empowerment	Places responsibility with authority, has bias for action, causes followers to feel powerful, shares decision making, is influenced by followers, acts collaboratively, maintains open communications, is in touch with followers, demonstrates high energy.
Values	Demonstrates commitment to learning, advocates quality education, values consistency, demonstrates sound judgment, builds openness and trust, has sense of humor, leads by example.

The presidents took seriously their role of facilitating others in their decision making; many presidents spoke of delegating responsibility and authority, and they were comfortable involving others in decisions and solving problems. They knew how to integrate the critical and innovative ideas of others into their own views. They listened and learned from others. They acted positively and energetically. Marilyn Schlack, the president of Kalamazoo Community College in Michigan, said:

I am a consensus leader. I gather together many points of view and let every single person know that he or she has an important role to play. My styles of leadership may change based on a situation: sometimes I'm caring and sometimes I'm directive. I tend to be inward and evaluate and assess what is going well and what needs to be changed in terms of greater effectiveness. Hopefully, I'm a growing leader. (Interview 1988)

The analysis of CEO interviews yielded thirty-four distinct behaviors that were factored into five distinct clusters. (The five clusters are listed in Table 2. The behaviors with significantly different strength scores are highlighted in this table.) Presidents revealed a combination of attributes along a continuum; therefore, any drawing out and separating of the parts could become an ineffectual examination of separate pieces, rather than an understanding of the whole. How-ever, in the analysis of the Transformational Leadership Behaviors, gender differences were revealed by item analysis.

In examining the separate behaviors, four were significantly higher for women: (1) risk taking or taking appropriate risks to bring about change, a *vision* behavior; (2) demonstrates caring and respect for individual differences, a *people* behavior; (3) acts collaboratively, an *influence* behavior; and (4) builds openness and trust, a *values* behavior. Two behaviors were found to be significantly higher for men: (1) rewards others contingent on their effort and performance, a *people* behavior; and (2) is characterized by a bias for action, an *influence* behavior. Significant behaviors for women were labeled the "feminine" factors of leadership; those significant for men were labeled the "masculine" factors of leadership.

"FEMININE" FACTORS OF LEADERSHIP

Women in this study were involved to a greater degree in taking risks (takes appropriate risks to bring about change) than were men. Leadership research speaks often of the transformational leader as a risk taker. Taking risks is keenly involved in the concept of *vision* and provides the edge that separates the leader from the follower. "Effective leadership takes risks—it innovates, challenges and changes the basic metabolism of the organizational culture" (Bennis and Nanus 1985, 52). Loden (1985) views risk taking from the perspective of the female leader and suggests that as women recognized that their roles were ac-commodating and unproductive, they began to venture out and take risks that the "silent voices" in the past would have never dreamed of doing: "When women are no longer willing to accommodate by playing their prescribed roles, the familiar rules suddenly begin to change: for feminine leaders the choice of remaining in the role or risking the dissolution of long-standing relationships built on that role is difficult but not impossible to make, but it does imply that women take greater risks" (233).

It is only conjecture that risk taking may have its roots in the social implications of expected roles; nevertheless, it offers an insight into the roles of managerial, but not transformational, women leaders. In an actual experience, one of the administrative team at Bristol Community College in Massachusetts had this to say about president Eileen Farley:

We had always talked about affirmative action, but we had made no real effort to actively recruit minorities to our campus. It was easy to point to our books and say, "See, there it is: we do have a policy on affirmative action!" But that was just lip service. Dr. Farley was willing to risk the ennui and, in some cases, the opposition against active recruitment for minorities in our community and college. She authorized a strong recruitment effort, began advertising, went on recruitment searches, used personal contacts in minority communities to encourage applications, and provided incentives for successful efforts. In the 1987–1988 school year, three new minority faculty and two minority administrators were hired. Others were hired in technical and support services. I'll give Dr. Farley credit; she took risks that no one else was ever committed to take. Now we're all proud of her efforts. (Interview 1988)

Adrienne Rich, the noted poet, speaks to the risks women take by changing "accepted" roles:

If I could have one wish for my own sons, it is that they have the courage of women. I mean by this something very concrete and precise: the courage I have seen in women who, in their private and public lives, both in the interior world of their dreaming, thinking, and creating, and the outer world of patriarchy, are taking greater and greater risks, both psychic and physical, in the evolution of a new vision. Sometimes this act involves tiny acts of immense courage; sometimes public acts which can cost a woman her job or her life; often it involves moments, or long periods of thinking the unthinkable, being labeled, or feeling, crazy; always a loss of traditional securities. Every woman who takes her life into her own hands does so knowing that she must expect enormous pain, inflicted from within and without. I would like my sons not to shrink from this kind of pain, not to settle for the old male defenses, including that of a fatalistic self-hatred. And I would wish them to do this not for me, or for other women, but for themselves, and for the sake of the life on planet Earth. (1979, 215)

We were not surprised to find a difference between women and men around the variable of *caring and respect for others* (demonstrates respect for individual differences). In most of the literature about women since the early 1980s, the concepts of caring and connection have been identified as the basis of a new model regarding moral development theory. The tenets of this theory are simple. When psychologists Ericson, Piaget, and Kohlberg made their contributions to the theory of moral development (or the stages of man's ethical development), they either disregarded the females in their study, or pointed to their behaviors as deviant, or they failed to study females altogether. In 1982, when Gilligan pointed out the deficit to Kohlberg and posited her own theory of the "different voice" of women in moral development theory, both Kohlberg and the American public listened. The matching feminine response to moral development was a caring and connection mode (to Kohlberg's justice-rights mode). Gilligan, subsequently, has been the subject of much conjecture and research, but the idea of "caring" and the connection mode of ethics have been widely accepted; even Kohlberg has modified and adapted his thoughts to include Gilligan's theory.

Catherine Cornelius, the president of South Florida Community College in Florida, talked about gender roles:

I've never believed that the brain of an individual has a sex. I think both sexes are capable of logical thinking and problem solving. But women tend to be more nurturing than males; they tend to be more concerned about people as people and realize that problems, such as bad working conditions, may stifle performance. I see those people as human beings who need comfort in the job. I also know that good working conditions lead to more productivity, but the bottom line is that we care and we take care of people so that they can take care of themselves. (Interview 1988)

Women displayed greater strength than did men around the variable of *acting collaboratively* (is able to cause followers to work together to solve problems). Chancellor Patsy Fulton, of Oakland Community College District in Michigan, talks about her presidency at Brookhaven Community College in Texas:

I believe Bennis when he talks about the fact that the leader must be able to articulate the mission and the vision. When I went to Brookhaven, I did a lot of listening. I still listen, and then I take what I hear and match it to my audience. Collaboration is the critical element of my presidency. Why must we think as a group? It is because of the students: we care about the students and what students need; our job is to support what they need. My leadership style is collaboration, participation, listening and thinking, and acting on what is ahead. (Interview 1988)

Finally, women demonstrated greater strength around the variable of *openness and trust* (builds openness and trust through personal and professional behavior). President Yvonne Kennedy, of S. D. Bishop State Junior College in Alabama, said:

I've never been able to separate my own values as a person from my values as a college president. My own personal values begin with integrity and trust; I believe that these are essential qualities for all individuals, but especially for a college president who must always be accountable to her faculty, staff, administration, and community. (Interview 1988)

The ancient philosopher Lao-tzu reminds us that all behaviors contain their opposites: that water wears away the rock, that spirit overcomes force, and that, if one wishes to prosper, she or he must be generous. He also suggests that the feminine outlasts the masculine and that the feminine surrenders, then encompasses and wins. Leaders are urged to see things backwards, inside out, and upside down; they are taught that all behaviors are both masculine and feminine, and together they form the conceptual whole (Heider 1986).

"MASCULINE" FACTORS OF LEADERSHIP

The men in the study demonstrated two behaviors more strongly than did the women: *rewarding others* (people orientation) and *acting positively* (influence orientation). Bob Parilla, the president of Montgomery Community College in Maryland, explained that rewarding others on the basis of excellent performance is absolutely necessary to the well-being of the college environment:

Originally when I came to Montgomery, there was lots of turmoil within and outside of the college. I sat down with community people and talked with the goal of rebuilding community confidence with and for our college. Things began to turn around in the community, and the "town and gown" antagonism died away. Things were not that simple internally. But we talked, too. And our rewards came from doing our job well.

Now, because we have so many excellent examples of fine work by faculty and staff, we have instituted a system of merit increases—good performance deserves a reward. (Interview 1988)

Gender differences, therefore, are critical to the study of leadership. And while the numbers of women who are community college CEOs remain fairly small, obviously their number is growing. If we examine, for example, the "pathways" to the presidency including the number of women who are in positions of administration, about 35 percent of those positions are currently being held by women (Vaughan 1986; Gillett-Karam, Roueche, and Roueche 1991). Moreover, two groups, the American Association of Women in Community and Junior Colleges, an affiliate of AACJC, and the Leaders Project (formerly known as the National Institute for Leadership Development), Rio Salado Community College, Arizona, are both critical access vehicles for women's leadership roles in community colleges. Finally, an examination of higher education community college programs demonstrates at least an equal number (if not a higher number) of doctorates being awarded to women.

It is not surprising that the dissertations of these students are examining the role of women as future leaders in the American community college. One of these studies (Kishi 1992) examines gender and use of power. Three categories of leaders' uses of influence and power were examined—commitment, compliance, and resistance. The categories measured the extent to which the leaders' followers, or their administrative teams, changed their behavior or attitudes to reflect their leader's influence or power. By tabulating the responses described in a questionnaire (taken by CEOs as well as administrative teams), Kishi found that gender differences emerged. Female CEOs were more likely to disclose information and to state explicitly their expectations of their followers; male CEOs, on the other hand, were more likely to appeal to the reasoning ability of their teams. When the administrative teams were able to evaluate their leaders, gender differences once again emerged. Female leaders were perceived as having the "power" to influence behavior but not attitudes; male leaders were thought to influence behavior and change attitudes. This finding was, at least to the current research, controversial—moral development theorists and gender researchers posit that female leadership is empowering and participatory. This would suggest that Kishi should have found that women's leadership measured along the dimension, commitment, where internal agreement by the follower occurs as the leader delegates and utilizes participative leadership by empowering followers. Kishi's study did not find this concept consistent with (perceived) female CEOs' leadership behavior. This ability to use power to change attitudes was seen exclusively as a male quality of leadership. Nevertheless, although women were seen as having a unidimensional use of power, they were valued as effective leaders. Further study of this phenomenon is under way (Gillett-Karam and Kishi forthcoming).

CONCLUSION

Hopefully, the more researchers examine leadership, the more they will begin to lay to rest the covert and socialized mental messages that women, as leaders, are ineffective or have aberrent styles of leadership. Traditional views that posited leadership as an exclusive male domain are non-holistic. Gestalt psychology suggests the importance of viewing concepts from holistic emphases: In the ambiguous figure drawing of the vase or faces, one initially sees it one way; and, although the figure may be seen in both ways, there is a tendency to argue that there is only one right or better way of seeing that image. This pattern of perceptual organization reflects historical emphasis on "the one right way of viewing things," and it is central to the current situation which finds so few women in leadership positions in American community colleges. Our research finds that effective leadership is more behaviorally derived than gender derived, and it is subject to the dynamics and interactions of people and institutions. In other words, leadership depends on situations, not gender. Judy Merritt, the president of Jefferson State Junior College in Alabama, spoke candidly about gender and leadership:

From my perspective, gender has had an important impact on my presidency. It has given me some opportunities for leadership that might have been denied me under other circumstances or during other times. I see gender, or female, leadership as a chance to install innovative leadership into the community colleges of America. I have perhaps viewed my involvement with "rose-colored lenses," but the results have been gratifying. My goals are the group's goals, and my vision is a shared vision. (Interview 1988)

REFERENCES

Alfred R., P. Elsner, R. LeCroy, and N. Armes. 1984. *Emerging roles for community college leaders*. New Directions for Community Colleges. San Francisco: Jossey-Bass.

Belenky, M., et al. 1986. *Women's ways of knowing: The development of self, voice, and mind*. New York: Basic Books.

Bennis, W., and B. Nanus. 1985. *Leaders: The strategies for taking charge*. New York: Harper and Row.

Gillett-Karam, R. 1988. *Transformational leadership and the community college president: Are there gender differences?* Ph.D. diss., University of Texas at Austin.

Gillett-Karam, R., S. Roueche, and J. Roueche. 1991. *Underrepresentation and the question of diversity: Women and minorities in the community college*. Washington, D.C.: Community College Press.

Gillett-Karam, R., and T., Kishi. Forthcoming. *Power and leadership: Women in the American community college*. New Directions for Community Colleges. San Francisco: Jossey-Bass.

Gilligan, C. 1982. *In a different voice: Psychological theory and women's development*. Cambridge, Mass.: Harvard University Press.

Heider, J. 1986. *The tao of leadership: Leadership strategies for a new age*. New York: Bantam Books.

Interviews with author. 1988.

Kanter, R. 1977. *Men and women of the corporation*. New York: Basic Books.

Kellerman, B. 1984. *Leadership: Multidisciplinary perspectives*. Englewood Cliffs, N.J.: Prentice-Hall.

Kishi, T. 1992. *Transformational leaders in community colleges: Power and influence by gender*. Ph.D. diss., The University of Texas at Austin.

Loden, M. 1985. *Female leadership: How to succeed in business without being one of the boys*. New York: Times Books.

Matlin, M. 1987. *The psychology of women*. New York: Holt, Rinehart and Winston.

Rich, A. 1979. *On lies, secrets, and silence: Selected prose—1966–78*. New York: Norton.

Roueche, J., G. Baker, and R. Rose. 1989. *Shared vision: Transformational leadership in American community colleges*. Washington, D.C.: American Association of Community and Junior Colleges Press.

Sargent, A. 1983. *The androgynous manager: Blending male and female management styles for today's organization*. New York: American Management Association.

Shakeshaft, C. 1987. *Women in educational administration*. Newbury Park, Calif.: Sage Publications.

Solomon, B. 1985. *In the company of educated women. A history of women and higher education in America*. New Haven, Conn.: Yale University Press.

Vaughan, G. B. 1986. *The community college presidency*. New York: American Council on Education/Macmillan.

Part 2

The Mission and Functions of the Community College

The Mission and Functions of the Community College: An Overview

Albert L. Lorenzo

As we approach the end of this century, community colleges in America find themselves at a point of intense reexamination, both from the public they serve and from the educators who shape their structures. This scrutiny is predictable and healthy, driven in part by the approaching 100-year anniversary of the two-year college in America, and in part by the need to reshape many of the institutions serving our society to better fit a new world order.

Built on the American values of universal opportunity and access to education, it is not only what community colleges are providing, but how they go about providing it, that is being called into question. Even functions as traditional as remediation, job training, and transfer preparation are becoming legitimate subjects for reevaluation.

For example, some taxpayers are beginning to ask why they should have to pay twice for educational preparation. Shouldn't high schools be held accountable for correcting past deficiencies rather than supporting remedial programs at community colleges? At the same time, what is the value of job-specific training in a world where job skills become obsolete in a matter of a few years? Would it be better to provide an occupational core curriculum and then let employers provide the specialized training? Or should the community college do both? And, finally, how can we design a single transfer curriculum that will meet the increasingly divergent transfer requirements of senior institutions?

All of these questions will, of course, have to be pondered within the context of growing resource limitations. Planning approaches have historically assumed that all current offerings could be preserved while funding for new ventures would flow from new increments of revenue. Such a philosophy is destined to fail in today's environment of diminished public funds and taxpayer unrest.

New concepts such as growth by substitution, resource reallocation, and systematic abandonment will have to become as much a part of tomorrow's planning as enrollment forecasting was to previous models. But regardless of the planning and decision-making models employed, the cornerstone of institutional progress will be a well-defined and well-understood mission statement.

Clearly, no one individual or group can provide the answers to all of the questions surrounding the emerging mission and role of America's community colleges. Further, and by design, the mission of each college should differ somewhat in order to reflect the unique needs and characteristics of the community it serves. Therefore, as our nation's communities become more diverse, it is logical to expect that our nation's two-year colleges will become more diverse as well.

A strength of the community college system in the United States is that these institutions are both a part of a national movement and a series of local responses to national issues. Key among those issues will continue to be the challenge of assuring the ongoing opportunity for accessible, affordable, and relevant postsecondary education to the broadest possible segment of the nation's population.

THE EVOLUTION OF AMERICA'S COMMUNITY COLLEGES

A review of the literature on the evolution of the comprehensive community college mission provides a good starting point for envisioning the future purposes of America's two-year colleges. It is from this established core of basic services that community colleges will continue to evolve. The following narrative, therefore, seeks to summarize those traditional functions and subsequently to identify some emerging issues that are likely to shape the role of America's two-year institutions in the century ahead.

The earliest notion of education dates back to primitive times when nomadic tribes constructed crude learning exercises to attempt to help a child become a productive and contributing member of the tribe. This process, say anthropologists, is called enculturation. Much later in civilization, Plato observed in his Laws that "education produces good men, and good men act nobly." Even to this day, the overarching mission for all of education remains somewhat the same: to develop individuals into fully functioning and contributing members of a society.

Higher education has a long history in America. Nine degree-granting institutions had been founded in the United States before the American Revolution. They were designed to offer the traditional liberal arts of Latin and Greek grammar, rhetoric, mathematics, and philosophy.

It was not until after the Civil War, however, that three environmental conditions began to transform thinking about higher education: (1) the rapid industrialization of the United States and the related mechanization of its agriculture, (2) increasing completion rates from high schools, and (3) the emergence of American research universities (Deegan and Tillery 1985).

The Morrill Act, passed in 1862, along with later amendments, solidified the concept of education "for the people" and established land grant colleges to provide practical, skill-based higher education in the United States. It was later recognized, however, that geography and cost were major barriers to attendance even at these institutions. So, around the turn of the twentieth century, the first junior colleges were established. Their purpose was to provide a lower-cost, more conveniently accessible alternative to the first two years of traditional university education.

With the introduction of the two-year college, the national education "system" as we know it today was completed. That system is made up of components that are intended to work together to serve all of the educational needs of American citizens: elementary and secondary education, mandated by law, provides basic education and literacy for all Americans; proprietary schools provide skill-based job training over short time frames; community colleges provide comprehensive skill training, upgrading, personal enrichment, and transfer credit; universities provide baccalaureate and higher degree programs to prepare students for vocations and professions; research universities foster scientific inquiry and innovation; and private and religious colleges provide strong grounding in philosophical and theological thought.

A SYNTHESIS OF THE LITERATURE

Much has been written about the broad mission of community colleges in America. The "comprehensive" mission includes five traditional components, defined in *The American Community College* as transfer-oriented education, career education, general education, remedial education, and community education (Cohen and Brawer 1989). In addition, the literature stresses the importance of student services as a support function critical to attaining educational objectives.

The Collegiate Function—Liberal Arts and Transfer Education

Most of the literature on community colleges points to a balancing of the transfer function with other diversified functions in what is known as the modern, comprehensive community college. The literature also characterizes the evolution of two-year colleges along "generational" lines.

The first generation of junior colleges, which provided primarily liberal arts and transfer education, played an important role through the late 1950s. These institutions assisted our nation's citizens in raising their sights beyond the goal of simply achieving a high school education. The principal curriculum objective of the junior college was to parallel the lower division, undergraduate collegiate experience.

The next generation, the community college, offered a wider array of programs including technical education, general education, adult education, and community services (Knoell 1982). The third generation, known as the "comprehensive community college," focused on broadening the clientele to be served. "No longer was it possible to say that a certain type of student was the norm," says Knoell. "The evolution into the comprehensive community college was characterized by a vast increase in the heterogeneity of the student body with respect to age, ethnicity, readiness or ability to do college-level work, previous educational attainment, interests and goals, and objectives being pursued" (Knoell 1982, 7).

Historically, then, the only mission component to be present in each phase of community college development was the transfer preparation function. Ironically, though, a variety of pressures arose in the 1970s and 1980s that may, in fact, have contributed to an actual decline in the numbers of community college transfer students. These factors, according to Knoell, include

1. Pressure on four-year institutions to improve access for ethnic minorities
2. Unemployment and underemployment of baccalaureate degree holders
3. Public attitudes questioning the costs and outcomes of a college education.

Recent reports on student intentions, however, signal a returning interest in transfer programs. There is a trend toward establishing formal transfer articulation agreements with senior institutions, and there is a heightened interest in providing bachelors degree completion programs on two-year college campuses. Taken collectively, these factors suggest a renewed emphasis on the liberal arts and transfer function in the years ahead.

Career Education

The terms vocational, technical, semiprofessional, and occupational education all variously describe career education in community colleges. All connote a process of orienting students to provide productive contributions in the workplace—and of providing employers with skilled workers.

Almost since their inception, however, career education programs have been the subject of controversy. On the one hand, they provide a means for post–high school age graduates to obtain job skills. On the other hand, it is often argued that students completing career education programs lack the necessary basic skills—writing, computational, and problem solving—to adapt to the rapid changes in the workplace.

All the while, community colleges continue to be the focus of increasing pressure from business and government for more effective job training programs. Five sources for this increasing pressure have been identified (Luther 1984):

1. The recession of the early 1980s precipitated a restructuring of industry in America, forcing changes to occur in months which ordinarily would have taken years.

2. Industrial processes in the United States lost their competitive position, bringing about the decline of many U.S. firms in relation to their world-class competitors.

3. There have been fundamental demographic changes in the work force, with large numbers of blacks, Hispanics, and women demanding opportunities in the workplace.

4. The information revolution has pressed workers to be computer literate.

5. The Japanese influence on the world market has meant a new focus on quality, work-force involvement, and lower prices.

While destined to remain an essential part of the mission of every comprehensive community college, however, career education lacks a clear direction. Predictably, there will be some movement away from sharply defined, skill-specific programs in favor of less specialized core curricula. This movement emulates the "generalization" of job classifications occurring in most workplaces. Similarly, there may be a need to extend program requirements beyond the traditional two-year time frame in order to accommodate the expanded volume of learning required to be "certified" as competent and "work ready" in some fields.

The future form of career education is likely to be most directly influenced by the ultimate economic and work-force strategies chosen by American competitors. "At present, the new economy is still a series of different possibilities contingent on a wide variety of choices. Once these choices have been made, the nation will be wedded to a dominant configuration of markets, strategies, organizational structures, job designs, and skill utilization" (Carnevale 1991). Similarly, once these choices have been made, the future role of career education will be much easier to predict.

General Education

General education is perhaps the most misunderstood aspect of the community college curriculum. Frequently, students enrolled in general education programs are perceived as unable to make a decision about a career direction, and too often such programs are thought of as "warehouses" in which to place students in transit toward some other endeavor. Instead, general education should be thought of as "the process of developing a framework on which to place knowledge stemming from various sources, of learning to think critically, develop values, understand traditions, respect diverse cultures and opinions, and most important, put that knowledge to use" (Cohen and Brawer 1989, 312).

After twenty years of curriculum emphasis on career education programs, general education may enjoy a renaissance of emphasis in many community colleges across the United States. According to the special report in *Business Week* (Bernstein 1988), the convergence of three dynamic forces has produced a quantum leap in the educational requirements for new jobs:

1. Technology is upgrading the content of most jobs.
2. Job growth is greatest in the high-skill occupations.
3. The way we work is changing, requiring an ever-increasing ability to integrate into the structure of a company, communicate effectively, and interact with others on the job.

It is the third item that may drive the renaissance of general education, for it is within the context of such programs that students without a well-defined career plan can sharpen their integrative and interaction skills and enhance their employability profile. But for general education to retain its right of inclusion among multiple mission components, it will be necessary to identify more succinctly the intended student outcomes.

Several recent studies of emerging work-force requirements may serve as a guide in formulating the objectives for general education or general studies programs. An example of such a study, conducted by the State of Michigan (Pestillo 1989), defined employability skills as

1. Communication, comprehension, and critical thinking skills
2. Dependability, goal setting, goal achievement, values clarification, and self-discipline skills
3. Interpersonal, organizational, negotiation, creativity, innovation, and leadership skills.

These and other functional characteristics may help to better define the expected outcomes of the general education curriculum.

Remedial Education

While it is often difficult to identify all the underlying causes, the irrefutable fact remains that a significant number of students enter our nation's community colleges underprepared to succeed in college-level course work. A part of the blame must be placed with the educational system itself. Although difficult to quantify, "available evidence suggests that academic achievement of students in schools and colleges registered a gradual improvement between 1900 and the mid–1950s, an accelerated improvement between the mid–1950s and the mid–1960s, and a precipitous, wide-spread decline between then and the late 1970s before stabilizing in the mid–1980s" (Cohen and Brawer 1989).

A study of Michigan corporate chief executive officers (CEOs), conducted by the Center for Community Studies at Macomb, showed that solid basic skills development is a clear expectation of the educational system. Entirely 100 percent of the business leaders polled expressed the need for more skill among graduates in the areas of reading, writing, and math, as well as competency in problem solving and computers (Center for Community Studies 1990).

Even though a solid foundation in the basic skills is a proven prerequisite for collegiate success and a clear public expectation, remediation still seems to be the focus of considerable debate. One issue relates to how well we are able to determine the need for remedial support. For example, assessment testing provides some indication of basic skill deficiency, but preliminary findings of a study at Macomb shows that assessment testing is not much more accurate than the grades received in remedial course work in predicting subsequent academic success (Thompson 1991).

Another issue is to determine if there should be a level below which community colleges should not be expected to remediate. Can colleges realistically cope with *any* level of reading deficiency? Or is there a level of deficiency below which the college cannot reasonably be expected to help?

A more recent issue, flowing directly from the growing pressure on resources, is whether remediation should be available without cost to the student needing it. Stated differently, what is the appropriate "package" of services that is included in a student's tuition? Should all students share the cost of remediating some students, or should that cost be borne by the student needing assistance?

Finally, faced with tight budgets, some states are questioning whether remediation is appropriate at the community college level at all. Some suggest that individuals with basic skill deficiencies should simply be referred to their original school district for remedial classes without cost to the college or an employer. If such an attitude ever became public policy, the remedial component would be deleted from mission consideration.

Community Education

Community education encompasses a wide range of activities at the community college, including adult education, continuing education, contract training, and community services. These offerings can be credit or noncredit, based on learning job skills or enhancing personal enjoyment, ranging from a one-hour workshop to a semester-long course and taught at a college facility or off site.

Gleazer (1980) sees community education as "the nexus of a community learning system, relating organizations with educational functions into a complex sufficient to respond to the population's learning needs." The Commission on the Future of Community Colleges (1988) reinforces this view:

The community college, at its best, can be a center for problem-solving in adult illiteracy or the education of the disabled. It can be a center for leadership training, too. It can also be the place where education and business leaders meet to talk about the problems of displaced workers. It can bring together agencies to strengthen services for minorities, working women, single parent heads of households, and unwed teenage parents. It can coordinate efforts to provide day care, transportation, and financial aid. The community college can take the lead in long-range planning for community development. And it can serve as the focal point for improving the quality of life in the inner city. (35)

That is an inspiring list. The reality, however, is that the funding systems in many states act as a disincentive to providing that nexus to the community learning system by not recognizing—and reimbursing—the costs associated with the extension of community education activities. A second problem associated with community education is the nature of specific courses to be offered. Such courses often provide "alternative" learning experiences but, by being nontraditional, call into question the validity of course content and social value. For this and other reasons, community service staff often feel like the stepchildren of the organization.

The future of community education is unclear at this point. Cohen and Brawer (1989) advocate a separation of community education from the traditional educational activities of a community college. The purpose would be twofold: to structure a funding mechanism that would support the community education arm and to address the ongoing relegation of community education to secondary status within a college.

There is, however, a unique aspect of community education. It is typically the most adaptable, flexible, and responsive of all the learning experiences offered by the college. These attributes most closely parallel the tenor of the times in corporate and community life. Community education could, therefore, become a low-risk source for curriculum experimentation and incubation.

It is clear, though, that some means must be found to assess better the economic and educational value of community education before a conclusion can be reached about its proportionate role within the mission of the modern community college.

LOOKING AHEAD

Community college educators are seldom at a loss for conjecture on the future of their institutions. "The debate concerning the possible futures for American community colleges has been smoldering ever since Arthur Cohen presented that 'heretical concept' in Dateline '79" (Norris 1989, 1). In *Building Communities*, the Commission on the Future of Community Colleges gave some collective insight into what may be expected. "The world may not yet be a global village," said the commission, "but surely our sense of neighborhood must expand . . . if students do not see beyond themselves and better understand their place in our complex world, their capacity to live responsibly will be dangerously diminished" (1988, 31).

As the context for life in America changes, it is highly likely that new aspects of community college mission will emerge. This sentiment is echoed by noted forecaster John Naisbitt who says that "in tune with trends toward convenience and value, forward thinking community colleges will broaden their curricula and enjoy continued growth in the years ahead" (1991, 7). Based upon emerging practices and changing societal needs, by the turn of the century, it is likely that three new elements will be incorporated into the missions of many American two-year colleges: customized education, advanced education, and adaptive education.

Customized Education

A national survey of two-year colleges conducted by Philip Day for the American Association of Community and Junior Colleges (1985) revealed that nearly three-fourths of all respondents offered specialized training programs for large private sector employers, and 80 percent of all the colleges reported involvement with local and state economic development offices.

The majority of this type of programming has to be customized in some way: course content, delivery system, calendar and/or sequencing. Although the volume at most institutions is still proportionately small in comparison to degree credit instruction, there is every likelihood that community colleges will be called upon more frequently to provide customized offerings.

As the demand for customized course ware grows, colleges should consider moving this type of programming from underneath the broad umbrella of community education into a more independent identity. Institutions with strong commitments to customization may want to signal that emphasis by moving quickly to create a specific reference to customized education within their mission statements.

Advanced Education

Community colleges were created to help overcome barriers to access in higher education. When the majority of college students were younger, more full time, more day time, and more mobile, providing convenient access to the first two years of college may have been enough. The profile of community college students has changed, however, The majority are now part-time students, attend in the evenings, are over the age of twenty-five, and must contend with geographic barriers. Such realities necessitate adjustments on the part of community colleges.

To accommodate fully the higher educational needs of this "new majority" of college students, community colleges are once again being called upon to remove a barrier to access—only this time it is access to upper division course work. For those prospective students beyond a reasonable commuting distance to a senior institution, the community college may become their only means for securing more convenient opportunities for degree completion programs.

A few national models for bachelors degree partnership programs have already emerged, and several states are studying the concept (Cage 1990). These cutting-edge relationships typically provide for all upper division course work to be offered on the community college campus, either in shared facilities or in space fully dedicated to the senior institution(s). As the relationship between higher education and higher wages becomes more direct, the pressure on community colleges to provide convenient opportunities for completion of advanced degrees is likely to grow.

Adaptive Education

The emerging global economy has forced a discussion of new standards for education in America. Individual schools and individual students should no longer be judged solely against a national standard, but rather against a world standard. Any institution striving for world-class status will have to ensure that its graduates have acquired a basic understanding of the ability to function within multiple cultures.

Community colleges across the United States are being asked to help their students see the world as larger than their own ethnicity, their own city, their own country. "Developing International Education Programs" (Fersh 1990) summarizes the task quite well: "Challenged and confronted now by the certainty that people increasingly will live in cultures that are less and less extensions of their pasts, we now have the opportunity and the need to be culture-creators as well as culture-inheritors."

We are also seeing community colleges become the institution of choice for many adults who are new to our nation. In many urban centers, English as a second language and related "enculturation" courses are experiencing annual double-digit enrollment increases. It is likely that this trend will continue wherever immigration is a significant source of population growth. So perhaps the newest expectation of our nation's two-year colleges will be to help individuals adapt to divergent cultures and ensure the maximum degree of "social fit," both at home and abroad.

INSTITUTIONAL QUESTIONS AND ANSWERS

Clearly, then, no one individual or group is likely to be able to provide universal direction to the future course of America's two-year colleges. Given the community-based nature of these institutions, the best choices will most often come from within the organizations themselves. But while it is difficult to propose generic answers, it is possible to frame a few global questions.

In considering a better way to describe the emerging purpose of our nation's institutions of higher education, members of the Pew Higher Education Research Program (1991) developed a list of three key questions related to society's expectations of America's colleges and universities. These questions can be paraphrased to apply more directly to community colleges as follows:

1. What are community colleges expected to deliver and to whom?
2. What differences should a community college education make in the lives of those who earn an associate degree?
3. How much responsibility should two-year colleges have for maintaining the nation's (or a community's) social fabric, securing its economic well-being, preserving its history and culture, and strengthening its attitude and beliefs?

Institutionally developed answers to these three far-reaching questions can provide a solid foundation for drafting a more contemporary mission statement.

One final set of comments relates to the context within which any reexamination of mission will occur. While it might seem unnecessary to contrast the circumstances and conditions of the 1990s with those of the 1960s, when nearly half of America's two-year colleges were founded, failure to internalize those differences may result in a mission review's falling short of its best possible outcome.

As we prepare for the turn of the century, we find that we are on the verge of a true global society, that most aspects of our population and infrastructure are aging, that the nature of families and households is continually changing, and that, although the prospects for women and minorities appear to be improving, the lot of many children is deteriorating. As a nation, we are diversifying and downsizing. The number of legitimate opportunities is far outpacing available resources, and the growth in human need seems to outdistance the limits of our compassion. Perhaps most perplexing, we are surrounded by compelling evidence of the need for change while at the same time many Americans are enjoying a high degree of personal comfort with the status quo.

Those who successfully fashion the community college mission statements of the future will have to find a way to balance tradition with innovation, and expectations with possibilities. They will need to know the roots of the "movement" and the emerging needs of our society. Most important, they will have to possess a deep respect for the inherent values of teaching, learning, and human potential.

REFERENCES

Bernstein, A. 1988. Where the jobs are is where the skills aren't. *Business Week* (September 19):104–6.

Cage, M. C. 1990. Michigan's "higher education mall" viewed as a model for other communities. *Chronicle of Higher Education* (September 19, 1A and 26A).

Carnevale, A. P. 1991. *America and the new economy.* Washington, D.C.: American Society for Training and Development and U.S. Department of Labor Employment and Training Administration.

Center for Community Studies. 1990. *Michigan 100 survey: Business leaders' views on education and training.* Warren, Mich.: Macomb Community College.

Cohen, A. M., and F. B. Brawer. 1989. *The American community college.* 2d ed. San Francisco: Jossey-Bass.

Commission on the Future of Community Colleges. 1988. *Building communities: A vision for a new century.* Washington, D.C.: American Association of Community and Junior Colleges.

Day, P. 1985. *In search of community college partnerships.* Washington, D.C.: American Association of Community and Junior Colleges.

Deegan, W. L., D. Tillery, and Associates. 1985. *Renewing the American community college.* San Francisco: Jossey-Bass.

Fersh, S. H. 1990. Adding an international dimension to the community college: Examples and implications. In *Developing international education programs*, ed. R. K. Greenfield. New Directions for Community Colleges, no. 70. San Francisco: Jossey-Bass.

Gleazer, E. J., Jr. 1980. *The community college: Values, vision, and vitality*. Washington, D.C.: American Association of Community and Junior Colleges.

Knoell, D. M. 1982. The transfer function—One of many. In *Improving articulation and transfer relationships*, ed. F. C. Kintzer. New Directions for Community Colleges no. 39. San Francisco: Jossey-Bass.

Luther, D. B. 1984. Partnerships for employee training: Implications for education, business, and industry. *New Directions for Community Colleges* no. 48. San Francisco: Jossey-Bass.

Naisbitt, J. 1991. Junior colleges gain new respectability. *John Naisbitt's Trend Letter* (September). Washington, D.C.: Global Network.

Norris, N. A. 1989. *Community college futures: From rhetoric to reality*. Stillwater, Okla.: New Forums Press.

Pestillo, P. J. 1989. *Workforce-ready . . . Michigan's solution*. Lansing: Governor's Commission on Jobs and Economic Development.

Pew Endowment. 1991. An end to sanctuary. *Policy Perspectives* 3(4) (September): Section A. Philadelphia: Pew Higher Education Research Program.

Thompson, D. R. 1991. *An exploration of the use of ASSET post-test scores to measure the effectiveness of remedial courses and to predict success in follow-up courses*. Warren, Mich.: Macomb Community College Information and Planning Systems.

Improving Transfer Effectiveness

Dorothy Knoell

DEFINITIONS AND DISTINCTIONS

The transfer function has two major components—admissions and articulation. They are interrelated and to a considerable extent interdependent, and the transfer function cannot be considered to be fully effective in either the community colleges or the baccalaureate institutions if either component is weak.

"Admissions" needs to be broadly defined to include related services such as outreach to potential students, counseling and advising, orientation, and student financial aid. The delivery of these student-oriented services, often provided by student services personnel, should be on a continuum from high school (or earlier) through the community college to the four-year institution to which the student transfers. On the other hand, "articulation" is defined here as the alignment of courses taught and programs offered at different levels to minimize duplication, overlap, and loss of time and credit by students as they move from one educational level to the next. Articulation activities involve faculty and other academic personnel more often than staff in student services although the assignment of an institution's "articulation officer" may be to either the academic or the student services sector of the institution's organizational scheme.

This chapter concerning the transfer function begins with a definition of transfer effectiveness and various attempts to measure it. It proceeds to a discussion of the kinds of evidence that are available to support claims that the admissions component of the transfer function is effective from the standpoint of the community colleges, the baccalaureate degree-granting institutions, and the constituencies in each. The second section presents example of programs, practices, policies, and services that have been implemented with the objective of increasing transfer effectiveness, with attention to special populations including groups that have been historically underrepresented in higher education. Finally, the issues surrounding the transfer of these groups are examined, along with those of transfer effectiveness.

TRANSFER EFFECTIVENESS

With increasing frequency, transfer effectiveness is being defined as the rate at which community college students transfer to baccalaureate degree-granting institutions. Beyond this simple definition, there are differences in the way such a rate is calculated—in the numerator, who is to be counted among the students who have in fact transferred; in the denominator, how to constitute the "transfer pool." Two major national endeavors that are focusing on defining and then computing a transfer rate are sponsored by the Transfer Assembly at the Center for the Study of Community Colleges (Cohen 1991, 1992) and the National Effective Transfer Consortium (Berman/Weiler Associates 1989). These efforts have been directed more toward finding a way to compute institutional, state, and national rates that (1) use data that are readily available and (2) produce credible results, rather than assessing the effectiveness of the transfer function under varying conditions.

Still other researchers have been less concerned with how to compute a transfer rate and have focused instead on analyses over time and of different cohorts. Among them are Grubb (1991), who has found decreasing rates of transfer over time, and Adelman (1991, 1992) who, like Grubb, used the National Longitudinal Study data base (NLS72) for his analysis. As summarized in *Setting the National Agenda: Academic Achievement and Transfer* (National Center for Academic Achievement and Transfer 1991), the rates, variously computed, are in the lower 20s and range from 20 percent (Grubb, 1980 high school graduates) to 29 percent (Grubb, 1972 high school graduates).

While there is a movement to use transfer rates as the measure of transfer effectiveness, states and colleges continue to show interest in assessing effectiveness in terms of numbers of students who transfer to four-year institutions— by gender, race/ethnicity, associate-degree status, and major field (Illinois Board of Higher Education 1992; California Postsecondary Education Commission 1991). Increases in numbers are assumed to be indicators of effectiveness, although particular rates may decline if the transfer pool increases faster than the flow of students. Number may, in fact, be of greater utility than transfer rates when the denominator for the rates is small or its composition unclear, or when special programs are being evaluated.

Changes in numbers and rates of transfer are only a first, inadequate step in assessing transfer effectiveness, with measures of performance after transfer of at least equal importance. These include persistence and time to graduation with a baccalaureate degree (often in comparison to "native" students who began work in the institution as freshmen), and transfer students from other types of institutions, and grade-point average after transfer (in comparison to the grade-point averages that these students earned in the community college before transfer and with those earned by native students). Still other analyses of transfer effectiveness compare the performance of transfer students who would have been eligible for university admission as freshmen on the basis of their high school record and test scores with that of students whose high school performance would not have qualified them for admission as freshmen. States with experience that may be useful to others in developing student data bases and then reporting with this kind of measure of effectiveness include California (University of California 1991), New York (State University of New York 1992), and Washington (Washington State Board for Community College Education 1989).

While most analyses focus on persistence and time to the baccalaureate degree after transfer, California has added a measure of productivity, which is the proportion of baccalaureate degrees that are awarded to transfer students from community colleges in comparison with the proportions awarded to native students and transfer students from other types of institutions (California Community Colleges 1989a). The analysis is performed by major field and gender and may be done by racial/ethnic groups as well.

Going beyond the single analysis of changes in numbers as a measure of effectiveness, two California researchers have been exploring the organizational environment of community colleges as it affects transfer effectiveness. Banks (1992) used both national and California data in her examination of environmental and organizational factors that influence transfer effectiveness, defined as institutional student credit and transfer rates. Results of her analysis indicate that about half of the college's transfer performance is influenced by environmental factors and the remainder by its organizational context. Environmental factors in the analysis of national data included unemployment rates and community income, percentages of full-time faculty and younger students, tuition, and expenditures per full-time equivalent (FTE) student. Organizational factors that were found to promote transfer in the six California colleges included in the study were faculty involvement in decision making, institutional commitment, course articulation with four-year institutions, and a comprehensive liberal curriculum.

McIntyre (1988) used transfer rates for more than 100 California community colleges to perform a regression analysis; the independent variables included fourteen student, college, and community characteristics. The factors that were found most recently to relate positively to transfer rates (at the 0.05 percent level or better) are as follows: number of full-time students, percent of full-time students under twenty-five years of age, the operation of a transfer center on the campus, total expenditures per average daily attendance (ADA), and a negative response on whether the college sent more than 10 percent of its transfers to one of three California state university campuses that restricted transfer admissions in the year studied.

Two factors were found to be significantly, but negatively, related to transfer rates: percent of full-time students who are Black or Latino and percent of full-time students who are male. Among the factors that were not found to be significantly related to transfer rates are the age of the college, its proximity to a public university campus, the population per square mile in the college's service area, and the percentage of instruction that is taught off campus.

Other Measures of Effectiveness

The "burden of proof" in assessing the effectiveness of the transfer function is most often on the community colleges, and, more specifically, on the students who actually transfer to four-year institutions and complete a baccalaureate degree program. As noted earlier, community colleges are thus judged by their transfer rate, the grades their students earn after transfer, and the percentage who persist and complete a baccalaureate degree. There are two additional ways of assessing the function—not yet documented in the research literature—both assume that transfer effectiveness is a shared responsibility of community colleges and four-year institutions and that responsibility for it does not begin or end at the point of transfer.

Current approaches to measuring effrectiveness assume that baccalaureate degree-granting institutions admit all community college applicants for advanced standing who have completed a minimum amount of transfer credit with a grade-point average (GPA) of C or better. Computations of transfer rates now make assumptions about eligibility to transfer and define the pool (denominator for the rate) in terms of a very small number of units earned in the community college of origin. In practice, many universities have higher, sometimes selective, standards and criteria for admission with advanced standing (i.e., associate of arts degree or fifty-six semester units with a GPA of C +). Given these conditions, the following are proposed as measures to gauge the effectiveness of a community college in preparing its students for transfer:

1. Percentage of students who complete the general education requirements that are needed for the baccalaureate degree
2. Percentage of students who complete an associate degree program that is designed for transfer
3. Percentage of students who complete thirty and sixty semester units of transfer credit with a GPA of 2.0, 2.5, 3.0, and better
4. Percentage of students expressing transfer goals at entrance who complete a transfer program with a satisfactory GPA
5. Percentage of students completing a transfer program with an appropriate GPA who complete an application for transfer, are admitted by a baccalaureate degree-granting institution, and transfer.

The effectiveness of the receiving universities also needs to be assessed, especially since the concept of a transfer rate is not applicable. The following measures are a few possibilities for assessment:

1. Percentage of initial applications that are completed, accepted for admission, and enrolled

2. Percentage of community college transfer credit for which baccalaureate degree credit is awarded and which satisfies degree requirements

3. Retention/persistence to the baccalaureate degree, compared with native students

4. Proportion of baccalaureate degrees awarded to transfer students from community colleges compared with other student courses and by gender, ethnicity, and field.

Opinions about Effectiveness

The opinions of users, providers, and observers of transfer programs and services are still another useful source of information in evaluating the transfer function. While used perhaps too often by community colleges as public relations devices, surveys of students, faculty, counselors, and others can yield insights into the strengths and weaknesses of various aspects of the transfer function. Interviews before and after students transfer may be more useful than opinion surveys in pinpointing problems and weaknesses in transfer programs and services. Topics for interviews and surveys would include curriculum as well as the counseling/advising process. Surveys of students who intended to transfer but did not might result in especially interesting data.

A national study of transfer and articulation, conducted when transfer from what were then "junior colleges" was being accepted as a primary function, included both student surveys and interviews (Knoell and Medsker 1965). These findings have been verified countless times in research ranging from doctoral dissertations to college-specific surveys: Community college students who transfer valued highly the instruction and services that they received at the community college, compared with those they encountered at the four-year institution.

Opinion surveys are used more frequently to evaluate specifically funded programs and services than to assess the effectiveness of ongoing programs. Such surveys seldom document effectiveness but, instead, yield information about how users, providers, and others regard the program.

SPECIAL PRACTICES, PROGRAMS, AND SERVICES

Massive federal, state, and foundation funds have been expended on special projects to increase transfer effectiveness during the past two decades, some of which have been awarded to community colleges, a lesser amount to four-year institutions, and some to consortia or partnerships of institutions to increase and improve the flow of transfer students. To this amount might be added the cost of increased articulation activities involving faculty and other academic personnel, most of which is not specifically budgeted since it is assumed to be part of the normal workload of the persons involved.

Federal funds for the student flow/admission component of the transfer function have come for the most part from the Fund for the Improvement of Postsecondary Education (FIPSE), which makes annual grant awards on a competitive basis. States with a strong commitment to improving transfer, especially for students from historically underrepresented racial/ethnic groups, have been appropriating categorical funds for pilot projects. What happens to their pilot programs and services after their effectiveness has been evaluated and the special funding has expired is not often clear, especially in times of severe budget constraints. In any case, "local" funds for special projects are defined as money in an institution's base budget that may be used either to institutionalize pilot projects or to establish new programs and services to replicate successful pilot projects developed elsewhere, or to initiate different approaches to improve transfer. California and Illinois appear to be leaders among the states in appropriating special funds for programs to improve transfer.

Ford Foundation Grants

The Ford Foundation made the improvement of transfer and articulation a priority program for funding in the 1980s, particularly in urban community colleges for students from historically underrepresented groups. Grants have been made for developmental, demonstration, evaluation, and research activities in colleges and universities, to individual researchers, and to organizations that in turn award grants to entities that undertake pilot projects to improve transfer. A full description of Ford Foundation activities appeared in a report written by the author (California Postsecondary Education Commission 1990). The following paragraphs give an overview of these programs.

Transfer Opportunities Program (TOP). In September 1983, the Ford Foundation awarded grants to twenty-four urban community colleges in fifteen states with large percentages of African-American and Latino students to assist them in strengthening their academic and support programs so that their students would be better prepared to move on to four-year institutions (Schaier-Peleg 1984). The Ford Foundation also funded the Academy for Educational Development and the Center for the Study of Community Colleges to conduct research on and an evaluation of TOP, and Networks at Bronx Community College to facilitate communication and information about the TOP experience to colleges in the program and to higher education generally.

Transfer/Articulation Program. The Ford Foundation made a grant to the United Negro College Fund (UNCF) initially in 1986 to make grants on a competitive basis to member institutions for the purpose of working with public community colleges with significant African-American student populations to develop transfer and articulation agreements. The major components of the proposals that have been funded during the three-year cycle of the Ford Foundation grant are (1) articulation agreements that set forth the conditions that each pair of institutions is expected to meet in facilitating student transfer, (2) faculty exchanges, and (3) plans and timetables for student transition to the four-year institutions. Although not all UNCF institutions are located in the south, many in the program are cooperating with community colleges in northern states that are some distance away (i.e., Cuyahoga Community College in Ohio). The program has been evaluated by an external consultant from North Carolina State University. As might be expected, students have not been able to transfer as soon after the start of the program as had been hoped, and considerable time during the first year or more of the project was spent on both campus visitations by faculty and staff and work on lower-division course articulation agreements.

Minority Student Achievement Project. The Ford Foundation made a grant to the State Higher Education Executive Officers (SHEEO) association in 1988 to conduct a competition for grants to state agencies for higher education planning and coordination for the general purpose of improving minority student baccalaureate degree achievement, with an emphasis on coalition building. Objectives the proposals were asked to address include strengthening the transfer function and developing or improving accountability. Grants to six state agencies (in Arizona, Colorado, Illinois, Massachusetts, New York, and Ohio) were made to accomplish a number of objectives related to the overall purpose of improving minority achievement. The program was evaluated by Nettles (1990), who concluded that it was successful from the standpoint of both SHEEO's execution of its plan for the project and the commitment of the states that participated in it to make it work.

National Center for Academic Achievement and Transfer. In 1990 the Ford Foundation made a multiyear grant to the American Council on Education to establish the National Center for Academic Achievement and Transfer for the purpose of examining, strengthening, and enhancing student transfer between two- and four-year institutions. It is concentrating on curriculum, teaching, and learning issues in an effort to increase transfer rates while ensuring a successful two-year college experience and an opportunity for advancement to the baccalaureate degree. The council sees the center as a key player in its continuing efforts to achieve equity for underrepresented ethnic groups in higher education in this country. The center has been awarding grants of $25,000 to twenty-five pairs of community colleges and four-year institutions, which are now serving significant numbers of historically underrepresented and other disadvantaged students, to be used to modify academic offerings or classroom practices to improve transfer.

A second phase of the program provides a small number of grants of up to $250,000 to develop a core curriculum to meet the general education or liberal arts needs of transfer institutions. The center has also developed a national policy statement and background paper on the importance of transfer in providing opportunities for low-income and underrepresented ethnic groups, with sections on what is known about transfer, strategies to improve it, and the need for an empirical base to assess improvement projects (National Center for Academic Achievement and Transfer 1991). The center also publishes working papers periodically in a newsletter titled *Transfer.*

Center for the Study of Community Colleges. The Ford Foundation has also been instrumental in providing support to the Center for the Study of Community Colleges, a nonprofit organization with close ties to, but independent of, the University of California, Los Angeles (UCLA) and the federally funded ERIC Clearinghouse for Junior Colleges. The Ford Foundation has made grants to the center for significant research related to the Urban Community College Transfer Opportunities Program and, most recently, to support a national Transfer Assembly on transfer data and definitions, a primary objective of which is to attempt to secure consensus about factors that should go into the computation of state and national transfer rates. The center, founded in 1972, has conducted national studies with grants from the National Endowment for the Humanities, the National Science Foundation, the Andrew W. Mellon Foundation, and the Carnegie Foundation for the Advancement of Teaching, as well as the Ford Foundation.

The Andrew W. Mellon Foundation with the Association of American Colleges

A survey conducted in 1983 showed that one-third of the institutional members of the Association of American Colleges actively recruited transfer students from community colleges although one-third of this group had no formal articulation agreements. An additional one-third were considering a policy change regarding the recruitment of transfer students; the remaining third expressed no such interest. Based on these findings, the association received a two-year grant from the Mellon Foundation to undertake a project that would uncover and overcome barriers to transfer, maintain enrollments in the four-year institutions, and increase access for community college students from the underrepresented groups. The final report of the project, published as *The Transfer Challenge: Removing Barriers, Maintaining Commitment* (Wechsler 1990), was intended to serve as a handbook to provide practical assistance to four-year institutions in their efforts to increase and facilitate the flow of transfer students into their programs.

Three principles for successful articulation emerged from the subgrants the association made to twelve four-year institutions working with thirty-four public community colleges: commitment on the part of the leadership of both two- and four-year institutions, comprehensiveness of effort, and institutionalization of the program. Five specific activities associated with these principles include presidential leadership, regular meetings of admissions and financial aid officers between the institutions, formal and informal exchanges between faculties, opportunities for community college students to visit four-year colleges, and regular consultation between staffs of learning development centers to share information on the characteristics of the transfer students.

California's Special Efforts

In a recent report on transfer and articulation, the California Postsecondary Education Commission (1990) stated:

Cognizant of the decreasing numbers of community college students who have been transferring to the University of California and the California State University since the mid–1970s, California's Governor and Legislature have provided funding for several pilot programs that are designed to reverse this trend, increase the number of transfer students from underrepresented ethnic groups, and reduce articulation problems for those who do in fact transfer.

Evaluation is very much a part of most of these specially funded efforts that remain in various stages of implementation. Demonstrable results in terms of increased numbers of transfer students are slow to appear since the transfer process itself is slow. . . . Numbers of transfer students still are an acceptable measure of the success of special programs. Progress in course and program articulation that increases persistence after transfer and reduces the time to the baccalaureate degree is more difficult to quantify but is scarcely less important than simply increasing the numbers who transfer.

The Transfer Centers Project. A commission report that called for community colleges to designate a central location on campus where transfer and articulation information and services might readily be available to students resulted in state funding for such centers. They are designed to do the following:

1. Identify and encourage students from underrepresented ethnic groups to transfer
2. Assist potential transfer students to prepare for upper division work
3. Assist transfer students in filling out applications for admission with advanced standing
4. Monitor and support the progress of transfer students through referrals to student services
5. Inform and motivate students
6. Involve faculty and staff in strengthening curriculum and articulation.

A 1989 report of Berman/Weiler Associates, *An Evaluation of the Transfer Center Pilot Program*, concluded that the program had been implemented successfully and had increased transfer rates, particularly to the University of California.

Evaluators calculated transfer rates by dividing the number of students who transferred to the University of California or the California State University by the community college credit enrollment, before and after the transfer center program was implemented, and for community colleges with and without state grants for transfer centers. The results suggest that the colleges with specially funded transfer centers experience a significant improvement (30 percent) in transfer to the University of California with a slight improvement over other community colleges in transfer to the state university system. However, the quantitative evidence does not allow cause-and-effect conclusions to be drawn from the standpoint of statistical analysis regarding differences or changes in rates.

Based on California's experience, the Illinois governor and legislature provided special funds in 1991 and again in 1992 as part of its Minority Articulation

Program to establish transfer centers in twenty-three urban community colleges (Illinois Board of Higher Education 1992). Short-term articulation grants were also made to public and private institutions to articulate programs and courses and to facilitate transfer, some of which funded university advisors to counsel students at the community college transfer centers. First-year evaluations of the transfer centers suggest that the centers are beginning to achieve their primary goals.

Project ASSIST. The Articulation System Stimulating Interinstitutional Student Transfer (ASSIST) is a microcomputer-based articulation and transfer system developed by staff at the University of California, Irvine, with the cooperation of the staff at Los Angeles Harbor College. Impetus for Project ASSIST came from a federally funded project to improve the articulation conducted by the Western Interstate Commission for Higher Education (1985). It is now in place on all University of California campuses, a majority of the state university campuses, and in many community colleges.

ASSIST was created to combat the problem of students' limited access to institutional information in planning to transfer, particularly the applicability of community colleges to university curriculum requirements. The system can provide students and their counselors or academic advisors with specific information about the transferability of community college courses to academic programs in any participating four-year institution and permits them to assess the student's progress toward satisfaction of degree requirements at any such institution. It also identifies community college courses that can be taken in lieu of university requirements. Finally, the system contains general campus information to help transfer students plan and make choices—information about deadlines, financial aid, majors, and so on.

Florida has developed the Student On-line Advisement and Articulation System (SOLAR), which involves high schools, as well as its colleges and universities (Palinchak 1988). It is designed to implement the state's Student Academic Support System (SASS) and, among other features, includes information about transfer procedures, admissions requirements, and special university majors. When fully implemented, it is expected to provide feedback on student progress in various majors, together with trends related to completion times and rates, grades, and other measures of student and institutional performance.

Puente. The Puente project is a statewide program that now functions on twenty-four community college campuses with the dual objectives of reducing the number of dropouts among Mexican-American/Latino community college students and increasing the number who transfer to complete a baccalaurate degree (California Community Colleges 1989b). Generally, few Mexican-American/Latino students transfer, but 40 percent of the Puente students who completed the program through 1986 have transferred to a four-year college or university.

Puente trains English teachers and Mexican-American counselors as teams to conduct one-year writing/counseling/mentoring programs on community college campuses. More than 1,300 professionals from the Mexican-American/Latino community serve as Puente mentors. Students and mentors are paired according to career and personal interests. Puente students take an accelerated writing program consisting of two courses—a one-term developmental writing course followed by a transfer-level English composition course—and remain with the same teacher for the entire year. The program, which uses group work to develop fluency and alleviate writing anxiety, emphasizes content over grammatical correctness at first. Puente students meet regularly with their counselors, who monitor their academic progress and help them make career and educational plans, and with their mentors, who serve as role models.

Special Programs for Underrepresented Students. In 1989 the Chancellor's Office for the California Community Colleges (1989a) published a comprehensive report that had been prepared for the Transfer and Articulation Committee of the Intersegmental Coordinating Council. The purpose of the survey was to develop an inventory of such programs, describe the characteristics and activities that contribute to their success, and provide information that could be used to replicate successful programs. The study found that, although a majority of the California community colleges have programs such as transfer centers that include components designed to improve transfer for students from underrepresented groups, fewer have programs with the specific purpose of facilitating the transfer of such students. It concluded that, while the community colleges have initiated many efforts in this area, most programs and practices are new, unproven, and in need of consistency, coordination, and evaluation.

Other University Programs. The University of California, Davis, has pioneered an effort within the university system to develop special Transfer Admission Agreements (TAAs) with community colleges, beginning with colleges in the area and now extending to campuses in all parts of the state. A TAA is a formal, written agreement that outlines the courses a student must take before transferring, states the GPA a student must earn, and lists specific requirements for limited-access majors. After a TAA is written, the student signs the agreement, along with the counselor and a Davis campus representative. These signatures guarantee that the student will be admitted to Davis in the major and for the term of choice, provided the student fulfills the agreement and applies for admission during the open filing period. A TAA may be written after the student has completed approximately thirty semester units of transferable credit or up to one year before the expected transfer.

The Center for Academic Interinstitutional Programs at UCLA initiated the Transfer Alliance Program (TAP) in 1985 in conjunction with the College of Letters and Science and the Office of Undergraduate Admissions and Relations with Schools as a means of strengthening the transfer function and the role of faculty in transfer in selected community colleges in the Los Angeles area, most of which enroll large numbers of students from underrepresented ethnic groups. The specific goals of TAP include

1. Stronger student academic preparation and curriculum planning
2. Focus on achieving the baccalaureate degree after transfer

3. Increased achievement of academic skills needed for success in the major

4. Faculty participation in all of the above (Ackermann 1989).

TAP publicizes the community college as a viable route to a baccalaureate degree with a letter sent to all applicants who are not admitted to UCLA as freshmen to inform them that they are guaranteed priority admission to the College of Letters and Science upon completion of TAP at a participating community college. While enrolled in TAP, students are provided meaningful links with UCLA that familiarize them with campus facilities and services. Expectations of commitment are clearly set forth for both UCLA and the community colleges that wish to participate in the program. These include a formal structure of an administrative, faculty, and student services liaison.

A third effort, the state-level office of the California Articulation Number (CAN) System, was first funded from the State General Fund in 1985 following the submission to the legislature of a report on the feasibility of a common course-numbering system for California's public postsecondary institutions (California Postsecondary Education Commission 1986). The report included an analysis of what other states were doing to establish such systems, most notably Florida, where it had been in statute for some time. Such a system had begun to develop in the Sacramento area a few years earlier.

CAN is a cross-referenced system to identify transferable lower-division courses that are commonly taught at both community colleges and four-year institutions in California. It does not replace an institution's own course numbers but, instead, adds a common number that includes a discipline-related prefix and a one- or two-digit number for each course. The common number does not imply commonality of content or methodology but is related to subject-matter requirements—that is not necessarily "equivalency" but a community college course taken "in lieu of" a university course in order to meet a particular requirement. The purposes of CAN are to promote transfer by simplifying the identification of transferable courses and the specific disciplines and programs to which they are transferable, to promote development of common methods of course identification, and to help identify courses with comparable content so that common competencies can be expected.

OTHER SOURCES AND RESOURCES

The literature of community colleges is replete with accounts of "this is how we did it" and, in some instances, "this is why we like it," usually with unpublished evaluations that are performed before special programs to improve transfer and articulation have had time to demonstrate their effectiveness. Such evaluations are further limited by their lack of attention to the issues of cost effectiveness (how much does it cost per student increase in number of transfers?) and cause effect (how much of the increase or improvement can be rightly attributed to the special program?).

In closing, attention is called to several compendia of accounts of special programs and services that may be useful. First there have been at least two national inquiries into the transfer function (Bender 1990; Knoell 1990), both of which focus on state programs and policies. A western regional report focuses on what works for minority students (Odell and Mock 1989), as well as do two additional California reports (California Community Colleges 1988; California Postsecondary Education Commission 1986).

From this analysis, it is obvious that a great deal remains to be done to find out what does and does not work, and at what cost, to increase the flow of transfer students to the baccalaureate degree, most especially in these times of fiscal constraints. The transfer function remains less effective for students from historically underrepresented groups than for Asian and white students, a concern that is shared by those who design and implement special programs. Practitioners and researchers alike will continue to look to the National Center for Academic Achievement and Transfer for both direction and enlightenment as the struggle continues to make the transfer function work.

REFERENCES

Ackermann, S. 1989. *An analysis of two UCLA transfer and retention programs: The transfer alliance program and the supergraduate program.* Los Angeles: University of California, Center for Academic Interinstitutional Programs.

Adelman, C. 1991. *Using transcripts to validate institutional mission: The role for the community college in the postsecondary experience of a generation.* Washington, D.C.: Office of Research, U.S. Department of Education.

———. 1992. *The way we are: The community college, an American thermometer.* Washington, D.C.: U.S. Department of Education.

Banks, D. L. 1992. Environmental and organizational factors influencing the community college transfer function. Ph.D. diss., University of California, Los Angeles.

Bender, L. W., ed. 1990. *Spotlight on the transfer function: A national study of state policies and practices.* Washington, D.C.: American Association of Community and Junior Colleges.

Berman/Weiler Associates. 1989. *An evaluation of the transfer center pilot program: Executive summary and recommendations.* Berkeley, Calif.: Berman/Weiler Associates.

California Community Colleges. 1988. *Successful teaching strategies: Instruction for Black and Hispanic students in the California community college.* Sacramento: Chancellor's Office.

———. 1989a. *Programs and practices that facilitate the transfer of ethnically underrepresented students.* Sacramento: Chancellor's Office.

———. 1989b. *The puente project.* Agenda item, July. Sacramento: Board of Governors of the California Community Colleges.

California Postsecondary Education Commission. 1986. *Progress in facilitating the transfer of community college EOPS students: A report to the legislature and governor in response to assembly bill 1114.* Sacramento: California Postsecondary Education Commission.

————. 1990. *Transfer and articulation in the 1990's: California in the larger picture.* Report 90–30. Sacramento: California Postsecondary Education Commission.

————. 1991. *Update of community college transfer student statistics: Fall 1990 and full-year 1989–90.* Sacramento: California Postsecondary Education Commission.

Cohen, A. M. 1991. The transfer indicator. *Transfer Working Papers* 2(2). Washington, D.C.: The National Center for Academic Achievement and Transfer, American Council on Education.

————. 1992. Calculating transfer rates efficiently. *Community, Technical, and Junior College Journal* 62(4):32–35.

Grubb, W. N. 1991. The decline of community college transfer rates: Evidence from national longitudinal surveys. *Journal of Higher Education* 62(2):194–217.

Illinois Board of Higher Education. 1992. *Undergraduate education: Transfer and articulation.* Springfield: State of Illinois Board of Higher Education.

Knoell, D. M. 1990. *Transfer, articulation and collaboration twenty-five years later.* Washington, D.C.: American Association of Community and Junior Colleges.

Knoell, D. M., and L. L. Medsker. 1965. *Factors affecting performance of transfer students from two- to four-year colleges with implications for coordination and articulation.* Washington, D.C.: American Council on Education.

McIntyre, C. 1988. Assessing community college-transfer performance. *Research in Higher Education* 27(2):142–162.

National Center for Academic Achievement and Transfer. 1991. *Setting the national agenda: Academic achievement and transfer.* Washington, D.C.: American Council on Education.

Nettles, M. T. 1990. *An evaluation of the SHEEO project: Challenge grants for state boards to improve minority baccalaureate achievement.* Denver, Colo.: State Higher Education Executive Officers.

Odell, M., and J. J. Mock, eds., 1989. *A crucial agenda: Making colleges and universities work better for minority students.* Boulder, Colo.: Western Interstate Commission for Higher Education.

Palinchak, R. S. 1988. Articulation Florida style. In *Enhancing articulation and transfer.* New Directions for Community Colleges no. 61. San Francisco: Jossey-Bass.

Schaier-Peleg, B., ed. 1984. *New initiatives for transfer students: Urban community college transfer opportunities program.* New York: Bronx Community College.

State University of New York. 1992. *Attrition and retention of full-time transfer students in first-time and baccalaureate and associate degree programs, including postsecondary opportunity students: Class of 1988.* Report Number 4–92. Albany: State University of New York, Office of Institutional Research.

University of California. 1991. *Report of University of California transfer programs and transfer plan for the California community colleges.* Agenda Item 302, Committee on Educational Policy (September 15). Oakland: Office of the Regents.

Washington State Board for Community College Education. 1989. *A study of the role of community colleges in the achievement of the bachelor's degree in Washington State: Results of the spring 1988 bachelor's degree survey.* Operations Report 89–1. Olympia: Washington State Board for Community College Education.

Wechsler, H. 1990. *The transfer challenge: Removing barriers, maintaining commitment.* Washington, D.C.: Association of American Colleges.

Western Interstate Commission for Higher Education. 1985. *Improving the articulation/ transfer process between two- and four-year institutions.* Boulder, Colo.

Synthesis of Literature Related to Tech-Prep Outcomes

Cassy Key

In the pursuit of happiness . . .

If George Baker is to be believed, 87 percent of U.S. workers spend about half their lives doing something they consider meaningless (1989–1990). It's no wonder productivity is low. Even though the U.S. Constitution guarantees a right to "the pursuit of happiness," few appear to be finding it in the workplace.

T. J. Asklund tells a different story. He considers himself a $15,000-a-year millionaire because he loves his job at Texas Instruments in Austin. But he had to work to get his current state of bliss.

When T. J. was nine, he partnered up with his big brother in a lawn-mowing business. They made good money. But after two years, T. J. got tired of doing something that did not interest him. So he moved on.

Then T. J. started working for his dad, who owned a laminated countertop business. The money was good, but when you are the owner's kid, you get to do the jobs no one else wants—just to prove you are not getting any special favors. So T. J. moved on.

He started doing maintenance and manual labor at a nearby resort. Later, he moved up to office work at the resort, including accounting. Then T. J. realized that unless he learned to communicate well with customers, he could never get into management. So he asked to be moved to the front desk. Although the money was even better at the front desk, he did not want to spend his future there.

One day, on his way to meet his girlfriend for lunch, T. J. had thirty minutes to kill. Armed with a career passport from his high school, T. J. went to Texas Instruments. Hopeful. He was ready to move along. TI hired T. J.—in fact, TI hired him at one step above entry level—only weeks after high school graduation. In high school, T. J. liked art, the principles of technology course, and the college electronics classes offered for college escrow credit. "It was a good deal—we could take about $300 worth of college courses free." T. J. thought the physics and electronics classes were fun because "you had to think and work at the same time and the problems were work-related."

As it turned out, the head of T. J.'s division at TI had helped design the course of study T. J. received—but the two never met until long after T. J. had been hired. Nevertheless, after less than six months at Texas Instruments, T. J. Asklund moved up. Now, after a year and a half at TI, T. J. has been promoted five times. He just enrolled in Austin Community College (fall semester, 1992).

"It really makes me feel good when someone with a bachelor's degree looks at me after I've solved a problem on the line and says, 'Hey, you really do know what you're doing.' I'm really lucky. TI not only gave me a job, they'll also help me with my college tuition and books. I couldn't afford it without them." T. J.'s expertise has him working on surface mount technology using a Fuji machine. In his spare time, T. J. also enjoys doing a little volunteer work. He's promoting something dear to him called tech prep. Why? T. J. says he wants to "give something back to the people who helped me get where I am today—and help other students like me know they can do it, too."

WHAT IS TECH PREP?

Tech prep is a synthesis of several education innovations which preceded it. In a nutshell, it is a plan to link individuals and institutions with similar education aims to produce a better skilled work force. Tech prep curricula, designed by teams of educators and employers, is meant for half of the high school population. It teaches skills to help students land marketable jobs in promising career fields. Students exit high school and the community college or technical school with three options—higher education, work, or both.

Tech prep is more than "two-plus-two." It is a lifelong career ladder, putting work experiences in tandem with schooling, nurturing mechanisms, and evaluation components. The tech-prep system dips into the middle school or junior high—perhaps even lower. Tech prep's work component starts with mentoring and shadowing in the early years and moves to apprenticeship, cooperative education, and other school-to-work transition mechanisms as the student becomes better educated.

The goal of tech prep is to provide the competencies needed for entry level into the most marketable jobs available—highly skilled occupations that require workers with a broad enough academic and technical base to be successful lifelong learners. These workers will be retraining and upgrading their occupational skills—perhaps making as many as seven to ten rather dramatic switches during their thirty-year careers. Since the community college or technical school will be doing most of that training, veteran workers may be taking basic academic skills on the low end and advanced technical skills on the high end of the tech-prep systems now being put into place all over the country. The aim of these programs is to provide more emphasis on the career choice process and to upgrade the exit competencies of 50 percent of at least high school students. These students will then move into community college curricula and exit with advanced skills and an associate's degree. Such aims for so many will require broad cooperation and collaboration throughout American society.

Although tech prep is an education innovation born from secondary level technical-vocational education, its promise is the renaissance of the U.S. economy. Therefore, tech prep is being built through consortia of high schools, community colleges, and government and community-based organizations, in concert with business, industry, and labor. And tech prep is significantly more than just "business as usual."

First, tech prep is not just a program, or a specific curriculum. Tech prep is a system of activities—activities already proven to produce successful students, but activities that heretofore have not been housed under one umbrella. Tech-prep systems include, in the middle school or junior high, student assessment that assists with career decision making, career-awareness instruction for students and their parents, monitoring of student success, a requirement for work site–based learning as part of the education plan, and a series of competency-based classes in sequences that lead to both work and college after high school. Tech-prep systems also include an evaluation component that links each academic program to business, industry, and labor and leads to ongoing refinement.

Tech prep's rigorous and holistic approach to creating a better qualified work force is housed in the technical-vocational high school/community college/technical school domain. Curricula frameworks integrate—and require the mastery—of both technical-vocational and mathematics, science, and communications skills. The mathematics, science, and communications courses are, however, taught differently. Teaching methodology is a hands-on and heads-on format tuned in to student learning styles and the Secretary's Commission on Achieving Necessary Skills (SCANS) competencies. Cooperative learning teaches team building. Each student's individual performance is measured using not only pencil-and-paper tests, but also team and skills testing. Course content is rigorous, and standards are high.

Tech prep offers students various incentives: (1) The system nurtures students through assessment, career awareness activities, and counseling, accommodating the needs of special populations (although tech prep is not a special populations act); (2) students get to take college courses free while still in high school; (3) students have an opportunity for smoother school-to-work transition since work is tied into the tech-prep curricula; (4) most program options leave open the opportunity for higher and higher degrees; and (5) the careers offered to tech-prep graduates boast better salaries and more job security than many other careers—even many careers that require a bachelor's degree.

By necessity, tech-prep career options are closely tied to the analysis of labor-market information. While long-term job forecasts are next to impossible to achieve in this rapidly transitioning and shifting economy, tech-prep curricula developers attempt to forecast high-demand occupations at least five years in advance, and business, industry, and labor lead the way in determining which competencies will be taught beginning with freshman high school students and continuing through the associate's degree—sometimes beyond. This way, a graduate can emerge not only with an associate's degree, which represents a state-of-the-art technical training, but also with a core of competencies that prepare the way for lifetime career development and higher education.

ARE TECH PREP AND TWO-PLUS-TWO ARTICULATION REALLY THE SAME THING?

The forerunner of tech prep was simply a curriculum arrangement called two-plus-two articulation. Research and a review of the literature suggest that two-plus-two articulation did not work very well most of the time. A broad review of the two-plus-two articulation phenomenon includes, by necessity, not only two-plus-two articulation outcomes, but also forays into the realms of organizational management, communication, change, and the adoption of innovation. A synthesis of research outcomes within these areas suggests that the secret of success to tech-prep implementation is as holistic as the tech-prep system itself.

Tech prep's raison d'être is clear: America's middle majority work force must significantly increase its skills. Pushed by a rapid escalation in global competitiveness and declining abilities in the backbone of the work force, Congress is serious. Congressional appropriations out of the 1990 Carl D. Perkins Vocational and Applied Technology Act were $63.4 million in 1991, which is why, in spite of tightening budgets and a growing national deficit, tech prep was allocated $90 million for 1991–1992. This faith in a program just getting off the ground carries with it high expectations for technical-vocational educators.

In terms of students, these are perilous times. Among the 97 percent of students who take a vocational course (Wirt 1991, 427), only 27 percent specialize in a vocation, and only about 1 percent select technical occupations (Parnell and Armes 1984, 4). Instead, over 40 percent of high school students are enrolled in general education (Parnell 1985, 37). About 13 percent of seventeen-year-olds are functionally illiterate—in spite of a growing awareness that 45 percent of current jobs and 55 percent of the net new jobs between now and the year 2000 will require some college (Bailey 1989, 12). The success of tech prep rests on a paradigm shift with ramifications throughout society; therefore, it will take much more than the hard work of technical-vocational educators to move tech prep from a Congressional mandate to institutionalization.

WHY WAS TECH-PREP SECTION WOVEN INTO THE 1990 PERKINS ACT?

Vocational education grew out of a concern for the human condition and the promises each generation had for the next (Swanson 1982). Yet the discrepancy between what today's entry-level workers must do and what they can do has been noted in one or more major reports each year, beginning with Boyer's 1983 report for the Carnegie Foundation, *High School: A Report on Secondary Education in America*.

In 1984 came Parnell's article, "Five Critical Issues"; Parnell and Armes' concept paper, *A Working Degree for America*; and the National Commission on Secondary Vocational Education's "The Unfinished Agenda."

In 1985 came the beginnings of state-level reports as well as Parnell's landmark book touting the benefits of tech prep, *The Neglected Majority*. In 1986, the Bureau of Labor Statistics and Office of Economic Growth and Employment published *Projections 2000*. In 1987, the Southern Regional Education Board published *A Progress Report and Recommendations on Educational Improvements* while Johnston and Packer's *Workforce 2000* and Berryman's studies and policy papers from the National Center on Education and Training were predicting higher-level skills new jobs would require.

In 1988 Berryman continued to point out the higher-level skills new jobs required. She was joined by a chorus, including One America, Inc.'s final report, *Case Studies in Technology-Oriented Job Preparation*; the Grant Foundation's *The Forgotten Half: Non-College Youth in America*; Cox's study of vocational education for the Research Triangle Institute; the U.S. Department of Labor, Education, and Commerce's joint study, *Building a Quality Workforce*; the International Technology Education Association's *Technology: A National Imperative*; and Parnell's treatise *The Role of the Community College in Shaping the Nation*.

In 1989, reports such as Daggett and Kadamus's "New Directions for Vocational Education at the Secondary Level" began popping up both at the state and national levels (Parnell and Ponitz, 1989). Even President George Bush began to emphasize education (remarks at the American Success Awards Ceremony, 11 September 1989), and Secretary of Labor Elizabeth Dole and U.S. Representative Jack Jennings began to push the notion of preparing the nation's work force through vocational education. At the same time, Natriello was publishing a study of rising employer expectations, and Wirt et al. were publishing *A Summary of Findings and Recommendations: National Assessment of Vocational Education*, which concluded that vocational educators had a long way to go to meet those rising standards.

By 1990, almost everyone agreed about the gap. The Commission on the Skills of the American Workforce published *America's Choice: High Skills or Low Wages*, and the Association of Community College Trustees advocated moves to make the major changes necessary to revitalize the economy. States took action. For example, Texas began a joint initiative involving the Texas Education Agency, the Texas Higher Education Coordinating Board, and the Department of Commerce, which is called Quality Work Force Planning. Even the nation acted through the Department of Education's National Goals for Education.

In 1991, vocational education and work force development, long relegated to backdoor, blue-collar status in the academic community, made it to the living room at last. The editors of *Phi Delta Kappan* targeted a special February issue to the Carl D. Perkins Vocational/Applied Technology Act. Technology education, with tech-prep systems acting as the change agent, had become a national imperative. Ironically, this turnaround comes at a time when vocational education enrollments are suffering widespread decline (Gray 1991, 437).

There are 4.3 million vocational education students in the United States (Rosenstock 1991, 434), and as Vaughan observed, "We are creating an educational meritocracy in which education and training are the only paths to economic success" (1991, 447). Yet only 7 percent of seventeen-year-olds can handle college-level science, only 6 percent can do the math, and closer to 5 percent are capable of college-level reading (Hart 1989, 238). Although global competitiveness has created a modern-day gold rush to modernize and increase enrollments in technical-vocational education, "mobilization" must occur first. That's where tech-prep systems enter the picture, pick and pan in hand.

WHAT INVESTIGATIONS HAVE IMPLICATIONS FOR TECH-PREP SYSTEMS?

Tech-prep–related studies include the topics of two-plus-two articulation, the integration of academic and technical education, the success or failure of technical-vocational programs, maximization of the change process, the adoption of change in education environments, student outcomes in two-plus-two articulation programs, curriculum development, employee success factors, institutional effectiveness, and the facilitation of communication, as well as organizational development, leadership development, and economic development practices.

A partial list of these studies includes Lewin 1951; Argyris 1964; Bennis and Nanus 1985; Scott 1985; Naylor 1986; Carnevale, Gainer, and Meltzer 1988; Leiken 1988; VanAllen 1988; and Cutright and Martorana 1989.

WHAT DOES RESEARCH SUGGEST ABOUT TECH-PREP SYSTEMS?

Although two-plus-two articulation and tech prep are not the same thing, much can be learned from two-plus-two articulation program outcomes and other related findings which can help ensure tech-prep success. For instance, research about state-of-the-art technical-vocational education shows holistic student development aims (Copa 1985). Tech-prep students will need a strong system of support services (Ames and Elsner 1983; Colwell 1988; McKinney 1988). Given sufficient student services and support systems, articulated programs were of great benefit to students and employers (Arnold 1987). As VanAllen explained, "If properly designed, two-plus-two programs can provide maximum continuity of instruction within and between educational institutions. The end product is a highly specialized and employable . . . technician. The . . . possibilities are only limited by educational resources and employment trends'' (1988, 18). Tech-prep systems incorporate such services into the overall plan.

Program survival, however, appears to be tricky. By 1976, the National Advisory Council on Vocational Education found evidence of ''planned articulation in slightly less than 40% of the states'' (Long et al. 1986, 2). As Long and his team pointed out, growing interest in articulation was evidenced by the increased attention given the subject in research, program reports, and position papers.

Mabry's (1988) ERIC overview concluded that the following were essential ingredients in top-notch articulation programs (see Warmbrod and Long 1986; Parnell 1985; Long et al. 1986; Fadale and Winter 1987; Arnold 1987):

1. Leadership from all top administrators

2. Involvement of high school and college faculty from the first stages of planning

3. Recognition and rewards for key participants

4. Relationships built on trust and respect which resist the tendency toward ''turfism''

5. Clear benefits to all parties

6. Formal, written agreements signed by all chief executive officers

7. Open, frequent, and clear communication (including counselors and constituents)

8. Competency-based curricula

9. Shared vision

10. Modest initial goals and openness to change.

McKinney's 1988 study of articulation, which included a literature review, questionnaires to 482 institutions, and visits to five exemplary sites, went deeper than earlier reports. McKinney's report suggested that institutional personnel had to exhibit ''team leadership'' on a continuing basis; that local leadership was more effective than state-level leadership; that student services such as remediation and transportation services should be provided; that programs should be promoted through students, teachers, and counselors; that the program coordination should not favor one institution over another; and that an individual should be employed full-time to coordinate consortium activities and that each institution should designate an individual as the two-plus-two coordinator.

McKinney (1988) also promoted the notions of formative and summative evaluation, shared facilities and equipment among institutions, and active youth organization involvement. Other recommendations by McKinney indicated that implementors should

1. Allow stakeholders to jointly develop goals

2. Have realistic goals

3. Construct the strategic plan and program evaluation processes using a team of stakeholders

   4. Show strong commitment from governing boards, chief executive officers, managers, teachers, counselors, and other staff

   5. Ensure that stakeholders are committed to overcoming barriers to effectiveness and efficiency

   6. Have regular meetings of all stakeholders

   7. Maintain a continuous flow of information to stakeholders and to students

   8. Engage in staff development

   9. Construct clear communication channels and designate responsibilities

  10. Share facilities and equipment when the student commute is not a problem

  11. Encourage staff visits to exemplary programs

  12. Let current students mentor prospective incoming students

  13. Utilize program alumni in recruiting and informing others about the program

  14. Have regular meetings among vocational and academic and secondary/postsecondary teachers

  15. Focus on improved educational programs and services rather than ''turfism''

  16. Develop jointly a competency-based curriculum . . . based on marketplace demands so that a logical sequence of instruction can occur

  17. Develop and use written agreements with specific goals and institutional responsibilities

  18. Assign a director

  19. Enlist state-agency policy support (summary of pp. xv–xvi).

McKinney's research revealed vast differences between the ideal and what happened in real life. McKinney found that, although they were perceived by practitioners as major program goals, ''relatively few programs reported high success in achieving increased service to students, program improvement, student retention, program cost reduction, and/or increased service to employers'' (32). Arnold (1987) suggested determining student eligibility standards for admission; developing joint curricula review processes, including extensive revisions of both secondary and college programs; developing guidelines for advising and counseling students throughout the program; planning for joint teaching assignments; sharing advisory committees between secondary schools and community colleges; planning and conducting an orientation program for all stakeholders; and developing a joint annual budget for all activities.

All researchers concurred with VanAllen's (1988) assertion that relevant programming should be developed in concert with high levels of student interest, a favorable labor market, and, to a lesser extent, external funding (22). Researchers also concurred that the secret to success was shared vision and that the level of success was directly related to the climate in which the programs were housed. Furthermore, researchers suggested that channels of communication be created and kept open—not just during program start-up, but for the long haul (Long et al. 1986; Radcliffe and Zirkin 1986; Warmbrod and Long 1986; Arnold 1987; Fadale and Winter 1987; Selman and Wilmoth 1989).

Moreover, in order for communication to occur, the organizational structure must streamline the communication process and allocate power and authority to a full-time coordinator (Young 1989). Many programs have sunk under the weight of cumbersome communication channels; and Young (1989), McKinney and Ballard (1987), and Key (1991) have advocated that Ouchi-like organizational structures, involving students, teachers, administrators, counselors, student affairs personnel (counselors), business, industry, labor, and community-based organizations, be involved in goal setting and planning from the beginning. Self-interest—or benefits to all parties—was another important component that was facilitated by such a structure.

Whatever the curricula framework, research suggested that tech prep must be more than a curricular connection (Ames and Elsner 1983; Arnold 1987; Mabry 1988; McKinney 1988; Selman and Wilmoth 1989) in order to succeed. Curricula should be embraced by high levels of student and community building activity, including assessment, career planning, remediation in basic skills when necessary, apprenticeship and job placement, student monitoring, and program evaluation (Cox 1981; Hall 1987; Flack 1988; Cook 1988; Weiss 1988). Many practitioners believed they should have spent more time on public relations in the beginning, since public relations is strongly connected to student recruitment and public attitudes. Several researchers noted that the "buy-in" of locals could not be coerced through state or federal edicts (Parnell 1985; Long et al. 1986; Warmbrod and Long 1986; Black 1988; Selman and Wilmoth 1989).

Successful implementation was also closely related to time and money. Although research about the implementation of change and the adoption of innovation suggests that change is best implemented incrementally (Watkins 1981), most tech-prep system start-ups have been rushed. Research further suggests that tech-prep coordinators must facilitate "routinization" by linking new facts with the old and creating order (Watkins 1981, 245). Hall and Hord's (1987) suggested checklist of activities to support change include developing organizational arrangements, training, consultation and reinforcement, monitoring, external communication, and information dissemination activities; an awareness of the stages of concern (including awareness, information gathering, information management, an understanding of consequence, collaboration with others, and refocusing for program refinement); and time to incorporate levels of use (nonuse, orientation, preparation, mechanical use, routine use, refinement, integration, and renewal). The pull of inertia within the education community will be a formidable adversary for tech-prep practitioners. Their best allies should be principals, who have the key role in shaping school culture (Deal and Peterson 1990) as well as the key role in facilitating change (Thomas 1978; Hall and Hord 1987).

Money is equally important. As VanAllen concluded, "Though no one doubts local economic needs would have propelled the effort regardless of external resources, without the $40,000, the 2 + 2 program would still be in the development phases instead of the implementation stage'' (1988, 20). VanAllen also pointed out that ''educational programming does not occur in a vacuum. On the contrary, it takes place in a dynamic setting. It is the result of many variables interacting in a complex social system'' (19). ''Establishing climate'' has costs— both in human and financial capital.

The need for additional human and financial capital in the establishment of two-plus-two articulation is also supported by LeBlane's 1987 summary of Arizona's vocational education plans; McKinney and Ballard's 1987 evaluation of Rhode Island Community College's articulated electronics program; and Ingram and Troyer's (1988) articulation handbook, among others. Since tech-prep's aims are more holistic than two-plus-two articulation, one might presume that the dollars required for implementation will be higher as well. Fortunately, Congress has responded. The tech-prep allocation went up $27 million from 1991 to 1992— from $63.4 to $90 million.

WHAT ENHANCEMENTS WILL HELP TECH-PREP SYSTEMS SUCCEED?

Ideally, the tech-prep system pipeline should be strategically planned to include K–12 curricula (International Technology Association 1988). Lally (1990) and Hall (1987) report that, although vocational students select career options based on interest, they often lack prerequisite knowledge. These skills can be developed during the first two years of high school. Therefore, although the law looks at tech-prep curricula as starting in the junior year of high school, it actually begins much earlier—at least by the ninth grade.

Successful tech-prep education plans (curricula frameworks) should not only integrate technical and contextually taught math, science, and communications competencies, but also involve as much work-related experience as possible. Indeed, the number of students who work in high school has grown to a clear majority (Stern, 1991, 3). Why not incorporate that experience into the education plan?

In Germany, for example, technical-vocational students spend two days per week working and three days per week in the classroom. Peters believes that such practices here in the United States might help educators know how students perform according to the needs of the workplace, instead of only how students do in relationship to each other on standardized tests (1990, 17–19). Stern (1991) agrees. In addition to ''the work ethic,'' work teaches critical thinking, problem solving, communication, science, and other disciplines (Shapiro 1988; Dole 1989).

Successful tech-prep systems will require increased attention to professional development among teachers (math, science, communications, and technical-vocational), counselors (middle/junior high school through college level), and administrators. Public relations is a prime consideration—starting internally and moving en masse externally. If Berryman (1987), Resnick (1987), Bailey (1989), and Natriello (1989) are correct in their suggestions about learning, entry-level-worker requirements, and education's relationship to the economy, educators must develop ways to link institutions to maximize human and financial capital. The goal is to restructure education, moving away from the mass production of students to a more flexible production era. In a time of shrinking budgets, educators must produce these highly skilled employees with the competencies of "customized" education—or craft training—at the cost savings of mass production. Academic and technological literacy must increase in tandem, and it will be no small task. But all over the United States, small pockets of tech-prep pioneers are plowing new ground. It is quite possible that the best thing one can do for this country—and for one's grandchildren—is to count oneself among us.

REFERENCES

Ames, W. C., and P. Elsner. 1983. Redirecting student services. In *Issues for community colleges in a new era*, ed. G. B. Vaughan and Associates, 139–58. San Francisco: Jossey-Bass.

Argyris, C. 1964. *Integrating the individual and the organization*. New York: Wiley.

Arnold, J. P. 1987. Articulating secondary and postsecondary occupational programs. In *Developing occupational programs*, ed. C. R. Doty, 57–64. New Directions for Community Colleges no. 58. San Francisco: Jossey-Bass.

Association of Community College Trustees. 1989. *Trustee leadership for institutional excellence: A trustee handbook for leading America's community colleges into the 21st century*. Annandale, Va.

Bailey, T. 1989. *Changes in the nature and structure of work: Implications for employer-sponsored training*. New York: Columbia University, Institute on Education and the Economy, Teachers College.

Baker, G. A. III. 1989–1990. Lectures from leadership and decision-making: Advanced leadership competencies. University of Texas at Austin, Community College Leadership Program.

Bennis, W., and B. Nanus. 1985. *Leaders: The strategies for taking charge*. New York: Harper and Row.

Berryman, S. E. 1987. *Shadows in the wings: The next educational reform*. Occasional Paper no. 1. New York: Columbia University, National Center on Education and Employment, Teachers College.

Black, M. 1988. *The community college–high school connection*. Farmington, N.M.: San Juan College.

Boyer, E. 1983. *High school: A report on secondary education in America*. New York: Harper and Row.

Bureau of Labor Statistics and Office of Economic Growth and Employment Projections. 1986. *Projections 2000*. Washington, D.C.: U.S. Government Printing Office.

Carnevale, A. P., L. J. Gainer, and A. S. Meltzer. 1988. *Workplace basics: The skills employers want*. Alexandria, Va.: American Society for Training and Development and the U.S. Department of Labor.

Colwell, S. M. 1988. The relationship of intellective and demographic variables to the academic performance and persistence of technical college students. Ph.D. diss., University of Connecticut.

Commission on the Skills of the American Workforce, 1990. *America's choice: High skills or low wages!* New York: Columbia University, National Center on Education and the Economy, Teachers College.

Cook, J. N. 1988. Working it out: A partnership venture between Greater Lawrence Technical High School and Northern Essex Community College. Ph.D. diss., Boston University.

Copa, G. 1985. *An untold story: Purposes of vocational education in secondary schools.* St. Paul: University of Minnesota, Minnesota Research and Development Center for Vocational Education, Department of Vocational and Technical Education.

Cox. J. L. 1988. *Vocational education study: Final report.* ERIC Document no. ED 261 037. Raleigh, N.C.: Research Triangle Institute.

Cox, M. A. 1981. The effect of an assessment: Voluntary placement system on student success at the community college. Ph.D. diss., University of LaVerne.

Cutright, P. S., and S. V. Martorana. 1989. Composing advisory committees for community-based adult education. *Community College Review* (Fall): 34–40.

Deal, T. E., and K. D. Peterson. 1990. *The principal's role in shaping school culture.* Washington, D.C.: U.S. Government Printing Office.

Dole, E. 1989. Preparing the workforce of the future. *Vocational Education Journal* (October): 18–20.

Fadale, L. M., and G. Winter. 1987. The realism of articulated secondary-postsecondary occupational and technical programs. *Community College Review* (Fall): 28–33.

Flack, S. A. 1988. Secondary and postsecondary vocational education in North Carolina. Ph.D. diss., Virginia Polytechnic Institute and State University.

Grant (William T.) Foundation. 1988. *The forgotten half: Non-college youth in America.* Washington, D.C.

Gray, K. 1991. Vocational education in high school: A modern phoenix? *Phi Delta Kappan* (February): 437–45.

Hall, G. E., and S. M. Hord. 1987. *Change in schools.* Albany: State University of New York Press.

Hall, N. W. 1987. The efficacy of program selection procedures for vocational high school students. Ph.D. diss., University of Oregon.

Hart, L. A. 1989. The horse is dead. *Phi Delta Kappan* (November): 237–42.

Ingram, M., and D. Troyer. 1988. *Secondary/postsecondary vocational program articulation handbook.* ERIC Document no. ED 298 336. El Paso: El Paso Community College.

International Technology Association, 1988. *Technology: A national imperative.* Reston, Va.

Johnston, W. B., and A. H. Packer. 1987. *Workforce 2000.* Indianapolis: Hudson Institute.

Kadamus, J. A., and W. Daggett. 1986. *New directions for vocational education at the secondary level.* Series no. 311. Columbus, Ohio: National Center for Research in Vocational Education.

Key, C. B. 1991. Building tech-prep systems geared for the twenty-first century. Ph.D. diss., University of Texas, Austin.

Lally, K. 1990. Eighth-graders lack direction. *Austin American-Statesman* (7 April).

LeBlane, C. 1987. *Arizona perspectives on vocational education, 1981–1989.* Phoenix: Arizona State Board of Directors.

Leiken, R. A. 1988. *Case study: 2 + 2 cooperative efforts.* ERIC Document no. 301 259. Cleveland: Cuyahoga Community College.

Lewin, K. 1951. *Field theory in social science.* New York: Harper.

Long, J. P., C. Warmbrod, C. R. Faddis, and M. J. Lerner, 1986. *Avenues for articulation: Coordinating secondary and postsecondary programs.* Columbus, Ohio: National Center for Research in Vocational Education.

Mabry, T. 1988. The high school/community college connection: An ERIC review. *Community College Review* 16(3):48–55.

McKinney, F. 1988. *Factors influencing the success of secondary/postsecondary vocational-technical education articulation programs.* Columbus: Ohio State University, National Center for Research in Vocational Education. ERIC Document no. ED 289 053.

McKinney, F., and M. R. Ballard, 1987. *Evaluation of the electronics advanced-placement implementation process at Rhode Island Community College.* Columbus, Ohio: National Center for Research in Vocational Education.

National Commission on Secondary Vocational Education. 1985. *The unfinished agenda: The role of vocational education in the high school.* Columbus, Ohio: National Center for Research in Vocational Education.

Natriello, G. 1989. *What do employers want in entry-level workers: An assessment of the evidence.* Occasional Paper no. 7. New York: Columbia University, National Center on Education and Employment, Teachers College.

Naylor, M. 1986. *Granting academic credit for vocational education.* Columbus, Ohio: ERIC Clearinghouse on Adult Career and Vocational Education. ERIC Document no. ED 275 887.

Office of Technology Assessment. 1988. *Technology and the American economic transition: Choices for the future.* Washington, D.C.: U.S. Government Printing Office.

One America, Inc. 1988. *Case studies in technology-oriented job preparation: Final report.* Washington, D.C.

Parnell, D. 1984. Five critical issues. *Community College Journal* (May): 40–41.

———. 1985. *The neglected majority.* Washington, D.C.: American Association of Community and Junior Colleges.

———. 1988. The role of the community college in shaping the nation: An education forum. *Conference Report Series* 2(2):1–4. Atlanta, Ga.: Carter Center.

Parnell, D., and N. Armes. 1984. *2 + 2 tech prep/associate degree program: A working degree for America.* Washington, D.C.: American Association of Community and Junior Colleges.

Parnell, D., and D. Ponitz. 1989. *Public policy agenda.* Washington, D.C.: American Association of Community and Junior Colleges.

Peters, T. 1990. The German economic miracle nobody knows. *Across the Board* (April).

Radcliffe, C. W., and B. G. Zirkin. 1986. *Vocational-technical education program articulation and linkages in Maryland.* Cantonsville, Md.: Maryland University, Maryland Institute for Policy Analysis and Research. ERIC Document no. ED 277 868.

Resnick, L. 1987. Learning in school and out. *Educational Researcher* 16(9):13–20.

Rosenstock, L. 1991. The walls come down: The overdue reunification of vocational and academic education. *Phi Delta Kappan* (February):434–36.

Scott, D. C. 1985. From homeless hogs to two-plus-two. *American Association of Community and Junior Colleges Journal* (August/September):14–19.

Selman, J. W., and J. N. Wilmoth. 1989. Articulation practices and problems perceived by vocational personnel in selected secondary and postsecondary institutions. *Journal of Studies in Technical Careers* 11(1):25–37.

Shapiro, B. V. 1988. Two-plus-two: The high school/community college connection. *NASSP Bulletin* 40 (December):30–36.

Southern Regional Education Board. 1987. *A progress report and recommendations on educational improvements in the Southern Regional Education Board States*. Atlanta, Ga.

Stern, D. 1991. *Combining school and work: Options in high schools and two-year colleges*. Washington, D.C.: U.S. Office of Vocational and Adult Education.

Swanson, G. 1982. Vocational education patterns in the U.S. In *Education and work: 81st yearbook of the National Society for the Study of Education*. Chicago: University of Chicago Press.

Thomas, M. A. 1978. *A study of alternatives in American education*, vol. 2: *The role of the principal*. Santa Monica, Calif.: Rand Corporation.

U.S. Department of Labor, Education, and Commerce. 1988. *Building a quality workforce*. Washington, D.C.: Office of Public Affairs, Employment and Training Administration.

VanAllen, G. 1988. Two-plus-two programming: A focus on student achievement. *Community College Review* 16(2):18–23.

Vaughan, R. J. 1991. The new limits to growth: Economic transformation and vocational education. *Phi Delta Kappan* (February):446–49.

Warmbrod, C., and J. Long. 1986. College bound or bust. *American Association of Community and Junior Colleges Journal* (October/November):29–31.

Watkins, K. 1981. Managing change: Roles and stages of concern of administrators for three types of higher education innovations. Ph.D. diss., Florida State University.

Weiss, G. A. 1988. Retraining and employment patterns of dislocated workers enrolled at a community college. Ph.D. diss., University of Pittsburgh.

Wirt, J. G. 1991. A new federal law on vocational education: Will reform follow? *Phi Delta Kappan* (February):425–33.

Wirt, J. G., L. Muraskin, D. Goodwin, and R. Meyer. 1989. *A Summary of findings and recommendations: National assessment of vocational education*. Washington, D.C.: U.S. Department of Education.

Young, J. C. 1989. The political arena of the community college president. Lecture, 15 November. University of Texas at Austin, Community College Leadership Program.

Synthesis of the Literature on the Community Services Function Assumed by Community Colleges to Meet the Needs of Local Communities and Citizens over the Life Cycle

Michael Mezack III

THE ROOTS OF COMMUNITY SERVICE/CONTINUING OR ADULT EDUCATION

The idea of education being directed toward persons throughout their lives is in many ways a rather recent phenomenon; however, the fact is that there is a rich background from which the concept has evolved. Americans from the very beginning have placed education in high regard, for indeed it is revealing that a college (Harvard) was founded only sixteen years after the Pilgrims landed at Plymouth Rock. One of the first accounts dealing with the education of adults was written by Cotton Mather in his "Essays to Do Good" (1710) in which he suggested the formation of adult discussion groups to discuss community problems (Gratten 1959).

Of course, the often mentioned Junto founded by Benjamin Franklin, in which a small group of his acquaintances met on Friday evenings to discuss and write essays on morals, politics, or Natural Philosophy, was indeed one of the seminal events in the development of adult/community education (Gratten 1959).

Other American events are worthy of note: Josiah Holbrook's Lyceums (1826), which provided public lectures on popular topics; John Lowell, Jr.'s, Lowell Institute established in his will in 1832 providing for public lectures on morals and religion; Peter Cooper's Cooper Union (1850) for the advancement of Science and Art for the working class in New York; and John H. Vincent's Chautauqua (1888), originally a normal school for Sunday school teachers which, over the years, has developed into a program dealing with a variety of topics directed toward children as well as adults. W. R. Harper introduced college-level correspondence to American higher education a century ago; and Thomas Davidson, in his 1898 essay "The Education of Wage Earners," made the point that vocational competence should be accompanied by an understanding of one's cultural heritage and that it is the difference in cultural understanding that separates class from class and not wealth and position. His Breadwinners University emphasized both professional training and cultural education (Gratten 1959).

Perhaps one of the most significant events that tied the American college to community service/education was the general extension movement. Until this time in America, adult/community education was either associated with religious education or promoted by individuals. In 1890 the American Society for the Extension of University Teaching of Philadelphia undertook to appropriate the English approach by establishing an independent organization to manage the service but drew upon the universities for teachers (Gratten 1959). The idea failed, though it provided a high quality of teaching.

Perhaps the most important events that moved the education of adults to the university's purview were the Morrill Acts of 1862 and 1890 which provided land, an annual appropriation, and provisions for the higher education of African-Americans. Although this federal initiative was intended to support the agricultural and mechanical arts, it came to be much more because the traditional colleges of the time were losing their influence, enrollments were declining, and new opportunities were competing with the traditional professions of the clergy, medicine, and law. Also, the developing nation needed all its citizens to be more knowledgeable.

Many states responded to the need not only to provide for the "education of the sons and daughters of the working class," but also to meet the educational needs of adults in the communities and rural areas of their service areas. No state, however, is as well known for its outreach as Wisconsin where, in 1885, the university inaugurated the famous "short course" in agriculture. Anyone with a common school education could take these short, noncredit courses. The state appropriated money for these farmers' institutes which were to be managed by the University of Wisconsin. "The Wisconsin Idea" was immediately successful, and a few years later, in 1903, President Charles R. Van Hise proposed professors be used as technical experts in other endeavors (Rohfeld 1990).

The colleges and universities began to move outside their "halls of ivy." In the mid-nineteenth century, the advancement of knowledge was accelerating at a more rapid pace than during any time previously. Moreover, the public was demanding increased access to this accumulating knowledge, and although at first it was agricultural knowledge that was sought, the public soon took an idea from the English and demanded that universities provide a wide variety of subject matter for public consumption (Rohfeld 1990). "The idea of extension caught like wildfire; and by the end of 1890 it is reported that more than two hundred organizations were carrying on extension in nearly every state of the union" (Rohfeld 1990, 24).

Perhaps no one makes a more eloquent case for adult/continuing education than Eduard C. Lindeman who, in 1926, talked about such things as "mature learning'' and ''lifelong learning,'' the interrelationship of learning with living—the idea that when we give up on educating our adults we have given up. One of the major influences on Lindeman was Bishop N.F.S. Grundrig who had established the Danish people's colleges (Warren 1989). These colleges were designed to make the lives of Danish farmers more interesting and to help ''close the yawning abyss between life and enlightenment'' (Lindeman 1961, xxix). Lindeman's message is clear: Education is not simply acquiring a skill but rather the total development of the individual. For indeed, education is not preparation for life but rather a lifelong endeavor. As he states, ''The whole of life is learning, therefore education can have no endings'' (5).

More recently, the most compelling reason for any college to become involved in community service/continuing education (CS/CE) is the exponential growth of knowledge and information (Fuller 1979, 2). The expansion of knowledge has not slowed; indeed, the ''educational half-life'' for most professionals continues to grow frightfully shorter and shorter. Moreover, the minimum skills and knowledge just needed to cope with the vicissitudes of daily life continue to increase for everyone at every level of society. It is clear that colleges can no longer expect that an initial education, regardless of how excellent it may have been, will serve an individual throughout a lifetime. Even more critically, for those who have stopped or dropped out of education somewhere along the K–12 continuum, the situation may be nothing short of desperate. Research confirms that those who have been successful in education will seek out more education while those who have not been successful in previous education will usually not seek additional education (Aslanian and Brickell 1980).

So, with such a rich philosophic and experiential background, to what extent have America's community colleges picked up on the idea that education need not be confined to the campus, nor be designed only for our youth, nor be confined to a narrow range of subject matter?

COMMUNITY COLLEGES AND COMMUNITY SERVICES

One of the most important events that helped shape the community colleges of today was the 1947 President's Commission on Higher Education which made recommendations for the development and expansion of the nation's community colleges (Levine 1978, 610). The challenge to ''assume new tasks'' was taken up quickly as reported by Bogue (1950), who suggested community colleges take on community service as one of their basic functions. But it was perhaps Edmund Gleazer who, as president of the American Association of Community and Junior Colleges (AACJC), pushed for the community college becoming the ''nexus of community learning activities'' (Cohen, Palmer, and Zwemer 1986, 382). ''To him, the institution was a resource to be used by individuals throughout their lifetime and by the general public as an agency assisting with community issues'' (Cohen and Brawer 1982, 252). The AACJC has been extremely supportive of the community education function in the nation's community colleges

(Cohen and Brawer 1982). There were those such as Alexis Frederick Lange who, in 1927, saw the junior college as the 13th and 14th grades, not as a service for adults in the community (Blocker, Plummer, and Richardson 1965). Blocker, Plummer, and Richardson pose the question, "[C]an the two-year college continue its adaptation to changing societal conditions and needs, or will it become a traditional and static institution with fixed and limited educational objectives?" (1965, 15). Actually, some of the so-called new tasks suggested by the 1947 President's Commission were not so new as they were underdeveloped and existed as peripheral to the mainstream activity of the community college. For indeed, there were the beginnings of adult education in evidence prior to the 1940s and 1950s.

During the 1920s and 1930s, some pioneering efforts were made in California to include adult education in the curriculum of the junior colleges, and in 1932 a Carnegie Foundation for the Advancement of Teaching report encouraged the development of adult education. During the early decades of the twentieth century, most adult education was given through the extension divisions of state colleges and universities. The report states that "the story of this change [was] from a collegiate-oriented institution to one providing diverse educational experiences for all citizens" (Center for the Study of Community Colleges 1986, 5). By 1960 nine out of ten community colleges were providing adult/continuing education (Hankin and Fey 1988).

Community service, an elusive term, is characterized and defined in many ways. According to Cohen and Brawer (1982), the participants usually have short-term goals, rather than degree or certificate objectives; they tend to be older, attending part-time; and they have a wider range of educational achievement. However, in this author's view, to give a single definition of community service would severely limit what one could consider to be classified as community service. For indeed, it is quite clear to those in the field that it depends on where one is as to what might be considered community service. Parsons states that although "CS/CE has been an integral component of the mission of the comprehensive community college for over a generation . . . there is still not a clear definition of what is considered community services" (1989, 3). I would like to suggest the approach Myran proposes: Community-based education, or community service, is really a value system and not courses, delivery modes, locations, or services.

It is a phrase that can be grouped with terms such as lifelong learning, life-centered education, the knowledge revolution, the communications age, the post-industrial society, and the learning society. None of these terms by themselves is very significant, but the value system they represent is powerful indeed. Regardless of the choice of terms, the basic values represented are:

1. Education can make a significant difference in the lives of all persons of all ages and backgrounds; all people have worth, dignity and potential.
2. Education is a means by which people can enrich and enhance their lives through

self-growth in various life roles such as those of worker, family member, citizen, and consumer.

3. Education is a recurring part of daily life, not an experiment set apart from daily life.

4. The community college has a responsibility to maximize the congruence between its services and programs and the educational needs and aspirations of all population groups in its service area.

5. The community college has a responsibility to function as an integral part of the fabric and rhythm of the communities it serves, and it should make a significant and positive difference in the quality of life in those communities. (1978, 1–2)

Under such a value system, it is clear why community service may take on so many meanings and why it is implemented in so many different ways. To turn a phrase, "community service appears to be in the eye of the beholder."

THE EVOLUTION OF COMMUNITY SERVICE

In a learner-centered approach to education, it is critical for the teacher/facilitator to have knowledge of adult development, learning styles, and the learning focus of the adult. There is a plethora of sources for those interested in learning more about adult development (Lewis and Caffarella 1990). Yet there appears to be an inertia within community colleges that keeps community service on the fringe of the institution. "[I]n spite of these realities, the prevailing attitude throughout much of Western society today appears to be that education is still the province of the young." Indeed, the statements given in support of "learning for life are nothing more than shallow rhetoric" (Fuller 1979, 1).

McCabe (in Eaton 1988) indicates that the primary role of the community college is to increase the quality of life; however, he suggests that the associate degree must have first priority and that community service/continuing education programming should have second priority. Thus it would seem there is the "tug and pull" between those who advocate meeting the wide range of a community's educational needs and those who state flatly that the community college cannot be all things to all people and thus should concentrate on a narrow range of educational programs.

The need for community services keeps growing due in part to the demands of our complicated society. Hankin and Fey indicate "that 126 million adults twenty-five years of age or older are in transition, moving from one state of adulthood to another" (1988, 153). Moreover, as proposed by Aslanian and Brickell (1980), 83 percent of all adults are involved in education because of a life transition of some sort. What is occurring then is that community service programs are becoming more critical in a society requiring so much change-oriented learning assistance, thus pushing providers, particularly community colleges, to establish and provide a wide variety of community service programming.

Examples of institutions responding to community service needs include a tremendous range of topics and activities such as business services (Bevelacqua 1983), adult literacy (South Plains Community College 1988), economic development (Gold 1982), parent education (Hare et al., 1987), single-parent education (Bromley and Moore 1987), family recreation (Beachler 1981; Ireland and Gegna 1983), development of a community resource center (Curtis and Stetson 1990), health issues, children's programs, senior citizens' education, art exhibits, theatre, festivals, and ethnic activities (Ireland and Gegna 1983).

A great deal of effort has been put into community service; nevertheless, as Matthews (1991) points out, community colleges are on the sidelines while a deadly game of poverty and missed educational opportunity is being played out in America. The underserved must be made ready to become a functional part of the nation's work force.

Efforts have been made to integrate the community service function more fully into the mission of community colleges (Flanagan 1981), to meet a broad range of educational needs in a community (Gordon 1986), and to meet the needs of business (Hamm and Tolle-Burger 1988; McDowell 1984).

The community service function is critical because it is often through these activities and programs alone that some residents of a community are served (Cutright and Martorana 1989). An example of such a group are those adults who are illiterate (Kazemek 1990; Johnston 1985). However, as pointed out earlier, not all segments of the population are equally attracted to educational programs. As a matter of fact, Merriam and Clark (1991) suggest there appear to be three dimensions which, when combined, help form the attitude adults have toward education: (1) the enjoyment of learning activities, (2) the importance of adult education, and (3) the intrinsic value of adult education. Moreover, the interaction among these dimensions forms a set of complex relationships between adults and their willingness or unwillingness to participate in educational activities. Further, we know that the learning experience must be valued by the learner and must result in some improvement in skill, ability, or self-worth or in some personal transformation (Merriam and Clark 1991). In other words, "[L]earning is a personal process" (Merriam and Caffarella 1991, 1).

THE FUTURE OF COMMUNITY SERVICE

Education is being touted as "the major public agenda issued into the 21st century" (Gayle 1990, 13). Gayle makes twenty predictions about what lifelong learning will be like in the twenty-first century. Some are very positive: Community colleges and technical institutes will be major factors in the growth of advanced technology; "lifelong learning will generate birth-to-death curriculum and delivery systems"; and education will be a key to economic growth. Others are not so good, such as the predicted increase in at-risk students and the forecast that one million young people will drop out of school each year. She suggests we invent the future and not react to it (13–14). Alan Pifer in 1974 at the AACJC convention went so far as to suggest that community colleges consider community leadership to be their primary role (Harlacher and Gollattscheck 1978).

A three-year project, funded by the Kellogg Foundation in 1971, had as its goal to determine to what extent CS/CE had become an integral part of twenty-nine Michigan community colleges. It found CS/CE to be in a developmental state, with substantial community support. However, the planning and research/evaluation functions lagged behind. Parsons (1989) reported that the presidents of the community colleges felt that the growth of CS/CE would be gradual but significant, but noted that each community college must design its own CS/CE program to be congruent with the pressing needs of its service area. He agrees with Myran (1978) that CS/CE must link its mission with that of the institution and "emphasize the centricity of teaching and learning and the importance of institutional effectiveness as measured by the outcomes of learning in the lives of students and the quality of life in the community" (Parsons 1989, 19).

Indeed, it is "through community-based programs [that] the community college becomes the community's college" (McGuire 1988, 63).

REASSESSING COMMUNITY SERVICE

Gollattscheck (1982) recommends that, if community colleges are serious about community-based education, they will need to make the collection of accurate and current data a priority, get involved in consortial arrangements, and encourage the study of how to improve community analysis. Nakamura suggests a paradigm shift from industrial age management "to a more personal and interactive information age leadership paradigm" (1989, 13). He suggests that only through enlightened leadership can the many internal and external problems be solved.

Gordon (1987) also suggests moving away from the industrial to the postindustrial information age. He further suggests that community service professionals must move to be more in line with their college's political mainstream so that, when decisions are made and resources are allocated, they will be more involved. To do so, community service professionals will need a well-developed knowledge base, skill in human relations, and refined conceptual skills. Fuller indicates that one of the driving forces behind the basic idea of the community college is that it should be "the vehicle for everyone to continue his or her education throughout life" (1986, 46). Harlacher states, "America has become a learning society with information its chief currency" (1988, 6). He further states that the movement will be from a linear life plan to a blended life plan, and he suggests that the community college, through its CS/CE function, is the most appropriate institution to assist the nation's adults with their lifelong learning needs.

REFERENCES

Aslanian, C. B., and H. M. Brickell. 1980. *Americans in transition: Life changes as reasons for adult learning*. New York: College Entrance Examination Board.

Beachler, J. A. 1981. *The community education project: Pittsburgh, Pa.* Presented at the Annual Conference of the National Council on Community Services and Continuing Education, Seattle, Wash., October 11–14, 1981. ERIC Document no. ED 219 095.

Bevelacqua, J. 1983. Management strategy for extending services to business. *Community Services Catalyst* 13(1):22–25.

Blocker, C. E., R. H. Plummer, and R. C. Richardson, Jr. 1965. *The two-year college: A social synthesis.* Englewood Cliffs, N.J.: Prentice-Hall.

Bogue, J. P. 1950. *The community college.* New York: McGraw-Hill.

Bromley, A., and M. Moore. 1987. *Focus on careers: A program for single parents or homemakers.* Final Report, Project no. 7–2D05. ERIC Document no. ED 285 985. Gainesville, Fla.: Santa Fe Community College.

Center for the Study of Community Colleges. 1986. *Community college involvement in the education of adults: Literature review and analysis* (First year project report). ERIC Document no. ED 270 168. New York: Carnegie Foundation for the Advancement of Teaching.

Cohen, A. M., and F. B. Brawer. 1982. *The American community college.* San Francisco: Jossey-Bass.

Cohen, A. M., J. C. Palmer, and K. D. Zwemer. 1986. *Key resources on community colleges.* San Francisco: Jossey-Bass.

Curtis, M., and N. Stetson. 1990. Community development through a community resource center. *Community Services Catalyst* 20(2):29–30.

Cutright, P. S., and S. V. Martorana. 1989. Composing advisory committees for community-based adult education. *Community College Review* 17(2):34–40.

Eaton, J. S., ed. 1988. *Colleges of choice: The enabling impact of the community college.* New York: Macmillan.

Flanagan, G. J. 1981. *The one-college concept and continuing education: The process of change from peripheral status to full integration.* ERIC Document no. ED 208 919.

Fuller, J. W. 1979. *Continuing education and the community college.* Chicago: Nelson-Hall.

————. 1986. *Community college curricula circa 1990: An anthology.* ERIC Document no. ED 273 324. Galesburg, Ill.: Carl Sandburg College Bookstore.

Gayle, M. 1990. Toward the 21st century. *Adult Learning* 1(4):10–14.

Gold, C. L. 1982. *Contracting with business and industry: Use your community resources.* ERIC Document no. ED 226 768. Escanaba, Mich.: Bay de Noc Community College.

Gollattscheck, J. F. 1982. Confronting the complexity of community analysis. *Community Services Catalyst* 12(1):7–11.

Gordon, A. 1986. Meeting the needs of the community through cooperation, collaboration, and community outreach. *Community Services Catalyst* 16(2):10–12.

Gordon, R. A. 1987. A renewed mission for community service educators. *Community Services Catalyst* 17(1):11–14.

Grattan, C. H., ed. 1959. *American ideas about adult education, 1710–1951.* New York: Columbia University, Teachers College.

Hamm, R., and L. Tolle-Burger. 1988. *Two-year colleges: Doing business with business (A handbook for colleges planning to serve commerce and industry).* ERIC Document no. ED 300 088. Washington, D.C.: Community Colleges Press.

Hankin, N. J., and P. A. Fey. 1988. Reassessing the commitment to community services. In *Renewing the American community college*, ed. W. L. Deegan and D. Tillery, 150–74. San Francisco: Jossey-Bass.

Hare, J. A., et al. 1987. *Curriculum guide for parent education programs*. ERIC Document no. ED 296 105. Pasco, Wash.: Columbia Basin College Parent Education Program.

Harlacher, E. L. 1988. The learning society: A vital role for community services and continuing education. *Community Services Catalyst* 18(2):6–8.

Harlacher, E. L., and J. F. Gollattscheck, eds. 1978. Editors' notes. In *Implementing community-based education*. New Directions for Community Colleges no. 21:vii–ix. San Francisco: Jossey-Bass.

Ireland, J., and M. Gegna. 1983. *The future management, funding, and scope of community services education within the Los Angeles Community College District*. ERIC Document no. ED 229 071. Los Angeles: Los Angeles Community College District, California Educational Services Division.

Johnston, C. W. 1985. *The adult basic education program: A technological approach to adult literacy education*. ERIC Document no. ED 264 918. Charlotte, N.C.: Central Piedmont Community College.

Kazemek, P. E. 1990. Adult literacy education: Heading into the 1990's. *Adult Education Quarterly* 41(1):53–62.

Levine, A. 1978. *Handbook on undergraduate curriculum*. San Francisco: Jossey-Bass.

Lewis, L. H., and R. S. Caffarella. 1990. Resources on adult development. In *Applying adult development strategies*, ed. M. H. Rossman and M. E. Rossman. New Directions for Adult and Continuing Education, no. 45:77–87. San Francisco: Jossey-Bass.

Lindeman, E. C. 1961. *The meaning of adult education*. Montreal: Harvest House.

Matthews, F. L. 1991. Revising the community college rhetoric. *Community College Week* 4(5):4.

McDowell, R. W. 1984. Community services' role in economic recovery. *Community Services Catalyst* 14(2):12–14.

McGuire, K. B. 1988. *State of the art in community-based education in the American community college*. ERIC Document no. ED 293 583. Washington, D.C.: American Association of Community and Junior Colleges.

Merriam, S. B., and M. C. Clark. 1991. *Lifelines: Patterns of work, love, and learning in adulthood*. San Francisco: Jossey-Bass.

Merriam, S. B., and R. S. Caffarella. 1991. *Learning in adulthood: A comprehensive guide*. San Francisco: Jossey-Bass.

Myran, G. A. 1978. Antecedents: Evolution of the community based college. *New Directions for Community-Based Education* 21:1–6.

Nakamura, Y. C. 1989. Student services in the tapestry of lifelong learning. *Community Services Catalyst* 19(3):12–13.

Parsons, M. H. 1989. *The past as prologue: Variables influencing the continuing development of community services in America's community colleges*. Presented at the Annual Conference of the National Council on Community Service and Continuing Education, Pensacola, Fla., October 11, 1989. ERIC Document no. ED 314 103.

Rohfeld, R. W., ed. 1990. *Expanding access to knowledge: Continuing higher education*

(NUCEA:1915–1990). Washington, D.C.: National University Continuing Education Association.

South Plains Community College. 1988. *LIFE: Literacy is for everyone. (Final report)*. ERIC Document no. ED 298 335. Lubbock, Texas.

Warren, C. 1989. Andragogy and N.F.S. Grundtvig: A critical link. *Adult Education Quarterly* 39(4):211–23.

Remedial/Developmental Education: Past, Present, and Future

Milton G. Spann, Jr. and Suella McCrimmon

REMEDIAL/DEVELOPMENTAL EDUCATION IN THE COMMUNITY COLLEGE

Traditionally, the community college has performed a number of curricular functions: college transfer preparation, vocational technical education, continuing education, community service, and remedial/developmental education (Cohen and Brawer 1982). With the breakdown of basic academic education at the secondary level, remedial/developmental education emerged in the late 1960s and early 1970s as a major function of community colleges and it remains so today. As long as the majority of students entering open-door community colleges continue to come from the lower half of the educational and socioeconomic spectrum, they will probably need heavy doses of effective remedial/developmental education.

Historically, remedial/developmental education has concerned itself primarily with the remediation of academic skill deficiencies. However, since the 1970s, the field has expanded to include all forms of learning assistance and personal development suitable to the needs of at-risk college students. Borrowing from a variety of theories and concepts of learning and human development, the field advocates placing the low-achieving learner at the center of the teaching/learning process, believing that, despite the extent of technology available, personal involvement with the learner and conscious attention to the student's developmental needs are essential if meaningful learning is to occur.

As an evolving field in the postsecondary sector, remedial/developmental education is still in a state of transition and is likely to be so well into the twenty-first century. While its philosophical roots are humanistic, its practices are quite diverse and often centered in the experience of its practitioners who come from a wide variety of backgrounds and do not have a set of clearly articulated assumptions about education.

The extensive curriculum of remedial/developmental education is perhaps the largest "hidden curriculum" in American postsecondary education. That is, remedial/developmental courses and services are frequently scattered throughout the institution with various administrative units responsible for a portion of them.

Whether these courses, services, and activities are brought together under one administrative umbrella or simply viewed collectively, they often affect, particularly in community and technical colleges, a significant portion (from 30 to 90 percent) of the student body (Richardson and Bender 1987). Educational assessment and demographic projections support the view that high percentages (from 25 to 30 percent) of students will enter America's postsecondary institutions with some academic, psychological, or physical challenge significant enough to impair their success if not compensated for or corrected (Hodgkinson 1985).

While the remedial/developmental function has become more acceptable to community college educators, it has drawn its share of critics. McGrath and Spear (1987) have discussed the politics of remedial/developmental education and have suggested that its presence in the community college has contributed to the perpetuation of a dual-class structure in American postsecondary education which has resulted in the tracking of the lower socioeconomic classes away from the professions and toward serving the lower-level technical and semiprofessional needs of society. Remedial/developmental education is identified as a contributing factor in the channeling of lower-class students toward the same relative position in the social structure their parents occupy and thus leaving the essential shape of the social structure unchanged. It appears that community colleges in general and remedial/developmental programs in particular may serve to lower the aspirations of individuals who have made the mistake of aspiring too high. Clark (1960) first described this process of lowering aspirations as the "cooling-out" function and believed it to be one of democracy's major problems—the consistency between encouragement to achieve and the realities of limited social mobility. Echoing Clark's observations, Zwerling described the community college counselor as playing the key role in redirecting low-achieving students away from aspirations to higher education and professions and toward the semiprofessional vocations more in keeping with their actual abilities. Test scores are frequently used to show the student that remediation is essential and "cast doubt on the students' feelings that they can do bona fide college work" (1976, 18). Zwerling also suggested that although remedial/developmental education may serve to remediate isolated low-level academic skill deficiencies, it usually fails to initiate the student into the intellectual community which has become necessary for access to the professions.

If community colleges are to remedy the cooling-out function, they must not only know how students learn and develop, they must also believe that these students can learn the higher-order thinking skills necessary for upward mobility in a modern society. Others would argue that teaching low-achieving students to think critically and reason carefully is beyond the scope of remedial/developmental education. Visionaries such as Curtis Miles at the Center for Reasoning Studies, Piedmont Technical College, and John Chaffee, director of Creative and Critical Thinking Studies at LaGuardia Community College, argue that higher-order cognitive skills are the very essence of a successful basic skills program and within the reach of most low-achieving students. Remedial/developmental programs of the future must move beyond rote learning, isolated skills training, and the memorization of isolated facts to a focus on learning how-to-learn skills and processes.

Regardless of what the critics say, there is little evidence that remedial/developmental education is declining in importance among community colleges or that it will do so in the future. In fact, the remedial/developmental function has become so pervasive that Richardson and Bender (1987) claim that the college transfer curriculum has now been displaced by this function. Accompanying the displacement of the transfer function has been the challenge of teaching the academically and psychologically underprepared college student, a challenge that Cohen and Brawer described as "the thorniest single problem for community colleges" (1982, 231).

HISTORY AND BACKGROUND

Helping underprepared students prepare themselves for college has been a feature of American higher education since Harvard opened its doors in 1636. The place of remedial/developmental education in the educational community proved increasingly tenuous, however, as higher education abandoned its roots in the more holistic English residential model of education for the research-oriented German model which prevailed following the Civil War. As faculty interest shifted from student to "whole-person" development to intellectual development, from religious to secular concerns, and from small intimate learning communities to larger, more complex institutions (Brubacher and Rudy 1976; Delworth and Hanson 1989), higher education struggled with the appropriateness of admitting students not adequately prepared for the college experience. The issue was often controversial and found expression through major reports and prominent speeches by educational leaders.

As far back as 1828, the Yale Report called for an end to the admission of students with "defective preparation" (Brier 1984). This sentiment was echoed in 1852 by the president of the University of Michigan, Henry P. Tappan (Maxwell 1979). Charles Elliot, on the other hand, stated in his inaugural address as president of Harvard that "the American college is obliged to supplement the American school. Whatever elementary instruction the schools fail to give, the college must supply" (1869). Harvard, along with others, instituted programs to remediate deficiencies, and by 1870 only twenty-three colleges reported no college preparatory program (Losak and Miles 1991).

After 1920 higher educational institutions left most of the preparation and remediation to the two-year college, but, prior to the 1960s, the success of remedial education programs must be questioned. Roueche (1968) found that as many as 90 percent of all remedial students in California community colleges failed or withdrew from remedial courses. A more recent study conducted by the National Center for Developmental Education showed examples of success in preparing low-ability students for successful entry into the college-level curriculum of choice (Spann and Thompson 1986). A few of the most successful programs have been able to prepare and then see graduate previously low-achieving students at rates equal to students not in need of remediation. Several community colleges in Ohio reported that the percentage of students using developmental services was greater among graduates than among the general student body, implying that students utilizing these services (i.e., preparatory courses, tutoring, and specialized counseling) were more likely to remain in college and earn a degree (Braswell 1978).

CAUSES OF POOR PERFORMANCE

Various reasons have been offered to explain the cause of poor academic achievement. Cross (1976) outlined several explanations for poor academic performance in the period between 1930 and 1980.

From 1894, when the first remedial course was offered at Wellesley College, until the 1930s, the perceived cause of poor performance was thought to be poor study habits. The typical response to this problem was to offer voluntary, non-credit courses or workshops. In the late 1930s and early 1940s, remedial reading courses, clinics, and workshops were added to the existing how-to-study courses. Students were placed in those courses based largely on a single test score. After 1945, millions of veterans swelled the ranks of colleges and universities, and their need for remedial/developmental education was extensive, particularly the need for counseling. Limited higher-education resources, along with an abundance of students seeking entry to college, produced increased political pressure to determine who was best suited for the college experience. Test results were used to separate ''underachievers'' from ''low-ability'' students with colleges admitting the more promising underachievers and rejecting most of the low-ability students as unsuitable for higher learning (Maxwell 1979). Many of these low-ability students enrolled in community colleges and technical institutes. With the passage of the Higher Education Act of 1965, the U.S. Congress provided greater access to more minority and, later, to handicapped students. Government-supported programs, particularly Upward Bound and Special Services, proved unusually effective in bringing the children of noncollege graduates to the campus. During this period (1940–1975), socioeconomic factors were regarded as the principle cause of poor academic performance, and compensatory academic and cultural enrichment programs were designed to bring deprived students into the mainstream of American society.

Today, we perceive the cause of poor academic performance as multifaceted and multidimensional, a combination of socioeconomic, cultural, and individual differences. Cognitive and affective dimensions of learning are increasingly diagnosed and treated. Particularly in large urban centers, student socioeconomic and sociocultural background is viewed as an important factor in planning and individualizing the program of study. Personality types, learning style, and other noncognitive factors may also be diagnosed and the results utilized in the development of a personalized learning plan for students.

THE PROFESSIONALIZATION OF REMEDIAL/ DEVELOPMENTAL EDUCATION

In the 1970s the numbers of students needing remediation sharply increased, and postsecondary institutions began to recognize and accept remedial/developmental education as a legitimate, even permanent, part of their mission. Programs were staffed by persons who accepted the challenge as a career opportunity rather than as a stepping stone to teaching regularly admitted students. Today more than 50 percent of those working in remedial/developmental education think of it as their career of choice. Referred to as developmental educators or learning skills specialists, they attend professional meetings and workshops on ways to teach, motivate, and assess at-risk students.

Beginning in the early 1970s, several professional organizations for remedial/ developmental education practitioners emerged. At the national level, there are two major organizations: the National Association of Developmental Education and the College Reading and Learning Association. Each organization hosts a number of state or regional chapters. Specialized practitioner and research-oriented publications, such as the *Journal of Developmental Education* and the *Review of Research in Developmental Education*, are published by the National Center for Developmental Education at Appalachian State University. Such other key publications as *Research and Teaching in Developmental Education* (New York Learning Skills Association) and the *Journal of College Reading and Learning* (College Reading and Learning Association) have been published since the mid–1970s. There are graduate-level programs specifically designed to prepare college-level remedial/developmental education professionals at Appalachian State University and Grambling State University.

STUDENT CHARACTERISTICS

The academically underprepared college student may be defined as one who fails to meet the established entrance criteria for a beginning college-level course or entry-level program of choice. Maxwell characterized underprepared students as those "whose skills, knowledge, and academic ability are significantly below those of the 'typical' student in the college or curriculum in which they are enrolled" (1979, 2). Low-achieving students tend to avoid what they perceive to be painful or threatening. For example, underprepared students who come to college with a weakness in reading, writing, or mathematics, when given a choice, will often put off taking the needed basic skills courses or try to bypass them. They may attempt to enroll in the regular beginning level course and thus try to avoid the pain of embarrassment and feelings of inadequacy they believe will come should they actually enroll in one of these courses (Maxwell 1979). Given the self-esteem issues associated with enrollment in basic skills programs, institutions should be more sensitive to the psychological dimensions of student behavior as they consider such things as the titles of basic skills programs, the numbering of basic skills courses, and the attitudes of basic skills faculty and staff.

Earlier, Pritchard and Bloushild (1970) researched the characteristics of low-achieving students and found the following: lack of academic potential, inadequate understanding of the work required for college success, failure to make studying the first priority, interference from psychological problems, failure to assume responsibility for learning and success, poor communication skills, and failure to select a college where they can be successful. Those descriptors are as valid today as they were in 1970.

Academically underprepared students are not the only at-risk students served by the modern developmental education or learning assistance program. Other at-risk populations include the learning disabled, the visually and hearing impaired, the mobility handicapped, the English as a second language student, the student-athlete, the returning adult student, and the first-generation college student. These and other at-risk populations may receive a variety of educational services, for example, counseling or instruction, designed to reduce the risk and maximize the potential for the successful completion of anything from a single course to a complete program of study leading to a certificate or a degree.

EVOLUTION OF TERMS

Historically, three terms—remedial, compensatory, and developmental—have dominated the literature and vocabulary of those concerned with the education of the academically underprepared college student. The term "remedial education" is based on the idea of a deficit in students' academic backgrounds. To remediate is to remedy the problem, to build the skills necessary for success in a college entry level course or program of study.

The term "compensatory education" is of more recent origin. According to Clowes (1982), this term emerged in precollegiate settings after World War II. In both England and America, compensatory education was associated with the lessening or removal of "environmentally induced" achievement deficits and later with the push to break the cycle of disadvantagement associated with President Lyndon Johnson's war on poverty. Compensatory education was essentially a middle-class response to a perceived cultural deficit in the educational and social background of lower-class persons. Compensatory education was designed to bring them into the culture of the middle class by providing a variety of educational, cultural, and personal growth experiences not available in their home environment.

In the 1970s "developmental education" became the preferred term among postsecondary faculty associated with courses and programs for academically at-risk college students. This term was first popularized by faculty at open-access colleges, particularly community colleges, and evolved from dissatisfaction with the negative connotations and limited meaning of the term remedial. The term developmental, at least in the context of the postsecondary developmental education movement, focused on the student's potential rather than the student's deficit. Since the goal of developmental education is a fully developed and fully functioning person, focusing on academic skills alone is insufficient if students are to make the transition to all-around effective students and involved citizens.

More recently, Losak and Miles defined developmental education as "those services and policies needed to help students develop the baseline academic intellectual and affective capabilities which are prerequisites to achieving their postsecondary educational goals" (1991, 22). This definition suggests a largely preparatory function and thus adheres strongly to the historical emphasis within the field. In the 1990 document *A Learning Assistance Glossary: Report of the CLRA Task Force of Professional Language for College Reading and Learning*, developmental education is given a threefold definition: "(1) a sub-discipline of the field of education concerned with improving the performance of students, (2) a field of research, teaching, and practice designed to improve academic performance, (3) a process utilizing principles of developmental theory to facilitate learning" (College Reading and Learning Association 1990, 3). The CLRA definition appears to turn away from the historical function and focuses instead on students as developing persons and on the principles of teaching and learning. It speaks to the learning and human development needs of all students at all levels rather than to the particular needs of the at-risk students.

An example of a definition with a distinguishing focus is the one offered in a recent study by the Southern Regional Education Board (SREB) of college-level remedial and developmental programs: "Remedial or developmental education refers to programs, courses, and activities designed specifically for first-time entering students who lack minimum reading, writing, or oral communications, mathematical, or study skills, and/or basic skills necessary to do freshman-level college work as defined by the institution" (Abraham 1986, 19).

STATUS OF DEVELOPMENTAL EDUCATION ACTIVITY IN THE UNITED STATES

A recent nationwide study of 546 randomly selected institutions conducted by the National Center for Education Statistics (NCES) (1991) described the current status of remedial/developmental education in community colleges. Results revealed that 90 percent of community colleges offered this type of education in 1989, compared with 88 percent in 1983. The data also indicated that 36 percent of all entering community college freshman enrolled in a remedial reading, writing, or math course. Of those freshmen taking these courses, 73 percent passed reading, 70 percent passed writing, and 65 percent successfully completed mathematics. On the average, two-year colleges offer 2.8 courses in each of these areas, with most colleges offering at least two levels of remedial/developmental work.

When asked how many faculty were involved in the teaching of remedial/developmental education courses, respondents failed to distinguish community college faculty alone. However, for all types of postsecondary institutions, nearly 31,000 taught one or more basic skills courses. These numbers were up considerably over the 26,000 faculty identified by the College Marketing Group of Winchester, Massachusetts, in 1985. However, the data did reveal the average number of persons in community colleges teaching basic skills courses. In the 139 two-year colleges surveyed, an average of 20 faculty members taught one or more remedial/developmental courses. Of those 20, an average of 11.5 were employed specifically to teach remedial/developmental courses, however, only 4.6 of them had degrees or credentials specific to remedial or developmental education.

CREDIT FOR REMEDIAL/DEVELOPMENTAL COURSES

When asked what kind of credit institutions offered remedial/developmental students, respondents to the NCES (1991) survey reported the following: among community colleges, 76 percent offered institutional or transcript credit in reading, 78 percent offered institutional or transcript credit in writing, and 79 percent offered institutional credit in mathematics. Among those community colleges offering degree credit for remedial/developmental courses, the data revealed that 14 percent offered degree credit in reading, 11 percent in writing, and 13 percent in mathematics. It is clear that institutional credit for remedial/developmental courses is offered more frequently than degree credit.

A comparison of data gathered in 1989 by NCES with data gathered by Cross (1976) in the early 1970s revealed a dramatic decline in the percent of institutions currently offering degree credit for remedial/developmental courses and a significant increase in those offering institutional or transcript credit.

LOCATION OF REMEDIAL/DEVELOPMENTAL PROGRAMS

In community colleges nationwide, NCES (1991) data revealed that 28 percent of remedial/developmental reading programs, 23 percent of writing programs, and 25 percent of mathematics programs were associated with a separate basic skills or developmental studies unit; while 55 percent, 63 percent, and 64 percent, respectively, were housed in traditional academic departments. Learning centers were the only other administrative unit to house these functions to any significant extent with 16 percent responsible for reading, 14 percent for writing, and 10 percent for mathematics. The trend since the 1970s has been to restore remedial/developmental course responsibility to the traditional academic departments.

EXTENT OF EVALUATION STUDIES

With increased demands for accountability from the public at large and by public agencies at the state and federal levels and with the growing need to determine the outcome or results of educational inputs, the evaluation of remedial/developmental programs is increasingly being emphasized. When Spann and Thompson (1986) reviewed documents from over 500 colleges and universities, they found evidence of ongoing written evaluation reports in less than one-third of all institutions submitting documentation. This study revealed a generally low level of sophistication in carrying out evaluation procedures and raised questions about the extent to which institutions were taking seriously the obligations they have to assess adequately their remedial/developmental courses and programs.

NCES (1991) data revealed that a variety of evaluation measures were used by community colleges including student opinion surveys, teacher effectiveness, student completion rates, and follow-up studies involving student grades, among others. It is evident that a significant majority were carrying on evaluation efforts, but it remains to be seen how sophisticated these studies are. At least one study of twenty-nine institutions in Michigan reinforces the perception that evaluation studies of remedial/developmental services in community colleges need improvement. This study, conducted by the Michigan State Board of Education (1990), produced several recommendations regarding the adequacy of current evaluation practices. The study recommended that community colleges improve records and data-keeping procedures to determine the impact of remedial/developmental services on various student populations and that they utilize stronger evaluation methods to determine the effectiveness of developmental efforts and incorporate the results into their decision-making process. Historically, evaluations of remedial/developmental programs have consisted of little more than solicited opinions and frequency counts. Comparative studies and investigations of student success in subsequent courses while seldom available are on the increase. We believe that more sophisticated studies will be required in the future.

RECOMMENDATIONS FOR REDUCING THE DEMAND FOR REMEDIAL/DEVELOPMENTAL ACTIVITIES

Two recommendations appear in the NCES (1991) study regarding ways to reduce the escalating demands for remedial/developmental education within the community college. One of the recommendations is to improve communications with high school students and their parents describing in various ways and through various means the knowledge, skills, and attitudes necessary for success in college. In 1989, 71 percent of all public colleges, including community colleges, reported that they were communicating with high schools about this subject. The second recommendation is that college and university personnel would benefit from attending organized workshops with high school faculty to discuss what a student must do to be ready for college. The NCES study found that only 24 percent of public college personnel have actually attended workshops of this type. In all cases, large institutions (5,000+) led the way in communicating and working with colleagues in the public schools.

In addition to NCES information regarding current practices designed to reduce the need for remediation, the SREB has offered eleven recommendations to help ensure quality undergraduate education and to reduce the number of inadequately prepared college students:

1. Require that higher-education institutions identify and implement statewide minimum standards and assessments for college courses that earn credit toward baccalaureate or associate degrees. These should represent a consensus by higher education on the basic academic skills students need to begin to study at the college level, especially in reading, writing, and mathematics.

2. Require secondary and postsecondary educators to work collaboratively to identify basic academic skills needed for college-level study.

3. Require students who do not meet minimum standards to take nondegree credit courses/programs that provide further preparation.

4. Require that minimum standards and procedures for placement and assessment be consistent statewide for all public institutions of higher education.

5. Recognize remedial/developmental education as an essential element of the mission of *all* public institutions of higher education that admit students who are not ready to begin college-level work.

6. Ensure that students not qualified to begin degree-credit study are within commuting distance of programs that will prepare them to qualify.

7. Initiate and maintain effective remedial/developmental programs that uphold institutional integrity and standards for quality undergraduate education.

8. Provide adequate funding for remedial/developmental programs, recognizing that it can require comparatively greater efforts and cost to develop instruction and programs for teaching students who are academically deficient.

9. Clearly state and make known to schools, high school students, and their parents the skills needed to pursue college-level course work.

10. Require that faculty and staff who teach remedial/developmental courses be fully trained and qualified.

11. Provide annual review and evaluations of remedial/developmental programs to ensure academic integrity and to ensure that students who complete those courses have competencies that are equivalent to entrance requirements for "regular" college-level students. (Abraham 1988)

CHALLENGES TO DEVELOPMENTAL EDUCATION

The field of developmental education currently faces an identity crisis. For the most part, it has little knowledge of its roots or a widely understood and articulated philosophy, a body of common knowledge, or a commonly accepted set of theoretical assumptions congruent with that philosophy. Like the academy, its guiding principles are largely based on folklore about "good education" and "good teaching" rather than on empirical evidence and a clear understanding of human needs. If the developmental education movement is to be a part of the reform so necessary in higher education, it must be willing to risk itself for the well-being of students and identify itself even more closely with an expanding list of basic skills and attitudes necessary for personal, academic, and vocational success in the twenty-first century. It is a field struggling with its identity with one foot in the traditionalist camp and one in the reformer camp. Its greatest challenge is to resist the call of acceptance and respectability and step forward as an articulate and enthusiastic representative for the long-term educational goals of the next century. Along the way it may raise the level of the dialogue regarding the art and the science of teaching, learning, and human development.

SUMMARY

This chapter attempts to lay the foundation for an understanding of the evolution of remedial/developmental education in the community colleges. A review of the historical context of remedial/developmental education in American higher education is used to set the stage for the dominant role played by the two-year college beginning in the 1920s.

The evolution of remedial/developmental education was influenced by increasingly complex reasons regarding the need for such services. These reasons parallel an increasingly sophisticated understanding on the part of social scientists about how persons learn, grow, and develop.

The field of developmental education was founded on the democratic ideals of justice, freedom, and opportunity for all citizens. The practice of remedial/ developmental education has not only been influenced by these ideals but also by metaphors like oneness, wholeness, and community. These powerful ideas make the field of developmental education a natural ally with those proponents of an egalitarian educational system. It is, therefore, understandable why the developmental educator has often been a protector and defender of the open-access college and why these educators may be among those persons best equipped philosophically and theoretically to deal with the coming demographic changes likely to bring large numbers of at-risk students into every level of education.

In spite of its belief in providing postsecondary education for all who can benefit, the adolescent field of developmental education faces an identity crisis. Will it succumb to the practiced values of the academy which make learning and student development a low priority, or will it take the lead in again making this the academy's first priority? Should the field choose the latter course, it may well become a major force in restoring the integrity of American higher education and thereby make the effective teaching of students the high priority it must become if the United States is to prepare its citizens for leadership and competition in the global society that is now upon us.

REFERENCES

Abraham, A. 1986. *A report on college level remedial/developmental programs in SREB states.* Atlanta, Ga.: Southern Regional Education Board.

————. 1988. *Remedial education in college: How widespread is it?* SREB Report no. 24. Atlanta, Ga.: Southern Regional Education Board.

Astin, A. W. 1984. Student involvement: A developmental theory for higher education. *Journal of College Student Personnel* 24:297–308.

Bliss, R. W. 1986. *Intellectual development and freshman English.* Paper presented at Project MATCH conference, Davidson College, Davidson, North Carolina.

Braswell, W. 1978. *Report on admissions and developmental education.* Columbus, Ohio: Ohio Board of Regents, p. 9.

Brier, E. 1984. Bridging the academic preparation gap. *Journal of Developmental Education* 8(1):2–5.

Brubacher, J. S., and W. Rudy. 1976. *Higher education in transition.* New York: Harper and Row.

Buerk, D. 1985. From magic to meaning: Changing the learning of mathematics. Paper presented at ISEM Workshop on Teaching and Learning Mathematics, Saint Paul, Minnesota.

Burnham, C. 1984. The Perry scheme and the teacher of literature. Paper presented at Conference on College Composition and Communication, Las Cruces, New Mexico.

Chaffee, J. 1992. Critical thinking skills: The cornerstone of developmental education. *Journal of Developmental Education* 15(3):2.

Chickering, A. W. 1969. *Education and identity.* San Francisco: Jossey-Bass.

Clark, B. 1960. The cooling-out function in higher education. *American Journal of Sociology* 65:569–76.

Clark, B., and M. Trow. 1966. The organizational context. In *College peer groups: Problems and prospects for research*, ed. T. M. Newcomb and E. K. Wilson. Chicago: Aldine.

Claxton, C. S., and P. H. Murrell. 1987. *Learning styles: Implications for improving education practices.* ASHE-ERIC Higher Education Report no. 4. Washington, D.C.: Association for the Study of Higher Education.

Clowes, D. A. 1982. More than a definitional problem: Remedial, compensatory, and developmental education. *Journal of Developmental and Remedial Education* 4(2):8–10.

Cohen, A. M., and F. B. Brawer. 1982. *The American community college.* San Francisco: Jossey-Bass.

College Reading and Learning Association. 1990. *A learning assistance glossary: Report of the CLRA task force of professional language for college reading and learning.* Minneapolis, Minn.

Copes, L. 1982. The Perry developmental scheme: A metaphor for learning and teaching mathematics. *For the Learning of Mathematics* 3:38–44.

Cross, K. P. 1971. *Beyond the open door: New students to higher education*. San Francisco: Jossey-Bass.

———. 1976. *Accent on learning: Improving instruction and reshaping the curriculum*. San Francisco: Jossey-Bass.

Delworth, U., and G. R. Hanson. 1989. *Student services: A handbook for the profession*. San Francisco: Jossey-Bass.

Drucker, P. F. 1989. How schools must change. *Psychology Today* 23:5.

Elliot, C. W. 1869. *A turning point in higher education: The inaugural address of Charles William Elliot as president of Harvard College, October 19, 1869*. Cambridge, Mass.: Harvard University Press.

Erickson, E. H. 1950. *Childhood and society*. New York: Norton.

———. 1968. *Identity: Youth and crisis*. New York: Norton.

Fetters, W. B. 1977. *Withdrawal from institutions of higher education*. National Center for Educational Statistics. ERIC Document no. ED 150 913. Washington, D.C.: U.S. Government Printing Office.

Glasby, M. K. 1985. An analysis of cognitive development and student profiles over three levels of mathematics courses at a selected community college (Perry scale). Ph.D. diss., University of Maryland.

Glasser, W. 1984. *Take effective control of your life*. New York: Harper and Row.

Haisty, D. B. 1983. The developmental theories of Jean Piaget and William Perry: An application to the teaching of writing. Ph.D. diss., Texas Christian University.

Havighurst, R. J. 1953. *Human development and education*. New York: Longmans, Green.

Heard, F. B. 1988. *An assessment of the Tennessee statewide school-college collaborative for educational excellence: The middle college high school*, ed. D. Practicum. Nova University: Fort Lauderdale, Fla. ERIC Document no. ED 294 637.

Heath, R. 1964. *The reasonable adventurer*. Pittsburgh: University of Pittsburgh Press.

Hodgkinson, H. L. 1985. *All one system: Demographics of education, kindergarten through graduate school*. Washington, D.C.: Institute for Educational Leadership.

Hunt, D. E. 1970. A conceptual level matching model for coordinating learner characteristics with educational approach. *Interchange* 1:68–72.

Katz, J., and N. Sanford. 1962. *The American college*. New York: Wiley.

Keniston, K. 1971. *Youth and dissent*. New York: Harcourt Brace Jovanovich.

Kiersey, D., and M. Bates. 1978. *Please understand me: Character and temperament types*. 3d ed. Del Mar, Calif.: Prometheus Nemesis Books.

King, P. M. 1982. Perry's scheme and the reflective judgment model: First cousins once removed. Paper presented at annual conference of Association for Moral Education, Minneapolis, Minnesota.

Kitchener, K. S., and P. M. King. 1981. Reflective judgment: Concepts of justification and their relationship to age and education. *Journal of Applied Educational Psychology* 2:89–116.

———. 1985. The reflective judgment model: Ten years of research. Paper presented at Beyond Formal Operations Symposium.

Kneflkamp, L., C. Widick, and C. Parker, eds. 1978. *Applying new developmental findings*. San Francisco: Jossey-Bass.

Kohlberg, L. 1969. Stage and sequence: The cognitive developmental approach to socialization. In *Handbook of socialization theory and research*, ed. D. Godlin, Chicago: Rand McNally.

————. 1972. A cognitive developmental approach to moral education. *Humanist* 6:13–16.

————. 1975. The cognitive developmental approach to moral education. *Phi Delta Kappan* 10:670–77.

Kolb, D. A. 1976. *Learning styles inventory technical manual.* Boston: McBer.

Lawrence, G. D. 1982. *People types and tiger stripes.* 2d ed. Gainesville, Fla.: Center for Applications of Psychological Type.

————. 1984. A synthesis of learning style research involving the MBTI. *Journal of Psychological Type* 8:2–15.

Levinson, D. J. 1978. *The seasons of a man's life.* New York: Knopf.

Loevinger, J. 1976. *Ego development: Conceptions and theories.* San Francisco: Jossey-Bass.

Losak, J., and C. Miles. 1991. *Foundations and context of developmental education in higher education.* Boone, N.C.: National Center for Developmental Education.

Marcia, J. 1966. Development and validation of ego-identity status. *Journal of Personality and Social Psychology* 35:551–58.

Maxwell, M. 1979. *Improving student learning skills.* San Francisco: Jossey-Bass.

McGrath, D., and M. B. Spear. 1987. The politics of remediation. In *Teaching the developmental education student,* ed. K. M. Ahrendt. New Directions for Community Colleges no. 57. San Francisco: Jossey-Bass.

————. 1991. *The academic crisis of the community college.* Albany, N.Y.: State University of New York Press.

Michigan State Board of Education. 1990. Survey of student assessment in Michigan's public community colleges. ERIC Document no. ED 320 624. Lansing: Michigan State Board of Education.

Myers, I. B. 1980. *Gifts differing.* Palo Alto, Calif.: Consulting Psychologists Press.

National Center for Educational Statistics. 1991. *College level remedial education in the fall of 1989.* Fast Response Survey System, 38, Washington, D.C.: U.S. Department of Education.

Neugarten, B. L. 1976. Adaption and the life-cycle. *Counseling Psychologist* 6:16–20.

Newcomb, T. M., et al. 1967. *Persistence and change.* New York: Wiley.

Perry. W. G. 1970. *Forms of intellectual and ethical development in the college years.* New York: Holt, Rinehart and Winston.

Piaget, J. 1964. Cognitive development in children. In *Piaget rediscovered: A report on cognitive studies in curriculum development,* ed. R. Ripple and V. Rockcastle. Ithaca, N.Y.: Cornell University School of Education.

Pritchard, R. W., and B. Bloushild. 1970. *Why college students fail.* New York: Funk and Wagnalls.

Project synergy: Software report for underprepared students. 1991. Miami: Miami-Dade Community College.

Reid, G. B. 1986. The use of the Perry scheme in the teaching of freshman English. Ph.D. diss., Memphis State University.

Richardson, R. C., and L. Bender. 1987. *Fostering minority access and achievement in higher education.* San Francisco: Jossey-Bass.

Roberts, G. H. 1986. *Developmental education: An historical study.* ERIC Document no. ED 276 395.

Roueche, J. E. 1968. *Salvage, redirection, or custody? Remedial education in the com-

munity/junior college. Washington, D.C.: American Association of Junior Colleges.

Sanford, N. 1966. *The American college.* New York: Wiley.

————. 1967. *Where colleges fail: A study of the student as a person.* San Francisco: Jossey-Bass.

Spann, M. G., and C. G. Thompson. 1986. *The national directory of exemplary programs in developmental education.* Boone, N.C.: The National Center for Developmental Education.

Van Hecke, M. 1985. The work of William Perry, part II: Teaching psychology to dualistic level students. *Illinois Psychologist* 24:15–20.

Wright, D. A., and M. W. Cahalan. 1985. Remedial/developmental studies in institutions of higher education: Policies and practices. Paper presented at the annual conference of the American Educational Research Association, Chicago, Illinois, April 1. ERIC Document no. ED 263 828.

Zwerling, L. S. 1976. *Second best: The crisis of the community college.* Boston: McGraw-Hill.

Challenges Facing the Urban Community College: A Literature Review

Robert Pedersen

Any attempt to synthesize the literature of the urban community college is hampered by the ambiguity and confusion that surround the use of the term "urban." This designation is sometimes applied narrowly, to include only the nation's largest and most disadvantaged urban centers; at other times, it is used broadly, to incorporate the relatively affluent and economically vital communities that ring many of the nation's dying core cities.

It would be a serious mistake to regard this ambiguity as simply an academic issue of semantics. The lack of consensus about the meaning of the term "urban" has, in fact, deprived this field of inquiry of a focus and a shared vision. It has resulted not only in a body of literature at odds over which community colleges rightfully should be designated "urban community colleges," but also in a literature that avoids synthesis in favor of the anecdotal, is frequently ambiguous toward urban students and their communities, and is seemingly incapable of setting its own agenda, responding instead to the issues and concerns raised by institutions largely insulated from America's urban crisis.

Recognizing the need to address the definition issue at the outset, this chapter will not only survey the literature of the urban community college, describing what are frequently divergent views on the nature and role of the urban community college, but also suggest possible strategies for achieving the following:

1. A more precise definition of the urban community college

2. Greater continuity and vision within the literature itself, primarily through a deeper appreciation of the urban community college's history, a less ambiguous response to urban students and their communities, and the replacement of anecdotal reporting by broad-based analysis of this institutional type

3. Greater control over the public policy debate surrounding the urban community college by the leadership of these institutions.

An aim of this review and its recommendations is to suggest the basis for a more focused and mature literature, characterized by shared purpose and vision, with clear guidance for policymakers as they strengthen and expand the role of the community college in meeting the challenges now confronting urban America.

DEFINING THE UNIVERSE OF URBAN COMMUNITY COLLEGES

State of the Literature

The nation's collective image of urban America has been fixed by media coverage of recent events in Los Angeles. The popular connotation of "urban community" is one that is densely populated, burdened by high levels of unemployment, divided by racial tension, unable to deliver basic social services, and evidences other signs of social decay. To a large degree, this vision of urban America has been shaped by the seminal work of sociologist William Julius Wilson (1987). Supported by the scholarship of Ricketts and Sawhill (1988), Kasadra (1989), and others, Wilson has popularized the identification of urban America with the nation's larger core cities. Even as the rest of America has experienced economic growth, argues Wilson and others, its urban centers have been victimized by the growth of a socially dysfunctional and alienated underclass, themselves victims of the export of low-skill industrial employment away from core cities to the American sunbelt and Pacific Rim nations. Thus, this identification of urban America with its core cities links "urban community colleges" to a mission of serving primarily the nation's growing underclass.

Unfortunately, other definitions of "urban America" have confused matters. The U.S. Census Bureau applies the term "urban" to a far broader range of communities than would fit within the framework advanced by Wilson and his followers. The Census Bureau classifies any community that supports a population of more than 2,500 as urban, regardless of its social or economic characteristics. Given the steady movement of Americans from farms and other rural areas over the last eighty years, and the emergence of a great many large, relatively affluent suburban communities, the Census Bureau now classifies virtually all Americans as urban residents. Simply on the basis of the Census Bureau's classification system, it would be perfectly reasonable for virtually all community colleges to claim, in some sense, to be urban, regardless of the social or economic characteristics of the communities they serve.

The community college body of literature has yet to signal which of these two competing definitions of urban should govern the categorization of community colleges. Even the most highly respected textbooks do not make specific reference to the urban community college (Cohen and Brawer 1982; Deegan and Tillery 1985; Vaughan 1985). A persistent misconception within much of the community college literature is that the nation's nearly 1,000 public community colleges are of a single and uniform type. The mistaken notion that generalizations can be made across the board is a continuing obstacle to the kind of meaningful typology that would allow for a focused understanding of the urban community college and the special conditions under which it operates.

While some writers have limited the definition of urban community colleges to those serving the distressed core cities, others have rejected such a restrictive definition. For Church, writing in *Urban Community College Report*, an urban community college is defined not by population density, ethnic diversity, or the concentration of industrial jobs within its service area. Rather, it is the presence of certain social conditions such as unemployment, dysfunctional behaviors, and structural economic change which justifies the designation as urban. Even though his own college serves a county in which farming remains a major industry, lacks a major city, and is approximately 85 percent white, Church nevertheless argues that his county's high levels of unemployment and the loss of industrial jobs allow him to claim about his college, "Clearly, we are urban too . . . We, too, care about inner city concerns and devote considerable resources to solving them" (Church 1992, 3).

Response to the Literature

The tendency within much of the community college literature to stress the institution's universal or common characteristics is no longer defensible at a time when social polarization and the death of our nation's core cities confront urban community colleges with challenges differing radically from those now facing the vast majority of community colleges. Continued insistence on such a universal view will only mask the extent and nature of the crisis facing urban communities colleges and, in the process, blind policymakers to the additional assistance these institutions will require from both public and private sources if they are to serve their communities adequately.

While virtually no community has avoided the modern social ills of unemployment, crime, and family disintegration, these alone do not warrant the designation of a community as urban, any more than they warrant this designation for its community college. As a growing body of works has documented, over the last two decades both the social and economic conditions of America's true urban communities—the nation's fifty or so core cities—have deteriorated dramatically, even as the ring communities surrounding these core cities have experienced dramatic economic expansion. This growing polarization of urban America and its ring communities is a study in marked contrasts. Increasingly, the ring communities of the nation's metropolitan regions have become home to white Americans, largely employed in managerial, professional, and skilled occupations. The primary beneficiaries of the economic boom of the last decade, these communities provide their residents with expanding job opportunities, well-funded community colleges, and a developing network of cultural institutions.

In contrast, during this same period, America's core cities have become home to a growing underclass, overwhelmingly minority, that enjoys neither stable communities nor the opportunities such communities can provide. This underclass, estimated to number 2.5 million even before the current recession (Mincy, Sawhill, and Wolf 1990, 451) are frequently young and reside in low-income homes headed by a single female with minimal formal education. Job prospects for core city residents with limited education are diminishing. Between 1970 and 1980 alone, New York City lost nearly 450,000 jobs that did not require a high school diploma; in Detroit, more than 100,000 such jobs were lost. Moreover, as Orfield and Ashkinaze's (1991) description of developments in Atlanta make clear, the potential for the underclass residents of a core city to gain access to the developing opportunities found in ring communities is frequently blocked by failure of public policy in the areas of housing, transportation, and education. The Commission on the Future of Community Colleges recently warned of the dangers inherent in these developments of the common life of the nation: "Thoughtful observers warn us that our society is afflicted by growing polarization. They report that there is a strong movement toward social and economic ghettos where young blacks and Hispanics, and members of other minority groups, such as Native Americans, are the most socially and economically disadvantaged" (1988, 9).

Clearly, those community colleges that must respond to the grave challenge now facing America's largest core cities, the *true* urban America, must not only recognize the uniqueness of this challenge, but also support the development of a literature that speaks directly and unambiguously to their common circumstance and to strategies for successfully meeting this challenge in an era of scarce resources. The *Urban Community College Report* (Church 1992) represents an important first step to this end and should be strengthened, but it should also work to stimulate a more extensive and complementary literature.

CONTINUITY AND VISION WITHIN THE LITERATURE

A Historical Perspective on the Urban Community College

Integral to any institution's sense of continuity and purpose are an understanding and an appreciation of its historical development. The urban community college is no exception to this rule. Unfortunately, in emphasizing the broad national forces that have shaped the community college, most histories of the movement have overlooked what were, in many instances, the unique parochial interests and concerns that governed the history of the urban community colleges.

The nominal attention paid to the urban community college in junior college historiography is understandable to some degree, given the relatively small number of junior colleges that were established in the nation's larger cities during the pre–World War I era. Most early public junior colleges were established in small cities located in rural areas of the Midwest and Far West, and a surprisingly high percentage of the few junior colleges established in larger cities either closed within a few years or were converted into senior colleges or universities.

Indeed, from what little historical record remains, it seems safe to conclude that the urban junior college's hold on public support was tenuous at best, and that it was, as a result, the frequent object and occasional victim of local opposition. One finds, for example, that a public junior college operated in Newark, New Jersey, from about 1919 to 1921, only to be closed, as was the junior college in Springfield, Massachusetts; the four junior colleges established in Los Angeles before 1920 were all closed the year that the Los Angeles Normal School became a branch campus of the University of California (*Junior College Journal* 1936, 33).

Certainly the most complete and instructive history of an early urban junior college is to be found in Smolich's unpublished dissertation (1968). Smolich's study of Chicago's ill-fated Crane Junior College describes an institution differing little from its modern urban counterpart. Those school officials who initiated the college program at Crane favored a vocational program, and were little interested in transfer or the professional aspirations of the early Crane students. The student body was, for the most part, poor, and was made up largely of recent immigrants, primarily from Russia. The college experienced difficulty in tracking its students after graduation and was uncertain how many, if any, transferred to senior institutions. By 1930 repeated conflict with the Chicago School Board over funding and the North Central Association's objections to the college's offering of remedial course work had led to the college's loss of accreditation (*Junior College Journal* 1931a, 205). While accreditation was eventually restored (the Chicago school system reduced teacher loads sixteen hours, eliminated remedial English offerings, and imposed more stringent entrance examinations), the college was nevertheless subsequently closed by the Chicago School Board as an economy measure (Dougherty 1983).

Those who believe that the challenges now facing America's urban community colleges—from cultural diversity and conflict, to remediation and testing, to political intervention—are of recent origin might do well to look to the history of Crane Junior College for consolation, if not inspiration.

The difficulties faced by the junior college in securing acceptance in urban America may be attributable to the opposition of civic leaders who, surprisingly, saw the junior college as an elitist venture designed to benefit the children of the affluent at public expense. Fields (1971), in his history of Baltimore Junior College, fully documents the extent and nature of this local opposition to a junior college. Fields' dissertation chronicles the resistance of Baltimore's local political leadership to various attempts to establish a public junior college in what was otherwise regarded as a progressive public school system. Fields highlights the 1927 decision of Baltimore's Mayor Broening to veto a measure creating a junior college in Baltimore on the grounds not only that the $100,000 cost was excessive, but also that the college would serve only the city's well-to-do.

Unlike their rural and suburban counterparts, many of the early urban junior/community colleges frequently faced pressure to expand into senior colleges. In light of recent discussions of Miami-Dade Community College's possible offering of the baccalaureate, the history of Detroit Junior College takes on a certain relevancy. As described by Strobel (1975), various community pressures led to the transformation of what was, at the time, the nation's leading junior college into Wayne State University. As a senior college, Wayne State University eventually adopted the norms of its sector and adopted restrictive admissions practices and a traditional academic program. The citizens of the Detroit region subsequently found it necessary to create an open-access, comprehensive community college: Wayne County Community College.

Finally, various sources also document that many urban junior colleges proved willing to accommodate the regressive social policies of their sponsoring cities. While urban community colleges now pride themselves on their accessibility to all, prior to the 1960s many urban community colleges maintained selective admissions policies (a practice whose legacy is to be found in their selective admissions policies for specific programs). Also, prior to the 1954 case *Brown v. Board of Education* numerous urban junior colleges were segregated. As noted by Brice (1949), major cities in several Southern and border states maintained dual junior college systems. One of the oldest, and possibly largest, of the African-American junior colleges was Houston Negro Junior College, and other examples can be found in Baltimore and Miami. As Brice noted, by 1948, the Kansas City area actually supported two public all-Black junior colleges, one on each side of the river.

While the urban junior/community college frequently struggled to gain and hold public support, it would be wrong to conclude that these institutions contributed little to the general development of the community college movement. It was, in fact, an urban junior college president, William Snyder of Los Angeles Junior College, who popularized the inclusion of occupational education within a comprehensive junior/community college curriculum. As Thornton (1972) observed in his discussion of the evolution of the junior/community college between 1920 and 1945, Snyder was the leading advocate of vocational education within the junior college, and he did much to gain acceptance of the comprehensive curriculum. For Snyder (1930), vocational education provided students with vision and sufficient skill ''to enable them to earn a living and to adjust themselves to the progress of the world.''

Reaction to the Literature

Historians of urban education, recognizing their failure to acknowledge the distinctive history of urban institutions, have enhanced our understanding of the urban elementary school through such works as *Educating an Urban People* (Ravitch and Goodenow 1981). The authorship of a comparable work focused exclusively on the urban junior/community college might well provide invaluable insight into the forces that have shaped this institution and, more specifically, explore the nature of opposition to the community college unique to the urban setting and of strategies for resolving this opposition.

AMBIGUITY IN THE LITERATURE'S RESPONSE TO URBAN STUDENTS AND THEIR URBAN SETTING

Criticism of sociologist Wilson's work has focused on its fundamentally ambiguous, even critical, view of urban America. While many core cities still remain vital centers of art and culture, and some have enjoyed success in promoting expanded employment opportunities, Wilson and others have focused public policy debate upon the disintegration of urban communities under the combined weight of economic restructuring and antisocial behavior. Wilson's urban America is dominated by crime and poverty, structural unemployment, drug abuse, and the disintegration of the family. To whatever degree one might reject such a portrayal, it would be naive to expect that the literature of the urban community colleges should escape entirely its influence and the widespread perception that urban America and all of its institutions are in crisis.

The ambiguity found in Wilson's work is clearly reflected in Temple's essay, "The Urban Community College" (1991). Temple sees "cities being consumed by pushers of crack cocaine, PCP and an alphabet soup of other drugs . . . I see babies having babies." He evidences little optimism in the capacity of urban community colleges to influence the disintegration of urban life, and he challenges the reader to cite one urban community college that is effectively meeting its community's needs when he poignantly asks, "Where are the programs? Where are the leaders?" Absent dramatic change, for which he offers no strategy and little hope, Temple concludes with a prediction of "the ultimate loss of an entire generation of Blacks, Hispanics, Asians and poor White Americans" (1991, 124).

Temple's generally pessimistic assessment of the urban community college's capacity to respond to the urban crisis is echoed by others. Pincus and Archer, for example, accuse the urban community college of failing to maintain an academic climate that emphasizes "intellectual rigor and critical thinking" (1989, 3). They assert that racial division and animosity is commonplace, in which "a generally hostile atmosphere characterizes relations between minority students and the predominantly white administration and faculty on many community college campuses" (20). This hostility prompts "self-destructive" behavior on the part of minority students and is exacerbated by minimal minority representation on most community college faculties.

Moreover, rarely does this literature characterize urban students in terms of positive qualities or attributes. Rather, students are described in terms of their deficits—academic, economic, and social—and the extent to which they differ from "traditional" students. To quote Elsner, "These are the single parents who come into our classes, who say they have been kicked out of their apartments because they cannot pay their rent. These are the students who cannot get their cars running in the morning, who cannot afford taxi fare. These are real, everyday problems for a normal community college student" (1991, 26).

Recalling the apologist descriptions of nineteenth-century settlement houses, this literature nevertheless presents the urban community college as the one last hope for students otherwise condemned to continued social marginality and an underclass existence. This sense is apparent in the description of a student in a recent issue of the *Urban Community College Report*. The student, we learn, "was one month from high school graduation when he got in trouble with the law and was sentenced to jail." However, through the intervention of his local community college, this student was redirected and earns a measure of social respectability. Under "a new program in Duval county [he] chose to participate in the Jobs for the Future Program at Florida Community College as an option to jail. He is now a student of Central Florida University in Orlando and plans to attend medical school" (Church 1992, 3). Importantly, this literature holds to the view that the urban community college somehow carries out its vital mission alone, without the support of other community-based social service agencies. As Elsner has observed, "Despite these looming social problems that exist around us, we [the community colleges] may be the only institutions in a position to respond—whether we are ready or not" (1991, 25).

Response to the Literature

In light of the recent events in Los Angeles, it would be absurd to diminish the challenges facing urban community colleges and their students. The crisis is very real, and solutions are not readily apparent. But those who work in urban community colleges also have direct experience of the positive contributions their institutions have made in the lives of students. The literature of the urban community college might take on a more constructive role if it were to move beyond its current reliance on simple descriptions of archetypical students and its sense of institutional isolation and undertake the kind of continuing, sector-wide research that will not only yield meaningful, if generally more complex, findings about the effects of this institution on its students, but also explore the interaction of the community college with other urban institutions—including churches, community-based organizations (CBOs) and small businesses—in promoting the access of the urban underclass to lives of opportunity and fulfillment.

RELIANCE ON THE ANECDOTAL IN DESCRIBING THE URBAN COMMUNITY COLLEGE

In the absence of a thorough and comprehensive description of the nation's major urban community colleges, the reader must rely on essentially anecdotal descriptions of individual colleges to gain an understanding of this institutional type. This tendency to the anecdotal, in lieu of inclusive and comprehensive, can be found as early as *This Is the Community College* (1968) in which Gleazer provides an interesting and, in many respects, insightful description of the various local interests that came into play in the creation of the St. Louis, Missouri, community college district. *Access and Excellence: The Open Door College* (Roueche and Baker 1987) provides another description of an urban community college. This work focuses exclusively on Miami-Dade Community College, which the authors propose as the "archetypical institution" not only for its "dynamic climate" but also for its visionary leadership. While certainly worthy of emulation, it is difficult to understand how the Miami-Dade model might be readily exported to other urban community colleges where core funding is uncertain and leadership unstable.

Possibly the most interesting of the anecdotal descriptions of an urban community college is Binzen's "La Guardia Community College" (1974). One distinguishing feature of this brief essay is that it is one of the few descriptions of an urban community college intended to serve a predominantly white community, the Long Island City area of Queens, New York. More than anything, it is useful in giving the reader a real insight into the degree to which presuppositions—largely unfounded—about the nature of urban population have shaped community college policy and practice. Chief among these assumptions (which also influenced thinking at La Guardia's sister college, Hostos in the Bronx) is that its intended students would more likely attend if they were offered a program unlike traditional higher education, but consistent with student experiences, values, and beliefs. For Binzen, La Guardia represented a clear break with the underlying principles of traditional liberal arts education, in that it offered an education intended not to change, but rather to affirm: Because its community was made up of industrial workers, the college was housed in a converted factory. Because the work ethic was strong, a college-wide cooperative education program was mandated. The goal of college planners was not student learning in any abstract or traditionally abstract sense, but the preparation of students for employment in occupations only slightly more prestigious than those of their parents.

Response to the Literature

Reliance on the anecdotal is characteristic of a literature lacking shared vision and common purpose. It would seem that a deeper appreciation of the common challenges, experiences, and achievements of the urban sector of the community college movement, gained through a fuller understanding of its history and its distinctive role within the complex urban context, will allow for a measure of generalization that will not only render anecdotal reporting irrelevant, but also allow for sector-wide policy assessment and recommendations. This development is of critical importance if urban community colleges are to secure the support of policymakers for the new program initiatives and revenues needed to address the urban crisis.

CONTROLLING THE LITERATURE'S AGENDA

A distinctive feature of the urban community college literature is that it has gained much of its force and direction largely from outside the urban community college's own leadership. With the exception of William Snyder, who played a major role in defining the place of vocational education within the community college curriculum, urban community college leaders have exercised only a secondary influence over the debate surrounding the sector's major policy issues.

This point is exemplified by the evolution of the concept of "open access." The now commonplace belief that the urban community college has a special responsibility to provide the urban underserved with access to higher education—regardless of their lack of academic preparation, diminishing career prospects, and uncertain commitment—is, in fact, a notion of relatively recent vintage. Even as late as the 1960s, public policy recognized only two barriers to access: distance and cost. As a result, state and federal policymakers generally considered the strategic placement of low-cost community colleges throughout a state as a sufficient response to the growing demands for access and equity. The selective admissions criteria and even the overt tracking systems (commonplace in California until the mid–1950s) used by many community colleges, including those serving urban America, were not considered barriers to access.

Historically, it was not at the instigation of urban community college leaders, but rather through the influence of such scholars as Cross, Medsker, and Tillery, that this concept of access was replaced by a more inclusive definition and the comprehensive, open admissions urban community college could emerge. In a truly revolutionary reconceptualization of access, Cross and others argued that ethnicity, gender, class, and, most critical, deficits of previous education were no longer legitimate barriers to community college admission. The acceptance of this far more inclusive definition of access by state and federal policymakers gave the urban community college a distinctive rationale that, in clearly differentiating its social role from that of the urban university, made its rapid growth through the 1970s possible. It was the rationale first articulated by Knoell, and not the arguments of urban community college leaders, that provided justification for the greatly expanded state, federal, and philanthropic funding of the inclusive mission of the urban community college.

In her seminal work, *Toward Educational Opportunity for All* (1966), Knoell introduced many of the core themes that urban community college leaders most often call upon to justify policies of open access and a comprehensive curriculum.

Knoell envisioned a "changing" society that would require increasing levels of formal education of all its citizens because to limit access to higher education on the grounds of outmoded notions of class or ability would effectively exclude large numbers of youth—and particularly those from underprivileged urban settings—from participation in this new economic order. For Knoell, the most appropriate instrument for achieving broader access would be the community college and, because it would serve a far broader range of students than had previously been attempted by higher education, it would need to offer the widest possible range of programs, particularly of a vocational nature.

Knoell's vision of the comprehensive urban community college not only provided a reasoned basis for the dramatic expansion of the City University of New York's reliance on the community college, but also inspired such works as *Breaking the Access Barriers* (Medsker and Tillery 1971), in which diversification of the community college instructional program was seen as essential to serving effectively the widely varying student needs of a truly accessible urban community college.

The works of Knoell, Tillery, and Medsker established the framework for much of the urban community college literature that would follow over the next decade. However, by the end of the 1970s, individuals outside the urban community college leadership, largely inspired by the Ford Foundation's developing interest in the revitalization of the urban community college's transfer function, would redirect the focus of this literature for a second time. Those urban community colleges that had taken their lead from the works of Knoell, Medsker, and others, and had expanded their range of program offerings to include a variety of terminal and vocational offerings, suddenly found themselves the object of an often critical literature that equated vocationalism with diversion, challenged the effectiveness of urban community colleges in providing underserved students with meaningful access to the baccalaureate and those positions of leadership for which it is a prerequisite, and called for fundamental changes in both institutional practice and values.

The sources and nature of the Ford Foundation's interest in the collegiate role of the urban community college has been documented in several works, including *New Initiatives for Transfer Students: Urban Community College Transfer Opportunities Program* (Schaier-Peleg 1984), *Transfer: Making It Work* (Donovan, Schaier-Peleg, and Forer 1987), and *Bridges to Opportunity* (Pincus and Archer 1989).

As a body, these works assumed that urban community college leaders had lost interest in the transfer function over the course of the 1970s and had directed institutional resources toward remedial education and terminal vocational programs. As a result, they argued, the urban community college was no longer an avenue to opportunity, but an obstacle to the baccalaureate and, more important, to the growing number of positions of influence and leadership for which college graduation was a prerequisite.

In addition to their descriptions of transfer-related Ford Foundation programs, these works typically included various policy recommendations. One theme common to the recommendations is that the chief barrier to student transfer, and particularly minority student transfer, is to be found in the "climate" of the urban community college. The failure of urban community college students to achieve the transfer goal in reasonable numbers can be traced, these works argue, to the urban community college's inability or unwillingness to foster an "academic" climate and a "vibrant" sense of community (Pincus and Archer 1989, 20). These recommendations also share the naive assumption that the urban community college, alone, is somehow equipped to counterbalance the many obstacles to success inherent to the lives of the urban underclass. In this belief, these authors share the same sense of institutional insularity reflected in the works of Temple and Elsner.

Within this Ford Foundation–inspired literature, but offering a somewhat more balanced view of the urban community college and the challenge it faces in promoting access to the baccalaureate, are two works by Richardson and Bender (1985, 1987). Without ignoring the criticisms of urban community college effectiveness, they clearly recognize that many of the current barriers to access are not solely of the community college's making. They note, for example, the diminished capacity of federal and state financial aid programs to meet fully the needs of poor students and the reluctance of many urban senior colleges and universities (where most urban community colleges would likely transfer) to work collegially with their community college partners. "[Urban] university officials are often unwilling to showcase their special programs for the urban underprepared" and, even more important, urban universities may believe that their own image problems are only exacerbated by close association with urban community colleges (Richardson and Bender 1985, 7).

In a series of recommendations, Richardson and Bender reveal a solid understanding of many of the dynamics that currently undermine the effectiveness of urban community college transfer programs. For example, they call for a clearer distinction within the curriculum between transfer and nontransfer courses, recognizing that the tendency to blur this vital distinction has come in part from attempts made by community colleges to improve state funding. But the key to any improvement in urban student transfer is to be achieved through an unprecedented sharing of responsibility for the student by both two- and four-year colleges.

Response to the Literature

The leaders of America's urban community colleges are at a critical threshold. At a time when their cities are engulfed in crisis, they can allow the community college literature to focus solely on those issues of moment to suburban community colleges—such issues as "total quality" and "globalization" and "business-industry partnerships." Or they can create a body of literature that addresses urban concerns from an urban perspective, offering leadership and guidance for a policy agenda that is sensitive to the unique concerns of urban institutions. If urban community colleges, as a group, are to achieve their full potential, they must focus their attention and energies on devising the very strategies Temple has outlined. In collaboration with other urban institutions, they must find ways to revitalize gravely polarized communities, overcome the deepening divisions of race, and replace the culture of violence that pervades many inner cities. And they must create their own literature to transform their otherwise individual and isolated successes into general practices while shaping a public policy context fully supportive of these efforts.

REFERENCES

Binzen, P. H. 1974. La Guardia Community College. In Laurence Hall and Associates, *New colleges for new students*. San Francisco: Jossey-Bass.

Brice, E. W. 1949. *A study of the status of junior colleges for Negroes in the United States*. Ph.D. diss., University of Pennsylvania.

Church, R. 1992. We're urban too. *Urban Community College Report* 3(4):3.

Cohen, A. M., and F. B. Brawer. 1982. *The American community college*. San Francisco: Jossey-Bass.

Commission on the Future of Community Colleges. 1988. *Building communities: A vision for a new century*. Washington, D.C.: American Association of Community and Junior Colleges.

Crane College reinstated. 1931. *Junior College Journal*. 1(9):566.

Deegan, W. L., and D. Tillery. 1985. *Renewing the American community college*. San Francisco: Jossey-Bass.

Donovan, R. A., B. Schaier-Peleg, and B. Forer. 1987. *Transfer: Making it work*. Washington, D.C.: American Association of Community and Junior Colleges.

Dougherty, K. 1983. The politics of community college expansion: The cases of Illinois and Washington state. Ph.D. diss., Harvard University.

Elsner, P. 1991. Institutional renewal. In *Conceptualizing 2000: Proactive planning*, ed. D. Angel and M. DeVault, 25–30. Washington, D.C.: Community College Press.

Fields, R. R. 1971. A case study of major educational changes in a two-year college: The democratization of Baltimore Junior College, 1947–1970, 78–82. Ed.D. diss., Teachers College, Columbia University.

Gleazer, E. J., Jr. 1968. *This is the community college*. Boston: Houghton Mifflin.

Kasadra, J. D. 1989. Urban industrial transition and the underclass. *The Annals* 501:31.

Knoell, D. 1966. *Toward educational opportunity for all*. Albany, N.Y.: State University of New York.

Los Angeles Junior College. 1936. *Junior College Journal* 7(1):33.

Medsker, L., and D. Tillery. 1971. *Breaking the access barriers*. New York: McGraw-Hill.

Mincy, R. B., I. V. Sawhill, and D. A. Wolf. 1990. The underclass: Definition and measurement. *Science* 248:450–53.

Orfield, G., and C. Ashkinaze. 1991. *The closing door*. Chicago: University of Chicago Press.

Pincus, F. L., and E. Archer. 1989. *Bridges to opportunity*. New York: Academy for Educational Development and College Entrance Examination Board.

Ravitch, D., and R. K. Goodenow. 1981. *Educating an urban people*. New York: Teachers College Press.

Report on Crane Junior College. 1931. *Junior College Journal*. 1(4):205.

Richardson, R. C., and L. W. Bender. 1985. *Students in urban settings*. Washington, D.C.: Association for the Study of Higher Education.

———. 1987. *Fostering minority access and achievement in higher education: The role of urban community colleges and universities*. San Francisco: Jossey-Bass.

Ricketts, E. R., and I. V. Sawhill. 1988. Defining and measuring the underclass. *The Journal of Policy Analysis and Management* 7(2):316–325.

Roueche, J. E., and G. A. Baker III. 1987. *Access and excellence: The open door college*. Washington, D.C.: Community College Press.

Schaier-Peleg, B. 1984. *New initiatives for transfer students: Urban community college transfer opportunities program*. New York: Ford Foundation.

Smolich, R. S. 1968. An analysis of influences affecting the origin and early development of three mid-western public junior colleges—Joliet, Goshen and Crane. Ph.D. diss., University of Texas at Austin.

Snyder, W. N. 1930. The real function of the junior college. *Junior College Journal* 1(2):77.

Strobel, E. C., Jr. 1975. Wayne County Community College: A history of its antecedents, establishment, and early development in the metropolitan Detroit setting. Ed.D. diss., Wayne State University.

Temple, R. 1991. Urban community colleges. In *Conceptualizing 2000: Proactive planning*, ed. D. Angel and M. DeVault. Washington, D.C.: American Association of Community and Junior Colleges.

Thornton, J. W., Jr. 1972. *The community junior college*. New York: Wiley.

Vaughan, G. B. 1985. *The community college in America: A short history*. Washington, D.C.: American Association of Community and Junior Colleges.

Wilson, W. J. 1987. *The truly disadvantaged*. Chicago: University of Chicago Press.

Rural Community Colleges: Meeting the Challenges of the 1990s

Anne S. McNutt

Across the country there are huge pockets of fast-emptying countryside. Some analyses of economic and social distress in those areas suggest America's own "third world" is in the making. Although the label "rural" applies to such a variety of geographic and economic settings that no sweeping characterization or prophecy fits them all, for the most part the nation's rural areas are older and poorer than urbanized America. And they are getting more so.

—Gimlin 1990, 414

Just as the label "rural" applies to a variety of geographic and economic settings, the label "rural community college" applies to a diverse group of community, junior, and technical colleges which face unique demographic and economic challenges in serving their communities.

The U.S. Census Bureau identifies as rural residents individuals living in towns of less than 2,500 population or in the open country. The 1980 census identifies 59,495,000 rural residents. At the same time, the population of the nonmetropolitan counties (counties that do not include an urban population center of 50,000 or more) was 57,115,000 (Gimlin 1990, 415). "Rural" in this discussion refers to both rural and nonmetropolitan areas.

Within the American Association of Community and Junior Colleges (AACJC), almost 600 institutions consider themselves to be rural and/or small. The Task Force on Rural Community Colleges was established in 1976 by the board of directors of the AACJC for the purpose of examining issues facing the community colleges that enrolled small numbers but served large geographic areas (Vineyard 1978, 29). It defined the rural community college as publicly supported, located in a population center of under 100,000, serving a vast geographic area, and having a programmatic thrust toward comprehensiveness. In 1979 about two-thirds of these rural colleges had fewer than 1,000 students (31). According to *A Summary of Selected National Data Pertaining to Community, Technical and Junior Colleges*, 25 percent of all public community colleges in 1990 were small, enrolling less than 1,390 students (AACJC 1990, 5).

While small/rural colleges constitute nearly half of the AACJC membership, their enrollments account for less than one-fifth of the community college students nationally. Perhaps this small student enrollment explains why the education community has focused its attention, funding, and research on urban and sub-urban areas (Margolis 1978, 62). Whatever the reason, for rural community colleges, "the professional literature reveals few solutions to problems, for these are the unmentioned institutions" (Vineyard 1978, 35).

THE RURAL COMMUNITY COLLEGE AND SOCIAL ISSUES

Despite the paucity of literature, these colleges constitute an important segment of higher education, and the issues facing them should be discussed within the framework of the broader issues facing American higher education. The most significant challenge confronting higher education today is financial. In an article called "Meeting the Challenge: Doing More with Le$$ in the 1990s," Hauptman (1991) maintained that the recession, along with a voter disinclination toward tax increases, suggests difficult times ahead for community colleges, which depend significantly on local revenues. *Campus Trends 1991* indicates "that financial problems are severe and growing" (El-Khawas 1991, 1). El-Khawas suggests that "doing more with less may be a phrase that is heard often during the early 1990s in higher education. Safeguarding quality and showing results appear to be part of that theme as well" (19–20). As a result, assessment activities are under way at most colleges. Eighty-eight percent of two-year institutions report assessment activity, and two-thirds of the two-year colleges have modified their programs or curriculum as a result of assessment (13–15).

Campus Trends 1991 identifies other key issues facing higher education. There has been a slowing in the trends for increasing numbers of women, minorities, and older faculty as well as a difficulty in hiring new faculty. While the labor market for college faculty in the 1990s will experience change, the changes will vary according to segmented markets (El-Khawas 1991, 7).

Increasingly scarce resources and demands of accountability from legislatures and the public will prompt more collaborative efforts within the education community (Hodgkinson 1985, 2). Ninety-two percent of the administrators at public two-year institutions identified collaboration with the high schools as a high priority (El-Khawas 1991, 16). The tech-prep program, a collaborative effort of two-year colleges and secondary schools, outlined by Parnell in *The Neglected Majority* (1985), is being implemented throughout the country.

Although a substantial portion of higher education literature is devoted to community colleges, a dearth exists concerning rural community colleges.

McMullen suggests that the rural college is "a last minority" and observes that while college and university faculty often work to reduce such social biases as racism and sexism, "a comparable enthusiasm in behalf of the rural minority has yet to emerge" (1979, 8). After a flurry of publication immediately following the work of the Task Force on Rural Community Colleges and continuing until the early 1980s, the literature is again relatively silent concerning rural community colleges. Margolis captured the depth of the problem, commenting that the bibliography included in the Task Force report was less than three pages, even though most entries were "only indirectly related to the rural community college endeavor" (1978, 63).

The Task Force's report incorporated five position papers on key topics: (1) equal opportunity for the small/rural college, (2) financing the small college, (3) small colleges and accrediting agencies, (4) federal and state constraints on small college programs, and (5) developing the literature and research support for rural community colleges (Vineyard 1978, 30). Focusing on equal educational opportunity, the report maintained that any division of financial resources based "upon equal funding per unit is an inequitable system" because it places the smaller colleges at a disadvantage in staffing, instructional equipment, libraries, space requirements and utilization, physical plant, administrative services, and student services. Funding should equalize educational opportunities by developing some means of "allowing for the higher costs of operation per unit within the smaller, rural community college" (1978, 37–39).

By suggesting ways to develop the literature and research base on rural community colleges, the Task Force "set the stage for further examination of the issues" (Fuller 1979, 17). At least one specific suggestion of the Task Force was implemented—that the AACJC's journal devote a future issue to rural community colleges and "make an effort to increase the frequency of articles of interest and applicability to the small, rural-based institutions" (Vineyard 1978, 42).

Created the year after the Task Force completed its work, the Commission on Small and/or Rural Community Colleges was begun in 1977 to advise the AACJC board on both "the immediate and long-range concerns of small/rural colleges. The Commission studies the particular problems and challenges confronting the small/rural colleges, develops advocacy papers, and suggests programs for the Association to meet these needs" (Gianni 1982, 48).

Devoted to that status of the rural community college, the October 1981 *Community and Junior College Journal* focused on "A Vital Component of the Delivery System" (Eaton 15–16), the financing of the rural community college (TenHoeve 17–20), the need for the development office in the rural community college (Higbee and Stoddard 21–23), serving sparsely populated areas (Lee and Strayer 24–26), leadership (Sullins 27–29), and "Doing More with Less" (Atwell 30–32).

A few years later, a series of essays in the *Community, Technical and Junior*

College Journal (1986/87) examined the challenges facing small, rural community colleges: student retention (Weiss and Bryden 26–27), image building (Young 27), the role of rural community colleges in economic development (Sharples 28), and faculty recruitment (Lidstrom and Conrad 29).

Exemplary Programs and Services published in 1991 by the Commission on Small and/or Rural Community Colleges of the AACJC highlights numerous programs in rural colleges, giving a brief description of the program, key concepts for success, and personnel requirements.

Within the demographic trends of the country as a whole, these for the rural population are distinctive. Rural areas "have a greater representation of children, relatively fewer young adults, a greater proportion of middle-aged persons" (Fuguitt, Brown, and Beale 1989, 115), and "a larger proportion of the elderly" (Brown and Deavers 1988, 14). Since 1960 the net migration of adults aged sixty and older has been toward rural areas. While older migrants are attracted to retirement and recreation areas in scenic and warm regions (U.S. Department of Agriculture 1990, 20), the retirees who move into rural areas are generally more affluent than the long-term rural elderly (Glasgow 1991, 27). The relatively few numbers of young adults in rural areas can be attributed to the pervasive outmigration of this group (U.S. Department of Agriculture, 1990, 20).

The age-sex composition of the rural population reflects the major demographic events of the twentieth century—the baby boom, the prolonged period of low fertility, and increased longevity. Trends in age and sex composition affect the nation's and community's economic life, but in a rural area adapting to a changing age-sex composition can be difficult because these communities have few fiscal resources to provide the necessary services (Fuguitt, Brown, and Beale 1989, 135–36).

Not only is America's rural population older, it is less well educated than its urban counterpart. In 1980 one in ten persons in the adult rural population had completed college—"about the same as the urban percentage a decade before" (Brown and Deavers 1988, 15). In rural areas only 26.5 percent of those adults aged twenty-five or older had completed one or more years of college; the corresponding figure for the urban areas was 40 percent (Kominski 1988, 2). The educational attainment of young adults living in rural areas is less than that of those living in urban areas not only because rural residents are less likely to finish high school or to attend college, but also because the better educated young adults migrate from the rural areas. As do those with the best skills, the better educated move to urban areas, leaving behind the young adults who are least likely to adjust to a changing economy. Thus, the poverty rate among young families in rural America has grown (O'Hare 1988, 12–13).

The gap between rural and urban incomes widened in the 1980s "primarily because rural incomes have declined in real terms" (O'Hare 1988, 8). Rural poverty has seemed more entrenched than urban poverty since 1980 because the poverty rates for the rural areas have remained higher, and individuals have been trapped below the poverty line for a longer time. In fact, by 1986, the poverty rate in rural areas had caught up with that of the inner cities (O'Hare 1988, 9–10; U.S. Department of Agriculture 1990, 16).

While poverty among children in the United States has increased dramatically, the increase has affected rural children disproportionately. By 1988 the poverty rate among children in rural areas was "almost one-third higher than that for children in urban areas" (O'Hare 1988, 11).

Although rural areas reflect racial and ethnic diversity, they contain a smaller percentage of the three largest racial or ethnic minorities than do urban areas. Major regional differences exist in the ethnic composition of the rural population, with the rural minority population largely concentrated in the southern third of the nation. In some of these rural areas, African Americans and Hispanics constituted significant percentages, sometimes a majority of the population. Of the ethnic minorities, the Native American is the lone exception to "the dominant metropolitan urbanism of racial minorities" (Fuguitt, Brown, and Beale 1989, 153–55).

The rural areas have been touched by the changing structure of American households—an aging population, the baby boom, lower fertility, and delayed marriage. Rural areas "have a higher proportion of married couple households with minor children, a smaller proportion of single parent families, and a much lower proportion of persons living alone" than do urban areas (Fuguitt, Brown, and Beale 1989, 172). Another distinctive feature of rural areas lie in the makeup of households headed by females. In rural areas they "are more likely to be maintained by widows and less likely to be maintained by separated or divorced persons" (Fuguitt, Brown, and Beale 1989, 177–180).

The farm-based economy that once distinguished the rural areas has declined in importance. Until December 1982, when the farm economy experienced tough times, so did the rest of the country. While the national economy came out of the 1979–1982 recession in December 1982, the farm economy remained in a slump—into 1987 (Gimlin 1990, 416–17). Less than one-third of the counties identified as rural in America are farming dependent. Almost as many rural counties draw at least 30 percent of their income from manufacturing as from farming, and in over half of the farm families at least one family member maintains a nonfarm job. The typical "family farms" producing $100,000 to $200,000 a year have been steadily disappearing (Gimlin 1990, 421).

Although many rural economies have industrialized, the industries attracted tend to be those requiring low-level skills, labor-intensive industries where jobs are declining in America (Fuguitt, Brown, and Beale 1989, 230–31). Lower levels of educational attainment in the rural areas may partially explain this trend (1989, 241).

The dramatic changes in the industrial sector of the American economy this century have also affected rural areas. During the 1980s all three key industrial sectors in the rural areas experienced downturns—agriculture, mining, and manufacturing (Fuguitt, Brown, and Beale 1989, 259). During the 1980s international competition, high interest rates, automation, and a reduced demand for manufactured goods disrupted industrial growth in the rural areas. Many industries automated or relocated in foreign countries, leaving rural areas with fewer jobs, with relatively unskilled work forces, and without the necessary infrastructure to rebuild (Rosenfeld 1983, 270). Because newer manufacturing industries require higher skills, they locate where a skilled labor force exists, relegating lower-paying service jobs to rural areas (Fuguitt, Brown, and Beale 1989, 432; Gimlin 1990, 415–16).

The inability to attract high-skill, high-paying jobs to the rural areas is tied to the lack of a skilled labor force. Regardless of industrial category or gender, employed rural workers have lower educational attainments, especially college education, than urban workers; therefore, rural areas have "a difficult time competing for high-skill, high-wage employment opportunities" (Fuguitt, Brown, and Beale 1989, 300). Recent outmigration from rural areas has also negatively affected the economy because those leaving in the largest numbers are the better educated young adults, the very people needed to revitalize the rural economies (O'Hare 1988, 5).

Because rural areas are diverse, ranging from wealthy areas beyond affluent suburbs to impoverished communities, their tax bases vary significantly. In many rural areas, lack of industry translates into lack of an adequate tax base. On almost any scale of national well-being, rural areas generally fall on the negative end of the scale—loss of hospitals, shortage of doctors, shortage of nurses, and high rates of poverty (Gimlin 1990, 417). Obviously, rural America has not escaped the "urban" crises of inadequate health care for the poor and homelessness (Lazere et al. 1989).

Rural America has a diminishing economic base to support public services, including schools (Ross 1988, 296). Perhaps this diminishing economic base may have contributed to Louis Harris's finding that teachers in rural areas provided fewer excellent ratings (38 percent) of the quality of education in their schools than did all but inner-city teachers (1989, 11). The high cost per student often prohibits rural schools from offering a wide range of advanced and specialized courses (National Commission on Agriculture and Rural Development Policy 1990, 25). Helge's national study of at-risk students found "that the social and economic strains facing rural students are at least as difficult as those facing inner-city youth" (1990, 1). The outmigration of young people to better jobs compounds this problem causing rural taxpayers to be reluctant to invest much-needed local tax dollars in education (National Commission on Agriculture and Rural Development Policy 1990, 25).

THE AGENDA FOR RURAL COMMUNITY COLLEGES

America's rural areas offer their community colleges substantial economic and demographic challenges. While rural areas face social problems similar to those of urban areas, rural communities lack the financial resources and the necessary infrastructure to address these problems effectively. For this reason, rural community colleges may represent even more valuable resources to their communities than do their urban counterparts. In facing these economic and demographic challenges, rural community colleges must determine what programs and services to provide for their communities.

Building Communities: A Vision for a New Century maintains that "the community colleges of the nation have an urgent mandate to fulfill—the building of communities" (Commission on the Future of Community Colleges 1988, 8). For rural community colleges, which frequently represent the only readily accessible higher education in their community, this mandate is indeed urgent (Sullins and Atwell 1986, 45; J. M. Eaton 1981, 15). To Americans residing in rural areas, community colleges, more than any other single entity, provide hope for improving educational attainment, hope for ensuring that individuals may reach their potential, hope for building the community, hope for a better trained work force, and hope for a better way of life. Community colleges may be the "ideal catalyst for addressing many of the problems of rural life" (J. M. Eaton 1981, 15). By providing graduates of their degree and certificate programs to industry, by offering customized training for industry, and by supporting small business development activities, community colleges assist in economic development (Donato 1988, 11). Whereas rural community colleges historically have been involved in economic development efforts to recruit new industry, as the economy changes, these colleges need to shift the focus of their economic development activities to cultivate small businesses.

For the foreseeable future, while rural community colleges engage in economic development activities, they will be facing dire economic times themselves. Managing and providing leadership for rural colleges through the 1990s will challenge even the most creative, talented president, for the 1990s promise to be "times of dramatic and painful change for many institutions" (Smith 1991, 26). Because of their small size and generally inadequate financial base, rural community colleges may find these times especially challenging.

Rural community colleges need to hire talented faculty and staff. Although rural areas hold special attraction for some individuals, these communities no longer are immune to the social problems of American society, and a lack of social ills can no longer be used as a recruiting point. West observed that rural colleges enjoy the advantages of "better living environments: clean air, unlittered public places, unjammed traffic, relative safety from crime"; these colleges also have a greater impact on the development of "a better quality of life for their home community" (1980, 212–13). In spite of these advantages, attracting competent faculty and staff to rural areas requires special efforts. Even though times of economic challenge tend to produce more individuals who will consider teaching positions, salaries at rural community colleges generally fail to compare favorably with those of urban colleges. However, the lower cost of living in most rural areas makes positions more attractive because this lower salary may actually provide more discretionary income than would a higher salary in an urban area. Furthermore, because of the small size of the administrative staff and the numerous administrative duties, administrators at rural community colleges would be wise to employ individuals who are generalists and who enjoy the variety of the administrative tasks.

Providing professional development activities presents a challenge for rural community colleges. Despite severe budgetary constraints and, in many cases, distance from the nearest university, these colleges still must ensure the professional growth of their faculty and staff. Teleconferencing, distance learning, and other technology-based instruction offer cost-effective means for providing professional development activities.

Facing limited budgets and increasing demands, rural community colleges must aggressively become involved in resource development. Traditionally, these colleges receive little funding from local sources because of the inadequate tax base (Nazari-Robati and Zucker 1981, 49). With a small number of students, many of whom come from the lower socioeconomic levels, these colleges collect limited tuition and fees. While community colleges have slowly become involved in fund-raising in the private sector, rural community colleges have seemed almost reluctant participants. The National Council for Resource Development of the AACJC can serve as a valuable resource to rural colleges as they seek private funding and additional federal and state grants.

Building collaborative working relationships with secondary schools and senior colleges is essential to rural community colleges. These relationships, however, must extend far beyond the traditional relationships between high schools and colleges if high school completion and college participation are to increase. Collaborative efforts involving resource sharing of faculty, classrooms, labs, and libraries should become the norm, not the exception. The current national movement to establish a tech-prep curriculum increases communication among the faculties of the colleges and the high schools, facilitates access to college, and builds on students' existing knowledge.

While rural community colleges are building the tech-prep program, they must simultaneously work to increase enrollment in college transfer programs because, in many rural areas, the community college represents the only accessible higher education. Unlike their urban counterparts, rural community colleges often must work with numerous senior colleges and universities located at great distances from their campus. On a national level, this issue for the rural college fails to receive adequate research and attention. Although the AACJC declared 1991 the ''Year of Transfer,'' for example, scant attention was paid to the transfer issue for rural community colleges.

With high illiteracy rates plaguing many rural areas, rural community colleges have an obligation to serve as the catalyst for addressing this problem. Whether this problem is addressed through adult education provided by the college or the public school system, through volunteers, through work-force efforts, through the Laubauch method, through computer instruction, or through a combination of methods, the severe illiteracy problem in rural America cannot be ignored.

In addition to serving as a catalyst to address illiteracy, to offering certificate and degree programs, and to providing training for business and industry, rural colleges serve three special constituents: the elderly, minorities, and women. Rural areas containing retirement communities find that today's affluent retirees are in better health and more frequently relish learning new skills. Over half of the colleges responding to the survey on which the *Community College Programs for Older Adults: A Status Report* (Doucette and Ventura-Merkel 1991) was based identified themselves as "rural." As the elderly population increases in rural areas, community colleges must broaden their programmatic offerings for this group. By the year 2000, the shortage of skilled workers will cause America to turn to retirees to help sustain the economy. Thus, in addition to the courses and programs normally offered, colleges will offer special programs for self-employment, second careers, career counseling, and job placement for retirees.

Because many minority students enter higher education through community colleges, rural community colleges must ensure that they attract, matriculate, retain, and graduate minority students. Since minorities constitute increasingly larger percentages of the new entrants into the work force, rural community colleges must provide the necessary technical training, career development, and job placement services for minorities. In addition, as women enter the work force in dramatic numbers and as they increasingly serve as heads of households, rural community colleges must address their special needs. While women's centers and women's studies offer valuable perspectives, rural community colleges must provide special support services including child care centers, job search techniques, and job placement.

Successful rural colleges will play several roles in their communities. By providing comprehensive educational programs and services, tailoring both credit and noncredit programs to the population, they will facilitate and develop leadership for their communities. Rural community colleges can address the need for leadership by working closely with their chambers of commerce and with business leaders. Second, by facilitating the development of small businesses, rural community colleges can serve as economic development centers of their communities. A third role is that of a center of cultural and civic life. Theatrical performances, concerts, and debates held at these colleges enliven and enrich the lives of individuals and the community.

SUMMARY

Moving toward the twenty-first century, rural America faces great challenges. "More than ever it is true that future changes in the demographic, economic and social structure of rural and small town America are associated with the ties that bind such areas to the rest of the national economic and social structure, and to the global system beyond our nation's borders" (Fuguitt, Brown, and Beale 1989, 437). Today rural colleges and rural areas need a clear, sharp focus on their importance, as well as their problems, and a commitment from the higher education establishment for research and support.

According to Hodgkinson, "Demography is destiny" (1986, 273). While demography alone does not constitute destiny, demographic challenges, economic challenges, and society's response to these challenges do. For America's rural areas to reach their potential, America must focus on and address the demographic and economic challenges in these areas, and community colleges must play a key role. For America's rural community colleges to fulfill their destiny, American higher education must devote attention and resources on this last minority—rural community colleges.

REFERENCES

American Association of Community and Junior Colleges (AACJC) 1990. *A summary of selected national data pertaining to community, technical and junior colleges: Community colleges, where America goes to college.* Washington, D.C.

Anderson, R. A., Jr. 1983. Small/rural roundup: Guidelines for roundup contributions. *Community and Junior College Journal* 54(1):43, 45.

Atwell, C. A. 1981. Doing more with less. *Community and Junior College Journal* 52(2):30–32.

Brown, D. L., and K. L. Deavers. 1988. *Economic dimensions of rural America.* Paper presented at the Rural Development Policy Options Workshop: Critical Issues and Options in Developing a New Rural Policy for the Nation. October 3–5, 1988. Brimingham, Ala. ERIC Document no. ED 304 256.

Castro, J. 1991. Condition: Critical. *Time* (25 November): 34–42.

Choate, P. 1982. *Retooling the American work force.* Washington, D.C.: Northeast-Midwest Institutes.

Commission on Small and/or Rural Community Colleges. 1991. *Exemplary programs and services 1991.* Washington, D.C.: American Association of Community and Junior Colleges.

Commission on the Future of Community Colleges. 1988. *Building communities: A vision for a new century.* Washington, D.C.: American Association of Community and Junior Colleges.

Donato, D. J. 1988. Economic development. In *Small-rural community colleges: Report of the Commission on Small and/or Rural Community Colleges.* Washington, D.C.: American Association of Community and Junior Colleges.

Doucette, D., and C. Ventura-Merkel. 1991. *Community college programs for older adults: A status report.* Laguna Hills, Calif.: League for Innovation in the Community College.

Eaton, J. M. 1981. A vital component of the delivery system. *Community and Junior College Journal* 52(2):15–16.

Eaton, J. S. 1991. Encouraging transfer. *Educational Record* 72(2):34–38.

El-Khawas, E. 1991. *Campus trends, 1991.* Higher Education Panel Report no. 81. Washington, D.C.: American Council on Education.

Fuguitt, G. V., D. L. Brown, and C. L. Beale. 1989. *Rural and small town America.* New York: Sage Foundation.

Fuller, J. W. 1979. The small rural community college. *Community College Frontiers* 7(2):14–17.

Gianni, P. C. 1982. Small/rural roundup: Colleges asked for problems, solutions. *Community and Junior College Journal* 53(1):48.

Gimlin, H. 1990. *The continuing decline of rural America*. Editorial Research Reports. Washington, D.C.: Congressional Quarterly.

Glasgow, N. 1991. A place in the country. *American Demographics* 13(3):24–31.

Greenwald, J. 1991. Permanent pink slips. *Time* (9 September):54–56.

Harris, L. 1989. *The Metropolitan Life survey of the American teacher 1989: Preparing schools for the 1990s*. New York: Louis Harris and Associates.

Hauptman, A. M. 1991. Meeting the challenge: Doing more with le$$ in the 1990s. *Educational Record* 72(2):6–13.

Helge, D. 1990. *A national study regarding at-risk students*. ERIC Document no. ED 324 178. Bellingham: Western Washington University, National Rural Development Institute.

Higbee, J. M., and R. L. Stoddard. 1981. Paving the way to prosperity. *Community and Junior College Journal* 52(2):21–23.

Hodgkinson, H. L. 1985. *All one system: Demographics of education—Kindergarten through graduate school*. Washington, D.C.: Institute for Educational Leadership.

———. 1986. Reform? Higher education? Don't be absurd! *Phi Delta Kappan* 68:271–74.

Kominski, R. 1988. *Educational attainment in the U.S.—March 1987 and 1986* (Series P–2, No. 428). Washington, D.C.: Bureau of Census, U.S. Department of Education.

Lazere, E. B., P. A. Leonard, and L. L. Kravitz. 1989. *The other housing crisis: Sheltering the poor in rural America*. Washington, D.C.: Center on Budget and Policy Priorities and Housing Assistance Council. ERIC Document 320 753.

Lee, J., and J. Strayer. 1981. Meeting individual needs in isolated communities. *Community and Junior College Journal* 52(2):24–26.

Lidstrom, K., and J. Conrad. 1986/87. What are the challenges facing small, rural community colleges today in faculty recruitment? *Community, Technical and Junior College Journal* 57(3):29.

Margolis, H. S. 1978. Rural academe. *Change* 10(6):62–63.

McMullen, H. G. 1979. The rural college: A last minority. *Community College Frontiers* 7(2):5–10.

National Commission on Agriculture and Rural Development Policy. 1990. *Future directions in rural development policy*. Washington, D.C.: U.S. Department of Agriculture.

Nazari-Robati, A., and J. D. Zucker. 1981. Resolving the financial crisis in America's rural community colleges. *Community College Review* 9(2):48–52.

O'Hare, W. 1988. *The rise of poverty in rural America*. ERIC Document no. ED 302 350. Washington, D.C.: Population Reference Bureau.

Parnell, D. 1985. *The neglected majority*. Washington, D.C.: Community College Press.

Rise of rural poverty. 1989. *The Futurist: A Journal of Forecasts, Trends, and Ideas about the Future* 23(1):45.

Rosenfeld, S. 1983. Something old, something new: The wedding of rural education and rural development. *Phi Delta Kappan* 65:270–73.

Ross, N. 1988. Rural America in the twentieth century: Implications for business education. *Journal of Education for Business* 64:293–99.

Sharples, K. 1986/87. What are the challenges facing small, rural community colleges today in economic development? *Community, Technical and Junior College Journal* 57(3):28.

Smith, P. 1991. Beyond budgets: Changing for the better. *Educational Record* 72(2):26–28.

Sullins, W. R. 1981. Leadership in the 1980s. *Community and Junior College Journal* 52(2):27–29.

Sullins, W. R., and C. A. Atwell. 1986. The role of small rural community colleges in providing access. *Community College Review* 13(2):45–51.

TenHoeve, T., Jr. 1981. To serve "even the last man in line." *Community and Junior College Journal* 52(2):17–20.

U.S. Department of Agriculture. 1990. *Rural conditions and trends.* ERIC Document no. ED 324 188. Washington, D.C.

Vineyard, E. E. 1978. AACJC task force report—The rural community college. *Community College Review* 6(3):29–45.

Weiss, M., and B. Bryden. 1986/87. What are the challenges facing small, rural community colleges today in student retention? *Community, Technical and Junior College Journal* 57(3):26–27.

West, D. C. 1980. Special role of small rural colleges. *Liberal Education* 66:212–13.

Young, J. 1986/87. What are the challenges facing small, rural community colleges today in image building? *Community, Technical and Junior College Journal* 57(3):27.

Part 3

Curriculum and Instructional Development in the Community College

Teaching for Learning: Instructional Development and Change in Two-Year Colleges

Albert B. Smith

From its beginning, the community college has been viewed as a teaching institution. The importance of good teaching and instruction has always been emphasized by planners of community colleges. Alexis Lange, dean of the University of California at Berkeley, for example, was especially influential in the development of junior colleges as teaching institutions in California. Lange was an early advocate of the "teaching" of technical subjects and some "terminal" programs in junior colleges. According to Cohen and Brawer, "[c]ollege planners never envisioned these institutions as the homes of research scholars" (1989, 148).

Leaders and observers of the community college movement have always reported that teaching was the main activity of the faculty of this institution. Eells called the junior college "a teaching institution 'par excellence' " (1931, 389). Thornton proclaimed instruction as the prime function and stated that it had to be better than the university because of the wider range of student abilities and their weaker academic records: "It is fair to say that most community college students are able to learn but are relatively unpracticed. Under good instruction they can succeed admirably, whereas pedestrian teaching is more likely to discourage or defeat them than it would the more highly motivated freshman and sophomores in the universities" (1972, 42).

More recently the American Association of Community and Junior Colleges (AACJC) Commission on the Future of Community Colleges reflected this emphasis on teaching and instruction in the community college when it set forth the goal that: "The community college should be the nation's premier teaching institution. Quality instruction should be the hallmark of the movement" (1988, 25). It also appears that community colleges have an excellent chance of becoming the leaders of the quality movement of the 1990s and beyond, much as they were the leaders of the access movement in the 1960s (Cross and Angelo 1989).

The report of the commission, *Building Communities: A Vision for a New Century*, defines community "not only as a region to be served, but also as a climate to be created." The commissioners also observed that "the theme 'Building Communities' is applied most appropriately to the classroom, where both intellectual and social relationships are strengthened and where students and teachers can be active partners in the learning process" (1988, 25). "Building community through dedicated teaching is the vision and inspiration of this report."

After focusing their attention on the quality of teaching and learning that takes place in two-year college classrooms and laboratories, this commission recommended, "Community colleges should define the role of the faculty member as classroom researcher—focusing evaluation on instruction and making a clear connection between what the teacher teaches and how students learn" (27).

There is substantial evidence to support the notion that community colleges have had a long history of instructional innovation and change. However, it is this writer's contention that community college faculty will need to place greater emphasis on "student learning" if they are to continue to be successful in their major and most important role. To do this, community college faculty will need to gain a greater understanding of the changing characteristics of their students, new learning theories and principles, and new strategies for motivating students. If teaching is defined as "causing learning," as some community college educators have proposed, it would seem appropriate for community college educators to focus less on teaching behaviors and more on "learning outcomes" in the 1990s and beyond.

The remaining sections of this chapter include a brief history of instructional innovation and change in U.S. community colleges, describe the increasingly diverse student body that now attends U.S. two-year colleges, and consider the future, including a discussion of some learning principles, a learning theory, and research on community college faculty that should be useful to community college faculty in future years.

HISTORY OF INSTRUCTIONAL INNOVATION IN U.S. COMMUNITY COLLEGES

There has been a continuing interest in various instructional approaches in two-year colleges. In 1969, Johnson surveyed community colleges throughout the United States to determine the degree to which various instructional strategies were used in these institutions. He found the following instructional practices were employed at many community colleges: (1) audiotutorial teaching, (2) instruction by telephone, (3) gaming and simulation, (4) computer-assisted instruction, (5) dial-access audio systems, (6) television, (7) programmed instruction, (8) cooperative-work-study education, (9) multistudent response systems, (10) use of film and radio, and (11) a multitude of other techniques.

This trend of instructional innovation and emphasis continued in two-year colleges throughout the 1980s (Cohen and Brawer 1989). For example, in 1985, the Wisconsin State Board of Vocational, Technical, and Adult Education (VTAE) reported that seventy-eight electronic technologies were in use in twelve VTAE districts. In the following sections, some of the better known instructional innovations in U.S. community colleges will be highlighted.

Television

Since the 1950s, when the City Colleges of Chicago organized a television college, many other community colleges have acquired licenses to offer credit-course instruction as well as cultural enrichment and entertainment programs for the general public. Colleges such as Dallas County Community College and Miami-Dade Community College now offer a wide range of televised courses.

The use of television instruction in two-year colleges has grown steadily in the 1980s and early 1990s, with open-circuit courses for college credit being one of the most popular options. In the 1980s, over two-thirds of the community college instructors in the United States had entry to media production facilities. Such college districts as Miami-Dade (Florida), Coastline (California), Chicago, and Dallas have become known for their excellent programming (Cohen and Brawer 1989).

Computers

The following forms of computers in instruction are found in most community colleges in the United States today: (1) computer-based instruction, (2) computer-managed instruction, and (3) computer-assisted instruction. Computer-based instruction, the use of specialized computer programs, such as models and simulators, is found in the teaching of business, economics, and engineering technology courses. Computer-managed instruction is being used to support teaching by administering tests and maintaining student records. Computer-assisted instruction, the presentation of linear and branching instructional programs, is found in the teaching of mathematics, business, and developmental education programs.

One community college that has taken full advantage of computer technology is Miami-Dade Community College (MDCC). Most of the reform programs in this college have been tied to sophisticated computer programs. One example of this is the RSVP (Response System with Variable Prescriptions) at MDCC. This computer-based instructional management system supports a great deal of individualization of the instructional program at this college.

RSVP is also responsible for the individualization of the Academic Alert letters. A total of 150 messages are written for the four campuses. Out of this pool, RSVP selects appropriate messages according to programmed decisions: "The possible combinations of the messages for students' letters add up to 26,878. In other words, the system can generate 26,878 unique letters if students' information is equally unique." (Roueche et al., 1987, 58)

This is but one of many hundreds of examples of how computers are being used by community colleges and community college faculties to improve teaching and advisement in America's two-year institutions. Computer technology will certainly continue to be an important tool for teaching and learning in the community college of the twenty-first century.

Cognitive Style Mapping

Cognitive style mapping is another instructional innovation that has been used by some community college faculties to determine each student's best mode of learning. Much of this cognitive style mapping began with the work of Joseph Hill in the 1970s at Oakland Community College (Michigan). Hill used his testing system to identify students' cognitive maps or preferred learning styles and then matched the students with instructors or classroom learning situations that would be most effective for the students (Cohen and Brawer 1989).

The learning styles literature (see Claxton and Murrell 1987 for a review) is based on the assumption that individuals can be described by certain psychological characteristics, traits, or styles that determine or influence the manner in which they perceive, organize, and react to different environmental experiences or stimuli. Villa and Lukes (1980) found that cognitive mapping resulted in greater retention, higher grades, and student satisfaction. However, Cohen and Brawer note that, while "some success in arranging college teaching to accommodate students' learning styles has been noted, . . . the concept has not taken hold as a major determinant of teaching method" (1989, 154). The problem seems to be that it is often too difficult for faculty members to change their teaching styles to meet a wide range of different learning styles.

Writing across the Curriculum

In a movement called Writing across the Curriculum by James Britton (1975), many community college teachers decided that only through writing can students develop and use higher-order thinking skills. This concept has achieved considerable popularity in community colleges in the 1980s and 1990s. A number of colleges have encouraged faculty members in a wide range of disciplines to require writing. Writing across the curriculum has been used at Somerset County College (New Jersey) and at Puma College in Arizona (Cohen and Brawer 1989).

In almost every community college, one can find some instructors who use writing to help students learn. However, it would appear that relatively few colleges have made it a requirement. In order to further encourage this movement, one author has recommended several principles to use in designing writing assignments that foster learning:

1. Assignments have to be at least stimulating enough to kindle expectation.
2. Writing needs to be frequent enough to maintain involvement throughout a course.
3. Writing assignments should be a means of comprehensive monitoring whereby students can check their own understanding.
4. It helps if students can apply information in some familiar content.
5. Finally, professors should make sure that students share their writing with others. (Tomlinson 1990, 35)

More research will be needed to determine the extent to which this instructional strategy is being used today in community colleges.

Supplemental Instruction

Because of the high number of at-risk students found in community colleges, this relatively new instructional approach, pioneered at the University of Missouri at Kansas City, is being used in a number of two-year colleges. According to Cohen and Brawer, supplemental instruction

is designed to teach students to read the texts and interpret the tests used in the academic classes they are taking. In these programs students work with tutors outside of class. A leader coordinates the work of the tutors with that of the instructors who have agreed to participate by encouraging their students to take advantage of the tutoring. (1989, 155)

This form of instruction, which is being used in colleges where dropout and failure rates in basic introductory courses have been very high, shows promise because it provides community college students with a way of increasing the learning skills that they will need in order to succeed.

Learning Resource Centers

While not often categorized as an instructional strategy, the community college library is certainly an important instructional service in two-year colleges. As far back as 1939 (Johnson), it was called the heart of the college. Today the community college library is not only a resource for independent study, but also, more and more, an adjunct to classroom instruction. In the 1960s and 1970s, libraries in two-year colleges underwent major changes and became learning resource centers (LRCs). Often the library remained intact, but facilities were added for a variety of study options including programmed learning, audiovisual learning, and computer-aided instruction.

The Technology of Instruction

In the last twenty years, we have witnessed an instructional revolution in two-year colleges, much of it with the motivation that individualization should be the goal in most, if not all instructional programs. The basic model of instructional technology includes "clearly specified learning outcomes or objectives, content deployed in relatively small portions, learning tasks arrayed in sequence, a variety of modes of presenting information, frequent feedback on student performance, and criterion tests at the ends of instructional units" (Cohen and Brawer 1989, 161).

Much support for this approach to instruction was given by Roueche in *A Modest Proposal: Students Can Learn* (1973). Roueche took the position that learning is best achieved through a series of programmed-instruction units that permits a student to learn at his or her own rate.

Today the most common applications of instructional technology have been undertaken by instructors of developmental education courses and the directors of learning resource centers. In the 1970s and 1980s, many community college instructors experimented with programs based on the concepts of mastery learning or competency-based education, two of the most popular forms of instructional technology at the time.

The intent of mastery learning is to help students gain a specified set of competencies presented in the form of learning objectives for students. Many researchers have been able to demonstrate that sizable cognitive and affective gains have been made by students when this teaching strategy is used. However, the concept and approach, firmly entrenched in two-year colleges, are not without problems. In many institutions, this teaching strategy has failed because of the high costs associated with the development of instructional materials and because of the amount of time it takes on the part of teachers.

Competency-based education is yet another instructional technology that is being used quite widely in community colleges. This approach depends on the specification of desired competencies, but it does not include all of the specific instructional approaches of mastery learning. Faculty members using competency-based education are most likely to be found in developmental courses, as well as occupational courses of study such as nursing education.

The Higher Education Coordinating Board of the state of Texas is requiring all technical programs to be competency-based programs. The process of developing a competency-based program, outlined for technical occupations faculty by the Dallas County Community College District in 1989, involves the following steps: assess the occupational needs of business and industry; perform a task analysis; validate the tasks identified; create a course matrix; develop learning outcomes; develop a course outcome; analyze outcomes among all program courses to prevent gaps and duplications; make necessary revisions; develop program outcomes; identify content outlines; identify instructional methodology and learning activities for each course; develop evaluation strategies and tools;

and format the final product (May 1990). It appears that competency-based technical education is likely to see even more widespread use in the future.

Other Teaching Strategies

This has been a very brief summary of some of the more prominent instructional innovations used in two-year colleges. Other teaching strategies used widely by community college teachers include (1) lecturing, (2) discussion, (3) student-centered instruction, (4) tutoring, (5) laboratory teaching, (6) case method, (7) simulations, (8) instructional games, (9) role playing, (10) personalized systems of instruction, (11) audiotutorial instruction, (12) programmed instruction, and (13) peer teaching, among others. The most effective community college teacher in the future is most likely to be one who employs a variety of teaching strategies—a necessity in any given community college course to meet the very diverse learning styles and characteristics of an ever-changing community college student population. This diverse student population, described in the next section, shows the challenges facing community college teachers.

THE DIVERSE COMMUNITY COLLEGE STUDENT POPULATION: A NEW CHALLENGE FOR COMMUNITY COLLEGE FACULTY

When the decade of the 1990s opened, more than 5 million students were enrolled in 1,408 two-year colleges in the United States (*The Chronicle of Higher Education Almanac* 1991). These students do not fit the traditional image of a college student as being an individual of about twenty years of age; going to college full-time; living on campus in a sorority, fraternity, or dormitory; and preparing for a career in one of the professions. According to Parnell (1990), this image may be accurate for some college students but certainly not for the majority of college students who attend community colleges. Increasingly, the student population is diversifying, and it is useful to examine some of the characteristics and trends that community college instructors will encounter in the future.

Community colleges enroll larger portions of older students than four-year colleges and universities. The average age of students in for-credit classes at public community colleges is now approaching thirty years of age—the model age is nineteen, and the median age is twenty-four. Fifty percent of the students in two-year colleges are older than the traditional college age cohort (eighteen through twenty-four). It can also safely be assumed that the noncredit students, another very large group of students in two-year colleges, make up an older cohort, with the average age well into the thirties (AACJC 1990).

Women represent an increasingly significant segment of the community college population. In the fall of 1970, women accounted for 40 percent of all students in community colleges; in 1989, they accounted for 55 percent of all students enrolled. The growing participation of women in community college education is reflected in associate degree statistics. Between 1975 and 1985, the number of associate degrees awarded to women increased by 49 percent. In contrast, the number awarded to men increased by only 6 percent (AACJC 1990). The dramatic story in the past twenty years of postsecondary education has been the large increase in women in higher education as well as women over the age of twenty-five.

Next to age and gender, the most important trend in the changing U.S. population is the growth of Black, Hispanic, and Asian populations. According to government figures for the fall of 1988, minorities made up 22 percent of all students enrolled in community, technical, and junior colleges. Of the students enrolled in the fall of 1988, 76 percent were white, 10 percent were Black, 9 percent were Hispanic, 4 percent were Asian, and 1 percent were Native American. In terms of higher education, as a whole, minorities are more likely to attend community, technical, and junior colleges than whites. Enrolling only 36 percent of the nation's white college students, community colleges enroll 54 percent of Native American college students, 42 percent of all Black college students, 56 percent of Hispanic college students, and 40 percent of all Asian college students (*The Chronicle of Higher Education Almanac* 1991).

As open-admissions colleges, two-year institutions enroll students with a wide range of educational goals and objectives. When researchers for the Carnegie Foundation for the Advancement of Teaching in a national study asked community college students to indicate "What is your primary reason for enrolling at this college at this time?," the students responded as follows: (1) 36 percent indicated "preparation for transfer to a four-year college or university," (2) 34 percent replied "to acquire skills needed for a new occupation," (3) 16 percent answered "to acquire skills needed for a current occupation," (4) 15 percent indicated "to fulfill a personal interest," and (5) 4 percent said "to improve basic English, reading, or math skills" (Commission on the Future of Community Colleges 1988).

There is an even greater variation among community college students than these statistics indicate, however, depending on the student's age and major or curriculum. For example, in the above mentioned study, 56 percent of the students who were twenty or younger said "preparation for transfer" was their primary educational objective, compared to only 16 percent of the respondents who were thirty-three or older. As for curriculum, 50 percent of all students in liberal arts and science classes indicated that they planned to transfer, compared to only 24 percent of the students in such applied courses as business, engineering technology, secretarial science, allied health, or criminal justice (AACJC 1990).

Degree goals of two-year college students also differ from those of students attending four-year institutions. Data collected from the *High School and Beyond* study validated the fact that community college students are less likely to aspire to baccalaureate or higher degrees than students at four-year colleges and universities. Of the high school seniors questioned in this research investigation, those planning to obtain a baccalaureate degree were more likely to attend a four-year college than a public community college (40 percent and 16 percent, respectively). Only 13 percent of the students who planned to achieve an advanced graduate degree attended a public two-year college; 69 percent went to a four-year institution (El-Khawas et al., 1988).

Community college students are also a very diverse group in terms of their academic abilities. On the average, two-year college students begin their college courses with lower levels of academic achievement than students at four-year institutions. Only 9 percent of high school seniors with an "A" average attend community colleges in the first year after high school; in comparison, 44 percent of these "A" students attend public four-year colleges, and 27 percent attend private four-year colleges (El-Khawas et al., 1988).

Since the beginning of the community college movement in America in 1901, much of the research in these two-year institutions has focused on the teaching process as opposed to the student learning process. With the growing diversity found in two-year college student populations, community college educators and researchers are now attempting to identify key factors related to the improvement of student learning.

A LOOK TO THE FUTURE: IMPROVING THE TEACHING/ LEARNING PROCESS IN COMMUNITY COLLEGES

Fortunately, a good deal of theorizing and research has already been done on the learning process, the implementation of which can prove useful to community college faculty and administrators who are interested in enhancing learning, reducing student attrition, and meeting the needs of an increasingly diverse student population. A great deal more research is needed at the two-year college level since most of the previous research on student learning occurred in public schools and in four-year colleges and universities.

In 1963, Goodwin Watson developed a list of basic learning principles which are still useful to community college teachers as a starting point for guiding their own and their students actions throughout the teaching/learning process in the most beneficial manner. The principles include emphasis on the importance of reinforcement and feedback; the negative consequences of sheer repetition, frustration, and punishment; the environment in which "learning by sudden insight" occurs; and some generalizations about such topics as memory and the importance of relevance in the learning process (Metos 1990).

In addition to these classic principles of learning, community college teachers are making use of even more recent theories to improve the teaching/learning process in their classrooms.

Figure 1
The Experiential Learning Cycle

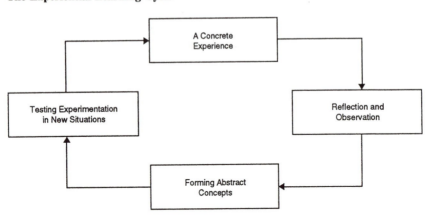

Source: Adapted from Svinicki 1990.

Current Learning and Teaching Theories: Ideas for Improving Community College Teaching

A simple yet powerful theory for instructional design is Kolb's (1981) experiential learning cycle, which proposes that learning moves through four phases: experience, reflection, abstraction, and experimentation (see Figure 1).
Kolb has defined learning as the process

whereby knowledge is created through the transformation of experience. This definition emphasizes several critical aspects of the learning process, as viewed from the experiential perspective. First is the emphasis on the process of adaptation and learning as opposed to content or outcomes. Second is that knowledge is a transformation process being continuously created and recreated, not an independent entity to be acquired or transmitted. Third, learning transforms experience in both its objective and subjective forms. (1984, 38)

This definition of learning is not a complex idea; it is very similar to the scientific method in general and to the active learning ideas developed earlier by Dewey, Lewin, and others.

To use the model in Figure 1 for instructional design, instructors should choose learning activities that lead to each of the four points of the cycle or model. For example, an instructor could begin by having students "experience" some concrete phenomena, such as in a laboratory, then ask the students to "reflect" in groups on what they had observed. Each small group could then be asked to provide an explanation that "abstracts" a general principle from what they had observed. Finally, the students could be asked to return to the laboratory to test their abstraction with an "experiment," which could then become the experience for another round of learning activities. This fairly simple model could be employed to create instructional sequences and learning activities for all manner of content (Svinicki and Dixon 1987).

Kolb has also developed a Learning Style Inventory (LSI). However, some community college educators, while supportive of many of Kolb's ideas, believe that knowing a student's preferred learning style may be little more than a scientific curiosity, unless the information provided can be employed to help a student reach his or her educational goals (Baker, Roueche, and Gillett-Karam 1990).

Baker, Roueche, and Gillett-Karam believe that Kolb's model of experiential learning "does not adequately describe the learning process the teacher uses to increase student performance" (1990, 127). They have built a conceptual framework for "teaching as leading" that is based on two assumptions: Excellent teachers adapt to student needs regularly and excellent teachers do not lower their standards. As with Kolb's experiential learning theory, their teaching as leading model involves a four-step process. These community college educators believe that teaching as leading involves "(1) influencing learners individually and in groups to set goals and (2) leading the learners toward goal accomplishment" (128).

Based on their research with 869 excellent community college teachers, Baker, Roueche, and Gillett-Karam (1990) found that community college teachers have a pronounced tendency in the way they interrelate with students and with content and the manner in which they conceptualize and activate learning experiences. They maintain that the interaction of these two tendencies creates the community college teacher's "teaching as leading style." These four styles are (1) supporter, (2) theorist, (3) achiever, and (4) influencer. Understanding these four dominant teaching styles should help community college teachers gain new insights into the teaching/learning process in two-year institutions.

Other learning theories that have been adapted for use by community college instructors include: (1) social learning, (2) personal growth theory, (3) cognitive development theory, (4) self-efficacy theory, and (5) expectancy-value theory. Each of these new theories, as well as such new teaching strategies as collaborative learning and classroom assessment, provides powerful new approaches for motivating students and increasing learning outcomes (Svinicki 1990).

In conclusion, it can be said that community colleges continue to be viewed primarily as teaching institutions, thus remaining true to their central mission in the twentieth century. However, if these two-year institutions and their faculties are to succeed in the twenty-first century, they will have to place a great deal more emphasis on student learning than they have in the past. The focus in community college teaching, as well as in all of higher education, needs to move away from teacher behavior to student behavior/learning. The successful community colleges in the twenty-first century will be colleges where faculty members can demonstrate that their teaching strategies are in fact "causing learning."

REFERENCES

American Association of Community and Junior Colleges (AACJC). 1990. *A summary of selected national data pertaining to community, technical and junior colleges.* Washington, D.C.

Baker, G. A., J. E. Roueche, and R. Gillett-Karam. 1990. *Teaching as leading: Profiles of excellence in the open-door college.* Washington, D.C.: Community College Press.

Britton, J. 1975. *The development of writing abilities.* London: Macmillan & Co.

Chronicle of Higher Education Almanac. 1991. Washington, D.C.

Claxton, C. S., and P. H. Murrell. 1987. *Learning styles: Implications for improving educational practices.* ASHE-ERIC higher education report no. 4. Washington, D.C.: Association for the Study of Higher Education, ERIC Clearinghouse on Higher Education.

Cohen, A., and F. Brawer. 1989. *The American community college.* San Francisco: Jossey-Bass.

Commission on the Future of Community Colleges. 1988. *Building communities: A vision for a new century.* Washington, D.C.: American Association of Community and Junior Colleges.

Cross, P., and T. Angelo. 1989. Faculty members as classroom researchers, *Community, Technical, and Junior College Journal* (April/May):23–25.

Eells, W. C. 1931. *The junior college.* Boston: Houghton Mifflin.

El-Khawas, E., et al. 1988. *Community college fact book.* New York: Macmillan.

Johnson, B. L. 1939. *Vitalizing a college history.* Chicago: American Library Association.

———. 1969. *Islands of innovation expanding: Changes in the community college.* Beverly Hills, Calif.: Glencoe Press.

Kolb, D. A. 1981. Learning styles and disciplinary differences. In *The modern American college: Responding to the new realities of diverse students and a changing society,* ed. A. W. Chickering and Assoc. San Francisco: Jossey-Bass.

———. 1984. *Experiential learning: Experience as the source of learning and development.* Englewood Cliffs, N.J.: Prentice-Hall.

May, G. 1990. *Competency-based education.* Typescript. University of North Texas, Denton.

Metos, T. H. 1990. *The human mind: How we think and learn.* New York: Venture Books.

Parnell, D. 1990. *Dateline 2000: A new higher education agenda.* Washington, D.C.: Community College Press.

Roueche, J. E., in collaboration with J. C. Pitman. 1973. *A modest proposal: Students can learn.* San Francisco: Jossey-Bass.

Roueche, J. E., G. A. Baker III, with P. L. Mullin and N. H. Omaha-Boy. 1987. *Access and excellence.* Washington, D.C.: Community College Press.

Svinicki, M. D., ed. 1990. Changing the face of your teaching. In *The changing face of college teaching. New Directions for Teaching and Learning,* no. 42 (Summer): 5–15.

Svinicki, M. D., and N. M. Dixon. 1987. The Kolb model modified for classroom activities. *College Teaching* 35(4):141–46.

Thornton, J. W., Jr. 1972. *The community junior college.* New York: Wiley.

Tomlinson, S. 1990. Writing to learn: Back to another basic. In *The changing face of college teaching*, ed. M. D. Svinicki. New Directions for Teaching and Learning no 42. San Francisco: Jossey-Bass.

Villa, R. E., and E. A. Lukes. 1980. A multiple system approach to applying the cognitive style of learning. *Community College Social Science Journal* 3(1):19–25.

Wisconsin State Board of Vocational, Technical, and Adult Education. 1985. *Three-year longitudinal follow-up study of Wisconsin VTAE graduates of 1980–81: Report of data from twelve VTAE districts*. ERIC Document no. ED 263 326. Madison: Wisconsin State Board of Vocational, Technical, and Adult Education.

The Historical Development of Academic Programs in Community Colleges

George R. Boggs and Judy J. Cater

From relatively modest nineteenth-century beginnings, the community college has developed from a "historical accident" (Cowley 1970) into the "characteristic educational institution of the United States" (Hutchins 1936). Its egalitarian and open-access mission and its community-responsive curricula are reflective of America's democratic ideals and values. The U.S. Bureau of the Census (1991) lists 1,436 community and junior colleges among the 3,658 institutions of higher education in America. Of the 1,436, the overwhelming majority, 984, are public institutions, offering a wide variety of classes, programs, and activities for the citizens they serve. While community colleges are no longer being founded on an average of one per week, as was true in the 1960s, the need for lower-division postsecondary education in transfer, occupational, remedial, and community service courses continues to grow.

FORERUNNERS OF THE COMMUNITY COLLEGE

Palinchak (1973) summarizes the nineteenth-century antecedents of the modern community college. Beginning around 1835, private academies with elements of both secondary and postsecondary curricula came into existence. Academies mixed transfer, vocational, and terminal education programs and included two-year normal or teachers' colleges as well as institutions for women and African Americans.

Academy graduates desiring to continue their education might receive lower-division credit when transferring to American colleges and universities. These academies gained prominence primarily on the East Coast and the Southern states; paradoxically, the eastern states were the slowest to develop what we now recognize as the modern junior or community college. In the latter part of the nineteenth century, curriculum reform developed as an important issue in American education. Cohen (1971) and Monroe (1972) chronicle the interest of late nineteenth-century educators in the reorganization of the American system of higher education. At this time, concerns were expressed about the future of higher education in the United States, especially in light of a growing population and increasing demands on the existing systems.

Those individuals regarded as the founding fathers of the junior college movement—Henry Tappan, W. W. Folwell, Edmund James, and William Rainey Harper—were significantly influenced by German models of education. Arguing that the first two years of collegiate education should be left to the secondary schools on the model of the German gymnasium, these men contended that the universities should be freed from undergraduate education to concentrate on upper division and professional curricula. Smaller, "weaker," private colleges would be encouraged to "decapitate" themselves, removing the final two years of collegiate education from their programs and becoming "junior" colleges. Strong four-year institutions would then drop the freshman and sophomore years. In the view of these educators, some students from the "junior colleges," as they were beginning to be called, would go on for additional study while others would terminate at grade 14.

While these ideas attracted a great deal of attention well into the 1930s, they generally were not implemented on a wide scale. Existing schools were unwilling to drop the freshman and sophomore years for both political and financial reasons. A notable exception occurred at the University of Chicago under William Rainey Harper. In 1892, President Harper separated the university into two divisions which, by 1896, were known as the Junior College and the Senior College (Brint and Karabel 1989). By 1900 the university granted an associate degree to those completing the first two years of work. Some students terminated at this point while others moved ahead into the more rigorous curriculum of the Senior College.

THE RISE OF THE PUBLIC JUNIOR COLLEGE

While private academies and junior colleges continued to flourish in the early years of the twentieth century, educators in the Midwest and Far West recognized the need for publicly supported institutions at the junior college level (Palinchak 1973). In 1901, under the guidance of William Rainey Harper, Joliet Junior College, the first publicly funded junior college, was founded in Illinois. Brint and Karabel (1989) describe the enabling legislation passed in California in 1907 that allowed local school boards to offer the first two years of college work. Strongly supported by President David Starr Jordan of Stanford and Alexis F. Lange, dean of the School of Education at the University of California, Berkeley, the junior colleges to come would take over the routine tasks of providing lower-division college course work, enabling Stanford and the University of California to concentrate on upper-division studies, graduate programs, and research.

Echoes of these ideas appeared fifty years later in the 1960 California Educational Master Plan.

In 1910, the Fresno Board of Education opened Fresno Junior College, the first publicly funded school of its kind in California. Others followed, generally as departments of high schools and administered by local school boards. As late as 1915, the majority of the early junior colleges, some 75 percent, were still private (Palinchak 1973). Education for transfer to four-year institutions continued to be the focus of these colleges, and their curricula were similar to those of the first two years of undergraduate studies.

In 1921, the first independent junior college districts were established, with a single institution serving several communities rather than a high school area. California took the lead in this process, creating autonomous local boards to oversee these junior colleges and removing them from the control of high school boards. Programs often mirrored those at four-year institutions, and the demand from students grew steadily.

The literature from that period (Koos 1925) presents a characteristic picture of the eighteen-year-old student who, for financial, social, or emotional reasons, was not ready to attend a university or four-year college and could be educated at low cost while living at home supervised by the family. At the end of the two-year course of study, that individual could expect to be accepted at a state school and given appropriate credit for work already completed. It is unclear from the research whether many of these students would otherwise have attended college, but it is clear that the impact, although important, is not as significant as it would become in later decades.

By 1930, California led the nation with 15,000 students in thirty-four junior colleges (Monroe 1972). This figure represented about half of all the students enrolled in California colleges at that time. Although California took the lead in the junior college movement, other states including Illinois, Texas, and Missouri also developed strong programs. Some states developed two-year institutions under the governance control of larger four-year colleges or universities. Serving as a pattern for separate public junior colleges for the rest of the country, California's 1921 district authorization was closely modeled by the state of Texas in its 1929 junior college enabling law (Brint and Karabel 1989).

THE GROWTH OF VOCATIONAL PROGRAMS

While educational programs continued at the freshman and sophomore levels, increased demands for occupational and vocational programs were heard throughout the 1920s. Despite the progress made in the early part of the century, higher education was still not commonly viewed as being "for everyone," and many of the junior college proponents undertook as their mission a "vocationalization" of the two-year curriculum. Preparation for effective citizenship would be a goal of two-year postsecondary education, as would training for "junior-college-appropriate" professions including accountant, bank teller, nurse, printer, watchmaker, and the like. Despite enthusiastic support from the University of California and Stanford, by 1930 only about one-sixth of California's community college students were enrolled in vocational programs. Studies during that decade show that the vast majority of students and their parents were interested in transfer education (Brint and Karabel 1989) and that these transfer students were more likely to come from a lower socioeconomic background than their counterparts at four-year colleges and universities.

However, the trend to add vocational programs to the curriculum continued. Most of the programs were established as a result of community demand, contributing a remarkably individual character to the curricula at each college. This vocationalization and responsiveness to the community eventually led to the present-day comprehensive community college. The balance between the numbers of vocational and transfer classes varies widely between colleges and reflects the needs and values of the communities they serve.

Questions regarding the emphasis placed on one or the other of the two primary missions of transfer and vocational education continue to the present time. However, the institutions seem quite capable of providing both of these sets of curricula. Students often shift from vocational to transfer courses of study and vice versa.

It is also interesting to note that some community colleges started as vocational or technical institutes and later developed into comprehensive institutions by adding the transfer or junior college curriculum. Although some states still maintained separate junior and technical college systems as late as 1992, in most parts of the country the two have been merged into single state systems of community colleges.

FROM THE GREAT DEPRESSION TO THE POSTWAR ERA

The coming of the Great Depression brought an unexpected boost to the community college movement (Brint and Karabel 1989). The pressures of economic hard times and the resulting high unemployment among all ages combined with the number of college-age youth available led states to establish sixty-five public junior colleges between 1933 and 1939. These schools were less costly to build and maintain than four-year schools and, in the pragmatic view of some, "kept late adolescents off the unemployment rolls and police ledgers" while providing them with a good general education (Brint and Karabel 1989, 54).

The end of the Depression and American involvement in World War II slowed the growth of the community college movement as America turned its eyes toward other goals. As the end of the war approached, Americans began to make provision for the millions of veterans expected to return home. Recognition of the debt owed to these service men and women was tinged with concern over their impact on an economy only recently recovered from the Depression. An expected drop in defense industry spending added to this concern as jobs in that sector could be lost as well.

A combination of idealism and simple pragmatism led to what may be seen as the single greatest piece of educational legislation enacted since the Morrill Land Grant Act of 1862. The Servicemen's Readjustment Act of 1944, popularly called the G.I. Bill of Rights, provided a host of benefits for veterans of World War II. Among these was financial aid for both vocational and liberal arts education programs designed to keep the returning veteran in the classroom and off the unemployment rolls. Hundreds of thousands of veterans who took advantage of this opportunity often became the first in their families to consider the possibility of higher education, much less attain it. Colleges and universities were flooded with new students and, in some cases, had no idea what to do with them all.

With this in mind, President Harry S. Truman, in 1946, established a Commission on Higher Education. The panel was chaired by George F. Zook, president of the American Council of Education (ACE) and a longtime friend of junior colleges (Monroe 1972). The Truman Commission's six-volume report, published in 1947, represents a dramatic change in the way in which America viewed access to higher education. Citing such barriers as economics, restricted curriculum, and racial and religious prejudices or quotas (Levine 1978), the final report stated, "The Commission does not subscribe to the belief that higher education should be confined to an intellectual elite, much less a small elite drawn largely from families in the higher income brackets" (Brint and Karabel 1989, 69). Education in the United States should be accessible and tuition free through grade 14.

THE COMMUNITY COLLEGE AND THE "DEMOCRATIZATION" OF EDUCATION

Central to the implementation of the Truman Commission's recommendations was the two-year college. Recognizing the need for and existence of institutions teaching the first two years of college course work, the Truman Commission also made recommendations concerning paraprofessional or vocational education as well as provision for community service and continuing education classes for local residents. The report used the term "community college" extensively, signaling a change from the purely transfer function of the junior college. In order to accommodate the large numbers of students this democratization of education would admit, the report recommended the establishment of a large number of community colleges throughout the United States.

Community college proponents were quick to respond to this challenge, and the postwar period represents an era of unprecedented growth for the movement. Brint and Karabel (1989) describe massive expansion in states such as California and the implementation of entirely new systems in states such as New York. Eastern and Southern states began to catch up with the Plains and Western states. A spirit of optimism and increased aspirations resulted from the expanding postwar economy. Brint and Karabel describe the new climate of opportunity that appeared to guarantee better jobs to students with college-level course work. Much of this course work was the transfer level with increasing recognition that students in community colleges were academically able to handle the same level of work as found in four-year institutions.

The sharp postwar increase in the birthrate (the baby boom), which followed the relatively low birthrates of the 1930s and early 1940s, meant that America's colleges would, as early as 1963, have to be prepared to absorb an increased number of potential students. Public education systems struggled to meet the impending onslaught of new students, and, throughout the country, many educational master plans were developed. Just as California continued to be a leader in the community college movement, the state's Master Plan for Higher Education was "widely viewed as a model in providing both broad popular access and the maintenance of academic excellence" to public higher education (Brint and Karabel 1989, 86). Developed with a great deal of input from University of California President Clark Kerr, the 1960 Master Plan recommended a three-tiered postsecondary educational system for the state. At the top was the University of California, which would accept students in the top 12.5 percent of their graduating classes. The California state colleges (now universities) would admit students from the top one-third of their graduating class. The remainder of students looking toward public higher education would be channelled to the community colleges which had no admissions requirements beyond high school graduation or being eighteen years old. Transfers to the University of California required a 2.4 grade point average (on a 4.0 scale); admission to the state colleges required a 2.0. Lower-division enrollment at the four-year institutions would be reduced from 51 to 40 percent with the remaining students diverted to the community colleges.

While the California Master Plan has long been regarded as a model system, providing both accessible and low-cost postsecondary education, it has been questioned and challenged. In 1991, only two years after the Master Plan was reaffirmed by the California legislature, leaders of the three segments in that state began to question whether the system could be maintained in the future. Resources available to public higher education were being restricted at a time when enrollment pressures were at record high levels.

Decisions made by public officials throughout the country continue to have a dramatic effect on access to postsecondary education. Program support, level of staffing, student tuition charges, and even which courses and programs will be offered are recurring issues of debate at both the local and state levels.

OTHER ROLES FOR COMMUNITY COLLEGES

One area that is often questioned by public officials and some professionals is remedial, or developmental, education (Brown 1981). Yet it remains one of the fastest growing areas of the community college curriculum. Even major universities have found it necessary to place some students into remedial classes to prepare them for college-level course work. At community colleges, remedial programs have developed to the point where they represent a major part of the curriculum. They prepare students for the transfer and vocational programs of the community college; furthermore, it has become common for community colleges to offer remedial courses to university students, often on the university campus.

The remedial function of the community colleges is also deeply rooted in the history of the movement. After 1920, colleges and universities tried to encourage other institutions to provide remediation (California Postsecondary Education Commission 1983). Richardson, Martens, and Fisk (1981) argue that the growth of community colleges was sought at least partially for that reason.

Until recently, there were few data to show the effectiveness of remedial programs. There are now some studies, however, that show a positive effect of both matriculation programs, which guide students into remedial programs, and the remedial programs themselves (Barr 1988; Boggs 1984a, 1984b, 1985a, 1985b; Slark, 1986, 1987a, 1987b, 1988). For such open-entry institutions as community colleges, both effective guidance or placement programs and effective remedial or developmental education programs have become necessities.

Over the years, community colleges have also served to help integrate new immigrants into America's democratic society by providing courses in citizenship and English as a Second Language (ESL). Students in ESL classes are among the most diverse on the college campus. In their turn, Europeans, Cubans, Vietnamese, Cambodians, and Latinos have constituted the majority of students in these programs. Like the remedial or developmental programs, they not only prepare students for further college course work, they also provide the skills needed for a higher quality of life in the United States.

Because of the important role played by community colleges in transfer education, the community college curriculum is often influenced by changes in the university segment. Reactions to such factors as student activism, equal opportunity efforts, and expanded access to education had resulted in decreased requirements throughout the curriculum in the period from 1960 to 1975 (Boggs, 1983). Starting around 1975, curricular reform at such prestigious universities as Harvard and MIT served as a harbinger of a movement toward a more restrictive policy of general education. General education, according to the Truman Commission, has come to mean those phases of nonspecialized and nonvocational learning that should be the common experience of all educated men and women. A task force of the California State University System in 1979 reviewed general education programs on the system's nineteen campuses and concluded that the programs had been left largely to unsupervised and virtually unrestricted choice, resulting in an accumulation of courses with no curricular coherence (Crooks 1979). The task force recommended the elimination of the "educational cafeteria" and an increase in general education requirements.

A similar lack of regard for a general education program existed in many community colleges in the 1960s and 1970s. Following the lead of the senior institutions, general education patterns have been restricted in the community colleges. Articulation agreements with various universities have led to patterns that are common at the university level. In fact, in the early 1990s, California's three segments of higher education were working to develop a common core program of general education for all of that state's college and university students.

Not as easily influenced by transfer universities are the curricula designed by community colleges to serve their communities. According to Lombardi (1978), adult basic education, adult education, continuing education, and community services comprise a group of functions, activities, and programs that, in the late 1960s and 1970s, grew more rapidly than the traditional functions of transfer and vocational education. Many of these programs developed as a non-state-supported fee-based part of the curricula in the public community colleges. Gleazer (1980) argues for a broadened mission of the community colleges to serve as resources and points of connection for their communities. He sees students as lifelong learners and community colleges as ideal institutions to serve their needs. In fact, he notes that the "two-year" terminology no longer fits the community colleges as institutions. Students fit their education around the needs of their families and careers, often taking well in excess of two years to complete their academic programs. Many students return to take individual courses even after they have received college or university degrees.

SUMMARY

Academic programs in community colleges have evolved from the limited junior college function envisioned by the founders of the movement to a comprehensive set of programs designed to meet the needs of a diverse group of students in the communities served by the colleges. Community colleges have taken on vocational programs, remedial and developmental programs, citizenship and ESL courses, community education courses, and adult education courses. These changes in academic programs are reflected in the change of the designation from the original two-year junior college or vocational institute to the ubiquitous "community" college. These colleges have proved to be the most flexible and community-responsive institutions of higher education in the world. The community college movement has spread across the United States and into other countries that have discovered their value. The academic programs of these dynamic colleges should continue to develop as they respond to the future educational needs of their communities. Despite their detractors, they indeed have become the characteristic institution of higher education in the United States.

REFERENCES

Barr, R. 1988. Student outcomes study, Year 3/math. ERIC Document Reproduction Service no. ED 321 782. San Marcos, Calif.: Palomar College.

Boggs, G. R. 1983. General education: Definition, purposes and implementation. *California Community College Trustees Forum* 2(3), Supplement.

————. 1984a. The effect of basic skills assessment on student achievement and persistence at Butte College: A research report. ERIC Document Reproduction Service no. ED 244 686.

————. 1984b. The effect of a developmental writing course on student persistence and achievement: A research report. ERIC Document Reproduction Service no. ED 244 687.

————. 1985a. Evaluation of remedial programs: Pilot study final report. ERIC Document Reproduction Service no. ED 263 963.

————. 1985b. Measuring the effect of developmental writing. *Inside English* 12(3):1–5.

Brint, S., and J. Karabel. 1989. *The diverted dream*. New York: Oxford University Press.

Brown, G. W. 1981. Quoted in M. G. Scully. Entrance rules tightened at some public institutions. *Chronicle of Higher Education* 23(15):1–3.

Brubacher, J., and W. Rudy. 1958. *Higher education in transition*. New York: Harper.

California Postsecondary Education Commission. 1983. *Promises to keep: Remedial education in California's public colleges and universities*. Commission Report 83–2. Sacramento: The California Postsecondary Education Commission.

Cohen, A. M. 1971. *A constant variable*. San Francisco: Jossey-Bass.

Cowley, W. H. 1970. Critical decisions. In *Twenty-five years 1945–1970*, ed. G. K. Smith. Washington, D.C.: American Association for Higher Education.

Crooks, J. B. 1979. History's role in general education. *Journal of General Education* 31(2):118.

Gleazer, E. J., Jr. 1980. *The community college: Values, vision and vitality*. Washington, D.C.: American Association of Community and Junior Colleges.

Hutchins, R. M. 1936. The confusion in higher education. *Harper's Magazine* (October):449–58.

Koos, L. [1925] 1970. *The junior college movement*. New York: AMS Press.

Levine, A. 1978. *Handbook on undergraduate curriculum*. San Francisco: Jossey-Bass.

Lombardi, J. 1978. Community education: Threat to college status? Topical Paper no. 68. Los Angeles: University of California, ERIC Clearinghouse for Junior Colleges.

Monroe, C. R. 1972. *Profile of the community college*. San Francisco: Jossey-Bass.

Palinchak, R. 1973. *The evolution of the community college*. Metuchen, N.J.: Scarecrow Press.

Richardson, R. C., Jr., K. J. Martens, and E. C. Fisk. 1981. *Functional literacy in the college setting*. American Association for Higher Education Research Report no. 3. Washington, D.C.: American Association for Higher Education.

Slark, J. 1986. *Student outcomes study, Year 1/writing*. ERIC Document Reproduction Service no. ED 286 566. Santa Ana, Calif.: Rancho Santiago College.

————. 1987a. *Student outcomes follow-up study*. Santa Ana, Calif.: Rancho Santiago College.

————. 1987b. *Student outcomes study*, Year 2/reading. Santa Ana, Calif.: Rancho Santiago College.

————. 1988. *Student outcomes follow-up study*. Santa Ana, Calif.: Rancho Santiago College.

U.S. Bureau of the Census, 1991. *Statistical abstract of the United States, 111th ed.* Washington, D.C.: U.S. Government Printing Office.

Educational Technology in Community Colleges

George Voegel

We shape our tools, then our tools shape us.

Marshall McLuhan

This chapter examines the role of educational technology on the teaching-learning process. Technology is viewed in this chapter as representative of a wide range of media; equipment (hardware); materials (software); support services, such as libraries and learning resource centers (LRCs); and conceptual processes, such as instructional development. For anyone who wants to delve into the background of such developments in the United States, Saettler (1968, 1990) has written two excellent resources on the history and development of technology in education from ancient times to microcomputer times. It is the intent of this chapter to focus on the role of such technology starting from the late 1950s and early 1960s, when the great community college expansion coincided with numerous shifts in the technology, and concluding with the early 1990s, when the community colleges have settled in and the technologies have blended into each other.

BACKGROUND

In the beginning, there was—chalk! Actually, there was more to it historically than that. In his two great works on technology in American education, Saettler (1968, 1990) goes back to the times of the ancient Greeks who used the term *techne* to mean an art, craft, or skill, and it was conceived as a particular activity and a kind of knowledge. Saettler asserts that if technology is to be understood, it needs to be ''seen as a system of practical knowledge not necessarily reflected in things or hardware'' (1990, 3). As examples of a ''system of practical knowledge,'' he describes the three-field crop rotation system during the Middle Ages in Europe which, without any ''tool'' impact, increased productivity and improved nutrition; the Peruvian prehistoric technology of raised-field agriculture which required no chemicals; and the division-of-labor concept in factory work.

In education, the system of knowledge concept had forerunners in such people as Abelard in the 1200s (who also influenced Saint Thomas Aquinas) with his scholastic method which played an important role in the rise of European universities. This method, which examined ideas in a systematic, rational way, provided a technique for sorting out the mass of traditional and irrational doctrines of that era. Later, Comenius (1592–1670), who wrote the classic *Great Didactic* and who developed the idea of *pansophia*, or system of universal knowledge in which a methodical procedure could be applied to all problems, also wrote *Orbus Pictus*. This well-planned book for children was illustrated with 150 pictures, each of which served as a topic for one lesson; thus, Latin and science teaching were accomplished by associating objective reality (the illustrations) with abstract cognate word symbols. As education became more broadly based and finally mandatory for grades K–12, Comenius's ideas were followed by those of other educational leaders who provided a variety of conceptual contributions, all dealing with what is known today as the teaching-learning process or, as Saettler called it, a system of knowledge about teaching.

The ''things'' technology in education came largely from societal factors external to education itself: for example, the shift from individual student notebooks, made from animal horns, to manufactured blackboards (slate boards), with the teacher using chalk (and controlling the presentation), which became the mass media approach of its day (Voegel 1986, 73). Except for a few flame-lit lantern slide projectors and hand-cranked phonograph record players, most of the things technologies came to rely on electricity.

Probably two of the most important breakthroughs in technology have been the development of thin-film plastics, which led to a variety of photo and movie films, overhead transparencies, and iron oxide–coated tape for audio, video, and computers, and the electronics of the transistor and microchip technologies. When these things came into educational use, they had a big impact not only on the materials and things, but also on the way in which content was presented and taught and on the way in which students were perceived to learn through the use of the application of these technologies.

From the early 1900s to the late 1960s, many technologies came and went. Often, some of these had to wait for the proper educational environment in order to thrive. For example, in 1913, Thomas Edison thought that movie films would make it possible to teach every branch of human knowledge and that schools would completely change in ten years. Exaggerated claims for the value and instructional usefulness of various forms of technology have been made through the years: radio in the 1920s, films in the 1930s, television in the 1950s, teaching machines in the 1960s, dial-access technology in the 1970s, and computers in the 1980s.

The skills *techne* also had some developments during this time. The concept of mastery learning developed in the 1950s by a team lead by Bloom (1956) was followed by Mager's (1962) instructional objectives and Skinner's behavioral science approach in the 1960s, which coincided with the application of the teaching machine. Postlewait developed the audiotutorial approach in the late 1960s and early 1970s, and then cognitive learning came in the 1980s. The *techne* of the 1990s is probably classroom research as espoused by K. Patricia Cross. These are all examples of nonequipment learning systems thinking.

As the discussion gets more specific on the use of the various forms of technology, it should be remembered that these things occurred within the larger context of education and American society itself, as perhaps represented by the tremendous expansion of the community colleges and technical institutes in the 1960s and 1970s.

THE LATE 1960s TO THE EARLY 1980s

Americans had been out in space and back; President Lyndon Johnson's Great Society and Congress were pouring money into various educational "titles" and expecting great things in return; 3M had perfected its inexpensive overhead transparency materials; transistors were being utilized to make electronic equipment smaller and more portable; the audio tape cassette was introduced without equipment incompatibility problems; and the start-up rate for community colleges was nearly one per week.

Older community colleges, such as the Chicago City Colleges in Illinois, already had a decade or more with television experience. Erickson and Chausow (1960) and Erickson et al. (1964) reported on the television experiences from 1956. The open-circuit television, which enrolled 1,261 students with a 65 percent course completion rate, provided access to those students who otherwise would not have taken the course. At Long Beach City College, in California, in 1968 a health education course enrolled 30 percent homemakers and 24 percent full-time employed, and the college concluded that they were reaching a different population than was found on the campus. Bainster (1969) described two history courses offered at Mount San Jacinto, in California, in which one used FM radio and a course manual and the other one, on campus, used tapes, filmstrips, and response sheets. Typical of most classroom media comparison studies, there was no difference in the level of learning of the students in the two courses.

While the LRCs at the newer colleges were struggling to define their emerging comprehensive service role—utilizing media, circulation, and media production—some were moving closer to a direct instructional support role. In 1970 Hunter described the system approach used at Meramec Community College, in Missouri, as based on the maximization of instructional methods to increase the students' potential to meet course objectives. At William Rainey Harper College, in Illinois, the comprehensive LRC was running institutional development sessions for faculty (Voegel 1970, 1971). In 1974 Holloway conceptualized the redesign of LRCs to include instructional development and television. By 1975 enough was being reexamined and reorganized that Peterson (1975) could conduct a lengthy study on LRC functions in the community colleges. LRCs were even using media on themselves with taped orientation tours (Vernon 1975). Terwilliger (1975) described ways in which an LRC could assist instructors in applying instructional technology to support curricular resources.

Because things seemed to be happening too fast for many colleges, there was a need for some to band together into consortia and for leaders to establish new organizational units within or affiliated with national associations. Goodwin (1988) wrote an overview of the League for Innovation (a nationwide consortium of community colleges) and reported that, in its beginning years (1968–1975), the league focused on curriculum and instructional issues before shifting to social issues (1975–1980). From the 1980s to the present, the League for Innovation has pioneered efforts to self-paced instruction and basic skills programs and, in recent years, has provided outstanding community college leadership on the instructional use of computer technology.

The efforts of a twenty-member community college consortium in southern California has served as a harbinger for television utilization (Gross 1972). Two television courses were offered: 8,000 students enrolled, and there was no difference in the learning results between these students and those enrolled in traditional classroom situations. The Dallas County Community College offered its first telecourse in 1972, and Kelly and McCabe (1972) have reported on Miami-Dade's national efforts to produce its first telecourse on the topic of the environment. At about the same time, a statewide LRC consortium was organized in Illinois (Weiss and Steinke 1986) through the leadership of Elgin Community College, William Rainey Harper College, College of Lake County, and College of DuPage. This Northern Illinois Learning Resource Cooperative (NILRC) started with a sharing materials approach between area LRCs, then went on to joint purchases of books and materials, and into sharing telecourse costs. It was later emulated by the founding of the Southern Illinois Learning Resource Cooperative (SILRC) and the Mid-Illinois Learning Resource Center (MILRC).

At the national level, the Community College Association for Instruction and Technology (CCAIT), formed in 1973, has held numerous regionally and nationally, electronically linked conferences on the issues of instruction and technology. It has provided valuable support in such efforts as conducting a critical review of the New Directions for Community Colleges issue on "Using Instructional Technology" (Voegel 1975). Affiliated with the Association for Educational Communications and Technology (AECT), it is currently linked with the American Association of Community and Junior Colleges' (AACJC) LRC Council.

Individual faculty classroom efforts in the use of instructional technology have always been numerous and varied. The literature probably represents only a small fraction of the total efforts made by community college faculties across the nation. Some representative projects are highlighted here. The use of individualized instructional systems at Hillsborough Junior College, in Florida, suggested that student mastery has increased at certain levels in various disciplines (Shanberg 1971). London (1972) used films to focus on social problems in the social science curriculum offered at Everett Community College, in Washington. Utz (1973) used more than 100 single-concept videotapes for remedial learning at Kingsborough Community College, in New York. At Bergen Community College, in New Jersey, Yonker (1973) described how the multiflexible language lab was used. Brantley (1974) compared the audiotutorial method with lecture-demo classes in physical science at Pensacola Junior College, in Florida, and found that the grades of the audiotutorial students were directly related to the amount of time spent in the labs. This result was found in almost all audiotutorial studies.

Kotnick (1975) used single-concept slide sets in chemistry for students with poor verbal and quantitative skills at Cuyahoga Community College, in Ohio. Parsons (1975) described the use of learning modules, audiotutorials, and contracts for the individual learners. Eleven years later, Parsons reported that the audiotutorial approach was still viable because it was software oriented and not equipment dependent (Voegel 1986, 78). Another software or *techne* approach used was cognitive mapping (Neil 1975) at Oakland Community College, in Michigan, where the students' learning styles were analyzed. Teaching and support services, such as the LRC, were supposed to develop appropriate teaching-learning methodologies around those styles.

Tengwall (1980) described a project conducted at Anne Arundel Community College, in Maryland, in which history was taught with an integrated media approach to learning and found that including media in the lectures can broaden students' perceptions. As an indication of the growing concern about adequate English as a Second Language (ESL) instruction, Peck (1981) used audiovisually enriched learning experiences to teach ESL students. Likewise, community colleges began to attend to business and industry training needs. Moore (1982), for example, described a short-term training project held at Chemeketa Community College, in Oregon, which used course modules on an open-entry/open-exit competency-based program. Wilkins (1984) at Bossier Community College, in Louisiana, used a slide-lecture method for introductory and educational psychology classes to avoid the "messiness of chalk dust." As an example of the contemporary concern about appropriate instruction on other cultures, Kehrer et al. (1990) described the use of international readers and films in the cross-cultural freshman composition at Valencia Community College, in Florida, which helped students gain insight into non-American cultures.

Other examples of instructional improvement relate to the process of using the technology rather than being discipline specific. Approaches, such as faculty training on instructional development and teaching strategies, the design and production of materials, and the organization of teaching based on the new technologies, lead to new ways of applying such technology to teaching and learning. For example, Anandam and J. Kelly (1981–1982) described the implementation of technology in education and commented that the three phases of extensiveness, effectiveness, and endurance in an innovation-diffusion process were being ignored. Roark (1983) reported how the Pensacola Junior College, in Florida, instructional program could be reorganized based on a model for integrating the library, educational media, and instructional development functions.

When the gasoline crisis occurred in the 1970s, some educators became concerned about the survival of the typical commuter community college student. Vander Haeghen (1979), at Coastline Community College, in Fountain Valley, California, analyzed the impact of telecourses and other forms of extended study on such students. He figured that, by not driving the average ten miles round trip to and from a campus, most students could save from $90 to $220 per semester. With about 10,000 students enrolled per year at Coastline and about 160,000 enrolled in telecourses nationwide, the 540 miles driven times the enrollments resulted in 86 million miles not being driven, or over 5.5 million gallons of gasoline being saved, in addition to lessening air pollution. As time wore on, telecourses were taken on the basis of timeliness and accessibility rather than on saving gas. Luskin and Small (1980) reported that Coastline Community College, which had opened in the fall of 1976 using diverse modes of instruction including television, became the model for community colleges "without walls."

In 1974 a radio and television consortium in Florida coordinated the use of broadcast media to offer credit courses (Hobbs, 1981). Brock (1975) described one of Dallas's first efforts at producing a national thirty-lesson telecourse in freshman composition. Lucas (1976) reported on the use of two-way interactive cable television for adult education offered by Spartanburg Technical College, in South Carolina, with encouraging results—the students felt that their teachers cared more about them. By 1979 Dallas had gone from one in 1972 to seven complete productions ("ITV Close-up" 1979). Enrollments went from 399 to 10,000 per year in eighteen courses with several delivery modes. Kressel (1980) conducted a survey of 1,300 two-year colleges on adult learning and the use of television. Results indicated that a variety of outlets were used, such as closed circuit television (CCTV) and public and commercial television; that the use of consortia was effective; and that the financial aspects considered both costs and revenues.

During this same time period, the computer, in its punched-card data entry mainframe, was beginning to make its presence felt. Actually, most of the newer colleges being planned or built were designing computer centers for their campus operations.

Howell (1964) reported on guidelines developed for data processing instructional programs in the Los Angeles junior colleges and recommended that each college should have its own data processing center. One of the early was mainframe-supported projects—Time-Share Interactive Computer-Controlled Information Television (TICCIT). This computer-assisted instruction (CAI) project with remote computer terminals at North Virginia Community College provided students with a color television screen, headphones, and keyboard. Peckham (1973), on the other hand, suggested that instructional programs need their own interactive system instead of just terminals off the mainframe. Wesolowski et al. (1973) studied twenty-six Florida community colleges with computer systems. Some of the information revealed that the larger community colleges had more computer applications but that there was no difference in the costs of applications of computer centers, memory core, budgets, and so on with the colleges that had similar student full-time enrollment (FTE) size. In the state of Washington, Howard et al. (1975) reported on a statewide study and plan for instructional computing for the state community colleges.

Individual colleges were also planning for wider applications of computer technology. Campbell et al. (1979) described the final computer plan of the Saddleback Community College, in California, which called for a large mainframe system with minicomputers wired into it. Carlson (1980) reported that computer equipment had been bought in 1978 at the College of DuPage, in Illinois, without a plan and suggested that the best approach was to rely on commercially developed and maintained software and to install a microcomputer lab for faculty to experiment with hardware and software. Veley et al. (1982) described a master plan for computers at Los Angeles Trade-Tech, in California, which had numerous minicomputers for CAD/CAM plus the use of the main computer system.

THE MID–1980s TO THE EARLY 1990s

By the mid–1980s, much of the early excitement of the comprehensive LRCs had worn off. The services became routine and expected by both faculty and students. While some LRCs were reaching out to incorporate the newer technology, such as cable television and telecourses, others were being asked to assume or create learning-assistance centers to help the low-achieving and underprepared students. Dale (1984) surveyed forty-six community college libraries/LRCs on the use of computers and found that many libraries were participating in computer cataloguing networks; were using computers for cataloging, circulation, and searching; and had begun to make computers available to students as a service. Wacker et al. (1985) described an instructional telecommunications system at Kirkwood Community College, in Iowa, which provided sixty hours of live educational programming weekly at over twenty locations through an interactive delivery system and other learning resources to off-campus learners. Chalfoun (1986) reported on the Community College of Vermont's direct library reference service to twelve sites via a Wide-Area Telecommunications Service (WATS) installed in the community colleges' library. Each site was also hardware and software equipped to access a teaching techniques information network.

In 1985 the CCAIT, in an attempt at organization renewal, started a short-lived quarterly journal on instruction, technology, and LRCs. In its first edition, Bock (1985) overviewed two decades (1964–1984) of library and LRC involvement with various technologies. This period saw a 500 percent increase in community college credit enrollments to five million and a like number in noncredit. From books, periodicals, and some microfilm, the college libraries/LRCs expanded into records, films, audio and visual tapes, and a variety of multimedia packages. In these two decades, approximately 500 new LRC buildings were constructed to accommodate these changing technological and service needs. Bock concluded that the LRC is the "combination of technology, processes, services, and people to meet the widest possible range of learning needs" (1985, 11).

The new television technology intruding on the local community college scene in the early 1980s was cable television. Changes in cable franchising at the community level precipitated a rush by cable companies to wire up. Often the community college was dragged into these franchise efforts by offers from cable companies to equip their television studios with the latest equipment and a free channel in exchange for making the college facility a local community production center. Holleman (1983) described a master telecommunication plan for Peralta Community College District, in California, in which a mix of broadcast and cable television, radio, instructional television fixed service (ITFS), microwave, slow-scan satellite television, and videodiscs was examined. Allen (1986) reported on Miami-Dade's (Florida) community-based television project using its own channel on local cable company television.

Purdy (1986) indicated that the challenge to faculty and administration was to produce quality telecourse materials using the best features of television for distant learners. Earlier, she had discussed quality television production standards as changing from single college development to multimarketing (Purdy 1983). Zigerell (1986) edited the AACJC Issues Series No. 3, which described nine case studies of using telecommunications to reach a variety of student clienteles. In 1990 Brey discussed a survey of telecourse use by the Instructional Telecommunication Consortium (ITC) members of the AACJC from 1986 to 1989.

Another component of television that was assimilated in the mid to late 1980s was satellite television. This became feasible due to lower receiving antenna (dishes) costs and the interest shown by some community colleges in being down-link sites (receiving the signal from the satellite on a prescribed frequency) for teleconferences for the local community and business and industry. Vander Haeghen (1986) discussed the satellite potential to reach new, educationally underserved populations. Parnell (1988) described the inauguration of the Community College Satellite Network of the AACJC as a vehicle for AACJC members to share satellite programming and become a national resource of information for teleconferences.

Two recent studies examine the status of telecommunications at the state level. In 1990 the State Board for Community College Education, in Washington, found that over 3,000 (366 FTE) from sixteen community colleges were enrolled in telecourses and gave them high ratings. Fifteen colleges also used teleconferencing networks for faculty/staff in-service training. Manley (1991) reported that thirty colleges in North Carolina offered telecourses to 1,350 students. Finally, Neal (1991) detailed the history of the R. Jan LeCroy Center for Educational Telecommunications in the Dallas Community College District. This center evolved into one with a national reputation for producing quality telecourses, working with twenty consortia and associations representing 500 institutions using its telecourses, and becoming the top supplier of telecourses for the Adult Learning Service of the Public Broadcasting Service (PBS).

Meanwhile, the microcomputer—the personal computer or PC as it came to be known—was introduced. Here, for the first time, was a piece of equipment that put digital computer power directly into the hands of the user. There were no legions of computer technocrats who spoke in "computerese" known only to themselves; the user was in charge and alone. This loneliness and detachment from the technocrats forced the users into two modes. First, the users became active learners in how to use this new powerful thing; second, the users, knowing they were on their own, began to huddle in user groups based mostly on the equipment type and linked up electronically through user networks and bulletin boards.

Appropriate software for education has been a continuing problem. Only a "calc" program, later known as a spreadsheet, and a hobby program on flying a small airplane were available at first. Next came word processing and data bases to complete the big three of software. Individual programs for community college students or for the adult learner were difficult to find.

On the demand side, in the 1980s, there was a sense of great urgency to order the hardware for labs all over the campuses. From 1987 to 1988, expenditures for academic computing increased by 9 percent in community college representing 43.7 percent of their direct instruction funds as compared to 3 percent and 33 percent, respectively, at universities. Anandam observed that "such trends signal a very important message to educators—that technology is a means to an end" and needs to be revisited periodically so that we do not lose ourselves in the "means" (Anandam, 1989, 423).

The various disciplines leaped into microcomputer use. Levin and Doyle (1983) discussed the advantages of the microcomputer in the writing/reading/study lab and pointed out uses for students in writing reports as well as for learning vocabulary and grammar and improving reading. At Pima College, in Arizona, Fincke and Wakefield (1983) reported on the use of the microcomputer to compile data for archaeology. In the business education sector, the growing availability of business application software was causing community colleges to promote more noncredit, short-term training opportunities in accounting (Hubbard 1985). Grzywacz-Gray et al. (1987) described the kinds of copy, font options, and so on that the Macintosh computers could accomplish for production, graphics, accounting, and advertising in community college journalism programs. Styne (1987) presented survey information that some community college instructors were skeptical about student interest in poetry. She cites two computer programs oriented to poetry writing as being very useful to help students write and enjoy poetry. As an example in the social sciences, Xidis (1988) explains how IBM and Apple computers at Johnson County Community College, in Kansas, were being used with CAI modules for each unit in the U.S. history survey course.

Other instructional areas were also being examined for computer applications. For example, Heermann (1984) outlined a plan for the use of microcomputers to provide learning opportunities for the adult learner. At Lima Technical College, in Ohio, Hanson (1984) described the use of the library as a site for ongoing computer education, particularly a computer literacy program. Roueche, Baker, and Roueche (1986) devised a macro model for a Low-Achiever Instructional System that incorporated assessment, placement, instructional prescriptions, content-based instruction (including instructional delivery), exit testing, and subsequent course articulation. In California, Robledo (1987) reported on a study conducted on the use of microcomputers in the learning disabilities (LD) programs of forty-three colleges which indicated, among the findings, that thirty-five of them use computers with their LD programs with a range of 1–5 per program; twenty-four felt that their faculty were not sufficiently computer knowledgeable; and twenty-seven indicated that some of their LD students had their own computers at home. In-service training, faculty development, and faculty attitudes were also concerns with this new microcomputer technology. Anandam and D. Kelly (1981) reported on the Exposure to Microcomputers (GEM) project conducted at Miami-Dade, which was developed to familiarize their faculty with microcomputers and to determine the potential of interactive video programming. Armistead et al. (1987) described the results of a national telephone survey of sixty community college faculty members on their opinions about microcomputers and concluded that faculty in all discipline areas agree on the value of computer use in the classroom. In 1988 a faculty attitude study was conducted at Oakland Community College, in Michigan, on computers (Austin 1988). In the 146 responses, 86 percent indicated a high level of interest in computer use, but only 20 percent felt they had a high level of computer literacy; 64 percent believed that computers were important to their discipline; 68 percent considered computer access at work to be important; and 37 percent owned home computers. There were some differences by disciplines in the results.

Microcomputer use has been discussed and surveyed at state and national levels. Dellow and Poole (1984) edited an entire *New Directions for Community Colleges* issue on the microcomputer revolution, which examined issues related to computer literacy, telecommunications, videodisc technology, microcomputer access, faculty workload, and curricular change. A few years later, in Virginia, a study was done to determine the extent of microcomputer/software use in counseling and career planning (Taylor 1987). Results from 174 high schools and 27 community colleges indicated that they had largely integrated microcomputers into the counseling process. In Alabama a survey was conducted by Martin and Dean in 1987 to assess the status of computer use in the forty-one two-year colleges. Results indicated that Alabama ranked below the national average in numbers of computers used; most computers were purchased with grant funds; 50 percent used IBM or Apple microcomputers, and the rest used a mixture; the junior/community colleges centralized computers in a lab, and the technical colleges placed theirs in the occupational facilities; instructional use was 70 percent word processing, spreadsheets, and data bases, 50 percent taught programming skills, and 25 percent were used in nonbusiness discipline areas; and teachers were generally not involved in developing computer programs nor were they consulted about purchases.

With the wide general interest and large funds involved with implementing microcomputers in the colleges, new ways to be effective and efficient came about in the form of master planning for computers. Maricopa County Community College District, in Arizona (Jacobs 1986), Johnson County Community College, in Kansas (Gentry 1987), and the College of DuPage, in Illinois (Wenger et al., 1987) have all developed comprehensive college-wide master plans of mainframe computers and microcomputers for administration and instruction.

In the late 1980s, EDUCOM (the consortium of colleges, universities, and other institutions founded to facilitate the introduction, use, and management of information technology in higher education) developed some teams or task forces to examine software initiatives. One project was a faculty-oriented brochure, *Software Snapshots 1989*, on computer software development, for which a second edition was printed by Miami-Dade and distributed by the League for Innovation.

The AACJC report entitled *Building Communities* (1988) addressed technology and teaching in the section on "The Classroom as Community." After describing a few of the advantages of using technology, the report suggests that each college should clarify the "assumptions on which its use of technology is based" (1988, 28) and that there should be a regularly updated plan and that faculty must be involved in technology priorities. It recommended that each college develop a plan for the use of technology, that proposed faculty incentive programs for adaptation of educational technology to classroom needs be implemented, that the AACJC set up a software clearinghouse, that colleges use technology to extend the campus, and that new uses of technology be explored.

The immediate future calls for greater collaboration between the technologists and educators. Perhaps the cognitive approach to the application of technology may represent such a possibility. As Saettler has pointed out, "It is not easy to predict the future of educational technology. Probably the easiest prediction to make is that things do not usually turn out the way they are predicted" (1990, 538).

REFERENCES

Allen, J. M. 1986. Cable television: Strategic marketing through community relationships. Paper presented at the annual convention of the California Association of Community Colleges, 15 November, Anaheim, California.

American Association of Community and Junior Colleges (AACJC). 1988. *Building communities: A vision for a new century*. Report of the Commission on the Future of Community Colleges. Washington, D.C.

Anandam, K., ed. 1989. Transforming teaching with technology: Perspectives from two-year colleges. McKinney, Texas: Academic Computing Publications.

Anandam, K., and D. Kelly. 1981. GEM. Guided exposure to microcomputers: An interactive video program. Miami, Fla.: Miami-Dade Community College.

Anandam, K., and J. Kelly. 1981–82. Evaluating the use of technology in education, *Journal of Educational Technology Systems* 10:21–31.

Armistead, L. P., et al. 1987. Impact of microcomputers on the community college faculty. *Community College Review* 15:38–44.

Austin, H. S. 1988. Results of faculty computing survey. Paper presented at the League for Innovation in the Community College Conference, "Computing across the College Spectrum," February, Toronto, Ontario.

Bainster, R. E. 1969. Comparison of two history instruction methods: Radio broadcasting and visual aids versus individualized instruction with audio-visual aids. Gilman Hot Springs, Calif.

Bloom, B. S., et al. 1956. Taxonomy of educational objectives. *Cognitive Domain* 1.

Bock, D. J. 1985. Learning resources: Two decades of technological progress. *CCAIT Journal* 1:10–11.

Brantley, W. T. 1974. A comparison of the audio-tutorial method with the lecture-demonstration method for producing student achievement in college level physical science survey classes covering physics and astronomy. Ed.D. diss., University of Southern Mississippi.

Brey, R. 1990. Telecourse utilization survey project third year report: Fall 1986–summer 1989. Research project of the Instructional Telecommunication Consortium. Washington, D.C.: American Association of Community and Junior Colleges.

Brock, D. 1975. Writing for a reason: A telecourse in freshman composition. Paper presented at the annual meeting of the Conference on College Composition and Communication. Saint Louis, Missouri.

Campbell, D. A., et al. 1979. The next step: A computer facilities master plan for Saddleback College. Final Technical Report, Mission Viejo, Calif.: Saddleback Community College.

Carlson, B. 1980. Developing a computer literate faculty at College of DuPage. Paper presented at the annual meeting of EDUCOM. Washington, D.C.

Chalfoun, E. 1986. Off-campus library services: Community College of Vermont. Paper presented at the Off-Campus Library Services Conference, Reno, Nevada.

Dale, D. C. 1984. Computers in community college libraries. *Community and Junior College Libraries* 3:17–26.

Dellow, D. A., and L. H. Poole, eds. 1984. *Microcomputer applications in administration and instruction*. New Directions for Community Colleges, no. 47. San Francisco: Jossey-Bass.

Erickson, C. G., and H. M. Chausow. 1960. Chicago's TV colleges. Final Report of a three-year experiment of the Chicago City Junior College in offering college courses for credit via open-circuit television. Chicago, Ill.: City Colleges of Chicago.

Erickson, C. G., et al. 1964. Eight years of TV college—A fourth report. Chicago, Ill.: City Colleges of Chicago.

Fincke, M. S., and L. Wakefield. 1983. Archaeologists dig computers. *Community and Junior College Journal* 53:36–37.

Gentry, H. R. 1987. Developing an Academic Information Resources Master Plan: A paradigm. Paper presented at the Role of Communications Technology Conference, San Francisco, California.

Goodwin, G., ed. 1988. *Celebrating two decades of innovation, 1968–1988.* Laguna Hills, Calif.: League for Innovation in the Community College.

Gross, L. S. 1972. A study of two college credit courses offered over television by the Southern California Consortium for Community College Television. Paper presented to the California Association for Educational Media and Technology, Newport Beach, California.

Grzywacz-Gray, J., et al. 1987. Desktop publishing: Its impact on community college journalism. *Community College Journalist* 15:5–12.

Hanson, C. D. 1984. Computer literacy in an academic library. *Community and Junior College Libraries* 3:3–11.

Heermann, B. 1984. Computer-assisted adult learning and the community college response. In *Microcomputer applications in administration and instruction*, ed. D. A. Dellow and L. H. Poole. New Directions for Community Colleges, no. 47, pp. 81–88. San Francisco: Jossey-Bass.

Hobbs, T. W. 1981. Seminole Community College working with twenty-seven other institutions. Local working paper. Sanford, Fla.: Seminole Community College.

Holleman, J. J. 1983. A master plan for the use of telecommunications for instruction and community services in the Peralta Community College District. Ed.D. Diss., Nova University.

Howard, A., et al. 1975. A plan for community college instructional computing. Paper. Olympia, Wash.: State Board of Community Colleges.

Howell, J. M. 1964. A feasibility study in efficient instructional use of digital computers. Report. Los Angeles, Calif.: Los Angeles Community College.

Hubbard, G. R. 1985. The need for a cooperative paradigm to meet business's key microcomputer training requirements. *Technological Horizons in Education* 12:100–103.

ITV close-up: The first six years. 1979. (May) Paper. Dallas, Texas: Dallas County Community College.

Jacobs, A. 1986. Master plan for instructional computing. Paper. Tempe, Ariz.: Maricopa Community College.

Kehrer, G., et al. 1990. Internationalizing freshman composition I and II through literature and film: A cross-cultural approach. *Community/Junior College Quarterly of Research and Practice* 14:359–70.

Kelly, J. T., and McCabe, R. H. 1972. An overview of the scope and a description of the components of man and environment television learning system. Paper. Miami, Fla.: Miami-Dade Community College.

Kotnick, L. J. 1975. Developing material for underprepared students. In *Using instructional technology*, ed. G. H. Voegel. New Directions for Community Colleges, no. 9, pp. 39–42. San Francisco: Jossey-Bass.

Kressel, M. 1980. Adult learning and public broadcasting. Report.

Levin, R., and C. Doyle. 1983. The microcomputer in the writing/reading/study lab. *Technological Horizons in Education* 10:77–79.

London, G. 1972. Exploring social issues through cinema. *Junior College Journal* 42:33–35.

Lucas, W. A. 1976. Moving from two-way cable technology to educational interaction. Paper presented at the National Telecommunications Conference, Dallas, Texas.

Luskin, B. J., and J. Small. 1980. Coastline Community College: An idea beyond tradition. Paper presented at the Conference of the American Association for Higher Education, Washington, D.C.

Mager, R. F. 1962. Preparing instructional objectives. Paper. Palo Alto, Calif.: Fearson.

Manley, F. 1991. Around the ITC. *Instructional Telecommunications Consortium Newsletter* (Spring): 5–7. Washington, D.C.: American Association of Community and Junior Colleges.

Moore, G. R. 1982. Short-term training: Where the action is. Position paper. Bakersfield, Calif.: Bakersfield College.

Neal, J. F. 1991. The history of the R. Jan LeCroy Center for Educational Telecommunications of the Dallas County Community College District. Ph.D. Diss., North Texas State University.

Neil, M. 1975. Cognitive style: A new aspect to institutional technology. In *Using instructional technology*, ed. G. H. Voegel. New Directions for Community Colleges, no. 9:73–80. San Francisco: Jossey-Bass.

Parnell, D. 1988. Community college satellite network of AACJC. *Community, Technical, and Junior College Journal* 59.

Parsons, M. H. 1975. MATC spells instructions. In *Using instructional technology*, ed. G. H. Voegel. New Directions for Community Colleges, no. 9:17–24. San Francisco: Jossey-Bass.

Peck, D. 1981. Insights into an audiovisual approach with adult ESL students. Paper presented at the annual conference of the Pacific and Asian American Educators Association, Honolulu, Hawaii.

Peckham, H. D. 1973. Computing in the community colleges: Fact and fancy. Paper presented at the annual conference of the Association for Computing Machinery, Atlanta, Georgia.

Peterson, G. T. 1975. The comprehensive learning center. In *Using instructional technology*, ed. G. H. Voegel. New Directions for Community Colleges, no. 9: 43–50. San Francisco: Jossey-Bass.

Purdy, L. 1983. Quality control in the design and production of telecourses. Paper presented at the annual conference of the American Association of Community and Junior Colleges, New Orleans, Louisiana.

———. 1986. Telecourses: Using technology to serve distant learners. In *Advances in industrial technology*, ed. G. H. Voegel. New Directions for Community Colleges, no. 55:3–12. San Francisco: Jossey-Bass.

Roark, D. B. 1983. Reorganizing toward instructional development. *Community and Junior College Libraries* 1:39–48.

Robledo, G. 1987. Microcomputer use in learning disabilities programs at California community colleges. Research project.

Roueche, J. E., G. A. Baker III, and S. D. Roueche. 1986. Access with excellence. In *Advances in instructional technology*, ed. G. H. Voegel. New Directions for Community Colleges, no. 55:29–40. San Francisco: Jossey-Bass.

Saettler, P. 1968. *A history of instructional technology*. New York: McGraw-Hill.

———. 1990. *The evolution of American educational technology*. Englewood, Colo.: Libraries Unlimited.

Shanberg, M. S. 1971. Individualized instruction systems. *Junior College Journal* 41:46–49.

Software snapshots: Where are you in the picture? 1989. Princeton, N.J. and Miami-Dade, Fla.: EDUCOM.

Styne, M. M. 1987. Poetry in English composition, with computers or without. Paper presented at the meeting of the City Colleges of Chicago Conference "Literature across the Disciplines: The Roles of Literature in the Community College," Chicago, Illinois.

Taylor, H. T. 1987. Microcomputer hardware and software directory: Guidance and counseling services in Virginia. Paper. Hampton, Va.: Thomas Nelson Community College.

Tengwall, D. 1980. Teaching history with media: A case study. Teaching guide developed for classroom use.

Terwilliger, G. 1975. Exploiting learning resources: A team approach. In *Using instructional technology*, ed. G. H. Voegel. New Directions for Community Colleges, no. 9:11–16. San Francisco: Jossey-Bass.

Terwilliger, G. 1988. TICCIT: Instructional technology's best kept secret. *Community and Junior College Libraries* 6:45–53.

Utz, P. 1973. Single-concept videotapes for college remedial learning. *Educational Technology* 13.

Vander Haeghen, P. 1979. Other benefits to telecourse students. Paper.

———. 1986. Satellites stop beeping and start teaching. In *Advances in instructional technology*, ed. G. H. Voegel. New Directions for Community Colleges, no. 55:13–20. San Francisco: Jossey-Bass.

Veley, V. F., et al. 1982. Master plan: The introduction of computer science and computer related instructional programs, 1982–1985. Report. Los Angeles Trade-Technical College.

Vernon, C. 1975. An individualized program for learning resource center orientation. Paper.

Voegel, G. H. 1970. A report of the beginning efforts in instructional development at William Rainey Harper College. Report.

———. 1971. The innovative diffusion center: A potential concept to accelerate educational change. *Audiovisual Instruction* (January):67–69.

Voegel, G. H. ed. 1975. *Using instructional technology*. New Directions for Community Colleges, no. 9. San Francisco: Jossey-Bass.

———. 1986. Instructional technology mix: Some considerations. In *Advances in instructional technology*, ed. G. H. Voegel. New Directions for Community Colleges, no. 55:73–82. San Francisco: Jossey-Bass.

Wacker, K. A. et al. 1985. The classroom and the library that cover seven counties. *Community and Junior College Libraries* 3:23–32.

Weiss, J. A., and R. G. Steinke. 1986. Change through cooperation: the NILRC model. In *Advances in instructional technology*, ed. G. H. Voegel. New Directions for Community Colleges, no. 55:21. San Francisco: Jossey-Bass.

Wenger, G. E., et al. 1987. College of DuPage institutional plan for computing. Paper.

Wesolowski, Z. P., et al. 1973. An analysis of computer utilization for administration and instruction in the Florida community college system. Paper based on a practicum submitted to Nova University.

Wilkins, S.A. 1984. The slide-lecture: An alternative to chalkdust? Paper. Bossier City, Louisiana: Bossier Parish Community College.

Xidis, K. 1988. Students, micros, and software: A new approach in history courses. *History Microcomputer Review* 4:15–20.

Yonker, F. H. 1973. Multi-flexible language laboratory. *NALLD Journal* 7:37–43.

Zigerell, J. 1986. Telelearning models: Expanding the community college community. Report. AACJC. Issue Series No. 3. Washington, D.C.

Part 4

Leading and Managing the Community College

Research and Practice on Shared Governance and Participatory Decision Making

Richard L. Alfred

Governance, closely related to concepts of administration, management, decision making, and leadership, is one of the most widely discussed and misunderstood subjects in community college education today. The published research on community college governance is beset with problems. Much of the work is descriptive in nature or is limited in scope and design; selected work is reflective of excessive dependence on organizational scholars such as Selznick, Cohen and March, Corson, Pfeffer, Pfeffer and Salancik, Mortimer and McConnell, and Baldridge. This focus on concepts that work well in theory, but not necessarily in practice, has contributed to ambiguity concerning what governance is and what it is not.

Governance may be defined as "the process for locating authority, power, and influence for academic decisions among internal and external constituencies" (Alfred 1985a). In its simplest form, governance may be defined as the "act of decision making." Three themes in this definition guide its application in community colleges: (1) historical patterns of decision making and the impact of these patterns on institutional culture, (2) differential involvement in governance among staff depending on position in the institution, and (3) a prevailing concern about the location of authority and power for decision making among different parties. These themes will be used to examine and synthesize the literature concerning shared governance and participatory decision making in community colleges.

An overview of the theories underlying shared governance and participatory decision making in community colleges is an appropriate beginning. Governance is complex under the best of circumstances. It can assume different forms depending on the institutional context and characteristics of the external environment. We know, however, that community colleges have moved through stages of development from establishment to maturity that involve increasing pressure for involvement in governance (Richardson 1976; Alfred and Smydra 1985; Deegan and Gollattscheck 1985; Slaughter and Broussal 1986; O'Hara 1990). With this in mind, the chapter moves from the historical context to current practice and a careful analysis of the benefits of shared governance. Attention is given to the governance models currently in use in community colleges, the nature and extent of faculty and staff participation in governance, and strategies for change to increase involvement in governance. The chapter closes with an examination of the future. What will be the shape of governance in community colleges? How will faculty and staff roles change? What new or different roles will leaders play in decision making?

THEORIES OF GOVERNANCE

Theoretical models to understand how governance works in colleges and universities have been developed by organizational theorists Weick (1976), Baldridge (1971), Cohen and March (1974), Corson (1975), Millett (1978), Mortimer and McConnell (1978), Pfeffer (1981), and a host of others. In general, they draw from the fields of sociology, psychology, political science, public policy, and anthropology and present a comprehensive approach to understanding how decisions are made in higher education institutions. These distinctive theories complement those developed in other disciplines, but distinguish colleges and universities as having organizational characteristics that set them apart. For example, postsecondary institutions are seen as having ambiguous and contested goals, fluid and situational participation in decision making, and fragmentation and conflict associated with differential goals pursued by staff. Although community colleges, in particular, have not been the subject of these models, a generic relevance exists as will be made evident in the following examples.

Cohen and March (1974) espouse a theory of governance in which goals are ambiguous and generous resources allow departments to go in different directions. Labeled "organized anarchy," decisions are the by-products of unplanned activity involving problems, decision makers, and preconceived solutions. Another model proposed by Baldridge (1971) views colleges and universities as miniature political systems with interest group dynamics and conflicts similar to those in other types of organizations. The key elements of this "political model" are fragmentation among internal interest groups, fluid and situational participation in decision making, and vulnerability to the external environment. A model centered around the relationship of the institution and external environment is the coupling theory proposed by Weick (1976). How individuals conceptualize what is happening in the environment around the organization is critical to how the organization then responds or does not respond. The responses of individuals are determined by their position within an organization. Ranks and positions are not equal in their power or access to power, and it is thus the perceptions of key decision makers that are critical to the operations of the organization. Finally, it is important to acknowledge the contribution of Likert (1967) in developing a continuum for governance running from autocracy or "rule by one" to participation or "rule by many." Likert believed that, as institutions matured, they operated on a cycle involving an inevitable transition from autocracy to participation in governance. In the parlance of modern-day organizational theorists, Likert's theory can be broken down into subtheories labeled Theory X (autocratic supervision allowing for minimal group influence), Theory Y (democratic supervisory style allowing for a considerable degree of group decision making), and Theory Z ("pure" democracy allowing for total group decision making and placing the supervisor in a rotational role with staff).

As community colleges have grown larger and more complex, they have come to contain all of these theories. For example, a president has responsibility for positioning the organization with the external environment and yet is at the top of a bureaucratic organization made up of layers of staff requiring coordination. Similarly, a department chair has a leadership role and yet is part of a consensus body (Silverman 1987).

TOWARD SHARED GOVERNANCE

In the early period of development (1950 to 1965), community colleges were small but growing organizations administered by leaders with seemingly unlimited authority reinforced by a board of trustees. Presidents made decisions with a small group of administrators and depended on an informal peer network to communicate the results of the decision process. As institutions grew in size and complexity, a pyramid structure for governance evolved in which power flowed from the president at the top of the organization through layers of staff—vice presidents, deans, directors, department heads, and faculty. The allocation of resources in the college budget came to be the primary mechanism of control for many presidents. Faculty maintained primary responsibility for decisions on courses, curricula, and matters that affected teaching and learning, whereas administrators maintained responsibility for decisions related to planning, coordination, and allocation of resources. The interests of students, faculty, administrators, and trustees were different, each holding unique goal sets and serving distinct constituencies. The result was the beginning of conflict between faculty and administrators regarding their roles in decision making. Issues were weighed in terms of their impact on group concerns, and the sheer mass of new staff in the institution made the availability of resources the critical factor in decision making.

Tightening resources and increasing pressure for representation in decision making changed the context for governance in the late 1970s and early 1980s. Community colleges that had assigned a strong administrative role to the president in their developmental years recognized that authority for decision making had been extended to new actors—coordinating boards, legislative committees, legislators, and the executive branch of government (Alfred and Smydra 1985). No issue generated more controversy in this period than that of the control of community colleges and who was to make the decisions on specific issues. A sharp increase in support from the state was accompanied by state-level monitoring, auditing, and policies that affected the programs and operations of most colleges. At the same time, faculty and staff began to push for meaningful involvement in decision making. Increasingly cognizant of the fact that collective bargaining could safeguard or improve working conditions, but could not guarantee involvement in strategic decisions, faculty began to establish alliances with influential groups to forge new approaches to governance. California Assembly Bill 1725—legislation spurring a move from ''participative'' to ''shared'' governance in California community colleges—provides an excellent example of what collaboration can do to change the inner workings of campus governance.

This brief overview of the evolution of governance in community colleges simplifies the complex set of actors, circumstances, and events that contribute to governance. There are contextual variables unique to colleges such as size, location, collective bargaining history, and so forth that determine the approach to governance. For example, a published study of the perceptions of forty-two top- and middle-level administrators at four community colleges concerning decision-making processes used at their college cited differences according to geographical location (Sagini 1991). Rural colleges relied on a consensus model, whereas urban colleges were more likely to rely on autocracy and rational models. Studies of the impact of collective bargaining and faculty associations on governance show that faculty have taken on certain management functions and rights (Walker and Polythress 1983; Decker et al. 1986).

A factor universal to community colleges, irrespective of context, is the movement toward participative decision making. As community colleges have become larger and more successful, attention has turned to the role of faculty in governance. Faculty leaders contend that continuing governance in a business-as-usual fashion with a minority of teacher activists participating in governance by means of collective bargaining will result in a strong adversarial presence in management-faculty relations and diminished institutional loyalty among instructors (Slaughter and Broussal 1986). The ideal scenario would involve faculty and staff participation in a broad range of institutional processes and a shift in the focus of professional roles from the periphery to the center of decision making and policy formation. To accomplish this goal, new governance paradigms have been presented to strengthen the self-esteem of faculty through involvement in administration, opportunities for professional development, and recognition of expanded roles in decision making (Floyd 1985; Schuster et al. 1989; O'Hara 1990; Alfred and Linder 1990; Alfred, Peterson, and White 1992). Effective community colleges will implement systems for continuous assessment and planning at all levels. In the process, faculty roles and work loads will change. Tomorrow's faculty members will do more than teach. They will forecast market conditions, plan and evaluate curricula, conduct research on student outcomes, build marketing and recruitment plans, lobby private-sector markets for resources, and perform other management functions as necessary to improve performance.

STRATEGIES TO ACHIEVE SHARED GOVERNANCE

As community college leaders and staff consider approaches and strategies for implementing shared governance, initiatives are under way at a number of colleges to expand faculty involvement in decision making. These initiatives have taken three different forms:

1. Changes in administrative structure to open governance to faculty and staff
2. Modification of institutional processes (goal setting, planning, assessment, etc.) to expand staff roles in governance
3. Utilization of special techniques to examine faculty and staff roles in decision making and to develop systems for shared governance.

Derived from a topical bibliography generated by the ERIC Clearinghouse for Junior Colleges, the college initiatives described for each of these forms have common features worth noting: They are designed to increase faculty and staff involvement in decision making; collective bargaining contracts will need to be modified; top-down approaches to decision making will change as the organization structure is "flattened" to involve additional parties; and the role of the chief executive officer will shift from one of "control" to one of "establishing direction" for the institution through planning and participative decision making. Due to space limitations, selected initiatives will be described for each form.

Structural Change

The Metropolitan Community College (Nebraska) instituted a College Advisory System (CAS) to replace its cumbersome governance structure of seventeen standing committees and numerous ad hoc committees (McBride and Devine 1987). The CAS is a voluntary, action-oriented, entirely open system, allowing for input from all sectors of the college community. It is not controlled by the administration, but rather it is composed of a steering panel and four subcommittees for business and personnel matters, the college's future, student services, and teaching and curriculum. All constituencies (i.e., faculty, students, administrators, and classified staff) of the college are represented on the appropriate committees. The steering panel meets once a month to review, discuss, and determine appropriate action for proposals received during the month. Proposals are submitted on simple forms requiring the initiator to state his or her idea or concern, indicate what brought about the request, suggest a solution, and provide supporting materials. Proposals that affect many individuals or areas are channeled to one or more of the four committees for further discussion and are then forwarded to the appropriate vice president for input and implementation.

"Housekeeping" proposals on clear-cut issues are submitted directly to an administrator. Efforts are made to complete all action on submitted proposals within twenty working days. As an advisory system, the CAS can make recommendations for change, but it remains the task of management to make the final decision and implement the idea. The college community is kept informed of all proposals submitted to the CAS through a weekly publication.

The Foothill/DeAnza Community College District (California) has given special priority to meeting the goal of shared governance in California Assembly Bill 1725 through changes in its governance system (Gulassa 1989). The college's success can be attributed to the climate for excellence created by its collaborative governance body, the District Budget and Policy Development Group (BPDG). This group includes representatives from the student body, faculty union, minority staff association, and directors of human resources and plant services, as well as college presidents, deans, and senate representatives. The district chancellor acts as referee. Decisions are arrived at collaboratively, and each member's presence and input is required at all meetings. Idea integration is used as the primary means of dealing with intragroup conflict. Although the chancellor and management retain administrative power, the emphasis is on consensus building and mutual respect for all interests represented.

The College of Marin (California) has adopted a model of collegial governance that involves the entire campus community in recommending the policies and procedures that determine the rules by which employees and students live (Stetson 1990). The model, which was designed by a task force representing faculty, staff, and students, is based on the U.S. government model of executive, legislative, and judicial branches. Its major components are an Academic Senate, a Classified Senate, a Student Senate, and a Senate Executive Board. Each of the three senates has two major roles: (1) to review and recommend district policies and college procedures and (2) to recommend appointments from its membership to college governance committees. The Senate Executive Board is composed of an equal number of representatives from each of the three senates. Proposal for new or changed policies or procedures travel through a number of committees before reaching the Senate Executive Board (comparable to a legislative conference committee), where the proposals are refined using suggestions from the three individual senates. The board of trustees has the final authority to veto or amend policies recommended to it by the superintendent/president, who serves as the chair of the Senate Executive Board. The superintendent/president has the authority to change recommended procedures if she or he feels they are not in the college's best interests. Through the collegial governance system, the College of Marin has established the Affirmative Action Committee, the Employee Development Committee, the Planning Committee, and the Instructional Equipment Committee. Since the model's implementation, forty-two policies and procedures have been recommended and approved.

At the Wytheville Community College (Virginia), the management style is collegial, while the management structure is bureaucratic (Snyder 1989). Formal bureaucratic structures exist for normal and routine communication and for policy decisions. However, faculty are encouraged to share their concerns with the president and other administrators without going through formal channels. Various mechanisms have been created to encourage "coalition management": (1) the Faculty Government Association has specific committees to address admissions and standards, affirmative action, curriculum, financial aid, improvement of instruction, and other areas; (2) the College Council, made up of students, staff, faculty, and administrative representatives, provides a forum for the discussion of ideas, concepts, and policy matters; (3) the loosely organized Support Staff Group communicates directly with the president on matters related to improvement of the work environment; (4) the president has appointed ad hoc committees and task forces to deal with such matters as the college calendar, faculty evaluation, long-range planning, and space allocation; (5) regular "town meetings" are held, involving all members of the college community; (6) all major documents, such as the "College Policies and Procedures Manual," are submitted to faculty in draft form for review and comment; and (7) a system to recognize publicly the contributions of faculty to community, professional, and college activities has been implemented.

Institutional Process

The Eastern Iowa Community College District (EICCD) recently completed a project involving staff at all levels to develop a collective image of what the community college should be in the coming century (Blong and Friedel 1991). The reasons for seeking this shared vision were to create institutional focus, foster commitment, build communication, and reaffirm the college's mission and beliefs statement. The efforts to develop a shared vision, termed the "2020 Vision Process," involved a series of all-day, in-service meetings, administrative retreats, a survey of the academic community, and the development of a series of environmental impact statements focusing on factors likely to affect the college in coming years. The process involved every college employee and resulted in the revision of EICCD's Mission and Belief Statements, the formulation of new goals and objectives, and the creation of specific implementation strategies to achieve the objectives. Among the new institutional goals identified were the following: (1) develop and maintain administrative and staff support dedicated to student learning; (2) recruit and retain students from diverse backgrounds; (3) encourage initiative, risk-taking, and individual responsibility; and (4) become an active partner in defining and addressing community and business needs.

The Riverside Community College (California) has initiated a strategic planning process designed to draw a larger proportion of the college community into institutional planning (Vail 1988). In the first meetings of the President's Strategic Planning Advisory Committee (PSPAC), fifty-eight faculty, managers, and support staff gathered to address questions concerning the college's mission, goals, and programs. The committee met each Friday afternoon to discuss case studies of successful and unsuccessful businesses. The presentations made by the college president and other members of the committee served as exemplars of good teaching. Between the large group meetings, smaller groups met to review the discussion questions on the week's case study or current topic. The discussion groups were expected to look at ideas from every possible angle, but not to produce any product. Instead, action groups made up of representatives of the discussion groups were formed to come up with such products as a list of what the college does best, or needs to do. Despite early resistance to the adoption of a business mentality, newly learned business and marketing concepts were applied to the college. The final outcome of the first PSPAC meetings was a series of statements about the college's "business," vision, and values.

The South Central Community College (Connecticut) received funding to develop a long-range planning process (Sturtz 1984). The process, modeled on the three-year planning cycle developed by the National Center for Higher Education Management Systems, used the college's existing organizational structure. A Planning Council was established as the pivotal committee for the planning process. In order to simplify and focus the planning efforts that had been initiated as part of a self-study process, the Planning Council undertook a five-phase process: (1) review and appraisal, which examined the role and scope of the college, developed planning assumptions upon which the institution's goals were prioritized, and provided information on the service region, college funding, student profiles, facilities and resources, staffing, programs and services, and governance; (2) divisional goals, during which faculty and staff met with deans and department heads to establish divisional goals; (3) reformatting, which involved a review of divisional goals and their statement as measurable objects; (4) approval by the president; and (5) renewal of the process. The broad-based goals and objectives that were articulated in the resulting planning document established priorities for budgetary expenditures and personnel allocations.

A quality/performance circles system model was implemented at the Lakeshore Technical Institute (Wisconsin) to promote greater participation by staff in decision making and problem solving (Ladwig 1983). All management personnel at the college were invited to participate in the process, and thirty-nine volunteered. Nonmanagement staff were allocated a limited number of openings, which were filled by ten faculty members and nine support staff. A study of the effectiveness of the model and of implementation procedures was conducted to investigate: (1) attitude changes before and after involvement, (2) differences in the attitude changes of management and nonmanagement personnel, and (3) variations in attitude changes of personnel with differing management styles. The study involved a presentation to all personnel regarding the quality/performance system model, a literature review on the model and measures of its effectiveness, a pretest and posttest attitude survey, and the administration of a management style inventory. The results revealed a significant change in the participants' attitudes toward institutional decision making and problem solving.

Following an eleven-month period of study, planning, and pilot testing, a project was undertaken at the Central Piedmont Community College (North Carolina) to implement quality circles—small groups of employees doing similar work who voluntarily met on a regular basis to set goals, identify and analyze problems, find solutions, and cooperate with management to implement solutions (Moretz 1983). The project's objectives were to orient line managers to quality circle concepts, establish an advisory committee, train facilitators and circle leaders, implement quality circles, produce instructional materials, build state-wide awareness of the concept, evaluate the project, and develop a plan for implementing quality circles in interested institutions. From July 1981 to November 1982, sixteen quality circle work groups, involving 200 of the college's employees, completed forty improvement projects, and seven task forces were formed to address specific problems. Over 1,700 professional staff, representing 250 colleges and public schools, attended presentations and workshops led by the project staff. An assessment of the project found that, although attitudes and problem-solving abilities improved significantly due to quality circle involvement, communication with administrators, students, and other work groups did not improve significantly.

In 1986, the Learning Resource Center (LRC) of the New River Community College (Virginia) initiated efforts to increase the level, quality, responsiveness, and adaptability of LRC services (Wilkinson 1989). Central to these efforts was an emphasis on employee involvement and empowerment intended to create an atmosphere of trust and teamwork, enhance employee problem-solving and decision-making capabilities, better use employee skills, improve communication between employees and among departments, develop leadership, improve job satisfaction, increase employee knowledge levels, and improve the level and quality of products and services. Employee involvement and empowerment were promoted through (1) exercises in self-awareness; (2) problem-solving training; (3) the initiation of a quality circle; (4) the use of a special project team to solve problems related to collection development, library automation, and staff; (5) presentations to top administrators; (6) the development of a five-year plan for the LRC; (7) weekly staff meetings; and (8) a yearly evaluation retreat. The success of the program was reflected in the behavior of front-line employees making more decisions, questioning methods, and seeking better solutions to problems. Employees indicated a high sense of job satisfaction, and the level and quality of products and services improved through expanded involvement in decision making.

Technique

The Baltimore County Community College (Maryland) used the Community College Goals Inventory (CCGI) to determine and compare the views of administrators, faculty, students, community residents, and business/industry officials regarding the actual and desirable goals of the college (Harrison 1985). Instruments for building consensus around organizational goals were viewed as a valuable tool for building staff commitment to institutional purposes and programs. Shared vision embraced in consensual goals was viewed as an important first step in building a system of shared governance.

The psychology faculty at the Community College of Allegheny County (Pennsylvania) used the Delphi technique to achieve consensus on twenty-two issues related to standardized course prerequisites and descriptions (Dailey 1988). The technique was viewed as providing a cost-effective method of geographically disbursed systems to reach consensus with advantages over meetings and polls.

FUTURE DIRECTIONS

Numerous issues will command attention in the future as community colleges confront new challenges. What elements of control should be maintained by state agencies? What should be reserved for local institutions? What new actors in governance will emerge in the future, and what role will they play in shaping institutional programs and finances? What further changes in institutional management will result from the trend toward placing more control in the hands of external agencies? What will be the effect of tightening resources on relationships within and between institutions? Can relationships of faculty to faculty and faculty to administrators be maintained in a period of intense competition for resources and spiraling demands for quality and cost efficiency? Will it be possible for institutions to "age gracefully" in the face of changing conditions?

New parties will emerge in community college governance over the next ten years. Power, authority, and influence in the decision process will be shared with external constituencies. The rising influence of these agencies will result in a governance system that might best be described as a political-bureaucratic model devoted to regulation and control. An increasing number of colleges, especially those that are part of a state system, will be placed in a management mode rather than a governance context. The increasing complexity of governance will not only demand a new breed of administrators, but also demand that administrators be individuals with far-reaching educational vision—that they be capable of interpreting community needs and expectations and adept at working with multiple constituencies, such as faculties, governing boards, state governments, and community groups, as well as representatives of other segments of education (Alfred and Smydra 1985).

To address these issues successfully, administrators will require sophisticated information about institutional characteristics and performance, as well as about changing community needs. At the same time, state agencies will place increasing pressure on community colleges to furnish information about institutional performance to guide resource allocation decisions. To respond effectively, community colleges will need to adopt governance systems that merge multiple information systems used by different groups into a single information system that can serve as a foundation for strategic decisions by policymakers both within and outside of the institution. This model for decision making, termed the "coordinated systems model'' will become an important feature of community college governance in the 1990s (Alfred and Smydra 1985).

The 1990s will be a decade of rapid growth in information systems used by community colleges, government agencies, and private-sector organizations. It will be a period in which decision makers become comfortable with the new technology and employ sophisticated information banks in making decisions about programs, students, resources, staff, and facilities. The future shape of governance can best be described as one of ''organizational dualism,'' in which multiple systems for decision making will be utilized by different groups (Alfred and Smydra 1985). In matters of academic affairs, organized faculty groups (through a representative senate, curriculum committee, or collective bargaining unit), private-sector organizations (through program advisory committees, presidential advisory committees, and personal influence networks), and state government agencies (through program approval mechanisms and resource allocation procedures) will have considerable influence over decisions related to degree programs, degree requirements, curriculum structure, course offerings, and admission standards. Administrative matters, such as fund-raising, budgeting, public relations, and institutional planning, will remain the province of trustees and administrators—but in direct relationship to the information networks and decision inputs of other groups. In short, it will be difficult for administrators to make major decisions—either academic or administrative—in isolation. The conjoined interests of internal and external constituencies and the increased capacity of these constituencies to shape institutional decisions through sophisticated information systems will be the driving forces underlying new initiatives in governance. Governance in this context will differ from earlier depictions because it will involve a much larger number of actors, many of whom are external to the institution.

Implementation of the coordinated systems model will involve the establishment of participative decision systems and the application of strategic information to ongoing institutional processes. One such process is the operating budget, which offers an excellent illustration of how shared governance can work. Administrators responsible for planning, research, and business operations will work with academic department heads and other cost center managers to collect, analyze, and input data into the decision spectrum at specific points in the budgetary process. The task of executive administrators (presidents, vice presidents, and deans) will be to assess economic, demographic, technological, and social conditions in the external environment to provide a foundation for development of the operating budget. Most likely, institutional research personnel and business officers will contribute to this assessment process by collecting information needed to establish revenue projections. These projections will be used by academic department heads and nonacademic managers to guide judgments about resource requirements in specific cost centers.

A potentially rewarding outcome of a coordinated systems model of governance will be consensus among internal and external constituencies regarding undesirable solutions to complex problems. When sophisticated information systems are brought to bear on a specific problem by multiple agencies, inappropriate decision alternatives will be quickly rejected from consideration. In this way the coordinated systems model should improve decisions, but it should also sharpen understanding on the part of faculty and administrators as to the utility of accurate data in the decision process.

In the decade ahead, community faculty, administrators, and external groups should be able to come together to improve decision making through coordinated information systems. It will be the task of administrators to present recommended decision alternatives to the governing board. If the choice proves correct, all parties to the decision process will profit through the experience. If the choice proves incorrect, faculty and administrators will question the wisdom of engaging external constituencies. The challenge to community college leaders is to achieve the first and avoid the second outcome.

REFERENCES

Alfred, R. L. 1985a. Governance and the community college mission. *Community and Junior College Journal* 55(6):52–53.

————. 1985b. Power on the periphery: Faculty and student roles in governance. In *Ensuring effective governance*, eds. W. L. Deegan and J. E. Gollattscheck. New Directions for Community Colleges, no. 49:25–39. San Francisco: Jossey-Bass.

Alfred, R. L., and V. Linder. 1990. *Rhetoric to reality: Effectiveness in community colleges*. Ann Arbor, Mich.: Community College Consortium.

Alfred, R. L., and D. F. Smydra. 1985. Reforming governance: Resolving challenges to institutional authority. In *Renewing the American Community College*, eds. W. L. Deegan and D. Tillery. San Francisco: Jossey-Bass.

Alfred, R. L., R. O. Peterson, and T. H. White. 1992. *Making community colleges more effective: Leading through student success*. Ann Arbor, Mich.: Community College Consortium.

Baldridge, J. V. 1971. *Academic governance*. Berkeley, Calif.: McCutchan.

Baldridge, J. V., D. V. Curtis, G. Ecker, and G. C. Riley. 1978. *Policy making and effective leadership: A national study of academic management*. San Francisco: Jossey-Bass.

Blong, J. T., and J. N. Friedel. 1991. *2020 vision: The EICCD moves into the 21st century*. ERIC Document no. ED 327 249. Davenport: Eastern Iowa Community College District.

Cohen, M. D., and J. G. March, 1974. *Leadership and ambiguity: The American college president*. New York: McGraw-Hill.

Corson, J. 1975. *The governance of colleges and universities*. New York: McGraw-Hill.

Dailey, A. L. 1988. Faculty consensus at a multi-campus community college through delphi. *Community/Junior College Quarterly of Research and Practice* 12(1):21–26.

Decker, R. H., et al. 1986. Faculty impact in institutional decision making in Illinois community colleges. *Community/Junior College Quarterly of Research and Practice* 10(3):241–59.

Deegan, W. L., and J. F. Gollattscheck. 1985. Ensuring effective governance. *New Directions for Community Colleges*, no. 49:1–5. San Francisco: Jossey-Bass.

Floyd, C. E. 1985. *Faculty participation in decision making: Necessity or luxury?* Washington, D.C.: Association for the Study of Higher Education/ERIC Clearinghouse on Higher Education.

Gulassa, C. 1989. *Collaborative governance in the Foothill/DeAnza Community College District: Management report 1988–89*. ERIC Document no. ED 322 965. Sacramento: Association of California Community College Administrators.

Harrison, W. L. 1985. Importance of planning institutional goals in the community college and extent of their congruence among constituents. *Community/Junior College Quarterly of Research and Practice* 9(3):187–95.

Ladwig, D. J. 1983. *Determining the effectiveness and evaluating the implementation process of a quality/performance circles system model to assist in institutional decision making and problem solving at Lakeshore Technical Institute*. ERIC Document no. ED 231 452. Ft. Lauderdale, Fla.: Nova University.

Likert, R. 1967. *The human organization*. New York: McGraw-Hill.

McBride, R. J., and S. Devine. 1987. *CAS works!* ERIC Document no. ED 290 523. Austin, Texas: National Conference on Teaching Excellence.

Millett, J. D. 1978. *New structures of campus power: Success and failures of emerging forms of institutional governance*. San Francisco: Jossey-Bass.

Moretz, H. L. 1983. *Quality circles in education: Final report*. ERIC Document no. ED 237 168. Charlotte, N.C.: Central Piedmont Community College.

Mortimer, K. D., and T. R. McConnell. 1978. *Sharing authority effectively: Participation, interaction, and discretion*. San Francisco: Jossey-Bass.

O'Hara, L. F. 1990. Faculty self-esteem: The 4th governance paradigm. *Community/Junior College Quarterly of Research and Practice* 14(2):149–54.

Pfeffer, J. 1981. *Power in organizations*. Marshfield, Mass.: Pitman Publishing.

Pfeffer, J., and G. R. Salancik. 1978. *The external control of organization: A resource dependence perspective*. New York: Harper and Row.

Richardson, R. C. 1976. The future shape of governance in the community college. *Community and Junior College Journal* 46(6):52–59.

Sagini, M. M. 1991. Planning models: The challenge of strategic imperatives in higher education. *Community/Junior College Quarterly of Research and Practice* 15(1):71–85.

Schuster, J. H., et al. 1989. *Governing tomorrow's campus: Perspectives and agendas*. New York: American Council on Education/Macmillan Publishing Company.

Selznick, P. 1957. *Leadership in administration*. New York: Harper and Row.

Silverman, M. 1987. *Models of organization and governance at the community college*. ERIC Document no. ED 284 606. Princeton, N.J.: Mid-Career Fellows Program.

Slaughter, R., and L. R. Broussal. 1986. *Collegiality and the California community colleges*. ERIC Document no. ED 277 414. Sacramento: California Association of Community Colleges.

Snyder, W. F. 1989. *Evidences of faculty centered management style*. ERIC Document no. ED 305 964. Washington, D.C.: American Association of Community and Junior Colleges 69th Annual Convention.

Stetson, N. E. 1990. *Collegial governance at College of Marin: A governmental model*. ERIC Document no. ED 318 494. Sacramento: California Association of Community Colleges.

Sturtz, A. J. 1984. *Institutional planning as a participative process: A community college self study.* ERIC Document no. ED 258 653. Albany, N.Y.: 11th Annual Conference of the Northeast Association for Institutional Research. October 13.

Vail, E. 1988. *Energizing an institution for excellence.* ERIC Document no. ED 303 194. Riverside, Calif.: Riverside Community College.

Walker, R. and J. Polythress. 1983. *Creating and implementing a faculty senate for a multi-campus community college.* ERIC Document no. ED 279 358. Dunwoody, Ga.: DeKalb Community College.

Weick, K. E. 1976. Educational organizations as loosely coupled systems. *Administrative Science Quarterly* 21(1):1–19.

Wilkinson, T. 1989. *Empowering employees for a new century.* ERIC Document no. ED 305 102. Washington, D.C.: American Association of Community and Junior Colleges 69th Annual Convention.

Linked in Governance: The Role of the President and the Board of Trustees in the Community College

Charles J. Carlsen and Robert Burdick

The literature on community colleges swells with monographs, articles, essays, and books on the relationship of boards of trustees and college presidents. Lacking, however, is a concise and universally accepted set of expectations and behaviors for those involved in this aspect of college governance. The mix of personalities—both of individuals and of institutions—ensures that styles of interactions will vary greatly.

Add into the equation the ever-changing pressures surrounding higher education, and the result is a situation that is far from static. Balancing short-term needs with long-term survival is a tricky proposition in any enterprise. In the community college business, then, those who ostensibly hold the reins of leadership—the board of trustees and the president—must demonstrate exceptional levels of flexibility and cooperation while making practical decisions, all the while allowing for occasional flashes of insight, inventiveness, and creativity.

There is general agreement that boards should operate in the realm of policy, and presidents in the realm of administration. But there are widely divergent styles of board-president management as well as a variety of approaches to policymaking and administrative activities. These differences have their origins in the history of lay governing boards, and they have excited no small amount of debate over the years.

Thorsten Veblen, writing in 1918, described trustees as quasi-literate businessmen—cunning, parochial, and meddling. Veblen said the life of a businessman prepares him neither to understand nor to respect disinterested scholarship (Foresi 1974). More recently, Clark Kerr accused trustees of being unduly enamored of trivial campus details (Alfred and Rush, 1985, 9). Trustees have enjoyed their moments as well. College administrators are decried for their rampant permissiveness, deteriorating academic standards, and molasses-like management processes. To add to the confusion, faculty often complain about lay governance and professional administrators in the same breath. Both are seen as unnecessary to the academic mission. Zoglin puts this in perspective:

Once upon a time, so the story goes, university faculties were self-governing communities of scholars, dispensing knowledge to the eager students who came to it at their feet. Only recently have lay governing boards and professional administrators insinuated themselves into the Garden of Eden, corrupting the natural relationship between teacher and student. The board of trustees is the arch-villain, a diabolical creation of American captains of industry bent upon running the university like a corporation. (1976, 9)

Zoglin notes further that, though this may be a widely held perception among faculty, it is not an accurate one. Cowley (in Zoglin 1976) has traced the history of lay governing boards and professional administration to as far back as the middle ages. Lay governing boards of the first American universities were far more autocratic and invasive than the usually benign and somewhat distant boards of today's major universities.

Lay governing boards originated in Italy in the thirteenth century, when university faculties petitioned local governments for charters and financial support. With financial support, however, came a measure of local control through the lay governing board.

Throughout the Renaissance, many European universities remained under ecclesiastical control, but many others, including those in Switzerland, Holland, and Denmark, adopted the Italian model of lay governance. This model worked its way north to Scotland and Ireland by the sixteenth century and essentially was exported to America with the early colonists (Zoglin 1976).

In 1642 Harvard's overseers forbade its scholars from traveling to another town without first receiving permission, fearing they might come in contact with ideas and viewpoints contrary to what the overseers wanted taught at Harvard. Since institutions in the colonial period were church sponsored, the question of what would be taught loomed large in the minds of these original trustees, many of whom were clergy (Zwingle 1980).

Many others were lay elders of the church. These appointive boards tended to administer every aspect of the academic endeavor, deciding what would be taught, how it would be taught, who would teach it, and who could learn it!

In the early part of the nineteenth century, as states began to charter their own universities, many also adopted the lay governing board model. Some states, such as Michigan, made a special effort to insulate their universities from the political process by adopting constitutional provisions that ensured a separation of the governing board from the legislature (Zwingle 1980). These boards also played a central role in administering their institutions.

Until the latter part of the nineteenth century, the growth of American colleges and universities was relatively slow. When the Morrill Act of 1862 established the system of land grant colleges, university enrollment was fewer than 50,000 students. However, the business expansion following the Civil War produced an unprecedented increase in institutions and enrollments, and the role and scope of the university began to change (Nason 1982).

During this period, boards began to be drawn from the ranks of business and the professions. Boards for public and private universities typically were appointive rather than elective. However, board governance of public universities in this period became more corporate and less paternalistic even though they continued to exercise a rigorous control over most aspects of their institutions.

At the same time, colleges and universities were becoming more complex, with many new disciplines and professional schools that reflected the economic and scientific revolutions occurring in post–Civil War America. Eventually, this growing complexity led to a decrease in the importance of the role of governing boards accompanied by the rise of strong presidents.

"Growth in size, in the range of instruction and in the problems of management created a need for more administration than busy trustees had time or talent to provide." Consequently, trustees began to delegate these functions to presidents. This process came about relatively soon as universities began to expand, but it was never fully realized in some institutions (Nason 1982, 4).

The turn of the century saw the rise of the great university presidents and the formation of the American Association of University Professors (AAUP). These two developments were reflections of the changes occurring in institutions of higher education. Presidents whose boards previously had attended to every administrative detail now found themselves faced with the task of the daily administration of increasingly specialized and decentralized institutions. Accompanying the increased responsibilities was an increase in power and visibility for chief administrators.

Faculty also were being asked to shoulder more responsibility—to hire new faculty in their respective disciplines and to decide on matters of curriculum. This new power led faculty to an increasing sense of professionalization. By forming the AAUP, faculty were simultaneously responding to and leading a movement that would result in new management orientation for American universities—a decentralized, collegial model of shared governance.

As part of this collegial model, university trustees turned their attention more toward a growing network of external constituencies and to pondering the long-range mission of their institutions. As the scope of education broadened, the role of the trustee became more that of a buffer to mediate among the various forces affecting the operation of the institution.

It was about this time that the first two-year colleges began to appear in the United States, and even though lay governance boards were beginning to move away from the day-to-day operations of institutions, their tradition of hands-on management would affect the fledgling two-year college movement.

When William Rainey Harper of the University of Chicago reorganized his institution in 1890 by separating the upper division, which he called the "university college," from the lower division, or "academic college," he launched the initiative that evolved into the American junior college (Foresi 1974). Harper considered the first two years of college more appropriately an extension of high school because of similarities in curriculum and teaching methods. He thought that by making the junior college a capstone to the high school experience, it would increase educational opportunity for many (Gabert 1991).

When the American Association of Junior Colleges held its second meeting in 1922, there were seventy public junior colleges in the United States. In 1907 California had created the first separate junior college districts, and by 1930 nearly half of the nation's public junior college students were in that state. Many of these early junior colleges were extensions of local high schools under the aegis of local school boards. Some states, such as Kansas in 1917, passed enabling acts that provided for local elections to approve the creation of independent junior colleges as well as special taxing districts to support them. In addition, locally elected boards of trustees were established (Gabert 1991). Since they were controlled locally, these boards were free to respond to community needs and to finance programs locally to meet those needs.

In 1947 the Commission on Higher Education, established by President Truman, endorsed the concept of college education for the general public. Public community colleges were promoted as an important vehicle for achieving this goal. In 1957 a follow-up commission, established by President Eisenhower, similarly concluded that community colleges provided the best way to meet the nation's critical need for higher education. These commissions paved the way for the growth of the community college movement in the 1960s (Gabert 1991).

By 1970 there were about 850 community junior colleges; by 1980 there were more than 1,000 with a total credit enrollment approaching 4 million. By 1990, the number of colleges was about the same, but enrollments had risen to more than 5 million, with another 4 million in noncredit programs. Over the next ten years, the number of institutions is not expected to change significantly, but enrollments are expected to be 20 percent higher (Gabert 1991).

Community college governance has evolved from both the public higher education model and the local school board model. Many community college boards are popularly elected, responsible to the citizens who voted to establish the community colleges. Community college boards differ from school boards in that they tend to be elected at-large from the community rather than by district. Those elected must understand the unique character of higher education, exercise a direct fiduciary responsibility for the public, and serve multiple constituencies. Some states have placed their community colleges within a state system of governance. These centralized models tend to usurp local authority and diminish presidential authority.

An average board numbers seven, and trustees usually serve staggered terms. Community college boards are generally defined as either "policy boards" or "working boards" (Hall 1981), and the management style of a board can affect the type of president chosen. A strong working board probably would not name a charismatic leader president. A strong policy board, on the other hand, just might seek out such an individual.

It is important to note, however, that boards are rarely all of one or the other type. Rather, they tend to be fluid. As trustees are replaced in the election cycle, the tone and orientation of a board can change. Consequently, most presidents and boards operate in a continuing state of flux that requires great flexibility on the part of all concerned. It is this dynamic that sets the tone for analysis of contemporary board-president relationships.

While there is general agreement that the board should influence policy, leaving administrative matters to the president, it is not always that simple. Obviously, boards set policy, operating on authority from state statute. But individual trustees can also be assets to presidents in administrative matters. Presidents can capitalize on board members' experiences by asking them their opinion as individuals on problems or concerns. This approach carries with it, however, both advantages and risks. A president seeking a trustee's advice on an administrative matter may indeed gain insight on that matter. But in offering that insight, the trustee may become convinced that the advice should be followed, and a president may inadvertently be encouraging involvement in administrative procedures.

Even so, the varying skills and abilities brought to their duties by trustees can provide a wise president a multitude of strengths upon which to capitalize. In some cases, substantial staff must be invested to orient and educate trustees so that they can deliberate effectively about the issues facing the institution. Educating board members about the institution does not necessarily encourage them to become overly involved in daily administrative matters. Quite the opposite. Well-informed trustees are likely to think more broadly and creatively about the institution's needs.

Successful strategies for presidents and trustees who value well-run public meetings include the following:

1. Identify potential problems by going over the monthly board agenda in some detail before each meeting. Advance discussion permits trustees to ask specific questions and minimizes public miscommunication. Meetings that flow smoothly result from preparation and planning.

2. Even when extensive information is provided in advance, the outcome of an administrative recommendation can remain uncertain. Successful trustees and presidents will postpone action on a proposal if it appears that there is confusion or dissention.

3. A good word for a job well done is as much appreciated by a president as it is a trustee. Successful trustees and presidents recognize accomplishments.

4. Master planning is, without question, one of the most important areas of board-president involvement. Regular sessions held throughout the year permit the board to engage in the planning process. By focusing on long-range issues, presidents and trustees add to their understanding of the institution and cement their partnership.

Another key to establishing effective board-president relationships is identifying common linkages to the community. Trustees and presidents begin to recognize how much they have in common when such linkages are brought into focus. Trustees, especially elected ones, serve as lightning rods for community opinion. So do presidents, although the input may come from different constituent groups.

Today's community college operates in a climate of intense public scrutiny, and it is subject to pressure from a wide range of special interests. Among the primary constituent groups of a typical community college may be its students, alumni, staff and faculty, taxpayer groups, community-based organizations, elected officials, business leaders, donors, and advisory committees. Each of these groups has its own agenda, and all must be heard if the college is to operate successfully.

Recognizing that presidents and boards alike must respond to requests, demands, and pressures, a strong communication link is essential if the institution is to be served effectively. A climate of trust between presidents and boards is a primary component of good communication. There are a number of ways that such an atmosphere of trust can be fostered:

1. Stay in touch by phone. Two or three calls a week are not uncommon. The subject can be college business, but it does not have to be. Sometimes a call is important just to keep communication lines open.
2. Provide reports on all issues of board concern. Brief, to-the-point communiques can be used to identify key administrative recommendations.
3. Allow access to staff. One-on-one sessions with key staff members are particularly effective in helping to build trust and confidence.
4. Recognize the personal agendas of trustees. Whether they be political or altruistic, effective presidents identify such ambitions and help trustees achieve their goals within the context of useful college activities.
5. Be patient. Presidents and trustees who exercise patience with each other will succeed in the public arena. Allow a time for transition, orientation, and learning about institutional processes.
6. Be truthful.

Other cooperative strategies can enhance and strengthen president-board relationships. Attendance at college events promotes visibility of the board, obviously, and demonstrates interest on the part of trustees. They may also participate on other deliberative bodies within the district, demonstrating the institution's interest and presence in the workings of the community. College advisory boards can also benefit from an active interest by trustees. When civic leaders, board members, and presidents work together, the college gains a powerful alliance.

Finally, some boards and presidents find retreats to be helpful in the planning/budgeting process. And those who cooperate in defining goals and far-reaching objectives extend the possibilities of their institutions beyond what they may imagine individually.

The lay governing board model has been effective in directing America's mass expansion of higher education, Nason (1982) argues, because there has been a climate of trust and consensus on the part of the major constituencies: faculty, administration, students, the public, legislatures, and alumni. Lay boards have helped insulate colleges and universities from the inherent conflicts of these constituencies. However, those who look to the future suggest that these and other, better strategies will be necessary to meet the political and economic challenges to education in the next century.

One continuing concern is the search for highly qualified trustees. Writing in 1969, Rauh warned that the remarkable growth of community colleges coupled with turnover on boards would present a potential shortage of qualified and effective trustees. He cited statistics compiled by the Association of Governing Boards of Colleges and Universities estimating the need for as many as 1,200 new trustees a year for community colleges. This presents a problem because most community colleges serve relatively contained communities, which limits the number of qualified trustees available.

Given, then, the need for a large number of trustees, a limited area from which to draw them, and a difficult trustee assignment, the first special problem of junior college trusteeship is to find an adequate number of qualified trustees—especially trustees whose backgrounds are sophisticated enough to recognize and honor the subtle relationship between trustee and management. (Rauh 1969)

Rauh's prediction has proved correct. The search for highly qualified trustees has never been more intense. Attracting and retaining outstanding board members is a priority of presidents and institutions nationwide. Without continuing excellent leadership, the local control of many community colleges may be imperiled in a restive political arena and regressive tax climate.

The increasingly complex nature of trusteeship and the inherent ambiguity in the position have led to a dualism in the role:

They [trustees] have formal power over education, but are actually cautious in the exercise of their power. They are homogeneous in social composition, but often unpredictable in behavior. They are concerned about receiving a representative sample of opinion from faculty and students, yet they shun direct representation of those groups on the board. They are omnipotent in policy-making, yet often reluctant to go beyond policy review. (Dominguez, in Alfred and Rush 1985, 7)

Zoglin, quoting from Mason, has noted that boards alone are in a position to establish ''some kind of balance or equilibrium between the needs of the social system which supports the institution and the needs of the individuals within the institution'' (1976, 90). Boards, in other words, must operate in the midst of conflicting societal opinions and pressures that attempt to influence how they do their jobs. The ability to withstand these pressures, do the homework, and make intelligent decisions is found in few individuals.

The fact that most trustees must stand for popular election further complicates the issue. "It is naive to assume that higher education is nonpolitical" (Richardson, Blocker, and Bender 1972, 40). "All of public education has become fair game in the political arena." Add into the equation the decidedly antipolitical mood in the nation, and the stress of having to campaign may further discourage those who would serve.

Trustees are acutely aware of this new public involvement in higher education. In an introductory comment to the Association of Community College Trustees (ACCT) Major Pronouncement: Common Concerns among Community College Presidents and Trustees, Jasiek wrote:

I think administrators can expect greater accountability to Boards and Boards, in turn, to the educational and community families because of the shrinking resources utilized to support education across the land. This is only part of the social evolution, and as the demands of all segments of society become more expansive there will be greater scrutiny of dollars expended in all areas of social activity. Perhaps this is unpalatable, but it is most necessary for the survival of quality education for all. (Jasiek 1976, ii)

Presidents and trustees who take the time to view their relationships in the context of history and in a spirit of cooperation may develop the resiliancy, the flexibility, and the determination to forge ahead in this uncertain climate, knowing that there are no textbook answers to their struggle, only the will to see their colleges survive and succeed in meeting the ever-growing needs of society.

REFERENCES

Alfred, R. L., and P. D. Rush. 1985. *Emerging trustee roles in community college governance*. Annandale, Va.: Association of Community College Trustees.

Baird, J. M. 1977–78. The tools of boardsmanship. *Trustee Quarterly* (Winter):4.

Carlsen, C. J. 1988. *Making boards presidential assets*. Leadership Abstracts 1.2. Laguna Hills, Calif.: League for Innovation in the Community College.

Foresi, J., Jr. 1974. *Administrative leadership in the community college*. Jericho, N.Y.: Exposition Press.

Fryer, T. W., Jr., and J. C. Lovas. 1980. *Leadership in governance*. San Francisco: Jossey-Bass.

Gabert, G. 1991. *Community colleges in the 1990's*. Bloomington, Ind.: Phi Delta Kappa Educational Foundation.

Hall, R. A. 1981. *Challenge and opportunity: The board of trustees, the president and their relationship in community college governance*. Annandale, Va.: Association of Community College Trustees.

Heilbron, L. H. 1973. *The college and university trustee*. San Francisco: Jossey-Bass.

Jasiek, C. R. 1976. A comment by C. R. Jasiek in G. Fontelle, *An ACCT major pronouncement: Common concerns among community college presidents and trustees*. Washington, D.C.: Association of Community College Trustees.

Moore, W., Jr. 1971. *Blind man on a freeway*. San Francisco: Jossey-Bass.

Nason, J. W. 1982. The nature of trusteeship. Washington, D.C.: Association of Governing Boards of Universities and Colleges.

Rauh, M. A. 1969. *The trusteeship of colleges and universities*. New York: McGraw-Hill.

Richardson, R. C., Jr., C. E. Blocker, and L. W. Bender. 1972. *Governance for the two-year college*. Englewood Cliffs, N.J.: Prentice Hall.

Taylor, B. E. 1987. *Working effectively with trustees: Building cooperative campus leadership*. ASHE-ERIC Higher Education Report no. 2. Washington, D.C.: Association for the Study of Higher Education.

Vaughan, G. B. 1986. *The community college presidency*. New York: American Council on Education/McMillan.

Zoglin, M. L. 1976. *Power and politics in the community college*. Palm Springs, Calif.: ETC Publications.

Zwingle, J. L. 1980. Evolution of lay governing boards. In *Handbook of college and university trusteeship*, ed. R. T. Ingram and Associates, 14–26. San Francisco: Jossey-Bass.

Leadership Skills for Participative Governance

Susan B. Twombly and
Marilyn J. Amey

In the last several decades, participative forms of governance have captured the imagination and practice of U.S. organizations. Beginning with corporations and more recently extending to colleges and universities, various forms of participation have made their way into organizational practice. Participative governance is frequently identified as the cornerstone of the most successful businesses in the United States.

Means of involving organizational members in some aspects of decision making have long been evident in community colleges, but until recently, systematic attempts to create participatory governance have not been so widespread. In fact, community colleges have earned the reputation of being hierarchical, highly bureaucratic organizations. The widespread existence of unions on community college campuses has perhaps exacerbated this perception. However, as community colleges have matured, and ways of engaging in organizational renewal have been sought, much attention has turned to participative decision making. Much of the recent writing on governance in community colleges has, in fact, dealt with some form of participation whether called collaborative decision making, total quality management, or some other name (Palmer 1985). Judging from information available in the Educational Resources Information Clearinghouse, many community colleges are implementing participative forms of governance at some level.

Effective participative governance systems require effective leadership (Kanter 1983). This chapter reviews the most important skills necessary for effective leadership for participatory governance. Because most advocates of participation also note that participation is not a magic ticket to organizational success, we also review dilemmas of participation and the skills necessary to avoid the pitfalls. True participative governance requires not only that the right skills be employed, but also that the entire organization be "re-visioned," and so this chapter begins with a discussion of re-visioning the community college as an organization.

LEADERSHIP SKILLS NECESSARY FOR PARTICIPATIVE GOVERNANCE

In thinking about the leadership skills necessary for participative governance, it is necessary to engage in what Adrienne Rich calls re-visioning: "The act of looking back, of seeing with fresh eyes" (Kolodny 1985, 59). Re-visioning involves a reconceptualization of community colleges as organizations, a willingness to examine assumptions about leaders and leadership, and an openness to new definitions of the roles of collegiate members including, but not limited to, faculty and administrators. With this in mind, we can begin the process of identifying requisite skills for participative governance. In so doing, we note that many of the skills required may have the same labels as those required in any form of governance, but they may mean different activities and behaviors in a participative situation.

Re-visioning the Organization

The first step in the re-visioning process involves thinking differently about community colleges as organization in the 1990s and beyond. As an organization, each college goes through several developmental stages, from birth to growth to maturity to renewal or decline (Gardner 1986). At each stage of the organizational life cycle, different leadership strategies and skills may be required or emphasized (Twombly and Amey 1991). Many of these leadership skills can be approached in a more or less participative manner. As Hudgins (1990) observes, most community colleges have moved through the first three stages of the organizational life cycle and are now facing renewal or decline as mature colleges. Effective renewal requires the involvement and investment of members throughout the collegiate community and, therefore, provides opportunities for participative governance.

A second step in re-visioning the organization involves recognizing that the community college is more than a hierarchical structure and set of procedures. The organization is a collection of members—administrators, faculty, students, trustees, alumni, and so on—whose investment, commitment, energy, and activity are the keys to effectiveness and the accomplishment of goals. The means of capitalizing on that investment and maximizing efforts is tied directly to governance. As Gollattscheck defines it, governance is the accumulation of decision-making processes used to establish policies and procedures concerning mission, goals, and objectives; how the institution should be organized to achieve its missions, goals, and objectives; and how it operates on a day-to-day basis (1985, 88). In today's community colleges, there is a movement toward a form of governance that mandates active involvement in those decision-making processes by members at all levels. Stetson (1990) calls it collegial governance; Cross and Ravekes (1990) might call it collaborative governance. Regardless of the name, true participative governance begins with a need to rethink many of the traditional assumptions about what leadership is, about who and where leaders are situated in organizations, and about what leaders do.

Re-visioning Leadership and Leadership Roles

Most advocates of participative governance begin from the premise that leaders are found throughout organizations, not just in traditional positions of authority. For example, in most of the writings on participative governance, there is far less discussion of organizational structure and positions of power than there is of organizational climate and the affective side of college life. If we can move away from the concept of leadership as hierarchy, authority, and power, we can move to one of leadership derived from connectedness and collaboration (Cross and Ravekes 1990). Leadership becomes interactive rather than top-down and unidimensional. "Leadership is not simply a matter of what a leader does but of what occurs in the relationship between a leader and others. . . . Leaders both shape and are shaped by their constituents" (Bolman and Deal 1991, 409). Leaders *help* to establish vision, standards, and organizational direction, and they are helped in this process by others in the college community. This process of mutual influence invites the use of new verbs and metaphors to capture the essence of leadership—weaver, cultivator, networking, and connecting (Amey and Twombly 1991).

When we view leadership as a process, we begin to focus on action and activity—leadership *for* something, leadership as the ability to accomplish something (Sergiovanni 1991, 134). Leffel et al. (1991) suggest that a focus on process is paramount to product quality and that such an emphasis requires the participation of everyone involved. Shifting organizational perspective from product to process also suggests a different approach to problem solving. In a product mode, leaders might look at substance issues alone for answers to problems, assessing quality and measuring institutional effectiveness. Deegan (1985) contends that community college leaders in the 1990s need to broaden their scope to include a comprehensive, integrated analysis of issues, going beyond outcomes assessment to include process analysis as well.

If leadership is a process instead of an outcome, and if leaders can exist throughout the community college, we must re-vision the roles of leaders. Leaders at different organizational levels may exhibit different leadership skills and be involved in different leadership activity to varying degrees (Kouzes and Posner 1987). This perspective allows for leadership to be enacted in new ways apart from those actions traditionally associated with college presidents. It allows college members to draw upon personal strengths, contributing to a leadership compendium. Part of re-visioning leadership then becomes the development of organizational partnerships and the pooling of members' talents and strengths in creative new ways (Lee 1989). Lee calls the leader a catalyst; Bolman and Deal (1991) use the word facilitator. In both cases, the focus of the role is not to get what the leader wants, but to empower others to achieve their organizational vision and goals. As facilitator/catalyst, the leader is able to foster high degrees of ownership and commitment to institutional objectives, and the tasks of organizational renewal can more easily be accomplished.

Communicating

The ability to communicate effectively has always been considered an important leadership skill. In participative governance, communication becomes particularly crucial since communication comes from and moves in all directions, often apart from formal administrative hierarchies (Anthony 1989; Gollattscheck 1985). As a result, the process of communicating becomes as important as the information being disseminated. Effective communicators have command of symbolic language (Bolman and Deal 1991). They paint word pictures, weave metaphors, and enable others to see and hear what is of value (Kouzes and Posner 1987). They repeat college myths, tell community stories, and participate in institutional rituals (Sergiovanni 1991). Aspects of symbolic communication are central to effective leadership and to maintaining the commitment and consensus that are the foundation of effective participative governance. This is a change from a primary emphasis on communicating information and vision.

There is also a personal dimension to communication that is important in participative governance. One means of maintaining commitment is acknowledging the efforts and involvement of members. Recognition needs to be freely and openly exhibited (Leffel et al., 1991). Yet to give praise requires a certain sense of self-knowledge and comfort level with others. Argyris (in Asplund 1988) explains that leaders who reveal multiple aspects of their nature and encourage subordinates to reveal theirs are capable of solving the power dilemmas that often arise within collegiate organizations. Examples of such scenarios include how to be strong while acknowledging dilemmas around us and how to assert opinions without becoming dominant and stifling input from others. The result of self-disclosure can be a deeper sense of openness, one that affords a level of honesty in information, full and timely disclosure, absence of manipulation, and access to decision making for members (Fryer and Lovas 1991). All of these components, though not without risk, are important to the development of a sense of shared purpose and governance.

Empowering Others

In a review of the literature from 1975 to 1985, Palmer (1985) found that, although most community colleges spoke of participatory governance, they meant simply providing individuals opportunities to sit on institutional committees. Effective participative governance means far more than arraying adjunct committee appointments as mechanisms for involving college constituents. Instead, participation needs to be reconceptualized to mean empowerment. Empowering means not only seeking participation in decisions but also giving individuals the influence to get things done (Kanter 1983). Those closest to the problem and the impact of the decision need to be centrally involved in determining processes, making decisions, and assessing effectiveness (Anthony 1989; Kanter 1983; Sherr and Lozier 1991). Members throughout the college community need to be given responsibility for input and decision making, and the freedom to exercise it.

Consensus and Team Building

Re-visioning the roles of members within organizations, engaging in open and symbolic communication, and empowering others are all important foundations for the next three leadership skills: consensus and team building, motivating, and maintaining commitment.

Leffel et al. (1991) found that, although most collegiate managers may see themselves as part of an administrative team, most do not see themselves as part of a leadership team. As a result, they may never have learned the skills required to facilitate an effective team. Restructuring into teams by itself is not enough to foster participative governance. Old loyalties have deep roots, and institutional subcultures are hard to abandon. Building communities and effective teams requires the ability to articulate visions, goals, and ideals; to create functioning teams aligned with the pursuit of common goals; to assume team membership, which may not always mean team leadership; and to educate constituents about consensus building, teamwork, information sharing, and shared decision making. Learning environments for members need to be provided where people can learn how to work together and depend on each other as a team. Total quality management, for example, and its use of quality circles or teams, is both a learning opportunity for developing teams and a mechanism for maintaining them (DeCosmo, Parker, and Beverly 1991). Cloud (1986) defines quality circles in community colleges as workers from the same area who meet once a month to discuss problems, set goals, investigate causes, recommend solutions, and take corrective action whey they have the authority to do so. Emphasis is placed on consensus building and mutual respect even though the president retains ultimate responsibility (Gulassa 1989). Quality circles allow for creative problem solving, which, in turn, has positive consequences for the group.

Leaders need to change their perspective from ''if you choose the right team you get an effective organization'' to ''if you create a good organization, you will get an effective team'' (Asplund 1988). In participative governance, the effective team is like the larger college of which it is a part—one that encourages participation and ownership and appreciates differences. The most important assumption of the team is that input and expertise from all staff are valued (Anthony 1989). Leaders build teams with spirit and cohesion, and teams truly believe that they can make a difference. Involvement in effective teams has been found to improve the quality of decisions and to heighten a sense of trust among college members, and it is highly positively correlated to satisfaction with job security, a sense of belonging, self-esteem, a sense of autonomy, and opportunities for self-expression (Gulassa 1989; Palmer 1985).

Motivating

All colleges and universities have mission statements, but they are not often the rallying point for faculty, administrators, or staff (Winter 1991). As a result, leaders have long looked for ways of motivating members. As in other forms of governance, a key factor is knowing what motivates community members. Members have to know how they fit in the organization and why they are important. The particular answers may vary as a function of the college's stage in its organizational life cycle. Things that motivate members in a new, developing community college are likely not to be the same as those motivating members in a mature college. Sergiovanni suggests that for mature colleges, particularly in periods of declining resources, it is even more important to emphasize intrinsic reward structures as motivators. "What is rewarding gets done" (1991, 139). It is important for the leader to not only identify institutional values, but also to facilitate members' opportunities to participate in what is rewarding for them.

In addition to identifying intrinsic and extrinsic motivators for members of the community college, the leader can personally serve as a motivator. In part, this is due to the interactive and interdependent nature of participative governance. Leaders need to have personal commitment, passion, and care. They need to embody the best of institutional purposes (Sergiovanni 1991). Because of the interdependent relationships of members in this kind of governance situation, trust is essential and serves as its own motivator. This is especially true when trust is manifested through delegating, involvement in decision making, facilitating creativity and risk taking, and developing creative partnerships (Bolman and Deal 1991; Leffel et al., 1991). People are motivated by believing that the leader stands for and does what they believe in; in this way, motivating becomes leadership by example.

Maintaining Commitment

The importance of individual commitment to participative governance means that a lack of involvement can derail efforts to create a participative structure. Maintaining commitment in a participative system, therefore, is of paramount importance and may require more creativity on a leader's part than is required for other administrative forms. Musselwhite (1990) identifies at least three ways to gain commitment: get people involved in problem solving, lead through expertise or competence, and present a solution and let others implement it. Each of these is found in participative governance as in many other forms of governance. The difference is that participative governance emphasizes options one and two, and relies less often on option three. It is not enough for the leader to rely on the commitment and actions of a faithful few, however. The leader must find ways of bringing into the process as many members as possible, while keeping those informed who are not currently active. As Deegan (1985) has emphasized, the quality of the commitment to a decision is the most critical factor in the fate of any project, far more important than the quality of any given dimension of the decision itself.

Maintaining commitment has never been easy. In participative governance, it is not only paramount; it is a particularly creative and time-consuming enterprise. Commitment is retained by inducing clarity in communication, consensus and team building, and shared purpose and meaning. Leaders manage meaning in their colleges by knowing what is of value to members and by reinforcing those values, often through symbolic communication (Sergiovanni 1991).

Balancing Structure and Autonomy

Perhaps one of the most difficult aspects of implementing participative governance is discovering how to balance structure and authority. Few authors or practitioners suggest complete abdication of decision-making responsibility by presidents or senior administrators. At the same time, most agree that partnerships in decision making, affording involvement, delegation of authority, and the power to implement, must be created among college members. Fryer and Lovas suggest that these partnerships require three important components: (1) responsibility and accountability are retained by organizational officials; (2) officials find means of incorporating the views and interests of everyone in their decisions; and (3) people are provided the means to achieve—they can decide, act, and react in serving their institution (1991, 149–50). The authors admit that implementing these three aspects of participative governance is not easy, but they insist that they are essential.

Part of the balance of structure and autonomy comes from two points made earlier. The first is that rethinking organizational structure to accommodate participative governance does not mean anarchy or abandonment of procedures for decision making. It may be even more important in this kind of governance setting to put various operating procedures and decision rules in writing so that those involved with implementation at all levels have sufficient support documentation. The second reminder related to balancing structure with autonomy is that keys to effective involvement are empowerment and communication. When members are adequately informed, when they share a common purpose and language, and when they have been actively involved in the conceptualizing of objectives, determining process, and problem solving, there is far less concern about delegating responsibility throughout the college.

Every organizational system requires maintenance. In participative governance, part of the maintenance of the system and the achievement of balance between structure and autonomy comes from the kind of culture that is created. If values are strongly held and shared, if teams are created that recognize their impact and importance to the college, and if communication is clear and consistent, the organization allows for greater autonomy because others will work in the best interests of the college. To this end, one of the greatest challenges and opportunities in a re-visioning of leadership is the role of the climate controller (Fryer and Lovas 1991, 14).

THE DILEMMAS OF PARTICIPATION

Participation is not necessarily "Ms. Lydia Pinkham's Organizational Elixir," however (Kanter 1983, 241). Participative governance will not magically solve all organizational problems or make a college immediately, or even necessarily more, successful (Bolman and Deal 1991). As important as knowing and employing the skills discussed above to implement participative governance successfully is recognizing the special dilemmas and pitfalls inherent in participation. It is through successful management of these participatory dilemmas that the effectiveness of participatory governance can be enhanced. The most extensive discussion of the dilemmas of participatory forms of decision making is found in Kanter's *The Change Masters* (1983). Because Kanter brings a wealth of organizational research and personal experience to bear on the problems of participation, the following discussion relies heavily on her analysis.

Participation poses five types of dilemmas that leaders must recognize and resolve: (1) the dilemmas of beginning, (2) dilemmas of structure and management, (3) dilemmas of issue choice, (4) dilemmas of teamwork, and (5) dilemmas of evaluation and expectations (Kanter 1983, 241–77). Each of these sets of dilemmas will be discussed in turn.

Beginning: Participation by Command

Clearly one of the most difficult dilemmas facing leaders is how to initiate participatory governance without ordering or commanding that it be done. This is especially true if the president or the board decides that faculty, administrators, and staff *will* create participatory decision-making processes; but the directors of these units, on whom the responsibility for success or failure depends, have little say in the matter. On the other hand, if a leader has to wait until every single staff member supports participatory governance it might take years to reach consensus. And so one of the key dilemmas facing leaders is finding a middle ground between imposing participatory governance and waiting for everyone to reach consensus. According to Kanter, it is almost inevitable that some people will be left out and others will feel left out of the decision to engage in participatory decision making. If, however, leaders can successfully engage colleagues through information, education, and pilot projects, participatory governance is likely to become accepted and owned by all and will eventually become part of the organization's culture. In a paper entitled "Laying the Groundwork for the Effective Implementation of Quality Circles in a Community College," Ruff (1984) stresses that failure to assess readiness and to provide adequate start-up and implementation planning are two of the reasons that quality circles, as a specific form of participatory decision making, fail. Midlands Community College avoided these two problems by assessing the climate and establishing an organizational renewal committee to plan the college's move to participatory governance.

A related dilemma facing leaders initiating participatory governance is doing it for the right reason. Beneficent presidents may view participation as a gift rather than a serious organizational process and expect faculty, administrators, and staff to be appreciative. This is what Kanter calls "The paternalism trap." Staff may be viewed as ungrateful if they are not as appreciative as expected, and the gift of participation may be withdrawn. Kanter says that "gifts keep the giver in control" (1983, 246).

The question of voluntariness is another dilemma faced by leaders. Should everyone have to participate? Should participation be mandatory or voluntary? If participation is voluntary, teams might not be representative. Although making participation mandatory is somewhat contradictory to the objectives of increasing participation, the nature of some decisions may not allow the leader the luxury of waiting until the right mix of people volunteer to participate. To resolve this dilemma, Kanter observes that it is important for leaders to establish criteria for representation and membership on decision-making teams. "On the one hand," she says, "it is important to handpick people for teams or task forces who have the skills and enthusiasm for carrying out the activities. On the other hand, it is equally important to avoid making participation simply another 'job' that people are assigned to" (247). In addition to avoiding coerced involvement on teams, leaders should avoid creating informal peer and administrative pressures that make it difficult for people to say "no" such as labeling nonparticipants negatively.

Structuring and Managing Participation

The goal of participative governance is to create decision-making processes in which faculty, administrators, and staff at all levels of the organization are empowered to participate in organizational decisions and to get things done. This suggests that traditional hierarchical organizational structures and reporting lines will be replaced with flat organizational structures in which power and responsibility are spread among all staff. However, for participative governance to work effectively, several dilemmas of structure must be addressed: the need for structure, delegation, reporting and accountability, and time.

Without some structure, people and groups may flounder unproductively. "It is important to establish for people, from the beginning, the ground rules and boundary conditions under which they are working: what can they decide, what can't they decide'' (Kanter 1983, 248). Participatory forms of governance do not serve as a substitute for leadership. Participation works best when there is clear leadership in the organization. The potential benefits of participation do not accrue in situations in which everyone has equal, but little, influence to get things done. Rather, successful participatory systems are dependent on empowering more people in the organization though effective leadership (1983, 249).

The opposite of having no structure is overstructuring. One of the ways this happens is by imposing a prepackaged set of formulas and rules just because these formulas have worked elsewhere. Barry Stein has referred to this as the "appliance" approach (in Kanter 1983, 249): buying a complete program or model, bringing it home, and plugging it in. Likewise there is a danger of overstructuring, precluding faculty and administrators from participating in important decisions. Quality circles are a form of participatory decision making particularly prone to this problem. Because total quality management and quality circles are relatively new to higher education, colleges may be inclined to "purchase" and import the quality circle notion from sources outside of the institution rather than educate organizational members thoroughly on the necessary concepts and skills (249).

This is an important consideration for community colleges since much of the recent literature on participatory decision making in this sector focuses specifically on quality circles as a means of increasing participation. In order for quality circles to work in community colleges, Cloud (1986) and Ruff (1984) suggest that the concepts must be understood fully by the institutional initiators. Comprehending the concepts will prevent replacing one structure with another for which there is no real understanding.

A second structural or leadership dilemma is that delegation through creation of participatory groups does not mean abdication of responsibilities for monitoring and supporting teams (e.g., Kanter 1983; Cloud 1986; Ruff 1984; Needham 1991). Although it is most common for senior level administrators to initiate participatory governance (Needham 1991), total quality management has also been initiated by enthusiastic mid-level managers (e.g., Cloud 1986; Ruff 1984). In this case, it is important that these initiators seek and develop the involvement and support of senior level administrators. The bottom line is that leadership and guidance do not decline in importance when forms of participatory decision making are implemented. Leaders must keep problems moving toward solution (Keyser 1988).

A third, and related, leadership dilemma is that of reporting and accountability (Kanter 1983). Interest in knowing results is an important way of demonstrating that the leader has not abdicated responsibility and interest. Absence of reporting requirements can suggest to participants that an issue is not sufficiently significant for them to waste their time. Although reporting and accountability are important, an atmosphere of inspection should be avoided.

Finally, participatory forms of decision making are time-consuming additions to already full faculty and administrative schedules. In order for participation to work, the time required must be provided and legitimized so as to not interfere with normal duties and responsibilities (Moretz 1983; Keyser 1988).

Issue Choice

Leaders must carefully choose the issues around which participation will occur at various levels in the college (Palmer 1985). As Kanter notes, "A common assumption by managers in debates about participation is that people want to be involved in the 'big decisions' about the overall management of their organization or other sweeping concerns" (1983, 253). Some research has shown that participation is more likely to be successful if people are involved in the decisions that most affect them (Kanter 1983; Palmer 1985; Keyser 1988). This poses a dilemma for college presidents who may be interested in initiating broad-based participation in the major decisions facing the college. One of the difficulties inherent in tackling large issues is that, in order to keep faculty, administrators, and staff invested in participation, some results have to be produced. Too much talk and too little action are likely to leave people frustrated and feeling that they are wasting their time. The smaller and more focused the issue, the more likely participants are to observe the results (Kanter 1983; Palmer 1985; Keyser 1988).

There also may be a temptation to assume that participation is itself sufficient reward to keep people motivated (Kanter 1983). Once the novelty of participation wears off, some sort of compensation must be provided in order to maintain participation at high levels. Colleges are seemingly particularly susceptible to this trap. After all, colleges already involve many faculty, administrators, and staff in decision making through committees for which the only reward is self-satisfaction and a line on one's vita. If participation is to become an institutional philosophy, involving as many people throughout the organization as possible, some sort of formal reward and recognition must be established at the beginning.

Teamwork

Teamwork is the essence of participatory governance. Several kinds of inequalities, about which leaders must be aware and be able to manage, can disrupt the team concept. These six common inequalities, familiar to anyone who has ever worked in groups, take on added importance in a truly participative governance environment: (1) "the seductiveness of hierarchy" (Kanter, 256), (2) a knowledge gap, (3) differential personal abilities, (4) seniority, (5) team politics, and (6) "the myth of 'team' " (Kanter, 262). It is quite common in groups for those with lower status or less knowledge to defer to those with more information, higher status, or greater seniority. Thus, normal organizational hierarchical decision-making patterns may be replicated in the team because those who participate most are already those who have highly visible roles in decision making. Therefore training in institutional and group process knowledge is essential for participation to work to its fullest (Ruff 1984; Needham 1991).

Add to these dilemmas, the normal politics of teamwork. Anyone who works in a college setting knows well the political factors that enter into decision making: Do gains from dropping self-interest in the name of cooperation outweigh the costs? Does an interest group form to dominate the interests of the group? What historical or contextual factors carry over to the group? Teamwork does not necessarily mean democratic decision making will prevail. Often these inequalities are accepted, maybe even valued in the interest of task completion, as part of normal committee and task force work in colleges. However, if the goal of participatory governance is to improve the effectiveness of the college by empowering faculty, administrators, and staff at all levels of the organization to participate creatively in decision making, the leaders must attempt to avoid or counteract team inequalities. This is sometimes made more difficult by what Kanter (1983, 262) calls the "myth of the 'team.' " Because teams can feel that they must act as if they are working perfectly as a team, their members may not be able or willing to admit and deal with potential problems.

Also, leaders must be aware that there are some things that teams do not do well. Although teams are frequently used to make decisions about program cuts in colleges, staff selections, and even promotion and tenure, teams are generally not in the best position to fire people, for example.

If participation has been introduced by senior administrators, there will probably be many teams working on various problems throughout the college, and the president, or his or her delegate, will coordinate and monitor the activities of these teams. Participation is also introduced by mid-level managers in isolated units on campus (Needham 1991). In either case, but particularly in the latter case, the activities of the teams must be linked to the activities of the entire college. Several important problems must be managed in order for this to happen successfully.

One of the inevitable problems is that of turnover. Good people leave, taking valuable experience and knowledge with them. Although this provides an opportunity for new people to get involved, it is sometimes difficult for new team members to join. This is particularly true if teams have been working long or well enough together to develop a team spirit. Newcomers, latecomers, or outsiders may be put off by group enthusiasm, and, perhaps more important, the group may lose time and momentum in bringing the new members up to speed. A more damaging situation can occur if the newcomer has the power to undercut the gains made by the previous work of the team (Kanter 1983). This discussion assumes that those leaving belong to the faculty, administration, and staff. There appears to be little discussion in the literature about what happens to participatory governance if the president, or another key leader, leaves the college.

Turnover raises the important question of decision repetition. That is, does a group rehash previous decisions when new members join the team? Because constant rehashing would be unproductive and dissatisfying to longtime participants, Kanter (1983) suggests that some decisions be "fixed" so that there is no need to remake them every time turnover occurs. If the benefits of participation are to be enhanced, then continuity and fixed, cumulative decisions must be balanced by the new: new people with new ideas and changes in the organizational context (Keyser 1988).

Teams can also become so enthusiastic about their own work that they lose sight of the larger organizational goals or even unintentionally work against them. Also team activities are often related to each other; consequently, the work of related teams needs to be coordinated. Moreover, a unit may have difficulty adopting plans developed by another team. The work of teams may "step on the toes" of administrators or unions (Keyser 1988). Those who have written about participative governance in community colleges have acknowledged the administrative resistance problem that must be avoided, but surprisingly they have not discussed the role of unions in participative decision making. Although some research has suggested that unions do not negatively affect faculty governance processes, such as senates, the relationship of unions to truly participative systems is unknown. These kinds of problems reinforce the earlier point that leaders cannot abdicate responsibilities for monitoring participatory processes. Rather they must be actively involved in managing participation (Needham 1991; Keyser 1988). Ruff (1984) goes so far as to suggest a need for a special office on campus to monitor quality circles. This may be an appropriate strategy in some circumstances, but the president of the college is more likely to be in the best position to monitor participation.

Finally, Kanter (1983) notes that it is as important to plan for the death of some groups and teams as it is to plan for the birth of others. One of the objectives of participatory governance is organizational renewal. This renewal cannot occur if teams become entrenched and fixed. She also notes that the level of intensity required of teamwork cannot constantly be maintained and that leaders must accept and plan for downtime (1983, 270).

Evaluation and Expectations

One set of dilemmas remains: evaluation and expectations. Participation will not create an organizational utopia. Social science research has shown, that satisfaction is a more likely outcome than increased performance (Kanter 1983, 273; Palmer 1985). Furthermore, in the beginning, a college may not have sufficient experience and knowledge to engage fully in participative decision making. As human resources are developed, a surplus of knowledge and experience may result, creating a need for leaders to engage in activities to keep participants challenged and to use knowledge productively.

Participatory governance will not automatically solve problems of gender and ethnic imbalance. Two aspects of this expectation merit discussion. First, although participatory models of governance and decision making are often linked with women's personality and style (e.g., Cross and Ravekes 1990), participation should not be viewed as a feminist agenda or a "women's only" form of governance. We have argued elsewhere, however, that because of societal stereotypes of women and minorities, images of leadership inherent in participatory governance are more accepting of women as viable leaders (Amey and Twombly 1991; Twombly and Amey 1991). The skills required of leadership for effective participative governance are not gender or ethnic specific and can be used by men and women of any race or ethnicity. Second, participatory forms of governance alone will not bring more women and minorities into a college nor will participation ensure, for some of the reasons mentioned above, that women and minorities in the organization will be full participants. Participative governance may, however, provide increased opportunities for women and minorities already holding positions in a college to become significantly involved.

Finally, there is what Keyser (1988) calls the encore problem: What is to be done when the initial enthusiasm wanes or when staff appetites for participation are whetted and there is a desire to take on larger tasks?

Some dilemmas of participation are specific to colleges (Keyser 1988). For example, colleges already have numerous ways for staff to become involved. Leaders must find effective ways of bringing these existing committees into the participative governance structure. In addition, according to Moretz (1983), college faculty, in particular, are prone to engage in too much philosophizing and not enough action. She notes further that the typical college calendar with semester breaks can disrupt team momentum.

CONCLUSION

Thomas Cronin (1987) once observed that virtually anything that can be said about leadership can be denied, disproven, and refuted. After reviewing the literature on participative governance, it seems possible to come to the same conclusion. Advocates speak highly of the value of inclusive decision making for increased commitment and motivation; critics bemoan the time involved in trying to reach consensus, its inapplicability to many of the real life decisions that are required in a collegiate setting, and the difficulty with maintaining commitment without results. Proponents of participative governance stress the merits of empowerment and team building for increasing organizational effectiveness; cynics argue that authority needs to be maintained and that teams only replicate the inherent hierarchical relationships and power structures that exist within the college. In any given community college setting, the realities of enacting participative governance may fall somewhere in between the two sides of the argument.

We have not presented a cookbook on participative governance but have tried to highlight the necessary leadership skills and the dilemmas of participation that leaders need to consider. Like governance models and administrative strategies that have come before it, participative governance is not a panacea for community colleges in the 1990s. It does not solve resource problems, make institutions more accessible to women and minorities, nor automatically make them more responsive to their environment. Unlike traditional bureaucratic structures or strategies such as management by objectives, participative governance does provide opportunities for working within current resource constraints and organizational limitations. It allows leaders to draw upon the talents and expertise of community college members for setting goals and objectives, solving problems, and creating alternatives. It affords to members throughout the college a different level of ownership, involvement, and commitment than many past approaches to governance. Perhaps most important, participative governance, and the principles that are basic to it, is a means for accomplishing the tasks of organizational renewal, which may be one of the greatest challenges facing community college leaders in the decade ahead.

REFERENCES

Amey, M. J., and S. B. Twombly. 1991. Re-visioning leadership in community colleges. *Review of Higher Education* 15:125–50.

Anthony, J. H. 1989. Therapeutic leadership. *Leadership Abstracts* 2:13.

Asplund, G. 1988. *Women managers: Changing organizational cultures*. New York: John Wiley.

Bolman, L. G., and T. E. Deal. 1991. *Reframing organizations: Artistry, choice, and leadership*. San Francisco: Jossey-Bass.

Cloud, R. C. 1986. Quality circles in the community college. ERIC Document no. ED 271 181.

Cronin, T. E. 1987. Leadership and democracy. *Liberal Education* 73 (2): 35–38.

Cross, C., and J. Ravekes. 1990. Leadership in a different voice. *American Association of Women in Community and Junior Colleges Journal*: 7–14.

DeCosmo, R. D., J. S. Parker, and M. A. Beverly. 1991. Total quality management goes to community college. In *Total quality management in higher education*, ed. L. A. Sherr and D. J. Teeter. New Directions for Institutional Research, no. 71:13–26. San Francisco: Jossey-Bass.

Deegan, W. L. 1985. Toward a new paradigm: Governance in a broader framework. In *Ensuring effective governance,* ed. W. L. Deegan and J. F. Gollattscheck. New Directions for Community Colleges, no. 49:73–82. San Francisco: Jossey-Bass.

Fryer, T. W., Jr., and J. C. Lovas. 1991. *Leadership in governance*. San Francisco: Jossey-Bass.

Gardner, J. W. 1986. *Tasks of leadership*. Leadership Paper no. 2. Washington, D.C.: Independent Sector.

Gollattscheck, J. F. 1985. Developing and maintaining governance. In *Ensuring effective governance,* ed. W. L. Deegan and J. F. Gollattscheck. New Directions for Community Colleges, no. 49:83–96. San Francisco: Jossey-Bass.

Gulassa, C. 1989. *Collaborative governance in the Foothill/De Anza Community College District*. In Management Report, no. 3. Cupertino, Calif.: Association of Community College Administrators.

Hudgins, J. L. 1990. Renewing a mature community college. *Leadership Abstracts* 3 (4).

Kanter, R. M. 1983. *The change masters*. New York: Simon and Schuster.

Keyser, J. S. 1988. Collaborative decision-making. *Leadership Abstracts* 1 (17).

Kolodny, A. 1985. A map for rereading: Gender and the interpretation of literary texts.

In *Feminist criticism: Essays on women, literature and theory,* ed. E. Showalter. New York: Pantheon Books.

Kouzes, J. M., and B. Z. Posner, 1987. *The leadership challenge.* San Francisco: Jossey-Bass.

Lee, M. 1989. Learning leadership. *Leadership Abstracts* 2 (20).

Leffel, L. G., et al. 1991. Assessing the leadership culture at Virginia Tech. In *Total quality management in higher education,* ed. L. A. Sherr and D. J. Teeter. New Directions for Institutional Research 71: 63–72. San Francisco: Jossey-Bass.

Moretz, L. 1983. Quality circles: Involvement, problem-solving and recognition. *Innovation Abstracts* 5 (12).

Musselwhite, C. 1990. Mysteries of leadership. *WKKF International Journal* Fall/Winter.

Needham, R. 1991. Total quality management: An overview. *Leadership Abstracts* 4 (10).

Palmer, J. 1985. Sources and information: Community college governance. In *Ensuring effective governance,* ed. W. L. Deegan and J. F. Gollattscheck. New Directions for Community Colleges 49: 97–108. San Francisco: Jossey-Bass.

Ruff, D. 1984. Laying the groundwork for effective implementation of quality circles in a community college. Paper presented at annual forum of the Association for Institutional Research, Fort Worth, Texas. ERIC Document no. ED 287 525.

Sergiovanni, T. J. 1991. *The principalship: A reflective practice perspective.* 2d ed. Boston: Allyn and Bacon.

Sherr, L. A., and G. G. Lozier. 1991. Total quality management in higher education. In *Total quality management in higher education,* ed. L. A. Sherr and D. J. Teeter. New Directions for Institutional Research 71: 3–12. San Francisco: Jossey-Bass.

Stetson, N. E. 1990. Collegial governance at College of Marin: A governmental model. In *Management Report,* no. 2. Cupertino, Calif.: Association of Community College Administrators.

Twombly, S. B., and M. J. Amey. 1991. Leadership in community colleges: Looking toward the second century. In *Higher education: Handbook of theory and research,* Vol. VII, ed. J. C. Smart. New York: Agathon Press.

Winter, R. S. 1991. Overcoming barriers to total quality management in colleges and universities. In *Total quality management in higher education,* ed. L. A. Sherr and D. J. Teeter. New Directions for Institutional Research 71: 53–62. San Francisco: Jossey-Bass.

Institutional Effectiveness as a Leadership and Management Process

Dwight A. Burrill

The mandate to assess the effectiveness of undergraduate learning in America was overwhelming in the decade of the 1980s, and its achievement is the challenge for the decade of the 1990s. Numerous writers have urged higher education to focus on outcomes (Richardson 1987, 40); provide meaningful, quantifiable data (Richardson 1985, 44); use relatively objective standards (McClenney and McClenney 1988, 54); and develop explicit statements of purpose (Ewell 1988). Ashcroft's 1986 report, which grew out of the 1985 National Conference of Governors, reflects the thoughts of elected officials at various levels. Ashcroft calls for ''systematic programs that use multiple measures to assess undergraduate learning.''

The response to this mandate has been the development and implementation of institutional effectiveness programs in a variety of community colleges and other institutions of higher education. Effectiveness, simply stated, means accomplishing a desired result. The Middle States Commission on Higher Education's framework for outcomes' assessment states, ''The deciding factor in assessing the effectiveness of any institution is evidence of the extent to which it achieves its goals and objectives'' (Simmons 1990, 6). Since goals and objectives in well-run organizations flow from the mission of the institution, an institution is effective if it accomplishes its primary purpose as stated in its mission. Conversely, to the extent that an institution fails to accomplish its stated purpose, it is less effective.

It is also clear that any discussion of institutional effectiveness must ultimately revolve around the issue of quality. The Southern Regional Education Board (SREB) states that the traditional measures of institutional effectiveness lack meaning (SREB 1987). According to the SREB, a ''quality gap'' exists in

American higher education. Quality entreats questions such as: How well are we doing? Are the outcomes we are trying to achieve desirable, valuable, and worthwhile? How can we do it better? This last question lies at the heart of the total quality management (TQM) movement.

This chapter focuses on two primary considerations. First, it provides a review of the framework of the institutional effectiveness programs as they have developed over the past decade. As such, this chapter devotes much of its attention to operational programs in lieu of purely scholarly and theoretical literature. Second, it demonstrates that the central concern with effectiveness naturally leads to a focus on quality and, from that point, to the issue of total quality management. Total quality management is likely to change the fundamental character of American higher education over the next decade.

THE FRAMEWORK OF INSTITUTIONAL EFFECTIVENESS

The National Alliance for Community and Technical Colleges provides a practical working definition for institutional effectiveness: "the process of articulating the mission of the college, setting goals, defining how the college and the community will know when the goals are being met and using the data to form assessments in an ongoing cycle of goal setting and planning" (Grossman and Duncan 1989, 5). This definition, as with many other process definitions of institutional effectiveness, contains profound questions that all higher education institutions are confronted with at least once every ten years, at the time of the review of their accreditation, and more often in well-managed organizations. Briefly stated these questions are (1) Why does this institution exist and what are its mission, goals, and objectives? (2) How does the institution know whether it is accomplishing its mission, goals, and objectives? and (3) What is the institution accomplishing in terms of mission, goals, and objectives? These questions, at the core of the issue of institutional effectiveness, speak to the processes of *planning, assessment,* and *outcomes,* respectively. Together these components form the basis for and describe the framework of the institutional effectiveness process.

Planning

Richardson asserts that institutional effectiveness begins with strategic planning (1988, 29). Hudgins also emphasizes the role of planning in the institutional effectiveness program at Midlands Technical College in Columbia, South Carolina (1990). Midlands Technical College defines planning as "a process which documents the intended purpose, direction and expected outcomes of the college and provides foresight for formulating policies, programs and services" (1990, 2). In a paper presented to the American Association of Community College Trustees, Allan Schurr, a trustee and former board chairman at Midlands, stated

Midlands' emphasized planning as the starting point of the college's institutional effectiveness program: "To establish a clear direction for our college, . . . Midlands designed a comprehensive plan . . . then established means to monitor our progress toward the plan" (Schurr 1991, 2).

The National Alliance of Community and Technical Colleges outlines a planning and feedback process for establishing an effectiveness program. The core of their recommendations focuses on the planning process: "[T]he mission statement of a college generates the definition of specific institutional goals that must be interpretable in terms of specific indicators" (Grossman and Duncan 1989, 5).

John Losak, in his introduction to the League for Innovation's monograph on institutional effectiveness, goes so far as to say that "institutions without an explicit and up-to-date mission statement probably cannot employ this approach." Losak outlines a detailed strategic planning process which "results in a straightforward statement of the priority activities of an institution" (Doucette and Hughes 1990, 4).

Effective planning requires that each institution state its reason for existence in a clear, simply defined mission statement. Effective planning further demands that the institution's governing board periodically revisit the mission statement to ensure that it continues to describe accurately the essence of the institution's purpose.

Once the mission statement is established, it can be divided into several major components. These normally take the form of general goal statements from which the organization can derive multiyear measurable objectives and from which stem annual measurable objectives. As a part of this process, the governing board must identify a few top-priority areas that reflect the core values of the institution. These priorities in turn guide the development of programs, schedules, policies, and procedures and the allocation of resources through the institution's budget. While there are differences in the wording and in the priority placed upon each area, most colleges agree that the number one priority is student learning, followed by (but not necessarily in this order) student access, constituent satisfaction (or perception), diversity, and human and physical resources.

At this time, the planning process is well developed at a number of community colleges. Howard Community College in Maryland reviews its intended priorities on an annual basis. The college has six priorities, three primary and three secondary. Currently its three top priorities are (1) teaching and learning excellence, (2) student access, and (3) customer service. Each of these priorities is then subdivided into a series of goals that are correlated to a group of indicators and activities (Heacock and Burrill 1992). Florida Community College at Jacksonville identifies its top three priority areas as (1) student success, (2) valued employees, and (3) innovation for excellence (Spence 1989).

In addition to established, college-wide goals, Midlands Technical College has identified six critical success factors that provide a structure for planning and evaluating the achievement of ongoing programs, services, and outcomes.

Midlands' critical success factors, based on a model developed by the Sloan School of Business at Massachusetts Institute of Technology and adapted by DeAnza College in California, are the "[k]ey things that must go right for the organization to flourish and achieve its goals" (Hudgins 1990, 6). These six factors are (1) accessible, comprehensive programs of high quality; (2) student satisfaction and retention; (3) posteducation satisfaction and success; (4) economic development and community involvement; (5) sound, effective resource management; and (6) dynamic organizational involvement and development (Hudgins 1990). These elements can be traced to the college's comprehensive mission statement, and Midlands is monitoring its critical success factors with indicators of effectiveness and defined performance standards.

These three institutions, as well as several others, have put solid, well-defined institutional effectiveness programs in place and have operated them successfully for the last half decade. Each of these effectiveness programs begins with an extensive planning process, a well-defined mission statement, and priorities and referents against which performance is judged.

When the planning process is well defined and operating smoothly, the institution can proceed to the assessment phase of institutional effectiveness. Only when the institution knows what it intends to achieve can it effectively begin to assess whether it has realized its goals.

Assessment

The most difficult conceptual problem in the institutional effectiveness process is the element of assessment. How does an institution measure its accomplishments? How does it operationalize the general priorities it established during the planning process phase? The complexity of this problem is best characterized by Heady in Miller's compendium of articles applying Deming's total quality management principles to higher education. Heady states, "It is one thing to apply statistical process controls to the manufacture of an automobile or the operation of a hotel; it is quite another to apply those processes to the education of a complex human being. As technologically sophisticated as are modern manufacturing processes, they pale in comparison with the intricacies of the learning process" (1991, 33).

Not only is human learning an immensely complex topic, this complexity is compounded by the fact that meaningful results often are not discernible for years after the classroom instruction is completed. By the time accurate findings regarding the effect of a particular learning or support process are available, several other processes may have been tried and discarded. One simple principle that we do know about learning is that the delay of response on performance, even by minutes, can degrade the learning process. And, responses from students that evaluate the effectiveness of a particular process are often delayed by years.

The essence of the assessment component of institutional effectiveness is to design a system that will provide information for higher education that will enable educators to learn quickly and efficiently what facilitates learning and what does not. The process is neither easy nor inexpensive, but it is absolutely necessary if we are to find ways to improve continuously the higher education system in America. The Southern Association of Colleges and Schools points out that "the assessment of organizational effectiveness essentially involves a systematic, explicit and documented comparison of organizational performance to organizational purpose" (Southern Association of Colleges and Schools 1985).

As noted, there is considerable agreement among community colleges on what the areas of strategic importance are. The taxonomy may differ from community college to community college; however, the conceptual components that support them are highly similar. There is also some agreement on what indicators (or measures) should be used to measure the performance of the strategic areas. There seems to be a set of commonly shared core indicators supplemented by a set of unique, institutionally specific indicators. The draft policy statement on institutional effectiveness of the American Association of Community and Junior Colleges (AACJC) captures the current consensus among community college leaders who are working on the issue of institutional effectiveness. The indicators found in this document are shown in Figure 1. These 20 indicators are grouped into three general categories: student performance, area performance, and organizational performance (AACJC 1992).

Student learning is without a doubt the most important priority for most community colleges. "The primary product of any educational institution is (student) learning in all of its manifestations, knowledge, attitudes and skills" (Bowen 1977). Since formal classroom teaching is a primary medium for transferring the culture's significant "knowledge, attitudes and skills" to those in society who want and need them, this process must be carried out effectively if society is to grow and prosper. A number of community colleges have made an effort to assess the accomplishments of their students in the classroom, but generally the approach has been an indirect one. A typical approach is described by Kreider (1991) at Mount Hood Community College in Oregon. The college's critical success factors are arranged into a matrix: "students" and "institution and functional area" (columns); "internal" and "external" (rows). The internal/ student cell includes such indicators as student completion of educational goals, achievement of career goals, course grades/GPA, student performance and assessment of cognitive outcomes, and student perception of noncognitive outcomes. The external/student cell includes attainment of a job related to curriculum, transfer, attainment of advanced degree, performance on certification and licensure examinations, and job success (Kreider 1991). These indicators are related to major themes found in Mount Hood's mission statement.

A more direct approach to assessing the accomplishments of the students was Project Cooperation which, under the auspices of the American College Testing (ACT) program, has carried out a pilot program of direct measurement of student competencies using ACT instruments. Eleven community colleges participated in the project in which several different models were used. Two models were

Figure 1
Areas of Institutional Effectiveness

STUDENT PERFORMANCE

Student access to programs and services
Assessment of basic skills for new students
Student placement at appropriate educational level
Student achievement of educational goals
Student achievement of career goals, including additional education (transfer and advanced degrees), job success, and licensure
Institutional student retention rates appropriate to student educational objectives
Student cultivation of social, personal, cultural and ethical values

AREA PERFORMANCE

Student use of and satisfaction with counseling and academic advising services
Student use of an satisfaction with library and academic support services
Student use of and satisfaction with cultural and social experiences
Community use of and satisfaction with college programs, services and facilities

ORGANIZATIONAL PERFORMANCE

Participation by staff in community agencies and organizations
Results of academic program reviews
Cultural diversity of staff and students
Institution-wide student retention rates
Student satisfaction with career students' preparation
Staff satisfaction with work and work life
Learning and developmental opportunities for all staff
Recognition of staff performance, service, competence, and creativity
Public perception and opinions of college performance

Source: AACJC, 1992, 2. Used with permission.

focused on the value-added theme, and two centered on a predictive research approach (Cowart 1990).

Lorenzo, in describing Macomb Community College's institutional effectiveness program, puts student learning measures under the heading of "achievement." He outlines three goals related to achievement: successful transfer, successful employment, and personal interests (Lorenzo 1989). The measure suggested by Macomb for these goals is a Comparison of Student Status to Student Intent. The source of data is student registration, MiSIS (a Michigan state data collection system), and follow-up studies.

At Midlands Technical College, Hudgins lists the areas of access and equity, general education, assessment of the major, and successful articulation transfer as indicators of "comprehensive programs of high quality." Midlands has developed definitions and standards for each indicator. Other success indicators Midlands uses are enrollment, retention, program completion, job placement, program capstone competencies, student technical skills, success in developmental/remediation programs, and employer/student/graduate satisfaction. The most important focus of the effort is students—their learning outcomes and their successes (Hudgins 1990).

Howard Community College, in Maryland, has developed a hierarchical information system by creating an additional level of conceptualization, by deriving goals for each of its priorities, and by assigning a number of alternative indicators to each goal. For example, the college identified four goals related to its number one strategic priority, teaching and learning excellence. The first goal, "Students will achieve their stated learning objectives," has six indicators associated with it: graduate's goal achievement, long-term success rates, employment in field, transfer goal achievement, student retention, and continuing education goal achievement. Institutional performance on each of these indicators is reported to the board of trustees on a periodic schedule, and standards are set and reviewed annually (Heacock and Burrill 1992). Other goals are concerned with student satisfaction with the quality of their education, evidence of student learning, and improvement of the teaching/learning process.

At Florida Community College at Jacksonville, Spence and his staff have identified a list of student success performance measures that relate to student learning: average GPA of transfers in Florida SUS (a Florida State data system), percentage passing CLAST (a state-wide competency test) on first attempt, percentage passing professional licensure, pre/post competency testing, and entry/exit requirements (Spence 1989).

Johnson County Community College, in Kansas, utilizes annual and three-year follow-up studies to collect data on the effectiveness of the college's programs: how well career students were prepared for employment, improvement in a variety of cognitive and noncognitive behaviors, achievement of educational goals, and progress in careers (Conklin 1990). Johnson County Community College also has conducted extensive work in assessing transfer success. Among the measures they use are performance on licensure exams and transfer success rates (Seybert, Kelly, and Doucette 1991).

A second major area of strategic importance is student access. Community colleges strive to enhance access and equity for their students and are committed to accessibility to higher education by persons in their service areas, especially traditionally underrepresented groups, disabled persons, and those students requiring financial assistance or academic support services.

Access to college begins before enrollment with the image of the college in the community. Students must first perceive the college to be a viable option in reaching their goals before they make a decision to enroll. Once students have made the decision to enroll, the process of moving through the institution must be made as free from barriers as possible. Smooth and efficient access to various college services is crucial. From admissions through testing, advisement, and registration, to the completion of learning programs and the eventual satisfaction of the students' educational objectives, systems for ensuring student success must be in place to assure continuity in providing access to quality education.

Some indicators of access currently used are total headcount enrollment (Lorenzo 1989), enrollment as a percentage of service area population (Spence 1989), and ratio of enrollment to service area totals by race and ethnicity, and age and service area locality (Heacock and Burrill 1992). The underlying logic dictates that ratios for all subgroups of interest be considered, for example, age cohort, gender, location, and income level, and these are under development at Howard Community College and other colleges as well.

Other essential priorities include the current concerns about customer service and diversity, as well as more traditional priorities such as resource management. For example, it is essential that community colleges continually strive to provide an excellent level of service that engenders loyalty and support among the constituents they serve. The way students and the general community perceive the college will be reflected in whether they continue their studies at college, recommend the institution to their families and friends, and continue to support the college. The diverse nature of the community college student population mandates a high level of individualized service including a responsive curriculum, efficient registration, flexible hours, and convenient class scheduling. Community colleges also must promote an atmosphere of service to coworkers. By encouraging this atmosphere, the college will better serve its external community and improve the morale of its staff.

The way in which information is gathered should also be considered. Should we use national or local sources? How unique should our data sources be? Howard Community College has used a series of alternative sources. For example, it uses a professionally administered image and reputation survey plus two internally developed instruments for assessing the satisfaction of institutional users. The first instrument is the Quality/Excellence Services Trends (QuEST) survey, which assesses the perceptions of internal users of services. The second, the Yearly Evaluation of Services by Students (YESS), surveys the perceptions of students and of users outside the organization (Leff and Burrill 1992). Macomb Community College uses telephone surveys (Lorenzo 1989). Mount Hood Community College uses student evaluations (Kreider 1991).

The assessment process allows us to convert data into usable information. However, the institutional effectiveness process requires one further conversion, that of information into action.

Outcomes

When referring to outcomes we are asking the question, "What is the institution accomplishing in terms of its mission, goals, and objectives?" While we may never be perfectly sure of our answer, given the enormous complexity of the question, the ultimate test of institutional effectiveness lies in our ability to convert information into meaningful actions. Understanding why the organization exists and assessing its performance are worthless unless the information is converted into actions that promote organizational change. It is at this juncture, the focus on utilization, that institutional effectiveness systems converge with other management functions and change the character of the institution. The selection of a set of activities, the allocation of resources to support those activities, the place of these activities in the structure and processes of the organization, and the long-term view of the process are significant elements in the outcome phase.

First, we should consider the joining of thought and action to produce outcomes—the appropriate channeling of funds and the flow of human resources resulting in a set of "activities" designed to achieve our desired institutional priorities. Consequently, institutional effectiveness requires that planning and budgeting be linked to achieve appropriate resource allocations to produce the desired institutional results (Calhoun 1991, 230). This linkage can have different connections requiring both broad allocations of resources to achieve institutional priorities as well as specific allocations of resources linked to individual actions (Grey, Spence, and Parker 1991, 109). The selection of activities can also happen in different ways. In some institutions, activities are determined in a top-down manner emanating from the executive management team or a planning council; in others, the form is a bottom-up selection of activities to attain institutional priorities. Of course, within either of these forms, numerous variations occur employing elements of each (Griffin and McClenney 1991).

An equally important consideration is how activities are adapted to the structure and procedures of an organization. How they become part of the operations of an organization can determine their success or failure and is closely linked to the way in which activities are assigned and where responsibility is located. For example, activities can be assigned to either organizational units or to individuals. Yet another way is to assign activities to committees. Of course combinations of the three methods are used as well. For example, Howard Community College has used both assignment methods recently moving away from unit plans (Heacock and Burrill 1992).

Reward and incentive structures already vary widely from system to system, and the way in which activities are assigned can also have implications for the way in which incentives and rewards are structured. Activities can be tied to material or intrinsic incentives (Nichols 1991, 28). For example, the success of activities can be a component of promotion in a system that uses merit promotion, or, in systems without merit promotion, the reward may be entirely intrinsic. These formulations are often the result of organizational constraints, in other words, existing personnel systems, apart from the institutional effectiveness model that is being employed.

The issue of rewarding performance for activities leads in turn to the question of a method to determine whether the activity was effective. That is, the activity itself must be evaluated and its degree of success rated. What criteria should be used? Activities can be linked to specific indicators or to more general goals or priorities. The level of linkage varies from system to system. Howard Community College ties its activities to more general goals rather than specific indicators. Additionally, activities can be judged together or apart from indicators all together. Whether an activity is judged as a success can be done in two ways. First, it can be judged in terms of its completion and second in terms of its intended effect. The former can occur without the latter, although we tend to link the two together (Suchman 1967). Howard Community College judges the success of activities based on their completion rather than on the outcome measure. In other words, activities are themselves evaluated apart from their impact on indicators. This approach promotes freedom of action and innovation.

Numerous other components can be considered when integrating outcomes into the overall organizational culture. However, perhaps most important, we need to consider the way in which the cycle of thought, assessment, and action is understood and sustained over the long term.

FROM PROCESS TO QUALITY

The selection of activities and their relationship to indicators or rewards is not the end of the story. How we view the entire institutional effectiveness process of planning, assessment, and outcomes is perhaps the most important point we must consider. We are engaged in an ongoing system that requires continual refinement over periods of time. However, this recognition involves more than just the acceptance of the repetitive nature of the process. Rather, it implies a fundamental shift in how we view the process of change and organizational learning.

When assessment has been carried out and standards have been set, the question becomes, ''Are we meeting our standards?'' If not, then we have an obligation to labor diligently to improve the organizations until they are met. If, on the other hand, standards are met, then we must establish higher ones. This continuous search for ways to improve our organizations is the first step in the process of ''total quality.''

Viewed in this manner, the institutional effectiveness process is the process of describing the level of quality at which we are operating. Institutional effectiveness indicators provide the standards and benchmarks against which we can judge our progress. Improvement, however, requires more than description of the history of the organization and where it is at the present. We must focus on ways to collect data and conceptualize information that can be used to guide us in continuously improving all aspects of the educational process, from the introduction of new learning techniques into the classroom to the painless registration of students. It is this pervasive attention to continuous improvement that characterizes the total quality management movement. Thus we come full circle from the Southern Regional Education Board's concern "that the traditional measures of institutional effectiveness lack meaning" and that a "quality gap" exists in American higher education (SREB 1987).

Total quality education, however, depends on two critical elements. The first, as we have just noted, is the continuous improvement process. The second, and equally important component, requires that the focus of the institution be on the customers—the students. Students have choices and they will exercise those choices. They will select the best value—the most quality they can get for the dollar. Deming's fundamental point is that price alone is meaningless (1986). Price is only significant in relation to the value obtained. For community colleges, which have long operated on the basis that "cheaper is better," the message is clear. The "cheaper is better" concept will no longer work with today's con-sumer-oriented students. Students will pay higher tuition if they feel the education they are receiving is worth the price of tuition. An example of this phenomenon can be found in the automobile industry. Very few of us can name the lowest priced car in America without considerable research; even fewer of us drives one. Most of us can, however, identify several excellent automobile values—automobiles with high quality at an acceptable price—in the American market-place. As educators we must deliver high quality at an acceptable price. We must look for every opportunity to reduce the cost of delivering our services, but never at the expense of quality.

The next decade will see a substantial restructuring of American higher ed-ucation, with some institutions excelling while other face decline. American students will exercise their power of choice. Those institutions delivering "value"—high quality at a competitive price—will be thriving in the year 2002. However, those institutions delivering mediocre quality even with very low tuitions will be withering away.

The obligation to the customer never ceases, for it will no longer suffice to have customers (students) who are merely satisfied. What will be required for institutions of higher education to thrive in the next decade is aptly described by Deming: "What is required is the loyal customer, the customer that comes back, waits in line, and brings a friend with him (or her)" (1989, 4).

REFERENCES

Alfred, R., and P. Kreider. 1991. Creating a culture for institutional effectiveness. *AACJC Journal* (April/May): 34–39.
American Association of Community and Junior Colleges. 1992. AACJC policy statement on institutional effectiveness. Draft. Washington, D.C.
Ashcroft, J. 1986. *Time for results: Report of the task force on college quality.* Wash-ington, D.C.: National Governors' Association.
Bowen, H. R. 1977. *Investment in learning: The individual and social value of American higher education.* San Francisco: Jossey-Bass.
Calhoun, H. 1991. Implementing institutional effectiveness in two-year colleges. In *A*

practitioner's handbook for institutional effectiveness and student outcomes assessment implementation, ed. J. O. Nichols, 228–38. New York: Agathon Press.

Conklin, K. A. 1990. Assessment of institutional effectiveness: Career student outcomes. *Community/Junior College Quarterly of Research and Practice* 14(4):349–55.

Cowart, S. C. 1990. *Project cooperation: A joint effort of community college educators and ACT to answer questions about institutional effectiveness and outcomes assessment.* Washington, D.C.: American Association of Community and Junior Colleges.

Deming, W. E. 1986. *Out of the crisis.* Cambridge: Massachusetts Institute of Technology, Center for Advanced Engineering Study.

———. 1989. Foundation for management of quality in the western world. Paper presented at a meeting of the Institution of Management Science, April, Osaka, Japan.

Doucette, D., and B. Hughes, eds. 1990. *Assessing institutional effectiveness in community colleges.* ERIC Document no. ED 324 072. Laguna Hills, Calif.: League for Innovation in the Community College.

Ewell, P. T. 1988. Institutional effectiveness: Issues and opportunities for community colleges. Presented to the annual meeting of the League for Innovation in the Community College, July, Charlotte, North Carolina.

Grey, P., C. Spence, and L. Parker. 1991. The effectiveness process: How policy strategic dollars and institutional involvement evolved into key outcomes. Presented at conference entitled Effectiveness and Student Success: Transforming Community Colleges for the 1990's. June, Toronto, Ontario.

Griffin, T., and B. McClenney. 1991. Finding the higher-ground: Strategic planning for effecting positive student outcomes. Presented at conference entitled Effectiveness and Student Success: Transforming Community Colleges for the 1990's. June, Toronto, Ontario.

Grossman, G. M., and M. E. Duncan. 1989. Indicators of institutional effectiveness. Columbus, Ohio: National Alliance of Community and Technical Colleges.

Heacock, R., and D. A. Burrill. 1992. Board of trustees information system. Columbia, Md.: Howard Community College.

Heady, S. 1991. *Applying the Deming method to higher education: Part three.* Washington, D.C.: College and University Personnel Association.

Hudgins, J. L. 1990. Education's quality assurance mandate. Columbia, S.C.: Midlands Technical College.

Kreider, P. 1991. American Association of Community and Junior Colleges 71st Annual Conference on Institutional Effectiveness and Student Success, April, Kansas City, Missouri.

Leff, B., and D. A. Burrill. 1992. Quality/excellence services trends (QuEST) and yearly evaluation of services by students (YESS). Columbia, Md.: Howard Community College.

Lorenzo, A. L. 1989. *Measuring institutional effectiveness.* Warren, Mich.: Macomb Community College.

McClenney, K. M., and B. N. McClenney. 1988. Managing for student success and institutional effectiveness. *Community, Technical and Junior College Journal* 58(5):53–55.

Nichols, J. O. 1991. *A practitioner's handbook for institutional effectiveness and student outcomes assessment implementation.* New York: Agathon Press.

Richardson, R., Jr. 1985. How are students learning? *Change* 17(3).

———. 1987. A question of quality. *AACJC Journal* (57)4.

———. 1988. Improving effectiveness through strategic planning. *Community College Review* 15(4).

Schurr, A. C. 1991. The role of the trustee in evaluating effectiveness. Midlands Technical College, Columbia, S.C. Paper presented to the Association of Community College Trustees, October, Biloxi, Mississippi.

Seybert, J. A., L. H. Kelly, and L. H. Doucette. 1991. Assessment of institutional effectiveness: The transfer function. Paper presented at the annual meeting of the American Educational Research Association, June, Chicago, Illinois.

Simmons, H. L. 1990. A framework for outcomes assessment. Philadelphia, Pa.: Middle States Commission on Higher Education.

Southern Association of Colleges and Schools. 1985. *Standards for accreditation*. Atlanta, Georgia.

Southern Regional Education Board. 1987. *Access to quality undergraduate education*. Atlanta, Georgia.

Spence, C. 1989. *Institutional assessment*. Jacksonville: Florida Community College at Jacksonville.

Suchman, E. 1967. *Evaluation research*. New York: Russell Sage Foundation.

Understanding the Many Contexts of the Two-Year College

Peter H. Garland

The bulk of the literature on two-year colleges focuses almost exclusively on the public community college and often more specifically on the comprehensive community college. Only brief mention is made of other forms of two-year education even in such comprehensive volumes as Cohen and Brawer's *The American Community College* (1982), Deegan, Tillery, and Associates' *Renewing the American Community College* (1985), and Cohen, Palmer, and Zwemer's *Key Resources on Community Colleges* (1986). For example, Cohen and Brawer define the community college as "any institution accredited to award the associate degree in arts or science as its highest degree" (1982, 5–6). That definition is inclusive of public and private, specialized and comprehensive institutions, including 250 private junior colleges. Little mention is made of the diversity of two-year colleges beyond this. For instance, only the finances of public two-year institutions are discussed.

The limited literature on other two-year colleges is particularly apparent in discussions of leadership (Roe and Baker 1989; Roueche and Baker 1984; Vaughan 1989; Amey and Twombly 1992). There has been, therefore, a gap in the literature which speaks to the various institutional contexts of leaders of two-year colleges and campuses.

The different forms of two-year education stem from different interests and goals at the time of their founding. Over time, two-year colleges have emerged from other educational institutions: lower divisions of senior institutions, post-secondary units of K–12 schools, or as specialized institutions in reaction to existing institutions such as technical colleges or junior colleges for women. Challenges for leadership of these often very different institutions reflect this diversity.

Different histories cause leadership for the broad array of two-year colleges to respond to a variety of traditions, cultures, decision-making processes, and governance structures. While the community college movement is renewing its call for active attention to the next generation of leaders (Elsner et al., 1984; Vaughan 1989; Martorana and Garland 1991), similar attention must be paid to the challenges of those who lead two-year colleges in other contexts.

This chapter focuses on the many contexts of two-year colleges and campuses and suggests the variety of challenges for leaders as a result of these different contexts. "Context" is used here to identify the missions, governance, and institutional cultures that define institutions and their programs, services, and operations. Contexts can be very different. For instance, two-year colleges and campuses may have comprehensive or specialized missions. Two-year colleges and campuses may be governed by their own board of trustees, a system or institutional board, or other governmental units. Levels of autonomy can be very different at two-year colleges and campuses, depending on their mission, structure, and culture. Similarly, the capacity of two-year colleges to respond to their communities may vary. Finally, different contexts lead to very different realities for two-year college leadership and, therefore, different needs for effective leadership.

An example of the diversity of two-year institutions can be illustrated by the institutions in Pennsylvania, where there are thirteen public community colleges, twenty-five two-year branch campuses of senior public institutions, nine independent junior colleges, one technical institute (established in the same manner as community colleges), and one state technical school administered by the Department of Education. In addition, there are some 330 private career schools at the postsecondary level, 88 of which are authorized to award the associate degree in one or more program areas. Many of these campuses share similar clienteles, offer similar programs, and even share missions; for others, the only similarity is the associate degree, and the differences are more striking.

Pennsylvania is not alone in having within its borders various providers of two-year education. Many states operate separate systems of public community colleges and public junior colleges (Alabama); technical colleges and community colleges (Connecticut, separate systems until recently); state community colleges and local community colleges (Michigan); and two-year colleges or university branches and community colleges (Alaska and Louisiana). Throughout the country, however, there are hundreds of two-year institutions and campuses that do not fit the mold of public community colleges which are the focus of the majority of recent literature on leadership, governance, and management.

THE EVOLUTION OF MULTIPLE INSTITUTIONAL CONTEXTS

Two-year colleges are a phenomenon of the twentieth century. Their evolution throughout this century is described by Tillery and Deegan (1985) as occurring in four distinct generations: (1) the extension of high school (1900–1930), (2) the creation of the junior college (1930–1950), (3) the establishment of the community college (1950–1970), and (4) the founding of the comprehensive community college (1970–mid-1980s). The fifth generation (mid-1980s–present) is described by the authors as a period of reflection and transition. As such, it may prove to be conducive to expanding our recognition of the varying needs of leadership at two-year colleges and campuses. Through these generations, prevailing images of two-year institutions have emerged. Similarly, different two-year college traditions, which are represented in the current array of colleges and campuses, have emerged.

In the first generation, splitting traditional baccalaureate education into upper and lower division enabled universities, on the one hand, and school districts and communities, on the other, to expand postsecondary opportunities. In this era, new traditions of community-based, postsecondary education were established, creating an opportunity for a variety of forms of two-year education to emerge, including public and private junior colleges, technical colleges, branch campuses, and community colleges. By 1930, 450 junior colleges were found in all but five states (Cohen and Brawer 1982).

During the next phase of the two-year college movement, from 1930 to 1950, Tillery and Deegan (1985) suggest that more efforts were made by states to influence the development of junior colleges. At the same time, pressures for local control sought to assert themselves in the governance of public community and junior colleges. The tradition of public two-year colleges was strengthened in this period.

The period from 1950 to 1970 witnessed a phenomenal growth in two-year colleges and campuses of all types. Public institutions began to outnumber private two-year institutions as states and localities endeavored to provide greater access to postsecondary education. Many states sought to accommodate increasing numbers of students by establishing branch campuses of existing senior public institutions while other states developed comprehensive plans for the development of public community college systems. The numbers of private junior colleges also grew. A number of governance patterns began to emerge—institutional or local community college boards, district or system boards, and university boards governed two-year colleges. Even state boards of education and departments of education found themselves in the business of running two-year colleges.

In the fourth generation (1970–mid-1980s), the comprehensive community college became the prevailing image of the two-year college and dominated the growing body of literature focused on two-year colleges. The comprehensive community college pursued a broad mission to serve not only as the nexus for community learning (Gleazer 1980), but also as a point of entry for higher education for previously underserved groups (disabled students, women returning to school, the academically underprepared, and immigrants).

The expansiveness of many two-year colleges brought ambiguity to the missions of the comprehensive community college and set the stage for the fifth generation in the mid-1980s. According to Tillery and Deegan (1985), concern has grown about defining institutional missions, the growth of programs, and the services that might best be left to other social service agencies. The constant and rapid pace of change in the first four developmental periods has led to a strong need to reflect on the mission, program, operations, and leadership of institutions in the fifth generation. Reflection on the purpose and future of two-year education may increase our awareness of the variety of traditions among two-year colleges and campuses and increase the potential to explore multiple futures.

GROWING LITERATURE ON LEADERSHIP, MANAGEMENT, AND GOVERNANCE

Through these generations, and particularly recently, the body of literature of leadership, management, and governance has grown. Cohen and Brawer (1982) suggest that more has been written about governance and administration than any other single aspect of community colleges. Coming, as much of it has, during the periods of public community college prominence, this literature reflects a community college bias. As such, this literature must be read with care by the leaders of the nation's two-year colleges and campuses.

This literature reveals a failure to reflect reality in three areas: (1) the diversity of two-year college traditions, (2) the multiple models of leadership needed, and (3) the governance and management concerns that are different from the comprehensive community college.

First, by focusing on the public community of the two-year college, we have neglected the diversity of traditions. After casual references to the variety of two-year colleges and campuses, most literature focuses on the leadership dimensions of public community colleges. Not surprisingly, writings by community college leaders (Gleazer 1980; Vaughan and Associates 1983; Vaughan 1989) talk about the demands on leadership of the public community college. More recent discussions of leadership, attempting to broaden the debate on leadership by focusing on new types of leaders (Roe and Baker 1989; Eaton 1988; Amey and Twombly 1992), remain targeted at community colleges. Certainly the demands of leadership in other two-year settings are somewhat unique.

Tillery and Deegan note the differences that exist between community colleges and junior colleges (1985, 13–14) and remind us that "individual colleges are not as much alike as the literature . . . might suggest" (16). Similarly, based on a broad study of leadership across institutional types, Baldridge et al. suggest that "governance and management vary systematically in different types of institutions" in such dimensions as governance and decision making (1978, 11). Seldom is there a discussion in the literature of the unique challenges of private junior college leaders, branch campus leaders, or specialized, technical colleges. For campus leaders within multiunit community college districts, more, but still relatively limited, attention to leadership is offered (Kintzer et al., 1969; Kintzer 1980, 1984).

Second, monolithic models of leadership fail to reflect the multiple models of leadership needed. Gleazer (1980) speaks of becoming an effective leader of a college expanding horizontally to become a nexus of community learning. Vaughan (1989) discusses the type of leader needed for maturing community colleges. These works reflect the prevailing belief that institutions are evolving in a similar fashion and therefore leaders must evolve similarly; they fail to reflect the variety of traditions, the multiple paths of evolution, and the diversity of demands on leadership present in the large array of two-year colleges and campuses.

In addition to recognizing variations in institutional settings writers, such as Amey and Twombly (1992), suggest the necessity of broadening the view of two-year college leadership to be more inclusive of the voices and style of women and minority leaders. Eaton (1988) and Vaughan (1989) also call for deepening the leadership pool and exploring more integrated, shared-leadership styles.

Third, the great concern of growing state control of two-year college operations fails to reflect the governance and management concerns of the variety of two-year college and campus leaders. Concern about the autonomy of the two-year college has been constant since state interest was defined early and the involvement of local and state officials in its expansion has been important. Certainly the growth of state involvement and direction of community college programs and operations has been well documented (Vaughan and Associates 1983; Tillery and Wattenbarger 1985; Martorana and Garland 1991); however, this is a phenomenon most troubling to public community college leaders. Increasing state involvement in community colleges can be of little relevance to leaders of private junior colleges or branch campus leaders. It is possible, in those states where state involvement restrains or limits community college expansion, that the erosion of local autonomy may be welcomed.

Leaders of the campuses that are part of larger systems, as well as presidents of independent junior colleges and specialized institutions, have other concerns. These leaders face such challenges as effectively advocating a two-year education mission within a larger, multiunit institution; clarifying the mission expansion of a specialized institution; and securing adequate resources for a tuition-dependent institution in an increasingly competitive student market. For these leaders, state control issues are but one of the many challenges of leadership.

TRADITIONAL SIMILARITIES ACROSS TWO-YEAR COLLEGES

Several reasons explain why we continue to think of two-year colleges and campuses as similar institutions. First, many share a founding belief of an educational alternative to traditional baccalaureate institutions or the desire of a community to provide educational opportunities for its citizens. Although two-year institutions have followed different evolutionary paths, the similar motivations that gave birth to the institutions have created a powerful bond (Fields 1962).

In addition, perhaps the most enduring similarity of two-year institutions, is the fact that they offer the associate degree as their highest degree. Although many offer courses and programs for transfer, degree level is a defining characteristic in American higher education (Cohen and Brawer 1982).

Third, two-year colleges and campuses share a common commitment to teaching and service, characteristics that have been integral parts of the two-year college philosophy since their inception (Vaughan 1989).

Fourth, the clienteles of two-year campuses are often similar to one another. Many institutions serve a geographically limited population of students who seek skills for employment and careers as well as entry to courses and programs leading to a baccalaureate degree and beyond. Two-year colleges of all types are generally credited with democratizing education (Medsker 1960).

Fifth, although communities vary widely in their needs, and thus in their demands on two-year institutions, responsiveness to community needs has been an identifying characteristic. Hankin and Fey (1985) describe the historical interest of the variety of two-year colleges in serving their communities.

DIFFERENCES AMONG TWO-YEAR COLLEGES

There are a number of areas in which significant differences emerge among the variety of two-year institutions. To understand the uniqueness of these institutions, one must understand (1) the institutional mission; (2) the levels of accountability; (3) the locus of control for decision making; (4) the acquisition of resources; and (5) the institutional culture.

First, the missions of two-year colleges are often quite different and, thus, the focus and efforts of each campus differ. Pennsylvania offers examples of some two-year college mission and purpose statements that reflect the variety of these institutions. The Community College of Allegheny County (CCAC), Pennsylvania's largest comprehensive community college, defines its mission in ways not unlike those of other public comprehensive community colleges:

The Community College is committed to providing an accessible, affordable college education, greater educational opportunity, comprehensive college programming and quality instruction in its classrooms. Its mission is to provide a high quality comprehensive community college program for the residents of Allegheny County. The program will include vocational-technical and career education, community services, developmental education, college transfer programs, as well as general education to enrich and enhance the student's life. The Community College of Allegheny County will seek to carry out its program with the most innovative and effective educational methods available, as economically as possible, at the lowest possible cost to its students and with full accountability to its constituents. The College will maintain an open door admissions policy and will conduct its program at multiple locations convenient to its students. (CCAC 1990, 2)

The mission of Manor Junior College (MJC), on the other hand, is more similar to that of a four-year liberal arts college with a strong religious tradition:

> The primary purpose of Manor Junior College is to provide its students with an education that is based upon the Judeo-Christian tradition. Manor believes that the ideals and values of this tradition are an integral part of human existence that give purpose and meaning to education and should illuminate every field of study and college life.
>
> Manor strives to provide its students with a personalized education that promotes a wide breadth of learning and enables students to develop fully as individuals. Manor professes that its students should possess an understanding of basic scientific, humanistic and ethical principles. To foster growth in these areas, students are encouraged to develop a sense of inquiry, critical thinking, and communication skills. (MJC 1991, 8)

Pierce Junior College (PJC) defines itself clearly as a two-year college with a focused mission: "Pierce has maintained a clear mission since its founding in 1865. That mission is, plain and simple, practical business education within the first two years of a strong collegiate educational program" (PJC 1990, 5).

With seventeen two-year branch campuses, Pensylvania State University (PSU) is a major provider of two-year education in the Commonwealth. The many branch campuses of Penn State operate within the broader mission of the university and therefore reflect the values of a large, prestigious, research-oriented institution (PSU 1991).

Clearly, the range in missions and purposes defines different operating styles, priorities, and administrative leadership. Leaders of those two-year colleges and campuses that are not comprehensive community colleges may share—at least in terms of mission—more in common with universities, liberal arts colleges, and special-purpose institutions.

Second, levels of accountability can be very different for the leadership of different two-year colleges and campuses. While all leaders are accountable to a variety of parties, formal levels of accountability differ by institutional context. The leadership of the comprehensive community college must deal directly with a governing board, local sponsors, and often state officials as part of the state system of community colleges. Leaders of independent junior colleges may report formally only to the institutional governing board. On the other hand, branch campus leaders may find themselves accountable to local advisory boards; provosts, deans, budget directors, and other university leaders (university relations, student affairs, etc.); and ultimately an institutional governing board and even a statewide coordinating board.

Third, the central administration in a multiunit institution may serve to facilitate or hinder the effectiveness of an individual campus. Campus leaders who are allowed to make decisions for their campuses within defined autonomy are able to respond to local needs with local actions. In his study of presidents, Kerr (1985) suggests that campus leaders within systems may actually be free to work more effectively with their constituencies because of distance from governing boards and bodies. For others, however, "central administration" exercises detailed authority over budget, program, and administration.

Fourth, competition for resources can vary across the variety of two-year colleges and campuses. Leaders of comprehensive community colleges find themselves advocating for resources in both state and local policy arenas, often competing with other educational institutions and organizations, along with other human service needs. This situation is perhaps most familiar to the leadership of urban, comprehensive community colleges who must argue for resources in the state capital and city hall, along with city schools, social and health services, and other public services. Vaughan (1980) and Hankin and Fey (1985) describe the competition for resources in the provision of adult education. Competition, while often intense, is largely interinstitutional and interagency.

Independent two-year colleges must compete with other colleges for students, for it is through student tuition dollars that most resources are acquired. Again, while competition may be intense, it remains interinstitutional.

For a branch campus leader or the leader of a multiunit community college district, competition is found both inside and outside of the institution. To obtain resources, the overall institution must first acquire adequate resources and then must allocate them across its many programs in a manner in which the two-year mission is recognized and supported. Kintzer, Jensen, and Hansen (1969) describe the conflicts inherent in the allocation process. In large universities, where the predominant goals may be graduate education and research, leaders of two-year education face a special challenge in advocating for and receiving adequate funding.

Fifth, different contexts for two-year colleges and campuses have enabled a variety of institutional cultures to emerge. Institutional culture, according to Kuh and Whitt, is

the collective, mutually shaping patterns of norms, values, practices, and assumptions that guide the behavior of individuals and groups in an institute of higher education and provide a frame of reference within which to interpret the meaning of events and action on and off campus. (1988, 12–13)

As such, culture is context bound, and precise definitions are elusive. In their review of the literature on institutional culture, Kuh and Whitt suggest seven features of institutional culture:

(1) historical roots, including religious convictions of founders, and external influences, particularly the support of the institution's constituents (e.g., alumni, philanthropic sponsors); (2) the academic program, including curricular emphases; (3) the personnel core, including faculty and other institutional agents who contribute to the maintenance of the institution's culture; (4) the social environment, particularly the influence of dominant student subculture(s); (5) artifactual manifestations of culture, such as architecture, customs, ceremonies, and rituals; (6) distinctive themes that reflect the institution's core

values and beliefs transmitted by the ethos, norms, and saga; and (7) individual actors such as charismatic leaders. (1988, 53)

Obviously, with the infinite variables possible, culture will vary from institution to institution. Large or multiunit institutions may foster several cultures.

THE CHALLENGE FOR LEADERSHIP

Every institutional leader faces challenges. A growing body of literature is concerned with leadership in higher education (Kerr 1985; Bensimon, Neumann, and Birnbaum 1989). Roueche and Baker (1984); Moore, Twombly, and Martorana (1985); and Vaughan (1989) provide thoughtful analyses on community college leadership. For those, however, who may find themselves moving between and among the variety of two-year contexts—community colleges, private junior colleges, branch campuses, or specialized institutions—additional considerations must be made to understand the effects context has on leadership.

To be effective at leading institutions and campuses, with often very different traditions, leaders must judge, clarify, assess, develop, and negotiate.

First, leaders must judge the accuracy of campus and institutional mission statements. Leaders moving across institutions must assess the "fit" of the mission statement and the appropriateness of programs and services to that mission. Kintzer (1980) found assessing and understanding the mission essential to leadership in all two-year college settings.

Second, leaders must clarify relationships. Each leader moving into a new context should seek to assess and clarify relationships. Vaughan (1989) suggests that it is an important task of leadership to clarify relationships with boards, professional organizations, and constituencies, as well as faculty, students, and other administrators. Kerr (1985) suggests that, within multicampus institutions and systems, a clear understanding of "who does what" needs to be established early so that campuses and central administration do not find themselves working at cross purposes.

Third, leaders must assess the culture(s) of which they are a part. For leaders moving from one two-year college context to another, it will be important, quickly and thoroughly, to understand the culture or cultures of which they are a part. A community college is not a private junior college, which is not a branch campus. The importance of having culture, strategy, and leadership overlap has been outlined by Chaffee and Tierney:

[W]hen identity is clear and coherent, all who are involved with the organization have a star to navigate by in their efforts to contribute to the group. They see what the organization is and, with consistent strategic leadership, they see where the organization is headed. (1988, 183)

Furthermore, Chaffee and Tierney suggest that the concept of organizational culture encourages practitioners to

- consider real or potential conflicts not in isolation but on the broad canvas of organizational life
- recognize structural or operational contradictions that suggest tensions in the organization
- implement and evaluate everyday decisions with a keen awareness of their role in and influence upon organizational culture
- understand the symbolic dimensions of ostensibly instrumental decisions and actions
- consider why different groups in the organization hold varying perceptions about institutional performance
- orchestrate innovation and change in the organization, mindful of how such change will impact on and be constrained by the culture. (1988, 9)

Fourth, leaders must develop effective advocacy strategies for the institution or campus. In his study of community college administrators, Vaughan (1989) found that presidents and other community college leaders feel they have not successfully promoted the community college mission. To leaders moving across contexts, different advocacy strategies will need to be developed particularly in the case of those moving in or out of multiunit institutions.

Fifth, if part of a larger institution or system, leaders must negotiate effective autonomy. In studying the multicampus context of two-year colleges, Kintzer (1984) found general support for most authority to be decentralized, particularly in terms of programs and faculty. However, Cohen and Brawer (1982) discuss the tendency for decisions to become more centralized over time in multiunit institutions. For leaders new to an institutional context, particularly those with limited experience in branch campuses or multiunit community college districts, care must be taken to assess relationships and negotiate effective autonomy.

THE CHALLENGE

To help the leaders in the large array of two-year colleges and campuses, scholars must broaden the scope of their research and begin to address more fully the various contexts in which two-year college leaders find themselves. First, they must recognize the variety of contexts that exist: comprehensive community colleges, public and private junior colleges, technical institutes, branch campuses, and multiunit community colleges. Differences between and among these institutions and the implications for leadership must become a more visible topic of research, debate, and informed discussion within journals, books, and professional associations.

Second, leadership development must broaden its scope to include those who will lead the various types of two-year institutions. According to Roe and Baker, "[W]ithout directed and individualized leadership training, we question how community college leaders can influence, shape and imbue values, beliefs and behaviors in their followers" (1989, 13).

REFERENCES

Alfred, R. L., and P. Kreider. 1991. Creating a culture for institutional effectiveness. *Community, Technical, and Junior College Journal* 61(5):34–39.

Amey, M. J., and S. B. Twombly. 1992. Re-visioning leadership in community colleges. *Review of Higher Education* 15(2):125–50.

Baldridge, J. V., D. V. Curtis, G. Ecker, and G. L. Riley. 1978. *Policy making and effective leadership*. San Francisco: Jossey-Bass.

Bensimon, E. M., A. Neumann, and R. Birnbaum. 1989. *Making sense of administrative leadership: The ''L'' word in higher education*. 1989 Higher Education Research Report no. 1. Washington, D.C.: ASHE/ERIC.

Chaffee, E. E., and W. G. Tierney. 1988. *Collegiate culture and leadership strategies*. New York: American Council on Education/MacMillan.

Cohen, A. M., and F. B. Brawer. 1982. *The American community college*. San Francisco: Jossey-Bass.

Cohen, A. M., J. C. Palmer, and K. D. Zwemer. 1986. *Key resources on community colleges*. San Francisco: Jossey-Bass.

Community College of Allegheny County (CCAC). 1990. *Catalog 1990–93 edition*. Pittsburgh, Pa.: CCAC.

Deegan, W. L., D. Tillery, and Associates, eds. 1985. *Renewing the American Community college*. San Francisco: Jossey-Bass.

Eaton, J. S. 1988. Love me, lead me, and leave me alone. In *Leaders on leadership: The college presidency*, ed. J. L. Fisher and J. W. Tack, 75–80. New Directions for Higher Education, no. 61. San Francisco: Jossey-Bass.

Elsner, P. A., R. L. Alfred, R. J. LeCroy, and N. Armes, eds. 1984. *Emerging roles for community college leaders*. New Directions for Community Colleges no. 46. San Francisco: Jossey-Bass.

Fields, R. 1962. *The community college movement*. New York: McGraw-Hill.

Gleazer, E. J., Jr. 1980. *The community college: Values, vision and vitality*. Washington, D.C.: American Association of Community and Junior Colleges.

Hall, R. A., and R. L. Alfred. 1985. Applied research on leadership in community colleges. *Community College Review* 12(4):36–41.

Hankin, J. N., and P. A. Fey. 1985. Reassessing the commitment to community services. In *Renewing the American community college*, ed. W. L. Deegan, D. Tillery, and Associates. 150–174. San Francisco: Jossey-Bass.

Kerr, C. 1985. *Presidents make a difference: Strengthening leadership in colleges and universities*. A report of the Commission on Strengthening Presidential Leadership. Washington, D.C.: Association of Governing Boards.

Kintzer, F. C. 1980. *Organization and leadership of two-year colleges: Preparing for the eighties*. ERIC Document no. ED 241 093. Gainesville: Florida State University, Institute of Higher Education.

———. 1984. *Decisionmaking in multi-unit institutions of higher education*. ERIC Document no. ED 242 362. Gainesville: Florida State University, Institute of Higher Education.

Kintzer, F. C., A. M. Jensen, and J. S. Hansen. 1969. *Multi-unit junior college district*. ERIC Document no. ED 030 415. Washington, D.C.: American Association of Junior Colleges.

Kuh, G. D., and E. J. Whitt. 1988. *The invisible tapestry: Culture in American colleges and universities.* 1988 Higher Education Research Report no. 1. Washington, D.C.: ASHE/ERIC.

Manor Junior College (MJC). 1991. *Catalog 1991–93.* Jenkintown, Pa.: MJC.

Martorana, S. V., and P. H. Garland. 1991. *State legislation and state level public policy affecting community, junior and two-year technical college education, 1989.* University Park: Pennsylvania State University, Center for the Study of Higher Education.

Medsker, L. L. 1960. *The junior college: Progress and prospect.* New York: McGraw-Hill.

Moore, K. M., S. B. Twombly, and S. V. Martorana. 1985. *Today's academic leaders: A national study of administrators in community and junior colleges.* University Park: Pennsylvania State University, Center for the Study of Higher Education.

Pennsylvania State University (PSU). 1991. *1991–92 Baccalaureate degree programs bulletin.* University Park: PSU.

Pierce Junior College (PJC). 1990. *Catalog 1990–91.* Philadelphia: PJC.

Roe, M. A., and G. A. Baker. 1989. The development of community college leaders: A challenge for our future. *Community College Review* 16(4):5–16.

Roueche, J. E., and G. A. Baker, eds. 1984. *Community college leadership for the 80's.* Washington, D.C.: Community College Press.

Tillery, D., and J. L. Wattenbarger, eds. 1985. *Ensuring effective governance.* New Directions for Community Colleges, no. 49. San Francisco: Jossey-Bass.

Tillery, D., and W. L. Deegan. 1985. The evolution of two-year colleges through four generations. In *Renewing the American community college,* ed. W. L. Deegan, D. Tillery, and Associates. 3–33. San Francisco: Jossey-Bass.

Vaughan, G. B. 1989. *Leadership in transition: The community college presidency.* New York: American Council on Education/MacMillan.

Vaughan, G. B., ed. 1980. *Questioning the community college role.* New Directions for Community Colleges, no. 32. San Francisco: Jossey-Bass.

Vaughan, G. B., and Associates, eds. 1983. *Issues for community college leaders in a new era.* San Francisco: Jossey-Bass.

A Synthesis of the Research on the Community College and the Legislative Process at the State Level

Donald E. Puyear

State-level organizational structures for governing or coordinating community colleges vary widely among the states. There usually is, however, a state board with governing or coordinating authority over community colleges and a state director for community colleges. The state director usually has responsibility for representing the community colleges before the legislative and executive bodies of state government and typically exercises some regulating or coordinating function on behalf of the state board with respect to the programs and services of the colleges. Most state directors have a staff which conducts research and analysis, among other responsibilities. This chapter reviews the type and variety of research on community college issues and on the legislative process that has been reported at the state level in recent years.

Procedure

The results reported in this chapter are based on a search of the documents indexed in the Educational Resources Information Center (ERIC) Clearinghouse for Junior Colleges at the University of California, Los Angeles (UCLA), conducted in the summer and fall of 1991, and a survey of state community college directors, conducted in the fall of 1991. The document search included eight separate searches of the ERIC data bases for documents in the following categories: (1) national comparative studies and general background articles; (2) state legislative issues; (3) state assessment issues; (4) documents on California, which is particularly active in state-level research; (5) student retention programs; (6) student attendance patterns; (7) accountability programs; and (8) long-range planning.

Since the ERIC system contains only journal articles and documents submitted by authors, a survey of community college state directors was conducted in September 1991 to locate additional research reports. Two forms of the survey letter were used. Both forms of the letter described the purpose of this chapter and the review of ERIC documents that had been conducted. For states not represented in the ERIC search, the request was made for any recent (1986 or later) papers or other publications on accountability, student outcomes, student retention and completion rates, long-range planning, organizational studies, legislative strategies, or anything else that might fit the general scope of this chapter. For states represented in the ERIC search, the request was for additional recent papers or other publications that may not have been submitted to ERIC.

The ERIC document search yielded the following: (1) eleven national comparative studies or general background documents, only one of which was identified with a particular state; (2) eleven documents on state legislative issues from nine states; (3) six documents from six states on state assessment issues; (4) fourteen documents on activities in California; (5) twenty-nine documents from eleven states on student retention programs; (6) ten documents on attendance patterns from six states; (7) twenty-nine documents on accountability from ten states, and (8) twenty-two documents from thirteen states on long-range planning. Some documents appeared in more than one search. In aggregate, 118 documents and twenty-five states were identified.

Responses to the survey request were received from twenty-one state directors; sixteen sent additional materials. The materials included fifty-four additional documents, excluding routine documents such as catalogs and annual reports, or documents that had been identified previously in the ERIC search. Responses were received from nine states that had not been represented in the ERIC search, including six responses that included materials. Between the ERIC search and the survey, documents were cited from thirty-one states; 172 documents were identified.

CONTENT REVIEW

The abstracts from the ERIC search and the documents submitted by the state directors were reviewed to identify the types of documents involved and the nature of their content. The results of this review are summarized below.

Types of Documents

The abstracts and documents were reviewed to find whether they could properly be characterized as state-level documents or research reports. Those produced as the result of a study by a state-level office or organization, or a study focusing on a single state, were considered state-level documents. This included university-based studies that featured a single state, but excluded studies that focused on nationwide or regional data. Studies conducted by college-level institutional research offices and dealing with matters within a single college, city, or district were also excluded from the statewide category. Documents were considered to be based on research if they involved the collection or systematic analysis of data or survey information. Documents that merely described or proposed some activity, policy, or institution were not included in this category.

All documents submitted in response to the survey of state directors and 75 percent of the documents identified in the ERIC searches were classified as state-level documents. Eighty-two percent of the ERIC documents and 67 percent of the survey documents were classified as research documents. For the combined pool of all documents, 83 percent were identified as state-level documents, 77 percent were research reports, and 62 percent were in both the state-level and research categories. All documents, whether or not they were classified as state-level or research documents, are included in the following topical discussions.

Accountability

Accountability includes a broad array of topics dealing with institutional effectiveness, student outcomes, quality standards, performance measures, compliance with state and federal mandates, and related topics. These topics have been of great interest to several state legislatures and regional accrediting bodies. It is not surprising, therefore, that the greatest number of documents identified in this study address some aspect of accountability.

Besides the documents identified in the ERIC searches on accountability and state assessment issues, a scattering of documents in the other searches and sixteen of the fifty-four documents submitted by the state directors dealt with accountability. Fifty-two documents were identified in these areas. Typical documents include an assessment model (California Community Colleges 1990); background papers (Roesler 1988; Smith 1989); commission reports (New Mexico State Commission on Postsecondary Education 1986); evaluation reports (Maryland State Board for Community Colleges 1990); articles (Piland 1987); and papers (Witt 1987).

Students

Student success is a major responsibility of any institution of higher education. It is particularly important to community colleges. Many issues related to student success were included in the previous section on accountability. The primary concerns of research reported are attendance patterns, retention, graduation rates, placement, and transfer. The extent to which particular racial, ethnic, or socioeconomic groups are served and the effect of specific programs on student success are also addressed.

There were thirty-eight documents relating to students and student services and forty dealing with student retention and transfer. Since these are not mutually exclusive categories, some, but not all, documents appeared in both categories. Typical documents include a retention resource manual from Alabama (Cantree

1985); a report on principles of effective retention (Tinto 1987); and state-level research reports (Puyear 1989, 1990) on retention and graduation rates. Much of the research on student success is conducted at the college level, and few college-level research reports (Garcia and Thompson 1990; Dillon 1990) were included in the ERIC searches.

Planning

State community college boards and state directors typically have a mandate to maintain a long-range plan for community colleges in the state. These plans can be quite sophisticated. Several futures commission reports have been issued, perhaps as a result of the approach of the twenty-first century, perhaps with the impetus of the publication of *Building Communities: A Vision for a New Century* (American Association of Community and Junior Colleges 1988). These reports differ from the usual long-range plans in that they consider broad themes and produce general recommendations rather than specific plans and projections.

Thirty-five planning documents, including futures commission reports and their responses, long-range plans, demographic projections, and similar documents, were identified. Typical of the long-range plans and futures commissions reports are those from Connecticut (Connecticut State Board of Trustees for Regional Community Colleges 1989), Maryland (Maryland State Board 1989), North Carolina (North Carolina State Department of Community Colleges 1989), and Virginia (Virginia Community College System 1988).

Legislation

While a considerable volume of state-level work is done in preparation for presentation to or in response to mandates from legislative bodies, little state-level research was found on the legislative process. The state directors do, however, participate in such research. Since 1975, S. V. Martorana and his colleagues at Pennsylvania State University have produced periodic reports on state legislation affecting community and junior colleges based on information provided by the state directors (e.g., Martorana and Garland 1986). The ERIC search and survey of state directors produced twenty-two documents dealing with legislation. Most of these documents are presentations to legislative bodies, listings of legislative priorities, or summaries of pending legislation. The California Postsecondary Education Commission's *Legislative Priorities* (1988) and the Arizona Community College Board's *Summary of 1991 Legislation Affecting Community Colleges* (1991) are typical of the documents identified in this category.

Politics

Politics are, of course, closely related to legislation. While the two categories could have been combined, it may be instructive to look at them separately.

Most of the eight documents identified as dealing with politics and the political process have a national focus, and many of them could more properly be called essays than research reports. The following articles are typical of the documents addressing the political process: Pedersen (1987) examines the relationship between state government in the junior college between 1901 and 1946; Dougherty (1988) discusses the politics of community college expansion; Garland and Martorana (1988) look at the interplay of political culture and participant behavior in political action; and Gordon (1988) provides observations from the perspective of a state legislator.

Finance

State directors and state boards work vigorously to enhance the financing of community colleges, but little research concerning this topic was found. As was discovered in the research of legislative matters, state directors participate in periodic surveys on community college financing. In this instance, Wattenbarger and his colleagues in the Institute of Higher Education at the University of Florida have been preparing periodic reports on community college financing since 1973. The most recent volume in this series (Honeyman, Williamson, and Wattenbarger 1991) provides an analysis of community college funding and expenditures in the 1987–1988 academic year.

Twenty-one documents were identified with community college finance. Fonte (1989) discusses financial governance patterns, and Bowen (1986) describes the need for statewide capital outlay planning. A study prepared for the State University of New York (Winter and Fadale 1991) describes the economic impact of community and technical colleges, and the Maryland State Board's strategic plan (1989), like most such plans, has a financial component. A Rhode Island Special Legislative Commission (1987) prepared a report on financing higher education in that state. These examples represent the range of documents on community college finance identified in this study.

Organization and Governance

The organization of community colleges and of the state-level structure to govern or coordinate them varies widely from state to state. While change in basic structure is usually slow, it is also continuous. The ERIC search and survey of state directors produced eighteen documents addressing organization and eighteen discussing governance. Twelve documents addressed both topics. Most of these were long-range plans and futures commission reports that discussed organization and governance along with other issues, but some documents addressed organization and governance more directly. When funds are scarce, as they have been in recent years, there is a renewed incentive to consider restructuring the colleges or state systems to produce economies. The restructuring of the Alaska system of higher education (Gaylord and Rogers 1988) is an extreme example. Nebraska's legislature recently considered the roles of community colleges in the state (Nebraska Community College Association 1991), and a group of higher education professors in Michigan (Raines et al. 1989) considered the future of higher education in that state.

Curriculum

Most state boards and state directors have some role in governing, coordinating, or regulating the curriculum at the community colleges within the state. Most of the seventeen documents found to address curriculum did so with other topics, and most were comprehensive planning documents. Among the documents dealing more directly with curriculum are the plans produced by the Washington State Board for Community College Education (1990), a paper describing changes to regulations governing the associate degree in California (Farland and Nussbaum 1988), an essay on curriculum as public policy (Kerschner 1988), and a study of the impact of contract courses in New York in meeting the needs of employers (Fadale and Winter 1988).

Faculty

Most of the thirteen documents dealing with faculty and faculty concerns were planning documents that also dealt with a variety of other matters. Notable exceptions to this generalization included a report of faculty and staff development in California (Walters and Howard 1990), a study of faculty replacement needs in New York (Winter, Fadale, and Kubala 1990), and a study on financing community colleges that included faculty compensation concerns (Rhode Island Special Legislative Commission 1987).

Teaching

There were but five documents dealing with teaching, and, except one (McHargue 1989), which dealt with incentives for improving undergraduate teaching, each document was a comprehensive planning document that addressed many topics. This is appropriate at the state level. While teaching is undoubtedly important, it is a topic best left to the individual colleges and the professional association. State-level involvement in teaching strategies is much more apt to create problems than progress.

OBSERVATIONS

Most state-level research is related to functions associated with state-level responsibilities: long-range planning, support for legislative initiative including funding, and responses to legislative requests for information or studies. Considerable state-level emphasis is, however, placed on the assessment of institutional effectiveness, including student success, which could arguably be considered an institutional responsibility. Little state-level research is directed toward faculty or instruction, which are also normally considered institutional responsibilities.

The preponderance of state-level research is directed toward some immediate product, such as producing a plan or making a point in support of legislation or funding. Rarely is state-level research directed toward gaining a better understanding of the institution of the community college. Fundamental research questions such as "What is happening in community colleges that works/does not work?" are largely neglected. There are some exceptions. California, Hawaii, Maryland, Michigan, New Jersey, New York, North Carolina, Texas, and Virginia have reported a scattering of basic research of this sort.

The states listed above plus Alaska, Connecticut, and Florida appear to conduct and report significant quantities of state-level research. Additional work was done in Arizona, Kentucky, Nebraska, Oregon, Rhode Island, and Washington, but it was apparently not reported to ERIC, since it did not appear in the search. Sixteen states either were not identified in the ERIC search or did not respond to the survey. While this does not show that they have done no state-level research, it does suggest that they have not placed any great emphasis on such work.

The general impression gained from this study is that, with rare exceptions, state-level research is seen more as a tool for persuasion than for gaining knowledge. This is unfortunate for, in those states with statewide data bases, the possibility of gaining essential knowledge about community college students and educational process is great. If the offices of the state directors do not have the resources or interest to pursue this potential, perhaps these data can be made available for research purposes to university researchers, or to others interested in this type of inquiry. With such access there is great potential for gaining new understandings—confirming good practices or dispelling myths, as the case may be.

REFERENCES

American Association of Community and Junior Colleges. 1988. *Building communities: A vision for a new century.* Washington, D.C.

Arizona Community College Board. 1991. *State community college board summary of 1991 legislation affecting community colleges.* Phoenix, Ariz.

Bowen, F. B. 1986. *The need for statewide long-range capital outlay planning in California: An issue paper prepared for the California Postsecondary Education Commission.* Commission Report 86–9. Sacramento, Calif.

California Community Colleges. 1990. *California community college accountability model.* Sacramento, Calif.

California Postsecondary Education Commission. 1988. *Legislative priorities of the commission, 1988.* Commission Report 88–2. Sacramento, Calif.

Cantree, B. J., ed. 1985. *Focusing on retention: A commitment to student success.* Montgomery: Alabama State Department of Postsecondary Education.

Connecticut State Board of Trustees for Regional Community Colleges. 1989. *Towards 2000: A long-range plan for the community colleges of Connecticut.* Hartford, Conn.

Dillon, P. H. 1990. *The myth of the two-year college: Length and variation in the time students take to complete associate degree requirements.* Los Angeles: Office of Research, Planning and Development, Los Angeles Community College District.

Dougherty, K. J. 1988. The politics of community college expansion: Beyond the functionalist and class-reproduction explanations. *American Journal of Education* 96(3):351–93.

Fadale, L. M., and G. M. Winter. 1988. *Impact of economic development programs in SUNY Community Colleges: A study of contract courses.* Albany, N.Y.: Two-Year College Development Center, University at Albany, State University of New York.

Farland, R., and T. J. Nussbaum. 1988. *Revisions to regulations strengthening the associate degree.* Sacramento: Office of the Chancellor, California Community Colleges.

Fonte, R. 1989. Financial governance patterns among two year colleges. Paper presented at the annual meeting of the Association for the Study of Higher Education, November 2–5, Atlanta, Georgia.

Garcia, R. Z., and V. Thompson. 1990. How long does it take to get a community college degree? The experience of spring 1987 graduates of the City Colleges of Chicago. Research paper prepared by the City Colleges of Chicago, Illinois.

Garland, P. H., and S. V. Martorana. 1988. The interplay of political culture and participant behavior in political action to enact significant state community college legislation. *Community College Review* 16(2):30–43.

Gaylord, T. A., and B. Rogers. 1988. Restructuring the University of Alaska statewide system of higher education. Paper presented at the annual international conference of the Society for College and University Planning, July 31-August 3, Toronto, Ontario.

Gordon, J. D. 1988. The Gordon rule: A state legislator fulfills his responsibility. In *External influences on the curriculum,* ed. D. B. Wolf and M. L. Zoglin, 23–30. New Directions for Community Colleges, no. 16. San Francisco: Jossey-Bass.

Honeyman, D., M. L. Williamson, and J. L. Wattenbarger. 1991. *Community college financing 1990: Challenges for a new decade.* Washington, D.C.: American Association of Community and Junior Colleges.

Kerschner, L. R. 1988. Curriculum as public policy. In *External influences on the curriculum,* ed. D. B. Wolf and M. L. Zoglin, 43–51. New Directions for Community Colleges, no. 16. San Francisco: Jossey-Bass.

Martorana, S. V., and P. H. Garland. 1986. *State legislation and state level public policy affecting community, junior and two-year technical college education, 1985.* University Park: Pennsylvania State University, Center for the Study of Higher Education.

Maryland State Board for Community Colleges. 1989. *Strategic plan for Maryland community colleges.* Annapolis, Md.

———. 1990. *1989 program evaluations.* Annapolis, Md.: Maryland Community Colleges.

McHargue, M. 1989. *Incentives for improving undergraduate teaching in the California community colleges*. Sacramento: Chancellor's Office, California Community Colleges.

Nebraska Community College Association. 1991. Excerpts: LB 247 Higher education committee reports related to roles of community colleges. Lincoln, Nebr.

New Mexico State Commission on Postsecondary Education. 1986. *Excellence and accountability: Report of the governor's task force on higher education reform*. Santa Fe, N.M.

North Carolina State Department of Community Colleges. 1989. *Gaining the competitive edge: The challenge to North Carolina's community colleges*. Raleigh: Commission on the Future of the North Carolina Community College System.

Pedersen, R. 1987. State government and the junior college, 1901–1946. *Community College Review* 14(4):48–52.

Piland, W. E. 1987. Evaluation of a state compliance system for community colleges. *Community College Review* 14(4):11–18.

Puyear, D. E. 1989. *Semesters, enrollment, and retention: The effect of converting from quarters to semesters on enrollment and retention in the Virginia community college system*. Richmond: Virginia Community College System.

————. 1990. *Persistence and graduation rates of full-time degree students enrolling for the first time in the fall quarter 1981 through the fall quarter 1986*. Richmond: Virginia Community College System.

Raines, M. R., et al. 1989. *Thinking together about the new century in Michigan higher education*. Project 90: A Priority Assessment from Professors of Higher Education within the Education Administration Department of the College of Education, Michigan State University. East Lansing, Mich.

Rhode Island Special Legislative Commission. 1987. *Toward excellence without extravagance: Report of the blue ribbon commission to study the funding of public higher education in Rhode Island including compensation of faculty*. Providence, R.I.: Rhode Island Special Legislative Commission.

Roesler, E. D. 1988. *Assessment of institutional effectiveness: A position paper prepared for the committee on the future of the Virginia community college system*. Richmond, Va.: Virginia Community College System.

Smith, K. B. 1989. *Critical success factors for the North Carolina community college system*. Raleigh, N.C.: North Carolina State Department of Community Colleges.

Tinto, V. 1987. The principles of effective retention. Paper presented at the fall conference of the Maryland College Personnel Association, November 20, Largo, Maryland.

Virginia Community College System. 1988. *Toward the year 2000: The future of the Virginia community college system*. Richmond: Committee on the Future of the Virginia Community College System.

Walters, J., and D. Howard. 1990. *Faculty and staff development: A report on AB 1725 activities with recommended guidelines and directives*. Sacramento: Board of Governors, California Community Colleges.

Washington State Board for Community College Education. 1990. *Washington community college program and enrollment plan: 1991 to 2000*. Olympia, Wash.

Winter, G. M., and L. M. Fadale, 1991. *Spring 1991 update: The economic impact of SUNY's community colleges and technical colleges*. Albany: Two-Year College Development Center, University at Albany, State University of New York.

Winter, G. M., L. M. Fadale, and T. S. Kubala. 1990. *A study to identify academic personnel replacement needs in SUNY community colleges and technical colleges, fall 1990*. Albany: Two-Year College Development Center, University at Albany, State University of New York.

Witt, A. A. 1987. Excellence through exit evaluation: The Florida experiment. Graduate seminar paper. Gainesville: University of Florida, Institute of Higher Education.

Wolf, D. B., and M. L. Zoglin, eds. 1988. *External influences on the curriculum*. New Directions for Community Colleges, no. 16. San Francisco: Jossey-Bass.

Entrepreneurial Management in American Community Colleges: Theory and Practice

William L. Deegan

American community colleges have been described as evolving in four generations (Deegan and Tillery 1985):

1900–1930	Extension of high school
1930–1950	Junior college
1950–1970	Community college
1970–mid-1980s	Comprehensive community college

The fifth generation of community colleges has not been completed, but it may eventually be known as the generation of the entrepreneurial college. Entrepreneurship has enjoyed a resurgence in American society generally—from large corporations to small, individual businesses—and the entrepreneurial spirit has also spilled over into the public service sector and is reflected in a growing number of proposals and calls for the use of more entrepreneurial activities as a supplement to other processes. "The need for innovation and entrepreneurship is clear. Public service institutions now have to learn how to build those qualities into their own systems" (Drucker 1985, 186).

Entrepreneurial activities are defined as those that help generate resources from external sources (such as contract training programs with corporations or the creation of private foundations to raise funds). Intrapreneurial activities (internal entrepreneurship, see Pinchot 1985) are activities that help reduce costs or increase productivity within the organization. Although the interest in entrepreneurship has gained great acceptance in American society generally, the term "entrepreneur" remains controversial in education. Advocates claim that the concept can lead to programs that will help generate resources from external sources while benefiting the community and the college, and that it can also lead to programs that can help reduce costs and improve quality and productivity internally. Opponents warn of the danger of leading the college into the wrong kinds of programs, of the potential for divisiveness, and of the potential to change community college value systems in ways that might have negative long-term consequences. In view of these controversies, the objectives of this chapter are to review briefly the emergence of management theory between 1965 and 1990, to review the concept of entrepreneurship in theory, and to present research findings about and suggest guidelines for the use of entrepreneurial management concepts in community colleges.

TWENTY-FIVE YEARS OF MANAGEMENT THEORY: 1965–1990

The search for more effective management and leadership has produced a number of distinctive concepts and theories of management that have influenced the way in which organizations of all kinds are managed today. As part of the research for this chapter, a review was made of the major management books (and the concepts they propose) that have been acknowledged to have been influential in shaping management practice over the past twenty-five years. Some of the concepts reported have endured, in one form or another, over several decades (for example, management by objectives); others, such as zero-based budgeting, appear to be on the wane. The following brief review of major management theories and concepts is presented to help set a context for the data that are reported in the third section of this chapter. The review is not intended to be comprehensive but merely to present an overview of each major approach.

Management by Objectives

Formal planning activities are relatively recent phenomena of American colleges and universities. Prior to the 1950s there was a great reluctance on the part of many academic institutions to plan formally. With the growth in both the number and diversity of institutions in the 1960s, the need for formal plans and state master plans became increasingly important. One of the first models adopted by higher education came from the business world—management by objectives. This model, which assumes rationality in planning, is based on the concepts of needs assessment, resource inventory, mission statement, goals, objectives, plans of action, evaluation, and feedback. Many argue that the basic model of management by objectives endures today in the form of strategic planning which became popular in the 1980s and continues in the 1990s.

The Program and Zero-Based Budgeting Approaches

As we moved from the era of growth in the 1960s into the accountability era of the 1970s, the interest in management theory shifted away from an emphasis on planning for growth activity to a greater focus on tying management-by-objectives plans to budgets. While some of this was always part of the management-by-objectives theory, the financial planning often took a back seat to the development of broad plans and program objectives for growth. As budgets tightened in the 1970s, program budgeting and, later, zero-based budgeting, became concepts important either as replacements for or supplements to incremental budgeting.

Japanese Management Theory

When American companies lost ground to Japanese management corporations in the 1970s, there was a tremendous growth of interest in Japanese concepts and practices. A number of books and studies that attempted to analyze the Japanese theories of management were published late in the 1970s and into the 1980s. Among the most prominent were Ouchi's *Theory Z* (1981) and *The Art of Japanese Management* (1981) by Pascale and Althos. As a result of these books, there was experimentation with such concepts as job circles, job rotation, and matrix organization, as well as a broad framework emphasizing the so-called soft "S's" (staff, style, skills, and superordinate goals) over what were called the hard "S's" (strategy, structure, and systems).

Excellence, Quality, and Leadership in American Corporations

As the interest in Japanese management grew, it stimulated an interest also in studying the American corporations that were successful in competing with Japan. A number of books, such as Peters and Waterman's *In Search of Excellence* (1982) and Deal and Kennedy's *Corporate Cultures* (1982), suggested approaches to management and leadership which had helped American companies to be successful. Among these were a bias for action, a closeness to the customer, the greater use of autonomy and entrepreneurship, an emphasis on productivity through people, a hands-on value-driven approach, an emphasis on basics, a simple form and a lean staff, and simultaneous loose-tight control properties. These concepts, along with an emphasis on building a successful culture that emphasizes quality and productivity, provided a predominant focus for many managers in the 1980s.

Strategic Planning in Education

Just as the business world encountered problems in management and competitiveness in the 1970s, higher education passed through a period of fiscal problems, demands for greater accountability, criticisms for wasting resources, and accusations of becoming an "organized anarchy" lacking direction and focus. As a response to these charges, Keller (1983) wrote an enormously influential book entitled *Academic Strategy*, which calls for colleges to get away from cumbersome, long-term planning models based on outdated concepts and to implement a strategy for a shorter, more realistic time frame. There are several distinguishing features of academic strategy: It is active rather than passive; it looks outward and is focused on keeping the institution in step with the changing environment; it is competitive, recognizing that higher education is subject to economic market conditions and to increasingly strong competition; it concentrates on decisions, not on documents and plans that sit on shelves; and it is a blend of rational economic analysis, political maneuvering, and psychological interplay. It is, therefore, participatory and highly tolerant of controversy. Strategic planning, which concentrates on the fate of the institution above everything else, continues to be an influential model for institutional planning in the 1990s.

TOWARD A THEORY OF ENTREPRENEURIAL MANAGEMENT

A recent milestone in the evolution of management theory came from a series of books that emphasized entrepreneurial management concepts. Entrepreneurship, which was a "dirty" word in the 1960s and a risky word in the 1970s, began to emerge in the literature of such writers as Peters and Waterman, Keller, and Deal and Kennedy, but in the mid-1980s a number of books specifically calling for entrepreneurship as a main theme emerged. Thus authors such as Drucker (1985), Pinchot (1985), and Naisbilt and Aburdene (1985) wrote books calling for entrepreneurial management in both profit and nonprofit organizations.

American institutions may be coming to the end of a twenty-five-year trend toward building bigger organizations. A movement is underway to "deinstitutionalize" America—both in the creation of smaller, more specialized businesses and in the search for ways to incorporate entrepreneurship in larger ones. Entrepreneurial management for large organizations is a concept in its infancy. While no generally accepted theory of entrepreneurial management in large organizations exists, a number of concepts are emerging which constitute a basis for building a theory of entrepreneurship for large organizations.

One fundamental of entrepreneurial management is the need to create a proper climate, or organizational culture, conducive to developing an awareness of opportunities for entrepreneurship. This means attention to organizational structure, funding, rewards, and incentives; a proper balance between control and freedom; and an active search for opportunities.

Once an organizational climate and an active search for opportunities are in place, a second key concept is that entrepreneurial activities, as much as possible, should be organized separately. For an organization to be capable of innovation, it has to create a structure that allows people to be entrepreneurial. It has to devise relationships that center on entrepreneurship, and it has to make sure that its rewards and incentives, personnel decisions, and policies all reward the right entrepreneurial behavior and do not penalize it. This means that the entrepreneurial and the new should be organized separately from the old and existing wherever possible. It also means that someone in the top levels of administration should be responsible for providing support and guidance for entrepreneurial initiatives in order to break down barriers and ensure a fair chance for new ventures.

A third concept essential to promoting entrepreneurship is the creation of a "venture capital" fund. Colleges should set aside a small percentage of their budgets (even if it means small cuts in some area budgets) to provide seed money for new ideas. This is especially important during the early stages of projects when costs exceed returns. Agreement on target results expected after one, three, and five years (and provision of adequate resources to meet those targets) will help in the development and management of effective entrepreneurial programs, and it will also help foster a critical analysis of the role these programs will play in the future of the college.

Related to the concept of a venture capital fund is a fourth concept—the need to consider what rewards and incentives will be provided to encourage and motivate staff to undertake new initiatives. This is a complex issue because the college does not want to encourage a rash of wild initiatives or reward people for failure, but neither does it want to penalize them or discourage them from trying. Each college will need to develop policies on rewards and compensation based on its unique traditions and culture, but the development of such policies is a key ingredient for a successful entrepreneurial program.

A fifth concept to help encourage entrepreneurship is an acceptance of the value of long-term versus short-term thinking. The "quick fix" often does not permit much time to pass before new projects are discarded. As with the venture capital fund, clarifications and agreement on project objectives and results to be expected after specified periods of time will help prevent unsuccessful projects from continuing, and it will also allow new projects sufficient development time to demonstrate their value to the long-term interests of the college.

A final concept is the need to ensure that projects are systematically evaluated. Too often innovation and entrepreneurship are described only on the "up" side—that is as projects are developing. Educators need to hear more about what works, what did not work, and why. There is much to be gained from sharing information about both successes and failures, and colleges should develop systematic evaluation programs to ensure that people learn from the past to help improve the future.

THE PRACTICE OF ENTREPRENEURIAL MANAGEMENT IN COMMUNITY COLLEGES

Given the evolution of management theory briefly described in the preceding sections, and the pressing problems of managing higher education institutions in the 1990s, a national survey was conducted in spring 1990 to determine the use and impact of key entrepreneurial management concepts in American community colleges. Of the 311 surveys mailed, 167 usable responses were returned, a response rate of 54 percent. The respondents were generally representative of American community colleges in terms of enrollments. There were no statistically significant differences between the sample and the institutions listed by enrollment category in the American Association of Community and Junior Colleges Directory. The survey sought to determine answers to two basic questions. First, what management concepts are being used in American community colleges and, second, what is the perception of the college presidents of the impact of those concepts on the colleges. Presidents were asked to report those entrepreneurial concepts they were currently using and to rate the success of those concepts they were currently using on a five-point scale ranging from very successful to moderately successful to not successful at all. For purposes of this chapter, only responses where the presidents were willing to say that a concept was *very successful* are reported.

Table 1 shows the kinds and the range of the use of the entrepreneurial concepts identified in the study.

As Table 1 shows, nineteen concepts were identified as being entrepreneurial— either designed primarily to generate funds from external sources or to reduce costs and increase productivity within the college. Most of the concepts are focused on internal activities. Several internal entrepreneurial activities, such as creating a special unit for innovation, creating a special fund for innovation, and creating new reward systems to encourage staff initiatives, are concepts highly recommended in the literature about entrepreneurial management. Among the least used concepts are matrix organization, quality circles, and job rotation, which have all been highly cited in the literature about Japanese management theory, and zero-based budgeting, which was a fad of the 1970s and early 1980s.

An important issue that these data suggest concerns the gap between the amount of strategic planning taking place institution wide (89 percent of the colleges) and the amount of strategic planning occurring at the departmental level (39 percent of the colleges). These data suggest that much strategic planning may not be translated into action beyond top management levels, an issue that individual colleges should examine as they try to determine the impact and effectiveness of their own strategic planning efforts.

The second part of the questionnaire asked the community college presidents to rate the impact of the various concepts used in their institution. They were given a five-point rating scale with choices that ranged from very successful through moderately successful to not successful. As might be expected, many presidents rated concepts as moderately successful. However, for the purposes of this chapter, only responses where presidents were willing to say that an entrepreneurial concept was very successful are included. Table 2 shows the percentage of presidents rating the various entrepreneurial concepts as very successful.

Many of the concepts at a success rating of greater than 50 percent or from 40 to 49 percent are entrepreneurial concepts that are geared primarily externally, especially to raise funds. The most successful internal entrepreneurial concepts

Table 1
A Framework of Entrepreneurial Concepts

	Community Colleges (%)
Most Used (> 60%)	
Strategic Planning (institution-wide)	89
Use of a College Foundation to Raise Funds	74
Began or Expanded a Contract Training Program	69
Use of Business Leaders as a Primary Advisory Group	64
Used in 40–59% of Community Colleges	
Used Special Units for Innovative Ideas to be Developed or Tried	57
Use of a Special Fund for Internal Innovation	45
Use of Futures Task Force (college-wide)	41
Used in 20–30% of Community Colleges	
Use of Strategic Planning in Departments	39
Hired More Staff to Write Grants (Full-Time)	34
Contracted for Services with Vendors from Outside the College	28
Used a Merit Pay System	27
Use of Futures Task Force (in department)	20
Used in Less Than 20% of the Colleges	
Matrix Organization (college-wide)	18
Used New Reward Systems to Encourage Staff Initiative	17
Used Zero-based Budgeting	17
Used Quality Circles	10
Used Matrix Organization (within units)	7
Used Job Rotation (within units)	6
Used Job Rotation (between units)	5

Table 2
The Perceived Impact of Entrepreneurial Concepts Used in Community Colleges

Concepts	Rated Very Successful (%)
> 50%	
Used Special Units for Innovative Ideas to be Developed or Tried	54
Began or Expanded a Contract Training Program	52
40–49%	
Use of a Special Fund for Internal Innovation	47
Use of a College Foundation to Raise Funds	45
Use of New Reward Systems to Encourage Staff Initiative	45
Use of Business Leaders as a Primary Advisory Group	42
Use of Zero-based Budgeting	41
20–39%	
Contracted for Services with Vendors from Outside the College	38
Hired More Staff to Write Grants (full-time)	37
Used Quality Circles	35
Strategic Planning (institution-wide)	34
Use of Strategic Planning (in department)	29
Use of Futures Task Forces (college-wide)	28
Matrix Organization (college-wide)	27
Used Job Rotation (between units)	22
Used a Merit Pay System	20
Less than 19%	
Use of Futures Task Forces (in department)	18
Use of Matrix Organization (within units)	17
Use of Job Rotation (within units)	10

were the use of special units for innovation, the use of special funds for innovation, the use of new reward systems to encourage staff initiative, and the use of zero-based budgeting, a concept that had low usage but apparently a high rating of success where it was used.

The other two categories of success ratings raise some interesting issues. Contracting with vendors from outside of the college for certain services, a concept that is receiving a good deal of attention and support in the literature of both education and public service management, received a rating of very successful by 38 percent of the college presidents surveyed, a high rating for a concept that is relatively new and controversial. A second issue that the data suggest is that strategic planning, either at the college-wide or department level, does not appear to be as successful as much of the literature would lead readers to expect it to be.

Finally, many of the concepts from Japanese management theory, such as matrix organization and job rotation, received relatively low ratings of success, as did the use of futures task forces in departments.

SOME PERSPECTIVES ON ENTREPRENEURSHIP IN AMERICAN COMMUNITY COLLEGES

The success and use of various entrepreneurial concepts will change depending on the traditions, the history, the financial status, and the organizational climate of a college. The primary objective of this chapter was to develop some baseline perspectives about the use and the impact of various entrepreneurial concepts. The data present a broad perspective on these concepts—on what is being tried and with what success. While the survey data need to be analyzed further through case studies and in-depth interviews, they do suggest some issues that might serve as a focus for analysis by community college administrators.

It seems clear that entrepreneurial approaches to management have emerged as a major force and complement to other, more traditional ways of doing business in community colleges. Most organizational and management theory in the past fifty years has been devoted to building bigger organizations: "bigger" translated as "successful." During the past fifteen years, however, a negative reaction has emerged to the unresponsiveness and ineffectiveness of many very large organizations. A consequence has been the search for ways to reduce the size and increase the effectiveness of large organizations by breaking them into smaller, more entrepreneurial units. This emergence of entrepreneurship in community colleges is part of the effort to "deinstitutionalize" large organizations that is taking place throughout American society.

As reported, the most used and most successful entrepreneurial activity is primarily geared externally, with concepts such as contract training, creating a college foundation, or the use of business leaders in planning and developing programs having both high use and high ratings of success. Internally, the use of special units for innovation, special funds for innovation, and new reward systems to encourage initiative are the concepts with the greatest impact.

A number of management fads of the 1970s and early 1980s (such as job rotation, matrix organization, and quality circles) now have low use and relatively low impact. The use of futures task forces at the department level fits into this category as well. Zero-based budgeting, a major fad of the 1970s, has declined in use, but it has a relatively high success rating where it is still used.

The study also raises several questions about the use and impact of strategic planning. As reported, there is a significant gap between the amount of strategic planning that occurs institution-wide compared with the amount of strategic planning that occurs at the department level. The rating of the success of strategic planning at both levels was also well below what one might expect given the volume of advocacy for the concept that has appeared in recent literature about college management.

One encouraging finding is that there is a good fit between much entrepreneurial management theory and entrepreneurial practice in community colleges. There is some consensus in the works of Drucker (1985), Pinchot (1985), and other writers about entrepreneurship that the concept is facilitated by effective planning and the development of an organizational climate, an active search for opportunities, a separate organizational structure, a venture capital fund, an agreement on rewards and incentives, a long-term emphasis, and a systematic evaluation program. The survey data on the use of these concepts suggest that many colleges are following theory quite closely, and a good deal of the theory is leading to successful practice.

In summary, given the educational climate of the 1990s, which appears to be one of increasing fiscal difficulties externally and increasing problems of quality and productivity internally, the concept of entrepreneurship seems to be emerging as a major complement to the collegial, political, and bureaucratic ways in which colleges have traditionally approached problems. Even though entrepreneurial activities may not reach large numbers of the college staff, they do seem to hold significant potential for both increasing resources from external sources and for reducing costs and improving productivity internally. While entrepreneurship may not be the most used management concept of the decade ahead, it may be one of the concepts that has the most impact on the academic productivity and fiscal stability of American community colleges as they enter their sixth generation.

REFERENCES

Deal, T., and A. Kennedy. 1982. *Corporate cultures*. Reading, Mass.: Addison-Wesley.
Deegan, W. L., and D. Tillery. 1985. *Renewing the American community college: Priorities and strategies for effective leadership*. San Francisco: Jossey-Bass.
Drucker, P. 1985. *Innovation and entrepreneurship*. New York: Harper and Row.
Keller, G. 1983. *Academic strategy*. Baltimore: Johns Hopkins University Press.

Naisbilt, J., and P. Aburdene. 1985. *Reinventing the corporation*. New York: Warner Books.

Ouchi, W. 1981. *Theory Z: How American business can meet the Japanese challenge*. Reading, Mass.: Addison-Wesley.

Pascale, R. T., and A. G. Althos. 1981. *The art of Japanese management: Applications for American executives*. New York: Simon and Schuster.

Peters, T. S., and R. H. Waterman. 1982. *In search of excellence, lessons from America's best-run companies*. New York: Harper and Row.

Pinchot, G. 1985. *Intrapreneuring*. New York: Harper and Row.

Part 5

Resource Development in the Community College

Resource Development in the Community College: The Evolution of Resource Policy Development for Community Colleges as Related to Support from Local, State, and Federal Governments

James L. Wattenbarger

The literature related to junior and community college finance has developed following a pattern similar to its historical evolvement. Because the early junior colleges were generally supported by public school systems, no special attention was given to their financial problems, except when there were not enough funds to carry out their programs. Thus the attention was focused upon internal budgets and the general support for public education. Articles in the *Journal of Higher Education*, memos to faculty, reports to the superintendent of the district, or reports to accrediting agencies when applicable constituted the type of written attention provided for finance.

The contributions of those highly respected researchers in the public school finance field such as Mort, Johns, Morphet, Cubberly, Zook, and others constitute the pertinent literature, but even they did not give very much special consideration to the junior college. The attention of researchers in community college finance followed the trends of junior college leadership as planning moved into community college statewide development, and a special literature on community college finance began to develop shortly after the Truman higher education report became influential (President's Commission on Higher Education 1947).

Since the community colleges were associated with the public school systems during this early period, the literature on public school finance still has pertinence to an understanding of community college finance. However, recent state concerns and changes in support patterns have resulted in grouping these institutions in the planning activities for higher or postsecondary education. Support for higher education has, in many states, been centered on annual or biannual negotiations with the legislature. Planning systems of higher education have increased state-level attention on formulas and state boards' ''middleman'' responsibilities. In addition, concern for the economic development of states has provided an increased emphasis upon support for the technical and career courses and programs in the community colleges as capstones to education and training begun in high school; these two-plus-two programs (tech-prep programs) call for considerations often omitted from discussions of support patterns at either level.

Almost all of the literature relating to financing community colleges assumes that the educational opportunity offered by the community colleges is a valid expenditure of public funds. Several studies have questioned whether this educational value is cost effective and enhances an individual's income when the level of education ends at the associate degree level, but to date few studies question the value of the education itself.

Studies have raised questions, however, about the necessity of maintaining low tuition asserting that equity is better served when higher fees are balanced by higher support for those with financial problems. Breneman and Nelson (1981), in particular, conclude that low tuition is "quite vulnerable on equity grounds." Garms (1972) suggested that a way should be developed to make the cost of attending a public community college comparable to the cost of attending a private institution.

Wattenbarger and Cage (1974) discussed state participation in the financing of community colleges based on criteria current in the 1950s and 1960s: public responsibility, equal opportunity, local control, state coordination, state support for operating expenses, state support for all programs, and state support for capital outlay (Arney 1969). These themes were incorporated into the criteria that developed during that time for evaluating state plans for the establishment of community colleges. Among the criteria were the following:

1. The state considers the community college level of education to be a part of the publicly supported system of education.
2. The state provides equal educational opportunity at the community college level for all who may benefit from this level of education.
3. Local support is an integral part of a state community college system in which each community college is governed by a local board.
4. The state has a unified approach to postsecondary education and, therefore, provides state coordination of a statewide plan for community colleges.
5. The state provides a partnership between the state and local governments in funding current expenses for community colleges.
6. The state provides financial support for all the programs that are offered by the community colleges.
7. The state provides a partnership between the state and local governments in funding capital outlay for community colleges.

Even though these criteria were not universally applied or even universally accepted by all state planners, most of the newly developing state systems that originated between 1950 and 1980 followed these or similar bases for financing the new community colleges. There were variations, of course, among the states. In some cases, there was full support from the state with no local taxes involved; in others, limitations were placed upon support for the community services/ continuing education courses. Some states witnessed constant rivalry between community colleges and previously established vocational-technical schools, and others saw a similar rivalry with the two-year branches of the four-year colleges and universities.

State officials were seeking a "magic" formula that would provide answers to the question: What is the best way to finance the community colleges? The American Association of Community and Junior Colleges established task forces and commissions to look into model legislation that would establish a "best" formula. Studies of normative practice were carried out. Patterns of financing were classified into a taxonomy that served to describe the variety of the fifty states within a framework of four categories: no formulas, formulas with no set amounts, formulas with a set rate or schedule of rates, and formulas with detailed procedural methodologies (Wattenbarger and Starnes 1976). However, in 1988, a new taxonomy was developed to describe the methods current at that time (Wattenbarger and Mercer 1988). This new taxonomy included three types of negotiated budget funding—cost to continue plus, formula plus, and a dual system of appropriation and allocation—and three types of formula funding— unit rate, grant plus, and cost based. Although states were represented in each of the six categories, there was a definite shift in the direction of negotiated budgets.

A series of status studies has been carried out with the cooperation of the Council of State Directors of Community Colleges by the Institute of Higher Education at the University of Florida. These studies provide statistics on the expenditures and methods of allocating funds in the various states. Recent state studies include studies conducted in Florida by Jones and Brinkman (1990) and in Nebraska by Brinkman and Jones (1991).

The economic value of education is of concern to those who influence policy decisions in the cities, counties, and states and at the national level (Alexander 1986). An integral part of this discussion is the extent to which the individual or society benefits from continued educational opportunities. The topic of access enters the discussion at this point (Hyde 1982; Zitewitz and Alfred 1983).

IMPLICATIONS OF RESOURCE ALLOCATIONS

When junior colleges were first developed in some states, the local tax structure was the major source of support for the public school system and, therefore, for the junior colleges as well. State minimum foundation program support for grades 1–12 was not used as a basis for equalization of educational opportunity. State law and policy concentrated upon compulsory education, textbook selection, and uniformity in the public schools. Junior colleges were not involved in compulsory education nor in any of the usual considerations for uniformity. Their requests for funds were directed toward the same local boards that operated the grades 1–12, but since their approaches to scheduling, teaching, employing personnel, and other budgetary questions were completely different from those used by the public school system, local school boards tended to approve the resource allocations with little intensive analysis. As long as the requests were reasonable, the boards were willing to approve.

The college deans (a title often used instead of president) assisted their siblings in the school system in such elections for local taxes as were needed. The competition for funds was with other district services or county services such as fire and police protection, county roads and city streets, sewage systems, and other local services provided through county government or through an overlapping special district board. College personnel were talking with their neighbors and their students and their students' parents about the need for resources. They were talking with individuals with whom they had daily contact and with whom they shared the results of the taxing decisions when they paid their own taxes.

They were also providing limited courses and the less expensive capital needs. In a number of instances, the college shared the high school building with other grade levels, and their academic courses did not require expensive equipment or laboratories. The college budget was simpler in a number of ways.

After World War II, when community colleges began to grow and communities began to discover that local taxation on real property was no longer the best way to tap the potential wealth, many changes in support for education occurred. The public school districts looked to the state for resources in addition to those local taxes that were increasingly difficult to obtain. There was a demand to establish new community colleges in districts separate from the grades K–12 districts and to redefine district lines with the community college as the sole institution in the district. Statewide planning for higher education recognized the community colleges as a part of the planning. The emphasis changed from local competition for the needed tax resources to the state legislature where resource allocation was focused upon many new concerns: universities, welfare, state health services, state highways, and prisons.

State planning was concerned with providing opportunity to all parts of the state using a governance structure that either coordinated or controlled the institutions. Budgets came under the surveillance of the state-level budget director, and comparisons were made with other colleges and with the universities. No consideration was given to raise the expenditures to the level of the universities, however. The emphasis was on the fact that the community colleges were less expensive than other colleges and universities. The legislatures wanted a state-level agent to hold responsible and established state boards to coordinate the community colleges or assigned them to existing state boards that had other responsibilities as well. In either instance, another type of budget review was taking place, and the focus was at the state capitol rather than the county courthouse.

Competition for resources involved state funds that were appropriated by the legislature, and each community college president (or chancellor) knew only a few members of the legislature (primarily those who represented the area of the state where the college was located). Gaining influence related to appropriations became a new type of lobbying, one that was in competition with experienced, often professional, lobbyists.

The community college leadership was also struggling for resources with other parts of the educational establishment and was in competition with universities as well as the public schools. In this arena, community colleges often came in third. Outside of education, however, the rapidly increasing social services were also struggling to obtain the resources that they needed to carry out their mandates. And in those states that maintained a local tax base (and many states still do), the local competition for resources continued the same rivalry as before.

Another new major source was the tempting ability to increase tuition fees or to establish a list of special fees. The famed low-cost-to-students theme of the earlier junior colleges became lost in these changes. Student fees were not always left up to local board decision: State board policy sometimes set the range of fees, or the legislature did it for them. When other sources failed to deliver, the local board increased the student fees.

A major shift in the search for funds from gifts and grants also became a necessity in many community colleges. For the first time, colleges appointed an individual to create a development staff and a college foundation. In some instances, the state legislature provided incentives, such as matching funds, to encourage the colleges to seek funds and the donors to provide them. In addition to the applications for grants from federal sources, colleges prepared grant requests that were presented to various foundations and held fund-raising events to encourage local gifts.

Neither of these latter two sources had a great effect upon the total budgets, however. Funds from gifts and grants were generally allocated for special purposes and categorical aid; high student fees decrease the total enrollment and encourage more part-time student attendance.

CONCLUSIONS ON THE COMMUNITY COLLEGE FUTURE

A recent study of community college finance observed that for the period from 1988 to 1990, an increase in community college tuition had not affected enrollment. It is probable that there is a level to which tuition may rise with no contrary effect on enrollment, but, beyond that, enrollment will begin to decline. Determining this level may have a significant effect upon the philosophy of the open door in the community college. The amount of financial aid will have little direct effect upon this marginal level.

Community college leadership still supports the major philosophical and equal opportunity principles that were basic to the early development of these institutions. Concern is still expressed for the benefits to society from the opportunity for its citizenry to continue education, and there is still endorsement for the encouragement of support from the public tax base. The sources of this support have changed as was noted above. These changes have nine implications for the future.

First, the combination of low tuition and financial aid has encouraged a diversity of students in the community colleges that has enabled these institutions to provide educational opportunity to many who would not have had such educational opportunity otherwise. If tuition increases beyond the marginal level and/or if financial aid is curtailed, this service to diversity in the student body will be likewise limited.

Second, the trend toward more state support will continue until in many states there will be complete support from the state as far as tax support is concerned. A result of this must be an increase in cooperation among the various levels of education. The public school districts will need state support in addition to the local tax support that has been a major factor in their financing; the university systems will continue to depend quite heavily upon state tax sources with a possible increase in funds from federal sources; the community colleges will depend upon state sources in order to provide equity and opportunity. These three levels will need to coordinate their efforts in order to gain adequate support from the legislative as well as the executive branches of state government.

Third, an unfortunate shift from general revenue as a source of support for education (and other state activities) to state lotteries may occur in a number of states. This shift is not a positive step in educational financing since it is a fluctuating source of income that is continually subject to legislative whims.

Fourth, state legislative emphasis upon accountability will have an impact upon many collegiate activities. Pressure to demonstrate efficiency through some state-imposed criteria will increase. One example will be the increased use of testing students as a way of measuring teaching effectiveness. Another will be to discontinue programs based upon some state-level evaluative criterion.

Fifth, at the same time, there will be an increased emphasis on assisting students to obtain marketable skills thereby aiding the total economic basis for the state. This should cause a careful examination of the allocation of resources within an institution, and some changes will develop as a result.

Sixth, colleges will seek ways to improve teaching through classroom quality controls that will be developed by the faculty. Faculty will place more emphasis upon the improvement of teaching and will take active leadership in evaluative activities related to the classroom.

Seventh, student success programs will provide a positive influence upon recruitment and retention of students who, by obtaining an advanced level of educational skills, will be better contributors to the socioeconomic life of the nation. This emphasis will also result from the accountability theme.

Eighth, increasing participation in decision making on the part of the faculty, the lower echelon administrative staff, the career staff, and the building maintenance staff will be necessary if budget limitations continue to increase. Budget limitations will force resource limitations that will require an understanding on the part of all employees in order to maintain quality despite the cuts. Participant perceptions can be effective for positive results or negative results, and these perceptions must be based upon a knowledge that comes with participation in the operational decisions affecting the college.

Ninth, the improved use of teaching technologies including such innovations as better applications in the use of media, more effective use of volunteers, differentiated staffing, improved evaluation procedures, and similar planned improvements will provide colleges with ways to get more service from the available resources at whatever level they exist.

The major conclusion that may be emphasized is that this level of education—the community college—is now a permanent part of the continuum of educational opportunity that will be available in the United States. A new and comprehensive paradigm for education has been developed, one that is based upon the understanding that education is a component of the life of each person for a lifetime.

REFERENCES

Alexander, K. 1986. The value of education. In *ASHE reader on financing higher education*, ed. L. L. Leslie and R. E. Anderson, 191–223. Lexington, Mass.: Ginn.

Arney, L. H. 1969. A comparison of patterns of financial support with selected criteria in community junior colleges. Ph.D. diss., University of Florida.

Breneman, D. W., and S. C. Nelson. 1981. *Financing community colleges: An economic perspective*. Washington, D.C.: Brookings Institution.

Brinkman, P. T., and D. P. Jones. 1991. *An examination of costs and productivity at the Nebraska technical community colleges*. Denver, Colo.: National Center for Higher Education Management Systems.

Garms, W. L. 1972. *Financing community colleges*. New York: Teachers College Press.

Hyde, W. 1982. *A new look at community college access*. Denver, Colo.: Educational Finance Center.

Jones, D. P., and P. T. Brinkman. 1990. *Report on funding of Florida community colleges*. Tallahassee: Postsecondary Education Planning Commission.

President's Commission on Higher Education. 1947. *Higher education for American democracy*. Vols. 1–6. New York: Harper and Brothers.

Wattenbarger, J. L., and B. N. Cage. 1974. *More money for more opportunity*. San Francisco: Jossey-Bass.

Wattenbarger, J. L., and P. M. Starnes. 1976. *Financing community colleges*. Gainesville, Fla.: Institute of Higher Education.

Wattenbarger, J. L., and S. L. Mercer. 1988. *Financing community colleges 1988*. Washington, D.C.: American Association of Community and Juniors Colleges.

Zitewitz, B., and R. Alfred. 1983. The paradox of the open door: Student turnaway in the community college. *Community College Journal for Research and Planning* 3(1):5–14.

The Development of a Structure to Link the Fiscal Function to Strategic Planning in Community Colleges

Byron N. McClenney

If one looks back to the great explosion of community and technical colleges during the 1960s, it is clear that the preoccupation was with facility plans, the establishment of revenue bases, and the development of personnel to deal with an emerging comprehensive mission. Less than thirty years after the boom, the call is for controlling costs and increasing productivity. Reducing costs while improving quality may, in fact, be the strategic challenge of the decade. The movement has been from exciting development to questioning and uncertainty. Zemsky asserts that colleges now "must become more disciplined in their programmatic investments, more capable of growth by substitution instead of addition" (1991, 7A).

From heady growth and incremental budgeting to calls for accountability, community colleges have joined the rest of higher education during a new period of intense scrutiny. Community college administrators now join their counterparts in doctoral institutions in focusing on financial issues as the greatest challenge (El-Khawas 1991, 19). The program of the 22nd Annual Convention of the Association of Community College Trustees (ACCT) (1991) illustrates the concern. Trustees and administrators heard from futurist Robert Theobold and participated in sessions on "Understanding the Budget Process" and "Strategic Decision Making." Proposals for new ways of thinking about planning have been issued (Angel and DeVault 1991) to encourage community college leaders to be more proactive to protect the things we value. Without a doubt, learning how to link strategic decisions to the allocation or reallocation of resources will be a priority during the 1990s as community colleges cope with the economic misery currently experienced throughout the country.

PATTERNS OF RESOURCE ALLOCATION

Most community and technical colleges in the early 1970s were using incremental budgeting approaches through which uniform percentages were applied to a previous year or period. Most institutions were experiencing growth so the incremental approach worked reasonably well. Many states and systems, however, began to impose some order through a variety of approaches to the allocation of resources. Whether to gain control of growth or to deal with stalled growth, the new approaches impacted community and technical colleges. Orwig and Caruthers (1980) reviewed the primary approaches:

Incremental budgeting: uniform percentages applied.

Formula budgeting: specific criteria utilized to make distributions.

Planning-Programming-Budgeting (PPBS): relative costs and benefits of programs calculated and utilized to allocate resources to the programs with the most favorable cost-benefit ratio.

Zero-base budgeting: every activity from base zero and ranking of decision packages justified.

Performance budgeting based on management by objectives: goal-driven budgeting.

These approaches and many other hybrid efforts attempted to introduce a rational, systematic method to translate plans into action. The shift for community colleges was from incremental budgeting without a link to planning to systems in which it was impossible to allocate resources without planning.

The complexity of the systems, which made it difficult to involve all units of an institution, and the volume of paper generated caused most of the efforts ultimately to fail over time. The notion of linking plans to budgets, however, was a thread picked up in the early 1980s as an important element. Work on how to link planning and budgeting effectively remains to be done in the 1990s (Marsee 1991).

Reactions to dire financial situations experienced during the 1980s have been summarized by Angel and DeVault (1991). Most community colleges have implemented some or most of the following actions: hiring freezes, across-the-board cuts, increasing tuition, increasing class size, curtailing services, discontinuing programs, delaying capital expenditures, and instituting long-term productivity studies.

Awareness of these actions led McClenney and Chaffee to ask the question, "Does the budget implement the important values?" (1985, 7). The case is then made that key values and strategic choices about future directions for an institution should have a direct link to the allocation of resources.

EVOLUTION OF STRATEGIC THINKING

Many community and technical colleges were engaged in the development of master plans for facilities in the early 1970s. They moved into long-range planning for programs by the mid–1970s and began to make a transition to strategic thinking by the end of that decade. Evidence that the transition in approach was complete in the early 1980s can be found in a review conducted by Palmer (1983). He reviewed forty-seven documents on strategic planning entered into the Educational Resources Information Center (ERIC) data base during the early 1980s.

The foundation for the transition was laid starting in the mid–1970s as organizations like the National Center for Higher Education Management Systems (NCHEMS) studied planning processes in numerous institutions. Kieft (1978) documented that planning should be based upon a clear mission and should be comprehensive, information based, and linked to institutional decision-making processes. Cope (1978) and NCHEMS (Kieft, Armijo, and Bucklew 1978) talked about the importance of planning being supported by the study of current programs and resources, and of both internal and external information. Van Ausdale's prerequisites for successful planning are top-level commitment, clearly defined procedures and schedules, and broad participation (1980).

A peak of activity for community colleges was seen during 1978–1979 as NCHEMS held regional sessions involving hundreds of community college participants (Armijo and McClenney 1978–1979), and almost every professional association meeting included planning as a program topic. The focus during this time was on how to make planning an integral part of an annual cycle of activity and on how to move beyond long-range planning without impacting the operational units of an institution. A typical five-year plan was seen as outdated after a year or two, and college leaders were looking for ways to implement plans. The search for linkages between long-range plans and operational plans became as important as the search for linkages between plans and budgets.

An indication of the maturing process evident by the mid–1980s can be found in a statement by Moore:

A systematic planning process enables rational consideration of environmental pressures and opportunities, consensus regarding a vision of where the institution wishes to go, and broad involvement of the campus community in determining how it should get there. The planning process becomes a gathering point for various institutional assessment activities, so that information can be integrated, plans for action developed, and priorities established. (1986, 59)

According to Taylor et al. (1991), ''[S]trategy is finding the paradigms that promote institutional aims and mission.'' The promotion of institutional aims amidst changing conditions and the uncertain future has now become critical to community colleges in the 1990s. Vincent states the challenges and the promise as follows:

Strategic planning leads to agreement on the college's mission and provides a broad vision of future directions. It endeavors to reveal the character of an uncertain future while also confronting a highly political environment both inside and outside the institution. (1991, 3)

Theobald and Admire extend the challenge for the 1990s by indicating that "ways must be found to introduce information about the rapidly changing world so that it becomes clear that old solutions will not work while helping people grasp current realities" (1992, 3).

THE CASE FOR LINKING STRATEGIES AND BUDGETING

What has emerged is a clear understanding that long-term or strategic thinking should influence operational planning and actions. Similarly, strategic and operational plans should influence the allocation or reallocation of institutional resources.

As Tierney has suggested, "In the best of all possible worlds, the allocation of resources would follow institutional priorities" (1981, 29). He goes on to suggest, however, that difficulties arise when there is a lack of consensus about priorities. While budgets have always served as control mechanisms and have always implemented choices between alternative distributions, the promising element is the potential to translate plans into action (Orwig and Caruthers 1980). The idea that an institution can understand itself and its environment and anticipate future changes is integral to the effort required during the 1990s and beyond.

Reinforcement of core values and development of a collective vision about future development were at the heart of the approach suggested by McClenney and Chaffee (1985) in an approach to linking planning and budgeting. Additional elements are now being suggested in a comprehensive look at important linkages. "Community colleges that will be effective under the entrepreneurial model will be those that integrate planning, accountability, and resource development" (Blong and Bennett 1991, 32). Keener, Ryan, and Smith (1991) talk about a development plan linked to mission development and clarity as well as strategic thinking about institutional development.

Ewell (1983) also linked the institutional effectiveness discussion to strategic thinking as he demonstrated the use of assessment to identify critical strategic issues that must be faced as institutions move toward goal achievement. The above-mentioned linkages were recognized by the Council for Advancement and Support for Education (CASE) in a handbook for community colleges, and its approach to strategic planning (McClenney 1989) stresses the importance of allocating or reallocating resources on the basis of plans. The Association of Governing Boards of Universities and Colleges (AGB) has even gone so far as to identify forty-two strategic issues under ten critical decision areas as a help to trustees who are struggling with the choices of the 1990s (Frances et al., 1987). Further, the AGB has provided a peer comparison which includes a case study on a community college including cost comparisons with forty-seven other community colleges (Taylor et al., 1991).

The agenda for community and technical colleges in the 1990s will clearly include a search for practical approaches to link strategic thinking and operational plans to the allocation of resources.

PRACTICAL APPROACHES TO LINK PROCESSES

A realistic approach to the assessment of internal and external realities is critical to any approach an institution may undertake to plan a desirable future. Among the important external realities are demographics, political and economic realities, social forces, and the impact of technology.

Among the important internal realities are enrollment trends, program mix, results of program reviews, studies of facility utilization, impact of tenure, student retention studies, collective bargaining trends, affirmative action results, organizational structure, and financial trends.

Although many other areas could be added to either list, it is important to suggest examples out of which may come the critical strategic issues to be faced if an institution is to continue developing. Out of the assessment activity focused on these examples and others should flow information for strategic decisions and guidance for operational planning (Shirley and Volkwein 1978).

Reports and studies by outside organizations can be helpful to supplement assessment work done by internal staff, but it is important that internal constituents view the work as credible. Among the most useful surveys to be done from time to time are the following:

Graduates
Nonreturning students
First-time enrolled students
Employers of graduates
High school seniors
Social service agencies
Economic development organizations
College faculty and staff
Professional associations.

Again, the list is not meant to be all inclusive, but rather to suggest examples of activity that might be part of an annual cycle of activity. What is learned from the assessment activity might be utilized to refine institutional mission, set or modify long-term goals, establish competitive position, and identify the critical issues facing the institution.

Utilization of focus groups or community advisory committees can be useful alternatives to written or telephone survey work. The important ingredient is that the institution have an ongoing commitment, preferably as part of an annual cycle of activity, to assemble useful information to guide the strategic thinking and resource allocation processes of the college. Timely presentation and discussion of this useful information is crucial to successful strategic decision making and budgeting. Theobald and Admire (1992) present a good example of an interactive process with a community through which a college refined its approach to service.

Since it is important to focus decision making on the critical issues, and since the credibility of the people translating data into useful information is crucial, the choice to use a representative group can ensure acceptance of its conclusions (Keller 1983). Many community colleges have found that using a representative planning council or committee can expedite the creation and updated versions of strategic plans as well as the identification of priorities to guide operational planning (McClenney and Chaffee 1985).

Timely preparation of summary papers or issue papers can also be useful in a process to involve all personnel or board members. If the papers draw tentative conclusions on the basis of the data, then reactions can be obtained to inform a planning council during its deliberations. Topics which have proven useful include institutional overview, population characteristics and trends, community economic and social priorities, enrollment trends and potential, faculty and staff survey results, finance and governance, and the impact of technology.

A set of recommended strategic choices, which should come from the planning group, may then become the strategic plan for the future development of the college. Equally important is the step of recommending priorities for the next year in the life of the organization. This is a vital link if strategic choices are to make any difference in the future. A limited set of priorities, perhaps three to six in number, drawn from the strategies can then provide guidance to the units of the college, as they plan for a specific year of operation. These priorities can also be utilized to make resource allocation decisions for that same year of operation.

While a representative council or committee can provide leadership for strategic thinking, operational plans must be prepared by the people who will do the work. With the recognition that strategies will not make a difference until they are incorporated into operational plans, all college units should be asked to follow the guidance provided by the strategies and priorities and to develop operational plans for a specific year. Useful elements in these unit plans are the following:

1. A summary of achievements or results for the current year that can serve as an evaluation of whether a unit did what it said it would do

2. Statements of desirable outcomes for the next year that are responsive to the strategies and priorities

3. A set of projections for a second year (or period) in a cycle of activity, based on the assumption that plans for the next year can be completed

4. A staffing and financial summary updated to reflect the major implications of the desirable outcomes.

An effort to consolidate these unit (department) plans by area (instructions, student services, and administrative services) can be an important next step, particularly if priorities for personnel, capital equipment, and capital projects emerge as a specific outcome. Since these three items make up more than 85 percent of most budgets, causing unit heads to reach agreement on these priorities by area can greatly simplify the budget process once it is launched. Similarly, a college plan can be consolidated through the interaction of area administrators.

A feasible schedule for the above-mentioned activities could be the following:

Weeks 1–6	Planning Council reviews available data and reports, then develops or updates strategies and recommends priorities to guide operational planning and resource allocation
Week 7	Planning workshop held for participants in the process
Weeks 8–9	Unit plans developed
Weeks 10–11	Area plans developed
Weeks 12–13	College plan completed
Week 14	Budgeting launched

Key to success in the operational phase is the dependence on intense activity during a brief period of time. If accompanied by brevity (page limits) in the documents produced, the process need not become a burdensome one.

Only after the unit heads receive feedback on their plans would work begin on line-item budget requests. Major requests would be supported in the plan, or they would not receive consideration. Priorities developed in area meetings would be honored if resources fall short of covering all requests. Equally important, resource shortfalls can lead to the creation of plans for revenue enhancement. Priorities for the development of grant proposals can easily flow from the overall process.

Conceptualization of the overall process could be as follows:

Strategic components: mission/values, strategies, priorities for next year

Operational planning (consolidated by area and college/district): achievements/results of current year, desirable outcomes for next year, projections for the future, staff and financial summary, priorities for personnel, equipment, and projects

Budgeting: allocation or reallocation of resources

Implementation of plans: programs and projects

Evaluation based on results: next round of achievements and results.

OVERCOMING BARRIERS

An institution must be prepared to face certain barriers if it undertakes systematic planning and budgeting. Among the most common barriers are fear of change, lack of time to plan, protection of "turf," bad attitudes based on earlier efforts, lack of commitment, lack of skill in establishing priorities, declining resources, and apathy.

The involvement of people at all levels of a college in an open process to develop a collective vision and priorities for future development will pave the way for breakthrough activity.

BENEFITS OF SYSTEMATIC DECISION MAKING

The redirection of resources (money, staff, space, and time) may be one of the few available mechanisms for maintaining a college capacity for strategic change in the 1990s. Shifts in the distribution of these resources may, in fact, be the only real indicators of institutional priorities. What is suggested is a process for wise decision making about the future directions for a college. It is a process through which conflicts between competing interests can be resolved on the basis of strategic choices. It is also a process through which each college unit is asked how it can contribute to the movement toward the fulfillment of a collective vision.

Those responsible for strategic decision making can ensure success by keeping in mind the following:

1. Stress a commitment to ongoing internal and external assessment
2. Schedule assessment or research activity to provide data and useful information at the appropriate time in an annual cycle of activity
3. Develop and enforce a plan for planning, including a simple format
4. Identify strategic or critical issues through assessment activity
5. Involve people at all levels of the college
6. See strategic thinking as guiding operational planning (next year) and see operational planning as guiding the allocation and reallocation of resources
7. Utilize approved plans to make decisions about staffing, equipment, programs, and capital projects.

CONCLUSIONS

In order to take full advantage of the linkages described, it is essential for an institution to reject incremental budgeting for increases or decreases in total resources. The culture to be created is one in which all involved endeavor to put resources against the most critical problems or the most important priorities. The fact that a unit had money for equipment last year should not necessarily mean money will be available for the same purpose next year. Vacant positions would not necessarily be filled in the same department or division. Reallocation of existing resources should be a possible outcome in every budgeting cycle.

Budgets have always reflected choices, but all too often they have been inadvertent choices. Patience and commitment are required when any institution undertakes the discipline of a systematic approach to planning and budgeting. Rational approaches in political environments can lead to significant struggles. Good answers can, however, come from shared struggles.

REFERENCES

Angel, D., and M. DeVault. 1991. Managing "McLean." *Community, Technical, and Junior College Journal* 62:27–29.

Armijo, F., and B. N. McClenney. 1978–1979. *Executive briefings*. Boulder, Colo.: National Center for Higher Education Management Systems.

Blong, J., and B. Bennett. 1991. Empty wells. *Community, Technical, and Junior College Journal* 62:30–33.

Cope, R. G. 1978. *Strategic policy planning: A guide for college and university administrators*. Littleton, Colo.: Ireland Educational Corporation.

El-Khawas, E. 1991. *Campus trends*. Washington, D.C.: American Council of Education.

Ewell, P. 1983. *Information on student outcomes: How to get it and how to use it*. Boulder, Colo.: National Center for Higher Education Management Systems.

Frances, C., G. Huxel, J. Meyerson, and D. Park, Jr. 1987. *Strategic decisionmaking*. Washington, D.C.: Association of Governing Boards of Universities and Colleges.

Keener, B. J., G. Ryan, and N. J. Smith. 1991. Paying attention pays off. *Community, Technical, and Junior College Journal*, 62:34–37.

Keller, G. 1983. *Academic strategy: The management revolution in American higher education*. Baltimore: Johns Hopkins University Press.

Kieft, R. N. 1978. *Academic planning: Four institutional case studies*. Boulder, Colo.: National Center for Higher Education Management Systems.

Kieft, R. N., F. Armijo, and N. S. Bucklew. 1978. *A handbook for institutional academic and program planning*. Boulder, Colo.: National Center for Higher Education Management Systems.

Marsee, J. A. 1991. Creating the winning edge. *Business Officer* (September): 55–57.

McClenney, B. N. 1989. Strategic planning. In *Marketing and development in the modern community college*, ed. J. Ryan and N. J. Smith. Washington, D.C.: Council for Advancement and Support for Education.

McClenney, B. N., and E. E. Chaffee. 1985. Integrating academic planning and budgeting. In *Strengthening financial management*, ed. D. F. Campbell, 7–19. San Francisco: Jossey-Bass.

Moore, K. M. 1986. Assessment of institutional effectiveness. In *Applying institutional research in decisionmaking*, ed. J. Losak, 49–60. San Francisco: Jossey-Bass.

Orwig, M. D., and J. K. Caruthers. 1980. Selecting budget strategies and priorities. In *Improving academic management: A handbook of planning and institutional research*, ed. P. Jedamus, et al. San Francisco: Jossey-Bass.

Palmer, J. 1983. Sources and information: Strategic management. In *Strategic management in the community college*, ed. G. A. Myran. San Francisco: Jossey-Bass.

Ryan, J., and N. J. Smith, eds. 1989. *Marketing and development in the modern community college*. Washington, D.C.: Council for Advancement and Support for Education.

Shirley, R. C., and J. F. Volkwein. 1978. Establishing academic program priorities. *Journal of Higher Education* 49:472–88.

Taylor, B. E., J. W. Meyerson, L. R. Morrell, and D. G. Park, Jr. 1991. *Strategic analysis*. Washington, D.C.: Association of Governing Boards of Universities and Colleges.

Theobald, R., and N. Admire. 1992. From concept to reality. *Trustee Quarterly* (Winter):5–10.

Tierney, M. L. 1981. Priority setting and resource allocation. In *Evaluation of management and planning*, ed. N. Poulton. New Directions for Institutional Research, San Francisco: Jossey-Bass.

Van Ausdale, S. L. 1980. *Comprehensive institutional planning in two-year colleges*, vol. 1: An overview and conceptual framework. Columbus, Ohio: National Center for Research in Vocational Education.

Vincent, W. E. 1991. Resolving the deficit dilemma. *Trustee Quarterly* (Fall):2–4.

Zemsky, R., ed. 1991. An end to sanctuary. *Policy Perspectives*. Pew Charitable Trusts, vol. 3., no. 4:1–7.

Building Budgets for Effective Resource Utilization

Roland K. Smith

THE COMMUNITY COLLEGE OPERATING ENVIRONMENT

The role played by America's community colleges in providing accessible educational opportunities to the U.S. populace has become increasingly important since the early years of the twentieth century. Growing from a nucleus of eight two-year colleges in 1900 to almost 700 by 1960 and to 1,227 by 1987, two-year institutions now enroll over 5 million students (Cohen and Brawer 1989).

Community College Expenditures

Although some diversity exists regarding the definition of community college expenditure categories, the delineation of academic versus administrative expenditures will serve adequately for comparative purposes. Clarification of the composition of these two major categories is provided by Cirino and Dickmeyer (1991).

They define academic expenditures as those connected with instruction, research, public service, and academic support (including libraries). Administrative expenditures are identified as including costs of student services, institutional support, and plant operation and maintenance. During the five-year period included in the Cirino and Dickmeyer study, community college annual median expenditures for academic and administrative purposes averaged 59.72 percent and 36.47 percent of total costs, respectively.

The 1986 median academic expenditure per credit for a full-time equivalent (FTE) student was $2,589. By 1990 that figure had increased 18.96 percent to $3,080 per credit per FTE student. Correspondingly, the per credit FTE student expenditure for administrative functions grew over this same period from $1,548 to $1,841, an 18.93 percent increase (Cirino and Dickmeyer 1991). The study does not speculate on the ingredients that influence cost increases in the academic setting, but some insight into the reasons behind the continuing year-to-year increases in academic costs is necessary for a comprehensive understanding of the resource-allocation process.

Some of these factors are outside the realm of control of institutions. They consist of "legacies from the period of growth, the spiraling costs of inflation, and the costs associated with government-mandated social programs and government regulation" (S. D. Campbell 1982, 9). Likewise, Hauptman (1989) poses moderated enrollment growth as one culprit in the major per student cost increases experienced during the 1980s. He theorizes that these costs would have moderated had that period's enrollment continued to expand rather than undergo the leveling effect that actually occurred.

Unlike the Hauptman (1989) study, which relates cost increases in part to longitudinal enrollment patterns, Hackney (1986) cites institutional location, institutional mission, and salaries necessary to attract and retain qualified faculty as the basic ingredients in the escalating cost environment in which today's colleges operate.

Despite the speculations and realities that continually escalating costs hold for the future of community colleges nation wide, the revenues available for the support of these institutions "are consistently higher than expenditures" (Cirino and Dickmeyer 1991, 32). Although the classes of revenues available to meet the needs of institutions have varied little over the past forty years, the relative contribution of individual revenue types has varied significantly.

Community College Revenues

The major revenue sources available to community colleges include student tuition and fees, and payments from state, local, and federal governmental authorities in the form of grants, cost reimbursements, direct appropriations, and local property taxes.

At their outset, in the early years of the twentieth century, public junior colleges received 94 percent of their financial resources in the form of local tax funds. The remainder was provided by students in the form of tuition and fee payments. During the early 1940s, state and federal funding entered the community college resource mix. However, local taxes continued to provide the majority of funds available to these schools. Beginning in 1965, the states became the major source of community college funding (Cohen and Brawer 1989, 128). That pattern persists today—approximately 52 percent of the typical 1990 community college's resources are provided by state and local appropriations; local sources provide 10 percent; and federal sources represent from 5 to 10 percent of the available funding (Cirino and Dickmeyer 1991, 32).

Clearly, the pattern over the years has been one in which states have maintained a practice of increasing their funding of America's community colleges. According to a recent study (Jaschik 1990), that trend continues despite the fact that the overall two-year rate of increase in state support of higher education dropped to a thirty-year low of 11.6 percent in 1990–1991. Senior colleges fared slightly worse (increasing 11.5 percent), but state support of community colleges increased by 16.8 percent for 1990–1991 compared to 1988–1989 (Jaschik 1990).

Contention for Resources

Although the prospect of higher education funding difficulties during the 1990s may have caught some observers off guard, the seeds for these financial problems were sown in the mid-to-latter 1980s. Jaschik pointed to "uncertainty about the national economy, brought about by last fall's stock-market crash; continued regional economic problems in states that depend for their revenue on agriculture, oil, or timber; and the reluctance of governors or legislatures to raise taxes in an election year" (1988, A1) as limitations to the availability of financial resources. The bitter fruits of economic downturn may yield a grim harvest for all in higher education. States which only a few years ago "were financing ambitious new higher-education programs to promote their state economies" face a future probably characterized by only minor program expansions (*Chronicle of Higher Education*, 24 Oct. 1988, a 21).

As if the direct consequences of a faltering economy were not enough, the decline in student enrollments experienced in community colleges, such as those in California, have a double-barreled negative effect. The immediate revenue reductions in the form of tuition decreases are compounded by the aftershock experienced when enrollment reductions are factored into state funding formulas (Fischer 1986). Neither can the subjective nature of the political process be discounted as a factor affecting the funding of higher education.

To that point, Benveniste proposes that further deterioration in revenue levels available to these institutions occurred "as their relative share of government allocation also declined" (1985, 183). For example, California's governor exercised an eleventh-hour veto that cut $68 million from that state's community colleges in 1985 (Fischer 1986). In a similar move, the governor of Texas vetoed $52 million in 1986–1988 funding earmarked for community college employee benefits programs. Also, under a worsening financial condition for the state of Texas, that same governor signed legislation in 1989 that expanded the resource base of several South Texas public colleges by making them part of the educational systems of the University of Texas and Texas A&M University (Mangan 1989).

CHALLENGES IN INSTITUTIONAL FINANCIAL MANAGEMENT

There is general acknowledgment among community college leaders that financial difficulties lie ahead for these institutions. By dedicating limited resources to increase program availability to a growing constituency, community colleges may be in danger of approaching certain operational limits.

Alfred (1985) notes the paradox that exists regarding the simultaneous decline in available resources with an ambitious commitment among community colleges to the following: open access, comprehensive mission, quality instruction, program responsiveness, and institutional renewal. It would seem that the very foundations upon which the contemporary community college was founded may be at serious risk.

Just when a philosophy of outreach appears to be essential, some colleges may turn farther inward. As the prospect of funding shortages becomes significantly more likely, there is an unfortunate tendency among institutions to "emphasize financial management as the end rather than the means to an end" (Campbell 1985, 3).

Indeed, a decline in the availability of economic resources apparently heightens institutional sensitivity to financial issues. Skolnik (1986) briefly summarizes the direct relationship between the weakening of an institution's financial situation and its leadership's emphasis on financial matters. Cohen and Brawer (1989) describe specific high-level steps that have been implemented by community colleges faced with the prospect of unbalanced budgets. Finally, Temple (1986) details institutional compromises effected in the face of financial difficulty and cautions against acts of academic hypocrisy that may be invoked in attempts to offset financial difficulties and enrollment declines.

Whether the intent is to emphasize financial management or to effect controls and restraints in response to the scarcity of funds, the consequences for academic management may be the same: First, the emphasis on financial issues can shorten the time frame available for the planning of academic responses to the crisis; second, the numbers of academic participants in the process probably will be directly proportional to the shorter time available to consider these vital issues; and third, the resulting tensions may encumber the quality of any subsequent financial plan. In such an environment, "the few academics who are co-opted into the decision-making process are caught in an intensive process and a series of emergencies which are not their version of the sweetness of academic life" (Benveniste 1985, 182).

While no more unfortunate course of action could be mandated or chosen by any community college, financial resources available to these institutions, whether in times of scarcity or plenty, require strengthened financial management. If the appropriate resource goals of effective utilization, maximization, and security are to be achieved, institutions must be in a position to determine the current status of vital performance indicators, to anticipate and develop strategies for the acquisition of additional resources, and to implement policies that protect and enhance the financial resource base.

Caution, however, is essential since institutional management directs its attention to these latter objectives. Cost accounting models have an appropriate role as one component of a comprehensive institutional decision-support system

(Kaneklides 1985), but they are no substitute for good management. Likewise, many institutional decision-making systems focus on the measurement of program efficiency in terms of decreased unit costs and increased student-teacher ratios, but they do not consider comprehensive program evaluation activities that measure effectiveness in terms of long-range outcomes and values of program offerings (Blong and Purga 1985). Further, a significant amount of time is expended by institutions, related external agencies, and auditors in measuring internal compliance with policies and procedures, in satisfying reporting compliance with applicable statutes, and in assessing financial compliance with applicable accounting rules and regulations. Compliance efforts are essential stewardship roles. They contribute to the preservation of revenues and enhance institutional credibility, but seldom do they provide new funds for the college's use. They cannot replace the accomplishments of a comprehensive development office that successfully raises "new resources in times of declining funds" (Luskin and Warren 1985, 85). Finally, institutions cannot rest on the plaudits that accompany a successful fund-raising campaign.

The 1970s, characterized by high inflation and high interest rates, caught most colleges by surprise. Reserves and endowments languished in idle accounts or in low-yielding securities while advances in the consumer price index ravaged all sectors of the economy. During this period, all institutions suffered the economic effects of double-digit inflation, but some emerged in better financial condition than others. Taylor and Greenway (1985) attribute at least a portion of the success of these colleges to prudent investment management. Whether the financial environment is characterized by inflation or stagnation, "there is great opportunity for the well-managed fund to appreciate beyond the point of inflation . . . [to] provide the college with still another source of increased resources . . . [through mastery of] a few ground rules of investment management" (Taylor and Greenway 1985, 88).

Resource Allocation Strategies

The massive physical expansion of American community colleges during the 1960s and 1970s has ceased, and student growth has moderated. However, community colleges continue to enroll more than 50 percent of the higher-education students in the United States. Facilities are in place and the demand for instruction continues, but the financial condition of these institutions has never been worse. Fundraising efforts have reached new levels, and a fresh consciousness relative to the identification and preservation of revenue sources is emerging. Although the economic futures of institutions of higher education are uncertain, the importance of these institutions to the future of the nation's economic prosperity is well understood.

Colleges are intensifying efforts dedicated to the preservation of existing financial resources and to the development of potential new revenue streams. In addition, these schools may experience important benefits by applying contemporary resource allocation strategies to the capital they currently hold.

The Qualitative Agenda

The commonplace financial difficulties evident in community colleges are the product of revenue reductions and cost increases generic to today's academic fiscal environment. It may be difficult to improve the immediate financial condition of these schools by attempting to increase revenues or decrease costs because neither is easily or painlessly done. However, it has been pointed out that other controllable variables may be at least partly responsible for the escalating educational cost/price spiral. Students of organizational financial theory do not agree on a common set of remedies to the current problems in educational finance. Although the ultimate task of resource allocation probably will be based upon highly sophisticated enrollment and financial models, certain fundamental concepts related to the quality of the process may be useful to all institutions.

One critic proposes that part of the problem may be attributed to shortcomings in the procedures used by institutions to allocate resources and develop budgets (Massy 1989). The key components of this author's recommendations call for an organizational climate in which deans, department chairs, and faculty perceive ownership of the budgetary process. Additional criteria beyond this significant degree of decentralization include incentives to promote efficiency and the availability for "modest reallocations of funds among major academic units when external conditions or institutional priorities change materially" (Massy 1989, 54).

Other organizational theorists point out that, although colleges may acknowledge the existence of reduced resource levels and recognize the need for spending cutbacks, the personnel at these institutions may have neither the experience nor the training necessary to implement large-scale retrenchment strategies (Ashar and Shapiro 1990). In the study cited, the relative merits of the rational choice and decision process models "in explaining retrenchment decisions" were examined, and the authors found a "systematic relationship between objective, evaluative data and policy decisions in time of financial stress." While the decision process model may be appropriate to normal conditions, "retrenchment increases reliance on rational procedures and . . . at least procedural rationality is maximized" through the use of the rational choice model in such circumstances (1990, 136–37).

Still others (Schmidtlein 1989; Foster 1989) suggest that, despite the financial condition of institutions or the qualifications of the staff, higher education generally has failed in its attempts to develop budgets based on well-conceived plans because of a general lack of acceptance of the fundamental linkages between planning and budgeting. These studies also implicate the uncertainty of the future, the difficulty of discerning opportunities and threats, politics, power distribution, and the costs of planning as impediments to an effective planning and budgeting cycle (Schmidtlein 1989).

Finally, Morrell (1989) proposes that quality budget planning and resource allocation strategies depend in large part upon the administrative initiatives (1) to communicate effectively information concerning the college's current financial situation, (2) to involve direct stakeholders in the development of the budget, and (3) to provide consensus-building opportunities among the various components of the institution. Mentoring participants from orientation to advocacy through active participation lends significant credibility to procedural outcomes.

Integrating Planning and Budgeting: Limiting Factors

The previously cited studies clearly suggest components necessary for linking the planning and resource allocation processes. However, institutions generally have not been successful in these efforts.

Reasons given for the lack of progress toward the institutional goal of relating the resource allocation function to a comprehensive planning effort vary. Gillis cites the lack of an "effective mechanism for translating fundamental policy decisions (in)to resource allocation decisions" (1982, 33) as one barrier. Bruegman suggests that the benchmark used to measure the results of planning efforts may be all wrong. He points out that institutional attempts to utilize conventional (commercial) planning methods that lead to bottom-line results do not apply because "the products of higher education are altogether different from the products of a private business" (Bruegman 1989, 20). Gates and Brown (1987) blame the reluctance of institutions to set priorities as one key deficiency in efforts to link the planning and resource allocation functions. Lisensky (1988) cites shortcomings in mission formulation, goal setting, evaluation procedures, and the will to effect remedies as common characteristics of fragmented planning-budgeting cycles. Schmidtlein suggests that some of the blame lies in the parochial attitude represented by "academics [who] value their professional autonomy and academic freedom" (1989, 22) more than they value the allocation of resources by budget office staff, regardless of the efficiencies involved. McClenney and Chaffee (1985) write that leadership may be the missing ingredient. They cite reactive nature, pessimistic attitude, and an absence of risk-taking behavior as characteristic of poorly integrated planning and budgeting systems.

Gates and Brown (1987) suggest three additional factors that affect higher education's ability to link the planning and budgeting processes. First, the perspectives necessary to accomplish these two functions are dramatically different. While planners must by nature look to the future, budgeters concentrate on controlling the present. In addition, the long-term goals characteristic of the planning function are in direct contrast to the more urgent political constraints faced by budget officials. Finally, planning's strength is gained through consensus whereas budgeting involves a bureaucratic process and quantitative goals.

Resource Allocation Techniques

Although the limitations inherent in efforts to link the planning and budgeting functions of higher education are well documented, ''theorists and practitioners for many years have maintained a quest for the secret to a successful linkage'' (Schmidtlein 1989, 9). Indeed, significant energy has been devoted to the development of planning systems, comprehensive budgeting approaches, and decision-making models. These results have gone far beyond the prospective attempts at a mere quest for consequential planning and budgeting systems.

While substantial diversity is represented in the approaches used, the essential first step directed at integrating the planning and budgeting functions emphasizes the necessity for a focused statement of ''needs and [strategies] filling them'' (Foster 1989, 25). Similarly, other theorists recognize that efforts to link planning and budgeting systems must be based on shared institutional priorities, goals, objectives, implementation strategies, and evaluative measures (Gillis 1982; Gates and Brown 1987; Bruegman 1989).

A second step requires the involvement of organizational units in the planning process. Plans should be developed by those responsible for their implementation (McClenney and Chaffee 1985; Lisensky 1988). Since plans probably will be forged through group participation they will not necessarily evolve without struggles related to the choices involved (McClenney and Chaffee 1985). Gates and Brown refer to the process of narrowing alternatives as one of ''gaining consensus on the substantive goals that the link between planning and budgeting is designed to achieve'' (1987, 54).

Third, the organization will need to adopt and utilize a decision model that guides the budgeting and rebudgeting process through the major fundamental choices that the institution must make. Gillis's program choice/resource compaction model represents one higher-order technique for strategizing the annual resource allocation process. Under this approach, each program or function supported by the college is first grouped into one of several categories reflecting that program's stage of development. Next, each program is then benchmarked against the current mix of institutional priorities. This step is intended to measure the extent to which the commitment necessary to move programs toward completion will mesh with established institutional prerogatives. Finally, each program's nature, staffing requirements, activity calendar, audience, and output are blended with revenue and expenditure estimates into a three-dimensional matrix intended to ''combine the attributes of many planning and budgeting systems'' (Gillis 1982, 36).

While Gillis's model initiates the resource allocation process through a stages-of-program development review, Gates and Brown's (1987) model identifies the institution's major budget alternatives and establishes a set of eight decision categories to be addressed during completion of the annual budget process. The strength of this model lies in the interface structured between the eight-step decision model and strategic plans, priority goals, and program plans leading to the allocation of resources at institutional and program levels.

IMPLICATIONS FOR INSTITUTIONAL MANAGEMENT

The financial future of the nation's community colleges has never been more clouded. Their ingrained commitment to meet an ever-expanding set of demands has been one major source of their strength, but that commitment is now challenged by a combination of resource constraints and expenditure requirements. Under such circumstances, the demands facing these institutions arise from problems related to their financial infrastructure and are compounded by the limitations imposed by external funding sources.

In this environment, all institutions are faced with the immediate need to analyze and modify, if necessary, their comprehensive mission statement. Next must come a thorough review of instruction programs and support services with regard for contribution to and applicability within the established mission statement. After program and support priorities have been determined, revenue sources should be quantified and matched against the action plan to itemize the extent and course of budgetary recommendations.

The ability of community colleges to retain their inherent resiliency in the face of multiple obstacles will serve them well in the difficult times that lie ahead. The future will be best addressed by those institutions that invoke a sense of community in the development of the strategies related to institutional mission, program priorities, and resource allocation.

REFERENCES

Alfred, R. L. 1985. Emerging issues in public policy and financial administration. In *Strengthening financial management*, ed. D. F. Campbell. New Directions for Community Colleges, no. 50. San Francisco: Jossey-Bass.

Ashar, H., and J. Z. Shapiro. 1990. Are retrenchment decisions rational? *Journal of Higher Education* 61(2):121–41.

Benveniste, G. 1985. New politics of higher education: Hidden and complex. *Journal of Higher Education* 14:175–95.

Blong, J. T., and A. J. Purga. 1985. Institutional research: A critical component of sound financial planning. In *Strengthening financial management*, ed. D. F. Campbell. New Directions for Community Colleges, no. 50. San Francisco: Jossey-Bass.

Bruegman, D. C. 1989. An integrated approach to academic, fiscal, and facility planning. In *Planning and managing higher education facilities*, ed. H. H. Kaiser. New Directions for Institutional Research no. 61. San Francisco: Jossey-Bass.

Campbell, D. F., ed. 1985. *Strengthening financial management*. New Directions for Community Colleges, no. 50. San Francisco: Jossey-Bass.

Campbell, S. D. 1982. Responses to financial stress. In *Successful responses to financial difficulty*, ed. C. Frances. New Directions for Higher Education, no. 38. San Francisco: Jossey-Bass.

Cirino, A. M., and N. Dickmeyer 1991. Two-year colleges finances stable. *NACUBO Business Officer* 24(9):29–33.

Cohen, A. M., and F. B. Brawer. 1989. *The American community college.* 2d ed. San Francisco: Jossey-Bass.

Fischer, R. 1986. California community college libraries: Spiraling downward. *Wilson Library Bulletin* 60(8):15–19.

Foster, E. 1989. Planning at the University of Minnesota. *Planning for Higher Education* 18(2):25–38.

Gates, L. C., and K. Brown. 1987. The eight-step decision making model: An institution's approach to linking planning and budgeting. *Planning for Higher Education* 16(4):53–62.

Gillis, A. L. 1982. Program choice/resource compaction. *Planning for Higher Education* 10(3):33–38.

Hackney, S. 1986. Under the gun: Why college is so expensive. *Educational Record* 67(2–3):9–10.

Hauptman, A. M. 1989. Why are college charges rising? *The College Board Review* 152:11–32.

Jaschik, S. 1988. Spending by states on higher education totals $36.2 billion. *Chronicle of Higher Education,* (19 October): al,a28.

———. 1990. States spending $40.8 billion on colleges this year: Growth rate at a 30-year low. *Chronicle of Higher Education,* (24 October): al,a26.

Kaneklides, A. L. 1985. Cost accounting for decision makers. In *Strengthening financial management,* ed. D. F. Campbell. New Directions for Community Colleges, no. 50. San Francisco: Jossey-Bass.

Lisensky, R. P. 1988. Integrating the control systems. In *Successful strategic planning: Case studies,* ed. D. W. Steeples. New Directions for Higher Education, no. 64. San Francisco: Jossey-Bass.

Luskin, B. J., and I. K. Warren. 1985. Strategies for generating new financial resources. In *Strengthening financial management,* ed. D. F. Campbell. New Directions for Community Colleges, no. 50. San Francisco: Jossey-Bass.

Mangan, K. S. 1989. Texas legislature approves merging some colleges with state's systems. *Chronicle of Higher Education* (17 May):a23, a32.

Massy, W. F. 1989. Budget decentralization at Stanford University. *Planning for Higher Education* 18(2):39–55.

McClenney, B. N., and E. E. Chaffee. 1985. Integrating academic planning and budgeting. In *Strengthening financial management,* ed. D. F. Campbell. New Directions for Community Colleges, no. 50. San Francisco: Jossey-Bass.

Morrell, L. R. 1989. The faculty and the framework budget. *Academe* 75(6):16–20.

Schmidtlein, F. A. 1989. Why linking budgets to plans has proven difficult in higher education. *Planning for Higher Education* 18(2):9–23.

Skolnik, M. L. 1986. If the cut is so deep, where is the blood? Problems in research on the effects of financial restraint. *Review of Higher Education* 9(4):435–55.

Taylor, C. E., Jr., and D. Greenway. 1985. Managing and investing college funds. In *Strengthening financial management,* ed. D. F. Campbell. New Directions for Community Colleges, no. 50. San Francisco: Jossey-Bass.

Temple, R. J. 1986. Weak programs: The place to cut. In *Controversies and decision making in difficult economic times,* ed. B. W. Dziech. New Directions for Community Colleges, no. 53. San Francisco: Jossey-Bass.

Community College Resource Development: Foundations and Fund-Raising

Lawrence Subia Miller

Community colleges now recognize that alternative funding sources (that is, beyond state revenues, local taxation, student fees, and tuition) will be a prerequisite to their success in the future. With the diminishing of the availability of external grants, two-year schools are looking to fund-raising to provide additional dollars.

The primary method for community college fund-raising comes through nonprofit foundations that obtain and distribute cash and other donations. Typically, funds are raised for student scholarships, faculty and staff development, capital construction or equipment, and for unrestricted operation use (Robison 1981; Ryan 1989a; Council for Aid to Education 1991a,b). Endowment and related funds are often the primary dollars available for the college leadership's unrestricted use. Indeed, "voluntary support frequently provides the margin of excellence, the element of vitality, that separates one institution from another and allows institutions to escape from the routinized sameness of fully regulated organizations" (Leslie and Ramey 1988, 115).

Private giving to American colleges has a history measured in centuries. Yet external foundations are new to community colleges. The exact origin of the first program for philanthropy at a community college is unclear, but junior college foundations were organized by the first decade of the twentieth century (Angel and Gares 1989; Duffy 1980; Sears 1990). More than 80 percent of the currently operating community college foundations began after the late 1960s (Hollingsworth 1983).

This chapter examines some of the considerations basic to fund-raising and foundations in relation to American community colleges. The material is presented in five areas: an overview of community college fund-raising; the historical development of community college foundations; the operations, strategies, methods, and techniques of foundations and development efforts; the factors that are associated with successful fund-raising in higher education; and the characteristics of donors and patterns of giving. Finally, some significant resources for community college advancement will be identified.

OVERVIEW

Although American individuals, corporations, and philanthropic foundations have continued to increase charitable donations yearly, fledgling community college foundations must operate in an increasingly difficult market for private funding. For the year 1988, the total amount given to all American tax-exempt causes was approximately $93.68 million (Harvey 1990). Still, the competition for the philanthropic dollar is steadily increasing as many other not-for-profit organizations turn to the same donor base. Therefore, community colleges who want to join the quest for donated resources will need to become far more effective at what is now generally termed "institutional development" or "institutional advancement."

While community colleges are only beginning to take foundation work seriously, other higher education institutions have been very successful in fundraising. Private universities and major state-supported research universities have set a course for success that community colleges would do well to follow. Data from the Council for Aid to Education, comparing community college foundations with the efforts of four-year institutions, presents a striking disparity in voluntary support between the top community colleges and four-year institutions. For the year 1989, the combined total of reported donations to the top ten community colleges was approximately $16.8 million. Yet, the tenth-ranked four-year school, the University of Minnesota, received about $100 million during the same period (Council for Aid to Education 1991a; Miller 1991). The Council for Aid to Education survey for 1990 reveals that the following two-year schools have been the most successful in terms of annual voluntary support:

Edison Community College (Florida)	$9,010,293
Miami-Dade Community College (Florida)	$5,201,085
New Mexico Military Institute (New Mexico)	$2,961,500
Maricopa County Community College (Arizona)	$2,516,601
Long Beach City College (California)	$2,383,312
Broward Community College (Florida)	$2,174,899
Dallas County Community College (Texas)	$1,588,471
Harrisburg Area Community College (Pennsylvania)	$1,458,689
Johnson County Community College (Kansas)	$1,382,741
Total	$28,678,591

Significantly, the total for the ten most successful community colleges has doubled in two years, and the council's total reported annual support for public two-year colleges went from $44.5 million in 1989 to $59.5 million in 1990 (Council for Aid to Education 1991a,13). These are indications that there has recently been a greater level of success in community college fund-raising.

HISTORICAL OVERVIEW

Voluntary giving is an important characteristic of American society. The private funding for higher education in this country can be traced to the very earliest colleges and universities (Angel and Gares 1989; Curti 1965; Broce 1979). Sears (1918) wrote the first systematic study of private giving to American colleges and universities. Although flawed by today's standards, his research has demonstrated that Americans have supported higher education through private gifts since colonial times. The early period of American education was one in which the institutions of higher learning were supported almost entirely by student tuition and private gifts. An illustration of this private philanthropy was the establishment of the first endowed chair in higher education at Harvard in 1721.

Although the Morrill Land Grant Act of 1862 established many state-funded colleges and universities, the philanthropy of individuals continued to be essential to the financial support of these new schools. Clearly, names such as Ezra Cornell, Leland Stanford, and Johns Hopkins are indicative of the tradition of philanthropy in American colleges and universities.

The first higher education foundation was established at the University of Kansas in 1893 (Sharron 1982). Alumni associations handled virtually all the fund-raising into the early twentieth century, but institutions such as Harvard, Yale, and Princeton led the way in creating separate fund-raising organizations (Pokrass 1989; Sears 1990).

After World War I, fund-raising professionalism at colleges and universities began changing the character of the appeals for money from charity to philanthropy (Brittingham and Pezzullo 1990). Federal income tax legislation with its exemption for charitable giving played an important role in motivating many individuals to give to higher education for reasons related to their personal finances. Although state support to education was well defined by the first third of the century, the importance of charitable contributions has continued to the present. In fact, the significance of alternative financial support for colleges and universities has never been greater than at present (Catanzaro and Arnold 1989).

Two-year public schools have had minimal development operations until very recently. A few reports of organized fund-raising date back to the first decades of the twentieth century (Duffy 1980; Angel and Gares 1989). Largely because of the perception that public junior and community colleges did not have the need to seek external financial support, little activity transpired until the explosion of community colleges occurred after World War II.

In 1965 a University of Texas research project was funded by the W. K.

Kellogg Foundation to seek information about philanthropy for public community colleges. It found that, for the period from 1960 to 1963, about 45 percent of the colleges surveyed received no voluntary support; in fact, most colleges indicated that, as tax-supported institutions, they did not solicit or expect gifts (Bremer and Jenkins 1965).

During the 1960s and early 1970s, while community colleges were expanding rapidly, they were also groping for their true identity. As a result, fund-raising was usually ineffective (Hunter 1987). While a 1974 study conducted by Luck and Tolle reported that less than half of the community colleges in the United States had foundations (Luck and Tolle 1978), by 1987 that figure was 53 percent (649 foundations affiliated with the nation's 1,222 community colleges) (Angel and Gares 1989). However, many college foundations have been passive, serving as little more than collection operations for people who contact a community college about a contribution. Ryan estimates that only 200 of America's community colleges are actively and professionally engaged in fund-raising (Ryan 1989a).

FUND-RAISING OPERATIONS IN COMMUNITY COLLEGES

Fund-raising is new for community colleges. Consequently, reported research on the efforts of foundations to generate new financial resources is also limited. In addition, the effectiveness of development efforts, how well it is done and at what cost, has not been measured in a standardized manner, so comparisons are often difficult. Brittingham and Pezzullo (1990) have described the research literature on development in higher education as limited and fragmented. In spite of the lengthy tradition of Americans giving to education, there has been a lack of interest toward scholarly research on the topic. As these authors suggest, fund-raising has not yet intrigued educational researchers.

With an increase in activity will come a body of literature specific to community college foundations. Currently, the amount of scholarly research on the subject is minimal, although the number of dissertations relating to community college foundations and fund-raising seems to be on the rise. The works of Bremer (1965), Luck (1976), and Degerstedt (1979) have attempted to look at the role of foundations across American community colleges. As the number of community college foundations has grown, more dissertations have taken a regional focus. For example, MacRoy (1970) and Webb (1982) both have examined New York community colleges; Hay (1987) has covered the southeastern United States; Blackledge (1988) has concentrated on two-year institutions in Alabama; Weinberg (1988) has studied Maryland schools; and Jenner (1987) and Nusz (1986) have looked at California's community colleges.

Fortunately, there is a substantial amount of literature that deals with the general topic of fund-raising, which contains some important references to fund-raising for higher education. Much of this material comes from practitioners— the development officers and foundation professionals who do the work of bringing donations to their organizations. Although not in the traditional vein of scholarly writing, this literature is extremely valuable. Many practitioner-authors are well versed in market analysis theory and institutional research, and the data they collect, analyze, and present can be obtained only through their pragmatic efforts.

In part, four-year colleges and universities have been successful in fund-raising because they employ experienced professionals and provide them with adequate resources. Operationally, community colleges are less experienced and have fewer resources. A study conducted by the Council for the Advancement and Support of Education (CASE) described characteristics of the development officers at two-year schools. Those in two-year colleges were less likely to be full-time fund-raisers, were younger, and had less experience on the job. In addition, although two-year development professionals were slightly better educated, they earned less than their peers at other educational institutions (For two-year colleges, little cause for optimism 1990).

A survey conducted of California community college foundations supports these conclusions. Only twenty-nine of the sixty-nine respondents were working for the foundation on a full-time basis. Seventy percent had been in their present job less than five years. Further, the wide diversity of backgrounds and professional experiences indicated "the lack of recognized, standardized training programs in fund raising and foundation management" (Community College Foundation 1989, 12).

Ryan (1988) identifies five reasons why community college development efforts have lagged behind. Community college leaders and their trustees have a fear of being rejected in their fund-raising attempts. Community colleges also tend to be stifled by the comparative success of four-year institutions. Ryan concludes that many CEOs are threatened by fund-raising or are unwilling to give it the time needed. Community colleges are often guilty of beginning fund-raising without an appropriate commitment of resources. Finally, the issues of mission and institutional vision are sometimes clouded when a foundation board becomes yet another player. "There is the fear of conflict between Trustees and Foundation Board members over College fundraising priorities, and there is the fear that College faculty will not be supportive of allocating the necessary resources to make the fundraising effort successful" (Ryan 1988, 7).

How do community colleges evaluate the worth of their foundation and institutional development operations? Clearly, the dollar amount is an essential measure, and the ratio of dollars collected to the costs incurred is another. Yet, there are other ways in which fund-raising can be a positive contributor to the college beyond money. Some are intangible and subtle, as in the goodwill generated by a successful scholarship fund drive. Other measures are more specific: Capital campaigns may yield donated buildings or equipment that would not otherwise be available.

To be effective, development (fund-raising) must be totally integrated into the mission and the culture of the nonprofit organization (Drucker 1990). Most prosperous development operations employ a systematic planning model in which the institution first determines what is to be done and then sets forth institutional goals that guide program decisions. Operational plans to accomplish goals are created, with appropriate allocation of support services and resources. It is critical to establish a system of evaluation for plan objectives through measurement and appraisal (Gianini 1990).

After the amount of money to be raised is determined, a college's development team will generate an overall strategy for fund-raising. The centerpiece is a statement of need, known in the terminology of fund-raising as the "case statement." A concise case statement is used to present compelling reasons why additional funding is needed and how it will be used. A strong case statement should do four things: create interest, arouse desire, secure convictions, and induce action (Fellows and Koenig 1959).

At this point in the process, it is necessary to identify and evaluate donor prospects. Colleges that are already heavily involved with the power structure of their service areas are clearly at an advantage. The prospects already close to the cause are important as first targets not only because they are likely to give, but also because other potential donors may be reluctant to give if the "natural prospects" do not contribute generously.

Start at the center and work out. The farther from the center, the weaker the interest. It is also necessary for one's best prospects to be active in the fund raising organization, where they receive maximum information and cultivation. Such prospects will quickly realize that they must make a gift before they can ask others to do so. (Broce 1979, 44)

Specific fund-raising activities are selected after mission, needs, priorities, feasibility, and potential donors are understood. Some of the common approaches for development include:

The capital campaign. Traditionally, the term capital was given to fund-raising that focused on building projects, as opposed to operational support. However, the term now is applied to major efforts for funding both capital and operations. What distinguishes capital campaigns are the dimensions of size, purpose, duration, and organization (Coldren 1982).

The annual fund. Donations obtained for direct, unrestricted operational support are often collected through the annual fund drive. Typically, such a drive takes place yearly and features such fund-raising techniques as donor clubs (such as the $1,000 per person "President's Circle"), direct mail solicitation, phone-a-thons, and special events (art auctions, poster sales, or gala dinners and breakfasts.) The personal participation of the institutional leadership is critical to annual fund development (Broce 1979).

Corporate and business support. Private-sector business may hold the greatest potential for increased financial support to community colleges. From 1984 to 1987, the amount of corporate giving to community colleges climbed from $10 million to $17.6 million. The percentage of the community college portion of all higher education corporate donations rose from 6.4 percent in 1984–1985 to 9.8 percent in 1986–1987 (Ryan 1989b). Stout found that community colleges can often appeal to business and industry for donations because of their association with technical education and training: "Some donors, especially those in business and industry, are enamored with the occupational orientation of the community college" (Stout 1973, 78). Ryan (1988) encourages community colleges to adopt the development models used in four-year settings, but to replace the emphasis on alumni giving with more effort in corporate philanthropy.

Deferred or planned giving. Donations that come through planned or deferred giving do not pass simply, or quickly, from the donor to the receiver. Planned gifts come in a variety of forms, each with specific legal and financial benefit to the donor. Simple bequests, life income trusts, insurance policies, or the donation of unrealized assets are possibilities. A very complex area legally and financially, deferred or planned giving promises to be an important development component. In general, this is not an area undertaken until annual and capital programs are well established (Walters 1987).

The process of institutional development is always improved by thoughtful evaluation. Certainly when dealing with donated dollars, the institution (through its foundation) has certain legal responsibilities for proper financial accounting. There is great benefit, however, to looking at the level of expenditures required to generate foundation income as a measure of efficiency. Further, the utility of gift revenues and, especially, noncash donations should be assessed.

There are significant differences between two-year community colleges and four-year colleges and universities. Development professionals need to be aware of the differences and to attempt to market their fund-raising in a manner that emphasizes the strengths inherent in these differences. The operational relationship between marketing the community college and the fund-raising effort is critical. The theoretical constructs and methodologies employed in marketing, such as needs assessment, market segmentation, and promotion, can provide the means to reach potential donors (Kotler 1975).

FUND-RAISING SUCCESS FACTORS

Ryan has conducted perhaps the most extensive investigation of development in American community colleges through a national survey of development operations (Ryan 1988; 1989a; 1989b). His survey found that over 80 percent of the institutional fund-raisers identified specific variables associated with successful fund-raising.

First, there must be strong involvement on the part of the college's CEO. Personal activism is essential, including communicating the college mission to the community of potential donors, identifying and planning for goals that are within the mission and can be achieved through alternative funding, and, quite literally, receiving donor contributions. Dr. Robert McCabe, president of Miami-

Dade Community College, in Florida, modestly described his role as being "the one who takes the check" (McCabe 1990).

Community college CEOs are increasingly aware that the external aspects of their leadership are linked to institutional advancement. Their challenge is to manage their college's resources in order to take advantage of alternative financial opportunities, and yet to maintain constant ties with their mission and goals.

Ryan cites the reputation of the institution as the second essential component of successful fund-raising. This touches on the distinction between a charitable contribution (motivations of pity, helping a needy cause) and philanthropy (making a positive difference to a worthy cause). "Donors want to give to a successful organization that makes good use of their money, not to a needy, desperate one" (Worth 1991, 43).

The talents and energy of the development officer and a professional staff were cited by Ryan's study group as a must for serious institutional advancement. A professional foundation staff is necessary for generating sustained, effective giving. Using a variety of skills and tools, from marketing to data base administration, a professional fund-raiser makes a major difference. One needs only to look at the large and well-supported development staffs at Harvard, Stanford, and Penn State to see that the institution's investment in development clearly pays off. A study conducted by the National Association of College and University Business Officers (NACUBO) showed that the dollar intake from a professional development staff exceeds its operational cost by a factor of ten (E. Ryan 1990).

Finally two essential points can be made about foundation boards of directors (Ryan 1989a). First, successful development through a foundation requires a board of directors with a composition that fits the donor community; second, those board members must be active in raising money. This means an active board made up of people who understand that their job is to get money and not to decide how it will be spent. The successful foundation board is usually composed of people who are themselves willing to give and to persuade others of the value of contributing to their local community college. Furthermore, a clear connection should exist between the foundation and key organizational elements of the college, especially marketing, institutional research, planning, public relations, alumni affairs, governmental relations, economic development, and grants administration. Mary Brumbach, president of the National Council for Resource Development, has suggested that a strong institutional cohesion, focusing on the college's mission and objectives, is an important aspect of resource development. When these elements work together, the result is internal "friend-raising" as well as fund-raising (Brumbach 1988).

Success in fund-raising requires an investment of time as well as dollars. Foundations and their activities should be seen as a long-range commitment, not a quick fix. Some community colleges have benefited by beginning on a limited scale with an outside consultant to initiate a major campaign or to handle prospect research (Miller 1991).

Creativity and persistence can be invaluable elements in development campaigns, especially for smaller institutions. Indian Hills Community College, a small, rural school in Iowa, has had a scholarship campaign that is totally funded by its own employees who give at a participation rate of from 97 to 99 percent (Hellyer 1988). Wilkes Community College, in rural North Carolina, has had great success with its foundation, raising over five million dollars in five years. According to their president, "Our size [2,500 FTE] and location became assets, not liabilities. Everything connected with the small rural institution is more personal, more well-known. . . . If the case is presented that the local givers should help the local college and provide local people with quality local educational opportunities, people respond. They come forward because they know that an investment at home pays dividends at home" (Daniel 1988, 66).

In contrast, the urban Community College of Philadelphia (CCP) has no foundation at all. Yet, CCP has had excellent results in grant writing and legislative initiatives, resulting in nearly five million dollars in nontraditional funding during one recent year (Eaton 1988).

The fact that success in obtaining alternative funding can be achieved through a variety of approaches is not surprising. American two-year colleges number nearly 1,300, and each has its own unique properties. Grants, fund-raising, economic development, and even more exotic methods of entrepreneurship are all appropriate in situations where they fit the institutional and community climate (Catanzaro and Arnold 1989; Mitzell 1988).

Several doctoral dissertations analyze various factors associated with community college fund-raising success. Duffy's (1979) study provided a basis for the evaluation of fund-raising success in the community college. Crowson (1985) and Hunter (1987) examined the community college foundation board and its role. Hollingsworth (1983), Paton (1983), Johnson (1986), Glandon (1987), Jenner (1987), and McNamara (1988) attempted to determine predictive factors associated with high levels of performance. Baxter's (1987) study is an analysis of the role of leadership in community college fund-raising. Henderson's (1988) dissertation looks at perceptions about the benefits of foundations for community colleges.

UNDERSTANDING THE DONOR

Although there is an important body of literature that describes fund-raising statistics and practices in higher education, much less is understood about donor behavior. This is especially so for the community college donor base. Why do people give to a cause? According to Soroker (1974), donors are motivated by five pressures: guilt, ego and the need to affiliate, self-preservation, belief in the cause, and as a reaction to pressure. Connolly and Blanchette (1986) and Lindahl (1991) suggest that Americans give as result of complex interactions between the donor and the cause.

In a study of donors who had made gifts in excess of $1,000,000, five factors emerged: belief in the merit of the institution, the objectives and plans of the school, institutional efficiency, competence of the institution's leadership, and tax advantages from philanthropic giving (Young 1980).

Harvey looked at the behavior of donors from a marketing point of view through "exchange analysis," defined as the activities performed and services provided by charitable organizations. Donor satisfaction is expressed through donor perceptions of three factors: the management of the organization, the services supported, and the fund-raising activities. Harvey suggests that an effective marketing approach to fund-raising is to select, or segment, and promote the issues most likely to strike a chord with potential givers. The character and relative importance of these dimensions point to alternative approaches to market positioning. The effectiveness and efficiency of fund-raisers can be expected to vary, depending on whether such organizations select market positions that are important in the view of the donors (1990, 33).

Leslie and Ramey's study (1988) using research university foundations is perhaps the most complete model proposed for understanding donor behavior specifically in higher education. They developed a complex model with eight independent variables along with a series of ratios that were designed to reduce extraneous error from variations in institutional size. The primary conclusion of this analysis was that the main predictor of alumni donation to the universities in the study was institutional prestige.

It is evident that, as community colleges move toward more sophisticated methods of fund-raising, the level of understanding of who their potential donors are, and how they can be motivated to give, will be better understood. At the local level, development professionals are already able to use consulting firms and computer data bases that assist in identifying potential donors. Fund-raising practitioners call this process "prospect research," and it enables institutions to ask for a gift that is both realistic in terms of the prospective donors' financial ability and consistent with his or her interests (Worth 1991).

RESOURCES

Several organizations and professional associations provide important resource bases for community college advancement. Conferences, publications, and networking opportunities available through these groups are very important.

American Prospect Research Association (APRA)

Council for the Advancement and Support of Education (CASE)

American Association of Fund-Raising Counsel (AAFRC)

Council for Aid to Education (CFAE)

Council on Foundations, Inc.

National Council for Resource Development (NCRD)

National Society of Fund Raising Executives (NSFRE)

Special mention should be made of the NCRD which, as a council of the American Association of Community and Junior Colleges, is dedicated to community college advancement.

REFERENCES

American Alumni Council Fund Committee. 1932. *An alumni fund survey*. Ithaca: N.Y.: American Alumni Council.

Angel, D., and V. D. Gares. 1981. Profiles of nine community colleges with successful foundations. *Community and Junior College Journal* 52 (3).

———. 1989. The community college foundation today: History and characteristics. In *Alternative founding sources*, ed. J. L. Catanzaro and A. D. Arnold. New Directions for Community Colleges, no. 68: 5–20. San Francisco: Jossey-Bass.

Any research is better than none. 1990. *Fund Raising Management* (June):36–40.

Baxter, V. L. 1987. Role of leadership in the development of successful California community college foundations: A case study of five California community college foundations. Ph.D. diss., University of LaVerne.

Blackledge, C. H. III. 1988. Characteristics of college-related foundations and private fund-raising in Alabama public two-year institutions. Ph.D. diss, University of Alabama.

Blocker, C. E., F. H. Bremer, and F. S. Elkins. 1965. *Philanthropy for American junior colleges*. Washington, D.C.: American Association of Junior Colleges.

Bremer, F. H. 1965. Philanthropic support for public junior colleges. Ph.D. diss., University of Texas at Austin.

Bremer, F. H., and F. S. Jenkins. 1965. Private financial support of public community colleges. *Junior College Journal* 36(7).

Brittingham, B. E., and T. R. Pezzullo. 1990. *The campus green: Fund raising in higher education*. ASHE/ERIC Higher Education Report no. 1. Washington, D.C.: George Washington University.

Broce, T. E. 1979. *Fund raising: The guide to raising money from private sources*. Norman: University of Oklahoma Press.

Brumbach, M. A. 1988. Resource development and faculty and staff development. In *Resource development in the two-year college*, ed. D. P. Mitzell. Washington, D.C.: National Council for Resource Development.

Carnegie Foundation for the Advancement of Teaching. 1989. The 1980s: A halcyon decade for voluntary support. *Change Magazine* (March/April).

Catanzaro, J. L., and A. D. Arnold, ed. 1989. *Alternative funding sources*. New Directions for Community Colleges, no. 68. San Francisco: Jossey-Bass.

Coldren, S. L. 1982. *The constant quest: Raising billions through capital campaigns*. Washington, D.C.: American Council on Education.

Community College Foundation and Network of California Community College Foundations. 1989. *Community college foundation survey*. Sacramento: Community College Foundation.

Connolly, M. S., and R. Blanchette. 1986. Understanding and predicting alumni giving behavior. In *Enhancing the management of fundraising*, ed. J. A. Dunn. San Francisco: Jossey-Bass.

Council for Aid to Education. 1991a. *Voluntary support of education 1990*, vol. 1: *National estimates and survey summary*. New York: Council for Aid to Education.

————. 1991b. *Voluntary support of education 1990*, vol. 2: *Detailed survey results by institution*. New York: Council for Aid to Education.

Crowson, J. C. 1985. Boards of directors of community college foundations: Characteristics, roles, and success. Ph.D. diss., University of Mississippi.

Curti, M. E. 1965. *Philanthropy in the shaping of American higher education*. New Brunswick, N.J.: Rutgers University Press.

Danbury, C. 1981. Strategies for fund raising when you are the new kid on the block. *Community and Junior College Journal* 52 (3):10–11.

Daniel, D. E. 1988. Wilkes Community College: A rural community college. In *Resource development in the two-year college*, ed. D. P. Mitzell. Washington, D.C.: National Council for Resource Development.

Degerstedt, L. M. 1979. Nonprofit foundations formed by public community colleges: Profile of their external funding. Ph.D. diss., Brigham Young University.

Drucker, P. F. 1990. *Managing the nonprofit organization: Principles and practices*. New York: Harper Collins Publishers.

Duffy, E. F. 1979. Evaluative criteria for community college foundations. Ph.D. diss., University of Florida.

————. 1980. *Characteristics and conditions of a successful community college foundation*. Resource Paper 23. Washington, D.C.: National Council for Resource Development.

Dunbar, M. K. 1987. The relationship of selected institutional and personal characteristics to the marketing attitude of community college faculty. Ph.D. diss., University of Maryland.

Eaton, J. S. 1988. Community College of Philadelphia: An urban community college. In *Resource development in the two-year college*, ed. D. P. Mitzell. Washington, D.C.: National Council for Resource Development.

Evans, N. D. 1986. Diagnosing a foundation. *Community and Junior College Journal* 57(1): 27–30.

Fellows, M. M., and S. A. Koenig. 1959. *Tested methods of raising money*. New York: Harper and Brothers.

For the record. 1991. *Community, Technical and Junior College Times* 3(18):3.

For two-year colleges, more cause for optimism. 1990. *CASE Currents* (September).

Gianini, P. C., Jr. 1990. Planning and resource development at Valencia Community College. Paper presented at the ACC 2000 speaker series, October, Austin, Texas: Austin Community College.

Glandon, B. L. 1987. Critical components of successful two-year college foundations. Ph.D. diss., Brigham Young University.

Hammersmith, V. 1985. The development of a survey instrument to profile donors to athletics. Ph.D. diss., West Virginia University.

Hargis, W. D., and C. E. Blocker. 1973. *A comparative study of philanthropy to American junior colleges: 1960–63 and 1968–71*. Harrisburg, Pa.: Harrisburg Area Community College.

Harvey, J. W. 1990. The fundraising product: Implications for market positioning. *Journal of Professional Services Marketing* 5(2).

Hay, D. F. 1987. Characteristics of philanthropic foundations in public two-year colleges in the southeastern United States. Ph.D. diss., Auburn University.

Hellyer, L. A. 1988. Indian Hills Community College: A rural multi-campus community college. In *Resource development in the two-year college*, ed. D. P. Mitzell. Washington, D.C.: National Council for Resource Development.

Henderson, E. 1988. The relative value and importance of perceived benefits of active foundations of public community colleges in the U.S. Ph.D. diss., North Texas State University.

Hollingsworth, P. 1983. An investigation of characteristics of successful community college foundations. Ph.D. diss., Pepperdine University.

Hunter, C. B. 1987. Fund raising from private sources in public community colleges using not-for-profit foundation boards. Ph.D. diss., West Virginia University.

Jenner, P. J. 1987. Factors associated with success of resource development programs at California community colleges. Ph.D. diss., University of San Diego.

Johnson, J. J. 1986. A profile of selected high- and low-performing nonprofit foundations in public community, technical, and junior colleges in the United States. Ph.D. diss., Virginia Polytechnic Institute and State University.

Kotler, P. 1975. *Marketing for nonprofit organizations*. Englewood Cliffs, N.J.: Prentice-Hall.

Leslie, L., and G. Ramey. 1988. Donor behavior and voluntary support for higher education institutions. *Journal of Higher Education* 59(2): 115–32.

Lindahl, W. E. 1991. Differentiating planned and major gift prospects. *Connections of the American Prospect Research Association* (Fall).

Luck, M. F. 1974. The characteristics of foundations and fund raising in public comprehensive two year colleges. Ph.D. diss., University of Southern Illinois.

———. 1976. Survey report: College foundations. *Community and Junior College Journal* 47 (2):34–35.

Luck, M. F., and D. J. Tolle. 1978. *Community college development: Alternative fund raising strategies*. Indianapolis: Rand R. Newkirk.

MacRoy, C. R. 1970. A study of voluntary support of public community colleges in New York State. Ph.D. diss., State University of New York at Buffalo.

McCabe, R. 1990. Miami-Dade's strategies to improve teaching effectiveness. Presentation to the Community College Leadership Program, November, University of Texas at Austin.

McNamara, D. L. 1988. Characteristics of an effective two-year college private fundraising program. Ph.D. diss., Oklahoma State University.

Miller, L. S. 1991. Community college foundations: Five factors for success. *The Bottom Line: National Council of Community College Business Officials* (Spring): 1–2.

Mitzell, D. P., ed. 1988. *Resource development in the two-year college*. Washington, D.C.: National Council for Resource Development.

Mulder, A. E. 1991. College fundraising numbers incomplete. *Community, Technical and Junior College Times* 3(18):3.

Nicklin, J. L. 1990. Tight budgets spur more 2-year colleges into fund raising. *Chronicle of Higher Education* 37(7):44.

Nusz, P. J. 1986. Development of guidelines for the establishment and operation of a California community college foundation. Practicum paper. Fort Lauderdale, Fla.: Nova University.

Paton, G. J. 1983. Correlates of successful college fund raising. Ph.D. diss., Stanford University.

Pezzullo, T. R., and B. E. Brittingham. 1990. The study of money: What we know and what we need to know about college fund raising. *CASE Currents* (July/August):44–49.

Pokrass, R. J. 1989. Alumni: Friends and funds for your institution. In *Alternative funding sources*, ed. J. L. Catanzaro and A. D. Arnold. New Directions for Community Colleges, no. 68. San Francisco: Jossey-Bass.

Pray, F. C., ed. 1981. *Handbook for educational fund raising*. San Francisco: Jossey-Bass.

Researchers advocate better reporting of charities' financial data to the public. 1991. *Journal of Philanthropy* 23(3).

Robison, S. 1981. The sky's the limit. *Community and Junior Journal* (November): 24–26.

Ryan, E. 1990. The cost of raising a dollar. *CASE Currents* (September).

Ryan, G. J. 1988. *Excellence in educational fund raising at America's community colleges and a key resource guide for educational fund raisers*. Rochester, N.Y.: Monroe Community College, Office of Institutional Advancement.

———. 1989a. The community college foundation today: Reasons for success. In *Alternative funding sources*, ed. J. L. Catanzaro and A. D. Arnold. New Directions for Community Colleges, no. 68. San Francisco: Jossey-Bass.

———. 1989b. Giving to community colleges. *Fund Raising Management* (July).

Ryan, J. S. 1991. Responding to donor signals. *Fund Raising Management* (June): 30–32.

Sears, J. B. 1918. *Philanthropy in the history of American higher education*. New Brunswick, N.J.: Transaction Publishers. Reprinted in 1990.

Sharron, W. H., Jr. 1978. *The development and organization of the community college foundation*. Resource Paper no. 18. Washington, D.C.: American Association of Community and Junior Colleges.

———. 1982. *The community college foundation*. Washington, D.C.: National Council for Resource Development.

Soroker, G. S. 1974. *Fund raising for philanthropy*. Pittsburgh: Jewish Publication and Education Foundation.

Stout, F. D. 1973. The untapped resource of revenue. In *Meeting the financial crisis*, ed. J. Lombardi. New Directions for Community Colleges, no. 2. San Francisco: Jossey-Bass.

Walters, L. 1987. Dollars equal the margin of excellence. *Southern Association of Community and Junior Colleges Occasional Paper* 5:2.

Wattenbarger, J. L. 1976. *The role of the professional educator as the college development officer*. Resource Paper no. 7. Washington, D.C.: National Council for Resource Development.

Webb, C. H. 1982. A policy relevant study of development programs at representative institutions within the State University of New York. Ph.D. diss., Michigan State University.

Weinberg, B. M. 1988. A profile of nonprofit foundations affiliated with Maryland public community colleges. Ph.D. diss., Vanderbilt University.

Woodbury, K. B. 1980. Establishing a foundation: A public institution, including the two-year college, may find that having a foundation aids fund raising. *CASE Currents* 6(4):18–21.

Worth, M. J. 1991. Prospect research, a tool for professionalism in fund raising. *Fund Raising Management* (June):43–44.

Young, J. H. 1978. Shotgunning for $. *Community and Junior College Journal* 49(3).

———. 1980. Resource development in the community college: A time to re-think priorities. *Community College Review* 8(1):24–26.

Part 6

Human Resource Management in the Community College

Human Resource Management Issues in Community Colleges

Glen Gabert

The employment decision is one of the most important any manager makes, and too little attention is focused on it in most community colleges. Administrators and college governing boards frequently do not place sufficient emphasis on the human resources function. What they fail to realize is that all of their plans for high-quality instruction and student support services will fail unless there are high-quality instructors, counselors, technical support staff, secretaries, custodians, and other employees to implement them. And too often the impact of an employment decision is considered only for the short term and not for its full course.

Most states provide tenure or continuing contract status for community college teachers after only a few years. There is little mobility for faculty, and significant numbers of teachers tend to stay in a school district from their time of appointment to their retirement. If a thirty-year-old teacher is hired at a starting salary of $25,000 and is granted a 3 percent raise every year until retiring at age sixty-five, the exit salary of that teacher will be $70,000 and that teacher's lifetime earnings, not counting any additional overload or summer school pay, will have been in excess of $1.5 million. Assuming a 30 percent additional cost for benefits (medical coverage, social security taxes, unemployment compensation, workers compensation, and other insurance), the district will have expended another half million dollars. Hiring an entry-level teacher is not a $30,000 decision; it is a $2,000,000 decision. Hiring a few science teachers is tantamount to constructing the building they teach in, and yet administrators and school boards often focus more energy in choosing lab furnishings than lab instructors.

The impact of that young teacher on students magnifies the importance of the hiring decision. If a thirty-year-old teaches five sections of twenty students each semester until retirement at age sixty-five, that teacher will have taught 7,200 students. A young teacher may teach a generation of students after the hiring manager has left the system or the school board that approved the hire has stepped down from office. The quality of a college's faculty and staff is as much a legacy of any president or dean or school board as is a new building on the campus.

There are no complete and current data on the total number of persons employed in community colleges. There are more than 1,400 community colleges in the United States and Canada, and it would be a safe assumption that their full-time faculty and staff number in the hundreds of thousands. If part-time and temporary employees are added, it is not unrealistic to assume that community colleges employ more than a half million people in the United States and Canada. The U.S. Department of Education estimated that more than 25 percent of U.S. colleges' faculties in 1987 were employed in community colleges (*Chronicle of Higher Education Almanac* 1991, 30). Despite the long-term cost impact of the decision to hire a community college teacher or the number of students that will be affected or the size of the community college labor force, relatively little empirical research focused on human resource management issues has been conducted.

Marchese and Fiori-Lawrence refer to the dearth of research in this area in the introduction to their 1987 report on academic searches (1987, iii). Kaplowitz also suggests areas for needed research in the conclusion of his 1986 ASHE-ERIC monograph on employment issues. It is interesting to read Cohen and Brawer's *The American Community College* (1989) with an eye to human resources management issues. This book has justifiably become a standard textbook for many university courses on community college education. It certainly provides information that any community college manager should know in order to understand what community college education is all about, but the book is virtually silent on the issue of human resources management and its importance for a successful operation.

The most reliable and ready source of information about employment issues in higher education is the Washington, D.C.–based College and University Personnel Association (CUPA). Its membership includes 4,000 personnel administrators who represent more than 1,300 colleges and universities. This organization has recognized the share of the higher education labor market employed by community colleges; as a result, its research and publications focus on issues pertinent to two-year colleges.

The CUPA publishes a quarterly journal and a semimonthly newsletter, *CUPA News*, which focuses on employment issues as well as association news. A typical *News* issue will review recent rulings of federal agencies such as the Equal Employment Opportunity Commission or the Labor Department's Wage and Hour Division. The *News* often carries an "Alert," which is an article on a proposed piece of legislation or agency ruling. Sometimes research conducted by consulting firms is reviewed, and a contact is identified for more information. The *CUPA Journal*, a quarterly "research" publication, is more scholarly than the *News*, but a review of the *Journal* indicates that most of the articles are reviews of practices and primary source materials rather than reports on original empirical studies. Annually, the CUPA conducts a comprehensive survey of compensation practices in U.S. higher education. The report gives salary ranges for almost 200 job titles for various institutional categories drawn from nearly 1,400 colleges and universities. Many colleges look to the CUPA report to price new job titles and to determine their competitiveness in the academic labor market.

The CUPA also publishes books and monographs. The 1988 *CUPA Practical Guide to the Employment Function* is an excellent example. It contains chapters on legal issues, employment processes, and employee relations issues as well as sets of model policy statements and forms. The CUPA publications tend to address nuts-and-bolts issues.

The Society for Human Resource Management (SHRM), formerly the American Society of Personnel Administrators, is the organization that speaks as the official voice of the human resources profession. While its sponsored research and publications often reflect the cutting edge and are of high quality, they usually focus on the issues of personnel in corporate America, and the community college practitioner must adapt the findings and recommendations to fit not-for-profit, locally based, teaching institutions that are for the most part small- to medium-sized employers. The research and publications of the SHRM are generally of first quality, and more community college administrators should become familiar with this organization and its activities. The SHRM publishes the *HR Magazine* monthly. Each issue is typically focused on a topic such as pensions, health insurance, compensation, recruitment, or training, providing an excellent overview of current research and practice in that area. One especially helpful feature of *HR Magazine* is "The Bookshelf," which carries brief reviews of new publications in human resources. *HR News*, also published by the SHRM, is issued more frequently and spotlights issues in the news.

With an increasingly complex matrix of laws governing employment, personnel-related issues probably constitute a major part of any school attorney's attention. One source of research information that is often overlooked by school officials is the National Association of College and University Attorneys, based in Washington, D.C. While the organization is focused on the specialized needs of college house counsel or of firms representing them, the association does conduct research and publish materials useful to the layperson. The organization's *Legal Issues in Faculty Employment* provides an excellent overview of controversial legal issues and includes essays on such topics as tenure, age discrimination, and drug testing.

The Employers Council on Flexible Compensation is a Washington, D.C.–based association that is one of the best sources of information on the complex network of laws governing employee benefits. Its newsletter, *CapitoLetter*, is a good resource. In addition, *Business and Health*, published by Medical Economics Publishing (New Jersey), is a monthly magazine devoted exclusively to health insurance and related employee benefits issues, and it often includes highly readable reports on recent research.

Professional consulting firms have become important resources as laws and regulations have become increasingly complicated and transitory. Many of the big accounting firms now have human resources consulting divisions. Johnson County Community College (JCCC), for example, located in the suburban Kansas City, Kansas, area, has used external consultants for personnel management issues three times between 1987 and 1992. Issues involved were its compensation and benefits programs, the establishment of a new pay system for nonfaculty, and the long-term planning and development of employee benefits programs.

The use of such external expertise is not unique to JCCC. Several of the large firms that specialize in human resources consulting publish periodic newsletters or information pieces, and often a personnel administrator need only write or call in order to be put on the mailing list. These newsletters typically review pending or new legislation and regulations, and may contain synopses of trends or research conducted by the firm. Sometimes full reports of the research are available for purchase. For example, Towers-Perrin (*TPF&C Monitor*) reported on surveys it conducted to determine the managers' level of awareness about such work-force issues as the needs of working women. William M. Mercer, Inc. (*The Mercer Report*) explained a study it had done on the effectiveness of praise versus financial incentives. A recent issue of *ACG Update*, published by the Alexander Consulting Group, was devoted to regulations published by the Internal Revenue Service for qualified retirement plans. An issue of the Grant Thornton *Benefits and HR Adviser* focused on issues related to providing benefits in an inflationary economy, eliminating sexual harassment in the workplace, and ways for improving manager training programs. Other worthy publications are the *Insider*, Andersen's *Compensation and Benefits Insights*, and the Hay Group's *Hay/Huggins Benefits Bulletin*.

Considerable research is conducted to investigate human resource and personnel issues in most community colleges. However, because these activities are focused on particular individuals, positions, groups, or issues in those colleges, the research is institution specific. Not unlike most institutional research, the results of these personnel studies are seldom of general enough interest to warrant publication. This may be one explanation for the lack of a large body of scholarly literature on many personnel issues. The methodologies used, particularly if they are innovative, may be more interesting than the research results.

Several human resource/personnel issues are frequently the subject of institutional research. Wage and salary studies are common. While the annual CUPA survey is useful, it cannot replace more specific issues. A community college, in order to be competitive, must have up-to-date information on the pay practices of other community colleges. Generic compensation studies like CUPA's can only identify trends and status in the broad marketplace. A community college will often need to do its own research for job pricing to provide information sufficient to determine external competitiveness. For classified positions at the

Johnson County Community College, for example, research is conducted on pay practices in the immediate county from which the majority of applicants are drawn; for faculty and administrative jobs, JCCC looks to other large suburban community college districts across the United States. Payroll is the largest single expenditure category in the operating budget of any college, and it is important that compensation decisions be data based.

Benefits surveys are also frequently conducted in house. Those responsible for human resources should know the components of an employee benefits program provided by companies with a similar number of employees in the community, of colleges and universities in the immediate area, and of community colleges in the state. The personnel office would want to know how the rate structures quoted to the college compare with rates of comparable employers in the area. The office would also need to have a sufficient understanding of its own claims experience to determine what vagaries that appear in the college's quoted rates are attributable to general inflation and trends and what are institution specific and attributable to claims history. Finally, the office should research and analyze benefits programs that have been negotiated in the area by any union or association that may represent an employee group at the college. Benefits are tantamount to a surcharge on the payroll—sometimes 25 percent or higher. Benefits costs increase faster than the general inflation rate. In Kansas, in recognition of this, the local school district can legally impose a separate millage just for employee benefits. If a community college is not conducting its own research on compensation and benefits, it had better start doing so.

A highly specialized type of personnel research, although few think of it as such, is the job audit. Typically a job audit consists of breaking a job down into its component parts by using employee and supervisor questionnaires, supplemented perhaps by actual observation of the employee at work. The parts of the job are then factored into a classification system that assigns weights on the basis of such factors as training and education required, responsibility exercised, nature of supervision given or received, authority over budget, consequence of error, or the nature of contacts with persons outside the immediate work area. Some pay programs consider working conditions or labor market factors. The weights assigned are added up for a composite rating which is the basis of assigning the job to a pay grade. Job audit research is important because it is the way a college decides whether its pay for a particular job is internally equitable and externally competitive. Failure to audit correctly can result in the failure to attract good applicants or retain good employees, or can even result in litigation focused on equal pay issues.

Frequently a community college will conduct its own research to learn about comparable human resource practices by local employers or peer institutions. At Johnson County Community College, for example, a study was done to identify the pay and special benefits afforded presidents at twenty other single-campus, suburban community colleges with comparable budgets and enrollments. Local employers were polled to learn how the Martin Luther King holiday was observed. Member community colleges in the League for Innovation in the Community College were surveyed to determine what number of sabbatical leaves they granted as a percentage of full-time faculty. Peer colleges were also asked to provide copies of their organizational charts for review when JCCC considered a possible reorganization. Peer colleges were surveyed concerning their human resources computer hardware and software systems, and follow-up site visits were scheduled to some campuses before a decision was made to purchase a new system. Yet another example was a survey of peer colleges to determine the extent to which they reimbursed candidates for faculty jobs for the expenses of going to a campus to interview. Occasionally institutions conducting this kind of research may share the results with survey participants.

There are many issues of common interest to community colleges that would be suitable fields for study and empirical research. Key among these concerns in the 1990s will be recruitment and selection, motivating and keeping current staff technologically up to date, control of benefits costs, and retirement programming.

An overview by Kaplowitz of issues involved in recruitment and selection point to the need for more empirical research in this area, especially on ''the process and dynamics of selecting and appointing one person from among several candidates; factors which can maximize the efficacy of interviews; [and] issues relating to the selection and subsequent success of internal vs. external candidates'' (1986, 86).

The *Search Committee Handbook* (Marchese and Fiori-Lawrence 1987) is a result of a series of short articles about candidate searches for the American Association of Higher Education (AAHE). Marchese and Fiori-Lawrence report that those pieces generated more reaction than anything AAHE had ever done, so they consulted the ERIC system to review the research. ''What it showed was sparse literature on search, mostly devoted to the selection of presidents (most of that not applicable since the presidential search has its own set of rules)'' (1987, iii). This discovery led to *The Search Committee Handbook: A Guide to Recruiting Administrators*, in which the authors give practical advice for setting up the search process, recruiting and screening applications, and selecting finalist candidates for faculty and exempt positions.

The CUPA's *Interview Guide for Supervisors* (1988) is also helpful for hiring managers. It contains a good synopsis of some of the legal issues such as EEOC requirements. The guide also gives some basic tips for setting up and conducting interviews and background checks. The guide applies to all hiring situations, not just searches for faculty and administrators.

The warnings about an imminent faculty shortage have been many and dire. A study conducted by the American Council on Education cited in the *Chronicle of Higher Education Almanac* (1991, 30) indicated that most community college respondents were not concerned about such a shortage and felt that any such impact would be limited to a few departments. It is probable that the faculty shortage is one issue that will not materialize for community colleges to the extent predicted, although some disciplines will be hard to staff and some community colleges will have difficulty for reasons unique to their location.

Recent research issues in recruitment and selection have revolved around questions such as: What are the traits that make a person a successful community college teacher? or administrator? or secretary? or support employee? What are those predictors of success for community college employment that can be identified beforehand?

The recent research of Baker, Roueche, and others has focused on those traits that appear to be commonly held among successful community college presidents (Roueche, Baker, and Rose 1989). Other studies they have conducted have targeted classroom instructors who have been recognized as master teachers. But, identified in theory, how are those traits accurately spotted in candidates for employment? What weight and consideration should be assigned such factors as personality traits, grade point average, professional preparation, and alma mater, for example? Are better teachers hired if faculty committees are employed or if student or alumni input is encouraged? Do requiring essays or micro-teaching tests of candidates provide this kind of success prediction information? For candidates who are currently employed elsewhere, to what extent can reference checks or site visits be used to gauge future performance?

Community colleges will be the most viable sector of American higher education in the next decade because their enrollments will increase more than those of four-year colleges and universities. Community colleges will be hiring more persons as a result of this growth, as well as because many of those teachers hired during the 1960s and early 1970s (when so many community colleges were established) will be reaching retirement age. Research issues relating to recruitment and selection are critical because a significant percentage of the faculty and personnel that will staff community colleges during the first quarter of the twenty-first century are being hired right now.

Related to recruitment and selection issues is staff orientation. How can a college initiate new staff not only with regard to institutional policies and procedures but more important to the mission of the college and to the needs of the community it serves? And, once initiated, how can that new employee's enthusiasm be retained and renewed?

Staff development is, of course, focused on far more than new employee orientation. There is little turnover of personnel in community college education compared with most profit sector employers. State and federal laws typically make it difficult to discharge faculty without being able to show clear and evident cause; employees in other categories usually have extensive due process rights as well. The leadership of any community college must operate on the assumption that the commitment of the institution to most employees is a long-term one. One challenge for staff development is to ensure that the commitment on the part of the employee is commensurate. Some staff development issues of particular significance for human resources and personnel have to do with keeping a faculty with little mobility motivated, focused on their jobs, committed to the organization, and technologically up to date. Managers need to know what strategies work best to accomplish these goals.

Compensation and benefits will also lend themselves to empirical research of more general interest than annual competitiveness studies. More specifically, there is a need to know the answers to these questions: Are some forms of pay more effective in promoting exemplary employee performance than others? Is there a better alternative than the traditional lock-step pay schedules common in so many schools and the annual across-the-board raise that goes with them? Is it possible to design a pay plan that recognizes and inspires better teaching? Benefits will continue to increase in cost annually into the foreseeable future, and the challenge will remain to juggle higher rates with reduced levels of coverage. Research issues may revolve around the search for new pay and benefits structures along with ways to include personnel in the formidable task of managing the cost of benefits.

Issues concerning retirement and separation from employment also need to be researched and reconsidered. Because so many community colleges were established and staffed over a short period of time in the 1960s and 1970s, their staff now tend to be in their late forties and fifties, and many will be approaching retirement age at one time. Add to this the greying of the population in general, the fact that people are living longer, and that for all intents the legal support for the mandatory retirement age has been removed, and the result is a heightened interest in retirement-related issues on community college campuses. Research needs to be done both on ways to best support staff who want to retire, and on ways to utilize an older staff not ready to retire.

The importance of the human resource function is coming to be realized by many community colleges. Human resource staff salaries as reported by the CUPA have risen higher than those of many other job categories. During the 1990s more research in this area will be undertaken as colleges realize the need to make data-based decisions on issues that are becoming increasingly complex.

REFERENCES

ACG Update. 1981– . Newburyport, Mass.: Alexander Consulting Group.

American Council on Education. 1991. *Chronicle of Higher Education Almanac*: Washington, D.C., p. 30.

Baker, G. A. III, J. E. Roueche, and R. Gillett-Karam. 1990. *Teaching as leading: Profiles of excellence in the open-door college*. Washington, D.C.: Community College Press.

Benefits and H.R. Adviser. 1991– . Chicago: Grant Thornton Compensation and Benefits Committee and Human Resources Group.

Business and health. 1983– . Montvale, N.J.: Medical Economics Publishing in consultation with the Washington Business Group on Health.

CapitoLetter. Washington, D.C.: Employers Council on Flexible Compensation.

Chronicle of Higher Education Almanac. 1991. Washington, D.C.

Cohen, A. M., and F. B. Brawer. 1989. *The American community college*. 2d ed. San Francisco: Jossey-Bass.

Compensation and Benefits Insights. Dallas, Texas: Arthur Andersen.

CUPA Journal. 1950– . Washington, D.C.: College and University Personnel Association.

CUPA News. 1974– . Washington, D.C.: College and University Personnel Association.

Employee Benefits News. 1987– . McLean, Va.: Enterprise Communications.

Hay/Huggins Benefits Bulletin. Philadelphia: Hay Group.

HR Magazine. 1956– . Alexandria, Va.: Society for Human Resources Management.

HR News. 1981– . Alexandria, Va.: Society for Human Resources Management.

Interview guide for supervisors. 3d ed. 1988. Washington, D.C.: College and University Personnel Association.

Kaplowitz, R. A. 1986. *Selecting college and university personnel: The quest and the questions*. Washington, D.C.: ASHE-ERIC.

Marchese, T. J., and J. Fiori-Lawrence. 1987. *The search committee handbook: A guide to hiring administrators*. Washington, D.C.: American Association of Higher Education.

The Mercer Report. 1979– . New York: William M. Mercer, Inc.

1990–1991 Administrative compensation survey. 1991. Washington, D.C.: College and University Personnel Association.

Roueche, J. E., G. A. Baker III, and R. R. Rose. 1989. *Shared vision: Transformation leadership in American community colleges*. Washington, D.C.: Community College Press.

TPF&C Monitor. New York: Tillinghast.

Wyatt Insider. 1991– . Washington, D.C.: Wyatt Company Research Center.

Management of Human Resources in the Community College

Helen M. Burnstad

The origins of staff development in community colleges can be traced to the early 1960s, when "some key people noticed that there was a need for in-service staff development programs in two-year colleges" (Smith 1989, 177). Mc-Keachie (1991) credits Michigan State University and the University of Michigan for establishing the earliest centers for faculty and staff development in about 1961.

During the 1970s, organizations such as the Professional and Organizational Development Network (POD) and the National Council for Staff, Program and Organizational Development (NCSPOD) brought together those who were interested in promoting staff development. Community college staff development officers have benefited from these and other organizations over the years. Betts, in *Energizing and Focusing the Movement* (1991), identifies numerous organizations that have provided assistance to community colleges.

The Program and Organization Development Network, founded in 1976, comprises faculty developers in four-year institutions. The POD sponsors an annual conference as well as annual publications including *To Improve the Academy*.

The NCSPOD, founded in 1977, is made up of about 700 professionals from a variety of venues: two-year and technical institutions, four-year institutions, and private practice. The organization sponsors a national conference each year as well as regional skills-building workshops. The organization's theme is "Promoting Institutional Vitality," and its extensive network of specialists promotes and enhances the profession.

The National Institute for Staff and Organizational Development (NISOD) is affiliated with the Community College Leadership Program at the University of Texas at Austin. Its major contributions to staff development are the annual

Celebration of Teaching Excellence Conference held since 1978 and the publication *Innovation Abstracts*.

Other organizations currently contributing to staff development through publications and conferences are the Community College Consortium—University of Michigan, University of Toledo, and Michigan State University—and the National Center for Research to Improve Postsecondary Teaching and Learning. Many other centers for teaching and learning at community colleges and universities produce publications as well. For a list of these, see the appendix in the POD publication, *A Handbook for New Practitioners* (Wadsworth 1988).

There are several key resources to which staff development professionals have turned over the years. *Staff Development in the Community College: A Handbook* (Hammons, Wallace-Smith, and Watts 1978) has been recognized as a leading resource, especially for those new to the field. In that handbook, the issues raised continue to be the same challenges facing community colleges today: staffing a development office, budgeting, gaining support from administration, and evaluating programs. In 1975, 1977, and 1981, Bergquist and Phillips published three handbooks for faculty development which provided a basis for defining the field, presented sample needs assessment documents, and identified methods for program evaluation. Bergquist discussed the development of the field at the 1985 POD Network–NCSPOD joint conference held in Delavan, Wisconsin. His article, "Reflections of a Practitioner: Ten Years of Professional and Organizational Development," printed in *To Improve the Academy* (1986), is worth review as a summary of his views on the field to that point and of the continuing challenges to those involved in staff development.

As staff development programs have evolved, other books have emerged as excellent resources, including *Achieving Results from Training* (Brinkerhoff 1987), *Innovation in the Community College* (O'Banion 1989), *Enhancing Faculty Careers* (Schuster, Wheeler, and Associates 1990), *How Administrators Can Improve Teaching* (Seldin 1990), and *Teaching Portfolios* (Seldin 1990). In addition, excellent material is available from the American Society for Training and Development (ASTD), which addresses competency, facilitation strategies, and evaluation issues.

Recent trends suggest that more emphasis on human resources development is needed. For example, *Building Communities*, completed by a blue ribbon panel sponsored by the American Association of Community and Junior Colleges (AACJC), states:

Every community college should have a Faculty Renewal Plan, one developed in consultation with the faculty. Such a plan should include campus workshops, faculty-led seminars, departmental and campus-wide retreats, participation in national conferences, short-term leaves, intercollegiate faculty exchanges, and sabbaticals. (AACJC 1988, 14)

Other proposals include setting aside at least 2 percent of the instructional budget for professional development; providing faculty with the opportunity for participation in national conferences and faculty exchanges; granting sabbaticals; setting aside an Innovative Teachers' Fund; and setting policy regarding the selection, orientation, evaluation, and renewal of part-time faculty (1988, 14).

What are the functions of a staff development program? What outstanding program elements have been recognized? What does the future hold for the staff, program, and organizational development function? This chapter presents a definition of terms, a review of selected outstanding program elements, and an examination of current challenges to staff development. Finally, it presents some possible future directions for staff development.

FUNCTIONS

For clarification of the scope of the NCSPOD, the terms "staff," "program," and "organization development" were defined by the NCSPOD board in 1989. But it is important for each college to determine the scope and mission of its own program, interpreting and tailoring the terms to its own purpose.

Staff development refers to programs designed to enhance the attitudes, skills, knowledge, and performance related to people in specific positions within the institution. While this function is usually synonymous with the training function in business and industry, most colleges provide voluntary programs for faculty and staff. Examples include training, development, or revitalization for faculty, classified staff, or management; mentoring programs; employee orientation programs; and workshops featuring topics such as resolving conflict, career development, team building, time management, networking, and human resources management.

Program development refers to programs designed to enhance attitudes, skills, knowledge, and performance related to the specific systems within the institution. Some examples include course design, literacy training, honors programs and graduate studies, technology use or information systems delivery, volunteerism, program evaluation, management training, wellness programs, and articulation. In addition, some consider curriculum development a part of program development.

Organization development consists of programs designed to enhance attitudes, skills, knowledge, and performance related to institutional effectiveness. Examples of these programs include strategic planning; integration of staff, program, and organizational development with the college mission; organizational evaluation; change; needs assessment; linkage with business and industry; recognition programs; and cultural diversity programs.

Faculty development refers to the programs that focus on the training, development, and revitalization of faculty. They are often comprehensive in that they include orientation, teaching skills training, recognition programs, career development programs, and preretirement planning programs.

Curriculum development refers to the programs that focus on the content of courses and their delivery. They may also include revision of general education requirements, prerequisite determination, and Develop a Curriculum (DACUM) processes.

With respect to the future of staff development, the NCSPOD believes that a comprehensive program must be organization wide. It should include orientation for all employees, both full- and part-time; it should provide appropriate training to address the changing academic environment; it should offer recognition strategies for all employee groups; and it should advance the mission of the college through a student-centered, research-driven approach. Realistically, this is an ambitious order for community colleges.

While there has been some writing about staff development—how to start a program and what the elements of a program are—no one model for all campuses has evolved. The NCSPOD position paper identifies three models: the comprehensive model, the faculty/classified model, and the faculty model (1991, 5–7). At the present, staff development is a full-time administrative position in some community colleges; in others, it is a position held by faculty with release time (as few as three credit hours). Unfortunately, at many others, no staff person has been designated for this role, and usually a vice president or dean is given additional responsibility for coordinating a program.

Smith concludes his chapter in *Innovations in the Community College* (1989) by citing the results of a program in which college presidents among others responded to the question, "What should be the priorities of institutional staff, program, and organization development during the next five years?" Writing in 1988, Smith listed the following priorities:

1. Expand the focus on total organizational development.
2. Involve CEO's and other major managers in the design and development of staff, program, and organizational development (SPOD).
3. Provide support and leadership for institutional management development programs.
4. Provide incentives for innovation and entrepreneurial activities.
5. Educate faculty and staff as change-agents and organization developers.
6. Promote student success through SPOD programs.
7. Promote commitment to community college philosophy by all faculty and staff.
8. Develop programs that emphasize individualized, personal and professional development activities.
9. Develop internal and external accountability measures for "service" programs.
10. Provide leadership in coping with managing and shaping change (in cooperation with management). (Smith, in O'Banion 1989, 197–98)

PRACTICES

Generally the literature says that a successful staff development program should be comprehensive, supported by administration, managed by a staff developer, constituent driven, adequately funded, evaluated periodically, and supportive of the organization's mission. Each year at its national conference, the NCSPOD recognizes the outstanding practices at member colleges by conferring an award for an exemplary single-campus program and one for a multicampus program. A review of the programs recognized in 1985–1986 reveals effective practices (Smith 1989).

Even more recently, single-campus organizations recognized have been Butte College in California, 1989; Johnson County Community College in Kansas, 1990; and the Community College of Aurora in Colorado, 1991. Butte College's commitment to their comprehensive program predates the California legislation and financing that has created the emphasis on staff development there in the past few years. One of the most outstanding aspects of the Butte College program is their alternative leave strategy which allows faculty to teach overload assignments without pay but "bank" time toward a future leave. The director of the program, Ernie Matlock, dean of instruction, says this approach has allowed faculty much more flexibility to update their skills and has served to enhance morale as well.

The Johnson County Community College program was cited for the comprehensive nature of its program as exemplified by the Staff Development Directory published by the Staff Development Center. Johnson County has had a full-time director of staff development since 1983. The JCCC staff development program is designed to follow the cycle of employment starting with orientation, providing skills training, encouraging professional and personal development, and recognizing service and success. Examples of some outstanding programs include recognition of faculty and staff for "Extra Efforts," an annual staff awards luncheon, orientation for all new employees, Master Teacher workshops, workshops and presentations by the JCCC faculty, in-service for all college employees, tuition assistance, computer training, an employee assistance program, special grants, wellness program, sabbatical leaves, and faculty exchange program. Further, the program is based on a career development model that begins with an Individual Development Plan.

The Faculty Development Program at the Community College of Aurora provides a comprehensive training model to support instructional excellence for all disciplines. The model encourages faculty to use experimental, student-centered teaching methods and helps instructors equip students with critical thinking and teamwork skills. Components of this program include a faculty mentor program, new faculty orientation, a self-paced course of effective college teaching, peer observation of an adjunct faculty, and faculty team projects. Mini grants, teaching consultations, professional development assignments, and a faculty resource center idea bank are also included. An outstanding international initiative was undertaken by the Community College of Aurora in developing and delivering a Faculty Development Institute beginning in 1991. This conference brings together faculty developers each summer to explore new teaching and learning initiatives.

El Paso Community College in Texas received the multicampus award in

1989. Its program is comprehensive and, for a number of years, has been led by a faculty member provided 100 percent release time. The program highlights included the "Round-up for Great Teachers" and "Wellness Weekends." They are currently working to establish a Southwest Faculty Consortium which will include schools in Texas, New Mexico, and Colorado.

No multicampus district received an award in 1990, but Austin Community College in Texas received the 1991 multicampus award for its comprehensive program administered by the Professional Development and Evaluation Office. Among the elements of this varied program are mini grants; a vocational/technical teleconference training network; faculty computer training, evaluation, and orientation programs; a professional development newsletter; a resource library; and workshops and seminars. A new service called Interaction Management teaches individuals specific communication methods to identify problems, to present possible solutions and identify the consequences of the alternatives, and to reach a mutual agreement of the solution.

There are numerous examples of outstanding staff development programs. Miami-Dade Community College, in Florida, is often recognized for its Teaching and Learning Project, a five-year project aimed at the improvement of the teaching/learning process. Each campus has a Teaching and Learning Center which provides all the staff development for the campus.

The Maricopa County Community Colleges in Arizona have long been active in staff development initiatives. They provided the leadership for the Women's Leaders Project as early as 1980, as well as the first international conference on adjunct faculty in 1988. More recently, they have provided the support for the development of the National Community College Chairs Conference and Academy.

Another approach to providing staff development programs has been through consortia arrangements. The state of Illinois has provided opportunities to faculty and staff of community colleges through "drive-in" conferences in the northern and the southern regions of the state. Combining resources is an advantage to all participating institutions. California institutions have also developed regional arrangements, including master teaching workshops, the support staff get-aways, the administrative conferences, and the cultural diversity projects. Other state systems support specific staff development initiatives, such as the University of Kentucky's Teaching Improvement Process. The Kentucky system consists of fourteen colleges. Since 1983 their program of teaching consultation has served over 400 faculty members.

The Kansas City area has a unique consortium. The Kansas City Regional Council for Higher Education (KCRCHE) is a formal consortium of nineteen higher education institutions. While the KCRCHE provides many services for its members, one of the strongest is staff development. The KCRCHE sponsors a separate series of workshops for faculty members, academic administrators, and support staff personnel. A recent initiative is the master faculty workshop, in existence since 1990.

A plethora of programs exists in community, junior, and technical colleges. The NCSPOD's current membership directory and human resource directory are both good resources for program models of particular interest.

PRESENT ISSUES

Although there are many outstanding staff, program, and organizational development programs in place, a number of issues continue to demand attention. The following eight items represent the most pressing and national in scope.

First, the maintenance of staff development programs is of concern. As the decade of the 1990s begins, many community colleges are facing budget constraints. This situation has resulted in difficult decisions in some schools. However, more and more administrators are recognizing the advantages of strong staff development programs and are protecting them from the whims of legislatures and budget officers. Recently, in California, a strong initiative to protect financing was successful.

Second, faculty development to serve underprepared students is receiving attention. As increasing numbers of students, who lack the skills to do college-level work, come to take advantage of the resources of the community college, the stress and strain affect faculty members who may be unprepared to meet the diverse needs of these students. Some programs suggested are advancing faculty training in student learning styles, learning strategies classes, and study skills. The classroom research concepts of Cross and Angelo (1988) are partially designed to assist faculty in learning what students are gaining in their classes and in providing timely feedback so that faculty can make the necessary changes to meet emerging student needs.

Third, cultural diversity agendas are important. Many community colleges are also facing the challenges presented by a more culturally diverse student body. The diversity comes from an increased number of immigrants, minorities, and older students, as well as first-generation college-bound students. Again, a challenge to faculty lies in the changing demographics of the classroom. Capitalizing on the new richness of the student population, developing new teaching methods to best meet students' needs, and assisting those students who are not native speakers of English demand staff development attention.

Fourth, vast changes are occurring in instructional technology. Computers are now commonplace in the education enterprise. Still some faculty are not computer literate, which presents a special problem when teachers work with students who have grown up in the age of technology. And the future holds even more challenges—more sophisticated computers, multimedia technology, and interactive videodisc technology, to name a few. As staff developers look to the needs of faculty for the next ten years, helping instructors stay abreast of computer technology is imperative.

Fifth is the need to serve all the needs of all the staff at community colleges. In addition to the traditional staff development activities of orientation, recognition, and training, new and evolving management systems are demanding unfamiliar skills and ways of interacting in the day-to-day workplace environment.

Sixth, the impact of institutional assessment must be considered. Staff, program, and organizational development initiatives will be extensively affected as state and federal programs mandate competency-based educational programs and measures of institutional effectiveness. Additional government accountability is also demanding more concrete evidence of success in all realms of higher education.

Seventh, preparation for institutional change is of concern. Organizational development will continue to challenge staff developers. Many community colleges are at an evolutionary stage where they must "renew or decline" (Lorenzo and Blanzy 1988). Presidents and administrators are examining systems and methods for revitalizing staff members and, therefore, the organization as a whole. Another issue facing community colleges in the near future will be the retirement of current faculty and administrators and the projected shortage of prepared replacements. Many colleges have a predominance of staff members who have been in the college for twenty years or longer. Orientation and integration of the new group of staff will present major challenges.

Eighth, there is a continuing need for training for new staff developers. Schools starting staff development programs are seeking ways of training those faculty and staff members charged with directing programs. Both the POD and the NCSPOD have recently published documents to assist with that training (Magnesen and Parker 1988; Wadsworth 1988; Lunde and Healy 1991). In addition, a number of workshops have been held for new practitioners at the national conferences as well as the regional NCSPOD workshops.

FUTURE ISSUES

While the present has many challenges, the future holds even more challenges for which planning must be undertaken now.

Institutionalizing staff, program, and organizational development is necessary. Unfortunately, some outstanding programs from the past are no longer in existence because the program was identified too closely with the single person who developed it. The staff development program should be both an integral component and a reflection of the college's mission, and, as such, it should be able to withstand personnel changes.

Further emphasis on organizational development is required. Lorenzo's writing has attracted the attention of many community colleges and has caused them to think about the need for revitalizing the staff as a part of institutional renewal and invigoration (Lorenzo and Blanzy 1988).

Distance learning and advanced technology must be examined. Change is so rapid that many personnel feel overwhelmed. The staff developer needs to work closely with the experts on campus to plan the necessary training and development as the new technologies are introduced.

The preparation and management of increasing numbers of adjunct faculty are vital. Because part-time faculty typically deliver from 25 to 50 percent of the instructional curriculum, successful colleges are finding ways to manage and develop these important resources.

The continuation of renewal programs for aging faculty is of importance. A multitude of social issues are involved, including the "sandwich generation" demands of caring for both parents and children, retirement issues, and wellness concerns.

Understanding and serving a global village become essential because rapidly changing world politics cannot be overlooked. Students and faculty alike must be prepared to understand and appreciate the shrinking world community. Staff development programs might include initiatives to internationalize the curriculum and to support faculty and staff in international travel and training.

The knowledge and skills of staff developers must be updated. The demand should be obvious. For staff developers to remain current in the multitude of issues facing community colleges, they must have available a wide range of activities to meet the increased demand.

SUMMARY

The evolution of staff development programs has taken place over the past thirty years. From the initial efforts to establish programs that served faculty needs, to the expansion of programs for all staff, to the current comprehensive programs that provide orientation, training renewal activities, recognition programs, and preretirement planning, the changes have been sporadic. Each institution is unique in the way in which it has embraced the needs of staff, program, and organization development.

The emerging realization is that efforts must be undertaken to integrate the staff development and program development efforts with the organizational development plan. The overwhelming vision for the future of community colleges is that staff development programs should play an increasingly important role in all aspects of campus life. The continuing success of community, technical, and junior colleges will be determined, in part, by how effectively administrators can integrate and blend the three areas with measures of institutional effectiveness.

REFERENCES

American Association of Community and Junior Colleges. 1988. *Building communities: A vision for a new century*. Washington, D.C.

Bergquist, W. H. 1986. Reflections of a practitioner: Ten years of professional and organizational development. *To Improve the Academy* :2–13.

Bergquist, W. H., and S. R. Phillips. 1975, 1977, 1981. *A handbook for faculty development*. 3 vols. Washington, D.C.: Council for the Advancement of Small Colleges.

Betts, L. J. 1991. *Energizing and focusing the movement: National organizations impacting community, technical and junior colleges*. Washington, D.C.: College and University Personnel Association.

Brass, R. J., ed. 1984. *Community colleges, the future, and SPOD*. Stillwater, Okla.: New Forums Press.

Brinkerhoff, R. O. 1987. *Achieving results from training*. San Francisco: Jossey-Bass.

Brookfield, S. D. 1990. *The skillful teacher*. San Francisco: Jossey-Bass.

Centra, J. 1976. *Faculty development practices in U.S. colleges and universities*. Princeton, N.J.: Educational Testing Service.

Cross, K. P., and T. A. Angelo. 1988. *Classroom assessment techniques: A handbook for faculty*. Ann Arbor, Mich.: National Center for Research to Improve Postsecondary Teaching and Learning (NCRIPTAL).

Gleazer, E. J., Jr. 1968. *This is the community college*. New York: Houghton Mifflin.

———. 1980. *Values, vision, and vitality*. Washington, D.C.: American Association of Community and Junior Colleges.

Hammons, J., T. H. Wallace-Smith, and G. Watts. 1978. *Staff development in the community college: A handbook*. Topical Paper no. 66. Los Angeles: ERIC Clearinghouse for Junior Colleges.

Lewis, K., ed. 1998. *Face to face*. Stillwater, Okla.: New Forums Press.

Lorenzo, A. L., and J. J. Blanzy. 1988. *A foundation for renewal*. Warren, Mich.: Macomb Community College.

Lunde, J. P., and M. M. Healy. 1991. *Doing faculty development by committee*. Stillwater, Okla.: New Forums Press.

Magnesen, V. A., and L. S. Parker. 1988. *How to develop, market and manage a comprehensive staff and organizational development program*. Chicago, Ill.: National Council for Staff, Program, and Organizational Development.

McKeachie, W. J. 1991. What theories underlie the practice of faculty development? *To Improve the Academy* 10:3–8.

Menges, R. J., and B. C. Mathis. 1988. *Key resources on teaching, learning, curriculum, and faculty development*. San Francisco: Jossey-Bass.

Miller, R. I., ed. 1988. *Evaluating major components of two-year colleges*. Washington, D.C.: College and University Personnel Association.

NCSPOD. 1991. *NCSPOD position paper*. Peoria, Ill.: National Council for Staff, Program and Organizational Development.

O'Banion, T. 1989. *Innovation in the community college*. New York: ACE/Macmillan.

Parnell, D. 1990. *Dateline 2000: The new higher education agenda*. Washington, D.C.: American Association of Community and Junior Colleges.

Schuster, J., D. W. Wheeler and Associates. 1990. *Enhancing faculty careers*. San Francisco; Jossey-Bass.

Seldin, P. 1990. *How administrators can improve teaching*. San Francisco: Jossey-Bass.

———. 1990. *Teaching portfolios*. San Francisco: Jossey-Bass.

Smith, A. B. 1989. Innovations in staff development. In *Innovation in the community college*, ed. T. O'Banion, 177–99. New York: ACE/Macmillan.

Task Group on General Education. 1988. *A new vitality in general education*. Washington, D.C.: Association of American Colleges.

Wadsworth, E. C. 1988. *A handbook for new practitioners*. Stillwater, Okla.: New Forums Press.

Whitman, N., and C. Roth. 1990. Evaluating teaching improvement strategies. *Journal of Staff, Program, and Organizational Development* 8(4):203–8.

Part 7

The Community College Faculty

The Preparation, Screening, and Selection of Community College Faculty Members

Elizabeth M. Hawthorne

The preparation, screening, and selection of faculty members in community colleges have been tied closely with the diverse historical roots of the community college in American education. While the role of the junior college has been widely discussed, the basic requirements for entrance to faculty status have remained consistent. Here the focus is on full-time, general education faculty in public two-year colleges. This chapter first examines the preparation of faculty members and the roles of the universities, the associations, and the junior and community colleges themselves. Second, the screening of faculty members through the mechanisms of certification and accreditation is discussed. Finally, the recruitment and selection of faculty are considered.

PREPARATION

Since community college faculty preparation programs have seldom become institutionalized, they have depended upon promotion by individual deans, faculty members, and foundations (Goodchild 1991). In the 1960s the Ford Foundation funded several programs that included teaching internships in participating community colleges (Kelly and Wilbur 1970). In addition, the Kellogg Foundation provided support for leadership programs across the nation, which produced many institutional and national leaders in the community college movement, but the dominant mission of these programs was administrator preparation.

The literature indicates continuing interest in acclimating faculty to the special characteristics of the community or junior college as well as ensuring their command of their fields and their ability to teach. Formal courses on the community college expanded throughout the 1920s and 1930s, with both faculty and administrators enrolled. By 1954 twenty-three colleges and universities offered an average of 1.8 courses with a range of from one to eight courses. Forty colleges and universities included the topic of the junior college in other courses (Colvert 1955). Indeed, "the emergence of the junior/community college was the raison d'etre for the development of several major higher education programs in the United States" (Goodchild 1991).

By 1969, Kelly and Wilbur (1970) and O'Banion (1971) reported that 100 programs were "aware of the two year college teacher's special graduate needs" (Kelly and Wilbur 1970, 59), but noted little innovation or institutional commitment to these programs. During the 1980s many such programs retrenched as the market for new faculty became limited when enrollments in two-year colleges leveled off and faculty mobility lessened. Courses offered that were directed to the needs of community college instructors were generally the prerogative of faculty members who, in large measure, had served as administrators in junior colleges.

In 1949 Koos noted that few instructors had ever taken a course on the community college (Cohen and Brawer 1989). Garrison in 1967 reported that "few instructors had had specific preparation for junior college teaching" (1967, 70). However, by 1970, Medsker and Tillery found that 33 percent had taken courses about two-year colleges (O'Banion 1971).

As the number and size of community colleges mushroomed, Gleazer reported that the American Association of Junior Colleges sought to mobilize the universities to establish preparation programs and offered guidelines (Johnson 1965). In order for the junior college to have excellence in teaching and learning, he recommended that

The immense academic and research resources of the universities must be pooled with the "laboratory" resources of the junior college. And this "mix" is possible only if the junior college administrator pays more than lip service to providing a viable "climate for teaching" and only if the university displays more than a fainthearted approach toward developing programs which are rigorous and realistic. (Johnson 1965, 28–29)

Reservations about the university training programs have persisted throughout the years. According to Scruffs, they were essentially too modest, reached too few faculty members, and often failed to give the graduate students experience in community colleges (O'Banion 1971, 90). Lumsden and Stewart found that "only 118 colleges and universities in the country offer graduate coursework specifically related to community and junior colleges" (1992, 44). Most of these appear to focus on administrator preparation; hence, one might conclude that their impact on the preparation of community college faculty is negligible. To be successful, university training programs need to link with community colleges to ensure that the education provided is consistent with the needs of the hiring institutions and their students. The nature of the linkage, however, is subject to debate.

Graduate programs are consistently seen as the villain in the preparation of faculty because of the overemphasis on research, the intense specialization within a discipline or field, the focus on the discipline over the needs of students, and the disdain (sometimes subtle, sometimes direct) for the "lower" stature of the community college. The clash of cultures between the university and the community college has a negative impact on the faculty of two-year colleges, dependent as they are on the universities for their advanced training.

Issues in Faculty Preparation

In the first fifty years of the junior college, faculty members were prepared much like secondary teachers (especially since many simultaneously served in both roles), except that in general the junior college instructors had more master's degrees (Koos 1925; Medsker 1960). The comparability to the preparation for secondary school teaching meant, too, that instructors had more professional education than traditional college instructors (Wahlquist 1931).

Reeves (1931) studied eight junior colleges in 1930 and noted the importance of regional accreditation as a factor in the degree attainment of faculty members. He found that the North Central Association of Colleges and Schools required the master's degree or equivalent, but that the Southern Association had less rigorous standards: A bachelor's degree was the minimum educational level expected, and fewer faculty members in the two-year colleges in that region had earned a master's or the equivalent. Similarly, Punke (1953) found geographical differences in the level of education of faculty at two-year colleges.

Since 1950 the pattern of academic preparation for teaching has reflected an increasing attainment of advanced degrees (Garrison 1941; Colvert 1955; Medsker 1960; O'Banion 1971; McCormick 1983–1984; Cohen and Brawer 1989). According to a 1984 Carnegie faculty study, 22 percent of the two-year college faculty members had earned doctorates, but these were often earned during their teaching careers in community colleges and not as preparation for their careers (Cohen and Brawer 1989, 71). (Given that the proportion of the faculty teaching in arts and sciences is smaller than in earlier studies because of the proliferation of the vocational and technical programs, the larger percent of faculty with doctorates does not fully reflect the proportion of the arts and sciences faculty currently holding doctorates.)

Over time additional themes concerning the preparation of faculty members for two-year colleges have emerged. First, the extent of degree attainment occupies the attention of most scholars (*Junior College Journal* 1931, 456; Koos 1947b). Related to this is the concern expressed by Medsker (1960) that faculty have degrees from quality institutions; that faculty hold degrees from a variety of institutions was a desirable situation reported by Eells (1934). Second, general education was and continues to be a significant issue (Pugh 1947). Stone (1958) deplored that faculty came to their positions with too narrow a specialization and lacked a concept of general education that integrated fields of knowledge.

The third theme is the specialized content, especially in the teaching areas.

In the early years of the junior college, 75 percent of public junior college instructors had majored in the field they taught, compared with 86 percent of the four-year college instructors (Eells 1931). In 1941 Garrison noted that, although most faculty members taught in areas of their major, they had typically earned only from thirty to fifty-eight credits in their major, which he deemed insufficient. Fourth, in 1941, when Koos looked at the relationship between what people taught and what their specialized preparation had been in those areas, he found that teaching across disciplines was common and that faculty had minimal preparation in their second and third teaching areas (Koos 1947a).

Fifth, professional education (including methods and curriculum) continues to be a major theme, one that reflects the middle ground that community colleges occupy—neither secondary, with its emphasis on methodological preparation, nor collegiate, with its emphasis on content and research (Garrison 1941; Pugh 1947; Dolan 1952). One is reminded of Koos's concern about finding a place for the junior college in American higher education. He reported in 1925 that early friends of the junior college asserted that "it would offer better instruction in these school years than is afforded in other higher institutions. . . . The more seasoned high school instructors selected for junior college work are more effective teachers than are the younger, less experienced instructors often employed in colleges and universities" (1925, 64). He argues that, in order to justify the "extension of the movement" on the basis of the purported teaching expertise, a dispassionate assessment of that assertion was essential. The result of his inquiry, based in part on the performance of the junior college transfers as compared with native university students, was that the better preparation of the college faculty was offset by the better teaching skills of the junior college faculty (Koos 1925). The current debate in university education on the value of teaching skills makes the discussion even more interesting. Eells (1931) and Garrison (1967) both found that faculty members themselves expressed a need for more professional education and strongly recommended the value of a broad general education for instructors instead of a narrowly specialized one.

Sixth, knowledge of the mission of the junior or community college as an institution looms large as a concern on the part of administrators, given the diversity of the student body and the resulting demands that places on the faculty (Stone 1958; O'Banion 1971; Fields, 1989). Additionally, Stone (1958) recommended a program that stresses learning by doing and problem solving, and O'Banion (1971) and Cohen and Brawer (1989), among others, have addressed issues of personal characteristics such as flexibility and commitment.

Finally, the type of degree and the graduate background deemed most beneficial for faculty in community colleges have both received attention. Eells (1934) discussed the Ed.D. degree for administrators and faculty in junior colleges, favoring it for the depth and breadth of knowledge it provided and the reduced emphasis on research. He favored the type of dissertation that would be an "organization" of knowledge rather than an original contribution to it. Johnson (1939) called for a specialized doctoral degree for junior college instructors—a degree in general education that included professional education. In this spirit, an experimental program at the University of the Pacific, which lasted for fifteen years under the leadership of the chemistry department chair and an education dean (Jantzen 1991), underscored the importance of providing some program that will allow faculty to remain current in their teaching fields and still pursue a doctorate that is not research focused (Jantzen and Cobb 1958). Jantzen (1991), states that "graduate work in education should also include advanced study in some liberal arts discipline." Kelly and Wilbur (1970), who reported that the master's degree was standard and that doctoral degrees were seen as too specialized for junior college teaching, looked with great expectations toward the emerging doctorate of arts, a degree that never gained legitimacy, yet seemed suited to the needs of community college instructors, allowing intensive study of academic areas as well as teaching methods appropriate for the diverse clientele of community colleges.

It is evident that, throughout the history of the two-year college in America, there has been an ongoing interest in the extent and type of preparation for community college teaching expressed in the literature, with a focus on the quality, quantity, and substance of that preparation (Dolan 1952; O'Banion 1971). Furthermore, different segments of higher education have different interests to be served. The debate continues.

SCREENING

Screening instructors is a regulatory process that controls access to the field and establishes minimum standards in preparation and accomplishment. Setting standards for instructors can be accomplished through state certification, accreditation, and professional association guidelines, or by common practice in a given state or region. Certification, as the term is used here, is an externally mandated set of requirements for entry into a professional field generally established by state governments or public universities. Unlike licensure, certification generally focuses on completion of specified educational requirements rather than successful performance on standardized tests.

In the mid–1930s, Eells (1935, 1936) reported that the American Association of University Professors in Michigan had recently discussed whether to have certification requirements for junior college instructors. In light of their subsequent enactment, Eells studied eleven states and two city systems (Chicago and Oklahoma municipal), which together represented 78 percent of the public junior colleges and 83 percent of the enrollment. Of these, seven states and both city systems required certification. Of the four states that had no required certification, Texas strongly encouraged certification comparable to high schools: twelve semester hours in education, six of which should be in secondary education. Mississippi had just passed the requirement of eighteen semester hours of professional training or successful college teaching experience. Georgia, in which eight of ten colleges were state controlled, was the only state studied that had absolutely no requirements, although no information was provided about the state of Oklahoma. The city of Chicago viewed their requirements as comparable to university requirements with expectations for sufficient academic training and an adequate amount of work in education (defined as fifteen hours). California, until 1988, had a junior college certificate which had more academic and fewer education requirements, but also had a secondary certificate which included more education course work that qualified people for junior college teaching.

Eells noted that the focus on standards was for college transfer programs and was generally imposed by the college sector. He queried whether standards should be imposed internally or externally. He stated that "there are broader possibilities for the junior college" that presumably the colleges themselves could best design (1931, 184). Eells later prepared the first major report on vocational education in the junior colleges which suggested the kind of "broader opportunities" he may have had in mind (Eells 1941a, 1941b; Engleman 1941).

The strong influence of collegiate instruction prevailed in early writings despite the fact that the predominant control of public junior colleges was the public schools systems. California, in fact, relied on teacher certification, a public school screening mechanism. Private junior colleges were less susceptible to state control. In contrast, the Association of American Colleges in this period recommended some professional courses be required of all college and university graduates desiring to teach at the college level. This is an idea rarely realized then or now (Eells 1934, 410).

As the country was moving toward World War II and the Great Depression was drawing to an end, Garrison (1941) found that a majority of instructors held some kind of certificate, but the administrators of the junior colleges did not require them when selecting faculty. The late 1940s was a period replete with direction setting and examination of the current state of junior college education and expectations for substantial growth (American Council on Education 1949).

In 1952 the Northwest Association of Secondary and Higher Schools instituted minimum standards for junior college instructors which differentiated requirements for transfer and vocational courses. "The primary interest is sound and inspirational teaching, rather than research" (Commission on Higher Schools 1952, 10). The requirements balanced general education, field of study, and professional education and experience (Martorana 1951). In 1960 Thornton reported that Illinois, Maryland, Michigan, Minnesota, New Jersey, and Utah had certification requirements. In 1970 Kelly and Wilbur reported that few states had laws on certification, employment, or tenure for postsecondary education faculty members. Those that did—Oregon, Washington, Arizona, Kansas, Florida, Missouri, and California—treated community colleges as secondary education (Bogue 1956; O'Banion 1971).

In 1960 Medsker reported that 62 percent of faculty favored certification. He concluded that those who have had to undergo certification tended to prefer that route over those who had not. In addition, he noted that certification requirements at that time generally included a supervised teaching feature.

By the end of the 1960s, the pattern of certification requirements with some variation included a master's degree in the teaching field (or a substantial number of graduate hours) and some teaching experience at the high school or college level (Kelly and Wilbur 1970). Certification standards rarely addressed the unique needs for the preparation of community college instructors, nor did they deal with knowledge of institutional mission.

Certification continues to find favor in some states, such as Arizona (Arizona State Board of Directors for Community Colleges 1989). States that have junior college certification are more likely to be those in which the junior college has been closely aligned with the secondary schools, in contrast to the university-related two-year colleges, for example, Pennsylvania and Ohio, or the state systems, such as North Carolina. In rare circumstances, credentialing has been raised as a discipline-specific issue (McCormick 1983–1984; Tew and Wheatley 1990).

Thus community college–specific certification has not been widespread, nor has it been uncontroversial. Stone (1958) suggested that accreditation processes should monitor the academic graduate preparation programs; this move would supplant the certification process's function of controlling programs. "An adequate teacher education program is the proper function of accreditation, not of certification," according to Stone (1958, 371). Later, the California State Board of Education Commission on Accreditation adopted this approach.

In 1988, after extensive statewide deliberation, certification was eliminated from California state standards (AB 1725 1988). In order for the colleges to blend into postsecondary education, requirements for faculty members in two-year colleges in California are now based on degree attainment, are determined by individual institutions within broad state guidelines, and allow for exceptional individuals—those without college but with clearly demonstrated skills for teaching—to be hired based on institutionally determined criteria. A major benefit to the new system is that material of faculty applicants no longer have to be processed in Sacramento, eliminating at least one bureaucratic level. In addition, philosophically, the practices of screening faculty are now akin to those in state colleges and universities, with the faculty of community colleges exercising more control over faculty hiring (Grosz 1989).

RECRUITMENT AND SELECTION

Recruitment involves the policies and the procedures of colleges to attract and select the most qualified instructional staff. Issues revolving around recruitment include (1) who is responsible within the organizational structure (Miami-Dade Community College District 1989), (2) the use of outside firms, methods, and sources (Coady 1990), (3) the specification of search strategies, (4) the packaging of special inducements, and (5) the ability to offer adequate salaries.

Although formal recruitment plans are not commonly used at two-year colleges (Reeves and Galant 1986), some do have elaborate and well-defined programs

(Recommendations 1989; Meznek and Grosz 1989; Phelps 1990–1991; Hahn 1990). Though screening, selection, and hiring are frequent activities of practitioners, little systematic attention has been paid to these topics in the scholarly literature.

Faculty selection criteria historically have focused on degree attainment and preparation in one's teaching field(s) with less attention given to teaching skills and knowledge of the community college, although administrators often view such knowledge as valuable (Koos 1925; Eells 1935; Cohen and Brawer 1989). Selection criteria for junior college faculty were first presented systematically in 1927: "capacity, training, technical expertise, character, personality, the pioneer spirit, intellectual integrity, physical as well as mental vigor and persistence in following teaching as a life work" (Morris 1927, 57).

By 1940 faculty members in community colleges came from teaching positions in high schools, colleges and universities, elementary schools, and junior high schools, in that order. Administrators tended to prefer junior college experience and were more in favor of the Ph.D. than the faculty. They also looked for "ability as a classroom instructor, professional growth, knowledge of subject matter and understanding of the educative process" (Garrison 1941, 36). The American Council on Education Conference in 1945 issued a strong statement addressing the expected need for more two-year college teachers. Among the recommendations were ways to make the career more attractive, along with encouragement for able two-year college students to go into community college teaching as a field (American Council on Education 1949).

Medsker (1960) found that the proportion of instructors with high school experience had decreased to 64 percent, and by the 1970s Cohen and Brawer (1989) found more faculty were coming from graduate programs, from business and industry, and from other community colleges. In the flush of rapid growth in the late 1950s and into the 1960s, little time was available to mobilize extensive formal search efforts because haste was a feature of the hiring process.

Of course, as the number of students fluctuates over time, the demand for faculty varies as well. After a period in the 1970s, when the number of new colleges dropped significantly and enrollments stabilized, the present situation is demanding a new crop of instructors since many of the faculty hired in the boom years of the 1960s are retiring. At the same time, demographic and political concerns are interjected into the hiring process, as attention has shifted to issues of equity (Linthicum 1989; California Community Colleges 1989; Hahn 1990) and adaptability to the community college clientele (Milligan 1988).

Since communication among faculty and administrators at two-year colleges and universities is largely confined to individual efforts, widespread changes are not likely (Hawthorne and Ninke (1991). However, the development of selected collaborative and consortial arrangements is changing the nature of the programs offering advanced degrees in which prospective and continuing faculty members might enroll. Community colleges have only sporadically sought to "create" new faculty members, for example, the recent collaboration between Miami-Dade and the University of Miami.

The California legislation AB 1725 gives considerable voice to the faculty by moving the selection of faculty from the hands of bureaucrats through the credentialing process to the hands of faculty through the Academic Senate. District-based decision making on hiring, with faculty playing a significant role, is more in line with higher education traditions and practices then the former process.

CONCLUSIONS

As the community college in the United States turns ninety years old, the state of preparation, screening, and selection of faculty is sporadic, ad hoc, and loosely tied to the needs of the institutions and their students. The chronicle presented here shows little progress has occurred amidst a lot of rhetoric. There is an urgent need for universities and community colleges, with the assistance of foundations, state governments and the federal government, and others, to design and implement programs that will ensure the highest quality education possible in two-year colleges.

REFERENCES

AB 1725: Bill Language, 1988. California (July).

American Council on Education. 1949. *Wanted: 30,000 instructors for community colleges*. Washington, D.C.

Arizona State Board of Directors for Community Colleges. 1989. *Annual Report to the Governor, 1988–89*. Phoenix, Ariz.

Bogue, J. P. 1956. The junior college world. *Junior College Journal* 27(7).

California Community Colleges, Office of the Chancellor. 1989. *Toward a new diversity: A state plan for affirmative action and staff diversity in the California community colleges*. Discussion draft. ERIC Document no. ED 302 301.

Coady, S. 1990. Hiring faculty: A system for making good decisions. *CUPA Journal* 41 (3): 5–8.

Cohen, A., and F. Brawer. 1989. *The American community college*. San Francisco: Jossey-Bass.

Colvert, C. C. 1955. Professional development of junior college instructors. *Junior College Journal* 25(8): 474–78.

Commission on Higher Schools. 1952. *Criteria for the evaluation of community or junior colleges*. Northwest Association of Secondary and Higher Schools. Mimeo.

Dolan, F. H. 1952. The preparation of junior college teachers. *Junior College Journal* 22(3): 329–36.

Eells, W. C. 1931. *The junior college*. Boston: Houghton Mifflin.

———. 1934. Accrediting standards. *Junior College Journal* (4)7.

———. 1935. Certification for junior college instructors. *Junior College Journal* 6: 75–76.

————. 1936. Desirable preparation of instructors for junior colleges. *Twenty-fourth yearbook of the National Society of College Teachers of Education*, 22–24.

————. 1941a. *Present status of junior college terminal education*. vol. 1. Washington, D.C.: American Association of Junior Colleges.

————. 1941b. *Present status of junior college terminal education*. vol. 3. Washington, D.C.: American Association of Junior Colleges.

Engleman, L. E. 1941. *The literature of junior college terminal education*. vol. 2. Washington, D.C.: American Association of Junior Colleges.

Fields, R. Interview with author. Tampa, Fla. 4 March 1989.

Garrison, L. A. 1941. Preparation of junior college instructors. *Junior College Journal* 11:135–41.

Garrison, R. H. 1967. *Junior college faculty: Issues and problems*. Washington, D.C.: American Association of Junior Colleges.

Goodchild, L. F. 1991. Higher education as a field of study: Its origins, programs, and purposes, 1893–1960. In *Administration as a profession*. ed. J. D. Fife and L. F. Goodchild, 15–32. New Directions for Higher Education, no. 76. San Francisco: Jossey-Bass.

Grosz, K. S. 1989. New roles for faculty under Assembly Bill 1725 (California). Los Angeles. Unpublished manuscript.

Hahn, T. C. 1990. *Future faculty development program*. ERIC Document no. ED 325 156. Chula Vista, Calif.: Southwestern College.

Hawthorne, E. M. 1990. Anticipating the new generation of community college faculty members. *Journal of College Science Teaching* 20(6): 365–69.

Hawthorne, E. M., and D. Ninke. 1991. A focus on university faculty service to community colleges. *Community College Review* 19(1): 30–35.

Jantzen, J. M. Personal correspondence with author. 23 December 1991.

Jantzen, J. M., and E. G. Cobb. 1958. A teaching doctorate degree for junior college instructors. *Junior College Journal* 29(4).

Johnson, B. L. 1939. Needed: A doctor's degree in general education. *Journal of Higher Education* 19 (February): 75–78.

Johnson, B. L., ed. 1965. *New directions for instruction in the junior college*. Occasional Report no. 7. Report of national conference, 15–17 July 1964, sponsored by UCLA, American Association of Junior Colleges, and the Accrediting Commission for Junior Colleges of the Western Association of Schools and Colleges.

Junior College Journal. 1931. Reports and discussion. 1(6): 456.

Kelly, D. K. 1990. *Reviving the "deadwood"*. ERIC Document no. ED 318 518. Claremont, Calif.: Claremont McKenna College.

Kelly, W., and L. Wilbur. 1970. *Teaching in the community junior college*. New York: Appleton-Century-Crofts.

Koos, L. V. 1925. *The junior college movement*. Boston: Atheneum Press.

————. 1947a. Junior college teachers: Subjects taught and specialized preparation. *Junior College Journal* (December): 196–209.

————. 1947b. Junior college teachers: Degrees and graduate residence. *Junior College Journal* (October): 77–89.

Linthicum, D. S. 1989. *The dry pipeline: Increasing the flow of minority faculty*. ERIC Document No. ED 307 950. San Francisco, Calif.

Lumsden, D. B., and G. B. Stewart. 1992. American colleges and universities offering coursework on two-year institutions: Results of a national survey. *Community College Review* 19(4): 34–46.

Martorana, S. V. 1951. Washington's teacher education plan related to preparation of community college instructors. *Junior College Journal* 22(3): 125–29.

McCormick, A. E., Jr. 1983–1984. The credentials of two year college sociology instructors. *Journal of the Association for the Improvement of College Teaching* (Fall-Winter): 29–44.

Medsker, L. L. 1960. *The junior college: Progress and prospect.* New York: McGraw-Hill.

Meznek, J., and K. S. Grosz. 1989. *Lists of disciplines to replace community college credentials.* ERIC Document no. ED 307 923. Sacramento: California Community Colleges, Office of the Chancellor.

Miami-Dade Community College District. 1989. *Recommendations concerning new faculty.* ERIC Document no. ED 313 079.

Milligan, F. G. 1988. *The vital role of faculty in developing successful relationships with business and industry.* ERIC Document no. ED 293 608. Las Vegas, Nev.

Morris, C. S. 1927. The junior college faculty. In *The junior college: Its organization and administration,* ed. W. M. Proctor. Stanford, Calif.: Stanford University Press.

O'Banion, T. 1971. *Teachers for tomorrow: Staff development in the community junior colleges.* Tucson: University of Arizona Press.

Phelps, D. G. 1990–1991. Access, equity, and opportunity. *Community, Technical, and Junior College Journal* 61(3): 242–45.

Pugh, D. B. 1947. Committee on teacher preparation. *Junior College Journal* 17(9): 388–91.

Punke, H. H. 1953. Academic qualifications of junior college faculties. *Junior College Journal* 23(7): 366–79.

Recommendations concerning new faculty. 1989. ERIC Document no. ED 313 079. Miami, Fla.: Miami-Dade Community College District.

Reeves, F. W. 1931. Survey of current methods of the inservice training of college teachers. *Junior College Journal* 1(4):213.

Reeves, R. A., and R. L. Galant. 1986. *An academic resource in low supply and high demand: A survey of community college recruitment plans of general education faculty over the next five years.* ERIC Document no. ED 273 334. Ann Arbor, Mich.

Stone, J. C. 1958. The preparation of the academic instructors for the junior college. *Junior College Journal* 28(7): 368–71.

Tew, W. R., and J. Wheatley. 1990. Credentials needed for teaching biology and chemistry in the community college. *Community/Junior College Quarterly of Research and Practice* (14)2: 67–82.

Thornton, J. W., Jr. 1960. *The community junior college.* New York: Wiley and Sons.

Wahlquist, J. T. 1931. The junior college and teaching efficiency. *Junior College Journal* 1(8): 479–80.

Maxims for Excellence in Teaching: Reaching the Underserved

Rosemary Gillett-Karam

As Plato reminds us, the object of teaching is to engage students in remembering, to encourage them to recollect by coaching and by allowing them to find their own courage to learn. Plato's notion that anybody can learn, that the good teacher draws out knowledge from the student, is one that over time has led to great debate and philosophical inquiry. What is central to this debate is who can be or who should be taught, who should do the teaching, and what should be taught. Thus, although the idea of teaching has an interpersonal dynamic, the structure of teaching has a more mechanical dynamic. Pedagogy as the art, profession, or study of teaching arouses the interests of all of us, and it demands that we look at both the interpersonal and the mechanical dynamics of teaching and learning.

One of the most controversial aspects of teaching in America today centers around the curriculum. Writers and modern prophets have raised an alarm which is being debated not only in academia, but in and through the popular media. Heuristics claiming "the closing of the American mind" and "political correctness" are being posited against "multiculturalism" and "diversity." National debates are taking place to discuss the direction America's new demography is taking us, and as we move from a nation that has always been Anglo-European dominant to one in which there is no single ethnic or racial majority, we are virtually at war about "what should be done." Educational institutions are at the nexus of this debate—public schools seem to be failing at everything they do, and senior institutions continue to rely on standards that are exclusive and restrictive. Community colleges, too, have been criticized for "diverting the American dream," for holding out promises that are patently false.

EXCELLENCE IN TEACHING

This chapter rejects the admonition that community colleges cannot produce quality in what they do. Furthermore, it posits that, through excellence in teaching and by allowing the teacher to be a leader in the classroom, it is possible to educate all students in these turbulent times even while addressing the issues of diversity. It is to the community college that this chapter turns to address the controversial issues of cultural diversity and a changing American demography. The Era of Developing Diversity (Gillett-Karam, Roueche, and Roueche 1991) refers to the critical role of community colleges, who must be pacesetters for multicultural identity. As technological advancements require a more sophisticated work force; as American demography challenges preexisting political, social, and economic patterns; as diminishing national boundaries bring the world's peoples closer together, our educational systems must be prepared for diversity. They must find advantages and value in diversity. Community colleges should be at the forefront of these shifting views, providing the higher education necessary to confront a changing world.

Diversity is a term that focuses on the ideas of pluralism, cultural diversity, and multiculturalism. Each of these terms suggests that "the one, like-minded view" of culture may be challenged by different and equally contributory views of culture; that, in fact, two or more cultures can coexist without one being qualitatively "better" than the other. While diversity suggests difference and distinctiveness, pluralism asks different groups "to explore, understand, and try to appreciate one another's cultural experiences and heritage" (Green 1989). This understanding leads to multiculturalism, or the transcendence over ethnocentrism, and the enjoyment of the contributions of the many, instead of the one. According to Ravitch, "The debate over multiculturalism follows a generation of scholarship that has enriched our knowledge about the historical experiences of women, blacks, and members of other minority groups in various societies. As a result of the new scholarship, our schools and our institutions of learning have in recent years begun to embrace what Catharine R. Stimpson of Rutgers University has called 'cultural democracy,' a recognition that we must listen to 'a diversity of voices' to understand our past and present" (1990, A–52).

The transcendence over ethnocentrism can be accomplished by strong leadership, especially leadership in the classroom. Many of the practices of excellent teaching in American higher education can be found at the community college (Baker, Roueche, and Gillett-Karam 1990). And it is these practices, combined with the need to address our rapidly changing student body, that this chapter addresses. The central focus of the community college has always been the student—thus, excellence in teaching, and not research, is the primary goal of community colleges: What is at the "heart of the matter" is what happens in the classroom. Quality teaching benefits all students. "Teaching and learning encompasses inquiry, pedagogy, educational theory, learning styles and preferences, and personal growth and development" (Green 1989, 133).

What Green and Ravitch are suggesting then is the designation and development of curricula that acknowledge and reward diversity in individuals, groups, and cultures. A curriculum that broadens students' horizons and enables them to appreciate different cultures, different modes of thinking and inquiry, and different values and aesthetics benefits all students. The role of the faculty, faculty leadership, and the receptiveness of individual faculty members to new ideas and their commitment to continued professional growth are essential to positive change.

What do we know about effective teaching? In *Teaching as Leading* (Baker, Roueche, and Gillett-Karam 1990), it is the teacher who accepts responsibility for the learning process and for motivating and influencing students to learn to learn. Teachers are urged to examine themselves to discover whether their predominant situational teaching style is as supporter, theorist, achiever, or influencer. Only by discovering their dominant teaching style can the teacher modify his or her behavior in the classroom to accommodate the readiness of students. While the supporter teaching style focuses primarily on student skill building development and self-esteem, the theorist teaching style mainly focuses on the science of learning, seeing learning as a systematic, programmatic process governed by rational choices. The achiever teaching style is one in which the focus is on subject matter, students see that the learning community is both demanding and competitive, but nonetheless a rewarding experience. The influencer demonstrates to students that performance is ultimately a personal experience and individual effort. In the teaching-learning cycle, students have varying developmental needs; the teacher as leader understands the contingent quality of teaching—that "the situation" must guide their teaching style. Not only are teachers leaders who recognize the importance of subject matter, but also their leadership ability allows them to motivate and influence student development.

MAXIMS FOR EXCELLENCE IN TEACHING

Six maxims of teaching excellence recognize the efforts of excellent teachers:

1. Engaging the desire to learn
2. Increasing opportunities for success
3. Eliminating obstacles to learning
4. Empowering through high expectations
5. Offering positive guidance and direction
6. Motivating toward independence.

These maxims are used to focus attention around the needs of the underserved populations in the community colleges. Notation should be made of the concept of underserved: This term acknowledges teaching as a service of the leader in the classroom. It is an admission of the servant-leadership concept (Greenleaf

1973) which emphasizes that all leadership must have accountability to and for the needs of the followers (i.e., students). Although many would argue this point, referring rather to the "underprepared" or "at-risk" students, these terms seem to focus on the "minority" social and economic status of certain students. Preference here is given to the term *underserved* primarily because of existing problems, and because of the overwhelming need to address and correct these problems in a rapidly changing world. In this chapter, the term minority refers to non-Anglo populations, namely, African-American, Asian, Hispanic, and Native Americans.

Observation and research around faculty attitudes and behaviors toward minority students suggest that, although teachers may demonstrate "good practices" (1) by encouraging student-faculty contact, cooperation among students, and active learning; (2) by giving prompt feedback and emphasizing time on task; and (3) by communicating high expectations and respecting diverse talents and ways of learning (Chickering and Gamson 1987), few instructors change their teaching methods—primarily because they emulate the traditional ways they were taught in their own undergraduate and graduate experiences. Many of these practices produce unconscious attitudes and behaviors, many of which are covertly discriminatory. More important, although a wealth of materials exists for good teaching practices, few training courses are available for college instructors—despite their discipline. Findings indicate a need for that training experience. Suggestions are that training programs teach teachers to teach and that exemplary teachers serve as models for teachers in these training experiences.

Teachers as leaders understand that only by recognizing the reality of the teaching situation can teachers modify their teaching behaviors. Situational teaching requires that the instructor become aware of the circumstances of the college environment, and that the instructor become a leader in the classroom, invoking the same direction, plans, and strategies that the CEO does for the entire campus. Thus, the exemplary college instructor plans for change, understands the environment or climate of campus and classroom, and implements that framework that allows modification of teaching style based both on student readiness and on the actual evaluated success or failure of the teacher's ability to motivate and influence students.

Engaging the Desire to Learn

Teachers must recognize a student's desire to learn: As such, they diagnose, communicate, and foster interpersonal relationships in their classrooms. They are aware of the research on cultural diversity, and they integrate that research with their ability to "draw out" the hidden potential and self-knowledge in their students. This is the role of the leader who encourages the courage of the follower—the courage for students to find what they need to know within themselves.

Several inflammatory discussions are resurfacing around the "nature" of racial-ethnic students and their "turning their backs on education" (Keller 1988–1989, 44). Keller reports that "college attendance rates and graduation rates for blacks actually declined in the 1980s, and most preferential treatment has not prevented the decline" (44). In this article, Black students are singled out as having low expectations and low priorities as far as higher education is concerned.

These accusations may have some foundation, but if this is an issue of sudden educational erosion among Blacks as Keller suggests, then educators must recognize their own responsibilities toward this immediate crisis. Nettles (1988) reminds us that American colleges enrolled 76,554 fewer Black undergraduates in 1985 than in 1976–a decline of 8.9 percent. Studies on culture would suggest crises cause us to reevaluate our practices and to direct change appropriate to environmental and societal need. Teachers should respond to Keller's accusation that the "lumping together of all minorities is intellectually questionable" and should address the issues of educational need based on individual experiences (Keller 1988–1989, 44). The issues that should be addressed include those around diagnosing student needs (underserved, and perhaps underskilled, students not only have different needs but also require innovative approaches to learning and development); communicating the importance, purpose, and goals of instruction as they relate to real-world situations and expectations; and providing a curriculum that allows student input and active student involvement.

Increasing Opportunities for Success

Helping to clarify learning goals and empowering students to achieve active learning contingent on effective performance are critical instructional strategies. The need to respect diverse talents and ways of learning involves a learning theory that individuals learn differently. Learning style refers to how students process and retain information, how they prefer to interact with their instructors and other learners, and their preferences for learning environments.

The relationship of gender, racial, and ethnic differences to learning styles creates controversy: Is it legitimate to associate learning style with gender, race, and ethnicity? Why are there differences? Various studies recommend teachers become more aware of how different cultural backgrounds affect communication and learning, but there is active disagreement as to whether cultural background should be singled out for attention. The danger lies in stereotyping; the dilemma lies in recognizing diversity without casting a stereotypical mold. Claxton and Murrell (1987) and Andersen (1988) indicate a relationship among culture, conceptual systems, and learning styles. Perceptual and cognitive differences have been demonstrated between different minority groups and the "dominant" culture—American educational values hinge on the male-oriented, Euro-American traditions.

Many researchers turn this issue to the nature versus nurture debate, maintaining that gender or race may influence preferred learning style because the style is either valued or reinforced by that group or the majority culture. The perception that women are collaborative learners, and not competitive, may be attributable to the fact that the dominant culture reinforces these tendencies in women and discourages them in men. Hale-Benson (1982) portrays Black children as more relational than analytical in their learning styles; others would say that these differences disappear when students are acculturated to the predominant analytic style of most schools.

Resistance to culturally based learning styles stems from the assumption that what is different from the norm is deviant, or less valuable. Learning styles, however, seem to be a question of preference rather than absolutes—good teachers allow students opportunities to exercise their own style while helping them to develop in other areas as well. A conceptual framework for a continuum of learning styles, such as that presented in *Teaching as Leading* (Baker, Roueche, and Gillett-Karam (1990), allows instructors a process of reexamining how students learn and assessing their own impact on student learning style. Personality, information processing, social interaction, and instructional preferences can be met; teaching should be situationally perceptive so that modification of style can occur based on student need. Classroom research about teaching and learning, in which instructors have students take a learning style inventory, and the Baker, Roueche, and Gillett-Karam (1990) TALI or Teaching as Leading Inventory, profit everyone. By employing such research, many of the obvious obstacles to student success are eliminated.

Eliminating Obstacles to Learning

Working to eliminate or at least reduce obstacles to learning is another strategic function of the teacher as leader; in this role, faculty are aware of the major barriers that confront the teaching-learning environment and work to eliminate or at least reduce them. Concentration here is on solutions; defining problems is not a sufficient goal of the exemplary teacher.

Richardson and Bender (1987) address the issues of minority participation in *Fostering Minority Access and Achievement in Higher Education*; their principle interest lies in the relationships between declining enrollments and the transfer function. Obviously, if women and members of ethnic and racial minorities are to succeed in our society—and to provide leadership and role models for future generations—the transfer function becomes paramount. We are reminded that the future looks very bleak if things continue in the present mode. The data demonstrate that we are experiencing little, if any, increase in numbers of these groups in positions of leadership in community colleges. Community college education provides opportunities for transfer and also beyond the transfer function.

Quality colleges and teachers work to reduce obstacles to learning by examining the status quo; by offering options to existing problems, such as language or reading skills deficiencies, and cultures whose norms do not ''value'' education in the same vein as does the ''dominant'' culture; and by addressing the issues of underrepresentation and underutilization of racial-ethnic minorities in the classroom, among the faculty and administration, and in positions of leadership in the community college. Examples at Miami-Dade Community College and at Borough of Manhattan Community College provide options, not accusations; provide and document successes, not failures, in overcoming and addressing obstacles for minority and gender issues in their communities and for their local populations.

Empowering through High Expectations

Questions such as the following may redirect attention to several issues: What are teachers' expectations of minority students? Do seemingly innocuous remarks by teachers appear sexist or racist to students? Do teachers call on minority students as frequently as majority students? Do teachers solicit the input of minority students as "spokespersons" or as individuals? (modified from Green 1989).

Research indicates that teachers form expectations on the basis of prior achievement, physical attractiveness, sex, language, socioeconomic status, and race-ethnicity (Good 1981; Brophy and Good 1984). Moreover, instructors may assume that minority students are grouped at the lower end of the ability continuum and have lower expectations of them—this leads to the self-fulfilling prophecy. Research shows differences in the way in which teachers interact with low achievers and high achievers. To the extent minority students are actually underprepared, or simply stereotyped as low achievers, they may be treated differently from other students—called on less frequently, given less time to respond to questions, interrupted or criticized more often, and given insincere or generalized praise (Green 1989). The assumptions instructors make about abilities and attitudes can and do differ for majority and minority students.

Students "pick up" on nonverbal clues, are intimidated by a predominantly white environment and dominant culture, and may view the instructor as an authority figure, not to be questioned. These are characteristics of cultural diversity and socialization by subgroup cultures. Cultural differences and norms may be demonstrated with eye contact—for some cultures, direct and sustained eye contact represents interest and engagement; for other cultures, it may represent disrespect; for others, it may imply personal or sexual interest (Byers and Byers 1972). For the minority student, these factors inhibit their participation, and faculty misinterpretation may exacerbate these issues. Pemberton (1988) demonstrates that, in the interaction between professor and student, what the instructor perceives as interest in the student, the student sees as his or her life "being ransacked for sociological evidence" of race.

Instructors model expected behavior—they "inspect what they expect." High expectations are themselves self-fulfilling prophecies; this is the so-called Pygmalion effect, and it can be demonstrated over and over again in social settings that seem desperate and unyielding. Surely, the achievements of Marva Collins demonstrate this fact, but so do the achievements of other "hopeless" cases; they remind us of the excitement of discovery for the love of learning. None of these cases is more powerful than Wright's (1945) discussion of the use of his mentor's loaned library card and how it opened his world to books and the world outside of his being a "black boy" from the South:

It had been my accidental reading of fiction and literary criticism that had evoked in me vague glimpses of life's possibilities. Of course, I had never seen or met the men who wrote the books I read, and the kind of world in which they lived was as alien to me as the moon. But what enabled me to overcome my chronic distrust was that these books— written by men like Dreiser, Masters, Mencken, Anderson, and Lewis—seemed defensively critical of the straitened American environment. These writers seemed to feel that America could be shaped nearer to the hearts of those who lived in it. And it was out of these novels and stories and articles, out of the emotional impact of imaginative constructions of heroic or tragic deeds, that I felt touching my face a tinge of warmth from an unseen light; and in my leaving [the South] I was groping toward that invisible light, always trying to keep my face so set and turned that I would not lose the hope of its faint promise, using it as my justification for action. (1945, 227)

Offering Positive Guidance and Direction

Increasing the opportunities for quality educational performance and success in college and recruiting and retaining minority undergraduates are essential for ensuring equity for minority citizens and for improving the learning environment for all students. A college degree provides increased employment opportunity as well as enhanced social standing. Anything less than full access for all citizens to this important credential is clearly unjust. Educational experiences should reflect the pluralism of our country and the importance of racial-ethnic minorities as individuals and cultures.

Between 1976 and 1986, the number of minority students in graduate schools grew by 40 percent: Hispanic and Native Americans doubled; Blacks did not grow at all; white students had a 10 percent growth. During that same period, the numbers of minority students as professional students doubled for Hispanics and Asians and increased 25 percent for Blacks; however, the numbers of Black and Hispanic graduate and professional students are still insufficient to achieve adequate representation in the professions and in faculty positions.

Both faculty and administration should be motivated to provide strategies to eliminate the gap between access and completion rates of minorities in higher education. Although this effort is made at the community college level, there are obvious implications beyond the two-year experience. Planning should be geared toward the acquisition of articulation programs aimed at both recruitment and retention; these programs are best complemented by admissions, academic support programs, and financial aid.

Planning. Work cooperatively with public schools to diagnose and correct conditions and current problems; sometimes this requires adaptation of junior high and high school curricula to accommodate college entry requirements.

Recruiting. Give careful attention to local schools, four-year institutions, and community colleges working collaboratively; recognize differences among and within minority groups; develop informational materials in languages other than English. Recruitment aimed at senior institutions is also critical: The graduate faculty network often excludes minority faculty members and faculty members at colleges with large numbers of minority students.

Admissions and Academic Support Programs. Consider high-risk minority students; use multiple criteria for admissions purposes; assist minority applicants in admissions procedures. Emphasize teaching and learning for all students; relate support programs to academic majors; provide trained, experienced teachers for underprepared students; integrate academic support programs with student service counterparts; provide peer counseling; provide an early warning system.

Retention. Create a hospitable environment for minority students; demonstrate the importance of support services for undergraduates. Graduate programs should support discipline-based minority student interest groups, such as ''Blacks in psychology,'' or ''Hispanics in engineering.''

Graduation. Help minority students understand how the graduate and professional school system work; develop financial incentives for departments such as increased minority fellowship funds or graduate assistantships, and annual affirmative action grants.

Financial Aid. Inform the student as early as possible about financial awards—preferably at the time of admission; provide more work-study programs and fewer loans to minority students; connect work-study programs to course and work-load decisions; provide budget counseling and emergency loan services. Graduate schools should provide minority students financial support packages that are adequate and guaranteed through the students' graduate careers.

Motivating toward Independence

Without heating up the controversy over curriculum, one could safely say that there is consensus around the overall purposes of a liberal education: An appreciation of humanities, sciences, and the arts, the promotion of ethical conduct, and the understanding of knowledge implementable in theory and practice are essential for undergraduate curriculum. The controversy begins to heat up around the interpretation, implementation, and relative importance of curriculum.

Moreover, there is agreement that curriculum cannot be static—new knowledge, changing conditions, and changing requirements of society all impact the curriculum at the college campus. Sometimes new information may render existing theories totally invalid or may point out the incompleteness of existing facts. In the last three decades, the college campus itself has drastically changed and has been dramatically challenged by the entrance of women, minority students, and older students. New areas of knowledge, new disciplines, and new educational issues have resulted. Not only did women's studies, African-American studies, ethnic studies, and area studies point out the omission of the curriculum to the experiences and contributions of large segments of society, but they challenged incomplete and unidimensional thinking. These shifts in curricula are not without their detractors, and some would suggest that not to recognize the critical need for such curricula in American higher education is "killing the spirit" of the learner (Smith 1990).

The current debate over curriculum centers on the question of inclusion of culturally pluralistic and global resources; it aims to ensure that all students understand the richness of history, art, and literature of women and racial-ethnic groups. This debate talks about "transformation" of the curriculum as it is now known—value and philosophical differences electrify the controversy. Efforts decry the "add-on" theory in which mention is made of cultural, racial-ethnic, or gender-related issues or contributions. Rather, inclusion of works and perspectives of women and minorities seeks to transform the curriculum and the entire teaching and learning process; it is meant to be a long-term process. Schuster and Van Dyne suggest that the current curriculum does not expose the "invisible paradigms which are the internalized assumptions, the network of unspoken agreements, the implicit contracts, that all the participants in the process of higher education have agreed to, usually unconsciously, in order to bring about learning" (1984, 417). Others would suggest that transforming the curriculum makes it too political (and less neutral); they claim that proponents of a transformed curriculum seek to distort it with politically motivated reform agendas.

The obvious framework for such curricula is one of an inclusionary change process. This reframing deemphasizes political debate and instead capitalizes on dialogue that incorporates new visions while protecting the existing curriculum. How to do it? McIntosh (1989), Green (1989), and Schuster and Van Dyne (1984) suggest directly confronting the exclusive curriculum through a series of phases that transforms the curriculum, integrating multicultural values and contributions. Some practical suggestions move the notion of the "add-on phase" to a more inclusionary policy that incorporates the "specialized" course, such as ethnic studies or women's studies, of which Smith says:

There are certainly positive aspects of "counter education run by women for women. There are strong moral imperatives. . . . There is passionate conviction . . . that women teachers take a far more personal interest in their students. They are the last utopians; they have revived the dream of a better, more humane society, not to be achieved this time by science or reason or objectivity, but by the keener sensibilities and nobler character of women" (1990, 289–292).

Eventually, the environment produces a breakthrough when a transformed curriculum is put into place, one that incorporates new knowledge and scholarship, new methodologies and new ways of teaching and learning and encourages new ways of thinking. Moving from strategies that transform the curriculum to strategies that increase representation of faculty and administrators on community college campuses seems to be a natural progression.

A diverse faculty is essential to a pluralistic campus. Faculty create the curriculum and determine the quality of the experience in every classroom. Currently, between 10 and 12 percent of faculty at community colleges across the nation are members of racial-ethnic groups. Between 1977 and 1985, Black faculty on college campuses declined from 4.4 to 4.2 percent of the total faculty; Hispanic and Native American faculty moved from 1.5 to 1.7 percent (1,000 more); and Asian faculty rose from 2.7 to 4.1 percent (7,000 more). Between 1981 and 1987, doctorates to minorities moved from 2,728 to 2,890, and concentrations of these degrees were in education. Minority faculty are less likely to hold tenure. Women are also less likely to hold tenure; and for both racial-ethnic minorities and women, there are substantial differences in salaries. The numbers of minorities choosing academic careers declined from 1975 to 1985. Only a small percentage of all administrators were members of racial-ethnic minorities (around 10 percent), and this figure includes all individuals who administer special minority programs in predominantly white institutions. Data demonstrate that these numbers have been relatively stable over the last ten years. Moreover, few of this small percentage of minorities are presidents, vice presidents, or deans; rather they are "assistant to" or connected to minority or affirmative action positions, opportunity programs, bilingual education, and student services. Often, the special minority programs are funded with soft money. (Data compiled from Mingle 1987; Carter and Wilson 1989; Linthicum 1989; Green 1989).

CONCLUSION

Excellence and leadership in teaching can be attributed to these maxims: engaging the desire to learn, eliminating obstacles to learning, increasing opportunities for success, offering positive guidance and direction, empowering through high expectations, and motivating toward independence. Although this chapter uses these maxims to point out the needs of women and members of racial and ethnic groups, the maxims are a result of what the best community college professors actually do to retain and motivate their students. The task that confronts all instruction around the issue of teaching and learning is to know the student, to promote active learning, and to motivate the student so that the learning experience becomes a transforming process. We are changing demographically and globally; excellent teachers are those who are prepared to meet these changes.

REFERENCES

Action Council on Minority Education. 1990. *Education that works: An action plan for the education of minorities*. Cambridge, Mass.: Quality Education for Minorities Project.

Andersen, C. J., et al. 1989. *1989–90 fact book on higher education*. New York: American Council on Education/Macmillan.

Anderson, J. A. 1988. Cognitive styles and multicultural populations. *Journal of Teacher Education* (January/February): 2–9.

Baker, G. A., J. E. Roueche, and R. Gillett-Karam. 1990. *Teaching as leading: Profiles of excellence in the open-door college.* Washington, D.C.: Community College Press.

Brophy, J. E., and T. L. Good. 1984. *Teacher behavior and student achievement.* Occasional Paper no. 73. ERIC Document no. ED 251 422. Bethesda, Md.

Byers, P., and H. Byers. 1972. Nonverbal communication and the education of children. In *Functions of language in the classroom*, ed. C. B. Cazden, V. P. John, and D. Hynes. New York: Academic Press.

Carter, D. J., and R. Wilson. 1989. *Minorities in higher education.* Washington, D.C.: American Council on Education.

Chickering, A. W., and Z. F. Gamson. 1987. Seven principles for good practice in undergraduate education. *Wingspread Journal* 9(2). Racine, Wisc.: Johnson Foundation.

Claxton, C. S., and P. H. Murrell, eds. 1987. *Learning styles: Implications for improving educational practices.* ASHE-ERIC Higher Education Report no. 4, Washington, D.C.: Association for the Study of Higher Education.

Education Commission of the States. 1987. *Focus on minorities: Synopsis of state higher education initiatives.* Denver, Colo.

El-Khawas, E., et al. 1988. *Community college fact book.* New York: American Association of Community and Junior Colleges and American Council on Education/Macmillan.

Gillett-Karam, R., S. D. Roueche, and J. E. Roueche. 1991. *Underrepresentation and the question of diversity: Women and minorities in the community college.* Washington, D.C.: Community College Press. AACJC.

Good, T. L. 1981. Teacher expectations and student perceptions: A decade of research. *Educational Leadership* (February): 417–22.

Green, M. F. 1988. *Leaders for a new era: Strategies for higher education.* New York: Macmillan.

———. 1989. *Minorities on campus: A handbook for enhancing diversity.* Washington, D.C.: American Council on Education.

Greenleaf, R. 1973. *Servant as leader.* Newton Center, Mass.: Robert K. Greenleaf Center.

Hale-Benson, J. E. 1982. *Black children: Their roots, culture and learning styles.* Baltimore: Johns Hopkins University Press.

Keller, G. 1988–1989. Review essay: Black students in higher education: Why so few? *Planning for Higher Education* 17(3): 43–56.

Linthicum, D. S. 1989. *The dry pipeline: Increasing the flow of minority faculty.* Washington, D.C.: National Council of State Directors of Community and Junior Colleges.

McIntosh, P. 1989. Curricular re-vision: The new knowledge for a new age. In *Educating the majority: Women challenge tradition in higher education*, ed. C. Pearson, J. Touchton, and D. Shavlik. New York: American Council on Education/Macmillan.

Mingle, J. R. 1987. *Focus on minorities: Trends in higher education participation and success.* Washington, D.C.: Education Commission of the States and the State Higher Education Executive Officers.

National Center for Education Statistics. 1990. Survey Report. *Trends in racial/ethnic enrollment in higher education: Fall 1978 through fall 1988.* Washington, D.C.: U.S. Department of Education, Office of Educational Research and Improvement.

Nettles, M. T., ed. 1988. *Toward black undergraduate student equality in American higher education.* Westport, Conn.: Greenwood Press.

Pearson, C. S., D. L. Shavlik, and J. G. Touchton. 1989. *Educating the majority: Women challenge tradition in higher education.* New York: Macmillan.

Pemberton, G. 1988. *On teaching the minority students: Problems and strategies.* Brunswick, Maine: Bowdoin College.

Ravitch, D. 1990. Multiculturalism, yes; Particularism, no. *Chronicle of Higher Education* 24 October 1990, A–52.

Richardson, R. C., and L. W. Bender. 1987. *Fostering minority access and achievement in higher education: The role of urban community colleges and universities.* San Francisco: Jossey-Bass.

Schuster, M., and S. Van Dyne. 1984. Placing women in the liberal arts: Stages of curriculum transformation. *Harvard Educational Review* 54(4): 413–28.

Smith, P. 1990. *Killing the spirit: Higher education in America.* New York: Viking Press/Penguin Books.

Wilson, R., and D. J. Carter. 1988. *Seventh annual status report on minorities in higher education.* Washington, D.C.: American Council on Education.

Wilson, R., and S. Melendez. 1988. Strategies for developing minority leadership. In *Leaders for a new era*, ed. M. Green. New York: Collier Macmillan.

Wright, R. 1945. *Black boy: A record of childhood and youth.* New York: Harper and Row.

Faculty Practices and Attitudes as Teachers and Scholars: A Review of Research

James C. Palmer

As the number of community colleges grew after World War II, so did the number of people who make or augment their careers as community college teachers. Historical data summarized by Cohen and Brawer show a tenfold increase between 1953 and 1987 in the number of faculty teaching at public and private two-year colleges—from 23,762 to 256,236 (1989, 77). Almost all of that increase is accounted for by teachers at public community colleges, which now employ about 94 percent of all two-year college faculty members and 42 percent of all faculty members teaching in America's public institutions of higher education (Snyder and Hoffman 1991, 218).

Despite the impressive size of this professorial group, community college teaching as a profession has yet to develop a distinctive nature, one that will provide its practitioners with a collective identity and serve as a frame of reference to be used by those outside the profession to understand its role and purpose. Over the years, several anchors for a professional identity have been suggested. The literature variously posits the community college faculty member as a pedagogical expert who builds courses and curricula around clearly defined behavioral objectives (Cohen 1973), as a scholar who brings currency and intellectual vitality to the classroom by remaining an active contributor to his or her discipline (Vaughan 1988), as a leader who motivates students to even higher levels of achievement (Baker, Roueche, and Gillett-Karam 1990), and as a "classroom researcher" who builds feedback mechanisms into teaching, thereby determining the extent to which students actually learn what is being taught (Cross and Angelo 1989; Commission on the Future of Community Colleges 1988). None has fully taken hold. During the 1960s, Garrison interviewed junior college faculty nationwide, observing that they "have yet to attain full professional identity or status" (1967, 76). Reviewing the literature over twenty years later,

Cohen and Brawer came to a similar conclusion: "Community college instruction has become a career in its own right. Its flowering awaits a more fully-developed professional consciousness on the part of its practitioners" (1989, 90).

In order to explore the unfinished nature of the community college teacher's professional identity, this chapter reviews prior research examining faculty attitudes and practices in two interrelated professional arenas: teaching and disciplinary scholarship. The tentative picture that results from this research, which includes both surveys of faculty and ethnographic studies of faculty life, shows a checkered pattern of professional initiative driven by an active minority who make notable contributions to instructional practice and engage in out-of-class scholarly work. The research also suggests ways in which the institutional culture of the community college and faculty attitudes toward their work may interact to stymie the professional initiatives of the remaining faculty who might otherwise establish a presence on campus that goes beyond the employee's obligation to teach so many hours per week.

FACULTY INITIATIVES IN TEACHING

Classroom teaching dominates the professional lives of community college faculty members. Findings from two recent national surveys, conducted by Astin, Korn, and Dey (1991) and by the Carnegie Foundation for the Advancement of Teaching (1989), show that, in comparison to colleagues at four-year colleges and universities, community college faculty spend more hours per week in the classroom, are more likely to view teaching as their primary interest, and are more likely to agree that teaching effectiveness should be the primary criterion for promotion (see Tables 1 and 2). While the majority of faculty members at all institutions view teaching as their principal activity, community college instructors appear to be more personally engaged in teaching, both as a day-to-day activity and as a personal interest. This is supported by several other surveys indicating that teaching and contact with students are considered by community college faculty to be among the most gratifying aspects of their work (Cohen 1974; Benoit and Smith 1980; Diener 1985; Riday, Bingham, and Harvey 1985; Stecklein and Willie 1982).

Yet further analysis of the national survey data presented in Tables 1 and 2 suggests that this engagement and interest in teaching does not translate into a distinctive institutional ethos of instructional experimentation and innovation. For example, the profile of instructional practices emerging in the national survey of faculty conducted by Astin, Korn, and Dey (1991) shows many similarities in the ways in which two-year and four-year faculty members teach. Traditional lecture and discussion, undertaken by teachers as a solo activity, prevail across institutional types. Only a minority of faculty experiment with computer-assisted instruction, although such experimentation is more common at community colleges than at four-year institutions, and few collaborate with colleagues in interdisciplinary work or team teaching.

Table 1

Teaching Activities and Attitudes toward Teaching: Selected Findings from a National Survey Conducted by the Higher Education Research Institute

Faculty Who	Public 2-Yr. Colleges %	Public 4-Yr. Colleges %	Public Universities %
Indicate that teaching is their primary activity	95	93	82
Indicate that teaching is their primary interest	70	30	12
Spend 13 or more hours per week on scheduled teaching	78	30	12
Spend 13 hours or more per week preparing for teaching	43	45	37
Had developed a new course in the last two years	64	69	67
Taught the following in the last two years:			
An honors course	11	16	20
A remedial course	29	13	7
An interdisciplinary course	24	34	34
A team-taught course	30	34	39
Used the following instructional methods in most or all courses			
Discussion	71	71	66
Computer-assisted instruction	19	12	11
Cooperative learning	29	27	23
Experiential learning	20	20	18
Group projects	15	17	16
Independent projects	32	36	34
Extensive lecturing	53	54	61
Used the following evaluation methods in most or all classes			
Multiple-choice midterms / finals	50	36	27
Essay midterms / finals	28	40	43
Short-answer midterms / finals	31	33	35
Multiple-choice quizzes	32	16	10
Term / research papers	20	33	36

Source: Astin, Korn, and Dey, 1991.

Table 2
Attitudes toward Teaching and the Academic Ability of Students: Selected Findings from a National Survey of Faculty Conducted by the Carnegie Foundation for the Advancement of Teaching

Faculty Who	2-Yr. College Faculty %	4-Yr. College Faculty %
Indicate that teaching is their primary interest	77	26
Indicate that teaching effectiveness should be the primary criterion for promotion	92	48
Agree that too many students ill-suited to academic life are now enrolling in colleges and universities	70	60
Agree that undergraduates with whom they have close contact are seriously underprepared in basic skills	85	70
Agree that most undergraduates do just enough to get by	63	51
Agree that there has been a widespread lowering of standards in American higher education	73	64

Source: Carnegie Foundation for the Advancement of Teaching 1989.

The differences that *do* emerge between the teaching roles of two-year and four-year college faculty lie in the nature of the students taught and in the assignments used to assess student learning. For example, community college faculty are more likely than four-year college faculty to teach remedial classes and to express dismay at their students' academic ability. In addition, community college faculty make more use of short-answer quizzes than written essays. These differences should not be overstated; because faculty at four-year colleges teach upper-division as well as lower-division courses, it is not surprising that they assign more papers and are less likely to teach at the remedial level. A more telling analysis would compare the teaching practices of community college faculty with the teaching practices employed by four-year college faculty in lower-division courses. Nonetheless, the picture that emerges is one of what Bowles (1982) calls instructional "conservatism" rather than instructional innovation, with community college faculty using traditional methods to contend with large numbers of students who do not have college-level literacy skills.

Surveys focusing specifically on community college faculty provide further evidence of this conservatism and point to potential weaknesses in instructional practice. Faculty respondents indicate that lecture and discussion remain the most frequently used instructional modes, although these traditional forms may be more prevalent in some disciplines (particularly the humanities) than in others (Bowles 1982; Keim 1989). In addition, short-answer tests are often used in lieu of more exacting writing requirements. National surveys conducted in1977, 1983, and 1985 by the Center for the Study of Community Colleges show that quick score tests or essay examinations are given more weight by community college arts and sciences teachers in the calculation of student grades than out-of-class papers (Brawer 1984; Cohen, Brawer, and Bensimon 1985).

Burnout is also a problem. When researchers turn their attention to factors that contribute to job satisfaction, they sometimes find that heavy teaching loads and poorly prepared students contribute to dissatisfaction (Hill 1983; Hutton and Jobe 1985; Keim 1989; Milosheff 1990). This supports Seidman's contention that there is a point of diminishing returns after which contact with students becomes more burdensome than gratifying (Seidman 1985, 1987). Finally, some research points to a misplaced sense of professionalism. For example, Cohen and Brawer (1977) conclude that most faculty view teaching excellence as a function of good interpersonal skills rather than expertise in instructional method and assessment. Cohen and Brawer draw a sharp distinction between the minority of faculty, who judge their worth on the extent to which students learn, and the majority, who define their value in terms of ''personal contact with students, resisting any suggestion that they align themselves with defined learning'' (1977, 107). The former experiment with instructional methods, gauging their effectiveness against student mastery of defined objectives. The latter relinquish the professional-client relationship in favor of an ethos that values one-on-one communication with students behind the closed classroom door rather than demonstrable student learning itself.

Ethnographic studies and interviews point to additional problems, suggesting that some faculty adapt to the frustrating aspects of their jobs by lowering academic standards rather than experimenting with instructional techniques. London's observations at a newly founded urban community college led him to conclude that many faculty members resigned themselves to the poor academic preparation of students and reduced their expectations of students accordingly (London 1978). In a more extensive study, Richardson, Fisk, and Okun (1983) observed classroom instruction at a community college (fictitiously named Oakwood Community College) for over two years, concluding that teachers watered down course reading and writing requirements in response to limited student literacy skills. A subtle process of negotiation between students and teachers led faculty to stress mastery of isolated facts rather than synthesis and contextual knowledge. "Over time," the researchers observed, "faculty members at Oakwood have come to view their students as possessing limited academic preparation and have adapted by preserving disciplinary content at the expense of literacy demands" (1983, 88).

Similarly, Weis's year-long study of an urban community college in New York led her to hypothesize that over time faculty accepted low student academic ability and aptitude as inalterable (Weis 1985a, 1985b). Adopting the view that only one or two students will succeed, the faculty Weis observed looked to collegial relations rather than to students for job satisfaction. As a result, the faculty gradually minimized their efforts in the classroom, decreasing the amount of course preparation time and relying increasingly on quizzes and short-answer tests. This, in turn, reinforced student behaviors that mitigate against academic achievement, further convincing faculty that their efforts to improve instructional practice and raise standards would have minimal results. In Weis's scenario, quality teaching is a casualty of the clash between student and faculty cultures.

Seidman's interviews with faculty also suggest a diminution of standards, though for different reasons (Seidman 1985, 1987). The faculty he talked with felt that insistence on challenging reading and writing requirements might isolate them from the college community, placing them at odds with administrators, who fear diminished enrollments; with students, who will register for other classes taught by less demanding instructors; and with faculty colleagues, who begrudge the perceived one-upmanship of those who cast their own instructional practices in a bad light. Concern for students also played a role. Contrary to what Weis observed, Seidman's interviewees maintained an ethos of "student-centeredness" and felt a sense of personal loss when a student dropped out. They felt torn between the maintenance of academic standards and the laudable ambitions of students who, however academically ill prepared, strove toward educational credentials that would improve their social and financial lot. All combined to create an institutional culture that exacts a heavy toll on faculty whose teaching imposes high demands on students.

These studies point to an institution at which purposeful teaching toward defined ends and at collegiate levels is difficult for many faculty members to sustain. This is not to deny the signal efforts individuals undertake to assess and improve their own teaching. Studies examining the practices of faculty recognized by peers or administrators as outstanding teachers testify to the initiative and imagination many teachers bring to the classroom (Baker, Roueche, and Gillett-Karam 1991; Easton et al. 1985). Nor is it to deny the success of numerous community college students who achieve their educational goals. What can legitimately be questioned is the meaning of the community college as a distinctive teaching institution. As in the four-year colleges, teaching at the community college remains a private enterprise conducted largely along traditional lines. Its practitioners seek gratifying relations with successful students but, more often than not, face the extraordinary pedagogical challenges posed by students who enroll with weak academic skills and attend for short periods of time. Discouragement and compromised standards may be common responses.

FACULTY INITIATIVES IN SCHOLARSHIP

The community college's emphasis on teaching and "student-centeredness" leads many to question the appropriateness of faculty work in disciplinary scholarship. From the earliest days of the institution, two-year college leaders have held as an ideal the notion of a faculty that has severed its ties with the discipline-based research of university graduate schools and has refocused its professional energy on student development. In 1918 Alexis Lange warned junior college leaders not to model their institutions after the university, arguing that the drive for research would overshadow student needs. "While the university professor is not expressly forbidden to educate young men and women, if he knows how," Lange observed, "his first and last duty is toward his subject" (Diener 1986, 69). During the growth years of the 1960s, Gleazer (1967) called on graduate schools to develop interdisciplinary master's degree programs specifically designed to prepare teachers who would accept and support the community college teaching mission. He feared that graduates of traditional, discipline-based master's degree programs would be dissatisfied with a community college career, identifying themselves with the scholarly enterprise of the university. The institutional culture of the community college is built in part on the pervasive belief that scholarly efforts outside of the classroom divert attention from teaching and constitute a disservice to students.

This heritage is reflected in the relatively small number of Ph.D. graduates hired by community colleges and in the limited rewards faculty receive for out-of-class scholarly work. Despite speculation that the number of faculty members holding the Ph.D. would increase (Cohen and Brawer 1977), only 19 percent of all full-time teachers at public community colleges hold this degree, compared to 69 percent at public comprehensive four-year colleges and 90 percent at public research universities (Russell et al. 1990). Few community college faculty members feel pressured by their institutions to publish; when asked by the Carnegie Foundation if tenure was difficult to obtain without publishing, only 6 percent of the nation's two-year college faculty responded affirmatively, compared to 77 percent of the four-year college faculty (Carnegie Foundation for the Advancement of Teaching 1989, 50).

Given the backgrounds of community college faculty and the limited incentives for publishing—not to mention high teaching loads—national surveys comparing two-year and four-year college faculty predictably show that the latter are much more likely to engage in research, publish, and deliver papers at discipline-based conferences. For example, Astin, Korn, and Dey (1991) found that 59 percent of the faculty at public universities and 33 percent of the faculty at public four-year colleges spent nine or more hours per week on research and scholarly writing. This compares to only 7 percent of the faculty at public community colleges.

The picture becomes more promising when the definition of scholarship is expanded, as Vaughan (1988) proposes, to include work on any product that requires systematic application of one's disciplinary knowledge and that is open to the criticism of knowledgeable peers. Under this definition, original research leading to a publication becomes but one form of scholarship, which may also encompass community service projects or the development of instructional materials and research reports for institutional use. For example, of the full-time community college faculty responding to a national survey conducted by Palmer (1992), 17 percent indicated that they had published an article in a professional or trade journal within the preceding two years, 5 percent indicated that they had contributed a chapter to an edited volume, 8 percent indicated that they had published textbooks or learning guides, and 7 percent indicated that they had published other works such as histories, plays, poems, or short stories. In contrast, 28 percent indicated that they had produced a research or technical report that was disseminated internally within the college or to outside clients, 26 percent indicated that they had produced unpublished textbooks or learning guides for use by colleagues at their colleges, 19 percent indicated that they had published brochures and other informational materials for the general public (such as pamphlets on prenatal care or household safety), and 11 percent indicated that they had produced informational materials designed to help area businesses, industries, or government agencies improve operations or increase their competitiveness. Yet, even here, faculty involvement is infrequent; of those indicating that they had worked on the development of these nontraditional scholarly products, most indicated that they had produced only one within a two-year period.

While the limited involvement in out-of-class scholarly work is well documented, its impact on the professional lives of community college faculty is not as well understood. Some community college faculty clearly embrace the historical skepticism of out-of-class scholarship, viewing its rejection as evidence of a professional commitment to teaching. For example, one respondent to Palmer's survey volunteered, in an open-ended response, that "the obvious must be stated: the principle mission of the two-year community college is *to teach*. I am here in large part because I consider that mission to be valid, important, and satisfying" (Palmer 1992, 63). Others struggle against the institutional diminution of out-of-class scholarship. Cohen and Brawer (1977) found that, although 29 percent of the humanities faculty they surveyed had ever published a journal article and only 12 percent had ever authored or coauthored a published book, 61 percent indicated that they would like to devote more time to research and professional writing.

London (1980) observed that isolation from their academic disciplines was a demoralizing element of the lives of many community college faculty members, diminishing one's sense of professional fulfillment. Seidman concluded that many of the faculty he interviewed "struggle[d] to maintain their scholarship and writing in an atmosphere that is at best ambivalent toward these activities and at worst somewhat hostile" (1985, 45). Palmer found that 72 percent of his respondents agreed that work on out-of-class scholarly activities would improve their teaching, and many resented what they viewed as a lack of institutional and collegial support for their scholarly work. One respondent, for example, noted, "Active hostility [toward publication] is found not only within the administration but also among faculty members who seem to associate research and publication with all that is evil in the university system. I would not like to be forced to publish, but I am very angry at the lack of toleration for those who do" (1992, 63).

This is a telling comment. That faculty scholarship remains alive despite a sometimes antagonistic institutional culture testifies to the enduring ties many community college teachers feel toward their disciplines. Yet scholarship, like instructional innovation, is the individual's prerogative, pursued as a personal endeavor rather than as a requisite of the profession. While some faculty members may embrace scholarly work, other feel that they can legitimately disclaim it. And in the absence of a strong commitment to instruction, the faculty member's professional identity may be cast adrift. In describing the community college professoriate, Cohen and Brawer state, "The lines of an *a*disciplinary group emerged, one that had abandoned the academic and not replaced it with anything of substance" (1977, 102).

HYPOTHESES AND FUTURE DIRECTIONS

Research on the professional roles of community college faculty must be interpreted cautiously. Surveys provide only gross indicators of faculty characteristics, attitudes, and practices, leaving the underlying patterns and causes of faculty behavior open to speculation. Ethnographic studies offer interpretations of actual faculty experience, but only within isolated contexts; until more of these studies are conducted in a variety of settings and with a consistent methodology, it will be difficult to generalize their findings to community colleges as a whole.

Nonetheless, two tentative hypotheses may be drawn from previous research in an attempt to explain the gap (evident in national surveys) between faculty attitudes toward the importance of teaching and scholarship and the extent to which faculty engage themselves as instructional innovators or disciplinary scholars. Both hypotheses posit barriers that may prevent the faculty member from making the transition from an employee teaching so many hours per week to a professional responsible for effecting changes in clients (students) and contributing to the larger scholarly community.

The first hypothesis speaks to the institutional culture of the community college, suggesting that many new faculty members undergo an acculturation process that diminishes faculty effort in instructional innovation and disciplinary scholarship. This is particularly evident in the studies conducted by London (1978), Richardson, Fisk, and Okun (1983), Seidman (1985, 1987), and Weis (1985a, 1985b), which portray the faculty as casualties of an acculturation process leading many new teachers to compromise their commitment to academic standards. Several factors may be involved in this process, including high teaching loads, institutional hostility or indifference to disciplinary scholarship, the weak academic backgrounds of students, the sociocultural gap between faculty and the students they teach, and an unstated though strong emphasis on maintaining enrollments and securing student success despite their marginal literacy skills. These factors may severely challenge the instructional and scholarly ideals of all but the most strong-willed individuals.

The second hypothesis has to do with the faculty members themselves. The literature suggests (with Weis as a notable exception) that many community college teachers view being with students in the classroom and exhibiting a sense of student-centeredness as fulfillment of their professional obligations. They view the act of helping students, and not documented student learning, as the primary measure of professional commitment. Where they exist, these attitudes provide a fuzzy sense of professional responsibility. When teacher-student interaction is viewed as an end unto itself, outside scholarship is extraneous, and the process and results of teaching as a professional intervention leading to student learning are of secondary importance (Cohen and Brawer 1977).

The extent to which these hypotheses actually explain faculty practice cannot be known without further research. This research should be undertaken because the demands made on faculty as scholars and teachers continue to rise, suggesting that the aborted nature of faculty professionalism implied in the hypotheses may be untenable in the future. Several trends point in this direction.

One is growing attention to curricular reform and the assessment of student learning. Without faculty involvement in these arenas, bureaucratic demands for data collection may overshadow academic needs for instructional improvement. Banta (1991), for example, cites several examples of college efforts to involve faculty in specifying general education outcomes and developing assessment programs that monitor institutional success in leading students to those outcomes. Only through these efforts, she maintains, can institutional outcomes assessment programs succeed. While some colleges begin planning these programs by selecting or developing assessment instruments, they in effect place the cart before the horse: "They cannot proceed very far along this path," Banta maintains, "without direction from a statement of expected student outcomes. That is, what do faculty hope students will know and be able to do as a result of their experience in the general education program?" (Banta 1991, 1). This view of faculty responsibility severely challenges the credibility of teachers who gauge their success in terms of gratifying relations with students rather than documented student learning itself.

A second factor is the contemporary debate about the nature of scholarship and its importance to professional development. While community colleges are not structured in ways that allow extensive faculty work in research and writing, the notion of a professional base built on faculty as disciplinary scholars may be gaining greater acceptance. Changing attitudes toward the scope of scholarly activity point in this direction; as college leaders recognize that original research is but one type of scholarship, the potential scholarly role of community college faculty increases (Boyer 1990; Commission on the Future of Community Colleges 1988; Vaughan 1988). Concern for faculty development and renewal has also heightened an awareness of the link between teaching and scholarship. Noting that scholarly activity builds faculty morale and helps teachers keep up with their disciplines, some community college leaders have argued for the establishment of procedures that encourage, recognize, and reward out-of-class scholarly work (Vaughan and Palmer 1991).

Finally, concerns for educational equity have also come into play, especially in relation to those community college students who plan to earn baccalaureate degrees. If inculcation into the traditions of inquiry and communication within the major is requisite to student success in attaining baccalaureate or higher degrees, community college faculty must view themselves as part of the scholarly community within their disciplines and teach in ways that help their students become part of that community as well (McGrath and Spear 1991; Ratcliff 1992). The disciplinary ties to this larger community are also emphasized in growing attention to transfer as an academic outcome that depends on the joint work and cooperation of two-year and four-year college faculty (Eaton 1990).

The professional identity of the community college teacher is not an either-or proposition, balancing the seemingly competing interests of teaching and disciplinary scholarship. Both are intertwined and vital to student success. As community college leaders face the prospect of replacing the generation of faculty who grew with the colleges after World War II, the more important issue is whether faculty will take professional responsibility for student learning within the disciplines and whether institutions will view and support faculty as professionals rather than employees. Without this shared sense of professional responsibility, community colleges may remain vulnerable to the breakdowns in faculty effectiveness illustrated in the writings of London (1978), Richardson, Fisk, and Okun (1983), Weis (1985a, 1985b), and Seidman (1985, 1987). To the extent that those breakdowns occur—an area that needs further study—the teacher's professional identity and effect will remain weak.

REFERENCES

Astin, A. W., W. S. Korn, and E. L. Dey. 1991. *The American college teacher: National norms for the 1989–90 faculty survey.* Los Angeles: Higher Education Research Institute, University of California, Los Angeles.

Baker, G. A. III, J. E. Roueche, and R. Gillett-Karem. 1990. *Teaching as leading: Profiles of excellence in the open-door college.* Washington, D.C.: American Association of Community and Junior Colleges.

Banta, T. W. 1991. Faculty-developed approaches to assessing general education outcomes. *Assessment Update* 3(2): 1–2, 4.

Benoit, R. J., and A. Smith. 1980. Demographic and job satisfaction characteristics of Florida community college faculty. *Community/Junior College Research Quarterly* 4(3): 263–76.

Bowles, C. R. 1982. The teaching practices of two-year college science and humanities instructors. *Community/Junior College Quarterly of Research and Practice* 6(2): 129–44.

Boyer, E. L. 1990. *Scholarship reconsidered: Priorities of the professoriate*. Princeton, N.J.: Carnegie Foundation for the Advancement of Teaching.

Brawer, F. B. 1984. A longitudinal analysis of community college humanities faculty. *Community College Review* 12(1): 14–20.

Carnegie Foundation for the Advancement of Teaching. 1989. *The condition of the professoriate: Attitudes and trends, 1989*. Princeton, N.J.: Carnegie Foundation for the Advancement of Teaching.

Cohen, A. M. 1973. Toward a professional faculty. In *Toward a professional faculty*, ed. A. M. Cohen. New Directions for Community Colleges, no. 1. San Francisco: Jossey-Bass.

———. 1974. Community college faculty job satisfaction. *Research in Higher Education* 2(4): 369–76.

Cohen, A. M., and F. B. Brawer. 1977. *The two-year college instructor today*. New York: Praeger.

———. 1989. *The American community college*. 2d ed. San Francisco: Jossey-Bass.

Cohen, A. M., F. B. Brawer, and E. Bensimon. 1985. *Transfer education in the American community college*. ERIC Document no. ED 255 250. Los Angeles: Center for the Study of Community Colleges.

Commission on the Future of Community Colleges. 1988. *Building communities: A vision for a new century*. Washington, D.C.: American Association of Community and Junior Colleges.

Cross, K. P., and T. A. Angelo. 1989. Faculty members as classroom researchers: A progress report. *Community, Technical, and Junior College Journal* 59(5): 23–25.

Diener, T. 1985. Community college job satisfaction. *Community/Junior College Quarterly of Research and Practice* 9(4): 347–57.

———. 1986. *The growth of an American invention: A documentary history of the junior and community college movement*. Contributions to the Study of Education no. 16. Westport, Conn.: Greenwood Press.

Easton, J. Q., E. P. Forrest, R. E. Goldman, and L. M. Ludwig. 1985. National study of effective community college teachers. *Community/Junior College Quarterly of Research and Practice* 9(2): 153–63.

Eaton, J. S. 1990. An academic model for transfer education. *Transfer Working Papers* 1(3). Washington, D.C.: National Center for Academic Achievement and Transfer.

Garrison, R. H. 1967. *Junior college faculty—Issues and problems: A preliminary national appraisal*. Washington, D.C.: American Association of Junior Colleges.

Gleazer, E. J., Jr. 1967. Preparation of junior college faculty. *Educational Record* 48(2): 147–86.

Hill, M. D. 1983. Some factors affecting the job satisfaction of community college faculty in Pennsylvania. *Community/Junior College Quarterly of Research and Practice* 7(4): 303–17.

Hutton, J. B., and M. E. Jobe. 1985. Job satisfaction of community college faculty. *Community/Junior College Quarterly of Research and Practice* 9(4): 317–24.

Keim, M. C. 1989. Two-year college faculty: A research update. *Community College Review* 17(3): 34–43.

London, H. B. 1978. *The culture of a commuity college.* New York: Praeger.

———. 1980. In between: The community college teachers. *Annals of the American Academy of Political and Social Science* 448: 62–73.

McGrath, D., and M. B. Spear. 1991. *The academic crisis of the community college.* Albany: State University of New York Press.

Milosheff, E. 1990. Factors contributing to job satisfaction at the community college. *Community College Review* 18(1): 12–22.

Palmer, J. C. 1992. The scholarly activities of community college faculty: Findings of a national survey. In *Fostering a climate for faculty scholarship at community colleges,* ed. J. C. Palmer and G. B. Vaughan. Washington, D.C.: American Association of Community and Junior Colleges.

Ratcliff, J. L. 1992. Scholarship, the transformation of knowledge, and community college teaching. In *Fostering a climate for faculty scholarship at community colleges,* ed. J. C. Palmer and G. B. Vaughan. Washington, D.C.: American Association of Community and Junior Colleges.

Richardson, R. C., Jr., E. C. Fisk and M. A. Okun. 1983. *Literacy in the open-access college.* San Francisco: Jossey-Bass.

Riday, G. E., R. D. Bingham, and T. R. Harvey, 1985. Satisfaction of community college faculty: Exploding a myth. *Community College Review* 12(3): 46–50.

Russell, S., R. S. Cox, C. Williamson, J. Boismier, H. Javitz, and J. Fairweather. 1990. *Faculty in higher education institutions, 1988.* NCES–90–365. Washington, D.C.: National Center for Education Statistics, U.S. Department of Education.

Seidman, E. 1985. *In the words of the faculty.* San Francisco: Jossey-Bass.

———. 1987. Merging access and excellence: The work of community college faculty. *Community, Technical, and Junior College Journal* 57(4): 43–45.

Snyder, T. D., and C. M. Hoffman. 1991. *Digest of education statistics.* NCES91–697. Washington, D.C.: National Center for Education Statistics, U.S. Department of Education.

Stecklein, J. E., and R. Willie. 1982. Minnesota community college faculty activities and attitudes, 1956–1980. *Community/Junior College Quarterly of Research and Practice* 6(3): 217–37.

Vaughan, G. B. 1988. Scholarship in community colleges: Path to respect. *Educational Record* 69(2): 26–31.

Vaughan, G. B., and J. C. Palmer, eds. 1991. *Enhancing teaching and administration through scholarship.* New Directions for Community Colleges, no. 76. San Francisco: Jossey-Bass.

Weis, L. 1985a. *Between two worlds: Black students in an urban community college.* Boston: Routledge and Keegan Paul.

———. 1985b. Faculty perspectives and practice in an urban community college. *Journal of Higher Education* 14(5): 553–74.

Part 8

Student Development in the Community College

Synthesis of Literature Related to Historical and Current Functions of Student Services

Don G. Creamer

There is a sixty-year history of literature pertaining to two-year college student service functions. The literature can be characterized in four ways: (1) It consistently points to the importance of student service functions relative to student success and to the achievement of institutional purposes; (2) it regularly reveals a fixed pattern of internal problems that prevents optimal delivery of services; (3) it periodically exposes severe criticism from scientific surveys of the overall effectiveness of student services; and (4) it rarely exhibits the use of research procedures for either program development or improvement. A reasonable conclusion can be reached from the literature about the vitality of student services in two-year colleges: The services historically have been important to the achievement of two-year college purposes, but they are not, and never were, ''the pivot, the hub, the core around which the whole enterprise moves'' as Collins (1967, 13) proclaimed they should be.

Literature shows that student service functions had a slow start in two-year colleges, despite some early claims that they were ''taking hold'' (Robb 1932). Robb reported that Koos made no mention of guidance in the junior college in a publication in 1924 and that Proctor recognized the guidance function in his book in 1927 by devoting only two pages to it. The next year, in 1928, Whitney dismissed the guidance function in his book with a discussion limited to five lines, but, four years later, Eells devoted an entire chapter of twenty pages to the guidance function (Robb 1932). This trend of guidance literature may indicate a slow ''taking hold'' of the concepts of student services in two-year institutions, but it also indicates the paucity of published thought on the subject prior to 1930. The neglect of the subject of student services in major publications was not over, however. In 1962, for example, Fields published a book on the community college movement and included only brief descriptions of guidance services and student activities offered at four community colleges cited as case studies (Fields 1962).

A major source of two-year college student services literature is the official journal of the American Association of Community and Junior Colleges (AACJC) (formerly the American Association of Junior Colleges). All AACJC's *Journal* issues, inclusive of volume 61, were reviewed to gain a sense of the place or the role of student services in the overall operation of two-year colleges. The proportion of articles in the *Journal* devoted to student services issues and concerns declined slightly from October 1930, when the first issue was published, to August 1980, as can be seen from three similar studies. Leunberger (1936) reported that 17 percent of the articles from 1930 to 1935 were devoted to student personnel. Twenty years later, Adams (1956) reported that 15 percent of the articles had been devoted to student personnel during the first twenty-six years of the *Journal*. Finally, Clowes and Towles reported in 1985 that 11 percent of the articles were devoted to issues of access and students during the *Journal*'s first fifty years (Clowes and Towles 1985).

These overlapping studies used somewhat different procedures to arrive at their findings, but their findings and other observations derived from the review of the sixty-year stream of student personnel literature in the AACJC's *Journal* leave one common impression. Student service functions always have received only modest attention in the *Journal* and they have faded farther into the background over time relative to other issues of concern to two-year colleges.

This literature review examined published reports that permitted revealing observations about (1) the role and functions of student services, (2) the forces that shape student service functions, (3) the effectiveness of student services, and (4) the prospects for the future of student services. Terminology of the profession, that is, what professionals call themselves, has changed over the past sixty years, from "student services" in the 1930s, "student personnel" in the 1940s, 1950s, and 1960s, to "student development" in the 1970s and 1980s. The changes reflect an ongoing identity crisis of the profession, and each term reflects certain political realities in the colleges. The historically legitimate term "student services" will be used in this review as an attempt to avoid most of the political issues relative to the use of other terms.

THE ROLE AND FUNCTIONS OF STUDENT SERVICES

It is not surprising that the first article to appear in the *Junior College Journal* pertaining to student services was concerned with vocational guidance (McAlmon 1931). The mission of two-year colleges mandated the preparation of students for occupations in the community, and there was a clear role for student services: "In order to give vocational guidance to junior college students it is necessary that institutions have information about occupations. Guidance is not so much a matter of counseling as it is a matter of preparing and presenting facts" (McAlmon 1931, 74). A more comprehensive definition soon replaced this narrow one, however. Through a flexible program, which would allow for individual differences, the "personnel organization" would create a supportive school environment in order to "stimulate and encourage the students" (Crawford 1932, 310).

This broadened view of student services foreshadowed the philosophical substance of the "Student Personnel Point of View" (SPPV 1937) published five years later, but it called only for the assignment of a chief personnel officer and faculty advisors to the service functions. Their tasks were to carry out a program of freshman orientation, a remedial program, a program for superior students, faculty advising, discipline, parent and high school relations, recruiting high school students, teaching, placement, and personnel records (Crawford 1932).

Early Program Forms

Junior colleges in the 1930s appeared to be searching for the form and substance of student services, having no prior legacy from which to draw. Still, certain functions appeared to have established early footholds in the overall program. Most notable of these early functions were vocational guidance (McAlmon 1931), student activities (Christensen 1933; Colvert 1948), and orientation (Worthy 1933; Bennett 1934). Throughout this early period, considerable literature was devoted simply to describing specialized functions and how they operated at a particular college in considerable detail. For example, Brintle (1933) described "the guidance interview" and "the guidance chart" showing how a particular college used the procedures, and Hilton (1938) described the functions of the dean of women in one college in great detail.

By the late 1930s, student services seemed to be taking on a more consensual and professional character. In 1937 Humphreys noted the "vital necessity" of the student personnel services function. Simultaneously, a consensus was developing about a definition of student services. One definition widely accepted by the profession and endorsed by Humphreys was crafted by Cowley (1936). Cowley said that "personnel work constitutes all activities undertaken or sponsored by an educational institution, aside from curricular instruction, in which the student's personal development is the primary consideration" (Humphreys 1937, 26). It might be noted that the "Student Personnel Point of View" was published originally in 1937 and that Cowley played a major role in writing the document.

Humphreys (1937) argued for a comprehensive program of student services, grounded in guiding principles, that included selection of students, orientation, educational counseling, vocational counseling, personal counseling, student health, financial help, placement, student activities, housing and boarding of students, personnel records, personnel research, and coordination of student personnel services. These activities and programs appeared to represent the mainstream of thinking about student service functions through the 1940s. Brumbaugh (1950) called for a similar set of comprehensive activities and programs at mid-century. His list of functions included counseling, physical and mental health, remedial services, administration of housing and food services, extra-classroom activities, financial aid, religious programs, and special counseling for married students. Lounsbury described the required functions as follows: "(1) directing students into study programs and future activities in line with their interests and abilities; (2) helping students adjust to the opportunities and demands of the college; and (3) insuring the optimal adaptation of the college program to the varying needs of students" (1946, 430).

Later Program Forms

By the mid–1950s, a fairly well-accepted list of activities and programs that made up a comprehensive program of student services was adopted operationally (Hardee 1961; Medsker 1960; Starr 1961; Yoder and Beals 1966). In a report by Feder (1958), the thinking of the Committee on Student Personnel Work of the American Council on Education was revealed. Their vision of a comprehensive program included "selection for admission; registration and records; counseling; health service; housing and food service; student activities; financial aid; placement; discipline; special clinics for remedial reading, study habits, speech and hearing; special services such as student orientation, veterans' advisory services, foreign-student program, marriage counseling, religious activities, and counseling" (Feder 1958, cited in Medsker 1960).

Without doubt, the most definitive list of student service functions for the two-year college was developed in the mid–1960s by the Project for Appraisal and Development of Junior College Student Personnel Programs established by the American Association of Junior Colleges and funded by the Carnegie Corporation of New York. The project team, chaired by T. R. McConnell, used the talents of selected student personnel leaders to define 24 essential functions, which were organized into seven categories: (1) orientation functions, including precollege information, student induction, group orientation, and career information; (2) appraisal functions, including personnel records, educational testing, applicant appraisal, and health appraisal; (3) consultation functions, including student counseling, student advisement, and applicant consulting; (4) participation functions, including co-curricular activities and student self-government; (5) regulation functions, including student registration, academic regulation, and social regulation; (6) service functions, including financial aid and placement; and (7) organizational functions, including program articulation, in-service education, program evaluation, and administrative organization (Collins 1967).

Literature since the mid–1960s makes no substantive modification to the list of operational functions used by the appraisal project team, although Cohen and Brawer (1982) show how specific functions temporarily have expanded or diminished depending on societal forces. More recent additions to the literature, relative to the essential activities of student services, reflect on the appropriateness of underlying concepts, such as a student development orientation (Brown 1972;

Cooper 1975; Creamer and Dassance 1986; Miller and Prince 1976), models for practice (Creamer 1989; Leach 1989; Keyser 1989; O'Banion, Thurston, and Gulden 1970), and a national agenda for action (NCSD 1990).

FORCES THAT SHAPE STUDENT SERVICE FUNCTIONS

Institutional purpose, educational philosophy, and historic events appear to be the major forces that have led student services to its current form and substance. Other forces such as institutional and societal contingencies and the nature of preservice preparation also play significant roles in determining the nature of student services in the two-year college, but the literature reveals no definitive picture of these effects.

Institutional Purpose

Obviously, institutional aims and objectives shape the nature of student services. Crawford (1932) recognized the importance of certain distinctive characteristics of junior colleges compared to senior colleges. These qualities included, according to Crawford, "the relatively small student body, the proportionately large number of students living at home, the close relationship with secondary schools, and the extent to which the junior college emphasizes the idea of preparation for citizenship in the home community" (Crawford 1932, 309). Traxler (1952) stated it simply: One of the essentials of an effective guidance program was to find its role in junior college objectives. More recently, Robbins (1972), writing about the influences on student services from inside the institution, acknowledged that the college's goals have a very direct influence on the student service practices.

Educational Philosophies

Nothing has influenced the nature of student services more than certain educational philosophies. Arising from the pragmatic and humanistic philosophy of John Dewey, most institutions in America accepted the obligation to educate the "whole student." The "whole student" philosophy was endorsed strongly by the late 1930s as shown by Brown and McCallister who argued that "[t]he philosophy underlying personnel service emphasizes the maximum development of the individual's whole personality" (1939, 179). The influence of neohumanists who recognized the duality of the development of personal and intellectual aspects also could be seen during this period as illustrated by Bonner who said that student services must promote a healthy or integrated personality, but that the work "goes hand in hand with the training of the intellect" (1935, 117). The influence of existentialists who supported the idea that learning fundamentally is the responsibility of the learner also was evident during the 1930s. This perspective is represented by Tyler who described the philosophy of student services at Sacramento Junior College: "The foundation of the work is to be found in the motto of the division; To help students to help themselves" (1935, 347). Popenoe also endorsed this view: "Guidance, like rational judgment, can never be implanted wholly from the outside. The most advantageous forms of guidance are those which are concerned primarily with the development and direction of self-direction and judgment" (1932, 373). Monroe described in detail the influence of educational philosophy on student services and spoke specifically about the influence of Dewey on the forces of egalitarianism of the 1970s:

[If] the whole person must be educated, then it was inevitable that a new personnel services be created if the expanded student body, drawn from the lower levels of society, was to be saved from academic failure and personal frustration. If the open-door college is to meet its responsibility to serve society in a democratic manner, the students need to be guided in their decisions and choices by a staff of professionally trained counselors. (1972, 154)

The most concrete evidence of the influence of humanistic and democratic values on student services can be seen in the publications called the Student Personnel Point of View (SPPV, 1937, 1949). The 1937 document, which contains the most quoted paragraph in the history of student services, describes the educational philosophy that underscored the value of assisting the student "in developing to the limits of his potentialities and in making his contribution to the betterment of society" (SPPV 1937, 49). Furthermore,

This philosophy imposes upon educational institutions the obligation to consider the student as a whole—his intellectual capacity and achievement, his emotional make up, his physical condition, his social relationships, his vocational aptitudes and skills, his moral and religious values, his economic resources, and his aesthetic appreciations. It puts emphasis, in brief, upon the development of the student as a person rather than upon his intellectual training alone. (SPPV 1937, 49)

The 1949 version added some additional objectives to the point of view, but, most notably, underscored the "education for a fuller realization of democracy in every phase of living" (SPPV 1949, 21). (For a recent overview of the role of philosophy in shaping student services in two-year colleges, see O'Banion 1989.)

Historical Events

Historical events influenced the nature of student services in two-year colleges in obvious ways by shaping the substance of dialogue with students and the nature of specific activities for student involvement. The dialogue and the activities were affected, for example, by economic conditions such as the depression of the 1930s, wars, major scientific achievements such as the launching of Sputnik in 1957, and social movements such as the civil rights movement of the 1960s and 1970s. Current issues such as the women's movement, increasing diversity and pluralism in society and on college campuses, and financial woes influence the form and substance of student affairs in subtle, but significant, ways.

Institutional Issues

Often institutional contingencies have affected the form, if not the substance, of student services. For example, from time to time, debates have arisen about the best organizational arrangement for student services. Berg (1972) proposed a reorganization of student services to align them more closely with instruction and make them more viable in curriculum development, although support of the overlapping purposes of guidance workers and teachers has been a recurring theme of the literature for more than fifty years. Typical calls for this arrangement can be seen in Madciff (1944) and Robinson (1960). Heise (1982) and Liston (1982) have offered a point-counterpoint argument detailing the advantages and disadvantages of administratively aligning student services with the academic program and of setting it up as a separate organizational unit. Consensus remains, however, as Medsker put it: "There is no one best way to organize and coordinate a college personnel program" (1960, 146).

THE EFFECTIVENESS OF STUDENT SERVICES

"The quantity and quality of personnel services in two-year colleges are not always considered commensurate with the need for them" (Medsker 1960, 143). This observation captures a recurring theme in two-year college student services literature. Whenever systematic examination or authoritative criticism of the functions occurred, serious reproach of the effectiveness of the services followed. This pattern can be illustrated by a report of the Student Personnel Committee of the American Association of Junior Colleges in 1952 (Humphreys 1952), by the report of a Carnegie Corporation–sponsored study in 1966 (Raines 1966), by the report of an Esso Corporation–sponsored study in 1971 (Matson 1971), and by a widely recognized comment by two distinguished community college educators in 1983 (Elsner and Ames 1983).

The Student Personnel Committee Study

While chairing the Student Personnel Committee of the American Association of Junior Colleges, Humphreys (1952) issued a report expressing concern over some apparent deficiencies in student services programs in junior colleges. The shortcomings listed included a shortage of programs adequately carrying out student personnel services; lack of recognition of the necessity of such a program; failure to develop testing and counseling aspects; a shortage of qualified staff and lack of training for that staff; and a "tendency for the head, or the assistant head, of some junior colleges to carry too much responsibility for detailed operations of student personnel services'' (Humphreys 1952, 382). Humphreys went on to suggest factors contributing to this situation: lack of acceptance of the personnel point of view, insufficient finances, lack of qualified personnel, lack of physical facilities, and insufficient time to implement and carry out a program.

The Carnegie Study

T. R. McConnell, chairman of the national advisory board for the Project for Appraisal and Development of Junior College Student Personnel programs, wrote, "The conclusion of these studies may be put bluntly: when measured against criteria of scope and effectiveness, student personnel programs in community colleges are woefully inadequate" (Collins 1967, 22). Raines reported the major findings of the Carnegie-sponsored study and said,

Three-fourths of the junior colleges in the country have not developed adequate student personnel programs. The counseling and guidance functions of student personnel work are inadequately provided in more than half of the colleges. Those functions designed to coordinate, evaluate, and upgrade student personnel programs are ineffective in nine out of ten institutions. (Raines 1966, 6)

The Esso Study

The Carnegie study recommended that a follow-up study be conducted to determine changes in student services and programs in the years immediately following their study. Matson (1971) conducted the follow-up in a study sponsored by the Esso Corporation. Though a few additions to services were noted, Matson claimed, "The variety or range of services provided in the colleges in the study has not appreciably increased or decreased since 1964" (1971, 52). The problems of providing expanded service as discovered in the Matson study seemed hauntingly similar to the problems reported by Humphreys in 1952: lack of support from faculty and administrators, need for improved competency of staff, inadequate facilities, and so on. Matson concluded,

Whether the student personnel functions will emerge as essential and contributing components in the colleges, as they struggle to meet the educational needs of a student population increasing in size and diversity, cannot yet be predicted with certainty. There is little doubt that other components of the college community, the faculty, administrators, and to some extent the students, are not entirely satisfied with the existing student personnel programs. (1971, 52)

Community College Educator Views

Finally, Elsner and Ames commented on the condition of student services. These widely respected and highly visible educators remarked:

No genuine consensus exists about the nature of, need for, or direction of community college student service programs. A model for change seems to elude most leaders. Those who believe that student services have never been needed more than at the present are also urging that such services be vigorously overhauled and reshaped. Others question the value and relevance of student services. Many student services professionals themselves feel beleaguered, unappreciated, and misunderstood. They do not feel that there is a promising future for them in times of tight budgets.

Leaders of community colleges and student personnel staffs agree on one point: student services need to be redesigned. The student services function needs an infusion of new ideas, new approaches, and a new reason for being. (Elsner and Ames 1983, 139)

With such compelling statements as these presented over a thirty-year period in the history of student services in the two-year college, it is impossible to conclude that the current condition is satisfactory in the eyes of community college or student services professionals. Yet, not everyone agrees with Elsner and Ames' conclusion that student services need to be redesigned.

PROSPECTS FOR THE FUTURE OF STUDENT SERVICES

The decade of the 1970s and the 1980s witnessed the emergence of even further applications of the humanistic and democratic values of Dewey, the coalescing of developmental initiatives in higher education, and a heightening recognition of the effects of fiscal, social, and political pressures on community colleges. The American College Personnel Association forged a plan for using developmental theory and practice to reform practices in colleges and universities (Brown 1972; Cooper 1975; Miller and Prince 1976), several student service professionals called for new models for practice or major reform of student services (Creamer 1989; Deegan 1984; Keyser 1989; Leach 1989; Matson and Deegan 1985; O'Banion, Thurston, and Gulden 1970; Schinoff 1982), and sensitivity to new realities for community colleges led to more calls for reform of student services (Deegan and Tillery 1987).

Tomorrow's Higher Education Project

With the emergence of a substantial body of developmental theory and research on the effects of college on students (Brown 1972), the American College Personnel Association provided impetus to a professional interest in refocusing the nature of student services. Miller and Prince (1976) presented new conceptual models for practice that drew upon developmental theory and called for a refocusing from an idea of simply delivering services based on student need to an idea of using those services more intentionally to influence student learning and development. This reconceptualization essentially called for a shift in thinking from means (services) to ends (student development) of education.

The literature of two-year college student services reflects the appeal of a developmental orientation for practice, but the most visible consequence of developmental initiatives in two-year colleges was a nearly wholesale shift in titles of chief student affairs officers in two-year colleges from such titles as dean or vice president for student services to dean or vice president for student development. The most evident application of a developmental perspective in practice is the use of the perspective as a rationale or justification for services and programs provided. (See the League for Innovation in the Community College 1987 for an example of this use.)

Calls for New Models of Practice

One of the earliest suggestions that two-year college student services professionals should consider a new way of doing business came from O'Banion, Thurston, and Gulden. Their proposal described an "emerging model" that called for a new role for student services professionals—the human development facilitator (O'Banion, Thurston, and Gulden 1970). This emerging model called for a new kind of professional in student services, one who personified the humanism of Maslow, Rogers, and Jourard. There is little evidence, however, that the emerging model has actually materialized in practice (Dassance 1984–1985).

Variations on the theme of the need for reform, and for specific suggestions for workable concepts to guide practice, came from Schinoff (1982), who articulated a systems approach to the delivery of student services, and from Keyser (1989), who described a model to achieve student success through student development services. Leach (1989) saw the ideal operation for student services as a consumer model, while Deegan (1984) called for multiple alternative strategies to revitalize student service practices. Matson and Deegan (1985) suggested that consideration be given to the divestiture of certain functions, contracting for others, and offering others for fees as any community agency might do. Finally, Creamer (1989) offered a contingency model for student development that would conform to variation in institutional mission, resources, and expectations and student talents and expectations for learning. His model contained three nuclei of professional activity: student and environmental assessment, program direction and teaching, and market and systems analysis.

Shaw (1989a, 1980b) called these discussions of professional problems and need for reform "psychobabble" (1989a, 74) and suggested that the future of student services calls more for renaissance than for reformation. She argued that student service professionals need to say goodbye to empty arguments and get on with building trust with faculty and administrative colleagues to meet student and institutional needs by returning to the basics enriched by a clear focus on student success and by new technologies.

Contemporary Publications

Recent literature on student services appears to have shifted from conceptual statements, like the calls for new models of practice that characterized the 1960s and 1970s, to aspirational statements that focus on leadership, contemporary realities of two-year colleges, and student success. Excellent examples of this type of student services literature can be seen in Keyser's (1984) monograph from a colloquium that focuses on issues of vitality of student development services and Floyd's (1987) monograph on leadership strategies. Other examples include a statement by the League for Innovation in the Community College (1987), focused on assuring student success, and a joint statement of the National Council on Student Development, Commission XI of the American College Personnel Association, and the Community College Network of the National Association for Student Personnel Administrators (NCSD 1990), which sets forth a national agenda for student services in two-year colleges. The national agenda calls for responses to increasing student diversity, contributing to institutional effectiveness, conducting research on student success, providing improved leadership, and assuring staff competency. One common feature of these literature forms is a focus on student success, an idea to guide practice that everyone in the two-year college can embrace regardless of disciplinary orientation or professional alignment.

SUMMARY

It would be an exaggeration to claim the existence of an expansive literature on two-year college student services. Instead, it must acknowledge that, at least during certain historical periods, such literature has been downright skimpy, even by quantitative standards. A more important acknowledgement, however, is that a serious qualitative differential exists between two- and four-year college student services literature. The literature on two-year college student services pertains in large measure to descriptive and analytic essays and occasional survey research reports, also descriptive in nature. By contrast, the literature of four-year college student services pertains increasingly to applications of theory in practice and includes the most advanced methods of behavioral science investigation. Perhaps the condition stems from the nearly universal practitioner orientation of two-year college student service professionals who do not see themselves as scholars and who are not encouraged or rewarded by their institutions to conduct research and report findings in professional journals. Whatever the reason, the quality of two-year college student services literature lags seriously behind that of four-year colleges.

This review of literature spanned the role and functioning of two-year college student service functions, the forces that influence the nature of two-year college student services, the findings of several survey research reports exposing certain weaknesses in program effectiveness, and the current nature of literature that suggests future directions for two-year college student services. The review revealed a historical portrait of professional educators who are assigned responsibilities that are vital to student and institutional success but who are struggling under chronic conditions of inadequate resources and colleague support in achieving their assigned duties.

REFERENCES

Adams, J. F. 1956. An analysis of the *Junior College Journal*: 1930–1956. *Junior College Journal* 27(4): 214–20.

Bennett, M. E. 1934. Trends in junior college orientation courses. *Junior College Journal* 4(7): 353–57.

Berg, E. H. 1972. Curriculum development and instruction: A proposal for reorganization. In *Student development programs in the community junior college*, ed. T. O'Banion and A. Thurston, 134–46. Englewood Cliffs, N.J.: Prentice-Hall.

Bonner, H. 1935. Personnel work at Ironwood Junior College. *Junior College Journal* 6(3): 117–21.

Brintle, S. L. 1933. A practical prediction and guidance chart. *Junior College Journal* 3(6): 300–303.

Brown, D., and J. M. McCallister. 1939. Personnel service at Herzl Junior College. *Junior College Journal* 9(4): 179–85.

Brown, R. D. 1972. *Student development in tomorrow's higher education: A return to the academy*. Washington, D.C.: American College Personnel Association.

Brumbaugh, A. J. 1950. Better student personnel services in junior colleges. *Junior College Journal* 21(1): 37–41.

Christensen, A. 1933. Student activities in public junior colleges. *Junior College Journal* 3(5): 251–54.

Clowes, D., and D. Towles. 1985. *Community and Junior College Journal*: Lessons from fifty years. *Community and Junior College Journal* 56(1): 28–32.

Cohen, A. M., and F. B. Brawer. 1982. *The American community college*. San Francisco: Jossey-Bass.

Collins, C. C. 1967. *Junior college student personnel programs: What they are and what they should be*. Washington, D.C.: American Association of Junior Colleges.

Colvert, C. C. 1948. Administering the student activity program. *Junior College Journal* 18(7): 394–99.

Cooper, A. C. 1975. Student development services in post-secondary education. *Journal of College Student Personnel* 16(6): 524–28.

Cowley, W. H. 1936. The nature of personnel work. *Educational Record* 42:218.

Crawford, S. C. 1932. A junior college personnel program. *Junior College Journal* 2(6): 309–13.

Creamer, D. G. 1989. Changing internal conditions: Impact on student development. In *Perspectives of student development*, ed. W. L. Deegan and T. O'Banion, 31–43. New Directions for Community Colleges no. 67. San Francisco: Jossey-Bass.

Creamer, D. G., and C. R. Dassance, eds. 1986. *Opportunities for student development in two-year colleges*. NASPA Monograph Series, vol. 6. Washington, D.C.: National Association of Student Personnel Administrators.

Dassance, C. R. 1984–1985. Community college student personnel work: Is the model still emerging? *Community College Review* 12(3): 25–29.

Deegan, W. L. 1984. Revitalizing student services programs. *Community and Junior College Journal* 54(8): 14–17.

Deegan, W. L., and T. O'Banion, eds. 1989. *Perspectives on student development*. New Directions for Community Colleges no. 67. San Francisco: Jossey-Bass.

Deegan, W. L., and D. Tillery. 1987. Toward a 5th generation of community colleges. *Community, Technical and Junior College Journal* 57(5): 36–40.

Elsner, P. A., and W. C. Ames. 1983. Redirecting student services. In *Issues for community college leaders in a new era*, ed. G. B. Vaughan and Associates, 139–58. San Francisco: Jossey-Bass.

Feder, D. D. 1958. The administration of student personnel programs in American colleges and universities. *Student personnel work*. Education Studies Series no. 6, 22(19). Washington, D.C.: American Council on Education.

Fields, R. R. 1962. *The community college movement*. New York: McGraw-Hill.

Floyd, D. L. ed. 1987. Toward mastery leadership: Strategies for student success. Summary of a report of a colloquium held at Columbia, Maryland, July. Iowa City, Iowa: American College Testing Program.

Floyd, H. W. 1936. The *Junior College Journal*: An analysis. *Junior College Journal* 6(5): 249–54.

Hardee, M. D. 1961. Counseling and advising in the new junior college. *Junior College Journal* 31(7): 370–77.

Heise, H. A. 1982. Student success attributed to placement of guidance on the academic side. *Community and Junior College Journal* 52(5): 14, 16.

Hilton, M. E. 1938. The functions of the dean of women. *Junior College Journal* 8(6): 281–86.

Humphreys, J. A. 1937. Personnel service in the junior college. *Junior College Journal* 8(1): 26–30.

———. 1952. Toward improved programs of student personnel services. *Junior College Journal* 52: 382–92.

Keyser, J. S. 1989. The student success systems model. In *Innovation in the community college*, ed. T. O'Banion, 70–97. New York: Macmillan.

Keyser, J. S., ed. 1984. *Toward the future vitality of student development services*. Summary report of a colloquium held at Traverse City, Mich., August. Iowa City, Iowa: American College Testing Program.

Leach, E. R. 1989. Student development and college services: A focus on consumers. In *Perspectives on student development*, ed. W. L. Deegan and T. O'Banion, 45–59. New Directions for Community Colleges no. 67. San Francisco: Jossey-Bass.

League for Innovation in the Community College. 1987. *Assuring student success in the community college: The role of student development professionals*. A statement of the League for Innovation in the Community College. Los Angeles.

Leunberger, H. W. 1936. The *Junior College Journal*: An analysis. *Junior College Journal* 6(5): 249–54.

Liston, E. J. 1982. Separation of academic and counseling functions fosters professional pride. *Community and Junior College Journal* 52(5): 15, 17, 32.

Lounsbury, J. L. 1946. Committee on student personnel problems. *Junior College Journal* 16(9): 430–31.

Madciff, E. I. 1944. The instructors in the guidance program. *Junior College Journal* 15(3): 126–28.

Matson, J. E. 1971. A perspective on student personnel services. *Community and Junior College Journal* 42(1): 48–52.

Matson, J. E., and W. L. Deegan. 1985. Revitalizing student services. In *Renewing the*

American community college, ed. W. L. Deegan, D. Tillery, and Associates, 131–49. San Francisco: Jossey-Bass.

McAlmon, V. 1931. Vocational guidance for commercial work. *Junior College Journal* 2(2): 74–77.

Medsker, L. L. 1960. *The junior college: Progress and prospect*. New York: McGraw-Hill.

Miller, T. K., and J. Prince. 1976. *The failure of student affairs*. San Francisco: Jossey-Bass.

Monroe, C. R. 1972. *Profile of the community college*. San Francisco: Jossey-Bass.

National Council for Student Development. 1990. *Student affairs professionals in two-year colleges: Priorities for the 1990s*. Washington, D.C.

O'Banion, T. 1989. Student development philosophy: A perspective on the past and future. In *Perspectives on student development*, ed. W. L. Deegan and T. O'Banion, 5–17. New Directions for Community Colleges no. 67. San Francisco: Jossey-Bass.

O'Banion, T., A. Thurston, and J. Gulden. 1970. Student personnel work: An emerging model. *Junior College Journal* 41(3): 6–14.

Popenoe, H. 1932. Orientation in the junior college. *Junior College Journal* 2(7): 371–74.

Raines, M. R. 1966. The student personnel situation. *Junior College Journal* 2(8): 427–34.

Robb, J. L. 1932. Guidance in the junior college. *Junior College Journal* 2(8): 427–34.

Robbins, C. J. 1943. Student activities make democracy live. *Junior College Journal* 13(8): 379–80.

Robbins, W. A. 1972. Influences from the inside. In *Student development programs in the community college*, ed. T. O'Banion and A. Thurston, 122–133. Englewood Cliffs, N.J.: Prentice-Hall.

Robinson, D. W. 1960. The role of the faculty in the development of student personnel services. *Junior College Journal* 31(1): 15–21.

Schinoff, R. B. 1982. No nonsense at Miami-Dade. *Community and Junior College Journal* 53(3): 34–35, 44–45.

Shaw, R. G. 1989a. Telling the truth, warming the heart: The future of student development in the community college. In *Perspectives on student development*, ed. W. L. Deegan and T. O'Banion, 73–84. New Directions for Community Colleges no. 67. San Francisco: Jossey-Bass.

———. 1989b. The future of student development in the community college. *Community, Technical, and Junior College Journal* 59(4): 45–48.

Starr, J. M. 1961. Guidance practices in selected junior colleges in the northwest. *Junior College Journal* 31(8): 442–46.

Student personnel point of view. 1937. In *Points of view*, 47–63. Washington, D.C.: National Association of Student Personnel Administrators.

Student personnel point of view. 1949. In *Points of view*, 21–46. Washington, D.C.: National Association of Student Personnel Administrators.

Traxler, A. E. 1952. Notes. *Junior College Journal* 22(6): 309–20.

Tyler, H. E. 1935. Student personnel work at Sacramento. *Junior College Journal* 5(7): 346–47.

Worthy, E. T. 1933. Orientation courses in junior colleges. *Junior College Journal* 3(7): 368–71.

Yoder, M., and L. Beals. 1966. Student personnel services in the west. *Junior College Journal* 37(2): 38–41.

Diversity Among Community College Student Populations

Howard L. Simmons

DEMOGRAPHICS OF COMMUNITY COLLEGE STUDENT POPULATIONS

Undeniably, most community colleges reflect the diversity of their immediate environs more than any other segment of higher education in America. Therefore, when anyone seriously studies or contemplates this truly American form of higher education, there is no logical escape from a focus on an institution that has increasingly become a part of the fabric of the community in which it exists in terms of a host of factors that define that particular community. Those factors include, but are not limited to, race, ethnicity, gender, familial status, socio-economic considerations, previous educational preparation, physical and learning disabilities, and business and industry demands. But as this chapter develops, it becomes clearer to the reader that not all factors in the diversity spectrum have required or elicited the same type of stimulus or response by community colleges.

However, it seems that the type of diversity that is written about most frequently and seems to elicit the strongest points of view and emotion is race, sometimes treated synonymously with ethnicity. And even though community colleges still enroll more racial minorities—with the one exception of the historically black colleges and universities—there is much more progress to be made in some communities in which these institutions are located. In actual numbers, however, "Hispanics [are] more likely than either African-Americans or Caucasians to enroll in a 2-year college" (National Center for Education Statistics 1991, 20).

Often characterized as egalitarian in terms of access and cost, community college student populations no longer serve only those who are economically and culturally disadvantaged; there is a growing diversity across economic lines and some worry that this very diversity may be threatened because of poor economic conditions and the need to curtail enrollment in some cases. More than a decade ago, Olivas concluded that "in this increasingly conservative climate programs designed to assure opportunities for minorities, always on the periphery of higher education interests, are threatened first. Not only are such programs viewed as nonessential, but few minorities are in positions where they have substantial impact upon budgets" (1979, 171).

Nevertheless, community colleges, particularly those in urban or nearby urban areas, still enroll students from racial and ethnic groups in relatively larger numbers than other types of postsecondary institutions in the United States (Cohen and Brawer 1989, 50).

Closely related to ethnic diversity among community college student populations is the added factor of native/target language for those whose primary language is not English; persons who fall into this category are often referred to in higher education circles as "linguistic minorities." Many community colleges have been prompted to offer bilingual programs and services. Community colleges with a broad range of such programs and services tend to be located in the Western and Southwestern states and in the large urban cities of the East (Hsia 1988, 12), especially since Hispanics, for example, "tend to attend institutions in centers of Hispanic population" (Duran 1983, 10). These include community colleges such as Hostos Community College of the City University of New York, which serves a large number of Puerto Rican and other Latin American students; the Los Angeles Community College District, the El Paso Community College, and the Maricopa Community Colleges, which serve large numbers of Chicano (Spanish-dominant) students; and the San Francisco Community College, which serves an array of Japanese, Chinese, and other Oriental language–dominant students. Although these other-than-English language–dominant students come from various racial and ethnic groups of the areas served by community colleges, they generally are Hispanics, Asian Americans, and Pacific Islanders. Thus, in addition to transcending some of the usual cultural barriers, these community college students must successfully remove their language barriers, often a real prerequisite to official matriculation for degrees or in preparation for careers. As a result, an increasing number of community colleges are responding to this phenomenon through a variety of teaching and learning strategies, including bilingual/bicultural approaches which focus on strengthening the student's primary language as well as providing the student with linguistic skills in English as the target language.

In terms of gender diversity in the community college, the enrollment of females surpasses that of males even in some of the traditional male curricula such as engineering and technology (Cohen and Brawer 1989, 39; NCES 1991, 44). One reason for this change is related to significant changes in the demographics of higher education in the United States. For instance,

In the final analysis, the sex ratio probably reflects community traditions concerning the position of the female in society, the employment opportunities for women, and the ethnic and racial patterns of female behavior rather than any inherent aversion to education on the part of the female student. (Munroe 1972, 187)

Another reason has to be a significant change in the attitude of female students toward science and technology as fields of study, as well as changes in the attitudes of the male-dominated scientific and technical fields toward the employment and promotion of women. Naturally, these attitude shifts have had some impact in changing the diversity of community college student populations as well as the overall student population in higher education. However, if one combines gender and race as factors in the diversity equation, there are some differences, for example, in the increase in African-American female students as opposed to a decline in the numbers of African-American male students enrolled in public community colleges.

Among other important factors of increased student diversity that community colleges have begun to address to a greater or lesser degree are those related to the physically and learning disabled and those related to various socioeconomic characteristics. Strategies for dealing with physically disabled students have principally involved actions of community colleges to achieve barrier-free campuses and to improve access. Of course, the passage of the federal Disabilities Act will no doubt accelerate efforts not only to provide better access, but also to develop unique programs, services, and policies that will result in a diversity of educational opportunity for those who are physically disabled or, in more contemporary parlance, differently-abled. This group includes, among others, those who are blind, deaf, or who have some other physical impairment. It is important to stress that some community colleges have for some time counted disabled students among their multifaceted diversities.

Early commitments to the differently-abled have usually come about because of enlightened leadership and the implementation of programs designed to sensitize others in the college community to the special needs of the physically disabled. Longo observed that "the diverse needs of physically disabled students required that the colleges adapt not only buildings and grounds but, more significantly, attitudes and curricula" (1986, 3).

In essence, the same principles—though not always with the same sense of urgency or commitment—have been applied to another group of community college students: the learning disabled. Nevertheless, there are numerous examples of ways in which community colleges are responding with increasing effectiveness to the needs of those who are learning disabled, not to be confused with those classified as needing remedial or developmental assistance. One writer describes some of the innovations and adjustments made by Ocean County College in New Jersey to serve the needs of physically disabled students better. She concludes her study by stating that "Ocean County College has shown that a little money and a lot of concern can go a long way in expanding educational opportunities for the disabled" (Longo 1986, 12).

HISTORICAL ROLE OF COMMUNITY COLLEGES IN SERVING DIVERSE STUDENT POPULATIONS

Perhaps one of the best ways to understand what I would describe as the "natural" diversity of student populations in community colleges is to peek at a small segment of the historical evolution of these colleges. More specifically, as the community college is profiled in the early 1970s, it is instructive to examine one of the traditions said to be shared with the public schools: The community college is expected to provide "universal opportunity for a free public education for all persons without distinction based on social class, family income, and ethnic, racial, or religious backgrounds" (Munroe 1972, 1).

Clearly, the early leaders in the community college movement were convinced that the community college was a missing link in the galaxy of higher education; its mission was to provide educational opportunities to a more diverse student population. It is likewise clear that the nature of this diversity has changed as the development of the modern community college as a truly American phenomenon has evolved. As particular groups in community college service areas have felt empowered or have sought empowerment, the spectrum of diversity in those specific communities has been generally reflected in the local community college. And, of course, some of this diversity over time has occurred because of the increasing assimilation of the community college as a serious provider of quality instructional programs in higher education. Today, transfer and articulation agreements with four-year colleges and universities suggest that the community college has been more effective in making its case. In addition, the ability of the community college to establish better liaisons with local business and industry has ensured a broadening of the diversity of students in terms of socioeconomic status and related educational objectives.

STRATEGIES FOR INCREASING DIVERSITY AMONG COMMUNITY COLLEGE STUDENT POPULATIONS

Not surprisingly, one of the simplest but sometimes most overlooked strategy for increasing diversity among community college student populations is the exploitation of the name "community" in community college. The importance of focusing on the concept of "community" in community colleges was stressed even during the period of rapid growth of community colleges in the 1960s and 1970s. One accrediting official who argued the value of the community college was convinced of the need to highlight "community" as an important focus of these colleges:

Every educational institution serves a constituency. . . . The constituency of a community college is the community, whatever that may be. . . . Typically, of course, in the two-year community college, the word *community* means a relatively small and reasonably well defined geographical area . . . [a] proper emphasis on the word *community* provides both the origin and the justification for tremendous diversity. (Meder 1966, 10)

However, a stress on community as representing the immediate environs of some community colleges limits certain categories of diversity, such as that relating to race and ethnicity, especially when residential patterns of the service area do not reflect any significant racial or ethnic diversity. But for those community colleges that view such circumstances as accidental, temporary, and inimical to their growth and development, there is usually assurance that the mission statements reflect the diversity desired, and special recruitment and admissions strategies are developed and implemented to increase racial and ethnic diversity. And even though the lack of significant racial and ethnic diversity in a community college service area may be attributable to early decisions made by community college founders—for either political or economic reasons—to acquire and develop sites away from more racially and ethnically diverse areas, most community college leaders today see racial and ethnic diversity as being important to a quality education for all students as well as critical to the maintenance of overall enrollments now and in the future. That is one of the reasons why accrediting bodies (e.g., Middle States Association, North Central Association, and Western Association) and national organizations (e.g., American Association of Community and Junior Colleges) have adopted policy statements on diversity within the last five years.

ACCOMMODATING THE DIVERSITY REPRESENTED IN COMMUNITY COLLEGE STUDENT POPULATIONS

While clearly diverse groups within community college student populations have some common characteristics and needs, it is also true that these same groups have unique characteristics and needs that community colleges must address by devising programs, services, and other strategies. Whether the characteristic or need is related to race, ethnicity, disability, or economic factors, a somewhat different response is usually required depending upon the particular circumstances involved. In fact, the mere act of accommodating diversity may well signal the need for changes in the attitudes and sensitivities of those in the host institution to new recruits from other diverse groups. To be sure, the very use of the term "accommodation" reflects much more than simply setting aside "space" for those students who figure in increasing the diversity on particular community college campuses. It also means that the community college has decided or has found it necessary to make a full panoply of changes in policies, programs, services, and human resources in order to accommodate the diverse elements represented in community college student populations. For example, when discussing what might be included in the design of technical programs to meet community needs, Olivas suggested that "minority community personnel needs should be considered in assembling heterogeneous classes" (1979, 179).

From the outset, these changes and adjustments in "campus cultures" of community colleges are initially reflected in the manner in which the institutions define their missions, formulate and implement recruitment programs, and set parameters for admissions. It is at this crucial point that eventual profiles of student populations are determined, both wittingly and unwittingly. The adoption of recruitment and admissions strategies is consciously done and, though the open-door policies of some community colleges can be a limiting factor, community colleges are often selective about admitting students into certain programs. The same holds true for recruitment efforts, since recruitment means that the college makes a special effort to find students who can benefit from its programs and services. Diversity in the form of race and ethnicity is addressed through a broad range of recruitment strategies and admissions programs. These, for example, may include targeting Blacks, Hispanics, American Indians, Asian Americans, or, for that matter, Russian or Polish immigrants. For example, the Harry S. Truman Community College of the City Colleges of Chicago and the Kingsborough Community College of the City University of New York have enacted special programs for the recruitment of Russian immigrants. Of importance is the fact that the linguistic minorities are accommodated through specially designed programs aimed at making these Russian language–dominant students more English proficient and more adjusted to American culture. A number of such programs existed long before the concept of *perestroika* was advanced by former Soviet Premier Mikhail Gorbachev.

Once recruited and admitted, culturally different students must have learning experiences that are consonant with their unique characteristics, needs, abilities, and interests. And while it is true that most community colleges making a commitment to diversity successfully implement programs and services that correspond to the special needs of these students, there are exceptions. As relevant today as were the prophetic words, more than twenty years ago, of a community college educator who probably best summarized how community colleges should respond to their new "constituencies on campus":

The college must respond to this new militancy in two ways. It must give special attention to the way each minority student (Black, Chicano, Native American, Puerto Rican, Oriental) differs from the traditional college student, for whom the present system of higher education is planned. And, at the same time, it must provide for the learning difficulties of this student as it provides for the learning abilities of honor students. (Moore 1971, 33, 54)

Particularly in those cases in which admission of culturally different students is coincidental to the overriding decision to shore up sagging enrollments, there can be higher than usual attrition because appropriate intervention strategies have not been implemented. For instance, the community college that cares about the development of all students recruited and admitted will often provide such students with "bridge" programs that focus on college adjustment; remedial, developmental, and compensatory courses; tutoring; personal and academic advisement; and other special experiences. These same institutions may well offer cultural sensitivity seminars for the benefit of their faculty, staff, and other students. Often, multicultural programming in terms of extracurricular activities round out special programs to address the needs of the full spectrum of diversity represented on the community college campus.

However, diversity in the totality of two-year college student populations is sometimes found in an entirely different form; that is, service to some student populations may, because of perceived need and special circumstances, be found in colleges devoted almost exclusively to a particular racial, ethnic, religious group, or gender. Pertinent as an example here is the tribal college in the United States, which was formed in order to preserve values and traditions.

COMMUNITY COLLEGE STUDENT POPULATIONS: 1990s AND BEYOND

As emphasized throughout this chapter, various forms of diversity have constituted one of the basic characteristics of community colleges since their early foundations, and increasingly diversity in terms of race and ethnicity is expected to figure prominently in community college student populations for the foreseeable future. That these forms of diversity are already realities in most of the largest metropolitan areas of the United States provides a glimpse of what the diversity landscape will look like by the year 2000. More important, community colleges and our American society, which supports them, will have to move far beyond questions of access and inclusion, and will have to focus their energies and resources on the improvement of the teaching and learning process for all students, regardless of their diverse qualities. This chapter concludes with a quote from an important study on minority participation. In its concluding section, devoted to various strategies for progress in improving prospects for minorities, the Commission on Minority Participation in Education and American Life included the following as one of its key recommendations:

Our fundamental goal is to erase the inequities that characterize the lives of minority Americans. By taking action now, we can make minority citizens *more visible physically* in every realm—in schools, in colleges and universities, in government, in the work place—and *less visible statistically*, as the conditions in which they live resemble more closely the conditions enjoyed by the majority. (ACE 1988, 21)

Having spent a considerable portion of my professional career teaching and administering in, writing and speaking about, and touting the community college, I am convinced that the community college as a sector has contributed much to whatever diversity exists in American higher education. Provided that there is continued commitment to the historic goal of reaching all citizens who can benefit from instruction, the community college will continue to be the pacesetter in American higher education in terms of truly diversifying its student populations and its work force.

REFERENCES

American Council on Education. 1988. *One third of a nation*. A report of the Commission on Minority Participation in Education and American Life (ACE/ECS). Washington, D.C.

Cohen, A. M., and F. B. Brawer. 1989. *The American community college* 2d ed. San Francisco: Jossey-Bass.

Duran, R. P. 1983. *Hispanics' education and background: Predictors of college achievement*. New York: College Entrance Examination Board, pp. 9–10.

Hsia, J. 1988. *Asian Americans in higher education and at work*. Hillsdale, N.J.: Lawrence Erlbaum Associates, pp. 123–27.

Johnston, J. R. 1980. Community colleges: Alternative to elitism in higher education. In *Questioning the community college role*, ed. G. B. Vaughan. New Directions for Community Colleges, no. 32. San Francisco: Jossey-Bass.

Longo, J. A. 1986. Adapting to diversity. ERIC Document no. ED 271 134. Paper presented at the annual meeting of the Conference on College Composition and Communication, 13–15 March, New Orleans, Louisiana.

Meder, A. E., Jr. 1966. *The community college in higher education*. A report on the conference on the Role of the Community College in Higher Education, ed. J. A. Stoops, 21–22 November, Bethlehem, Pennsylvania, Lehigh University.

Moore, W., Jr. 1971. *Blind man on a freeway: The community college administrator*. San Francisco: Jossey-Bass.

Munroe, C. R. 1972. *Profile of the community college*. San Francisco: Jossey-Bass.

National Center for Education Statistics. 1991. *The condition of education 1991*; vol. 2: *Postsecondary education*. OERI/U.S. Department of Education. Washington, D.C.: U.S. Government Printing Office.

Olivas, M. A. 1979. *The dilemma of access: Minorities in two year colleges*. Institute for the Study of Educational Policy. Washington, D.C.: Howard University Press.

Marketing the Vision: A Structured Approach to Marketing Higher Education

Starnell K. Williams

Most community colleges have a clear vision of their purpose and deeply held beliefs about their mission in the community. Every president can describe in detail the worth and dignity of the institution. However, if those to be served are unaware of the opportunities offered by the college, or if the entry process is so mysterious that its walls seem insurmountable, the institution will not reach its full potential.

In the decade of the 1990s, shifting economic trends have focused the common agenda of the nation's community colleges on the predicament of how to do more with less. According to the National Council for Marketing and Public Relations, an affiliate council of the American Association of Community and Junior Colleges, it is now crucial that the varied aspects of marketing be directly related to the institution's mission. Further, marketing objectives must be prioritized, managed efficiently, and tied to institutional outcomes (Jones 1992).

When the community college establishes an effective marketing structure and implements a strategic plan that includes influencing the perception of the public, adopting customer-oriented practices, and ensuring accountability in services, the momentum of increasing community response will serve as evidence that the institution has successfully brought its vision to the people (Williams 1988).

The movement to influence, and therefore manage, enrollments owes its popularity to the increasing competition among institutions and the need to attract students that will remain satisfied with their choices (Hossler 1988). It also appeals to the logic of recruiting with a new direction and efficiency (Aslanian 1988) usually associated with the marketing perspective of corporations. The recruiting and public relations functions of colleges, which did not necessarily work in tandem in the past, for example, are finding a unity of philosophy and purpose. The desired result is a synergy of purpose ultimately yielding increased enrollments (Hossler 1984).

Recognizing the need to become more aggressive and efficient as marketers, colleges are seeking private-sector corporate professionals to mastermind their marketing functions (Alsop and Abrams 1986). The changing patterns of student demographics necessitate a corporate approach to marketing because of the increasing diversity in the client base.

Increasingly, society values and, in some cases, the workplace demand continued higher education beyond the traditional degree-seeking years. Therefore, while the pool of "traditional students" may be striking, student enrollments are holding steady or, in some cases, expanding. In fact, the largest potential student segment now receiving attention from the educational community is adult learners, or those students in the over-twenty-five age group which includes women reentering the system and individuals making career shifts (Felicette 1988; Aslanian 1988). The 1989 edition of the *Digest of Educational Statistics* documents a 15 percent increase in college students under the age of twenty-five and a 114 percent rise in students over the age of twenty-five between 1970 and 1989. Considering these statistics, higher education is obviously penetrating new markets. Colleges must examine their structures with new objectivity to address better the demands of these new student sources. The resulting competition among institutions has created a buyer's market that has awakened many colleges to the need to market their product in traditional corporate terms (Discenza, Ferguson, and Wisner 1985; Weathersby 1980). This means defining and unifying the marketing function within the college and making a commitment to abandon vague or symbolic activities that have been called marketing over the years.

The growing awareness that the expansionist period in American higher education is over (Brubacher and Rudy 1976) has prompted many institutions to redefine their mission, to institute strategic planning models, and to clarify their market position (Shuman 1987). In addition to rewriting mission statements and streamlining admission procedures, institutions are taking a hard look at their images in the community and the way in which they are perceived by a variety of population segments (Topor 1986). The linkage of enrollment patterns to client perceptions follows the consumer-oriented philosophy of businesses recognized for their excellence and success (Peters and Waterman 1982).

In higher education, as in business, there are three major approaches to addressing the potential consumer. An institution may be sales driven, production driven, or market drive (Smith 1988). In the case of a sales driven model, success is measured by head count and credit hours; students are recruited without regard to their suitability; and low enrollment courses are routinely canceled and popular ones are heavily funded. In a production-driven model, huge lecture style classes prevail; classes are taught at all hours; support services are limited; and high dropout rates are ignored. These two approaches are given using deliberately extreme examples that qualify them as more responsive to the needs of the institution than those of the student. In support of Hossler's enrollment management theories, a third, market-drive approach is implied.

CONSUMER-DRIVEN EDUCATIONAL MARKETING

The purpose of leading an institution toward a customer-based marketing approach is the desire to eliminate confusion in the mind of the client. Competitive marketing as a part of higher education has seen a quiet revolution. Historically, deliberate attention to the image and reputation of a school was avoided, but an image existed nonetheless in the minds of the public who came in contact with the institution (Topor 1986). The advancement of a college's reputation and the enhancement of its image in the marketplace by the use proactive recruiting and public relations techniques and campaigns are parts of a repositioning strategy that has evolved over the last decade within higher education.

In general terms, marketing can be defined as the process of transferring the product from the producer to the consumer (Kotler 1984). Educational marketing is unique because the product to be transferred is intangible, and its value is difficult to quantify. Marketing the vision of a college becomes a quest to create in the mind of the client an understanding of the value of learning and an appreciation of the facilities, faculty, and staff offered by a particular college. The feeling of stability, dignity, and accomplishment must be conveyed to the customer by transferring information about how the institution can benefit the individual. To do this effectively, the college marketing plan should both reach into the past and look toward the future, examining historical enrollment trends and anticipating environmental and economic changes yet to happen. The dual tasks of anticipating and responding are closely tied to the success of all enterprises that wish to compete effectively in the marketplace (Abell 1978).

GOALS AND PURPOSE

With the commitment to a marketing philosophy must come the responsible consideration of what goals the college hopes to accomplish from the use of marketing dollars and staff. The purpose of any marketing effort should stem from the institution's deep commitment to inform the population to be served about the opportunities offered to them. Certainly this effort can become an elaborate mix of targeted information pieces, recruiting presentations, and media messages, and it can be tallied by the numbers of community contacts and the increasing enrollment figures. It has been demonstrated in many institutions that, if the niche exists for the college to operate, then patterned corporate marketing will indeed increase enrollments and bring higher retention rates as the result of a greater understanding of the educational product. More than these results, however, the institution should consider why it wants to grow and why it matters how many students are served. The ultimate strength of successful marketing comes from the intrinsic institutional commitment to deliver services to the community to enhance the economic and social circumstances of the people. Were this not the case, colleges would employ creative and proactive marketing and recruiting activities only in times of low enrollments, thus exhibiting a production-driven philosophy. Even if the institution's funding is based on a formula that factors in growth to yield financial support, it would be sad indeed if community colleges were to spread the message of accessible opportunity only for the sake of institutional growth.

STRATEGIC PLANNING

When colleges begin to subscribe to true enrollment management/marketing practices, the need for accurate research data bases should be the first concern (McIlquham 1988). Useful marketing data can be found disguised as institutional research, perhaps in the form of the careful records that have been faithfully kept by the office of research and analysis and the admissions office. These data should become the basis of situational analysis, the first step in marketing an institution. Institutions should resolve in the simplest terms who they are and what they were established to accomplish. This analysis can be incorporated into ongoing self-study, or it may be the function of a task force to identify certain critical success factors essential to the well-being and viability of the school. Based on strategies supported by IBM and other corporations, it is extremely helpful to isolate from five to ten factors that are absolutely necessary, and therefore critical, to institutional success (Hickman and Silva 1984). These elements can become the basis for the marketing message. The purpose of the effort should always be to clarify what is most important to the mission of the school. All institutional marketing should be based on the college's established priorities for the future.

Taking into account the demographic blend of both traditional and mature students and their life goals, target markets can be identified and procedures implemented to build a strategic marketing plan. Just as an institution is wise to respond to the specific learning needs of all of its client segments through its program diversity, multisegmented markets require varied communication approaches. Depending on the designated message and which constituents are targeted, the appropriate media delivery system should be chosen to convey the information (Argenti 1988). Essential to any communication is understanding who is to be addressed and through what method of communication they are most likely to be reached. That is why a complete understanding of potential student profiles is essential to any marketing effort. It should be determined where current and past students are living, what age groups they fall into, and what departments attract which type of students. Along with demographic understanding, marketing should take into account its amplifier, psychographics, the study of life-styles and social influences. Employment characteristics and economic indicators also affect the climate in which the students live and therefore have direct bearing on their choice of a college and how a message directed to influence them will be received.

The planning process essential to good institutional marketing is based upon ongoing environmental analysis, tracking of general enrollment patterns, changes in current market shares, general age shifts, minority enrollment patterns, and nationwide economic trends. Useful comparisons can be made by accruing information such as the following:

- Between 1985 and 2000, an additional 40,000 students over twenty-five years of age will enroll annually in colleges and universities; 80 percent will be part-time students (Keane 1985).

- In 1990, 50 percent of all new jobs in America required education beyond high school. According to the American Society for Training and Development, by the year 2000, 75 percent of all workers currently employed will need such training (Roe 1989).

- Close to 85 percent of America's work force in the year 2000 is already in the work force today (Hudson Institute *Workforce 2000* 1987).

- Approximately 63 percent of new entrants into the U.S. labor force between 1985 and 2000 will be women, and 30 percent will be minority (Cetron et al. 1990).

- Up to 4 percent of the labor force will be in job retraining programs in the 1990s to upgrade skills and knowledge to keep pace with changing technology and changing demands of the workplace (Cetron 1988).

- Employment in the services sector will be the healthiest of all industries, increasing 54.8 percent from 1986 to 2000. Providing much of this surge will be business, health, and human services and educational services (*S.C. Industry and Occupations Projections: 1986–2000*, 1990, 2).

By polling internal and external groups, marketing can determine areas of weakness or opportunity. Random sampling of students currently enrolled is an important source of close to the customer information. External research reveals short- and long-term demands as well as market penetration.

This process can be tedious, or it can be enlightening, depending on the ability of the college to visualize the way the college is seen by those outside of its influence and to identify ways of reaching the minds of the unserved. Data accumulation, however, can go only so far in finding the right pathway. Instincts and intuition of marketing professionals who are familiar with the character of the community and the college should also be considered.

The institution must remember to ask why students are attending college. For the first time, in January 1987, *The Chronicle of Higher Education* listed the response "To get a better job" as the number of one reason American freshmen entered college. Eighty-three percent of those polled were chiefly interested in their future careers and saw college as a means of attaining a more positive position in that regard.

Distinctive characteristics of the institution should be carefully identified, possibly as part of an executive staff retreat or faculty/staff task force. If the institution cannot agree upon its own best characteristics, they cannot be presented as an incentive to those who are not yet familiar with the college.

Analysis of competing institutions' marketing strategies yields valuable information on what tactics work and which are less than successful. Even if the college has no nearby competition, examination of successful marketing techniques of regional sister colleges should be considered as a resource. National professional organizations hold developmental workshops in many accessible cities for the purpose of supporting college marketing activities. These can be instrumental in aligning the institution with effective proactive marketing strategies. If assessment of the college's marketing program and its staff participation is needed, colleges should consider bringing aboard a consultant to troubleshoot the existing process and make impartial recommendations for restructuring and reassessing the use of targeted marketing funds to be more effective.

Armed with this type of understanding of the situation, the marketing effort should follow the basic guidelines of corporate marketing adjusted to be relevant to higher education. *Place*, *price*, *product*, and *promotion* are traditional elements of corporate marketing that can be superimposed on an educationally oriented matrix (Goodwin 1988).

Place obviously refers to an institution's facilities, but in relation to the customer's way of thinking, it also deals with commuter proximity, in the case of working adults, as well as off-campus courses, evening programs, or weekend college to entice those who are occupied during the day. Borrowing from the University of Wisconsin's rationale, the campus borders are no longer a quadrangle with ivy-covered walls. Place also refers to methods of delivery. Electronic transmission and distance learning are revolutionizing traditional definitions of place.

Price, of course, means tuition in the marketing context, but tuitions may be allowed to fluctuate in response to time frames and incomes. Thirty percent of two-year college students and 50 percent of four-year students receive state, federal, or institutional financial aid (Parnell 1988). Traditionally "price" has meant the financial realities of attending college. But there are other elements surrounding the price of attendance. The "cost" of negative experiences, logistical hassles, and incompatible images are all prices that may be too high for potential students to pay. Accessibility to information about admission, financial aid, and the location and length of assessment are all part of the payment facing an incoming student. These are not sums of money, but the marketing function of an institution should address these kinds of prices. As well, the "hassle factor" to enter the college may in fact be the most costly in terms of student persistence.

In the marketing of colleges and universities, it is easy to confuse the term "product" with the number of graduating seniors. The students should not be thought of as the institution's products, but rather quality education is the item that should be marketed. This is a very important distinction when considering that in enrollment management and in the marketing of the institution, the goal is to influence the potential student to choose a product that is of high quality, of good value, and suitable to his or her particular circumstances. By marketing the best in course content, the best learning format, and the best student services, it is more likely that enrollments will increase. Looking internally, the college must ask itself if it is offering what its client wants and if the quality and format are all that they should be.

Marketing must be response as economic development shifts to a more global perspective. By concentrating on the growth possibilities of certain career fields and by urging the college to structure its curriculum to meet the retooling needs of the country and changing client interests, the marketing leadership can be proactive in keeping the institution's products on target with the community needs.

MARKETING STRUCTURE AND LEADERSHIP

Once research defining the customer is in place, a comprehensive plan implemented through leadership expertise should create a marketing process that is right for the institution and the community. A centralized marketing model has been demonstrated to have substantial merit for effective institutional marketing that is deliberate and aggressive and corresponds to corporate America.

The restructuring of existing services according to the definition of what marketing will mean within the institution's culture must begin with the support of courageous presidents. Transformational leaders and risk takers are needed to disband traditional eclectic committees and to unravel reporting structures that tend to deliver conflicting messages with overlapping efforts and limited results. Instead, a reliable method for input from every sector of the college in the form of an advisory group should be established where information flows freely into a marketing unit, and philosophy and implementation practices are disseminated. This ensures contemporary, pragmatic information exchange between marketing and academic and support functions without allowing critical marketing decision making to be an auxiliary responsibility (Williams 1988).

A streamlined and effective corporate marketing strategy demands that a college place its confidence in a marketing program and structure designed under guidelines set forth by the president and planned and implemented by a professional marketing and recruiting staff. Keeping the college's marketing program on campus is important in maintaining an institutional memory that cannot be purchased from even the most expensive public relations or marketing firms. The college's chief marketing officer must have the power and the courage to impose standards of design, content, and established corporate identity on the products and messages that the college sends into the community. This is by no means an easy task. Ideally, the president of the institution will be the chief advocate of the centralized marketing division and will help to secure the support of the entire college.

Focusing all external communications of the institution, especially those involving the preenrollment functions, to speak to the community in one voice with a strong, purposeful message is a key element in successful marketing practices. When sources of student contact are all a part of a marketing unit, it is easier to bring an image based on the collge's vision to the public's eye. The public will notice the difference in measures that eliminate confusion, duplication of efforts, and errors in information received.

In pragmatic terms, a collge's recruiting, community relations, access and equity, publications, public information, advertising, public relations, and especially student information staff should all be under the auspices of the marketing unit. To expand the pattern of pre- and postenrollment functions as a part of marketing, some institutions should also consider including the college's foundation, alumni relations, financial aid, and institutional research offices in the model.

Building a spirit of enthusiasm and team cooperation is not the least of the internal responsibilities of the college's marketing function (Hillman 1986). A shift toward quality marketing brings about a certain pride of performance that is assuredly contagious. As an advocate of quality, the college's marketing unit must implement its programs based on the corporate marketing model and the guidelines of statistical research. Importantly, "quality" is understood as strict conformance to agreed-upon standards (Crosby 1984). In higher education, customer awareness through quality marketing is a guiding force behind a successful enrollment management program.

COMMUNITY POSITIONING

The truism "perception is reality" aptly describes the initial stages of client interest in a school. Awareness of that image and control of the feelings that are being transmitted to the public in a consistent, specific way are increasingly a major part of the marketing function of educational institutions.

Before any tactics are begun, before any budget dollars are spent, nothing should be done without first deliberating how best to influence the behaviors of those to whom the college's message is to be delivered. In other words, the simple question is: "What can be said that will possibly make any difference?" A trap to be avoided is spending money on clever and creative ideas that will have minimum influence on the targeted population.

Securing a corporate identity is paramount in deliberate image enhancement and the creation of positive public perception. In this type of marketing climate, institutional brochures become visual value statements and college literature the personification of the vision that the college and its leadership have embraced.

For instance, visual identification with the subjects portrayed in photographs sends a strong message. Using a representative demographic mix in college viewbooks, catalogues, and other literature matters a great deal to the success of the initiative in encouraging client response.

One well-received targeted mailing featured a group of very visible high school athletes and student leaders from each of the area's secondary schools in the cover photograph. The mailing, sent to all of the college's service area high school juniors and seniors, commanded the attention of the subjects' peers and provided a 15 percent response rate for more information to the college. An example of poor visual planning is a financial aid brochure that carried no minority students in its photographs in a region where minorities made up a large percentage of financial aid recipients. In the marketing of the college, sensitivity to the client should be an underlying factor in all materials.

Professional design, typography, photography, and writing of all institutional outreach pieces and recruiting literature is essential. The realm of good design is a specialized area that is invaluable in solidifying the quality image of the college. Nothing will speak louder to the community than poor quality graphics, meaningless choices of colors and designs, out-of-focus photographs, or too much text in material that must compete for attention beside the flash and polish of corporate advertising. Judgments are made by the image of the information that is held in the hands of potential students and their parents. The time it takes for the crucial first impression to be formed is less than three seconds. The public expects the same polished level of advertising that sees every day from corporate America.

ACCOUNTABILITY IN MARKETING

Once the marketing process is established, its effectiveness can be validated by enrollment increases, retention studies, tabulation of community contacts, and community image surveys. The use of multiple institutional effectiveness indicators as part of the public message about the college should not be overlooked when identifying powerful marketing tools.

Effectiveness measurements of marketing and recruiting programs are based on community response to materials and the increasing numbers of students who choose to enroll at the college. It is essential to include with every outreach, whether it is a mailed brochure or a high school visit, a mechanism for responding to the college. There is no other way to establish a two-way conversation with the community. The ability to evaluate the effectiveness of the outreach is tied to the response it produces.

Examples of tracking indicators of promotional effectiveness are the coding of inquiry response cards and phone calls, recording of monthly inquiry response totals, and follow-up studies comparing responses to applications to admitted students. These data will be of absolutely no use without the focused structure that allows significant decisions to be made. Again it is apparent that the college needs to empower the marketing office to assimilate the information and make choices. As with all institutional effectiveness information, response statistics must not be considered a stand-alone activity. All assessment measures must enter the bloodstream of the institution to be effective (Ewell 1991).

Traditionally, media outreach is measured by reach and impressions, but these figures can be misleading when evaluating the effectiveness of the approach.

While a great many people may be exposed to a marketing effort, the responses obtained by those who may benefit from the service offered can be quite low. That is why the number of community contacts the institution receives is more important in the long run than the number of media slots purchased.

Truly, institutional effectiveness, as it applies to marketing and recruiting, is best evaluated by the answers received instead of the messages sent. Practitioners who have not adopted comprehensive corporate models of planning, execution, and evaluation may point to the number of times they have run an ad or even the number of column inches they have purchased as evidence of their marketing expertise. In a time when funding requires effectiveness, presidents are no longer willing to accept this accounting of the use of marketing dollars.

The allocation of limited budget dollars to the marketing function is an area of institutional concern. While the corporate model often sees from 5 to 20 percent of available funds set aside for marketing activities, educational marketing dollars are rarer, typically from 1 to 2 percent of the institutional budget. Under these circumstances, it becomes a matter of carefully made choices where and how the marketing budget is spent. The menu of possible choices is long and expensive. Deciding what the college's message is to be and determining what effect it is intended to have are essential to successful participation in the marketplace. Making deliberate choices and above all saying "No" to extraneous good ideas is an art form when combined with responsible resource management practices.

What difference does it make when a college markets effectively? Over time, institutional image matters to the community in the most basic returns of enhanced economic prosperity and cultural potential. The value of the feelings that students have about the institution, and consequently share with others, is expressed by increased participation and interaction between the college and the community and by a mutual sense of pride. Even if enrollment growth were to be discounted as a primary marketing result, marketing the vision remains essential because it influences the way people conceptualize the value of the institution and quantify the quality of its facilities, faculty, and academic programs. At that point of accomplishment, the vision becomes a reality.

REFERENCES

Abell, D. F. 1978. Strategic windows. *Journal of Marketing* (July): 21–26.

Alsop, R., and B. Abrams. 1986. *The Wall Street Journal on marketing*. Homewood, Ill.: Dow Jones-Irwin.

Argenti, P. A. 1988. Professional interest. *CASE Currents* 6:42–45.

Aslanian, C. B. 1986. Mainstreaming of adults on American campuses. Speech presented at the National Council on Community Service and Continuing Education awards luncheon of the American Association of Community and Junior Colleges, 13–16 April, Orlando, Florida.

———. 1988. Enrollment management without adults: Only half the story. In *The ad-*

mission strategist, ed. S. MacGowan. New York: College Entrance Examination Board.

Brubacher, J. S., and W. Rudy. 1976. *Higher education in transition*. New York: Harper and Row.

Cetron, M. 1988. Long-term trends affecting undergraduate education into the 21st century. Paper presented at the National Education Conference, 28 September, Kansas City, Missouri. Arlington, Va.: Forecasting International Ltd.

Cetron, M. J., W. Pocho, and R. Luckin. 1990. *Into the 21st century: Long-term trends affecting the U.S.* Special report. Bethesda, Md.: World Future Society.

Crosby, P. B. 1984. *Quality without tears*. New York: McGraw Hill.

Discenza, R., J. M. Ferguson, and R. Wisner. 1985. Marketing higher education: Using situation analysis to identify prospective student needs in today's competitive environment. *National Association of Student Personnel Administration Journal* 4:18–25.

Ewell, P. T. 1991. Assessment and public accountability—Back to the future: *Change* (November/December): 12–17.

Felicette, L. 1988. Surprising survey results about recruiting reentry women students. In *The admission strategist*, ed. S. MacGowan, 43–48. New York: College Entrance Examination Board.

Goodwin, G. 1988. Innovations that serve new clientele. In *Celebrating two decades of innovation*, ed. G. Goodwin, 27–52. Dallas: League of Innovation.

Hickman, C. R., and M. A. Silva. 1984. *Creating excellence*. New York: New York American Libraries.

Hillman, J. 1986. Remarks at the convention of the Association of Community College Trustees, 15–19 October, San Diego, California.

Hossler, D. 1984. *Enrollment management: An integrated approach*. New York: College Entrance Examination Board.

———. 1988. Enrollment management: College recruitment philosophy for the eighties. In *The admission strategist*, ed. S. MacGowan. New York: College Entrance Examination Board.

Hudson Institute. 1987. *Workforce 2000—Work and workers for the 21st century*. Indianapolis: Hudson Institute.

Jones, K. 1992. President's report. *Counsel*. 2. Denver, Colo.: National Council for Marketing and Public Relations, 2.

Keane, J. G. 1985. Higher education: Some trends stressing the need for strategic focus. *Continuum* 45(2): 88–100.

Kotler, P. 1984. *Marketing management analysis, planning and control*. Englewood Cliffs, N.J.: Prentice-Hall.

McIlquham, J. 1988. Develop a powerful database management system for your institution. In *The admission strategist*, ed. S. MacGowan, 16–18. New York: College Entrance Examination Board.

Parnell, D. 1988. The importance of pell grants. *American Association of Community and Junior Colleges Letter* 294:3.

Peters, T. J., and R. H. Waterman. 1982. *In search of excellence*. New York: Harper and Row.

Roe, M. 1989. Education and U.S. competitiveness: The community college role. Austin: University of Texas at Austin, IC Institute.

Shuman, C. H. 1987. What effective market analysis can do for you. *Catalyst* 2:5–13.

Smith, L. N. 1988. Marketing management perspectives. Paper presented at the Marketing Higher Education to Adults conference of the College Board Association, March, Washington, D.C.

South Carolina industry and occupations: Projections: 1986–2000. 1990. Columbia, S.C.: S.C. Employment Security Commission, Labor Market Information Division, 2.

Topor, R. S. 1986. *Institutional image: How to define, improve, market it.* Washington, D.C.: Council for the Advancement and Support of Education.

Weathersby, G. 1980. Statewide coordination of higher education: Three perspectives. *Change* 7:18–24.

Williams, S. K. 1988. Marketing the community college. Presentation at the Association of Community College Trustees Regional Conference, 1–3 June 1989, Charleston, South Carolina.

Williams, T. E. 1986. Optimizing student-institution fit. In *Managing college enrollments*, ed. D. Hossler, 35–46, San Francisco: Jossey-Bass.

Student Assessment in the Community College and the Use of Technology in Testing

Karen L. Hays

The community college system in America has opened the doors of education to many who otherwise would not have had such opportunities. This commitment to accessibility has not diminished since the inception of the community college system. In 1978 Lukenbill and McCabe wrote, "With the spread of community colleges having open admissions policies, however, many students with deficiencies in basic skills have enrolled in college programs. This is especially true of urban community colleges which draw students with very different backgrounds and educational experiences" (1978, 43). Some community colleges responded to the educational diversity of their students by implementing programs to assess the skills of entering students. The evolution of assessment programs in community colleges has occurred rapidly, with a variety of instruments and a variety of delivery techniques currently in use. With an increasing number of states requiring the assessment of entering college students, and with the educational diversity of our students, the assessment program may prove to be the centerpiece of activities that enables colleges to achieve their educational mission.

HISTORY OF ASSESSMENT

The history of intelligence testing in this country is founded in the work of three psychologists: Henry Goddard, Edmund Huey, and Lewis Terman. In the early 1900s Goddard, Huey, and Terman revised Alfred Binet's intelligence scale which had been developed to identify children who would benefit from schooling (Resnick 1982). These intelligence tests were understood to be a measure of scholastic ability and were a precursor to the development of group-administered examinations (Astin 1991; Horrocks 1964).

During this same time period, the use of aptitude testing began expanding into other arenas. A proliferation of testing programs in American elementary, junior, and senior high school systems was occurring, and in the military during World War I U.S. Army recruits were tested in order to classify draftees and to select officers (Astin 1991). While these tests were not used for admissions decisions, they were used to group students or U.S. Army recruits more homogeneously and to assess programs (Resnick 1987).

The College Entrance Examination Board was developed in 1899 to initiate aptitude testing as a component of the admission criteria for universities (Resnick 1982). During this same period, the community college system began with the first public two-year-college, Joliet Junior College, in 1901. By 1922, thirty-seven states had created 207 junior colleges; by 1930, 70,000 students had enrolled (Cohen and Brawer 1982). This system of higher education now has an enrollment of well over 5 million students (Chronicle of Higher Education 1991).

The proliferation of aptitude testing can be readily observed. Resnick (1987) reports that colleges have used testing instruments as part of the admission requirements for over seventy years. During the early 1920s increased emphasis was placed on developing standardized aptitude tests required for college admission decisions. By 1926 the College Board introduced the Scholastic Aptitude Test (SAT) as an alternative method for screening college applicants (Resnick 1982). Popularity of the SAT for admission testing grew after World War II. In 1959 the American College Testing Program (ACT) was offered as an alternative to the SAT. The SAT and ACT remain the most widely used aptitude tests for admission to institutions of higher education today (Eckland 1982).

A review of the literature describes several reasons why community colleges have implemented assessment programs. Astin (1991) writes that the institution's values are reflected in the data collected and are used to achieve the goals of the college or university. Astin also has stated that community colleges place a higher priority on serving members of the community and, therefore, that the assessment practices should promote serving that population. The National Governors' Association Task Force on College Quality in 1986 promoted assessment as a mechanism for measuring the quality of education and whether colleges were spending their resources appropriately (Hutchings and Marchese 1990).

Hutchings and Marchese (1990) described the data collected by the American Council on Education, which indicated that 87 percent of two-year colleges have implemented assessment programs. The American Council on Education also reported that 42 percent of the responding institutions indicated that their states now mandated some assessment requirements; a majority of institutions have implemented locally designed tests to respond to assessment needs. Most of these basic skills assessment instruments focus upon identifying the student's current ability in reading, writing, and computation (Hanson 1990).

COMMUNITY COLLEGE ASSESSMENT PROGRAMS

The three most prevalent reasons for the existence of community college assessment programs today are (1) state legislative mandates, (2) facilitation of course placement decisions that are responsive to the diversity in the educational backgrounds of students, and (3) a step in the student flow model that enables the college to be accountable to the public.

Legislative Mandates

While most state legislative bodies currently promote the use of assessment activities in colleges, several states, including California, Georgia, New Jersey, Tennessee, Texas and Florida, already require or are considering entry-level testing as a requirement for all students (Morante 1987). One argument for statewide mandated tests is to define and agree to a uniform minimum standard of proficiency among colleges.

In addition to entry-level testing, the state of Florida requires that all students in a public institution (or those receiving state financial aid) successfully complete the College Level Academic Skills Test (CLAST) in order to receive an associate in arts degree or be admitted as a junior in a public university. This test was implemented in order to measure the level of student achievement in computation and communication skills at the point of completing two years of college. Minimum passing score requirements have been raised three times since the initial cut score requirement was determined in 1984. Much has been written about the impact of rising minimum score requirements of this single measure of student performance on minorities and students who have a native language other than English (Astin 1991; Fenske and Johnson 1990; Morris and Belcher 1990).

Response to Diversity

Community colleges provide educational and training opportunities to many people. Accessibility, however, encourages a diverse student population in terms of educational backgrounds and experiences. Many community colleges, therefore, have used basic skills assessments for course placement decisions that enable faculty to work with a more homogeneous student population in their classrooms. Palmer (1987) describes the assessment program in a community college as providing a mechanism to sort students. By doing so, colleges may identify each student with one or more skill deficiencies and offer a sequence of courses that will increase the student's chance to achieve educational goals. Using a standardized placement tool enables the advisor and student to make effective course enrollment decisions. "Common testing has a way of assuring that common learning has occurred and of assuring the public and the legislators who represent the public that the goals, values, and objectives that have been deemed important and appropriate are in fact demonstrably achieved in an objective manner" (Losak 1987, 26).

Public Accountability

Astin (1991) reports that the SAT and ACT have been used to measure the effectiveness of school systems, but score reports indicate a decline in the national scores since the 1960s. Declining test scores was one of the factors determining the at-risk status of the nation as cited in the National Commission on Excellence in Education's "A Nation at Risk" (Astin 1991). During this same period, colleges and universities became more dependent upon public funding and began to experience a decline in public confidence (Resnick 1987). Losak writes that "there is evidence that the initiation of such a testing program conveys a message of positive educational value to many constituencies in higher education, including students, faculty, and lay citizens" (1987, 26). Hirsch (1987) supports this philosophy and adds that assessment programs can be used to measure the effectiveness of programs and whether the goals of the college and state are being met.

The *Miami Herald* (Wheat 1992) described a report to the Florida House Postsecondary Education Committee which exemplifies how the identification of the skill level of students in high school and postsecondary education highlights the public perceptions of the educational system. An aide to the Florida Commissioner of Education was reported as having said that providing remedial education in community colleges is the price paid for maintaining the open door. One state legislator suggested that this was due to the lack of a broad enough college preparatory curriculum in the high schools. Several legislators now want high schools to integrate these courses into the general curriculum so that more students will be prepared for college work. However, some members of the committee fear that this college preparatory focus in the curriculum would create an increase in the dropout rate, already one of the highest in the country. While many school districts actively strive to decrease the dropout rate, one legislator was quoted as saying that we should not be concerned with this issue, since these students are a drain on the system. It is clear that the debate concerning the perception of effectiveness and goal achievement of school systems will continue.

ASSESSMENT ISSUES

The use of assessment instruments for course placement decisions is on the rise in the community college system. According to Morante (1987), all students should be tested at the time of admission to determine appropriate course placement. While many states now promote the concept of student assessment by public institutions, most allow the college to determine the instrument to be used and how the results will be interpreted (Astin 1991). Many colleges have developed their own instruments or have selected a placement test already on the market since the SAT and ACT alone are not appropriate measures of basic skills competencies (Morante 1987). The SAT and ACT measure the capability of students to achieve; basic skills assessments provide information about the current proficiency of a student.

With the decision to implement an assessment program, many issues arise (Knoell 1983). Who should tested? What competency level is expected when considering placement in college-level courses? What sort of remediation programs are in place? Should one instrument be used irrespective of the program or personal development goals of each student? Other issues may include the test delivery method, budgetary concerns, and the college's ongoing commitment to an assessment program. If student assessment is considered to be a vital component of the college structure, related concerns and issues should be the object of evaluation, scrutiny, and, if necessary, revision, as the institution grows and changes to meet current student and community needs.

An example of how one institution has addressed assessment issues over time is found at Miami-Dade Community College, one of twenty-eight public community colleges in Florida. Miami-Dade was founded in 1960 with an opening enrollment of 2,025 students. Today, Miami-Dade comprises five campuses and has a systemwide credit student head count per term of over 55,000 students. Miami-Dade has the largest foreign student population of any college or university in this country. The student ethnic profile is 53.3 percent Hispanic, 25.5 percent white non-Hispanic, 19 percent Black non-Hispanic, 2.1 percent Asian, and 0.1 percent American Indian. During the 1990–1991 academic year, 122,166 students (credit and noncredit) were served.

Course placement testing was implemented at Miami-Dade in 1960. During the first educational reform undertaken in the late 1970s, greater emphasis was placed on the assessment of basic skills at the time of entrance to the college. In the fall of 1980, the college began using the Comparative Guidance and Placement (CGP) test. Results were used to advise students into appropriate courses although students were not required to follow the advisement. In 1981 mandatory placement into remedial courses for students scoring below a cutoff score was implemented. The computerized on-line registration system was programmed to support registration into required courses. Beginning in 1985 colleges and universities were mandated by the Florida legislature to use one of four entrance tests: the SAT, ACT, Assessment of Skills for Successful Entry and Transfer (ASSET), or Multiple Assessment Programs and Services (MAPS). The state also required the use of common placement scores and enrollment in college preparatory courses for those students scoring below the cutoff score. Miami-Dade chose the MAPS as the assessment tool and continued to require mandatory course placement based upon test results.

In 1987 the South Campus began using the Computerized Placement Test (CPT) developed by the Educational Testing Service for the College Board. Miami-Dade, Central Piedmont Community College (in North Carolina), and Santa Fe Community College (in Florida) were pilot test sites for the CPT. Currently, all five campuses of Miami-Dade use the state-approved CPT as the entrance assessment. The flexibility in using computers for the assessment process has had an enormous effect upon improving the admission, advisement, and registration process for students. Students may now submit an application for admission and are immediately directed to the Campus Assessment Center to complete the CPT. After watching a brief orientation video, students are referred to an advisor in possession of their test scores and course sequencing pathways document. Once advised, students may register for courses. With the Assessment Center open year-round, and with on-line telephone registration, it is possible to spread the testing and advising work load more evenly across the term. The result is better service for students. On South Campus, a student who completes the assessment in January may register for the spring, summer, or fall term.

Over 10,000 students completed the computerized entrance assessment during 1991 on the South Campus of Miami-Dade. Miami-Dade requires that all degree-seeking students complete the assessment prior to registering for courses, and all nondegree-seeking students who have registered for more than fifteen credits must be tested. Students who score below the established cutoff scores are required to complete developmental course(s). Several additional courses are recommended to students who may need to continue improving their skills and study techniques.

In 1989 the New Directions project, initiated as the second educational reform, sought to review a variety of assessment and curriculum issues across the Miami-Dade district. Changes in minimum CLAST standards, along with an interest in updating the general education curriculum, precipitated a review of the entrance assessment scores and associated course placement decisions. In the fall of 1991 courses that had been previously recommended to students but not required were now included in the mandatory course placement criteria. Since mandated placement into developmental courses was instituted, enrollment in these courses has steadily increased. Currently over 65 percent of all new students score below the minimum on one or more of the subtests. The New Directions project committees are concerned with providing the necessary remediation programs that ensure student success, while also providing an array of college-level courses that attract and retain superior students.

Miami-Dade has recently embarked upon a second assessment program for students enrolling in Postsecondary Adult Vocational (PSAV) programs. PSAV programs are noncredit, short-term programs designed to provide entry-level skills in vocational areas. Students enrolled in PSAV are required to complete an assessment program. Miami-Dade has chosen the Test of Adult Basic Education (TABE) to assess the basic skills level of students in PSAV programs. This assessment program will be offered to thousands of students who seek short-term programs for entry or reentry into the work force. The state of Florida also requires any necessary remediation for students enrolled in these programs.

While some colleges have had an assessment program in place for many years, the concept of placement testing in the community college is rapidly expanding. Most entrance assessments in community colleges, whether in-house developed instruments or standardized assessments, are administered in a paper-and-pencil format. Until 1987 Miami-Dade used the MAPS as the required assessment instrument and this was delivered in group sessions using test booklets and answer sheets that were machine scored. Test booklets were reusable for quite a few administrations, and the cost for answer sheets was minimal. Although the answer sheets were machine scored, the test scores for each student were recorded by hand and entered manually into the student's record on the mainframe computer. There were several major disadvantages in administering such a program at the South Campus of Miami-Dade since each fall term an average of from 5,000 to 6,000 new students must be tested. Coordinating such a large testing program and maintaining the integrity of the test were challenging at best. The end of each large test session placed a heavy burden on other areas of the college as they tried to serve large numbers of students efficiently. In a program of this size, there is very little flexibility in making necessary time, staffing, or location changes in the testing program.

USE OF TECHNOLOGY

There may be some advantages in using group-administered paper-and-pencil tests; however, the focus in the future clearly will be on the use of computer technology in the delivery of tests. Some of the critical issues articulated when discussing the viability of a computerized testing program focus upon the following areas: cost factors in creating an assessment center, efficiency in testing students, the advantage of adaptive testing, student feedback, and flexibility in the assessment program administration.

Cost Factors

One of the first questions usually asked concerning the development of a computerized assessment center is the cost as compared to the traditional testing methods. Schinoff and Steed (1988) conducted a cost analysis comparing expenses of the CPT to those incurred with administering the paper-and-pencil assessment at Miami-Dade, South Campus. Personnel costs, equipment expenses, and testing fees were the three areas of expenses addressed in this report.

Administering the MAPS on the South Campus of Miami-Dade necessitated hiring one test administrator and two proctors for each test session. Students were tested on a walk-in basis; each session lasted approximately two and one-half hours. Sessions were scheduled for fall, winter, and spring/summer registration periods with approximately ninety-five sessions scheduled, for example, during a fall registration. Administrative costs in hiring, training, and supervising personnel, publicizing test dates, and preparing pay rosters were not included in determining personnel costs. During a five-month period in 1986, the total number of hours worked by testing personnel was 977. Dividing the salary of examiners and proctors by the number of students tested yielded a cost per student of $1.47. During a similar time period in 1987, the personnel cost for the CPT was determined. Part-time personnel were used to staff the center, with the average salary (in 1987) of $5.25 per hour. The total number of hours worked by testing personnel more than doubled in order to improve student access to the required entrance assessment. The cost per student was determined to be $1.88. However, since the number of students fluctuated during this five-month period, it is helpful to review the costs incurred during one of the busiest months. In July 1986, the cost per student with the paper-and-pencil administration was $1.45; in July 1987, the cost per student for the CPT was $1.49 (Schinoff and Steed 1988).

The most expensive component of the start-up cost for an assessment center is computer equipment. The number of stations required is determined by the number of students to be assessed per year and the uses of the computer for other testing services. Schinoff and Steed (1988) estimated that twenty-five stations were satisfactory for a year-round, walk-in operation for South Campus. Other hardware expenditures to consider include installing network capabilities so that each computer may connect to the college mainframe computer, enabling transmission of test scores directly to the mainframe computer. Further, networking each computer station to a testing file server is advantageous as the capabilities of testing via the computer expand.

Testing fees were also compared by Schinoff and Steed (1988) since the direct cost for the entrance assessment is paid by the college. Administering the MAPS (paper and pencil) was minimal, estimated at $.25 per student, and supported purchasing booklets and answer sheets. The cost per subtest on the CPT is $.75, for a total of $3.00 per student. Students who wish to complete the ACT, ASSET, or SAT (the only other tests approved by the state of Florida to meet entrance testing requirements) must pay the direct cost. The cost for those tests ranges from $2.50 to $12.00 per student.

Efficiency

Use of the CPT has been instrumental in significantly improving the flow of students through the admission, testing, advisement, and registration process at Miami-Dade. In one visit to the campus, a student may apply for admission, complete the CPT, receive test scores, and meet with an advisor. The availability of testing on demand has been advantageous for the nontraditional students who may work full-time and have many personal commitments (Webb et al., 1988). Part-time hourly employees staff the center, so that the hours of operation are determined by the demand expected. Hours may be extended during critical registration periods and reduced during traditionally slower time periods.

In addition to the improved student flow, computerized testing on terminals dedicated to this use provides maximum security of the instrument. By using technology, there is no chance of misplacing a booklet, and no problems with storing large quantities of materials.

Adaptive Testing

One of the most significant advantages in using the computer for testing is the availability of adaptive tests. With a larger number of items in the test bank, the adaptive test offers each student different test questions. This is accomplished by the computer basing subsequent questions upon the answer of the previous question. Item response theory enables the computer to select questions covering a wide range of ability and determine test scores that may be compared among the population tested (Rounds, Kanter, and Blumin 1987). Ward (1988) reports that adaptive tests require fewer questions to measure the skills of those tested thus shortening the amount of time needed for testing per student.

Student Feedback

When the CPT was first implemented at Miami-Dade, there was genuine concern that students would resist wanting to be tested via computer. Would older students, perhaps with little or no experience with computers, request paper-and-pencil testing, and would students complain about a new form of testing? In order to collect this information, a student feedback survey was administered on random days in a four-month period in 1987, using a survey authored and distributed at Santa Fe Community College during their pilot program. At Miami-Dade, the student responses indicated that 68 percent of students preferred the CPT to paper-and-pencil tests, 17 percent preferred the paper-and-pencil test, and 15 percent indicated no preference; 95 percent thought the CPT was very easy or reasonably easy to use; and 61 percent felt no pressure to complete the test quickly (Schinoff and Steed 1988).

Flexibility

Using the computer for the delivery of an assessment program permits great flexibility in providing services for students and faculty. The scheduling needs of students can be easily met in an assessment center with an adequate number of terminals available. As demand increases at certain times of the year, the hours of service can expand to accommodate the students who must be tested. On typically slow days, groups of high school students, or students in special programs, may be brought in to complete an early registration process. With increased accessibility for students, there is less chance that students who apply for admission will not follow through with the testing, advisement, and registration process.

The use of permanent part-time proctors enables the development of a cadre of well-trained staff who work a regular schedule, thus eliminating the potential for last-minute staffing problems associated with scheduled testing sessions. Proctors are able to answer questions efficiently and generate test scores quickly for each individual student, reducing the anxiety that may occur in large group, time-testing sessions.

The use of the assessment center can easily be expanded to include other computerized tests. One example of using the computer to meet a local testing need is Miami-Dade's development of an English placement test for students whose native language is other than English. National testing agencies are now pilot testing computerized versions of examinations for use on college campuses. Clearly, within a few short years, the computerized assessment center will be essential to both the campus and the local community.

CONCLUSION

Many new developments are on the horizon because of computerized testing capabilities. With sufficient numbers of terminals, students may provide greater amounts of information about their backgrounds and needs that will assist college personnel in developing relevant programs. It is possible for students to enter information about their educational and career plans, complete the entrance assessment and vocational interest inventory, use an interactive computerized college orientation program, and obtain interpretive test score results in very little time. Moreover, such a center can offer a myriad of other tests to students and to the community in a low-cost, efficient manner.

Community colleges are often characterized by their innovations in programs and services that meet the needs of an ethnically and educationally diverse student population while concurrently satisfying state mandates. It is essential that we not only collect data about our students, but also use the information to generate new academic paradigms that address the challenges we face in our communities.

REFERENCES

Astin, A. W. 1991. *Assessment for excellence: The philosophy and practice of assessment and evaluation in higher education*. New York: American Council on Education/ Macmillan.

Chronicle of Higher Education. 1991. *Almanac*. Washington, D.C.: Chronicle of Higher Education.

Cohen, A. M., and F. B. Brawer. 1982. *The American community college*. San Francisco: Jossey-Bass.

Eckland, B. K. 1982. College entrance examination trends. In *The rise and fall of national test scores*, ed. G. R. Austin and H. Garber. New York: Academic Press.

Fenske, R. H., and E. A. Johnson. 1990. Changing regulatory and legal environments. In *New futures for student affairs*, ed. M. J. Barr, M. L. Upcraft, and Associates. San Francisco: Jossey-Bass.

Hanson, G. R. 1990. Improving practice through research, evaluation, and outcome assessment. In *New futures for student affairs*, ed. M. J. Barr, M. L. Upcraft, and Associates. San Francisco: Jossey-Bass.

Hirsch, P. M. 1987. The other side of assessment. In *Issues in student assessment*, ed.

D. Bray and M. J. Belcher, 15–24. New Directions for Community Colleges, no. 59. San Francisco: Jossey-Bass.

Horrocks, J. E. 1964. *Assessment of behavior.* Columbus, Ohio: Charles E. Merrill Publishing Company.

Hutchings, P., and T. Marchese. 1990. Watching assessment: Questions, stories, prospects. *Change* 22(5):12–38.

Knoell, D. M. 1983. Serving today's diverse students. In *Issues for community college leaders in a new era*, ed. G. B. Vaughan and Associates, 21–38. San Francisco: Jossey-Bass.

Losak, J. 1987. Assessment and improvement in education. In *Issues in student assessment*, ed. D. Bray and M. J. Belcher, 25–29. New Directions for Community Colleges, no. 59. San Francisco: Jossey-Bass.

Lukenbill, J. D., and R. H. McCabe. 1978. *General education in a changing society.* Dubuque, Iowa: Kendall/Hunt Publishing Company.

Morante, E. A. 1987. A primer on placement testing. In *Issues in student assessment*, ed. D. Bray and M. J. Belcher, 55–63. New Directions for Community Colleges, no. 59. San Francisco: Jossey-Bass.

Morris, C., and M. J. Belcher. 1990. *What factors predict differences in CLAST performance among community colleges?* 90–12R. Miami, Fla.: Miami-Dade Community College, Office of Instructional Research.

Palmer, J. 1987. Sources and information: Student assessment at community colleges. In *Issues in student assessment*, ed. D. Bray and M. J. Belcher, 103–112. New Directions for Community Colleges, no. 59. San Francisco: Jossey-Bass.

Resnick, D. P. 1982. History of educational testing. In *Ability testing: Uses, consequences, and controversies*, part 2, ed. A. K. Wigdor and W. R. Garner. Washington, D.C.: National Academy Press.

————. 1987. Expansion, quality, and testing in American education. In *Issues in student assessment*, ed. D. Bray and M. J. Belcher, 5–14. New Directions for Community Colleges, no. 59. San Francisco: Jossey-Bass.

Rounds, J. C., M. J. Kanter, and M. Blumin. 1987. Technology and testing: What is around the corner? In *Issues in student assessment*, ed. D. Bray and M. J. Belcher, 83–93. New Directions for Community Colleges, no. 59. San Francisco: Jossey-Bass.

Schinoff, R. B., and L. Steed. 1988. The computerized adaptive testing program at Miami-Dade Community College, South Campus. Monograph. In *Computerized adaptive testing: The state of the art in assessment at three community colleges.* Laguna Hills, Calif.: League for Innovation in the Community College.

Ward, W. C. 1988. Using microcomputers for adaptive testing. Monograph. In *Computerized adaptive testing: The state of the art in assessment at three community colleges.* Laguna Hills, Calif.: League for Innovation in the Community College.

Webb, N. A., M. Gay, D. A. Rhoden, and J. Tripp. 1988. Computer adaptive assessment testing at Central Piedmont Community College. Monograph. In *Computerized adaptive testing: The state of the art in assessment at three community colleges.* Laguna Hills, Calif.: League for Innovation in the Community College.

Wheat, J. 1992. Students enter college unprepared, study says. *Miami Herald* (17 January): 10A.

The Role of Student Services in the Response to Reduced Support

Jane E. Matson

The two-year college will soon celebrate the centennial of its first appearance on the postsecondary education scene in the United States. Since its inception the two-year college has provided essential services to students in addition to classroom instruction, as indeed have all collegiate level institutions. Because of the nature of the two-year college population, student services over and beyond the essentials have traditionally been provided. These services have historically been considered an integral and highly significant part of the college. Medsker defined the role well when he stated:

A college may have a plant, a faculty, and a curriculum; but unless there is an orderly way of admitting students, some method of assisting them to appraise themselves and to plan their educational and vocational program accordingly, some means of assuring enriching experiences through campus social interaction, and some attempt to center attention on the individual rather than on the group, the college is an impersonal shell in which students are not conditioned for optimum learning. (1960, 41)

The specific definition of what activities are included in these services, commonly identified as student personnel services, will differ from college to college, reflecting the differences in student composition, the patterns of organization, and the assignment of responsibility for a variety of functions and services. A generic definition, however, can be set forth based on an examination of practices in various two-year colleges. Commonly included in this definition are the following functions: admission, records, orientation, counseling, assessment, financial aid, placement, student government, and activities. The operational definition of each of these areas may include a variety of specific activities, widely varying in some cases from college to college. It is not uncommon to find included under the rubric of student personnel services such functions as recruitment, precollege information, athletics, health services, academic regulation, foreign student programs, articulation, and some facets of evaluation and research in addition to those listed above. As is true of all aspects of the two-year college, the assumption of responsibility for specific services, and their allocation to administrative units of the college, has evolved over a period of time. As the two-year college has carved out a place for itself in the world of postsecondary education, this niche has changed in configuration in response to the range of economic and social pressures that it has been subjected to over the years.

The range of services provided for students is not static or fixed. As the two-year college assumed new functions over the years, the nature of the student population changed markedly. This in turn gave rise to changes in the nature of the student services provided. For example, in the early days of the two-year (or junior) college, it was often considered an extension of the secondary school. This institution evolved into an equivalent of the first two years of a four-year college or university. The needs of these students differed markedly from the needs of the students who participated in the eventual evolution of this institution to one concerned with the meeting of a broad range of community needs, including the vocational preparation of a work force, remedial education for the underprepared, and broadly expanded adult education services, in addition to the traditional preparation for transfer to a four-year institution. As significant changes occurred in such student characteristics as age range, ability levels, educational goals, and patterns of community participation, it was necessary to make changes in the nature of the services provided by the college in the area of curriculum as well as in the student services areas.

Public two-year colleges or community colleges, as they came to be identified, reflecting the shift of focus to serving the broader community, experienced phenomenal periods of growth during the 1960s and early 1970s. In the decade between 1965 and 1975, the number of publicly supported colleges more than doubled. At one time during this period, colleges were being established at the rate of one per week across the country. During this time of rapid growth and expansion, financial and community support were readily available. The key words were "growth" and "larger." New programs were introduced in areas of curriculum and student services, frequently without adequate planning or preparation. As the number of colleges and enrollments increased, student services expanded proportionately.

A landmark study, undertaken in the mid–1960s, attempted a national appraisal of student personnel programs in two-year colleges, under the auspices of the American Association of Junior Colleges (now known as the American Association of Community and Junior Colleges) with financial support from the Carnegie Corporation of New York. This was the first time that an entire sector of postsecondary education had undertaken an appraisal of a single major function of its institutions. The final report of the National Committee for Appraisal and

Development of Junior College Student Personnel Programs defines the basic student personnel program as "a series of related functions designed to support the instructional program, respond to student needs and foster institutional development" (1965, 15). The study grouped the major student services functions into five major units: (1) admissions, registration, and records, (2) placement and financial aids, (3) student activities, (4) guidance and counseling, and (5) administration. While the specific activities carried on under each of these units have changed as the two-year college has evolved, the categorization of student services has remained remarkably consistent over the three decades that have passed since the study was completed.

In a synthesis of the final report to the Carnegie Corporation, Collins (1967) reported that the data compiled in the study reflected broadly based inadequacies in the student personnel programs found in the sample of two-year colleges included in the study. The sample consisted of forty-nine colleges with enrollments of more than 1,000 students and seventy-four colleges with smaller enrollments.

While the study has never been replicated, it seems reasonable to assume that the quality of student personnel services improved with the advent of the federally supported training programs authorized by the National Defense Education Act and followed by the Education Professional Development Act in the late 1960s and early 1970s. The development of training programs specifically designed for two-year college personnel, and implemented in four-year colleges and universities across the United States, undoubtedly had a significant impact on the quality (and quantity) of student services provided in two-year colleges during this period.

While the taxonomy of student services may have remained relatively consistent, the change in the nature of the student population has been marked and has necessitated concomitant changes in the services provided. Among the most significant shifts in the nature of the student population are the following:

1. A marked increase in the proportion of older students who come to the colleges with substantial life experiences, including employment in a wide variety of occupational fields. It has been estimated that the average age of two-year college students ranges from twenty-five to thirty years in contrast with the typical recent high school graduate student of some years ago.

2. An increasing proportion of women who are returning to formal education after an absence of some years while engaged in homemaking or child-rearing activities and with little or no paid work experience.

3. Significant numbers of students who either through design or necessity are changing their career direction and need to acquire new skills to make them employable in the current labor market.

4. An increasing proportion of part-time students who are unwilling or unable to make a full-time commitment to education.

5. In addition to these groups, an increased diversity of student populations in terms of cultural backgrounds, language facility, and physical disabilities.

The influx of student with these characteristics into the traditional community college has heightened the importance of the student services areas. The appraisal of education needs, the shared responsibility with the instructional staff for the maintenance and success of these students, places an increased responsibility on the student services areas involved in the assessment of student needs and the design of educational experiences appropriate for meeting those needs. It becomes even more important for the achievement of a college's goals and objectives that the student services areas work in close partnership with the instructional areas. The ultimate success of the college requires a close coordination of these two areas.

For a variety of reasons, the rate of growth of community colleges both in number of colleges and enrollment began to decrease in the late 1970s and early 1980s. It should be noted that the number of private or independent colleges began to decrease as early as 1965 and continued to decrease both in number of colleges and enrollments through 1990. While the number of public colleges continued to increase through 1990, enrollments were sporadic, showing a decline in the fall of 1983 through the fall of 1985, followed by small increases in 1986, 1987, and 1988 (National Council for Marketing and Public Relations, 1991). In part, this slowdown in the rate of growth was caused by changing demographics plus the fact that the United States had been more or less blanketed with two-year colleges, especially in the more heavily populated states.

Related to this decline in the rate of growth, funding sources began to diminish and it became evident that some reassessment of the role and function of these institutions in the American structure of education was essential. Shrinking financial resources not only made it necessary to review the structure and function of a college in terms of the total concept of education, but also forced each sector of the college to review its own effectiveness in relation to its goals as well as those of the total institution.

The assessment of the quality of student services has too often been neglected, and a well-established system for measuring outcomes has not been developed. One effort to define and establish criteria by which to evaluate the role of student services professionals in the achievement of student success in the community colleges has been reported by the League for Innovation in the Community Colleges (1987). A broader perspective on assessing institutional effectiveness in community colleges was proposed by the League for Innovation in Community Colleges in 1990. The earlier publication focuses on recommendations for processes and procedures that contribute to the achievement of a higher level of student success. The 1990 publication emphasizes a broader approach to the assessment of institutional effectiveness. Both of these approaches can be of value to a college that is attempting to design a system of measuring the extent to which its students have achieved success or to assess the overall effectiveness of the college operation. Each of these is predicated on the existence of a clear and explicit statement of the various missions of the institution. Without that, any reasonably accurate assessment cannot be accomplished. It is also essential that the variations among colleges in terms of missions, goals, and objectives and the consequent differences in priorities among colleges be fully taken into account.

Alfred, Peterson, and White (1992) have provided leadership in the definition and analysis of student success as a factor in measuring the effectiveness of community colleges. In a recent study, done under the sponsorship of the Community College Consortium, practices contributing to student success in community colleges have been described and assessed. The findings, in general, reveal that quantitative factors (e.g., enrollment growth, program expansion, and resource acquisition) are more likely to be used as indicators of effectiveness in community colleges. On the other hand, qualitative factors (e.g., student satisfaction, faculty and staff satisfaction, and the identification and solution of problems) are considered important factors but are not as likely to be used extensively to determine effectiveness. Success practices directly related to classroom instruction (e.g., entry testing and placement) are more likely to be used in community colleges than those practices related to academic support (e.g., new student orientation). Even less likely to be used are collaborative programs involving other schools or external agencies. It may be inferred from these findings that community colleges, when attempting to assess effectiveness, are more concerned with and attach greater importance to success practices directly related to classroom instruction and academic policy. Student personnel staff need to be aware of this as they develop programs within restricted budget parameters.

For the most part during the 1960s and 1970s, increases in resources to be devoted to student services staff or programs were justified on the basis of increases in enrollment rather than on any critical analysis or evaluation of the services provided. The lack of an effective evaluation system and the absence of any well-defined statement of priorities have resulted in student personnel services becoming an early target when a college is looking for areas to be cut. Examples can be found where student services became an early focus of retrenchment. It was the perception of some administrators that the adverse effects of absorbing major budget cuts in the student services areas would not be readily visible. At New York City Community College, for example, budget cuts resulted in threatening the survival of student services in the mid–1970s (Sussman 1977). There is also the feeling in some areas of the college that, by cutting student services, the instructional program (viewed by some as the most crucial and essential services offered by the college) can be protected. A case can be made that this shortsighted approach largely ignores the need in an open-door institution for a system for distributing students among the available instructional programs in some appropriate and organized manner. The functions of admissions, records, registration, determination of the need for financial aid, and counseling, which usually belong to the student services area, cannot be eliminated or drastically reduced without serious consequences to the effectiveness and efficiency of the college. If response to the need for reducing services is to be realistic, it seems essential that a college must be considered as a total entity with interrelated functions rather than as a collection of disparate parts.

The existing literature regarding the reduction of services in times of financial adversity consists largely of descriptions of strategies proposed or actually used for coping with the need to reduce expenditures. These are recommendations of administrators based largely on theoretical predictions of what actions would cause the least damage and result in the least painful accommodation to reduced resources. The relation between the recommendations and the previously established goals and objectives of the services targeted for cuts and/or elimination are often not clear. There have been some examples of efforts to anticipate the need for reduction of budgets by the development of a strategic plan to be used as a basis for decision making when cuts become necessary. Gonzales and Keyser (1984) describe a plan designed for Linn-Benton College (Oregon) which calls for the determination of environmental trends and the identification of planning assumptions that can serve a guidelines for making decisions regarding the future of the college. These guidelines could be used when resources become limited and reductions in cost are required. For example, in the student services area, it is suggested that cost may be reduced by the development of a system of mail and telephone registration and the use of a system of mandatory advisement and placement in courses (1984, 31).

It is significant to note that, while most of the available literature is related to possible courses of action in preparation for responses to diminished financial support, there is little reporting of the effects of these actions on the college. There appears to be little information available about what impact the actions taken might have had on the overall effectiveness of the college in achieving its goals and objectives. In other words, what difference did it make in the overall operation of the college to cut or reduce services, discontinue curricula, limit enrollment, or undertake any of the other steps suggested in response to decreasing financial support? Without some evaluative data it is impossible to know whether the means taken to cope with budget restrictions inflicted serious damage on the college or resulted in more or less acceptable accommodation or adaptation. Without such information even more serious damage may not be avoided if future reductions in funding are experienced.

In an earlier discussion of student services and reduced financial support, Matson (1978) pointed out that the *real* priorities of a college are reflected in its budgetary decisions. Student services are too often budgeted by using the previous year's allocation as a starting point and adding to it (or taking from it) according to some more or less rationally established criteria. This procedure will not work in a period of shrinking resources. As a budget plan is developed, and in today's world that most often involves reduced resources, some means of measuring the impact on the efficiency and effectiveness of student services should be available in order to make decisions that will be most beneficial (or least harmful) to the college's goals. This requires some measure of the effectiveness of the various programs given the various levels of funding.

Students seeking services from community colleges need and deserve the best efforts on the part of the college to develop appropriate programs to meet their needs. Anything less than an all-out effort would deny the promised commitment of the community college to the postsecondary education system in the United States. Reduced resources make it more difficult to succeed in achieving the stated mission of any college. It is hoped that, with the mustering of the creative potential of those dedicated to the community college philosophy, even reduction of resources may provide the motive and the means of improving community college student services programs.

REFERENCES

Alfred, R. L., R. Peterson, and T. White. 1992. *Making community colleges more effective: Leading through student success.* Ann Arbor: University of Michigan, Community College Consortium.

Collins, C. C. 1967. *Junior college student personnel programs: What they are and what they should be.* Washington, D.C.: American Association of Community and Junior Colleges.

Gonzales, T., and J. Kyser. 1984. *Strategic planning for Linn-Benton Community College: President's perspective.* Albany, Oreg.: Linn-Benton Community College.

League for Innovation in Community Colleges. 1987. *Assessing student success in the community college: The role of student development professionals.* Laguna Hills, Calif.

———. 1990. *Assessing institutional effectiveness in community colleges.* Laguna Hills, Calif.

Matson, J. E. 1978. Reduction and student services. In *Coping with reduced resources,* ed. R. L. Alfred, 53–60. New Directions for Community Colleges, no. 22. San Francisco: Jossey-Bass.

Medsker, L. L. 1960. *The junior college: Progress and prospect.* New York: McGraw-Hill.

National Committee for Appraisal and Development of Junior College Student Personnel Programs. 1965. A report to Carnegie Corporation of New York.

National Council for Marketing and Public Relations. 1991. A summary of selected national data pertaining to community, technical and junior colleges. Greeley, Colo.

Sussman, H. M. 1977. Retrenchment in Brooklyn. *Community and Junior College Journal* 47 (7):38–41.

Part 9

External Forces and the Community College

The Articulation Function of the Community College

Carolyn Prager

ARTICULATION HISTORY

Articulation is a commonly perceived self-evident "good." From a public policy perspective, it promises benefits deriving from better coordination and utilization of existing or scarce resources. As the "middleman" in higher education (Kintzer 1973), the community college occupies a critical link on the articulation chain as both a receiver and feeder of students to and from other educational providers. These include, but are not limited to, high schools, colleges and universities, proprietary institutions, and the military. This chapter will synthesize some of the factors reflected in the literature affecting community college relationships to these educational providers.

Despite their commonsense appeal, articulation efforts involving community colleges have waxed and waned historically for a variety of reasons, some structural and some functional. The loosening of governance ties to the public schools, for example, which undermined the concept of K–14 education at the local level, has certainly affected the structural relationship of community colleges and public schools just as the creation of separate boards governing community and state colleges in many states or systems has affected their relationship. The assumption of functional missions more comprehensive than the delivery of transfer education alone has just as certainly diminished the intrinsic ties to the senior colleges.

In the absence of sustained public planning, community colleges have proliferated since the 1960s in an educational environment lacking systematic designs, mechanisms, and mandates fostering articulation. The history of articulation since the 1970s has been compensatory of necessity, representing attempts to create and sometimes impose such designs, mechanisms, and mandates somewhat after the fact. During the 1970s, some states, most notably Florida and Illinois, began to address two- to four-year articulation through statewide policies and procedures. In 1974 Georgia promoted a Core Curriculum Formula and New Jersey a Full Faith and Credit policy; in 1975 Massachusetts devised a Transfer Compact, Nevada a University System Articulation Policy, and Oklahoma an Articulation Plan. By the mid–1970s, at least seven states, and by 1990 at least thirty, had focused to one degree or another upon articulation, primarily at the credit transfer level. Having formulated policy, few states, however, have been able to conduct follow-up studies to examine implementation or effectiveness.

While state-level articulation efforts in the early to mid–1970s were characterized by concern for transfer from associate to baccalaureate degrees in the arts and sciences, the local level was more concerned in the same period with secondary and postsecondary occupational program articulation. In 1976 the National Advisory Council on Vocational Education surveyed its state counterparts and reported that almost 40 percent of the states responding to the survey could cite examples of secondary/postsecondary occupational program articulation. Meanwhile, Bushnell (1978) reported that many local educators saw vocational education articulation between secondary and postsecondary institutions as a matter of enlightened self-interest. As a result, Bushnell concluded that voluntary interinstitutional cooperation was a more powerful change agent than state mandate or incentive.

Most major studies of articulation reflect some degree of ambivalence about the wisdom or efficacy of external intervention to promote articulation, noting that articulation occurs best in a cooperative interinstitutional mode. Yet these studies dedicate most of their text in the main to examination of state or system policies, practices, and results, reflecting the reality that state intervention in promoting articulation has been a major, perhaps the major, catalyst of change through the 1980s (see, for example, Kintzer and Wattenberger 1985; Kintzer 1989; Bender 1990; Knoell 1991). Kintzer (1989) describes four patterns of statewide articulation patterns. Only one depends upon voluntary interinstitutional or intersegmental agreement (as used, for example, in Alabama, Alaska, Idaho, North Dakota, Vermont, and Wisconsin).

The other three patterns are more top down. One is by legislative or constitutional mandate, typically assuring transfer to the associate degree program in arts or science but not in applied science (as found, for example, in Colorado, Florida, New Jersey, and Texas). Another is through policies that localize responsibility for transfer within a system governance unit focusing upon transfer student services (e.g., Arizona, Kentucky, Nebraska, New York, and Virginia). The third is through articulation agreements involving primarily vocational-technical education in states with two-year public technical institutes or with other postsecondary vocational-technical education institutions (e.g., Delaware, Maine, Ohio, and Oregon).

ARTICULATION TO OTHER COLLEGES AND
UNIVERSITIES

Community colleges have a hierarchical rather than a structural connection within higher education. This connection depends currently upon a single phenomenon, the necessity of student transfer from the community college to earn a bachelor's degree. Given current realities, the ties that bind derive more from transfer than from common funding or governance relationships within higher education. Because of the hierarchical nature of the transfer relationship, however, upward articulation suffers from tension conveyed by the concept of "upper" and "lower" division study (Knoell 1991), especially as the latter is understood by two different institutional types.

Richardson and Bender (1985, 1986) have explored the concept of conflicting institutional cultures as an articulation barrier in their studies of minority student progress to the baccalaureate. In their landmark study, Knoell and Medsker (1965) analyzed the general failure of state systems to take articulation into account in master planning with consequent effects upon the quantitative and qualitative participation of community college students in baccalaureate study. Driven by public and legislative concern over the protection of student movement between public higher education institutions without loss of credit, however, state agencies have attempted to compensate for cultural and typological differences by emphasizing articulation technology and mechanics. Noting the shift from local to state-level articulation activity in the 1980s, Bender (1990) classifies this activity into four categories: statewide articulation agreements, state-level articulation/transfer bodies, transfer student services, and performance data/feedback systems. Bender (1990) and Knoell (1991) provide multiple examples of recent state initiatives in these directions.

These approaches have not always realized their own potential, usually because of inadequate fiscal support. Bender (1990) points out that few states, for example, have dedicated the resources necessary to involve faculty in curriculum alignment of two- and four-year programs. Palmer (1987) points out that, for fiscal reasons, few states have been able to convert existing data bases designed to count students for accounting purposes to information systems capable of analyzing student flow, persistence, and performance. That fact alone diminishes the potential within transfer compacts, since most states and institutions thereby lack the capability of monitoring or measuring the outcomes of these agreements.

State-fostered articulation agreements mainly attempt to bridge the sectors by reaffirming the university parallelism of the first two years of the undergraduate curriculum, whether completed in a two- or four-year context. As a result, they usually support only the associate in arts or science (if general education based) as legitimate transfer coinage. Students who have taken some or all of the same general education courses as the arts and science graduate usually fall outside of the transfer compact. This includes students who attempt transfer before graduation as well as applied science graduates, easily more than 50 percent of all students who "transfer" (Cohen and Brawer 1982; Prager 1988).

Such accords tend to be built upon course distribution models that ignore competencies in the search for course equivalencies or comparability (Bender 1990). As early as 1972, Willingham signaled two limitations with this approach. The first derives from its mechanical simplicity, which could "sabotage educational continuity" by allowing the two- and four-year programs to develop separate criteria. The second lies in its failure to encompass existing and emerging specialized curricula that "must span the upper and lower division" (1972, 17). As career education has materialized in the intervening years, the failure to address the articulation of vocational programs also courts the danger that four-year colleges may be tempted to develop four-year tracks in fields that traditionally have been the province of the two-year colleges, thereby undermining the public stake in articulation (Knoell 1991).

In the absence of a federal role in college-to-college articulation (except for military personnel), accreditation bodies are the only other global entities capable of developing articulation mandates and promoting articulation practices at two- and four-year institutions with the added virtue that they could do so according to principles agreed upon by those they represent. The regional accreditors could do so by requiring examination of articulation practices and activities as part of institutional self-study and external review, but they do not do so as a matter of course (Prager 1992). The specialized accreditors could do the same and raise the standards for general education courses and competencies in two-year occupational-technical curricula in ways that would ease the transfer of applied science graduates (Prager 1992). Both Bender (1990) and Knoell (1991) suggest that accrediting agencies "with no apparent commitment to articulation" (Knoell 1991, 60) sometimes contribute unwittingly to faculty misunderstandings and undercut state and institutional articulation efforts.

Meanwhile, two- to four-year curriculum continuity continues to suffer from the absence of a theory of curriculum articulation serving transfer with sufficient flexibility to allow for institutional differences called for by Cohen and associates in the early 1970s. In response, Willingham set down eight "deductive principles," including those revolving upon questions of the complementary objectives of two- and four-year programs and the nature of "substantive continuity" (1972, 16) within disciplines. Over a decade later, however, Richardson and Bender (1985) find little evidence of improvement in addressing curriculum articulation in this or any other fashion, especially at urban institutions.

At present, the closest we have to a theory of curriculum articulation involves the transferability and assessment of competencies in addition to earned credit. If blanket acceptance of the associate in arts or science moves too far in the direction of avoiding discussion of commonly agreed upon competencies, blanket competency testing runs the danger of subjecting the community colleges and their graduates to special forms of scrutiny, unless applied equally to all students who wish to undertake baccalaureate track studies, native and transfer. So far, the literature reveals few large-scale attempts to articulate lower and upper division education based upon assessment of competencies, except for the American Assembly of Collegiate Schools of Business validation exam guidelines to be imposed on transfer but not native students (Robertson-Smith 1988) and Florida's College-Level Academic Skills Test (CLAST) for all students who wish to pursue the junior year at a public college.

ARTICULATION TO PROPRIETARY SCHOOLS

Proponents of increased articulation between community colleges and proprietary schools argue from a public policy perspective aimed at better coordination of all resources in the educational marketplace. Peterson (1982) suggests that public interest rather than market forces should dictate the level of cooperation between the public two-year colleges and proprietaries. Wilms (1987) stresses that the latter educate almost 1.2 million, or three-quarters of all, postsecondary vocational students annually. Referring to them as "strangers in their own land" (1987, 10), he calls upon the higher education community to work with the for-profit sector on formulation of a model of cooperation adaptable to each state's unique environment.

Some groundwork has been laid. The Middle States Association provides policy directions on questions to be asked about transfer and articulation to commission evaluators who assess proprietary postsecondary degree-granting (but not other degree-granting) institutions (Kintzer 1989). The National Association of Trade and Technical Schools commissioned and published Lerner's thoughtful comprehensive articulation manual in 1987. At the state level, Maryland's Board of Higher Education adopted a transfer policy in 1983 affecting its independent postsecondary schools and community colleges which Kintzer (1989) suggests could be a model for other states. The policy contains guidelines for developing agreements that protect the award of college credit and the community colleges' evaluation of academic elements such as course outlines, textbooks, faculty, facilities, testing and grading, and so on. Efforts indicative of state interest in improving articulation between the two sectors appear to be under way also in Pennsylvania, Florida, Texas, Illinois, and Kentucky (Lerner 1987).

Peterson (1982) maintains that proprietary schools now meet tests similar to those met by other postsecondary institutions through accreditation and eligibility for public subsidy such as federal and state student financial aid and job training program funds. Despite this, arguments used sometimes to justify community college reluctance to translate postsecondary training by proprietary institutions into college credit often echo those of some four-year institutions in rejecting orderly relationships with associate degree–granting colleges. In addition to faculty reservations about associating with schools that aim to make a profit, these arguments include staff elitism mirroring that of the faculty, reluctance to evaluate alternative delivery modes such as competency-based education, and simple inertia (Naylor 1987; Lerner 1987).

Because of the "strained" (Kintzer 1989, 58) relationship between private postsecondary and community colleges, there is limited evidence of actual community college–private postsecondary collaboration. Peterson (1982), Naylor (1987), Lerner (1987), and Robertson-Smith (1990), however, document specific instances of informal and formal local cooperation. These are usually either contractual relationships in which the proprietary school offers specialized instruction to community college students or a credit transfer one whereby its graduates continue their education at a two-year college. To these should be added the possibilities inherent in dual enrollments, facilities sharing, and student enrichment (Lerner 1987).

ARTICULATION TO THE MILITARY

Community colleges serve thousands of military personnel and their families every year through local, national, and international programs such as the Servicemembers Opportunity Colleges (SOC), the Community College of the Air Force, the U.S. Army's AHEAD project, and the U.S. Navy's Afloat College.

According to a 1988 survey of seventy-two two-year colleges conducted by the American Association of Community and Junior Colleges, 42 percent provided formal educational training of some sort for members of the armed services (Day and Rajasekhara 1988). The Chicago City-Wide College alone has reported serving more than 20,000 servicemembers and their dependents annually at European sites and another 25,000 at air bases and on ships (Warden 1985). In addition, community colleges award credit for learning acquired in the military, guided by American Council on Education publications such as the biennial Guide to the Evaluation of Educational Experiences in the Armed Forces. On a more critical note, Palmer's study of articulation arrangements for military personnel concludes that most do not easily accommodate those who do not follow a "linear path" (1989, 15) to the degree, especially in the case of servicemembers who seek credit for military education and training.

This otherwise remarkable record owes much to the existence of community college efforts to promote a global articulation model through the SOC, by far the largest and most comprehensive effort designed for mobile members of the military. Founded by the American Association of Community and Junior Colleges (AACJC) in 1972–1973 and now cosponsored with the American Association of State Colleges and Universities in cooperation with eleven other associations of higher education, the military services, and the Department of Defense, the SOC involved 772 institutions of higher education in spring 1990, of which 48 percent were two-year institutions. Between 1987 and 1991, almost 25,000 students with associate degrees graduated from SOCAD and SOCNAV–2 programs offered at more than 270 army and 100 navy installations worldwide.

A concise explanation of how the SOC system works is provided in Miller

(1984) and in Pratt and Karasik (1984). In the SOC model, member colleges belong to curriculum networks. The SOCAD colleges currently support about thirty and SOCNAV–2 about fifteen networks in technical, interdisciplinary, and general studies. A student receives an official agreement regarding curriculum requirements from one college, which serves as the "home" college for the purposes of awarding the degree, fulfills a minimum residency requirement, and then completes the degree through courses delivered by any college in the network. Participating colleges guarantee acceptance of each other's credits in transfer, a key program component (Servicemembers Opportunity Colleges 1989).

As the only higher education articulation system that is national in scope, the SOC model merits greater study. Despite the temptation to embrace the SOC fully as a model of "articulation that really works" (Pratt and Karasik 1984), it should be noted that the SOC does exhibit some of the same strains as civilian models when it comes to two- to four-year program articulation because of its emphasis upon career-technical offerings. Colleges and universities in the bachelor's networks guarantee acceptance of only 45 percent of the credit requirement for the higher degree from a related degree (Servicemembers Opportunity Colleges 1989). Only the general education portion of the associate degree will transfer where vocational course work does not apply to the baccalaureate (Kintzer and Wattenberger 1985). Still, the SOC system responds better to career program articulation than do many civilian models in the sense that it provides assurances about the transferability of associate degree credits to students up front, even in vocational curricula.

ARTICULATION TO HIGH SCHOOLS

In the 1960s, community colleges tended to belong to K–14 system responding to common local and state governance authorities (Kintzer 1973; Knoell 1991). As a result of the Higher Education Act of 1972, requiring designation of a state commission for higher education planning and coordination, the community colleges were shifted away from a structural connection to the elementary-secondary sector. Other factors contributed as well to the weakening of ties at the local level including the revolving door nature of open admissions in the 1960s and early 1970s, increasing high school credit by examination, expansion of secondary vocational programs, and, as always in potential articulation situations, outright indifference (Kintzer 1973).

Formal recognition that true access and equity requires quality education and that excellence in higher education requires excellence in secondary education is a phenomenon of the early 1980s (Boyer 1980; Friedlander 1982). The notion of the marginal open-admissions college is implicit in that of the marginal high school at the interface of two cultures, one of childhood and compulsory education and the other of adulthood and voluntary education (Payne 1989). Caught between the seemingly incompatible demands of preserving access and quality

(Vaughan 1984; Roueche and Baker 1987), community colleges have had to move beyond seeing themselves as a product of uncontrollable social forces producing and burdening them with less college-ready students to seeing themselves as change agents working with the schools in ways that help reduce each other's academic marginality.

An AACJC study indicates that, by the mid–1980s, the majority of two-year public colleges were involved in some kind of collaborative programming with public high schools (Parnell 1985). A glance at two ERIC reviews of high school/ community college articulation, one at the beginning and the other at the end of the decade, however, suggests how that interface has been changing to include a wider range of students and mutually beneficial activities than ever before. Friedlander's article (1982) focuses on programs with high schools, many of them initiated by universities, designed to improve academic preparation and heighten student interest in liberal arts education or to increase community college enrollments of the academically gifted. Focus upon the gifted and talented, which is typical for this phase of public school–higher education reconnection (Lieberman 1985), is reflected in community college investment in scholarships, honors classes, seminars, accelerated programming, summer programs, and college-level courses for better prepared high school students (e.g., see programs referenced in Whitlock 1978 and Friedlander 1982).

While community colleges continue to sponsor similar programs and activities, they do so for a more diverse student population in more diverse delivery modes with greater attention to the interinstitutional dynamics of articulation by the late 1980s. The 1989 ERIC review essay written by Mabry documents activity within six areas. Much of it is truly collaborative, involving the secondary school and community college in (1) dual or joint enrollment programs, (2) faculty and facilities sharing, (3) advanced placement programs, (4) college preparatory programs, (5) curriculum articulation, and (6) interinstitutional communication. Community college attention to these functions requires varying degrees of direct involvement with high school students as well as counselors, teachers, and administrators.

In their attempts to reach the disengaged as well as more engaged students, community colleges and high schools have reached deeper into the student pool for enrollments in dual or joint courses typically taught by college faculty or high school teachers appointed as the college's adjuncts. DeKalb Community College in Georgia offers general education courses to the top 20 percent of high school seniors (Crews and Pierce 1986). Kingsborough Community College in New York reaches students with 65 to 80 percent high school averages through its College Now program. A limited body of evidence suggests that low and moderate achieving students do no worse and sometimes do better in college settings than they did in public school (Greenberg 1985).

Middle College in New York is the most renowned example of community college efforts in ''reconnecting youth'' (Newman 1985) by working directly with at-risk high school–age students. A joint enterprise with the New York City

Board of Education, Middle College and its newer counterpart for English-as-a-second language students, the International High School, embrace cooperative education internships to increase student self-esteem and connection to the community as well as course work delivered on the La Guardia campus (Lieberman 1985, 1986; Lieberman et al., 1989). With Ford Foundation support, the Middle College has been replicated at other community college sites throughout the country (Cullen and Moed 1988).

Advanced placement (AP) relationships are also changing to accommodate a broader range of students. According to a 1989 National Council for Occupational Education (NCOE) survey, 82 percent of the 205 two-year institutions responding had advanced placement agreements of one form or another with secondary schools. Typically, secondary students earn advanced placement through College Board AP testing, institutional exams, or college-level work completed in high school (Stoel 1985; Mabry 1989). Advanced placement need not be geared to the most academically gifted, however. Big Bend Community College in Moses Lake, Washington, for example, has developed competency-based testing that enables high school students or adults with automotive work experience to enroll in its automotive program without having to restudy what they have already learned (Buche and Cox 1986).

Parnell (1985) maintains that the "neglected majority" of high school youth neither prepares for nor aspires to baccalaureate degree study. Instead, they leave high school without education and training suited to an increasingly sophisticated technological workplace. In responding to the unmet educational needs of the neglected majority, community colleges have reformulated the high school–community college connection through technical-preparatory programs. The two-plus-two tech-prep approach is designed also to accommodate work-force requirements for more technologically sophisticated workers by integrating the 11th through 14th year of occupational-technical curricula.

According to the NCOE survey (1989), 37 percent of the responding two-year institutions had tech-prep programs in place in 1989. The Community College of Rhode Island's program is representative. In the high school component, general education or vocational students prepare for college career programs by taking Principles of Technology, English (with an applied communication component, where available), and math in the 11th and 12th grades as well as other courses in a defined sequence (Mamaras 1990). Successful completion of the high school component guarantees acceptance into the community college occupational or technical curriculum, successful completion of which culminates in the associate degree.

Although regarded by some as formulating too narrow a role for the community college in higher education (DiCroce 1989), tech-prep became virtually a national community college mission statement promoted by the AACJC during the Parnell years. It is now reflected in federal legislation. Although limited to career education, Title III, Part E of the new Perkins Act represents the first major federal initiative promoting strong comprehensive links between the high school and two-year college sectors in a systematic and sustained manner. Its passage is spurring increased commitment at local and state levels to two-plus-two artic-ulation backed by federal allocation of $125 million for such programs in FY '92. North Carolina, for example, recently announced plans to expand the tech prep/associate degree program to all public school and community college service areas as a means of increasing the percentage of students who graduate from high school from either a college or tech-prep curriculum (*Community College Week*, January 20, 1992, p. 4).

BEYOND HIERARCHICAL ARTICULATION

As currently conceived, articulation is usually flawed at the conceptual level by notions of "upper" and "lower," of "junior" and "senior," and of "sec-ondary" and "postsecondary." These are all hierarchical constructs implying that approval authority rests with the superior institution. In *An End to Sanctuary* (1991), the Pew Higher Education Research Program challenges the higher ed-ucation community to question why only the senior institutions should continue to speak for the collegiate curriculum when community colleges have the greater experience with nontraditional/new majority learners. The Pew paper asserts that, at present, however, few "presidents of four-year institutions would suggest that something of genuine interest could be learned from the community college down the road and that the result might be a more sustained rate of articulation between the two institutions" (1991, 3A).

As Knoell (1991) observes, collaboration "implies a more equal sharing of responsibility" than does hierarchical articulation. The emergence of occupa-tional-technical specialization at the high school and two-year college levels has helped spark more collaborative downward forms of articulation and greater collaboration in curriculum development among high schools, community col-leges, and the senior institutions. At the four-year colleges, inverted degree or capstone bachelor's completion programs, two-plus-two programs, dual admis-sions programs, and consortial delivery programs for community college oc-cupational-technical graduates can obviate the need for dependency on transfer pacts protecting only arts and science graduates (Prager 1988; Thomas 1988).

As the pivotal sector in education, the community college has the greatest potential to both promote and profit from collaboration beyond articulation.

REFERENCES

American Council on Education. Biennial. *Guide to the evaluation of educational ex-periences in the armed services*. New York: Macmillan.

Bender, L. W. 1990. Executive summary. In *Spotlight on the transfer function: A national study of state policies and practices*, ed. L. W. Bender. Washington, D.C.: Amer-ican Association of Community and Junior Colleges.

Boyer, E. L. 1980. Quality and the campus: The high school/college connection. *AAHE Bulletin* 32(9):5–6, 11.

Buche, R., and C. Cox. 1986. Development of a competency-based articulated program, Big Bend Community College and area high schools: Final report. ERIC Document no. ED 256 434. Moses Lake, Wash.: Big Bend Community College.

Bushnell, D. S. 1978. *Cooperation in vocational education*. ERIC Document no. ED 164 052. Washington, D.C.: American Association of Community and Junior Colleges and the American Vocational Association.

Cohen, A. M., and F. B. Brawer. 1982. *The American community college*. San Francisco: Jossey-Bass.

Crews, W. C., and J. R. Pierce. 1986. Public school systems and community colleges: A successful collaboration. *School Counselor* 34(1):32–34.

Cullen, C., and M. G. Moed. 1985. Serving high-risk adolescents. In *Insights from studies on collaboration*, ed. J. E. Lieberman, 37–49. Long Island City, N.Y.: La Guardia Community College.

Day, R., and K. Rajasekhara. 1988. Keeping America working: Profiles in partnership. Keeping America Working Series no. 4. ERIC Document no. ED 293 582. Washington, D.C.: American Association of Community and Junior Colleges.

DiCroce, D. M. 1989. Community college mission revisited: Three recent approaches. *Review of Higher Education* 12(2):177–80.

Friedlander, J. 1982. Working with the high schools to strengthen community college programs. *Community College Review* 10(1):9–17.

Greenberg, A. R. 1985. High school students in college courses: Three programs. In *Insights from studies on collaboration*, ed. J. E. Lieberman, 69–84. Long Island City, N.Y.: La Guardia Community College.

Kintzer, F. C. 1973. *Middleman in higher education*. San Francisco: Jossey-Bass.

———, ed. 1982. *Improving articulation and transfer relationships*. New Directions for Community Colleges, no. 39. San Francisco: Jossey-Bass.

———. 1989. *Articulation and transfer: A review of current literature on statewide and interinstitutional program models and trends*. ERIC Document no. ED 311 946. Trenton, N.J.: New Jersey Department of Higher Education.

Kintzer, F. C., and J. Wattenberger. 1985. *The articulation/transfer phenomenon: Patterns and directions*. Washington, D.C.: American Association of Community and Junior Colleges.

Kirkbride, E. B. 1985. Merging multiple systems: Process and problems. In *Insights from studies on collaboration*, ed. J. E. Lieberman, 101–11. Long Island City, N.Y.: La Guardia Community College.

Knoell, D. M. 1991. *Transfer, articulation, and collaboration: Twenty-five years later*. Washington, D.C.: American Association of Community and Junior Colleges.

Knoell, D. M., and L. L. Medsker. 1965. *From junior to senior college: A national study of the transfer student*. Washington, D.C.: American Council on Education.

Lerner, M. J. 1987. *Articulation manual: A guide for transfer of credit between educational institutions*. Washington, D.C.: National Association of Trade and Technical Schools.

Lieberman, J. E. 1985. *Insights from studies on collaboration*. ERIC Document no. ED 258 641. Long Island City, N.Y.: La Guardia Community College.

———. 1986. Middle College: A ten-year study. ERIC Document no. ED 271 153. Long Island City, N.Y.: La Guardia Community College.

Lieberman, J. E., ed. 1988. *Collaborating with high schools*. New Directions for Community Colleges no. 63. San Francisco: Jossey-Bass.

Lieberman, J. E., et al. 1989. A status report on the international high school at La Guardia Community College. ERIC Document no. ED 303 216. Long Island City, N.Y.: La Guardia Community College.

Mabry, T. 1989. The high school/community college connection: An ERIC Review. *Community College Review* 16(3):49–55.

Mamaras, J. 1990. 2 + 2 program guide: 2 + 2 tech-prep associate degree program. ERIC Document no. ED 317 251. Paper.

Miller, A. 1985. Servicemember opportunity college. *Community and Junior College Journal* 55(5):42–44.

National Advisory Council on Vocational Education. 1976. *Articulation: A study by the National Advisory Council on Vocational Education*. ERIC Document no. ED 133 434. Washington, D.C.

National Council for Occupational Education. 1989. *Occupational program articulation: A report of the study prepared by the Task Force on Occupational Program Articulation*. Monograph Series 12(1). Wausau, Wisc.

Naylor, M. 1987. Articulation between secondary and postsecondary schools, overview. ERIC Digest no. 64. ERIC Document no. ED 282 095.

Newman, F. 1985. Reconnecting youth: The new wave of reform. In *Insights from studies on collaboration*, ed. J. E. Lieberman, 5–12. Long Island City, N.Y.: La Guardia Community College.

Palmer, J. C. 1987. Bolstering the community college transfer function: An ERIC Review. *Community College Review* 14(3):53–63.

———. 1989. Articulation between degree programs. In *Problems faced by military personnel in pursuing higher education programs: A study with recommendations*, ed. J. C. Palmer et al. Pensacola, Fla.: Defense Activities for Nontraditional Education Services.

Parnell, D. 1985. *The neglected majority*. Washington, D.C.: Community College Press.

Payne, J. L. 1989. The high school/college interface: A new challenge for the community college. *Community College Review* 16(4):22–27.

Peterson, J. H. 1982. Community college and proprietary school relationships within the educational marketplace. In *Improving articulation and transfer relationships*, ed. F. C. Kintzer, 51–57. New Directions for Community Colleges, no. 39. San Francisco: Jossey-Bass.

Pew Higher Education Research Program. 1991. An end to sanctuary. *Policy Perspectives* 3(4):1–5.

Prager, C., ed. 1988. *Enhancing transfer and articulation*. New Directions for Community Colleges, no. 61. San Francisco: Jossey-Bass.

———. 1992. Articulation and transfer. Mitigating elitism from within. In *Prisoners of elitism: The community college's struggle for stature*, ed. B. W. Dziech and R. W. Vilter. New Directions for Community Colleges, no. 78. San Francisco: Jossey-Bass.

Pratt, L., and B. Karasik. 1984. SOCAD: Articulation that really works. *Community and Junior College Journal* 54(8):37–39.

Richardson, R. C., and L. W. Bender. 1985. *Students in urban settings: Achieving the baccalaureate degree*. ASHE-ERIC Higher Education Research Report no. 6. Washington, D.C.: Association for the Study of Higher Education.

———. 1986. *Helping minorities achieve degrees: The urban connection*. A report to the Ford Foundation. Tempe: Arizona State University.

Robertson-Smith, M. 1988. Accreditation and articulation of business programs. In *Enhancing transfer and articulation*, ed. C. Prager, 57–71. New Directions for Community Colleges, no. 61. San Francisco: Jossey-Bass.

———. 1990. *Articulation models for vocational education*. Columbus, Ohio: ERIC Clearinghouse on Adult, Career, and Vocational Education.

Roueche, J. E., and G. A. Baker. 1987. *Access and excellence: The open-door college*. Washington, D.C.: Community College Press.

Servicemembers Opportunity Colleges. 1989. Servicemembers Opportunity Colleges: Serving the voluntary higher education needs of the military services. Washington, D.C.

Stoel, C. F. 1985. History of the high school connection. In *Insights from studies on collaboration*, ed. J. E. Lieberman, 12–23. Long Island City, N.Y.: La Guardia Community College.

Thomas, G. 1988. Transfer relationships between two-year and four-year technological programs. In *Enhancing transfer and articulation*, ed. C. Prager, 49–55. New Directions for Community Colleges, no. 61. San Francisco: Jossey-Bass.

Vaughan, G. 1984. The community college at the watershed: Balancing open access and quality. *Change* 16(2):38–44.

Warden, D. 1985. We go where they go. *Community and Junior College Journal* 55(5):42–44.

Whitlock, B. W. 1978. *Don't hold them back: A critique and guide to new high school–college articulation models*. ERIC Document no. ED 147 414. New York: College Entrance Examination Board.

Willingham, W. W. 1972. *Transfer to the upper division*. Washington, D.C.: American Association of Higher Education.

Wilms, W. W. 1987. Proprietary schools: Strangers in their own land. *Change* 19:10–22.

Expanding Partnerships Between Community Colleges and Business/Industry as a Tool for Economic Development

Tony Zeiss

Scarcely anyone involved with America's community colleges or America's businesses today would deny the obvious benefits of integrating education with business. In fact, both educators and business executives appear to be seeking partnerships with each other more often than ever. Community college representatives, from the governing board chair to the technical instructor, seem to recognize that the needs of business and industry present special opportunities for their colleges and their programs. Business owners, managers, and human resource officers clearly recognize that training services from community colleges are a vital part of their effort to compete in an increasingly competitive marketplace. In the face of declining resources, colleges are turning toward companies in search of new resources, potential allies, and new enrollments (Gold 1981, 10). For the same reason, businesses are looking toward educational institutions in search of research, training, and ultimately increased profits. This synergistic relationship of community colleges and business and industry began with the origin of the community-junior college concept but has greatly accelerated during the past decade. This practical and cooperative union between education and business has established a compelling sense of renewed purpose among community colleges and is creating a landscape of shared opportunities and values among educators and business persons alike.

INTERNATIONAL MARKETPLACE DEMANDS

As the United States shifts its foreign and domestic attentions toward competing in the international marketplace, education-business integration will become especially important. Our preoccupation with political ideologies and their defense will transcend to increasing concern about our standard of living and overall economic health. Eventually, we will export our education and training expertise to "most favored nations" to help ensure their economic vitality as well. In the meantime, however, it is painfully clear that America's businesses and industries must become more competitive worldwide. Frankly, Americans are faced with a clear challenge—if we want to live well, we must produce well; if we want to produce well, we must educate well. Indeed, all sectors of our society seem to acknowledge the need for a seamless relationship between education and business supported fully by all levels of government. The motivation behind this flurry of national activity is the recognition that people and their abilities to produce are what ultimately drives our economy, not corporate structures and not government.

Our ability to empower all of our people with the knowledge and skills to be productive is what we must be about. As we proceed in this last decade of the twentieth century, human development, the most important need of our society, will rise to the top of our national agenda. There is a clear and ever present danger that we might ignore this challenge. To do so would be to guarantee a reduced standard of living and the development of a large underclass population with little or no middle class and an elite upper class. Parnell outlines this problem by explaining that "two converging forces, a skilled worker shortage and the development of a permanent under class, are bearing down upon the United States" (1990, 103). Parnell continues to explain that a major challenge for the 1990s will be to solve this problem by engaging our colleges and universities to the fullest.

Perhaps no report outlines our current need to develop a more educated population and a more skilled competitive work force than *America's Choice: High Skills or Low Wages*. This report, produced in 1990 by the National Center on Education and the Economy, succinctly outlines the problem of maintaining our standard of living in the increasingly competitive global arena. More important, it defines five major challenges and provides practical recommendations for meeting each. The report concludes that America is headed toward an economic cliff, and we will no longer be able to generate economic growth because the education and training levels of our people are non-competitive. Clearly, the time has come for the business, education, and governmental communities in this country to work together if we hope to solve this most recent and potentially most dangerous American challenge.

It is obvious that community colleges must develop and provide the programs and services to assist business and industry with the competitive demands of the world marketplace. The literature reveals that most community colleges are involved with the business sector, but the degree of involvement is dependent upon a variety of circumstances. Institutional priorities of the governing board and the president, local economic conditions, and the availability of state subsidies for economic development activities all contribute to the extent of a college's involvement in this arena. Nevertheless, the literature indicates that service to business clients has been widely accepted as a part of the community college mission (Palmer 1990, 44–46). Historically, the vocational education sector of community colleges has always been based upon cooperation and integration with business. There is some convincing evidence that the first colleges in history were established to develop learned workers. It was a century ago that American industrialists influenced and assisted in the establishment of Johns Hopkins and Cornell to provide studies in business vocations (Tate 1981). Unfortunately, the relationship between business corporations and higher education began to shift from one of curricula integration to one of financial support. It has been observed that budget problems and the related threat to educational quality should cause corporations to continue to support higher education institutions. At the same time, however, colleges should recognize that "corporations, unlike foundations, are not created for the purpose of making contributions to education. . . . They exist primarily to produce goods and services . . . to earn profits" (Smith 1984, 11).

Community colleges are uniquely suited, both by mission and by geographic location, to contribute significantly to America's ability to compete worldwide. The literature demonstrates that local initiatives to assist business and industry have been eminently successful and that the business and government communities are recognizing community colleges as the strong suit in economic development.

COMMUNITY COLLEGES' OPPORTUNITY

The time is ripe for community colleges to get deeply involved in the economic development activities of the communities they serve. The governors of the United States and her commonwealths have developed a strategic plan for stimulating our economic competitiveness. This plan, called Excellence at Work, which was developed through the National Governor's Association (*Business Week* 1991), calls for four major initiatives: (1) redesigning structures in the workplace to encourage specialization, flexibility, and greater employee involvement; (2) training and retraining the existing work force to keep pace with rapid technological changes; (3) providing new workers with the education and job skills needed to adapt to changing marketplace requirements; and (4) giving employees the support they need to manage the challenges of both work and family life.

It should be noted that community colleges in particular are well suited to help the United States meet each of these goals. The nation's 1,250 two-year colleges have the geographic advantage and the ability to be pro-active in meeting these goals in a timely manner. In effect, community colleges have a marvelous opportunity to emerge as the nation's most significant contributor to human and business development. Through the help of two-year colleges, our country and her people will be able to compete with and outproduce other countries. It would be tragic if community colleges missed this opportunity to increase their stature and identity among people, the business community, and the government.

Obviously there is a risk involved for colleges that become aggressive leaders in local economic development activities. Failure in this highly visible arena could cause long-term damage to the reputation of the college. However, to avoid getting involved with this major American challenge could be even more damaging. Hundreds of community colleges have been involved in a variety of economic development activities and are reaping wonderful benefits in reputation, financial support, enrollments, equipment, and even buildings. Many other colleges are just beginning to become pro-active in meeting their own community's economic needs. In any case, the momentum appears to be gaining throughout the country, and the community college movement is becoming more visible and more powerful every day.

Most community colleges use the expertise of scores of business and industry professionals to serve as program advisors to ensure instructional validity and integrity. In many respects, this direct integration of business with vocational training has been the secret to the success of community colleges across the nation. The relationships that develop between the training programs and their respective industry or business often involve financial support, scholarships, equipment gifts, and other assistance provided to the college beyond curricula advice. In turn, the associated businesses or industries have an available source of well-trained employees with the specific skills needed by their companies. In many cases, these companies begin to depend upon the college in a broader fashion. Worker upgrade training in both academic and technical skills has become a major demand in recent years, for instance. In some respects, it is difficult to separate the community college mission from the needs of business and industry today. Community colleges, apart from other forms of higher education, seem to recognize that their educational services must not exist in a vacuum. With the ever-increasing demands of corporate America and the applied missions of community colleges, it appears safe to assume that this country's two-year colleges will be developing even stronger ties with the business community.

Direct services to business and industry by community colleges are expanding in many ways. Apart from the traditional integration with business in the design of curriculum, today's colleges are involved with business creation, business expansion, business recruitment, and business retention. Indeed, federally financed Small Business Development Centers have surfaced among community colleges all across the country to assist emerging and existing business owners. Many colleges are heavily involved in workplace training which includes academic, technical, and even basic literacy education. More aggressive colleges also provide customized assessments to assist businesses with their employment activities and provide management training to assist with employee retention. Other colleges also provide government procurement training, import-export training, and compliance training for governmental regulations such as those required by the Occupational Safety and Health Administration. A synthesis of the literature testifies to the broad scale and remarkably successful economic development of business-related initiatives that are occurring at community colleges throughout America today.

SYNTHESIS OF THE LITERATURE

Much has been written about the general topic of education-business integration, especially within the past decade. As the economy of the United States evolved into a long-term recession and as the international marketplace thrust us into a McLuhan-like "global village," it became evident that the whole issue of a healthy economy is dependent upon our ability to develop the potential of our citizens. Businesspersons, governmental officials, and educators have come to recognize the fundamental importance of human development. It is equally clear, especially with community-based colleges, that their human development services and instructional programs must be need driven.

Need-Driven Services

Recent literature on this topic indicates that a large number of the country's two-year colleges and technical schools are client focused and pro-active. Local needs and conditions, both internal and external to the college or school, are driving educational services. This integrated approach is uncharacteristic of the more typical historical academic view which held that education should give people "what they need." Business people, on the other hand, expect education to give them "what they want." It is now recognized that a collaboration of business and education leaders can help society to reach its highest potential and accomplish the greatest good (American Association of State Colleges and Universities 1987, xi).

Gathering a composite national picture of community college services to business and industry is difficult. The literature, although abundant, is based primarily upon case studies or successful local models (Palmer 1990, 43). To categorize the collective business services of community colleges is further compounded because of terminology. One college will use the term "economic development" inclusively while the next college will divide its services into "business recruitment," "business partnerships," or "customized training services." In any event, the researcher will inevitably discover that all business services provided by community colleges are need driven and usually prepared in a manner specified by the company being served. In effect, it appears that community colleges are seizing the opportunity to evolve as America's most probusiness, community-centered educational institutions.

Numerous books, reports, and monographs that feature some very successful models of community college services to business have been produced within just the past five years. Most of these publications are descriptive and easy to read. A brief review of the titles of these publications indicates that community colleges are leading the way in (1) small business development, (2) customized assessment, (3) customized training, (4) employee retention training, and (5) workplace literacy training. In addition to these business services, many colleges have become directly involved with the industrial recruitment activities of the communities they serve. Those colleges that have become involved with the recruitment of jobs for their communities have, in effect, evolved into truly community-based institutions. Instead of simply supplying trained workers for employers, they also help to create and attract jobs for their students. This trend to become more focused on the needs of employers and more concerned with the needs of the communities served may signal a permanent and comprehensive integration of business and community into the mission of all community colleges in the country.

Models of Effective Initiatives

The recognition that American education should become more responsive to the needs of business led to the development of the Business-Education Forum, an affiliation of the American Council on Education. This forum, founded in 1978, published a report which outlined an action agenda to revitalize the American economy (Smith 1984, 3–4). Although this report focused primarily upon the contributions universities should make, the appeal to become lifelong partners with business and industry applies as well to community colleges. Other entities, such as the National Center for Research in Vocational Education, then located at Ohio State University, produced applied research and provided examples of how to deliver the services alluded to in action agendas such as that outlined by the Business-Education Forum. In the National Center's 1981 publication titled, "Sharing Resources: Postsecondary Education and Industry Cooperation," 219 exemplary business-related services programs are presented. Each of these programs is presented in a standardized format designed for easy replication (Warmbrod et al., 1981). It is curious to note that use of the research descriptor "education-business partnerships" before 1985 would produce a sizable number of university-based partnerships with industry. In fact, entire directories were often published to demonstrate what was then occurring in the way of education-based partnerships. For example, one directory, published in 1983, featured business partnerships by over 200 higher education institutions, and less than 15 percent were community colleges (Fenwick 1983, 166–68). Since 1985, most of the literature produced by this descriptor features community and technical colleges. It is not surprising that partnerships between business and education have increased. Handbooks and government reports (i.e., "Nation at Risk," published in 1983 by the National Commission on Excellence in Education, and the National Center on Education and the Economy 1990 *America's Choice: High Skills or Low Wages*) have helped to draw the attention of both educators and business people to the utility of such partnerships. Education has become everybody's business, and, as a result, partnerships have multiplied since the report, "Beyond Business Education Partnerships: The Business Expense" was published (Lund 1988, 4). Since the early 1980s, the American Association of

Community and Junior Colleges (AACJC) has encouraged the publication of its member colleges' contributions to the business sector as a means to enhance both the image and the quality of services of community colleges. In fact, this association has published several notable works on economic development in the broad sense with a particular emphasis on exemplary partnerships with the business community. Among these are *Doing Business with Business: A Handbook for Colleges Planning to Serve Commerce and Industry* (Hamm et al., 1988); *Community Colleges and Economic Development: Models of Institutional Effectiveness* (Katsinas 1989); *A Portfolio of Community College Initiatives in Rural Economic Development* (Thomas 1989); *Economic Development: A Viewpoint From Business* (Zeiss 1989); and *Creating a Literate Society: College, Business, Community Partnerships* (Zeiss 1991).

Of course, hundreds of journal articles, reports, and other publications have been published about the growing partnerships among community colleges and businesses. A summary overview of the literature reveals some common themes which characterize a majority of these exemplary initiatives. Although most community college–business partnerships are teaching focused, some colleges do engage in applied research, especially in communities where university research capabilities are not available. Midland College, for example, assisted the communities of Midland, Texas, and Big Spring, Texas, in researching current business and customer trends to promote business growth within these existing communities (McCarty 1990, 2). It is projected that direct product or processes research will probably remain with research universities, but community colleges have become important resources for the collection and analysis of specific business-related needs and for general data collection and synthesis for local economic development planning (Katsinas 1988, 29). Furthermore, an increasing number of community colleges are becoming directly involved in industrial recruitment, employee retention, and small business development. The respective opportunities for community colleges are limited only by the needs of their service area communities and by their ability to be imaginative and pro-active in this broad arena.

The following basic characteristics are most common among those community colleges that are deeply involved with their community's businesses. These colleges (1) are client centered, (2) customize their curriculum and provide flexible delivery systems, and (3) provide diverse services. It is presumed that they also have the full support of their board and their president in their business partnerships.

Client-Centered Services

Virtually every community, junior, or technical college that is successful has recognized the value in being a client- or student-centered organization. Those institutions that have become successful in the economic development business have simply used this same client-focused philosophy in the development of partnerships with business and industry. In effect, successful colleges embrace a vendor-of-services attitude that places the needs of their clients, whether students or businesses, as their top priority. All instructional programs and service-related activities then become need based and need driven.

A sterling example of this client-centered attitude was exhibited by Pueblo Community College in Pueblo, Colorado, and its involvement with the Mc-Donnell-Douglas Corporation. In 1987–1988, this college was provided the challenge of developing a work force for a new McDonnell-Douglas assembly plant. The plant would assembly the Delta II rockets which would become the nation's primary satellite delivery system. The college had two immediate tasks: (1) how to select the best possible workers and (2) how to provide the best possible training for those workers. After a great deal of planning with the company's human resource people, the college researched all available assessment systems and elected to use a commercially produced, criterion-referenced, computer-based system together with a locally designed structured interview. The results of this client-based prescreening system were so successful that the McDonnell-Douglas Corporation adopted the system for the whole corporation (Moorman and Zeiss 1990, 73–78).

Gulf Coast Community College, in Panama City, Florida, illustrated this client-centered disposition in its relationship with a five-state area chain of convenience stores and supermarkets. This partnership evolved from the need for Sunshine-Jr. Stores, Inc., to reduce employee turnover. The costs associated with employee turnover are tremendous and especially so in the service industry. Gulf Coast Community College, with the help of a Sunshine State Skills Grant (Florida), worked closely with company officials to research the factors that were contributing to the attrition problem and to develop and implement an action plan to correct the problem. This research-based project eventually caused a restructuring of the company's organization and the implementation of some very successful training activities. Employee turnover for the company was reduced by 26 percent, which is 39 percent below the average for the convenience store industry (Cardenas et al., 1989, 89–96). Massachusetts Bay Community College in Wellesley, Massachusetts, demonstrated its ability to be client centered by developing a model English-as-a-second-language (ESL) program for a large food distribution center. The Filen Natick Distribution Center was experiencing an increasing number of non-English speaking workers; this problem was compounded by the differences among three distinct cultures represented by those workers. By working with the company and its workers' union, Massachusetts Bay Community College was able to produce some impressive results in this complex situation. Its success was attributed to the fact that the training tasks were primarily job related (Luoto 1991, 45–51).

Literally thousands of client-centered college-business partnership success stories are available in the literature. Some intriguing examples demonstrate a broader focused approach. For instance, many community colleges, like Lake Michigan College at Benton Harbor, Michigan, and Godsden State Community

College in Godsden, Alabama, have established business-related centers to assist with their service area's entire economic development efforts (Katsinas 1989, 26–30, 33–50). The workplace literacy program conducted by the Colorado State Board for Community Colleges and Occupational Education, one example of a statewide effort, represents a program that serves the entire state with literacy training at the work site. Other colleges, like Miami-Dade Community College in Miami, Florida, have entered the international arena by serving the training needs of firms and nations beyond the borders of the continental United States (Katsinas 1989, 50).

Without exception, all successful college-business partnerships and successful college economic development efforts exhibit a strong client-centered, need-driven philosophy. Community, junior, and technical colleges are embracing this basic posture when developing and delivering services to both campus-based students and corporate employees.

Customized Curriculum and Flexible Delivery

The community colleges that develop successful partnerships with business and industry inevitably design industrial training programs tailored to the specific needs of their corporate partner. Further, they are prepared to deliver the training according to the wishes of the company. Most community colleges seem willing to provide training at the workplace and during the hours convenient to the employer and employees. It is also noted that the colleges that are consistently successful in providing training for business and industry have recognized the difference between comprehensive occupational education and industry-specific training. Colleges are designed to provide a formalized educational experience, whereas in-plant training should be considered as a short-term activity to improve worker productivity. The college experience includes training but also provides the larger human skills such as problem solving, communication, human relations, and the associated theoretical bases involved (Hamm et al., 1988, 81). Astute college trainers recognize industries' short-term interests in productivity and, over time, persuade company officials to broaden their perspectives to allow the college to develop and deliver a more comprehensive training package to company employees. In most instances, the company that recognizes the success of one training activity will be eager to identify additional training or educational needs which the college partner might satisfy. This growing relationship provides an excellent opportunity for the college to begin developing a more comprehensive and planned educational experience for the company's employees. In this manner, theoretical, analytical, and communications skills will eventually be added to the employees' technical skills, thereby providing the company with a fully educated and more productive work force. This more "generic" conceptualization and delivery of technical-vocational skills should be acknowledged for its importance in providing long-term solutions to worker skills deficiencies (Powers et al., 1988, 43–44).

In fact, in-plant spot training may well provide the vehicle needed for higher education to reach the workers of America and provide the academic, general, and technical skills necessary for successful international competition. Many workers are too busy working or are not inclined to upgrade their education and training of their own volition. Further, most plant managers are concerned with the immediate rather than long-term needs of their workers. However, there is good evidence that American employers are becoming increasingly interested in the overall basic academic skills of their workers (Nuventures Consultants, Inc., 1990, 37–42). The flexible, client-centered nature of community colleges provides an opportunity to make Americans even more productive through comprehensive, lifelong training.

Front Range Community College, located in Westminster, Colorado, has been using its ability to provide customized training with a flexible delivery system to aid many companies in a comprehensive fashion. To do this, the college employs two primary working principles:

1. Partner with the organization to identify and address factors that may impair the ability of the organization to manage change, whether or not these factors are typically regarded as training activities. This component of training delivery is generally referred to as organizational development.

2. Partner with the organization to emphasize training applications that will strengthen the company's capacity for self-management and independent conduct of training (Burns et al. 1989, 79).

Two specific companies, Oceanarium Products and Design, Inc., and Hunter Douglas, Inc., were featured in a recent publication as examples of how a college could provide comprehensive educational services to business and industry (Burns et al. 1989, 79–87).

Community, technical, and junior colleges throughout the country are providing customized training services in various degrees of complexity across the continuum from "spot training" to "generic or comprehensive training." California's community colleges are seen as a $2.5 billion resource to public and private sector business, and their legislature supports the importance of contract training with business (Ramirez 1989, 1, 4). Community colleges in Illinois see their missions in the same flexible, probusiness manner. They are engaged in creating "partnerships with commerce and industry including community college business centers, customized job training, enterpreneurship instruction and consulting services, industrial retention and attraction activities, contract procurement assistance, technology transfer, labor/management councils, and small business incubators" (Illinois Community College Board 1989, 1).

In all cases reviewed in the literature, the willingness to provide customized training, however comprehensive, through a flexible delivery system was a common theme of community colleges with industrial partnerships. The ability to determine the needs of a company and to design and deliver training to meet those needs is an essential element of successful college-business partnerships.

Diverse Services

A third common theme among successful college-business partnerships is the ability of the college to provide a wide diversity of services. Essentially, these colleges are willing to create programs and services to meet the ever-changing needs of the businesses and industries they serve. Further, most, if not all, of these services are directed toward jobs and productivity. Virtually all of these partnership-related activities fall within one of four basic economic development activities: (1) job attraction, (2) job creation, (3) job expansion, and (4) job retention.

Many colleges have elected to get directly involved with industrial recruitment. Their presidents are generally members of the local economic development entity, participate in an ongoing strategic planning process, and are members of the job recruitment team. In addition, most of America's community, junior, and technical colleges recognized the need to assist small businesses during the 1980s. Indeed, the federal government, via the Small Business Administration, initiated funding for a national network of small business development centers in 1980. Because of their probusiness attitude and broad geographic locations, two-year colleges were especially well positioned to establish these centers on their campuses. Today, the community colleges' small business development centers are extremely active in job creation, expansion, and retention. These centers provide one-on-one assistance to aspiring entrepreneurs by helping them develop business plans, secure loans, and generally develop their business.

Certainly, the customized assessment and training services offered to business by community colleges impact all four of these fundamental job-related areas. Lorain County Community College, in Elyria, Ohio, for example, has developed a state-of-the-art Advanced Technology Center and has established an industrial park on campus to help attract and support business. Des Moines Area Community College, in Des Moines, Iowa, helped attract and then trained 900 workers for Greyhound Lines, Inc. (Hamm et al., 1988, 121–22). The College of Lake County, in Grayslake, Illinois, initiated a center for economic development in 1982 and now provides a variety of services to approximately 450 different businesses each year. Most notable is its government contract procurement assistance to local businesses. This program helped local businesses to win over $9 million in federal contracts during 1987 (Hamm et al., 1988, 123–24). Pueblo Community College, in Pueblo, Colorado, is credited with attracting a 750-job American Express telemarketing firm to its community by designing a unique assessment and training program that reduced annual employee attrition rates from up to 300 percent to below 10 percent (Zeiss 1990, 37). Guilford Technical Community College, in Jamestown, North Carolina, has been lauded for its customized training services which helped attract and prepare 2,000 workers for an American Express Regional Operations Center (Hamm et al., 1988, 125–26). Clearly, the diversity of services and the ability to create new services to meet new business needs have propelled our two-year colleges into a most important asset for our communities and their businesses.

CONCLUSIONS AND FUTURE DIRECTIONS

Community, technical, and junior colleges represent the mainstream of human development for America's business community. Clearly, the community college movement has caught the attention of business, government, and the people of this country. In many respects, these colleges have created their own destiny— a destiny to be the foundation of America's work force and her ability to compete internationally. In other respects, the maturation of this country and the shift of other countries to a free market economy have demanded a practical, business-focused educational system which community and technical colleges were best suited to meet. In any event, the demand to integrate education and business is driving curricula and educational delivery systems like never before. Both the business community and two-year colleges recognize the utility, if not the necessity, of business-education partnerships. Ed Primozic, an IBM executive, observes that business leaders are calling for a shared vision with educators. Educators, he maintains, must view business, government, and their communities as customers just as they view students as customers (Primozic et al., 1991).

New Markets for Community Colleges

Community, junior, and technical colleges across the nation are recognizing the benefits of working directly with corporate America. As our economic base shifts from manufacturing to information and services, the demand for more highly skilled and lifelong-educated workers is increasing. In effect, we are moving into the age of human development. This situation presents myriad opportunities for community colleges. The benefits of education for workers, their companies, and their communities are apparent. But the direct benefits to the colleges that provide the instruction are often overlooked by the uninitiated. Many colleges are realizing substantial budgetary support through contracted services with industry, through state student reimbursements, through direct company donations, and through a host of other state and federal support programs. Some colleges track their increased local and state general fund support to their business and industry activities. Many colleges have developed sophisticated advanced technology centers which are fully supported by the industries they serve. Indeed, equipment and even buildings are being provided to colleges by the private sector (Chrestman 1991, 35).

Aside from the direct financial benefit of education-business partnerships, the rewards of an enhanced institutional image cannot be overlooked. A college's image affects its very being. Student enrollments, community support, and internal morale are all influenced by the way in which a college is perceived.

Those colleges that have already become closely linked with business and industry attest to the value of being seen as community-based and pro-active institutions.

Where are the new markets for two-year colleges? All around us! America's businesses, large and small, are desperately seeking well-trained workers. Sweeping changes in the economic systems of foreign countries present new international markets for education, and the new international trade pacts will begin to present additional opportunities for colleges. The Soviet Union, for example, has recently been sending technical educators to the United States to learn about our technology training and our adult education programs. The concept of lifelong education, as well as the free market system, is completely alien to them. Japan, Mexico, and China also regularly send education delegations to study our two-year colleges firsthand. Here at home we need to assist with the development of more multinational companies to increase our collective ability to compete internationally. As Phil Burgess, president of the Center for New West, recently stated, "We're on the edge of a major global expansion and there is a tremendous role for community colleges to help get small and medium sized businesses involved in international trade." Further, two-year colleges must stay abreast of changing markets and be pro-active with their educational services. For instance, our number one export industry today is tourism, which recently surpassed agriculture (Burgess 1991). In short, no other American higher education system is better positioned to find new business clients and new markets for their services.

Future Directions

The entrepreneurial spirit appears to be very much alive and well as evidenced through business–higher education partnerships. During this time of economic change and stress, a commendable effort is being made in this area (Powers et al., 1988, 237). Based upon this review of the literature regarding education-business partnerships, the die is cast. Community colleges seem to have created a renewed sense of purpose, a purpose that includes the needs of business, as well as the more traditional needs of students. In fact, the expectations of the communities and businesses we serve will cause two-year colleges to reexamine their mission and adopt a broader, more flexible vision. The modern community college will integrate fully with its sister educational entities, its community, and the businesses of that community.

A recent Colorado business services report summarizes this trend: "The boundaries between the techniques for training the traditional student and a specific group of employees at a workplace may dissolve. Community colleges will begin to see their instructional roles as a continuum, with the traditional student on one end, and the business clients who contract for training their employees on the other" (Kantor 1991, 16).

For decades, community colleges have been the avenue of entry for individuals, irrespective of age or preparation, to pick up their lives and move forward.

In the future, more and more people will take this course. It is predicted that more retired people will return to the work force and to college. In addition, retraining will become necessary for existing workers. To meet these changing needs, community colleges will have to redefine their role as one that provides access to local businesses (Ramirez 1989, iii).

REFERENCES

American Association of State Colleges and Universities. 1987. *The higher education–economic development connection: Emerging roles for public colleges and universities in a changing economy.* Washington, D.C.

Burgess, P. 1991. Keynote address, International Trade Conference, 12 November, Pueblo Community College, Pueblo, Colorado.

Burns, M., et al. 1989. Expanding a business: Oceanarium products and design and Hunter Douglas, Inc. In *Economic development: A viewpoint from business*, ed. T. Zeiss, 79–87. Washington, D.C.: American Association of Community and Junior Colleges.

Cardenas, M. G., et al. 1989. Effective expansion through reduced turnover of employees. In *Economic development: A viewpoint from business*, ed. T. Zeiss, 89–96. Washington, D.C.: American Association of Community Junior Colleges.

Chrestman, C. 1991. ATC's partners for economic and community development. *Community, Technical, and Junior College Journal* 62 (2):35.

Fenwick, D. C. 1983. *Directory of campus-business linkages: Education and business prospering together.* New York: American Council on Education/Macmillan.

Gold, G. G. 1981. *Business and higher education: Toward new alliances.* San Francisco: Jossey-Bass.

Hamm, R., et al. 1988. *Doing business with business: A handbook for colleges planning to serve commerce and industry.* Washington, D.C.: American Association of Community and Junior Colleges.

Illinois Community College Board. 1989. *Preparation for employment: Programs at Illinois public colleges.* ERIC Document no. ED 305 971.

Kantor, S. L. 1991. Direct services to business delivered by Colorado community colleges. Ph.D. diss., University of Denver.

Katsinas, S. G. 1988. Towards a new perspective on community college involvement in economic development. *Community College Journal for Research and Planning* 6(1&2):29.

———. 1989. *Community colleges and economic development: Models of institutional effectiveness.* Washington, D.C.: American Association of Community and Junior Colleges.

Lund, L. 1988. *Beyond business/education partnerships: The business experience.* Conference Board Research Report no. 918. New York: The Conference Board, Inc.

Luoto, G. 1991. Filene's workplace education project. In *Creating a literate society*, ed. T. Zeiss, 45–51. Washington, D.C.: American Association of Community and Junior Colleges.

McCarty, N. M. 1990. *Big Spring and Midland business retention and expansion survey.* ERIC Document no. ED 322 959.

Moorman, J. W., and T. Zeiss. 1990. Expanding a business through successful employee selection. In *Economic development: A viewpoint from business*, ed. T. Zeiss, 73–78. Washington, D.C.: American Association of Community and Junior Colleges.

National Center on Education and the Economy. 1990. *America's choice: High skills or low wages*. Rochester, N.Y.

National Commission on Excellence in Education. 1983. *A nation at risk*. Washington, D.C.

National governor's association: Excellence at work. *Business Week*. 28 January 1991: 77–78.

Nuventures Consultants, Inc. 1990. *America's changing workforce*. La Jolla, Calif.

Palmer, J. 1990. *How do community colleges serve business and industry?* ERIC Document no. ED 319 443.

Parnell, D. 1990. *Dateline 2000*. Washington, D.C.: American Association of Community and Junior Colleges.

Powers, D. R., et al. 1988. *Higher education in partnership with industry*. San Francisco: Jossey-Bass.

Primozic, E., et al. 1991. *Strategic choices: Supremacy, survival, or sayonara*. New York: McGraw-Hill.

Ramirez, K. M. 1989. *Economic development and the role of community colleges: Contract education in review*. ERIC Document no. ED 326 277.

Smith, R. B. 1984. *Corporate and campus cooperation: An action agenda*. Washington, D.C.: Business-Education Forum, American Council on Education.

Tate, P. J., ed. 1981. *Business and higher education: Toward new alliances*. New Directions for Experiential Learning, no. 14. San Francisco: Jossey-Bass.

Thomas, M .G., ed. 1989. *A portfolio of community college initiatives in rural economic development*. Washington, D.C.: American Association of Community and Junior Colleges.

Warmbrod, C. P., et al. 1981. *Sharing resources: Postsecondary education and industry cooperation*. Columbus, Ohio: National Center for Research in Vocational Education.

Wells, D. J. 1991. Managing technology: A vision for the 22nd century. *Community, Technical, and Junior College Journal* 62(2):51.

Zeiss, T., ed. 1989. *Economic development: A viewpoint from business*. Washington D.C.: American Association of Community and Junior Colleges.

———. 1990. Employee retention. *Community, Technical, and Junior College Journal* 60(4):37.

———. 1991. *Creating a literate society: College, business, community partnerships*. Washington, D.C.: American Association of Community and Junior Colleges.

Enhancing the Image of the Community College Through Public Relations

Charlotte A. Biggerstaff

Few American institutions have allowed the development of an image that is as multifaceted and paradoxical as that of the community college. A uniquely American product, the two-year institution has been both applauded and maligned. While advocates praise its diversity, social commitment, and innovation, detractors criticize it as second class, fragmented, and lacking in quality.

Despite this broad range of opinion, what really counts is how the institution is perceived by its various constituencies. Sadly, the community college for the most part is still not seen as a "real college." Savage noted that some twenty years after a community college opened in his hometown, high school seniors still taunt one another with remarks like, "If you can't go to college, go to Lakeland" (1989, 3). Clearly, for a large segment of the college-going public, educational quality is directly related to institutional selectivity.

Given this sentiment, one of the most pressing problems facing community colleges nationwide is how to alter such a misguided, deeply rooted perception. As college costs escalate, enrollment caps become more commmonplace, and students demand more for their money, consumers will increasingly expect their community colleges to satisfy a host of educational needs. In preparation, community colleges must begin to act in their own best interests. They can no longer be satisfied with an image that conveys lesser quality. In a competitive environment, large numbers of students who feel they have "settled for less" need to be convinced otherwise. Community colleges must begin to foster and nurture an image that makes sense if they are to command attention and ultimately change perceptions.

So, just what kind of image is appropriate for an institution that is reaching maturity? Generalizing from a study of two-year institutions in New York, Townsend (1986) concluded that the image most community colleges prefer is still that of "comprehensiveness." Such an image implies a broad range of programming and services, an academic orientation, and a strong sense of responsibility to the local community. Few community colleges would argue that this does not describe their overall mission. However, many have failed to convey this comprehensive image and have become disheartened at their continued second-class status. Perceptions are, after all, very slow to change.

If community colleges wish to enhance their image on the national as well as the local front, they must become actively engaged in shaping public opinion. If they are to insist that they are "comprehensive," they must infuse the term with appropriate, positive symbolism. If they want to be perceived as a significant source of quality learning experiences, they must accent student success and achievement. And finally, if they are to achieve a consistent, positive image of themselves, they must identify and continually address their goals, foster ownership among internal constituencies, and communicate their message to all relevant publics.

How can an effective public relations program help? First, it is important to understand two fundamentals: (1) Identifying institutional purpose and goals is basic to the development of image and (2) it is only through accurate *communication* that this identified message creates meaning for others. Communication theory asserts that for meaning to be conveyed, there must be a sender, a receiver, a message, and a means of transmission (Cutlip, Center, and Broom 1985). If any of these elements is missing, full and effective communication cannot occur. Furthermore, to the degree that external factors impinge upon the communication flow, any message may be altered. Thus, as the primary "means of transmission," an effective public relations effort involves the review, organization, and interpretation of messages as they flow back and forth between a college and the community. Clearly, this kind of transmission process is *central* to the creation and maintenance of a meaningful, consistent institutional image.

THE IMPORTANCE OF A CONSISTENT IMAGE

As community colleges find themselves competing with a growing number of special interest groups for scarce resources, there is much to be said for building a solid national image. According to Alfred and Weissman, institutional "stature" often develops on a "macro" as well as "micro" level through a process of association, such that "the gains established by one institution or set of institutions [become] those of another" (1987, 1). Similarly, the Commission on the Future of Community Colleges noted that "community colleges and the nation's future are inextricably interlocked" (Commission on the Future of Community Colleges, 1988, 49). Clearly, collaboration rather than competition is the means to effective change on the national front. Only then can the visions, energies, and experiences of all these institutions come together to create a perspective of the community college that transcends the image of any single institution.

According to Parnell (1986), the national community college image depends upon how well these institutions develop initiatives to deal with environmental change. Parnell reported that the American Association of Community and Junior Colleges (AACJC) has developed a policy that focuses on improving the national image by (1) ensuring that the associate degree implies quality, (2) forging links between high schools and community colleges that raise the level of technical preparation, (3) developing partnerships that benefit both education and business and industry, and (4) building public understanding by attracting national media attention. This kind of effective promotion is essential to improving perceptions of the role and scope of community colleges across the country.

Such an effort must be successful at the local level as well. It is impossible to overstate the importance of a strong base of community support. However, often, the more a college attempts to relate to the needs of its various constituencies, the more fragmented its image becomes. Community colleges that succeed in a highly competitive marketplace work diligently to ensure that their "comprehensive" nature is perceived as an asset rather than a liability (Harper 1982; Savage 1987). At the same time, successful institutions also position themselves for "distinction" by capitalizing on their uniqueness (Bryant 1982). An effective public relations program can bring these two seemingly dissonant goals into harmony.

THE VALUE OF PUBLIC RELATIONS IN MARKETING AND IMAGE BUILDING

Increasingly, community colleges have turned to educational marketing to help them better manage their enrollments. In so doing, they have become more aware of how accurately their image advances the values and vision of their institutions. Kotler and Fox have defined educational marketing as the "effective management by an institution of its exchange relations with its various markets and publics" (1985, xiii). This implies that marketing-oriented institutions scan the environment for emerging opportunities, identify various constituencies, develop goals and strategies to satisfy the needs of different publics, deliver products and services of appropriate quality, evaluate their efforts, and revise their marketing program as needed.

However, as many institutions have discovered, unless there is a planned program that calls attention to college offerings and successes, many opportunities go unbidden and achievements pass unnoticed. Harper (1982) noted that being "good and valuable" is simply not enough. Public relations efforts must tailor messages to specific segments of the population and identify appropriate channels for relaying them (Bryant 1982; Trent 1981). In so doing, the college conveys an enduring image of caring and concern for the individual.

Effective image builders play a major role in shaping public opinion. But it takes constant effort to analyze needs, interpret services accurately, and monitor perceptions. If a community college is to develop an image of integrity, consistency, and reliability, the public relations effort must nurture support by marketing "reality" rather than "ideality" (Topor 1986; Trent 1981). Ciervo put it well: "Credibility is to an institution what morality is to the individual" (1986, 122). In short, the better informed the public is about what its college actually stands for, the more likely it is to see the institution as reputationally sound. Therefore, an effective public relations program not only strives to communicate vision and commitment through image, but also does whatever it can to foster a dynamic interdependence between the institution and its environment.

CRITICAL ISSUES IN COMMUNITY COLLEGE IMAGE BUILDING

With the public demanding accountability and demonstrated effectiveness from its nonprofit institutions, community colleges are in a strong position to gather favor. As Keener, Ryan, and Smith (1991) have noted, few educational institutions are so well situated geographically—directly in the center of their marketplace. The need to build a consistent and positive image takes on added significance when the clientele is the immediate neighborhood. Along the way to achieving this desired image, however, community colleges often encounter a host of challenges to their intent—challenges that *must* be addressed from a clear understanding of institutional purpose, vision, and value. At each critical juncture, successful institutions are turning more and more to public relations to enhance their image while maintaining integrity.

Image management is essential to continued institutional success through time. Whether the goal is creating, maintaining, or restoring an image, a strategic public relations program can help ensure that the following key advancement issues are addressed: (1) alignment of external and internal perceptions, (2) identification and clarification of vision to diverse publics, (3) balancing comprehensiveness and distinctiveness, (4) managing the impacts of change, (5) developing and executing an effective image-building strategy, and (6) maintaining integrity in a competitive environment. The impact of an effective public relations effort on the management of each of these issues is worth reviewing.

Aligning Internal and External Perceptions

One of the most important issues facing image builders is how to develop a support base in which college attitudes, beliefs, and values are in harmony with those of the community. First of all, the literature is emphatic that commitment to institutional purpose must undergird all that a college says and does. According to Harper (1982), before perceptions in the external environment can be shaped, there must be appreciation, understanding, and support within the college itself. Similarly, Muller (1986) has claimed that a college's external reputation is strongly affected by the level of internal commitment and morale. In short, if a college fails to achieve an *internally* unified and positive sense of itself, it cannot expect to convey a viable image to its varied publics.

Positive alignment of internal values, attitudes, and behaviors is not enough to create a consistent image, however. An effective public relations program must also monitor, respect, and nurture perceptions in the *external* environment in order to manage the free flow of communication and identify impediments to harmonious exchange relations. According to Kopecek (1980), the primary purpose of any public relations operation is to interpret the activities of an institution to the community and to help predict and interpret the pulse of the community to the college. Monitoring public opinion is vital to serving and satisfying the community if an institution is to remain effective and viable (Johnson 1982). This open-systems approach to public relations is echoed by Pavlik (1987) and Alfred and Weissman (1987), who have suggested that institutional image is the end result of interaction among environmental forces, organizational attributes, communication outputs, and ongoing feedback. Thus, one of the most important functions of an effective public relations program is the management of this interdependent relationship so that positive perceptions of the institution become a significant by-product.

Identifying and Clarifying Vision

Community colleges also struggle to isolate a common vision, which is even more difficult to articulate than it is to experience. Clearly, in order to project a unified image, a college must first have a strong sense of its primary purpose, which is fully understood and capable of being articulated. According to Olins (1990) in his writings about corporate identity, this understanding of purpose must be consistently affirmed in everything an organization stands for and embraces, including its products, structures, and behavior. Thus, community college attributes must reflect and significantly enhance a sense of purpose, if identity and vision are to become enculturated and fully communicated.

However, to expect a public relations operation to singlehandedly *create* as well as communicate an image that brings diverse collegiate attributes into focus is to misunderstand its role and devalue the power of institutional identity. According to Topor (1986), *all* aspects of an institution contribute to building a cohesive, coordinated image. The role of an effective public relations operation is to communicate the image by isolating appropriate strategies for various constituencies of the institution so that all believe the message and become advocates for a common vision. No doubt, this is a lofty and ambitious goal, but it is vitally important for loosely coupled, highly diverse organizations like community colleges.

Balancing Comprehensiveness and Distinctiveness

Another key issue community colleges must manage if they are to enhance both their national and local images is the apparent dichotomy between the desire to be perceived as comprehensive in mission and the need to be distinguishable from the competition. Although there is sizable support for an image of comprehensiveness, the multiplicity of programs and functions implied therein makes it difficult to become identified with a distinctive vision. Perhaps the challenge, then, is to find ways to develop a broader tolerance for the coexistence of *both* images.

There is some evidence in the literature that this approach may be gaining favor. As the movement toward quality and student success gathers momentum nationally, community colleges are capitalizing on opportunities to distinguish themselves in new and exciting ways. For example, Roueche and Baker (1987) found that certain community colleges, while remaining true to their comprehensive mission, are distinguishing themselves as providers of access *with* excellence. Similarly, Hankin (1989), in a review of more than thirty community colleges, discovered a variety of highly innovative programs that attend to conditions in the external environment.

A comprehensive image is difficult to communicate to a widely diverse public. According to Templin (1989), more and more community colleges are employing marketing strategies to get their message across. By assessing their stature within the environment and constructing an image based upon this assessment, they highlight institutional purpose, character, and strength relative to need and target audience.

Since community colleges have been reluctant to relinquish their comprehensive image, an effective public relations strategy must break this message down so that each market segment can distinguish and make sense of the qualities directed specifically at it. In so doing, image builders better "position" the community college in a competitive marketplace, carving out a distinctive *and* comprehensive niche in the educational mainstream.

Managing the Impacts of Change

Another challenge facing community colleges is how to manage image optimally in an ever-changing environment. Fortunately, a central location in the marketplace positions these colleges to observe readily significant change impacts and to adapt appropriately. Once an impact is identified, a plan should be developed to manage the relationship between what is emerging and what has gone before. According to Templin (1989), strategic management of change depends upon an institution's ability to convey an image of adaptability while maintaining a "core character." Ensuring this delicate balance is an important goal of any sound public relations effort.

Unfortunately, the literature indicates that many institutional responses to environmental change are merely cosmetic. While visibility and enrollments may initially increase in response to a slick advertising campaign, high attrition and dissatisfaction are frequent by-products of "quick-fix solutions" (Kotler and Fox 1985). According to Caren and Kemerer (1979), colleges would be better advised to examine their internal structures and processes for adaptability, to develop a comparative advantage over the competition, and to minimize the distance between mission and need. In so doing, they will more likely maintain creative, healthy institutions over the long haul. And, for community colleges, the comprehensive image makes good sense as subtle shifting occurs and benefits continue to match needs.

The role of image makers in managing change is central to success. According to Savage (1987), effective public relations strategies must be carefully crafted to convey the values and beliefs that undergird mission, in order that any change in program emphasis aligns with purpose. As an institution positions itself to meet emerging needs, the public relations effort should be identified as a key leveraging strategy for shaping image, so that internal and external perceptions are enhanced in times of change.

Developing and Executing an Image-Building Plan

Once an institution has determined the image it wishes to convey, it must develop a plan for communicating that image. The literature is very clear on one point: *Effective* image building does not just happen. According to Alfred and Weissman (1987), it is the product of a highly complex interaction of environmental forces, institutional attributes, and influential processes. To the extent that a college can effect change in one or more of these components, it can be said to "manage" its image or otherwise influence its development.

Determining the Image. Perhaps the most important step in image enhancement is defining the image to be conveyed. A case has already been made for striking a balance between an image of comprehensiveness and one of distinctiveness. However, creating a consistent, unified image while maintaining this balance is, as Johnson (1986) has pointed out, particularly difficult when audiences are so extraordinarily diverse. Perkins (1986) has suggested a plausible alternative—an "aggregate" image comprising several "themes" that reflect what a college is, what it does, and why it does what it does. The image created would summarize various institutional attributes and appeal to multiple audiences. Whatever the approach, any viable image should command the support of most internal constituents and satisfy the external community as well.

Identifying the Publics and Selecting Communication Strategies. The next step in a successful image-building endeavor is the identification and segmentation of various audiences and the isolation of appropriate strategies for communicating the desired image to each group. For community colleges, these audiences generally include lawmakers, influential community members, prospective students, parents, high school counselors, donors, and competitors, among others. The literature argues that solid research into the economic, social, and political nature of these publics, as well as their attitudes, perceptions, needs and interests, is essential to any successful image-building effort (Harper 1982; Johnson 1986; Kotler and Fox 1985; Romine 1982). Once this information is known, it falls to public relations personnel to identify the best channels for communicating institutional beliefs, strengths, and attributes to multiple audiences, such that the messages received are uniform, positive, accurate, and above all meaningful. In fact, institutional well-being depends on determining who must be addressed, why they are important, what they think of the institution, what they must be convinced about, and how they can be reached.

In the educational arena, it is not enough to create a slick advertising campaign with a uniform theme and common visual elements. According to Johnson (1986), an ''eclectic'' model that treats audiences as discrete groups with different reading levels, content interests, and cultural values would be more appropriate for a community college. Furthermore, Romine (1982) has suggested that the approach to communicating with multiple audiences should be more program oriented than promotional; that is, the way to reach an adult market is to develop programs that appeal to older persons and market certain special features. And, finally, regardless of the specific audience to be addressed, image builders must make every effort to internalize and fully communicate an institution's most essential values, philosophy, and character.

Players, Responsibilities, and Planning. Public relations is everyone's job. According to Keener, Ryan, and Smith (1991), institutional image is a product of the integrity, credibility, and involvement of college trustees, president, faculty, staff, and students. Image is reflected in everything an organization does, and commitment that runs deep goes a long way toward embedding common understanding among multiple constituencies.

Still, according to the literature, institutional image ''turns'' on the accessibility, enthusiasm, and commitment of certain key players, most notably the college president. Trust in the president's judgment and expertise is critical to followers' commitment (Whisnant 1990). And, according to Kopecek (1980) and Romine (1982), no one plays a more significant public relations role that the chief executive, who sets the tone, establishes the structures, and allocates the resources. In other words, the president and public relations are inseparable.

Certainly, the president bears primary responsibility for managing major public relations efforts both inside and outside the institution. However, the second most influential person on a college campus may well be the person *formally* assigned responsibility for advancing the institution's image—the chief public relations officer. The literature consistently contends that the president and this officer must work hand in hand, thinking globally, sharing the same vision, taking in environmental cues, and shaping perceptions (Romine 1982; Savage 1987). The responsibilities of the chief public relations officer are comprehensive and include environmental scanning, marketing, publicizing, writing, designing, managing crises, advising, and evaluating (West 1985). While it is obvious that a host of factors impinge upon image development, the power of certain key individuals to influence perception cannot be underestimated. How an institution positions itself in the marketplace will be seen as a symbol of the president's vision and will reflect on the quality of the public relations effort.

While a number of different image-development programs are in use, the best plans generally begin with a definition of college philosophy and educational approach and end with an evaluation of how well the message was communicated. According to Bryant (1982), a well-conceived image-development plan derives ultimately from awareness of community needs and interests, focuses on convenience to the consumer, and identifies areas of potential growth. Savage (1987) also mentions the importance of pro-active efforts and a collective vision of a long-term image. Townsend (1989) and Templin (1989) claim that analysis of institutional strengths for market positioning and alignment with external conditions are also key ingredients. In summary, an effective image-building program must (1) research environmental perceptions and attitudes, (2) study the institution and be able to articulate its competitive advantages, (3) develop an image-building plan that is clearly a team effort, and (4) evaluate and refine the image as necessary.

Maintaining Integrity and Credibility

The last issue to be addressed relates to the ethics of the public relations profession. According to Cutlip, Center, and Broom (1985), "credibility" is one of the most important aspects of image, and the "climate of belief" that it fosters is a measure of customer confidence in an institution's performance. Unfortunately, in a time of growing financial constraint when competition for scarce resources intensifies, principles and ethics often fall by the wayside, and colleges may become compulsively positivistic. Ciervo (1986) has cautioned against such behavior, claiming that colleges so obsessed will destroy their credibility over time and pay the price in the long run.

As more and more institutions employ marketing and image-building techniques to distinguish themselves from their competition, public relations professionals are advised to bear in mind the importance of "truth in advertising." Since image depends heavily upon institutional quality, false advertising may indeed accelerate failure. Put another way, providing accurate information about an institution generally creates more harmony within the service environment than attempting to "persuade" thinking (Heath and Nelson 1986). The key to ensuring credibility over time, then, is to establish ethical standards designed to govern the ways in which an institution's best qualities are accurately and meaningfully publicized to its widely diverse audiences.

LOOKING AHEAD

The future of image enhancement in the community college is strongly dependent upon how well the public relations function is integrated into strategic planning efforts. The public relations role is as central to ascertaining what it is that community college publics want as it is to telling them what is available.

To ignore this important function is to shortchange not only an institution's image but also its entire reason for being.

More than ever, successful image development will continue to be significantly affected by how well certain key issues are managed. First, colleges with an eye to the future should analyze current perceptions for alignment with institutional mission and goals so that they can accurately interpret the messages that flow back and forth between environments. Second, colleges must determine how well their purpose and vision are reflected in everything that is done so that messages are communicated accurately and consistently. Third, forward-thinking community colleges will recognize that, in order to develop a competitive edge, they will need to distinguish themselves in the marketplace without sacrificing the comprehensive image that has sustained them and made them so readily adaptable to change. Fourth, it is critical that colleges develop public relations programs that monitor image for accuracy, segment audiences and determine appropriate communication strategies, and identify key players and responsibilities. And, finally, as more and more pressure is brought to bear, community colleges must meet their competition head on, without compromising the integrity of their mission in their struggle to access essential resources.

The community colleges that attend to these critical issues and acknowledge the importance of credibility over time will be more likely to thrive in a changing environment. In addition, the more artfully they distinguish themselves, the more likely they will be to create an image that closely matches intent. And, finally, as success accrues and breeds constituent confidence, resources and reputation can be expected to follow.

REFERENCES

Alfred, R. L., and J. Weissman. 1987. *Higher education and the public trust: Improving stature in colleges and universities*. ASHE-ERIC Higher Education Report no. 6. Washington, D.C.: Association for the Study of Higher Education.

Bryant, P. S. 1982. Enrollment management—A priority. In *Advancing the two-year college*, ed. P. S. Bryant and J. A. Johnson, 33–40. San Francisco: Jossey-Bass.

Caren, W. L., and F. R. Kemerer. 1979. The internal dimensions of institutional marketing. *College and University* (December): 173–88.

Ciervo, A. V. 1986. Emphasizing professionalism, performance, and productivity. In *Handbook of institutional advancement*, 2d ed., ed. A. W. Rowland. San Francisco: Jossey-Bass.

Commission on the Future of Community and Junior Colleges. 1988. *Building communities: A vision for a new century*. Washington, D.C.: American Association of Community and Junior Colleges.

Cutlip, S., M., A. H. Center, and G. M. Broom. 1985. *Effective public relations*. 6th ed. Englewood Cliffs, N.J.: Prentice-Hall.

Hankin, J. N. 1989. What makes the community college distinctive. In *A search for institutional distinctiveness*, ed. B. K. Townsend. New Directions for Community Colleges no. 65. San Francisco: Jossey-Bass.

Harper, W. A. 1982. A rationale for effective community relations. In *Advancing the two-year college*, ed. P. S. Bryant and J. A. Johnson, 3–9. New Directions for Institutional Advancement, no. 15. San Francisco: Jossey-Bass.

Heath, R. L., and R. A. Nelson. 1986. *Issues management: Corporate public policy-making in an information society*. Beverly Hills, Calif.: Sage.

Johnson, J. A. 1982. Views and challenges. . . . Now and beyond. In *Advancing the two-year college*, ed. P. S. Bryant and J. A. Johnson, 105–8. New Directions for Institutional Advancement no. 15. San Francisco: Jossey-Bass.

———. 1986. Advancement strategies for two-year colleges. In *Handbook of institutional advancement*, 2d ed., ed. A. W. Rowland, 706–21. San Francisco: Jossey-Bass.

Keener, B. J., G. J. Ryan, and N. J. Smith. 1991. Paying attention pays off: How to market resource development. *Community, Technical, and Junior College Journal* 62:34–37.

Kopecek, R. 1980. *The role of the collegiate office of public information in the 1980s*. Washington, D.C.: American Association of Community and Junior Colleges.

Kotler, P., and K.F.A. Fox. 1985. *Strategic marketing for educational institutions*. Englewood Cliffs, N.J.: Prentice-Hall.

Muller, S. 1986. The definition and philosophy of institutional advancement. In *Handbook of institutional advancement*, 2d ed., ed. A. W. Rowland. San Francisco: Jossey-Bass.

Olins, W. 1990. *Corporate identity*. Cambridge, Mass.: Harvard Business School.

Parnell, D. 1986. Shaping the environment. Paper presented at the annual national convention of the American Association of Community and Junior Colleges, Orlando, Florida.

Pavlik, J. V. 1987. *Public relations: What research tells us*. Newbury Park, Calif.: Sage.

Perkins, D. R. 1986. Interpreting the institution to external constituencies. In *Handbook of institutional advancement*, 2d ed., ed. A. W. Rowland. San Francisco: Jossey-Bass.

Romine, L. 1982. Managing community college public relations: An overview. In *Advancing the two-year college*, ed. P. S. Bryant and J. A. Johnson, 21–31. New Directions for Institutional Advancement no. 15. San Francisco: Jossey-Bass.

Roueche, J. E., and G. A. Baker. 1987. *Access and excellence: The open-door college*. Washington, D.C.: American Association of Community and Junior Colleges.

Savage, D. D. 1987. Public relations and marketing. In *Marketing strategies for changing times*, ed. W. W. Wilms and R. W. Moore, 75–81. New Directions for Community Colleges no. 60. San Francisco: Jossey-Bass.

———. 1989. Images of community colleges for the twenty-first century. In *A search for institutional distinctiveness*, ed. B. K. Townsend, 3–10. New Directions for Community Colleges no. 65. San Francisco: Jossey-Bass.

Templin, R. G., Jr. 1989. Using what an institution learns in the search for distinctiveness. In *A search for institutional distinctiveness*, ed. B. K. Townsend, 59–65. New Directions for Community Colleges no. 65. San Francisco: Jossey-Bass.

Topor, R. S. 1986. *Institutional image: How to define, improve, market it*. Washington, D.C.: Council for Advancement and Support of Education.

Townsend, B. K. 1986. Preferred directions and images for the community college: A view from the inside. *Research in Higher Education* 25:316–27.

———. 1989. A search for institutional distinctiveness. In *A search for institutional distinctiveness*, ed. B. K. Townsend, 23–32. New Directions for Community Colleges no. 65. San Francisco: Jossey-Bass.

Trent, R. L., ed. 1981. *Public relations in the community college*. Washington, D.C.: Council for Advancement and Support of Education.

West, P. T. 1985. *Educational public relations*. Beverly Hills, Calif.: Sage.

Whisnant, T. W. 1990. The presidential image: Key to effective leadership. *Community College Review* 17:10–14.

The Impact of Proprietary Schools on the Viability of Community Colleges

Jon A. Hittman

The effect of proprietary schools on the viability of community college poses an interesting conceptual dilemma. While both are considered postsecondary institutions, tradition suggests that these entities emerged to satisfy two separate and distinct needs.

Proprietary schools are defined as educational institutions (trade and technical, business, cosmetology, and barber schools) "which are privately owned and managed, and which in addition to being service oriented, are profit motivated" (Fulton 1969). Historically these schools have focused on vocational training. Proprietary school owners respond to marketplace demands for trained labor by providing short-term instruction in specific subjects with immediate employment for the graduate as the prime objective (Shoemaker 1973). By contrast, the original function of the junior/community college was to provide liberal arts education. Community colleges structured their curricula in the university image and established the "collegiate function" with transfer to the university as the primary goal (Cohen and Brawer 1984). Given this historic disparity in function, it is not surprising that a 1975 study (Erwin) noted that most proprietary schools do not compete directly with community colleges for students.

Since the publication of the Erwin study, the educational environment has changed significantly. There has been a dramatic shift in the mission of community colleges and a change in the autonomy of proprietary schools. External forces, such as the economy, work-force requirements, and legislation have had a profound effect on the viability of both community colleges and proprietary schools. The change engendered by the shifting environment has, to a certain extent, diminished the clarity of the differentiation between them and has fostered an atmosphere of competition.

The remainder of this chapter will (1) describe the historically dissimilar roles of proprietary schools and community colleges, (2) describe the specific features that have traditionally distinguished community colleges from proprietary schools, (3) explain how these features have been affected by watershed events, and (4) conclude with some of the effects of these events upon community colleges and proprietary schools.

HISTORICAL ROLE OF THE COMMUNITY COLLEGE

The predominantly twentieth-century and purely American phenomenon known as the community college has its roots in the university system. The purpose of higher education has always been debated from various perspectives. There is loose agreement, however, that the first two years of postsecondary education are preparatory. This notion, combined with the effects of population growth and increasing demands on education, created fertile ground for the development of the public junior/community college concept. Rapid growth in information and population in the late nineteenth and early twentieth centuries began to pressure the system of higher education. Between 1870 and 1900, the U.S. population doubled, while university enrollment increased by 450 percent. Universities confined their enrollment to students who had demonstrated the academic skill to prosper in an academic environment committed to scholarship and research. But many students with and without preferred academic skills demanded acceptance.

As a solution, a four-year university education was divided into two levels. The first two years were labeled the "college," and the second two years were called the "university." It was not until 1892 that William Rainey Harper, president of the University of Chicago, made this concept a reality. Harper established the Academic College (the first two years) and the University College (second two years). He later changed the names to Junior College and Senior College, respectively. Harper was instrumental in establishing the first public junior college by convincing the Joliet, Illinois, school board to expand the Joliet High School curriculum to include the 13th and 14th grades. This gave birth to the modern public junior/community college movement.

Harper's purpose in establishing junior colleges was to provide the University of Chicago with a ready supply of academically capable students while reducing the population of students who were academically inadequate. The time, effort, and problems associated with the student selection process were exported to the junior college.

During the early 1900s, legislation in California allowed public, secondary school boards to offer postgraduate courses to "approximate the first two years of university study." Further legislation provided public funds to support the junior college system. The popularity of the two-year, publicly funded, post-secondary community college grew from these beginnings.

HISTORICAL ROLE OF THE PROPRIETARY SCHOOL

The documented history of proprietary education in the United States is understandably limited because proprietary schools (1) are organized in various ways making their for-profit status difficult to determine, (2) are operated on a profit motive, which has been spurned by the traditional academic community, (3) have not previously been perceived as a threat to traditional segments of postsecondary education, and (4) have not previously been genuinely recognized and included in planning and policy-making activities (Carr 1980). Despite a dearth of research, there is agreement that correspondence instruction was the first type of proprietary training to be offered in the United States. According to Katz (1973), the *Boston Gazette* carried the following statement regarding the instruction of shorthand in 1728: "Any persons in the country desirous to learn this art may by having the several lessons sent weekly to them, be as perfectly instructed as those that live in Boston." Proprietary resident schools became relatively common in the middle of the eighteenth century. Classes were conducted in places of business, or sometimes at the homes of the proprietors, who also were instructors.

Historically, proprietary schools have been dependent upon the marketplace for income. Rapid industrialization in the United States provided a favorable environment for these schools. Other factors contributing to their growth have been (1) a student and employer market base that has not been traditionally courted or served adequately by public institutions (Carr 1980) and (2) the inefficiency of the American apprenticeship system for business and occupational training (Tonne 1954).

The phenomenon of multiple schools with a single corporate structure began to evolve as early as 1850 with the establishment of Bacon's Mercantile Colleges. These schools, founded by R. C. Bacon, were located in several Midwestern cities, including Madison, Cincinnati, and Cleveland. The Bryant-Stratton chain was organized in 1852 by H. D. Stratton and H. B. Bryant. By the end of the Civil War, the chain had grown to more than fifty schools in almost as many cities. This growth can be attributed to the development and employment of effective advertising campaigns, to the delivery of high-quality training using a uniform system of instruction and textbooks, and to the fact that the schools filled an important need not addressed by public education.

During the late nineteenth and early twentieth centuries, career growth for women was an important but relatively unheralded contribution of proprietary education (Lee and Merisotis 1990). The Civil War forced businesses to employ women as clerks, but they often lacked business training. As a result of the introduction of the key shift typewriter and the Gregg shorthand method, proprietary schools identified women as an untapped student market. Prior to the Civil War, most women who wanted to work were directed into teaching.

In the 1970s and 1980s there was a surge in the growth of proprietary school popularity. Proprietary school success has been attributed to the traditional characteristics of flexibility and specialization of service (Carr 1980) which have been enhanced by the relative autonomy afforded proprietary schools because of their private, for-profit structure.

SUMMARY OF TRADITIONAL ROLE DISTINCTIONS

Traditionally, community colleges have been considered slow and nonflexible. On the other hand, proprietary education has been considered flexible, providing training for new technologies as soon as they develop (Clark and Sloan 1966). One explanation for this disparity is that community colleges provide education whereas proprietary schools deliver training. Education is a slow, highly individual, lifelong process—but training is not (Wilms 1973). Training can be done quickly and effectively.

Proprietary schools are by definition private, for-profit entities existing in the marketplace and dependent upon tuition for revenue. As such, they traditionally have been more autonomous and subject to less governmental and accrediting body oversight than traditional public postsecondary institutions.

SPECIFIC TRADITIONAL DIFFERENCES

Funding

Sources of funding is the most obvious characteristic that distinguishes traditional public junior/community colleges from proprietary schools. Public institutions receive revenue from both public (local taxes, state and federal funding) and market (tuition and fees) sources. Proprietary schools traditionally have been dependent solely upon the marketplace for revenue. As a result, most proprietary schools have well-developed recruiting and placement functions (Simmons 1975).

Curriculum

Original curricular offerings of public junior/community colleges were primarily collegiate academic studies in preparation for the universities. Early occupational training delivered by the public junior/community college was preprofessional: pre-law, pre-medicine, and pre-engineering. Eells (1931) reported that, in 1929, proportional enrollment in California public junior colleges was 80 to 20 in favor of the collegiate academic studies over the pre-professional education.

Operating from the assumption that the length of a program is directly related to its quality, state departments of education, regional accrediting bodies, and professional groups have a prescribed length and course content (Wilms 1975). This assumption produces rigid course scheduling and curricular offerings.

Totally dependent upon the marketplace for income, proprietary schools have aggressively sought to identify and address the unmet needs of business and industry. Therefore, early proprietary programs were truly occupational in nature, and subjects that did not directly contribute to job skills were minimized. Traditionally, successful proprietary schools exploited differences between the offerings at community colleges and at their own institutions. The following distinct characteristics of proprietary school offerings have emerged:

1. Flexible program and course schedules designed to increase accessibility (Belitsky 1969)

2. Flexible curricula designed to make it easy for the student to enter, exit, and reenter, thereby increasing the probability of enrollment and completion (Erickson et al. 1972)

3. Flexible instruction to accommodate special student needs for individual attention, help, and encouragement (Kincaid and Podesta 1966)

4. Sensitivity and responsiveness to changes in level of demand for trained manpower and an emphasis on curriculum objectives (Katz 1973), that reflect current hiring criteria (Simmons 1975)

5. Unique occupational training programs that public colleges are seldom willing or able to offer.

Decision-making Process and Governance

Owners or corporate-level management generally make the critical decisions in proprietary schools. In community colleges, the decision-making authority is more broadly distributed among boards of trustees, administrators, and faculty organizations.

The two sectors also differ in motivations behind the decision-making process. The critical success factor of profitability is a primary consideration that strongly influences private school owners and managers. Decisions regarding equipment and facilities, program offerings, and faculty salaries are made with profitability as a crucial criterion.

While fiscal matters are of a high priority in public junior/community colleges, they are influenced by different circumstances. Lay boards, academic departments, and tenured faculty are all stakeholders in the decision-making structure. Their views must be considered. With the exception of large corporate chain schools, the private, for-profit schools benefit from a more streamlined decision-making process.

Instructor Qualifications and Compensation. The proprietary schools that offer direct training for jobs tend to employ faculty based primarily upon experiences related to the jobs for which the students are to be prepared (Gilli 1976). These instructors establish themselves as trainer models rather than as traditional teachers. In these institutions, educational background is not of primary relevance, and many instructors are hired from industry. In fact, many are also found to be concurrently employed in a field related to the one in which they are teaching (Wolman et al. 1972). The proprietary institutions offering degrees are notable exceptions. In the case of degree-granting institutions, the faculty education requirements are comparable to those in public colleges.

Regional accreditation is a requirement for public colleges, and these institutions are bound by the standards of the various regional accrediting bodies. As a result of these educational standards, community college faculty are more likely to hold degrees.

It is difficult to draw comparisons regarding compensation for the instructors employed by the two types of institutions. Salaries of proprietary school faculty might not represent their total earnings, and they are more likely to work a standard year instead of a nine-month academic year. However, proprietary school teachers tend to be less well paid, in general, than community college instructors (Belitsky 1969).

Community college faculty are more likely to have salaries set through the collective bargaining process. They also enjoy more job security or contract assurances, such as tenure.

IMPORTANT EVENTS ALTERING THE DISTINGUISHING CHARACTERISTICS

The Servicemen's Readjustment Act, commonly known as the GI Bill, was early legislation that affected the role of the community college and the autonomy of the proprietary school (Conrad and Cosand 1976). The GI Bill provided financial support for returning World War II veterans who wished to pursue postsecondary education, and, in all, 7.8 million veterans benefited from this program at a total cost of $14.5 billion (Tiedt 1966). At the end of the Korean War, an additional 2.25 million veterans received financial assistance through the GI Bill (Tiedt 1966).

The GI Bill encouraged the development of the career education function of the community colleges. As the veterans returned from war, they created a greater demand for noncollegiate vocational courses than for traditional transfer courses. The community colleges moved to fill the need for this vocational/technical type of curriculum. The GI Bill set the precedent for future, broad-based federal assistance for postsecondary education institutions, including proprietary schools.

For proprietary schools, eligibility to participate in the veterans program required federal and appropriate state agency approval. The immediate impact of the approval process was minimal because the criteria varied from state to state. The importance of this precedent is that, although eligibility was allowed, it was contingent on the implementation of an approval process.

Legislation at the state level also significantly affected the growth of the vocational function of the community college. As early as the late 1940s, Texas lawmakers enacted legislation requiring that community colleges offer a minimum of 40 percent of their courses in the so-called ''terminal'' (occupational) fields to qualify for state aid (Bogue 1950). The Vocational Education Act of

1963 and subsequent amendments in 1968 and 1972 greatly increased the federal funds available for career education, thereby encouraging the community colleges to alter their mission to include a greater emphasis on vocational training (Cohen and Brawer 1984).

Further encouragement for vocational education came from state and local governments, which matched these federal funds on a multiple basis. An example is the Illinois system which gave $6 from state and local governments for every federally appropriated dollar to community college districts after 1974, provided that 50 percent of the programs offered were in vocational education (Davenport et al. 1976). As a result, 1,871 of the statewide curricula were vocational in nature (Illinois Community College Board 1976).

THE 1972 HIGHER EDUCATION ACT AMENDMENTS

Amendments to the Higher Education Act in 1972 established the Basic Educational Opportunity Grant (BEOG, later renamed "Pell Grants" for Senator Claiborne Pell) and the Student Loan Marketing Association (Sallie Mae). The amendments were designed to increase middle-income and economically disadvantaged students' accessibility to higher education.

The 1972 amendments included proprietary schools in the definition of "eligible institutions," making them full partners with traditional higher education in respect to receipt of student aid (Lee and Merisotis 1990). Now proprietary and public postsecondary students are considered equally for federal financial aid based on financial need.

In an effort to ensure delivery of quality education, Congress made access to federal financial aid contingent upon certain fundamental requirements, including (1) state authorization or licensure for the institution, (2) accreditation by an Education Department–recognized entity, and (3) adherence to U.S. Department of Education regulations. These requirements had little impact upon community colleges because they were already subject to mandatory quality assurance scrutiny due to the public financial support (local taxes, state and federal funding) they received.

Though full partnership with traditional higher education in student financial aid matters enabled proprietary school students access to funding, it also brought additional state and federal regulation for proprietary institutions. Increased oversight and regulations have reduced their capacity for flexibility and market responsiveness. As a result, proprietary schools have developed some of the characteristics of public community colleges.

Because proprietary schools are market driven, they have implemented successful recruiting strategies, and their student population is generally considered to be "high risk" (poor, female, and minority) students (Lee and Merisotis 1990). Thus, they receive a disproportionate share of the funding made available by the amendments to the 1972 Higher Education Reauthorization Act. For the same reasons, proprietary school students have a disproportionate share of the guaranteed student loan defaults. Proprietary schools, whether they deserve it or not, have become the lightning rod in the guaranteed student loan default debate. The issue of guaranteed student loan default is too complex to address here, but it should be noted that recently passed legislation (ability-to-benefit and student right-to-know), as well as currently pending legislation designed to reduce loan default, has affected community college programs.

CHANGES IN ROLE, MISSION, AND AUTONOMY

As the "baby boom" generation ages, a dwindling work force, underprepared to function productively in a technology-oriented, fiercely competitive global marketplace, follows. While vocational and technical training have always been a component of the community college mission, this role has taken on greater significance as the colleges respond to a changing economic climate.

As a result, community colleges are becoming more responsive to industry training needs by providing more focused job-specific training. Offering this "training" rather than traditional "education" allows community colleges to be more competitive with proprietary schools. This new focus streamlines the decision-making process and reduces the response time because, in most cases, training courses do not require board of trustees or state higher education board approval.

Since general education is not normally required in training-oriented courses, the length of the course or program can be reduced. Also, the instructor qualifications are less stringent. This enables community colleges to employ part-time instructors who are concurrently employed in the private sector. The advantage of this is that these instructors are familiar with state-of-the-art equipment and techniques used in industry.

Flexibility, job-specific training conducted by instructors from the field, and market responsiveness now being demonstrated by community colleges to support the economic development mission have long been considered proprietary school strengths.

Proprietary school leaders recognize the current work-force dilemma confronting business and industry and most are well positioned to respond. However, eligibility for and utilization of federal financial aid programs have changed their operations.

Proprietary schools have traditionally depended upon student-paid tuition and fees for revenue. While this is still true, proprietary school *students* have become increasingly dependent upon Title IV aid since the passage of the 1972 Higher Education Reauthorization Act. This federal aid, available in grants and loans, finances the eligible student's education. According to a recent study, 78 percent of proprietary school students receive federal assistance of some kind (Merisotis 1991). A U.S. Department of Education study (1989) revealed that proprietary school students accounted for 36.7 percent of all those who borrowed and 36.4 percent of the total dollars borrowed in the guaranteed student loan program during FY '89. As proprietary school students receive greater portions of the federal assistance money, less is available for community college students. The increasing use of federal financial assistance by proprietary school students has resulted in a concomitant escalation in institutional regulation and oversight by governmental agencies. Proprietary schools are more closely scrutinized and must provide greater documentation of accountability then ever before. Now the proprietary sector's traditional competitive advantage is diminished because flexibility and response time to customers is impaired by required compliance with regulations and reporting procedures.

CONCLUSIONS

Current trends suggest that proprietary schools can be expected to seek degree-granting authority in increasing numbers (Lee and Merisotis 1990). More schools will pursue and obtain regional accreditation and strive to develop transfer agreements with high schools (two-plus-two programs) and traditional higher education institutions.

The need for a highly trained and productive work force is acute (National Center on Education and the Economy 1990). It is unlikely that this competitive environment will negatively affect the viability of vigorous and healthy community college programs. But as legislators, state agencies, and college administrators respond to demands for accountability for the expenditure of tax dollars, programs with low completion and placement rates will be scrutinized, and some will face closure.

The continued effectiveness of existing community college programs might be enhanced by collaborating with proprietary schools to meet regional educational and training needs. The inherent expense and duplication of service caused by competition can be mitigated through cooperation. Models of cooperation exist in which proprietary schools provide skills training and community colleges provide the general and theoretical education in applied associate degree programs. This strategy is particularly sensible for community colleges when specialized and expensive equipment is required to complete the student's training. State agencies of higher education can encourage and coordinate these collaborative efforts. In an environment where (1) training and retraining of the work force is becoming a critical need, (2) the cost of education is rising, (3) state and federal financial support for education is dwindling, (4) proprietary schools are adopting a more traditional educational model, and (5) community colleges are becoming more entrepreneurial, cooperation seems a prudent alternative to unbridled competition.

REFERENCES

Belitsky, A. H. 1969. *Private vocational schools and their students: Limited objectives unlimited opportunities*. Cambridge, Mass.: Schenkman Publishing.

Bogue, J. P. 1950. *The community college.* New York: McGraw-Hill.

Carr, D. 1980. *The impact of accreditation and degree status on proprietary business, trade, and technical schools in New York State.* Ann Arbor, Mich.: University Microfilms.

Clark, H. F., and H. S. Sloan. 1966. *Classrooms on main street.* New York: Teachers College Press.

Cohen, A. M., and F. B. Brawer. 1984. *The American community college.* San Francisco: Jossey-Bass.

Conrad, C., and J. Cosand. 1976. *The implications of federal education policy.* Washington, D.C.: American Association for Higher Education.

Davenport, L. F., et al. 1976. Vocational education in the 1980s. Paper presented at annual meeting of the American Association of Community and Junior Colleges. Washington, D.C. ERIC Document no. ED 124 249.

Eells, W. C. 1931. *The junior college.* Boston: Houghton Mifflin.

Erickson, E. W., et al. 1972. *Proprietary business schools and community colleges: Resource allocation, student needs, and federal policies.* ERIC Document no ED 134 790.

Erwin, J. M. 1975. *The proprietary school: Assessing its impact on the collegiate sector.* ERIC Document no. ED 145 791.

Fulton, R. A. 1969. Proprietary schools. *Encyclopedia of educational research,* 4th ed., ed. R. Ebel. Toronto: Macmillan.

Gilli, A. C. 1976. *Modern organizations of vocational education.* University Park: Pennsylvania State University Press.

Illinois Community College Board. 1976. *Curriculum enrollment summary in the public community colleges of Illinois: 1975–76.* Springfield, Ill.: Illinois Community College Board.

Katz, H. H. 1973. *A state of the art study of the independent private school industry in the state of Illinois.* Springfield: Illinois Advisory Council on Vocational Education.

Kincaid, H. V., and E. A. Podesta. 1966. *An exploratory survey of proprietary vocational schools.* Palo Alto Calif.: Stanford Research Institute.

Lee, J. B., and J. Merisotis. 1990. *Proprietary schools: Programs, policies, and prospects.* ASHE-ERIC Higher Education Report no. 5. Washington, D.C.: George Washington University, School of Education and Human Development.

Merisotis, J. P., ed. 1991. *The changing dimensions of student aid.* New Directions for Higher Education, no. 74. San Francisco: Jossey-Bass.

National Center on Education and the Economy. 1990. *America's choice: High skills or low wages.* Rochester, N.Y.

Shoemaker, E. A. 1973. Community colleges: The challenge of proprietary schools. *Change* 5(6):71–72.

Simmons, H. C. 1975. A descriptive of degree granting proprietary schools and their relationships to the development of community colleges in Pennsylvania. Ph.D. diss., Florida State University.

Tiedt, S. 1966. *The role of the federal government in education.* New York: Oxford University Press.

Tonne, H. A. 1954. *Principles of business education.* 2d ed. New York: McGraw-Hill.

U.S. Department of Education. 1989. *FY 1989 guaranteed student loan programs databook.* Washington, D.C.

Wilms, W. 1973. A new look at proprietary schools. *Change* 5(6):6–7, 80.

———. 1975. *Public and proprietary vocational training: A study of effectiveness.* London: D. C. Heath and Company.

Wolman, J., V. M. Campbell, S. M. Jung, and J. M. Richards. 1972. *A comparative study of proprietary and non-proprietary vocational training programs.* 2 vols. Palo Alto, Calif.: American Institutes for Research.

Part 10

The Future of the Community College

A Synthesis of the Literature on Understanding the New Vision for Community College Culture: The Concept of Building Community

Stephen K. Mittelstet

In his well-known work on the history of ideas, Lovejoy (1960) acknowledges the difficulty and complexity of synthesizing the history of an idea. This is especially true, according to Lovejoy, not just because in the course of time persons hold "all manner of conflicting beliefs under one name," but also because any one of these persons, as a rule, holds under that one name "a very mixed collection of ideas." The mixed collection of ideas within each person and throughout time combine to form a conglomerate which bears a single name and which supposedly constitutes some kind of unity (1960, 4). Even though community colleges have a rather short history and the notion of colleges' building community an even shorter one, the problems of understanding the community college culture and the notion of building community are still fairly complicated. Terms like "college culture," "college community," and even "community college" are equivocal and ambiguous, thereby creating much possibility of confusion. With that in mind, I endeavor throughout this chapter to use such terms in ways that clarify rather than obfuscate. At the very least, my hope is to write nothing that adds to ambiguity and equivocation. After providing a brief background of and context for the issue of building community, this chapter reviews major higher education writings on the topic and then shows how these works reflect a more general shift in consciousness within the community college culture. After detailing a few of the problems associated with shifting to a new vision of community, several commitments, which we in community colleges must make if we are going to build and foster community, are offered.

One of the interesting ironies regarding community colleges is that, all too often, they lack many aspects of community. This is not to say that the colleges lack a sense of the local areas that they serve. In the historical development of the community college, the concern for serving the needs of the local community has been a defining characteristic of the community college movement. In fact, the transition from the use of the term "junior college" to the term "community college" was primarily related to the notion that community colleges would be "more vitally involved in the community than was true of the older junior colleges" (Wattenbarger 1982, 982). Throughout their history, community colleges have been unquestionably committed to addressing the needs of the local community. In fact, it was once suggested that criteria could be established to determine the degree to which a community college progressed toward the goal of being an ideal college. All of these criteria were directly related to how well the college was fulfilling community needs (Valade 1958).

In saying that community colleges lack a sense of community, I am not suggesting that most community colleges have failed in this important aspect of their mission. In saying that they lack a sense of community, I use the term "community" as it is defined by the Commission on the Future of Community Colleges (1988). In the commission report the term "community" is defined not only as the local region served by the college, but also "as a climate to be created" (1988, 7). In a very important way this new manner of defining the term is an invitation to reexamine the way we in community colleges think about ourselves, our mission, and our vision. Certainly, as the commission's report points out, the community college "can reaffirm its mandate to respond to local needs" (35); however, in addition to serving the local community, we may now also envision as central to our mission the responsibility for building and fostering community in a broader sense. This larger sense is one which "encompasses a concern for the whole, for integration and collaboration, for openness and integrity, for inclusiveness and self-renewal" (7). This broader understanding of community not only has implications for the way we think about our role in the community, but also it demands of us a new vision that is, to say the very least, a challenging ideal for which to strive. Implicit in this conception of community (and therefore the new ideal of a community college) is the challenge of building and fostering community—a challenge that involves efforts to create a climate at the macro level of the local, national, and world community and also at the micro level of interpersonal relationships from the classroom to the board room.

Of course, this understanding of community and the role of education in creating a climate of community is, at least in some sense, an idea as ancient as the Greek *paideia*, which had as an education aim "the production of good citizens, sound in both body and character" (Nussbaum 1985, 7). The end of education was the preparation for a particular form of life, embedded in social practices and relationships within the community. It was clearly understood that individual feeling or understanding was not the aim of *paideia*, but rather social, communal, and political action (Else 1969, 803). While Socrates and Plato certainly did argue for individual self-inquiry, never—according to the these Greek philosophers—should the enterprise of self-examination or any other sort of study be pursued in a way that separates it from the end of living a good human life in a community (Nussbaum 1985, 13).

A contrasting view of education probably reached its fullness in the Enlightenment—a view that placed less emphasis upon community and more emphasis upon individual freedom. This freedom was linked to tolerance, egalitarianism, and individual volition rather than obligations to community. In addition, the ideal of freedom of intellect realized in the pursuit of knowledge became a goal that was sought for its own sake (Kimball 1986, 121). Enlightenment thinkers generally shared the ideal of an individual search for truth regardless of the effect upon community. Certainly American life and, therefore, American higher education has been dominated by this latter view. Bellah and his colleagues (1985), for example, have shown that regardless of the different views taken during the last two centuries in America, the underlying pattern has been consistent—a pattern characterized by individualism. Rather than building community, the aim of education in America has been typified by the desire to create individuals who are autonomous, independent, and self-sufficient.

The new vision of building communities in colleges is more comprehensive than the Greek idea of education, with its demands to be instrumental in the service to the community, and more demanding than the extreme individualism that has characterized modern American education for years. While much has been written about educational climate, the comprehensive nature of the concept of building community and the challenge to higher education to make building community the unifying principle in higher learning are perhaps best expressed in two recent reports: *Building Communities: A Vision for A New Century* (Commission on the Future of Community Colleges 1988) and *Campus Life: In Search of Community* (Carnegie Foundation for the Advancement of Teaching, 1990). Both of these works make significant contributions to the concept of building community and, therefore, are deserving of careful attention.

The commission report sees the building of communities as "an urgent new mandate" (1988, 9) for community colleges that recognizes "not only the dignity of the individual but also the interests of community" (6). This task is made particularly difficult, given the longtime mission of community colleges to serve all those who wish an education. As the report points out, in the next decade and beyond, community colleges will have the pressing challenge of affirming community while meeting the obligation to serve an even greater diversity of students. Creating a climate that enhances teaching and learning is a difficult challenge even when there are few obvious differences among the members of the community. Given the increasing numbers of community college students of widely varying ages, diverse backgrounds, different cultures, various stages of college academic readiness, and the strong commitment on the part of community colleges to help students from all segments of the community succeed, the challenge to building community is even greater. In essence, the commission report points out that, if community colleges are going to build community successfully, they must be places "where people confront the stranger in each other and in themselves, and still know that they are members one of another" (Palmer 1981, 125). Thus, building community from diversity, according to the commission report, is a challenge that most be met or else "America will become a socially and economically divided nation. The spirit of community will be lost" (1988, 10).

The commission report also points out the critical importance of faculty in the building of community. Obviously, as students become more diverse, teaching will not get easier. If community colleges are going to build community successfully, then each community college must "commit itself to the recruitment and retention of a top quality faculty and to the professional development of these colleagues" (1988, 13). If community is to be built from diversity, then renewal, faculty development, and selection of new faculty must be focused upon creating a campus environment that is characterized by greater appreciation of difference. In order to accomplish this, the "percentage of faculty members who are black, Hispanic, and Asian should be increased" (13). In addition, for community college faculty to serve as mentors and models for their students, they must collectively represent the diversity of the students that they serve, and they must demonstrate an understanding of and appreciation for diversity.

While diversity is a fact of our college communities and learning to acknowledge and to value difference is an essential part of becoming educated, community must also be characterized by commonalities. The commission report argues that, as we respond to diversity, we should be guided by clear goals. At present "the curriculum is too fragmented, and learning at some institutions, has become compartmentalized"; it is "through a curriculum with coherence" that a community can be built (15). The report offers four academic goals that the nation's community colleges should vigorously pursue:

- First, all community college students should become proficient in the written and the spoken word.
- Second, all students should learn about the human heritage and the interdependent world in which they live.
- Third, the community college should offer first-rate technical education and career-related programs to prepare students for working in the information age.
- Finally, the community college should make available to adults a rich array of short term and continuing education courses to encourage lifelong learning and help students meet their social, civic, and career obligations. (15)

All of these academic goals, of course, relate directly to the larger goal of building and fostering community. Language is the foundation of reality and interaction within any community, and it is through the use of language that traditions are shared and sustained. Bellah says that in an important way communities are constituted by their past, and in order to remember that past, "a community is involved in telling its story" (Bellah et al., 1985, 153). The college curriculum is, in a sense, the collective history of the larger community in which the college exists. Language is essential for the communication of this history; however, although proficiency in the use of language is necessary, it is not sufficient for building and fostering community. If the community is to be strengthened by the retelling of its story, then the history communicated must be truly a collective autobiography—the curriculum must honestly express diverse perspectives. In the past many voices and perspectives have been excluded from the curriculum.

The commission report concludes by stating that strengthening general education for students "is one of the most urgent obligations community colleges confront" (1988, 17). The goal of every community college in the nation, according to the report, should be to "provide a core experience of common learning" (18). However, it must be acknowledged that the core curriculum will not build or foster a diverse community unless it not only provides students with essential knowledge about their own heritage, but also encourages students to move beyond their own narrow interests into a deeper understanding and appreciation of the interdependent world in which they live.

Furthermore, if community colleges are going to teach students to overcome their narrowness, then colleges must first model this behavior by overcoming departmental narrowness. For example, the report suggests that colleges should make more efforts to integrate technical and career studies with the liberal arts; at present these departmental boundaries are too infrequently crossed. At the heart of community building in higher education is helping students to make connections and integrate their knowledge (19). The commission report acknowledges also that education as a preparation for work "has been a key component of the community college mandate from the first" (19); however, "that by affirming both technical and liberal learning, the prospects of broadening work preparation would be enormously enhanced" (21).

Community colleges, perhaps more than any other institution of higher learning, have made lifelong learning an essential part of their mission. According to the commission report, "a community college's success in building community will be measured, at least in part, by how often its students return to college" for refresher courses, preparation for career changes, and for life-enhancing personal development courses (22). Working in concert with the local community external to the college to address the lifelong learning needs of the community is a "special mandate" of the community college that must be met "if community is to be affirmed and continuously renewed" (23).

If the academic principles suggested in the commission report are to be realized, then teaching and learning in the classroom must be the foundation upon which community is built. It is the conviction of the commission "that the theme *Building Communities* is applied most appropriately in the classroom, where both intellectual and social relationships are strengthened and where teachers and students can be active partners in the learning process" (25). To accomplish this, each classroom should be a community that is a microcosm of the larger college community. In short, colleges must have classrooms where all students and teachers are active partners in the teaching-learning process and where diverse groups of students work collaboratively to learn, to develop, and to grow. In addition, the commission suggests that teachers must support their teaching with the appropriate and effective use of technology. The goal should be to use technology as a means to an end, rather than an end in itself. "The challenge for the community college will be to build partnership between traditional and nontraditional education, letting each do what it can do best" (28).

Without doubt, many classes within community colleges have been and continue to be outstanding models of community. Often this happens even when there is little or no community in the college as a whole. However, for community colleges to build and foster community effectively, the college beyond the classroom must itself be a community in which academic life and nonacademic life are inextricably connected. According to the commission report, "[C]reative ways must be found to extend the discourse, build relationships, and stir a spirit of shared goals" (30). In a true learning community there must not be separation and isolation between curricular and cocurricular activities. What is urgently needed are "people who are committed to the building of community—not just in the classroom, but in the financial aid office, the committee room, and the coffee shop, as well" (30). Building community involves commitment to the institution as a cultural entity, with not only a shared vision but also shared traditions, stories, and celebrations which are a part of the communal life of colleagues and students alike.

Community colleges have a long history of geographical restriction; that is, they have been closely tied to the needs of their service areas. The commission report asserts that this kind of parochialism is no longer an option. Community building will require that students are led to understand international connections, global perspectives, and the importance of partnerships with people and cultures other than their own. The report also recommends that there is great value for students in programs of service to the local community. A service program, according to the report, "adds special dimensions to the preparation for a career" (32). In short, the best preparation for students, and an essential element of community building, is the ability to think globally and act locally.

As has always been the case, the local community external to the college is of utmost importance; however, a successful attempt to build community will involve an authentic partnership—a community college responding to the needs of the local community and a local community transformed through the action and leadership of the college. Connections beyond the college—"with schools, industry, business, social agencies, and policy groups—will become a key strategy in the building of community" (35).

Without doubt, the challenge offered in the commission report is demanding, and success will come only through strong, creative, innovative leadership. As the report points out, leaders from all campus groups must be willing to adopt new models for decision making and governance (42). There will be little hope for community unless the divisions that exist between different segments of the college can be bridged by a shared commitment to the community as a whole. The commission report provides community college educators with a pervasive and demanding vision for a new century; however, I see it also as a document which offers meaningful guidance and significant hope. For, if—as the report says—"these goals are vigorously pursued, the community colleges of the nation will fulfill, in new and creative ways, their traditional mission as 'colleges of the people' " . . . and will meet the challenge of building community "in the classroom, on the campus, and around the world" (49).

The urgent need to build community on college campuses is addressed also in the special report issued in 1990 by the Carnegie Foundation for the Advancement of Teaching entitled *Campus Life: In Search of Community.* This report suggests that the need to build community on America's college campuses is the greatest challenge facing higher education today. The report proposes that six principles be adopted as a formal "compact" for our college campuses—principles that inform decision making, establish a framework for governance, and "taken together define the kind of community every college and university should strive to be" (1990, 6). The six principles are that every college or university be a purposeful community, an open community, a just community, a disciplined community, a caring community, and a celebrative community (8).

A purposeful community is one "where faculty and students share academic goals and work together to strengthen teaching and learning on the campus" (9). This principle is fundamental to the others and, like the Commission on the Future of Community Colleges' report (1988), suggests that community begins in the classroom with faculty and students as active partners in the teaching-learning process. The Carnegie report also says that, in a purposeful community, learning will extend beyond the classroom and into the entire life of the campus, so that a coherent curriculum is supported by a commitment to learning in cocurricular and extracurricular activities, as well. In short, pervasive, integrated learning is the hallmark of a purposeful campus community (1990, 16).

An open community is one "where freedom of expression is uncompromisingly protected and where civility is powerfully affirmed" (17). The quality of communication measures the quality of the college, and if the college is to be an open community, communication must be characterized both by taking care in the clarity of expression and by showing care for all members of the community; that is, communication should be both clear and civil (17). Obviously, many colleges and universities are attempting to cope with the sometimes contradictory values of supporting free expression and providing a safe environment for all members of the community. In a 1989 survey of college and university presidents almost half responded that sexual harassment and racial intimidation were moderate to major problems on their campus (18). (One must keep in mind, of course, that this response is from the perspective of a group dominated by white males, who may not be, in some cases, highly sensitive to gender and racial bias.) As campuses become increasingly diverse, communication, according to the Carnegie report, must be viewed as a "sacred trust," where care in speaking and listening is valued, where offensive language is "vigorously denounced," and where one "can expect everyone to respect the rights and dignity of everyone else" (23).

A just community is one "where the sacredness of each person is honored and where diversity is aggressively pursued" (25). The Carnegie report points out that participation rates for minority students dropped in the 1980s and strongly recommends a renewed effort to provide opportunities for these students; however, the report also says that "the issue is more than access; it has to do with the lack of support minority students feel once they have enrolled, and there are alarming signals that racial and ethnic divisions are deepening on the nation's campuses" (26). If the community is going to be just, then appreciation and understanding of difference must be seen as integral to a well-rounded education, and multicultural perspectives must be deeply valued.

A disciplined community is one "where individuals accept their obligations to the group and where well-defined governance procedures guide behavior for the common good" (37). The report points out that, on most campuses, whereas rules governing academic requirements are spelled out in great detail, the rules regarding nonacademic behavior are ambiguous at best. The report suggests that all campuses should have a code of conduct for students that defines the standards of behavior in both academic and social situations. The report concludes that, in order to have community, a college or university must be a place where "individuals acknowledge their obligations to the group" (46). According to the report, honor codes provide a "powerful message about how honesty and integrity form the foundation of a community of learning" (46).

A caring community is one "where the well-being of each member is sensitively supported and where service to others is encouraged" (47). The Carnegie report saw caring as the key to campus community. The way that people relate to one another and the sense of belonging that is experienced by students are crucial to building and fostering community on campus. The report points out that many students feel a sense of connection to smaller subgroups within the campus community, but that, although these groups are important, they are not sufficient for building community. In fact, these subgroups often pull students away from a common agenda and discourage students from connecting with the institution as a whole. The report did find, however, the students at two-year colleges tended to experience our institutions as more caring, concluding that "community colleges are . . . especially good at building a spirit of community" (53).

Finally, a celebrative community is one "in which the heritage of the institution is remembered and where rituals affirming both tradition and change are widely shared" (55). The report suggests that community "must not only be created but created continually" and that "rites, ceremonies, and celebrations" help to build community and give students a feeling of belonging to something of worth that endures (55). According to the report, the "challenge is to instill all rituals and ceremonies with real significance—and fun as well'' (55). This can be accomplished in a variety of ways: orientations, special convocations, commencements, special events, and other events that connect the campus in community. The report also points out that, as colleges and universities become more inclusive and more diverse, celebrations must not only mark tradition, but also recognize change and innovation (60).

The call for community building in both of these important higher education reports may well reflect a response to a modern shift in consciousness which has been written about extensively in numerous works outside of higher education. For example, Eisler (1988) expresses this change with great clarity in what she calls the cultural transformation theory. Eisler draws a distinction between two radically different models of society. The ''dominator'' model is characterized by ''ranking''; that is, in the social structure some individuals—popularly termed ''patriarchs''—are powerful over others. This model is typified by a hierarchic and authoritarian system that is ultimately conducted through the use of force. Eisler sees this model as now ''reaching its logical limits'' (1988, xx).

On the other hand, the ''partnership'' model is characterized by ''linking''; that is, a social structure in which interconnectedness is recognized and valued, and where power is defined as caring and affiliation (193). Furthermore, difference and diversity are ''not equated with either inferiority or superiority'' (xvii). In short, Eisler's transformation from a dominator to a partnership society is a metamorphosis that entails new ways of thinking, feeling, and acting—ways that are consistent with the values needed to build communities in higher education: inclusiveness, integration, collaboration, cooperation, diversity, caring, and partnership.

The physicist Fritjof Capra (1982) provides another example of the current transitions in worldview that have implications for our notion of community building. According to Capra, ''[A]s individuals, as a society, as a civilization, and as a planetary ecosystem, we are reaching a turning point'' (1982, 33). Capra believes that twentieth-century physics, which has undergone a conceptual revolution, provides a model for the changes in values and attitudes that are needed in social institutions. Our institutions, according to Capra, have been based on the philosophy of Descartes, the scientific methodology of Bacon, and classical Newtonian physics, which used a mechanistic image of the universe, an image in which nature—seen as feminine—was to be dominated and controlled. Now, modern physics provides a revolutionary new worldview which, contrary to the mechanistic view, can be best characterized by ''words like organic, holistic, and ecological'' (178). Capra says that ''the conception of the universe as an interconnected web of relationships'' is a major theme that recurs throughout modern physics (87).

Like Eisler, Capra sees the decline of patriarchy with its ''excessive self-assertion'' and value for ''power, control, and domination of others by force'' as fundamental to this cultural transition (44). According to Capra, ''[P]romotion of competitive behavior over cooperation is one of the principal manifestations of the self-assertive tendency in our society'' (44). What is needed is a new vision of reality with new forms of social organization based upon an ''awareness of the essential interrelatedness and interdependence of all phenomena'' (265). These new social organizations would emphasize, among other things, holistic relationships, variation, flexibility, renewal, openness, and harmony. All these are characteristics seen as integral to building and fostering community on our campuses.

Just as the transformations outlined in these two works suggest new possibilities for being in community, other recent works contain similar themes that have implications for community building on campuses. *Habits of the Heart* (Bellah et al., 1985) talks about a new ''social ecology'' or ''moral ecology,'' which would involve our being deeply aware of our ''intricate connectedness and interdependence'' (1985, 289). There are destructive consequences that have been brought about by the human failure to recognize our interrelatedness. By putting individualism and one's own advancement ahead of the common good, we have failed to build and foster community. In order to recover our social ecology, we must learn to link our personal aspirations with those of the group. Rather than resolve differences through power and manipulation, we ''could move to ameliorate the differences that are patently unfair while respecting difference based on morally intelligible commitments'' (187). Such a social ecology cannot be brought about by merely fine-tuning our current institutions; it ''involves a deep cultural, social, and even psychological transformation'' (289).

In a Difference Voice (Gilligan 1982) gives an account of the different ways in which males and females structure relationships—differences that lead to different views of morality and self. For women, relationship is translated into an image of network or web, thereby providing a ''nonhierarchical vision of human connection'' (62). Furthermore, care is an essential activity associated with relationship, ''of seeing and responding to need, taking care of the world by sustaining the web of connection'' (62). For men, however, relationships are seen through the image of hierarchy; that is, affiliations are usually seen as being characterized by dominance, subordination, and self-assertion. Given this, men develop the attitude that relationships should be governed by or protected by rules (46). These different images of relationship—hierarchy and web—suggest, of course, radically different visions of institutional structure. Clearly, seeing relationship as web rather than hierarchy provides an image of community that is more affiliative, cooperative, and creative.

Peters and Waterman (1982) in their popular management book *In Search of Excellence*, although not speaking directly about ''community,'' do suggest that excellent companies have a unique ''culture.'' This culture is characterized by many of the values and attitudes expressed above: more collaboration, less hierarchy, more shared decision making and individual control of one's destiny, less rational analysis, and more caring in the human relationships within the company. In fact, Peters and Waterman acknowledge that they are suggesting a "paradigm shift" away from the "rational model" of management (1982, 42). Upon close examination of their ideas about corporate culture, what they are really suggesting is a transformation from a more analytic, scientific, mechanistic, dominator model to a more interconnected, holistic, ecological, partnership model similar to that discussed and described by Eisler, Capra, Gilligan, Bellah, and others. Furthermore, we can see also the reports by the Carnegie Foundation and the Commission on the Future of Community Colleges are calling for transformations in campus life that clearly are consistent with this same shift.

I personally take this new paradigm as a valuable model for how we in community colleges can make meaningful attempts to build and foster community; however, many problems and questions must be addressed. Just as any major shift in consciousness creates tension, anger, conflict, and insecurity—all of which seem at odds with the goal of building communities—this transformation is no exception. What in the long run has great potential for creative and constructive changes on our campuses may be threatening and destructive in the interim. This is not surprising, given that—in some sense—any kind of transformation entails destruction of the old way of being and doing. Destruction of the old order to make room for the new always presents difficulties and challenges to the community. Given the current status of campus life at community colleges, the challenges are enormous.

When we consider, for example, the amount of caring and affiliation expressed and experienced on our campuses, there may be considerable room for improvement. We often judge ourselves in relative terms; that is, we say that we in community colleges are generally much more caring than those at large colleges and universities. We hear from our former students (and we are quick to point out to others) that at these institutions students are given little personal attention and often feel like they are merely numbers. In his work *The Neglected Majority*, Parnell says that providing a caring environment is one of the major elements of the opportunity-with-excellence philosophy of community colleges (1985, 92). However, if we are going to make meaningful changes in our campus communities, I think that we in community colleges must resist the temptation of making institutions, which are so often bereft of caring, the standard by which we judge ourselves.

Other issues also cloud the picture. To explain the lack of community at our colleges, I have hard the rationale used that community college students spend very little time on campus. However, as the Carnegie report says, "the spirit of community must be measured, not by the length of time on campus, but the quality of caring" (53). As we seek to build and foster community, I think we must be willing to evaluate honestly how truly caring are our institutions. Occasionally I hear colleagues speak of the problem of "pampering" students, suggesting that we do students a disservice when we do not prepare them adequately for what they will face in the "cold, cruel" reality of the "real world." However, there is certainly a distinct difference between coddling and caring. Too often, I fear, we justify a lack of caring by viewing nurturing as "soft"—

something to be the specific responsibility of counselors, or other student services personnel. Can we really justify showing our students a lack of caring in order to prepare them for a lack of caring at some later date? I think we should ask how can we reasonably expect to make the "real world" (in which we as individuals have such limited influence) more caring, unless we are prepared to make our own work group, our own classroom, and our own institution a caring community. Yet, many argue that this is "tough love," a good example of caring. One can see that even when there is agreement and resolve to be a caring community, there is still great possibility of disagreement about what exactly it means to be truly caring. In a sense, this question takes us back to the issue of the two different models of reality discussed above.

The literature suggests that the paradigm shift from one model of reality to another could be characterized as a shift from "masculine" ways of knowing, feeling, and acting to "feminine" ways of knowing, feeling, and acting. While in actuality the values and attitudes of caring, affiliation, connectedness, collaboration, integration, and the others associated with this new model are not gender specific, they may well be gender related. In may be that more women than men possess the values and attitudes that help build and foster community. Whether or not women are more likely to possess these values and attitudes, several problems still exist which would inhibit transformation. Not the least of these problems is that, when the issue is couched in language that suggest a bias against males, there is a strong likelihood of resistance and defensiveness on the part of men. Even more complications emerge when one considers that leadership positions in community colleges are overwhelmingly occupied by males. Furthermore, assuming that our institutions have historically tended to be governed in a patriarchal and hierarchical manner, then it seems likely that some of the women who have managed to rise to leadership positions are those who have learned best how to function within a hierarchical model. In short, the problem is how can we move from an authoritarian, hierarchical system to a more collaborative, caring community when many of the leadership positions may be occupied by individuals who function well within the old paradigm?

The same problem exists, although perhaps to a lesser degree, within our classrooms. Over half of community college faculty are men. Again, while there are certainly notable exceptions, our classrooms are frequently characterized by values and actions associated with the aforementioned "masculine" model. While many classrooms are communities that express a value for caring, collaboration, and shared decision making, these appear to be the exception rather than the rule. Once again, the question is how we can hope to bring about change when faculty are comfortable and have experienced some measure of success with the old, traditional, authoritarian ways of being in the classroom.

When we turn to the problem of building a community that is diverse and multicultural, the problem is even more complicated. About 90 percent of the faculty and managers within community colleges are of the ethnic majority. With leadership and faculty that is so monocultural, how can we hope to build a multicultural community where diversity is aggressively valued and pursued? Given the demographic changes projected for the coming years, and inasmuch as "community colleges are the major points of entry for minority students . . . and for new immigrants to the United States" (Green 1988, 21), then we can be certain that our classrooms will continue to become more and more diverse at a much more rapid pace than will our faculty and management. Given these realities, we must ask how we will be able to build diverse, multicultural communities.

Even in the most ideal situations, where virtually everyone within the institution agrees that change is needed and desirable, there are still considerable difficulties to overcome. To cite but one example, how can an institution move to a shared governance and shared decision-making model when such behaviors are counter to the prevailing campus culture? How can such a change be managed when few are sure what shared governance entails or how actually to go about it?

Theobald has written that we are currently living in the "rapids of change." "[W]e cannot slow down the changes coming to our culture, our society, our families, ourselves" (1987, 11). I believe, however, that we can negotiate these rapids and make significant progress in building and fostering community on our campuses if we will commit ourselves fully to several key notions—ideas that are consistent with transformation but are also, I believe, fundamental to our calling as educators.

First, we must be committed to dynamic self-renewal. Change is a given. To paraphrase the philosopher Heraclitus, everything changes except change. As we have noted, change is not only ongoing, it is also rapid. The issue for community colleges is not whether we will change; the real issue is how ably we manage change. There is a difference between change and innovation. The word "change' means to make different, whereas the word "innovation" means to make new. When we are committed to self-renewal, we are committed to innovation. For example, changing the ethnic and gender makeup of our communities is a clear and urgent need; however, this change alone is not enough. A commitment to dynamic self-renewal involves seeing such a change as an opportunity to make the community new. This means doing much more than merely providing more access to women and people of color into the old community. Rather, it means that the community welcomes the renewal that comes with the different perspectives, worldviews, feelings, and values these new members bring with them to the community. Inclusiveness into an existing model or framework is merely the shadow of inclusion. Authentic inclusiveness involves transformation of the old form into new ways of thinking, feeling, and acting. A commitment to dynamic self-renewal means the community views every such change as an occasion for rebirth.

The pathway to self-renewal of the community is found through a strong commitment to communication. This is the second key idea that must govern our attempts to build and foster community. The word communication and the word community share the same Latin root, *communis*, meaning common. The only way that we can hope to share a life in community is through an uncompromising commitment to authentic and honest communication. Communication is difficult in the best of situations. Certainly it is much more difficult when we attempt to communicate across our differences. Although we may not be able to step outside of our own cultural framework when attempting to communicate, we can be ever cognizant of the fact that we are bound by and limited to that conceptual framework. This means that we would be aware that what we think is transpiring is merely an interpretation of reality, not reality itself. Furthermore, we must accept the fact that honest and authentic communication will not always be pleasant. Palmer has written that "our image of community forces people to hide their disagreements instead of getting them in the open where we might learn from them, where the problem might be worked through" (1981, 120). Working through disagreements and differences will always build community if our communication is characterized by caring, which leads to the last key idea that must direct our attempts to build and foster community.

We must be wholly committed to our calling as educators. I have on numerous occasions heard the derivation of the word "education" incorrectly identified as *educere*, which means to bring forth or bring up. In actuality "education" is derived from the Latin *educare*, which means to care for and to cause to grow. We can see that the values we have associated with building communities are really inseparable from education itself. Caring is not one of the ways in which we can act as we attempt to educate; it is an essential, integral aspect of education.

We grow when we develop new frames of reference and when we can celebrate difference—not just intellectual differences, but differences in culture, gender, ethnicity, physical abilities and challenges, nationalities, religions, age, political beliefs, orientations, and values. Understanding and appreciation of diversity enriches us all. Through our increased understanding of and appreciation for new and different perspectives, we stretch our own limited boundaries—we grow. Valuing diversity is not a sideline for educators; it is our mission; it is, in fact, education. Building and fostering a diverse community does not mean for any one of us that we must learn more about "them" or vice versa. Valuing diversity must never be seen as a we-they dichotomy. Great diversity exists among the members of any single ethnic group, among the members of both genders, among us all. A diverse, multicultural community is not just some of us; it is each one of us. Valuing difference is a lifelong, developmental quest for each one of us, working together in community.

The phrase "lifelong learning" has long been popular in community college circles; however, too often I fear, our actions indicate we give only lip service to the concept. Our calling as educators is in fact a call to our own lifelong growth and development. In the final analysis, if we are going to build and foster community with our students, with the local communities external to the campus, and with each other, then we must make sure that lifelong learning is our way of life; we must answer our personal call to education with a resounding "yes!"

Even as I consider the difficult problems and tremendous challenges that face community colleges as we seek to build communities, I am able to look to the future with hope. My hope is grounded in several observations about community colleges in America. First, we are fortunate to have strong, innovative leadership at the national level. National community college organizations have helped to create a new vision for our colleges and also have provided valuable resources to move toward that vision. The establishment of creative leadership development programs for women and people of color is but one of many examples of how national organizations are helping to address the challenge of building community. My hope is also sustained by the fact that community colleges are by their very nature and design highly flexible. Surely within all higher education, community colleges have proven to be the most adaptable. Community colleges have a history of responding rapidly to new demands and challenges. Quite literally, courses and programs have been developed overnight in order to respond to the needs of the community. If we can bring that same flexibility to bear regarding the issue associated with building and fostering community, we can be confident of success. Perhaps the greatest cause for my hopeful attitude abides in the fact that community colleges have an abundance of individuals of great caring and commitment. Martin Luther King, Jr., said of our age, "[T]his may well be mankind's last chance to choose between chaos and community" (1967, 223). I am confident that the caring, committed individuals who have given their lives to the work of community colleges will answer the call and will lead us toward a choice for community.

REFERENCES

Bellah, R., et al. 1985. *Habits of the heart: Individualism and commitment in American life.* New York: Harper and Row.

Capra, F. 1982. *The turning point.* New York: Bantam Books.

Carnegie Foundation for the Advancement of Teaching. 1990. *Campus life: In search of community.* Princeton, N.J.: Princeton University Press.

Commission on the Future of Community Colleges. 1988. *Building communities: A vision for a new century.* Washington, D.C.: American Association of Community and Junior Colleges.

Eisler, R. 1988. *The chalice and the blade.* San Francisco: Harper and Row.

Else, G. 1969. The old and new humanities. *Daedalus* 98(2):803–6.

Gilligan, C. 1982. *In a different voice.* Cambridge, Mass.: Harvard University Press.

Green, M. F. 1988. *Minorities on campus: A handbook for enhancing diversity.* Washington, D.C.: Community College Press.

Kimball, B. 1986. *Orators & philosophers: A history of the idea of liberal education.* New York: Teachers College, Columbia University.

King, M. L., Jr. 1967. *Where do we go from here: Chaos or community?* New York: Bantam Books.

Lovejoy, A. O. 1960. *The great chain of being: A study of an idea.* New York: Harper.

Nussbaum, M. 1985. Historical conceptions of the humanities and their relationship to society. In *Applying the humanities*, ed. D. Callahan, A. Caplan, and B. Jennings, 3–28. New York: Plenum Press.

Palmer, P. J. 1981. *The company of strangers*. New York: Crossroads Publishing.

Parnell, D. 1985. *The neglected majority*. Washington, D.C.: Community College Press.

Peters, T., and R. H. Waterman. 1982. *In search of excellence*. New York: Harper and Row.

Theobald, R. 1987. *The rapids of change*. Indianapolis: Knowledge Systems, Inc.

Valade, W. J. 1958. The community college ideal. *Junior College Journal* 28:332–36.

Wattenbarger, J. L. 1982. Junior and community college education. In *Encyclopedia of educational research*, ed. H. Mitzel, 982–88. New York: Free Press.

New Wave Students and the Community College

Laura I. Rendón and
James R. Valadez

One of the most striking changes for postsecondary education has been occurring for nearly twenty years now, slowly at first, but with ever-increasing acceleration. Over the past decade, the American community college has been experiencing a large-scale transformation in terms of the racial and ethnic composition of its student population. From a largely Caucasian, traditionally college-aged student body, many community colleges are now enrolling more and more "new wave" students—immigrants and students of color. This vivid transformation mirrors the growth of new wave Americans, new people who are altering the demographic profile of this nation (Cetron and Davies 1989; Quality Education for Minorities Project 1990).

The overwhelming tide of this "new wave" student body has had a profound effect on community colleges, especially in regions of the country with large minority communities. In some of America's major cities, such as Los Angeles and San Antonio, the term "minority" has lost its statistical meaning, for people of color are the majority. This chapter will discuss (1) how demographic trends have contributed to enrollment shifts in institutions of higher education, (2) the factors that account for the growth of students of color in community colleges, and (3) the implications of the continuing transformation of the student body for the restructuring of community colleges.

DEMOGRAPHIC TRENDS

Demographic trends provide an important context for analyzing shifts in the profile of students entering the educational system. During the ten-year period between 1980 and 1990, minority groups fueled the growth of this nation. While Caucasians grew by 9.8 percent, African Americans grew by

13.2 percent. Native Americans grew by 37.9 percent, and Hispanics grew by 53 percent. The most dramatic growth was registered by Asian/Pacific Islanders who grew by 107.8 percent during that ten-year period. Two external factors are precipitating the process of change. First, about 9 million people immigrated to the United States in the 1980s, twice as many as in the preceding decade. About 84 percent of the immigrants are from Asia, the Caribbean, and Latin America. Second, the birthrate among people of color is far higher than that of Caucasians. Among African Americans, it is double the national average; among Hispanics, it is quadruple the national average (Cetron and Davies 1989).

These new wave Americans have no doubt contributed to the increasing pool of new wave students. The growth of new wave students can be detected by examining population trends in the eighteen-to-twenty-four-year-old eligible cohort. Table 1 indicates that prior to 1980, eighteen-to-twenty-four-year-old minority students numbered less than 4 million. During the 1980s, however, students of color enjoyed phenomenal growth, from about 4.6 million students in 1980 to 7 million students in 1990. In 1980, the cohort of eighteen-to-twenty-four-year-old minority students accounted for nearly 16 percent of the college-age population, but by 1990, the cohort had grown to about 27 percent. While the absolute numbers of minority students will decrease between 1985 and 1995, a quick rate of recovery is expected. By the year 2000, students of color are projected to constitute about 30 percent of the college-age population and nearly 40 percent in 2025 (Mingle 1987).

According to a report released by the Quality Education for Minorities Project (1990), currently about 20 percent of the nation is Alaska Native, Native American, African American, or Hispanic. Yet, this is only the beginning. By the turn of the century, one out of every four Americans will be Hispanic, African American, Asian, or Middle Eastern. By around 2015, Hispanics will be the largest minority group in America and around 2030, people of color will make up more than half of the American population, with European Americans becoming just one more segment of a multicultural nation made up of new wave Americans (Cetron and Davies 1989). As early as 2000, minorities will be the majority in fifty-three of America's largest cities.

But the future of higher education is already here, and it can be documented by examining enrollments in the K–12 sector. Between 1968 and 1986, the number of Caucasian school children fell by 16 percent, but the number of African American children increased by 5 percent, and the number of Hispanic children grew by a phenomenal 100 percent. Already, Mississippi and New Mexico have "majority minority" public schools, and California and Texas are poised to join that list. Today more than 30 percent of students in public schools—some 12 million—are minority. And twenty-two of the twenty-five largest central city suburb districts are predominantly minority. These students are growing older, and they now represent the nation's potential supply of college students.

Table 1
College-Age Population (18–24), Selected 1950–2050

Year	Total (in thousands)	Caucasian	Minority	Minority Percent
1950	16,075	14,186	1,889*	11.8*
1960	16,128	14,169	1,959*	12.1*
1970	24,712	21,532	3,180*	13.0*
1975	27,735	23,775	3,959*	14.3*
1980	30,081	25,415	4,666	15.5*
1982	30,344	23,074	7,270	24.0
1983	30,054	22,736	7,318	24.3
1984	29,476	22,181	7,295	24.7
1985	28,715	21,491	7,224	25.2
1990	25,777	18,768	7,009	27.2
1995	23,684	16,753	6,931	29.3
2000	24,590	17,062	7,528	30.6
2025	25,447	15,468	9,979	39.2
2050	25,659	14,278	11,381	44.4

*Does not include Spanish-origin population if they were classified as "Caucasian" rather than "African American and other" in the survey data.

Note: Minority 1982–2050 arrived by subtracting "Spanish-origin" from "Caucasian" and redistributing to "African American and other."

Sources: 1950–1970: U.S. Bureau of the Census; *Current Population Reports*, Series P–25, No. 311, p. 22; No. 519, Table 1; No. 704, Table 8; No. 880, Table 1; No. 870, Table 1; No. 917, Table 1; as reported in 1986–87 *Fact Book on Higher Education*, American Council on Education, page 4. 1975–1980: *Current Population Reports*, Series P–25, No. 917, Table 1. 1982–2050: *Current Population Reports*, Series P–25, No. 922, Table 2; No. 995, Table 2.

SHIFTS IN COLLEGE ENROLLMENTS

The impact of the nation's growth of ''new wave'' Americans can be detected throughout higher education. Table 2 illustrates that throughout higher education institutions, the proportionate share of Caucasian student enrollments has been steadily dropping, from 84.3 percent in 1976 to 81.1 percent in 1988. Conversely, the proportional representation of minority students has steadily increased, from 15.7 percent in 1976 to 18.9 percent in 1988. Therefore, much of the growth in overall college enrollments for minorities occurred during the 1980s—a period when fully 46 percent of new wave immigrants were Asian and 40 percent come from Latin America. Although noticeable drops can be noted for African American students, Hispanics and Asians increased their proportional representation during the 1980s. Conversely, a steady rate of proportional representation can be noted for Native American and Alaska Native students.

Similar patterns can be seen in Table 2 when analyzing proportional representation of students in the two- and four-year college sector. In four-year institutions, Caucasians have decreased their proportional representation, from 86.6 percent in 1976 to 83.6 percent in 1988. During the same time period, minorities increased their proportionate enrollments from 13.4 percent to 16.4 percent. Again, African American students appear to have lost proportional representation, and the representation of American Indians and Alaska Natives has held steady. Thus, most of the gains in four-year colleges can be attributed to Hispanic and Asian and Pacific Islander students.

An analysis of proportional distributions in the two-year college sector reveals similar trends. Again, Caucasians have lost ground in their enrollment distribution, dropping from 80.2 percent in 1976 to 77 percent in 1988. Yet, proportional enrollments of minorities during this period increased from 19.8 percent to 23 percent, with Hispanics and Asians and Pacific Islanders accounting for much of that growth. The proportion of African American students in two-year colleges has decreased, and the proportion of Native American and Alaska Native students has held steady.

Yet another way to analyze college enrollment shifts is to examine the absolute number of students attending higher education. Table 3 reveals that, although all ethnic/racial groups have increased their sheer numbers in two- and four-year colleges, African Americans and Caucasians have grown least, and Asians and Hispanics have registered dramatic enrollment growth. However, these data should not be misinterpreted to indicate that minorities are well represented in college. For example, Caucasian students increased their proportion of college entrants from 1981 to 1985, despite decreases in the number completing high school. Yet, for African Americans and Hispanics, the reverse trend is true. Losses in the proportion of African American and Hispanic students entering college have occurred even in the face of increases in the overall number completing high school. To illustrate, Orfield and Paul (1987–1988) assessed educational opportunities for minorities in metropolitan Chicago, Los Angeles,

Table 2
Percent Distribution of Students in Higher Education by Institutional Type and Race/Ethnicity: Fall 1976–Fall 1988

	1976	1980	1982	1984	1986	1988
All Students						
Total	100.0	100.0	100.0	100.0	100.0	100.0
Caucasian, Non-Hisp.	84.3	83.5	82.9	82.5	81.6	81.1
Total Minority	15.7	16.5	17.1	17.5	18.4	18.9
African American, Non-Hisp.	9.6	9.4	9.1	9.0	8.9	8.9
Hispanic	3.6	4.0	4.3	4.5	5.1	5.4
Asian/Pacific Is.	1.8	2.4	2.9	3.3	3.7	3.9
Nat. Amer./Al. Native	0.7	0.7	0.7	0.7	0.7	0.7
4-Year						
Total	100.0	100.0	100.0	100.0	100.0	100.0
Caucasian, Non-Hisp.	86.6	85.7	85.5	84.9	84.1	83.6
Total Minority	13.4	14.3	14.5	15.1	15.9	16.4
African American, Non-Hisp.	8.7	8.7	8.3	8.3	8.2	8.3
Hispanic	2.5	3.0	3.1	3.3	3.7	3.8
Asian/Pacific Is.	1.7	2.2	2.6	3.0	3.5	3.8
Nat. Amer./Al. Native	0.5	0.5	0.5	0.5	0.5	0.5
2-Year						
Total	100.0	100.0	100.0	100.0	100.0	100.0
Caucasian, Non-Hisp.	80.2	79.8	78.9	78.5	77.5	77.0
Total Minority	19.8	20.2	21.1	21.5	22.5	23.0
African American, Non-Hisp.	11.2	10.6	10.5	10.3	10.1	9.8
Hispanic	5.5	5.7	6.2	6.5	7.3	8.0
Asian/Pacific Is.	2.1	2.8	3.4	3.7	4.0	4.1
Nat. Amer./Al. Native	1.1	1.1	1.1	1.0	1.1	1.0

Sources: U.S. Department of Education, National Center for Education Statistics, *Full Enrollment in Colleges and Universities*; Integrated Postsecondary Education Data System (IPEDS), *Full Enrollment Surveys*. Table prepared February 1990.

Table 3
College Enrollments by Racial and Ethnic Group, 1978–1988

	1978	1988	% Change
Native American	78,000	93,000	+ 19.2
4-Year	35,000	42,000	+ 20.0
2-Year	43,000	50,000	+16.2
Asian	235,500	497,000	+111.3
4-Year	138,000	297,000	+115.2
2-Year	97,000	199,000	+105.2
African American	1,054,000	1,130,000	+7.2
4-Year	612,000	656,000	+7.2
2-Year	443,000	473,000	+6.8
Hispanic	417,000	680,000	+63.1
4-Year	190,000	296,000	+55.8
2-Year	227,000	384,000	+69.2
Caucasian	9,194,000	10,283,000	+11.8
4-Year	6,027,000	6,582,000	+9.2
2-Year	3,167,000	3,702,000	+16.9
Foreign	253,000	361,000	+42.7
4-Year	201,000	302,000	+50.2
2-Year	52,000	60,000	+15.3
All	11,231,000	13,043,000	+16.1
4-Year	7,203,000	8,175,000	+13.5
2-Year	4,028,000	4,868,000	+20.1

Source: *The Almanac of Higher Education*, 1991, Chicago: University of Chicago Press.

Atlanta, Houston, and Philadelphia. The researchers found that "African American and Hispanic enrollment in two and four-year institutions dropped relative to each group in proportion to the high school population, while Caucasian enrollment increased" (1987–1988, 57). The researchers concluded that barriers such as poor high school preparation, increasing college costs, and inadequate assistance to unprepared students continued to impede African American and Hispanic access to two- and four-year institutions.

The concentration of students of color in two-year colleges is documented in

Table 4
Enrollment by Type of Institution, 1988

	Total	American Indian	Asian	African American	Hispanic	Cau-casian	Foreign
Public							
4-Year	42.5%	36.0%	42.3%	39.7%	31.7%	43.3%	50.2%
2-Year	35.4	51.6	39.4	38.3	54.6	34.1	15.6
Private							
4-Year	20.2	9.5	17.6	18.4	11.8	20.7	33.3
2-Year	2.0	2.9	0.8	3.6	1.9	1.9	0.9
Total	100.0	100.0	100.0	100.0	100.0	100.0	100.0

Note: This table shows, for example, that although 42.5 percent of all students were enrolled at 4-year public institutions in 1988, only 36.0 percent of American Indian students attended such institutions.

Source: U.S. Department of Education, 1990.

Table 4. Two-year institutions are especially important for Hispanics who have traditionally used the colleges as a means to initiate college-based programs of study and for Native Americans who have their own network of tribally controlled two-year institutions. About 56.5 percent of Hispanics attending college in 1988 were clustered in two-year institutions, and 54.5 percent of Native American students in college attended two-year colleges. It is reasonable to predict that community colleges will continue to educate large proportions of "new wave" students. The immigration of large numbers of Asians and Hispanics is likely to continue well into the twenty-first century (U.S. Census Bureau 1989). The southwestern United States will be the area most affected, but other regions of the country, such as the southeastern United States, are facing unexpected waves of Hispanic immigration (*Raleigh News and Observer*, 25 August 1991). Table 5 reflects the fact that thirty-three states now enroll 30 percent or more minorities in the two-year college sector, and twenty-three states enroll more than 40 percent of minorities in the two-year college system.

Table 5
States with 30 Percent or More Minority Enrollment in Two-Year Colleges (by percent), 1986

State	4-Year Institutions	2-Year Institutions
Alabama	53	47
Alaska	38	62
Arizona	30	70
California	35	65
Colorado	48	52
Connecticut	61	39
Florida	46	54
Hawaii	57	43
Illinois	37	63
Kansas	58	42
Kentucky	70	30
Maryland	59	41
Mississippi	59	41
Missouri	66	34
Montana	54	46
Nebraska	63	37
Nevada	41	59
New Jersey	59	41
New Mexico	52	48
North Carolina	58	42
North Dakota	48	52
Ohio	67	33
Oklahoma	62	38
Oregon	56	44
Pennsylvania	64	36
South Carolina	60	40
Tennessee	67	33
Texas	53	47
Utah	61	39
Virginia	62	38
Washington	42	58
Wisconsin	55	45
Wyoming	29	71

Source: Chronicle of Higher Education Almanac, 6 September 1989, 8.

FACTORS ACCOUNTING FOR MINORITY ENROLLMENT GROWTH

The Early Years, 1920s–1950s

From the very beginning of the community college movement, the goals of the institution have been enmeshed in the promise to provide an opportunity for higher education for the masses of American people. The early years of the community college movement produced only modest results as reflected in the low enrollment figures. Available data indicate that, by 1920, only 8,100 students were enrolled in community colleges in the United States (U.S. Office of Education 1944). The first publicly supported junior colleges were created primarily with a mission of offering transfer education, occupational programs, and post–high school terminal programs for students who sought to enter jobs and prepare for family living. Consequently, the 1920s and 1930s were a period of increased interest and popularity of the community colleges. By 1930 there were 55,000 students enrolled in community colleges in the United States. During the Depression years, especially, the community college experienced significant growth, and by 1940 there were approximately 150,000 students enrolled in the community college system (Brint and Karabel 1989).

Much of the growth in the 1930s took place in three states: Illinois, Texas, and California. In fact, these states enrolled two-thirds of all community college students. The growth was not limited to these states, of course. New colleges were emerging in most of the United States but primarily in the established centers of community college activity: Minnesota, Iowa, Kansas, and Oklahoma (Brint and Karabel 1989).

The community colleges provided a relatively inexpensive way for students to attend college at a time when the nation was in the throes of the Great Depression. Coincidentally, and not insignificantly, the nation was experiencing rapid population growth. High schools were producing unprecedented numbers of graduates, but unfortunately for these students, the prospects for jobs were limited. This combination of factors was a major influence in the increased popularity of community colleges in the 1930s.

The community college enrollment surge continued during the 1940s, especially after World War II with the advent of the GI Bill of Rights. By 1950 enrollment in community colleges had increased to 217,000 students. The introduction of the GI Bill was a precursor to events that began to unfold in the post–World War II era and continued to the present day. Before World War II, the community colleges were primarily Caucasian, middle-class institutions (Brint and Karabel 1989). After the war, students who never considered the prospect of a college education now had the opportunity and financial wherewithal to enter college. Available data indicate that in the ten years after the war, one-half to two-thirds of the new students were from lower middle- and working-class backgrounds (Brint and Karabel 1989; Clark 1960).

The 1960s and Beyond

It was after World War II that the colleges expanded their mission to accommodate more students so that all American citizens, regardless of ability or background, could avail themselves of an equal opportunity for a college-based education. Junior colleges became community colleges, adding (1) community services, an array of cultural and educational programs that did not lead to transfer, and (2) remedial studies, programs designed to remedy the academic skills of poorly prepared high school graduates. When the colleges became "people's colleges," they underwent a major philosophical shift from institutions providing a traditional college preparation to flexible colleges that prepared students to find a job, adapt to life, and get the most for their money in a short time period, without leaving home and without having to give up a full-time job. The very nature of the broad mission and flexibility increased the diversity of the community colleges' clientele. Older students became attracted to tuition reductions and special classes for senior citizens. Working students were encouraged by easy attendance on a part-time basis, by classes offered at off-campus centers, and by the lack of rigid requirements to complete programs in a given span of years. Students with weak academic skills liked the fact that the college open doors meant easy entrance with no selective admissions criteria. Minorities and low socioeconomic students were lured by the colleges' close proximity to home, inexpensive tuition, and the opportunity to "try out" college-level work (Rendón 1984; Cohen 1985).

As working-class students, minorities, immigrants, and other nontraditional students began to enter the community college, the institution itself began to undergo a dramatic transformation that had an impact on the colleges' purpose. In the beginning, community colleges were promoted as institutions that provided the means for individuals to achieve upward social mobility through higher education. However, as more and more nontraditional students entered two-year colleges, concern arose about whether community colleges could indeed help students who were attempting to cross class boundaries in a highly stratified society (Karabel 1986). Community colleges touted the notion that an educational system formed on democratic ideals would lead students up the ladder of success, but that promise was cloaked in a social system that resisted change. Some claimed that the ambitions of many low socioeconomic status students were not developed and encouraged, but were in fact "cooled out" (Clark 1960). Critics of community colleges maintained that students, primarily working-class or minority students, were identified by testing or other methods and sorted into either academic or vocational tracks. In effect, critics claimed not only that the community college was not providing the means for upward social mobility, but also that the existence of two-year colleges made it possible for society to preserve higher status positions for students judged to be more capable and to reserve lower status jobs for those deemed less able, most of whom were working-class and minority students (Rendón 1991).

As minority and other nontraditional students expanded the rolls of community colleges, the demands for financial aid also increased. The increased availability of student financial aid beginning in the 1960s was a major attraction for the more economically disadvantaged students. Student assistance programs were relatively rare in the period before the 1970s. In fact, financial aid programs were found in fewer than half the states in 1970. By 1980 nearly all the states had programs. Federal student loans and work-study grants rose from less than $120 million in 1979 to nearly $450 million in 1978 (Breneman and Nelson 1981).

In addition to increased financial aid, the general spirit of the post–civil rights era of the late 1960s offered encouragement to minorities and opened the possibility for many to pursue higher education. Institutions became more aware of increasing the diversity on their campuses, and resources were made available to recruit and finance minority student education. To go along with an improved social climate, new legislation forced institutions to open their doors and provide resource for encouraging minority participation. The 1964 Civil Rights Act, of course, was the bellwether and was followed closely by the 1965 Affirmative Action Executive Order, the 1971 Basic Educational Opportunity (Pell) Grant, and the 1972 *Adams v. Richardson* decision by the U.S. Supreme Court dismantling segregation in higher education (Wilson 1986). The civil rights–related legislation signaled an era of encouragement and support for minorities. The community colleges were viewed as institutions that could provide for minorities the means for participating in the system of higher education and for having the potential to improve their social and economic conditions. The improved social climate for the 1960s seemed to be part of a nationwide phenomenon of changing attitudes, in which disadvantaged people were asserting their rights, calling for an end to war and oppression, and demanding equal opportunity for a chance at the American dream (Wilson 1986).

The infusion of financial aid programs and an improved climate for social justice, combined with a phenomenal increase of open-door two-year institutions located within easy access to minority population centers, dramatically increased the numbers of minorities in the nation's community colleges. The overall student population in community colleges was also booming. In 1960 there were 451,000 community college students. By 1970 that number increased to 1.6 million, and by 1980 there were 4.5 million students enrolled in community colleges (U.S. Department of Education 1990).

The explosion in the popularity of the community colleges is especially noteworthy for multicultural student populations. Community colleges still appear to provide the promise for the improvement of the social and economic standing of minorities and disadvantaged people. How that promise can be translated to reality remains an unfullfilled challenge. The 1990s again bring new students to community colleges. These new wave students, mothers and fathers, sons and daughters who have immigrated to this country in record numbers, are reason again for the colleges to examine their mission and programmatic offerings.

RESTRUCTURING COMMUNITY COLLEGES: IMPLICATIONS OF NEW WAVE STUDENT ENROLLMENTS

Although community colleges now serve as the principal gateway to higher education for the nation's new wave students and in many states constitute the primary point of college entry for the great majority of all students, there is concern that the community college may also be the point of exit for many college students. What little hope there is for upward social mobility for students of color may lie in the hands of community colleges. That is an enormous responsibility and one that cannot be taken lightly. The campus enrollment shift—from a predominantly white student population to one that is multicultural in nature—calls for a diversity restructuring program leading to improvements in mission, governance, curriculum, instruction, student support services, and faculty development.

Mission and College Goals

A diversity restructuring plan should be a plan of action based on the college's mission and goals. Does the college mission need to be revised? Where does the college want to be relative to improving the rate of retention and transfer for multicultural students? What should students know when they graduate from specific programs of study? What is needed to help the college be recognized as an exemplary multicultural community college? These are but some of the key questions administrators and faculty should address as they come to the table to prepare a diversity restructuring plan of action. These goals should also serve as benchmarks by which to assess the progress a college is making toward creating an exemplary multicultural campus.

Shared Governance

Good faith efforts do not work. Leadership from community college presidents and chief executive officers is needed to implement a diversity restructuring program that is in line with a multicultural campus. Leaders must convey to faculty, staff, and students that creating a campus that recognizes, values, and respects difference is a priority. Yet this is only the beginning. Participatory college management will be needed, in which administrators share power with faculty, support staff, and community representatives to build a strong college community. Through shared governance, it will be possible to help transform the college into an exemplary campus that values diversity in student, faculty, and staff representation, as well as in teaching and learning practices.

A Curriculum of Inclusion

Currently there is a heated debate about the college curriculum that is centered on the often misunderstood and misused concept of "political correctness." On the one hand, those who defend the traditional canon of the curriculum argue that the classics—the "great works" of literature, science, and history—should dominate what is taught. On the other hand, multiculturalists believe that the college curriculum should be more inclusive of the contributions that people of color have made to history, science, art, and literature. What is probably needed is for both camps to find a common ground, a pluralist view that avoids the separatist extremes of each school of thought. College teams composed of faculty, administrators, and students should review the college's course offerings with an eye toward designing a curriculum of inclusion—one that builds on the strength of the traditional European-centered curriculum. At the same time, the curriculum should reflect the merits of the contributions of people of color so that all students learn about the pluralism and diversity that are reshaping America.

Ethnic Styles of Learning

The learning styles of multicultural student populations are only beginning to be understood. Yet there is increasing evidence that a passive classroom environment, in which faculty rely too much on the lecture method and adopt the linear model of teaching where information flows only from faculty to students, may be inappropriate for women and students of color (Belenky et al., 1986). Community college faculty should assess their students' learning styles, as well as their own teaching styles, to determine how they can adjust the classroom environment to foster student learning. Faculty development programs will be needed to train instructors to assess learning styles and teaching styles, as well as to help faculty employ varied and active teaching techniques such as debates, demonstrations, interactive video, simulations, and case studies.

Mentoring Programs

Research indicates that students who make connections have an easier time making the transition to college life (Blackwell 1983; Clewell 1987). Mentoring programs that pair students with faculty and administrators, a well as those that connect students with their peers, need to be established. Yet, mentoring should not be the responsibility of minority faculty alone. Both minority and majority faculty and staff must share the responsibility of helping all students adjust to their college environment and to persist in college until their educational goals are fulfilled.

Faculty and Staff Diversification

Increasing the representation of Hispanic, Asian, African American, and American Indian faculty and staff will be increasingly important as more and more new wave students take advantage of community college academic and vocational-technical programs. It is important that these students find a critical mass of faculty and staff that they can turn to for mentoring and for the support they will need to integrate into the social and academic fabric of the institution.

Receptive Campus Climate

Community colleges must work vigorously to ensure that the campus climate is one that values and respects cultural diversity. Recently, students of color have been the victims of racial slurs, caricatures, and insensitive remarks from students and faculty. These incidents point to the need for creating a positive, nurturing campus climate where all students learn and grow while respecting diversity of backgrounds and opinion. Courses and seminars should address issues of race relations, policies should prohibit racial and sex discrimination, and staff development programs should be designed with an eye to sensitize faculty, counselors, and administrators to the concerns of multicultural students. In short, what is needed is not one or two exemplary programs, but a holistic, campus-wide effort that turns the college into an exemplary multicultural campus.

CONCLUSION

The ever-increasing, inexorable speed in which new wave Americans have found their way into this nation is being felt throughout higher education and especially in community colleges which remain attractive to large numbers of nontraditional student populations. Ever-shifting enrollments are creating a majority/minority student reversal that drives the need for faculty, counselors, and administrators to rethink the policies and conventions that have been accepted practices in community colleges. Futuristic ways of thinking are needed about how two-year colleges can best address the transformation of the college into a multicultural student campus. This will require new leadership styles, creating governance structures that foster community building, innovative ways to teach and to assess student learning, inventive ways of creating a curriculum of inclusion, and new ways of attracting and retaining a multicultural faculty and staff that reflect the changing profile of students. The hopes and dreams of new wave students include finding success in mainstream America. To help new wave students find the American dream, community colleges must adapt to new challenges brought by new wave students. To the extent that the colleges fulfill this critical responsibility, it will be possible to gauge whether or not community colleges can truly make a difference for the very students the colleges purport to serve best.

REFERENCES

Belenky, M. F., B. M. Clinchy, N. R. Goldberger, and J. M. Tarule. 1986. *Women's ways of knowing*. New York: Basic Books.
Blackwell, J. E. 1983. *Networking and mentoring: A study of cross-generational expe-*

riences of blacks in graduate and professional schools. Atlanta, Ga.: Southern Education Foundation.

Breneman, D. W., and S. C. Nelson. 1981. *Financing community college: An economic perspective*. Washington, D.C.: Brookings Institution.

Brint, S., and J. Karabel. 1989. *The diverted dream: Community colleges and the promise of educational opportunity in America*, 1900–1985. New York: Oxford University Press.

Cetron, M., and O. Davies. 1989. *American renaissance*. New York: St. Martin's Press.

Clark, B. 1960. *The open door college: A case study*. New York: McGraw-Hill.

Clewell, B. C. 1987. *Retention of black and Hispanic doctoral students*. Princeton, N.J.: Educational Testing Service.

Cohen, A. M. 1985. The community college in the American educational system. In *Contexts for learning*, ed. C. Adelman, 1–16. Washington, D.C.: National Institute of Education.

Cohen, A. M., and F. B. Brawer. 1989. *The American community college*. San Francisco: Jossey-Bass.

Karabel, J. 1986. Community colleges and social stratification in the 1980s. In *The community college and its critics*, ed. L. S. Zwerling. San Francisco: Jossey-Bass.

Mingle, T. R. 1987. *Focus on minorities. Trends in higher education participation and success*. Denver, Colo.: Education Commission of the States and the State Higher Education Executive Officers.

Orfield, G., and F. Paul. 1987–1988. Declines in minority access: A tale of five cities. *Education Record* 68(4)/69(1):79–85.

Quality Education for Minorities Project. 1990. *Education that works*. Cambridge: Massachusetts Institute of Technology.

Rendón, L. 1984. *Involvement in learning: A view from the community college perspective*. ERIC Document no. ED 255 268. Washington, D.C.: National Institute of Education.

———. 1991. Eyes on the prize. Students of color and the bachelor's degree. *Transfer Working Papers* 3(2):1–10.

U.S. Census Bureau. 1989. *The Hispanic population in the U.S. March, 1985*. Washington, D.C.: U.S. Government Printing Office.

U.S. Department of Education, Center for Statistics. 1990. *Digest of education statistics*. Washington, D.C.: U.S. Government Printing Office.

U.S. Office of Education. 1944. *Statistics of higher education 1939–1940 and 1941–1942*. Washington, D.C.: Department of Health, Education and Welfare.

Wilson, R. 1986. Minority students and the community college. In *The community college and its critics*, ed. L. S. Zwerling. San Francisco: Jossey-Bass.

A Paradigm Shift to Team Leadership in the Community College

Sandra C. Acebo

The concept of a "paradigm shift" derives from Kuhn's analysis of creativity in *The Structure of Scientific Revolutions* (1962). Kuhn maintained that every field of science has a "formal paradigm," composed of cultural rules defining methods of inquiry and standards of evidence in the field. Over time, the paradigm becomes depleted and few discoveries are made. Instead, practitioners begin to observe that anomalies that should not occur according to the paradigm do in fact occur, as well as events that cannot be explained by the paradigm. If scholars in a particular field become capable of adopting a fundamentally different conception of their paradigm, if they undergo a major "paradigm shift," then their field may be propelled into a period of great creative energy and progress.

Most American organizations are rethinking the way they see themselves and their employees. The quality revolution, the advent of the information age, and the pressure of international competition are waking us up to the benefits of honoring collective rather than individual accomplishment. "It's just not possible any longer to 'figure it out' from the top, and have everyone else following the orders of the 'grand strategist.' The organizations that will truly excel in the future will be the organizations that discover how to tap people's commitment and capacity to learn at all levels in an organization" (Senge 1990, 4).

The future of our nation may depend upon our ability to transform the dominant leadership paradigm successfully in a way that is uniquely American. Certainly the community colleges have much to contribute toward this end, but we also have much to learn. While many colleges have made good progress in increasing participatory governance, power struggles and accountability issues often ensue when the basic mental model of leadership remains top-down, and the vision of shared leadership and shared accountability has not come into full focus for the organization. An important task of leadership is to see the shift through to successful completion. This will require thoughtful and intentional change of staff members' fundamental and most deeply held expectations about who their leaders are and what they do. Leaders themselves must come to terms with a new reality, one in which the very skills that made them so successful may now be paralyzing their organization's ability to face the future. The struggle with such contradictions is a classic component of a paradigm shift.

CHANGING OUR MENTAL SET

The movement toward shared governance and participatory management in the community college should be seen in the context of a broader, nationwide effort toward quality improvement (Peters 1988; Reich 1987). While we continue to lead the world in cutting-edge scientific discoveries and Big Ideas, they quickly travel abroad where they can be implemented more cheaply and effectively. Or, in cultures that embrace collective entrepreneurship, like the Japanese, they are adapted and improved to achieve competitive advantage. The message is: "If America is to win in the new global competition, we need to begin telling one another a new story in which companies compete by drawing on the talent and creativity of all their employees, not just a few maverick inventors and dynamic CEO's" (Reich 1987, 80).

However, the new story can be hard to get across when the culture, national or organizational, holds on to its old paradigms. As Reich points out, most Americans would rather think that Lee Iacocca saved Chrysler than know the truth—that a large team of people with diverse backgrounds and interests joined together to rescue the ailing company. There has been a historically strong cultural bias for individual freedom and individual responsibility, firmly rooted in Western thought and further ingrained in America by the needs of a frontier society. With the advent of industrialization, the hero lived on in the legends of Ford, Sloan, and Watson. If successful, the corporate hero climbed alone to the top of the hierarchy, where the job was to have the vision, set the targets, and make sure the chain of command exercised appropriate control all down the line. The model was this: The people at the top plan and think; those at the lower levels do the work.

The reality of life for the modern organizational hero is quite different. Numerous studies indicate that American middle managers spend from one-third to one-half of their time in group activity, and top managers spend 60 percent. We are not so different from the Japanese in this regard. "The difference, primarily, is that we have a much more negative attitude toward it" (Pascale and Athos 1981, 127).

This "bad attitude" is caused by the friction between cultural norms and the necessity to change—to expand the leadership repertoire and to harness the collective wisdom of our people. Deep down, our hero is still Ted Turner surrounded in his CNN office by signs reading, "Lead, follow, or get out of the way." In contrast, the work *group* is the basic building block of Japanese organizations, and the prime qualification of a Japanese leader is acceptance by the group (Pascale and Athos 1981; Ouchi 1981). Japanese organizational charts show only collective units, not individual positions or titles or names. The group's harmony and spirit are the main concerns of the leader. The circle, not the pyramid, is more expressive of the Japanese leadership mentality.

OUCHI'S THEORY Z

Ouchi (1981) was among the first to hammer on the old paradigm. He distinguished between the features of the more successful companies (Type Z) and the less successful companies (Type A). In Type A organizations, the allocation of resources, evaluation of performance, and other important matters are decided on the basis of quantifiable, measurable criteria; in Type Z organizations, it is a distinctive philosophy of management that supplies the underlying premises for decision making. The organization derives a sense of its own uniqueness from a common understanding of both the purpose and appropriate methods of management that best serve the particular organization. A second difference involves competition *versus* cooperation. Type A organizations stress expertise and specialization; Type Z organizations reward coordination and integration. The result is that in Type A organizations, for example, departmental competition may preclude sharing of knowledge and resources. Teams and individuals in Type Z organizations, on the other hand, more willingly make short-term sacrifices for one another, knowing that in the long run equity will be restored.

FROM THE PYRAMID TO THE CIRCLE

A model of the paradigm shift from the Type A to the Type Z organization could be described as a shift from the pyramid to the circle (Scott and Jaffe 1991). The pyramid is reflected in the layout of a traditional organization chart: one leader at the top, and followers at the bottom. By contrast, the circle is a series of coordinating groups or teams, linked by a center, rather than a top. Differences in the two forms and cultures may be summarized as follows: In the pyramid, decisions are made at the top. Obedience and loyalty are demanded. Each person is responsible only for the individual, clearly defined "job." Change is slow and rare and comes only from the top. In the circle, responsibility, skills, and control are shared. Work teams are flexible. People work cooperatively. Change occurs quickly in response to new challenges.

In the pyramid, feedback and communication are from the top down. People focus attention upward; the person above is responsible for each worker's results. Managers say how things are done and what is expected. In the circle, giving and receiving feedback is a key personal skill for all employees. Individuals manage themselves and are accountable to the whole. Power comes from the ability to inspire, not from position. Managers are the energizers, connectors, and facilitators of their teams.

TEAMWORK

A key aspect of the new paradigm is the power of the team as opposed to the individual, a concept not totally alien to the American consciousness. Team building and team training are crucial in the movement to improve quality (George 1987; Hardaker and Ward 1987; Scholtes 1988; Spanbauer 1987). "When you ask people about what it is like being part of a great team, what is most striking is the meaningfulness of the experience. People talk about being part of something larger than themselves, of being connected, of being generative" (Senge 1990, 13). Francis and Young define a team as "an energetic group of people who are committed to achieving common objectives, who work well together and enjoy doing so, and who produce high quality results" (1979, 8). Indeed, the most important value of the team is that it can produce results: Through the diverse talents of its members, an end product will be created that is beyond the capability of the members acting individually.

A healthy team has an emotional tone of vitality and mutual enjoyment. This group energy has been called "synergy," indicating that the whole is more than the sum of the parts. A mature team has learned how to handle feelings of aggressiveness, competitiveness, or hostility. Issues of control, leadership, procedures, organization, and roles have been worked out. Openness is expected, confidences can be shared, personal difficulties can be worked through, and risks can be undertaken.

While the concept of a team is easily grasped, and most people have experienced at least some aspect of the power of the team, the collegial setting has precious few of them. Instead, we have an abundance of committees. "Committees are not teams, but likewise, neither are department head groups, dean's groups, cabinets, or boards of trustees, for that matter" (Barwick 1990, 33). The language of teamwork is often applied to these groups, but the behavior is something else. Russell Baker described the committee as "a mutual protection society formed to guarantee that no one person can be held to blame for a botched job that one person could have performed satisfactorily" (Barwick 1990, 34). According to Senge's pungent analysis (1990), most "teams" actually operate below the level of the lowest IQ in the group. The result is "skilled incompetence," in which people in groups grow incredibly efficient at keeping themselves from learning. We seem to be much better at talking teams than at doing them. Why?

One problem is that we fail to differentiate among the types of teams. In *Game Plans*, Keidel (1985) suggests a simple set of choices based on a simple question: What kind of teamwork is required? Is the dominant model baseball, football, or basketball? In most organizations, one kind of teamwork will dominate, but the three types are structurally and functionally quite different from one another. Distinctions among them illustrate how the term "working as a team" can have entirely different meanings to different people. According to Keidel, organizations that resemble baseball teams have a common feature: Their players enjoy considerable autonomy. Baseball is a highly individualistic sport that calls for only occasional or situational teamwork. Coordination is achieved through the design of the game. Player management is the management of individual heroes—of independence. Football, on the other hand, demands systematic teamwork. "The football field is analogous to a factory, with the moving ball/line of scrimmage representing product flow through the workplace" (1985, 8). Coordination is achieved through planning and hierarchical direction by the head coach and the staff. Player management in football is the management of dependence, of an asymmetrical relationship between planners and doers. The true hero is the coach.

In basketball, the team must be able to function as a unit without precise direction by the coach. "Because of the speed and flexibility required in basketball, coordination has to come from the players themselves, as a group" (10). The hero is the team. Whereas the dominant challenge in baseball is to get the players right, the challenge in football is to get the plan right, and the challenge in basketball is to get the process right. "The best teams understand their dominant challenge and organize to meet it" (15).

The football-type organization has its strengths: protection against high-cost failure, crisis-response capability, consistency, and coherence. But in an uncertain, rapidly changing environment, the central planning of a football organization is often of limited usefulness. Relying on the chain of command for integration does not work because too many things are happening at once; the hierarchy is easily overloaded. The baseball organization approach of disregarding integration is simply too expensive because it duplicates resources. "Only a basketball organization can achieve real-time integration in a dynamic environment" (65).

All three types of teams are found in a community college organization structure. In *The Structuring of Organizations* (1979), Mintzberg maintains that most school systems, general hospitals, and social work agencies share a common organizational structure which he calls the "professional bureaucracy." This structure hires trained professionals and gives them considerable autonomy. The "operating core" of independent professionals is the key structural aspect of the professional bureaucracy, like the baseball organization. Choosing the players is therefore extremely important. However, the professional bureaucracy is more democratic than a baseball team. The teacher, working alone, somewhat isolated from colleagues and superiors, has broad discretion over what happens behind the closed doors of the classroom. "In fact, not only do the professionals control their own work, but they also seek collective control of the administrative decisions that affect them, decisions, for example to hire colleagues, to promote them, and to distribute resources" (1979, 358). Controlling these decisions requires control of the middle line of management, which professionals do by assuring that these positions are filled with "their own." And a great deal of administrative work is done by the professionals themselves, work that is coordinated by a "plethora of committees" (358).

The power of an effective administrator in the professional bureaucracy or baseball organization is in selecting the players and in helping the professionals move their projects along, individually and in groups. "Knowing that the professionals want nothing more than to be left alone, the administrator moves carefully—in incremental steps, each one hardly discernible . . . [to] achieve over time changes that the professionals would have rejected out of hand had they been proposed all at once" (365).

In contrast, support units in a professional bureaucracy, such as student services, library services, and maintenance, are likely to be managed from the top—like a football organization—or what Mintzberg calls a "machine bureaucracy." As a consequence, parallel administrative hierarchies emerge, one democratic and bottom-up for the professionals, and a second, top-down for the support staff. Conflicts arise. "[H]ence, these two parallel hierarchies are kept quite independent of each other" (361), sometimes right up to the highest levels.

A consequence for the community college organizational structure is that the top management "team" probably consists of individuals holding differing concepts of what a team means. The vice president for instruction may operate as the manager of a baseball team; the vice president for student services and the business manager act as football coaches; the president, if astute, is trying to meld them all into an effective basketball team! It is a small wonder that the true power of the team is seldom realized at the top level of college leadership.

Indeed, a key challenge for the college president is "managing interdependence" among individuals with great strengths and very different styles. Top management must function like a basketball team—Mintzberg's adhocracy (after Toffler in *Future Shock*, 1970). According to Mintzberg, "Adhocracy is not competent at doing ordinary things. It is designed for the extraordinary" (1979, 463). The adhocracy is the structure for environments that are becoming more complex and demanding of innovation, with technical systems that are becoming more sophisticated and highly automated. "It is the only structure now available to those who believe organizations must become at the same time more democratic yet less bureaucratic" (360).

DOWNSIDES TO THE NEW PARADIGM

A common characteristic of a paradigm shift seems to involve a high mortality among the early adopters. The change is going well, people are excited and involved, but suddenly the change reaches a plateau or even goes into reverse. An example is the early success of quality circles in American colleges and businesses, and their subsequent failure in many cases. Senge (1990) points to the failure of quality circles as a perfect example of the "limits to growth" structure.

Senge explains this phenomenon as beginning with an amplifying process set in motion to produce a desired result. It creates not only a spiral of success, but also inadvertent secondary effects that eventually slow down the process. In the case of quality circles, the activity begins to lead to more open communication and collaborative problem solving, which in turn builds enthusiasm for more quality circles. "But the more successful the quality circles become, the more threatening they become to the traditional distribution of political power in the firm" (1990, 99). Managers graciously acknowledge workers' suggestions but fail to implement them. Union leaders fear that the new openness will reduce adversarial relations and therefore the need for the union. They play on workers' apprehensions of being manipulated by managers. Paradoxically, the more aggressively quality circles are promoted by the leader, the more stonewalling takes place. Rather than pushing harder, advises Senge, "you must identify and change the limiting factor" (101). Thus, where quality circles have succeeded, they have been part of a general change in managerial-employee relationships. Genuine efforts have been made to redistribute control, thereby assuaging mutual managerial and union concerns over loss of control. Senge's message is that every "growing action" has a counterbalancing "slowing action," which must be identified and dealt with if growth is to continue.

Middle management is frequently seen as a limiting factor in the paradigm shift from the pyramid to the circle. Their work is changed drastically when the organization's orientation is shifted from vertical (hierarchical) to horizontal (fast, cross-functional cooperation). Thus, we must "reconceive the middle management job as one of facilitator and functional-boundary smasher, instead of expert and guardian of functional units" (Peters 1988, 366).

An important slowing action for the paradigm shift as a whole is the lack of understanding and training in teamwork and group processes. This is a subject that most Americans have never studied in a formal way. As Gardner pinted out in a recent interview, "We train young people for individual performance. . . . The important thing is 'Me and my SAT. The way I write the equation, or my capacity to do that essay.' . . . When you get into industry, you have to have teams. Then some executive is trying to repair the omissions of 30 years in that youngster's life, and make him or her understand that we have to work together, we have to get the job done" (1992, C–3).

MODELS FOR CHANGE

Birnbaum summarizes various leadership and organizational models in higher education, including the bureaucracy, the community of scholars, and the political model, and points out that "while they are all different, the theories and models do have several ideas in common. They picture the leaders as heroic figures . . . they presume that leaders exist in a world that is rational, linear, and essentially certain" (1988, 141).

Between 1975 and 1985, however, new organization theories were developed that "in fact do try to alter our perceptions of reality" (142). These new ideas, which have been referred to as symbolic, cognitive, or cultural theories, view organizations as cultural creations—not discoveries—of those who work in them. Analysts in this tradition are Deal and Kennedy (1982), Schein (1985), and Weick (1979). Problems are analyzed in terms of what is right, not who is right.

Senge (1990, 341) reports asking groups of managers to imagine that their enterprise is an ocean liner. "What is their role?" Most answer "captain," while others say "helmsman," "engineer," or "social director." But, Senge claims, these are all eclipsed in importance by the role that no one thinks of—the designer of the ship. "It is fruitless to be the leader in an organization that is poorly designed." Yet, because good design work is so invisible, because it is not the center of the action, many leaders pay it little mind. "Those who practice it find deep satisfaction in empowering others and being part of an organization capable of producing results that people truly care about" (341). This is a new model of leadership, but it is also very old. To paraphrase Lao-tzu: The bad leader is the one whom the people despise. The good leader is the one the people praise. The great leader is the one to whom the people say, "We did it ourselves."

CONCLUSION

Most colleges are experimenting with ways to involve staff at every level in building a vision of service to students and to the community, and developing innovative, cost-effective ways of providing that service. Cross-functional teams are becoming the basic organizational form. Most presidents expect their top leadership to perform as a fluid, dynamic team in the best basketball tradition, while appreciating the need for simultaneous football structures for the support staff and baseball structures for the faculty.

The best news is the excitement that accompanies the advent of important change—a shift is occurring—the workplace is becoming qualitatively different. Senge calls this awareness "metanoia," literally a shift of mind. It means re-perceiving the world, extending our capacity to create, and becoming part of the generative process of life. It means true learning, and becoming a true learning organization. That is our future as we become leaders of the new paradigm.

REFERENCES

Barwick, J. T. 1990. Team building: A faculty perspective. *Community College Review* 17(4):33–39.

Birnbaum, R. 1988. The reality and illusion of community college leadership. In *Colleges of choice*, ed. J. S. Eaton, 135–53. New York: Macmillan.

Deal, T. E., and A. A. Kennedy. 1982. *Corporate cultures*. Reading, Mass.: Addison-Wesley.

Forsyth, T. 1991. The culture of governance: A study of organizational culture and congruence in six California community colleges. Ph.D. diss., University of California, Los Angeles.

Francis, D., and D. Young. 1979. *Improving work groups*. La Jolla, Calif.: University Associates.

Gardner, J. 1992. Interview in San Francisco Peninsula *Times Tribune*, 26 January 1992: C–3.

George, P. 1987. Team building without tears. *Personnel Journal* (November):122–29.

Hardaker, M., and B. K. Ward. 1987. How to make a team work. *Harvard Business Review* (November–December):112–19.

Jessup, H. R. 1990. New roles in team leadership. *Training and Development Journal* 44(11):79–83.

Kanter, R. M. 1983. *The change masters*. New York: Simon and Schuster.

Keidel, R. W. 1985. *Game plans*. New York: Dutton.

Kuhn, T. 1962. *The structure of scientific revolutions*. Chicago: University of Chicago Press.

March, J. G. 1984. How we talk and how we act: Administrative theory and administrative life. In *Leadership and organizational culture*, ed. T. Sergiovanni and J. E. Corbally. Urbana: University of Illinois Press.

Mintzberg, H. 1979. *The structuring of organizations*. Englewood Cliffs, N.J.: Prentice-Hall.

Ouchi, W. G. 1981. *Theory Z*. Menlo Park, Calif.: Addison-Wesley.

Pascale, R. T., and A. G. Athos. 1981. *The art of Japanese management*. New York: Simon and Schuster.,

Peters, T. 1988. *Thriving on chaos*. New York: Knopf.

Reich, R. B. 1987. Entrepreneurship reconsidered: The team as hero. *Harvard Business Review* (May–June):77–83.

Roueche, J., and G. Baker. 1987. *Access and excellence*. Washington, D.C.: Community College Press.

Schein, E. H. 1985. *Organizational culture and leadership*. San Francisco: Jossey-Bass.

Scholtes, P. R. 1988. *The team handbook*. Madison, Wisc.: Joiner Associates, Inc.

Scott, C. D., and D. T. Jaffe. 1991. From crisis to culture change. *Healthcare Forum Journal* 34(3):33–41.

Senge, P. M. 1990. *The fifth discipline*. New York: Doubleday.

Spanbauer, S. J. 1987. *Quality first in education . . . Why not?* Appleton, Wisc.: Fox Valley Technical College Foundation.

Weick, K. E. 1979. *The social psychology of organizing*. 2d ed. Reading, Mass.: Addison-Wesley.

Strategic Management of Community Colleges in a Dynamic Environment

Gunder Myran and Linda Howdyshell

DEFINITION: MATCHING REQUIREMENTS AND PERFORMANCE

The institutional processes that deal with strategy making in the community college may be brought together under the umbrella concept of strategic management. Strategic management in the community college is defined as the array of future-shaping processes that result in decisions on the mission, vision, and plans of the institution; provide for staff, governing board, and community involvement in shaping institutional strategy; create and implement institutional strategy; create and implement institutional development systems; and provide for the assurance of institutional quality. The basic purpose of strategic management is to optimize the match between student and community educational requirements and the performance of the college in meeting those requirements. The processes are aligned in such a way that the results should build awareness, support, and continued utilization of the college's services by all stakeholders: students, potential students, taxpayers, employers, governmental units, labor organizations, and other educational institutions.

CHARACTERISTICS OF STRATEGIC MANAGEMENT

The following is a description of the integrative, leadership, planning, and choice-making characteristics of strategic management in community colleges.

Strategic Management and Systems Thinking

Strategic management involves the *integration* of various future-shaping processes and levels of strategy making. The college as a whole is continuously redesigned and re-created in response to changing environmental dynamics. Strategic managers think about the entire college as a system and apply what Senge calls systems thinking: "Business and other human endeavors are systems. They, too, are bound by invisible fabrics of interrelated actions. Since we are part of that lacework ourselves, it's doubly hard to see the whole pattern of change. Instead, we tend to focus on snapshots of isolated parts of the systems, and wonder why our deepest problems never seem to get solved" (1991, 424).

Strategic managers learn to think about the whole organization in relation to the educational requirements of students and communities. A strategic thinker would likely address questions such as:

1. How much do I understand about the educational requirements of my students (or groups in the community)? What more do I need to know?

2. How much do I know about the staff competencies and institutional resources now available to meet the educational requirements? What more do I need to know?

3. To what extent do current programs and services meet the educational requirements of the community? What needs to change? How would it be changed?

Strategic Management and Leadership

Strategic management is a *leadership function* as distinguished from an operational function. Using the analogy of a ship, strategic management deals with the design and steering of the ship, rather than keeping the boilers running or planning the menus in the galley. Strategic management and operational management operate along a continuum and are interdependent. The effective functioning of the college depends on the success of both working together.

Strategic management takes place at all levels of the college; therefore, persons at all levels must engage in continuous learning about their community and the college itself by contributing to strategy making. There is no one grand strategist; rather, the college focuses on building collective aspiration and vision. Senge expresses it this way:

It is no longer sufficient to have one person learning for the organization, a Ford or a Sloan or a Watson. It's just not possible to "figure it out" from the top, and have everyone else following the orders of the "grand strategist." The organizations that will truly excel in the future will be the organizations that discover how to tap people's commitment and capacity to learn at all levels of the organization. (1991, 7)

Strategy making is done by leaders at all levels of the college. The leaders think about the educational needs of their students or potential students, assess the gap between those needs and present college programs and services, and then take steps to close that gap. Sometimes closing the gap requires the leverage of a long time period to develop the needed commitment, skills, and resources. In other cases, quick action is both possible and urgently needed. Sometimes institutional study and action are required; in other cases, a department or office is empowered to develop and implement the necessary strategy.

Strategic Management and Strategic Planning

Strategic management encompasses strategic planning, but it is a more inclusive concept. It includes the various institutional systems through which decisions and choices are formulated and implemented determining the destiny of the college. Since these critical decisions take place in all areas and at all levels of the college, strategic management provides a framework that guides daily decision making as the college moves toward its preferred future.

Strategic management as a concept evolved out of strategic planning. King and Cleland (1987) believe that formal strategic planning processes and techniques are useful but not sufficiently robust and comprehensive to encompass all the strategic thinking, entrepreneurial, and leadership dimensions that are necessary if an organization is to create its own future rather than to react to changing times. As a result of environmental uncertainty and dynamic social and economic changes, managers have moved from a total reliance on strategic planning to a more comprehensive approach, the management of strategy. Thus, strategic management overcomes some of the shortcomings of strategic planning:

- The tendency of such planning to isolate departments or divisions and ignore institutional politics and self-interest
- The slow response of traditional planning processes to environmental uncertainty and rapid social and economic change
- The failure of traditional planning processes to empower leadership at all levels of organization.

Strategic management is based on the assumption that strategic planning will be used in combination with other management techniques that deal more effectively with environmental uncertainty and the internal culture.

Strategic Management and Choice Making

Strategic management is ultimately *choice making*. Any successful organization today focuses on superior performance in a few mission-oriented areas. Certainly the community college has learned that it cannot be "all things to all people." Since the human, financial, physical, and information resources of the community college are limited, choices must be made about how to respond to community opportunities and environmental threats. In fact, strategic planning, and then the more comprehensive concept of strategic management, was first used in community colleges because leaders needed mechanisms for prioritizing needs and strategies in the face of increasing environmental demands and limited resources.

ELEMENTS OF STRATEGIC MANAGEMENT

Strategic management encompasses an array of institutional future-shaping processes. The following represent elements of strategic management.

Cluster A: Mission, Vision, and Strategic Planning

Element 1: Shared Mission. The fundamental element of institutional strategy is a shared commitment to the mission of the community college among staff members, governing board members, and community stakeholders. For example, the mission of Washtenaw Community College (Ann Arbor, Michigan) is to "make a positive difference in peoples' lives through accessible and excellent educational programs and services." This statement undergirds all planning and other strategic activities. Because the mission statement is both rememberable and memorable, it is easy for decision makers to keep in mind as a constant influence on daily decisions and actions.

Element 2: Shared Vision. A shared vision is built on the foundation of the mission statement among staff members, governing board members, and community stakeholders. The mission statement is basically timeless, although some modification could occur if dramatic social or economic changes mandate; however, the vision statement needs to be reviewed periodically and changed as conditions indicate.

The statement of the college's vision provides a future target or beacon as the college's mission is pursued during a set time period. An example of a vision statement follows: By the year 2000, Everypersons Community College will be a major educational resource engaged at the frontiers of community life, pushing forward the horizons of individual growth and community improvement. The college will accomplish this vision by:

1. Serving as a primary resource in creating a world-class work force capable of competing in an international marketplace
2. Minimizing disjunctives in access and service to all citizens, particularly those from low-income backgrounds, by networking with other educational agencies and groups
3. Serving as leader, catalyst, and community researcher in defining and solving community problems
4. Continuously striving to enhance the outcomes of learning for all individuals and groups.

The vision statement is a proclamation of a "stretch" future—one that will be compelling and motivating for those involved—and yet feasible. A vision statement is a decision about the future that those involved feel ownership of and are committed to create, not a "pie in the sky" statement used for public relations purposes. The vision statement articulates basic institutional strategy and serves as a guide to more detailed strategic planning.

Element 3: Strategic Planning. Strategic planning is a decision-making process. It involves an assessment of threats and opportunities in the external environment and the related strengths and weaknesses of the organization as a basis for determining the future direction of the college. A strategic plan is a statement about the destiny of the college at a selected point in the future, usually three to ten years, and the means by which to get there. A strategic plan answers fundamental questions about the future of the college:

1. Who should the college serve? Who can it serve?
2. What programs or services should the college provide now and in the future?
3. What geographic area should the college serve?
4. Should the enrollment of the college grow, stabilize, or decline in the future?
5. What should the resource development strategy be?
6. What configuration of staff talents and structure is needed in the future?
7. What institutional, divisional, departmental, and office weaknesses need particular attention in the future?
8. What programs or services are particularly distinctive and therefore need special nurturing?

Cluster B: Staff, Executives, and Governing Board Involvement in Strategic Management

Element 4: Staff Empowerment Concepts and Processes. The concepts and processes that enable all staff groups (faculty, administrators, office professionals, technicians, custodians, maintenance personnel, etc.) to be effectively involved in strategy making include:

1. Principles of collaboration and participation: A key step to staff empowerment is agreement on the principles that guide involvement in strategy making. These principles include mutual trust and respect, understanding of roles, understanding of the modes and processes of the decision making to be used, and the structures for collaboration and participation. All-staff involvement in developing these principles, making a commitment to them, and learning to use them is essential to moving toward greater staff empowerment.

2. Shared governance structure: Involvement in strategy making requires an all-staff "influence" structure that interacts with the "authority" structure of the governing board. This influence structure consists of administrators to whom the governing board has delegated authority and bargaining groups that have authority based on contractual arrangements. This influence-authority structure is designed to involve all staff groups in strategic deliberations and, where possible, make strategic decisions on a consensus basis. The structure typically involves several governance committees corresponding to areas of institutional strategy, such as curriculum development, teaching and learning, finance, and community relations, and a central coordinating council or senate.

3. Staff professional development: Since it has taken community colleges decades to evolve the traditional centralized approach to strategy making, it will take several years to evolve a new, more participative approach. A critical support for the transformation to this new approach is professional development activities for all staff groups. In-depth education of all staff groups in the philosophy, skills, and methods of participative strategy making is essential to the success of this new approach.

4. Cross-functional communications: A key ingredient of participative strategy making is communication and team building across functional areas. Office and departmental groups must move outside their "boxes" to work "between the boxes" on strategy making that requires cross-functional cooperation.

Element 5: Executive Leadership. Senge (1991) describes the role of leadership as continuously increasing the capacity of the organization to create its best future. The president and other executive leaders are no longer the "lone rangers" outlining grand strategies for the rest of the organization to follow. They serve to motivate, facilitate, and integrate staff, governing board, and community stakeholder involvement in the organizational learning process and resulting strategy making. Executive leadership continues to play a pivotal role in developing and advocating the college mission and vision and in guiding the interface between the community and the college.

The leadership competencies required to function effectively in a new participative paradigm are outlined in the next section of this chapter.

Element 6: Policy Development. The primary strategic roles for the community college board of trustees or governing board members are to (1) serve as the representatives of the community in articulating and prioritizing community educational needs, (2) interpret and legitimize strategic initiatives of the college to community groups, and (3) act as the final deliberative body, in cooperation with the president and staff, to determine the general future directions of the college. The strategic actions of the governing boards are captured in strategic plan documents and policy statements.

Cluster C: Strategic Institutional Development Processes

Element 7: Academic Development. As we look to the new century, the academic programs and services of the college will undergo continuous change in response to community, national, and international circumstances. Academic programs and teaching are at the center of community college life, and so strategic academic development will be vital to the success of the college in the years ahead. Components of academic development include curriculum development, advancement of teaching, instructional design, academic standards, articulation, learning resources, and continuing education.

A key to strategic management is the development of these components in a way that results in integrated academic strategies. These strategies must in turn be the driving force for the college's resource planning and other strategy-making systems.

Element 8: Constituency Relations. In the past decade, several specialized administrative functions, which have strengthened relationships with various community constituencies, have emerged in the community college:

1. Community outreach centers
2. Regional campuses or centers
3. Enrollment planning, including student recruitment
4. Business-industry centers
5. Foundations
6. Community relations offices
7. Community services offices

From a strategic perspective, it is very important to integrate these various functions within a constituency relations framework. These functions play a vital role in strengthening the college's adaptiveness as community educational needs change. A second major reason for integration is to provide increased opportunity for faculty and other staff groups to be involved in assessing constituency needs and in developing future strategies to respond to these needs.

Element 9: Organizational Design. Organizational design refers to the way in which the college is structured to accomplish its work. Organizational design includes both vertical components (administrative structure and academic divisional/departmental structure) and horizontal structures (governance committees, administrative committees, electronic communication systems, and cross-functional problem-solving teams). The organizational design should permit the institution to carry out its mission, vision, and strategic plans effectively. For this reason, the organizational design must be studied periodically and changes made as necessary. Currently, several community colleges are moving to a flatter administrative structure to improve all-staff communications and increase faculty and other staff involvement in strategic matters.

Element 10: Management of Organizational Resources. The human, financial, physical, and information resources of the college must be managed to have maximum impact on the mission, vision, and strategy of the college. If the college's strategy making is not the driving force for resource allocation, then the primary strategic tool of the organization is the annual budget. From a strategic point of view, the key role of resource management is to develop and allocate future resources to create the capacity for the college to achieve its preferred future.

Element 11: Effectiveness Program Focusing on Student Outcomes. Community colleges are moving away from the traditional credentialing emphasis of higher education toward a new emphasis on learning outcomes. Effectiveness defined by measurable outcomes in the lives of students will be the primary way the quality of community colleges will be judged in the future rather than the number of degrees and certificates granted. Steps in an effectiveness program include the following:

1. The identification of indicators of student success (completion rates, grading patterns, job placement, career advancement, persistence in a university transfer program, satisfaction with college services, etc.)

2. The measurement of student learning against the standards established by effectiveness indicators

3. The feedback of the measurement results to use as a basis for continuous organizational learning and improvement. Feedback on the strengths and weaknesses of student academic achievement is essential for ongoing strategy making.

An effectiveness program should include, in addition to student success indicators, community success and staff success indicators. The essential strategic question is whether value has been added to the lives of students, the quality of life in the community, and the work life of the college staff as a result of the investment of organizational and community resources and energy.

While the effectiveness program is described here as a separate strategic element, it will operate best when integrated into strategic and annual planning processes.

Element 12: Continuous Quality Improvement. Continuous quality improvement (CQI), referred to in the private sector as total quality management, is a recent addition to the strategic management processes of the community college. CQI is a management concept that (1) uses student or customer requirements as the basis for institutional improvement and (2) empowers staff teams at all levels to make plans and solve problems. CQI is most effective when integrated into the governance, planning, and effectiveness processes of the college.

Perhaps the greatest contribution of CQI to community college strategy is the central idea of making improvements based on the customers' requirements. By providing an in-depth way for the college and its units to identify its customers and their service requirements, CQI shifts assessment and planning away from internal bureaucracies, politics, and self-interests to the students and community groups being served.

A second contribution of the CQI concept is the emphasis on involving all levels of staff in problem solving and improvement through the use of cross-functional problem-solving teams. Thus, these teams provide a way to enable staff in all areas of the college to improve procedures and systems and, as a result, better serve students and the community.

SYNTHESIS OF THE LITERATURE ON STRATEGIC MANAGEMENT

This section is organized into three parts to provide a summary of insights regarding strategic management resulting from a review of related literature. First, the role of strategic planning in strategic management is examined. Second, evidence of the need to utilize strategic management is summarized. Then, the leadership competencies required for strategic management are highlighted: (1)

institutional vision, (2) institutional empowerment, (3) political leadership, and (4) institutional conceptualization and survival.

Strategic Planning

Merely adopting the concept of strategic planning did not necessarily result in successful implementation. It was clear, by the late 1980s, that strategic planning did not always live up to its promise. For every three institutions that started a strategic plan, two soon fell away from it and went back to business as usual (Jones 1990, 52). This may have been caused by frequent reliance on incremental approaches, the increasing number of external economic and political decisions that were future shaping, employee groups desiring to participate in strategic decisions, and an increasing need to define the scope of the community college mission (Myran 1983, 17).

The weakness of strategic planning may be remedied by using the broader concept of strategic management, since this increases organizational responsiveness to community dynamics and provides staff at all levels with opportunities to participate. According to Makridakis and Heav, if a strategy is to be useful it must:

1. Be used proactively
2. Accept our limited ability to predict environmental changes
3. Take into account the organizational, political, and psychological dimensions of corporate life
4. Be accepted by a majority of those concerned with strategy as a realistic tool for dealing effectively with the future. (1987, 7)

Need for Strategic Management

Community colleges may be one of the few social institutions able to respond to the urgent need to build unity and a sense of community in our diverse society. Elsner asserts that it is the responsibility of community college educators to know what the conditions are in our local communities and, through a process of "social entrepreneurship," integrate with other education providers and social agencies to reconstruct and rebuild communities (1991, 26). Cross and Fideler (1989) conclude that the challenge for community colleges in the coming years will be to balance flexibility and responsiveness to social change with institutional integrity and a continuing commitment to the communities they serve.

Deegan, Tillery, and Melone report that delineating roles in resolving the mission dilemma of community colleges, evaluating the quality and outcomes of their programs, and planning are vital for achieving public accountability. Alternatively, community colleges can watch dwindling dollars produce diminished quality across the board in the continuing pursuit of the all-things-to-all-people philosophy (1985, 287). Parnell also believes that the crucial question for community colleges is, "Is your school or college chasing excellence or cultivating excellence?" (1985, 171). It is clear that no college will succeed by settling for mediocrity across the board or by letting some elements of the community college mission slide into disrepute through neglect and lack of attention to standards of performance. "Quality of education is the central challenge to community colleges in their fifth generation; it can only be achieved if there is central agreement on mission" (Deegan, Tillery, and Melone 1985).

Strategic Leadership Competencies

Strategy making as the key process for achieving change is only as effective as the skill of those who lead the effort. It will be necessary for college executives to learn and practice strategic management skills in order to provide leadership in a period of dynamic change. These essential strategic leadership competencies are categorized below:

1. Institutional vision
2. Staff empowerment and transformation
3. Political leadership
4. Institutional conceptualization and survival. (Duncan and Harlacher 1991, 41).

Institutional Vision and Shared Mission. Defining the mission and vision of the institution is the first and most fundamental component of strategic management. The purpose of a mission statement is to set out the nature, shape, and character of the institution. To carry out the mission, the president inspires, nurtures, and stimulates the birth of a shared vision. It is the leader's job to keep that shared vision in front of everyone constantly, as the driving force behind the institution's activities. It is the dimension of a shared vision as the foundation for planning and implementation that defines true strategic management (Roueche and Baker 1987, 120).

Executive leadership has the responsibility for accomplishing change in the institutional culture as a prerequisite for effective implementation of strategic goals. In addition, executive leadership must engage in change management techniques such as creating readiness, overcoming resistance, and institutionalizing change.

According to Roueche and Baker, "Excellent leaders in educational institutions are not merely competent. Rather, they have a vision of what the college ought to be and work to instill an identifiable culture among the inhabitants of the organization" (1987, 120). The major competencies in their leadership model are (1) having a sense of direction, (2) a structure for implementation, and (3) a sense of personal commitment (115).

Staff Empowerment and Transformation. The task of leaders is to teach all staff self-leadership and to provide them with the opportunity to practice self-leadership in the workplace (Manz and Sims 1989). Many community colleges have a participatory governance structure involving people in the decision-making process. The president and others recognize that the president has the right and responsibility to make decisions by rules, regulations, and contracts; this results in a bureaucratic governance structure meshed with a collegial model. The result is a governance model that is participatory in nature but with clear lines regarding how decisions are made. "A danger is a lack of understanding on the part of some presidents regarding how to remain a strong leader while involving the appropriate people in making decisions" (Vaughan 1986, 91).

Strategic decision-making processes must be truly participatory, involving those who will be expected to carry out its mandate in a meaningful way. A successful strategy needs to evoke the kind of synergistic teamwork that will produce sound, strength-giving answers to the many problems faced by the organization. These strategies must be vision led and rely on the commitment of all staff members (Blake and Mouton 1988, 252).

Strategy is more than a compilation of unit plans. It should be a device to integrate units and enable the institution to capitalize on synergies so the "whole of the organization is more than its parts" (*Business Week* 1984, 62). This synergistic teamwork is the product of an open, trusting, innovative culture. Pascale's *Managing on the Edge* cites reasons why Honda Motor Corporation has been so effective in creating this environment:

1. No single point of view dominates its decision making.
2. Information on performance gets circulated widely.
3. Rewards are equitably distributed.
4. Degree of trust is fostered by adherence from top management on down to a common set of values (*Business Week*, September 14, 1984, 136).

Political Leadership. The conceptualization of organizations as environmentally interactive systems suggests that differences in environments require differences in the way in which organizations are structured and managed. Lawrence and Lorsch (1967) concluded that the uncertainty of environmental conditions was reduced by information clarity, the certainty of causal relationships, and quick feedback regarding the organization's activities.

Ulrich and Lake (1990) propose that, in the 1990s, a company's success will depend not only on ability to meet customer needs but also on how well an organization's internal processes work to meet external demands. By combining its processes with its ability to meet customer expectations, the organization succeeds from the inside out. Traditional means of gaining competitive advantage must be supplemented by organizational capability or the ability to manage people to gain a competitive advantage. "Building organization capacity focuses internal organizational processes and systems on meeting customer needs and ensures that the skills and efforts of employees are directed toward achieving the goals of the organization as a whole. Employees become a critical resource for competitiveness that will sustain itself over time'' (1990, 2).

Institutional Conceptualization and Survival. At the macro level, environmental conditions influence the degree to which any organizational structure can be effective. A volatile environment, which provides uncertain or unreliable information, mandates less organizational structure. Conversely, stable environments, which provide reliable information, require more structure. Organizational infrastructure must be reconceptualized and designed to replace the disruptive effects of control by fear and threat with understanding and insight. Bypassing the behavioral dynamics embedded in the institutional culture assures that the changes brought about through participatory structures will be temporary (Blake and Mouton 1988).

The challenge for the president will be to assume the role of social architect, mobilizing participants in whatever cultural change is appropriate for the organization's future survival and success. This new leadership style requires that managers' roles at all levels be transformed, with more time spent initiating problem solving among team members, absorbing internal and external information to ensure the best possible decision making and, pushing decisions downward for greater efficiency (Vogt and Murrell 1990).

In summary, the competencies required for strategic management are distinctive from traditional leadership models. Executive strategists must integrate through a participatory effort the various institutional processes, including strategic planning, through which the choices or decisions that determine the destiny of the college are formulated and implemented.

CONCLUSION

To provide directional leadership in a dynamic, volatile environment, strategic planning is important but not sufficient. To continuously strengthen the match between the educational requirement of individuals and the community and the capacity of the college to meet those requirements, several other future-shaping processes are needed: shared mission, shared vision, strategic planning, staff empowerment concepts and processes, executive leadership, policy development, academic development, organizational design, constituency relations, management of organizational resources and policy development, an effectiveness program focusing on student outcomes, and continuous quality improvement.

Strategic management is the umbrella concept that designs and integrates these processes in such a way that the educational requirements/institutional capacity match is maximized. Through using strategic management processes, staff members at all levels increase their knowledge of student, community, and institutional needs. This organizational learning provides the basis for shared strategy making. Strategy management is ultimately about choice making. In a period of rapid social and economic change, a vast array of signals about educational needs bombard the college; choosing those signals that closely relate to the college's mission and then developing and implementing responsive strategies is the core of strategic management. Through strategic thinking about the college's present and anticipated future position in relation to its external environment, the college uses the leverage of time to redesign and reshape itself so future conditions in the community are matched by the new and emerging strategies of the college.

The community college strategist rejects the "if it ain't broke don't fix it" bromide. In a dynamic environment, as someone has said, "When it's broke, it's too late to fix it." An effective community college must anticipate future conditions and invest time, energy, and resources in "fixing it before it's broke." This requires risk taking and flexibility, since no amount of planning can anticipate the sudden social and economic shifts that take place in communities and nations.

Strategic management is about shaping the future of the college, not predicting the future. It is about choosing a preferred future that can serve as a beacon to guide the college to that future. It is about guiding daily decision making that moves the college toward that preferred future. In-depth knowledge about students, the community, and the college kindles creative strategy making. The ultimate goal of strategic management is providing superior service to students, the community, and the staff.

REFERENCES

Bass, B. M. 1985. *Leadership and performance beyond expectations*. New York: Free Press.

Blake, R. R., and J. S. Mouton. 1988. In *Corporate transformation*, ed. R. Kilmann, T. Hand, and J. Covin and Associates. San Francisco: Jossey-Bass.

Burns, J. M. 1978. *Leadership*. New York: Harper and Row.

Chaffee, E. E. 1990. Strategies for the 1990s. In *An agenda for the new decade*, ed. L. Jones and F. Nowotnay. New Directions for Higher Education, no. 70: 59–66.

Cross, K. P., and E. F. Fideler. 1989. Community colleges mission: Priorities in the mid–1980s. *Journal of Higher Education* 60: 209–16.

Deegan, W. L., D. Tillery, and R. J. Melone. 1985. In *Renewing the American community college: Priorities and strategies for effective leadership*, ed. W. L. Deegan and D. Tillery. San Francisco: Jossey-Bass.

Duncan, A. H., and E. L. Harlacher. 1991. The twenty-first century executive leader. *Community College Review* 18 (4): 39–47.

Elsner, P. 1991. In *Conceptualizing 2000: Proactive planning*, ed. D. Angel and M. DeVault. Washington, D.C.: American Association of Community and Junior Colleges.

Galbraith, J. R. 1977. *Organizational design*. Reading, Mass.: Addison-Wesley.

Jones, L. W. 1990. Strategic planning: The unrealized potential of the 1980s and the promise of the 1990s. *New Directions for Higher Education* 780: 51–57.

King, W. R., and D. I. Cleland. 1987. In *Strategic planning and management handbook:*

The evolution of strategic planning and management, ed. W. R. King and D. I. Cleland. New York: Van Nostrand Reinhold Company.

Lawrence, P. R., and J. W. Lorsch. 1967. *Organization and environment: Managing differentiation and integration*. Cambridge, Mass.: Harvard University, Graduate School of Business Administration, Division of Research.

Litwin, G. H., and R. A. Stringer. 1968. *Motivation and organizational climate*. Boston: Harvard Business School.

Makridakis, S., and D. Heav. 1987. In *Strategic planning and management handbook: The evolution of strategic planning and management*, ed. W. R. King and D. I. Cleland. New York: Van Nostrand Reinhold Company.

Manz, C. C., and H. P. Sims. 1989. *Superleadership*. New York: Berkeley Books.

McClelland, D. C. 1975. *Power: The inner experience*. New York: Irvington.

Myran, G. 1983. *Strategic management in the community college*. San Francisco: Jossey-Bass.

Parnell, D. 1985. *The neglected majority*. Washington, D.C.: Community College Press.

Peters, T. J., and R. H. Waterman, Jr. 1982. *In search of excellence: Lessons from America's best run companies*. New York: Harper and Row.

Riggs, R. O., and M. Akor. 1992. *Community/Junior College Quarterly* 16 (1): 57–75.

Roueche, J. E., and G. A. Baker III. 1987. *Access to excellence: The open-door college*. Washington, D.C.: American Association of Community and Junior Colleges.

Senge, P. M. 1991. *The fifth discipline: The art and practice of the learning organization*. New York: Doubleday.

Tichy, N. M., and M. A. Devanna. 1986. *The transformational leader: Molding tomorrow's corporation winners*. New York: John Wiley.

Ulrich, D., and D. Lake. 1990. *Organizational capability: Competing from the inside out*. New York: John Wiley.

Vaughan, G. B. 1986. *The community college presidency*. New York: American Council on Education/Macmillan.

Vaughan, G. B., and Associates, ed. 1983. *Issues for community college leaders in a new era*. San Francisco: Jossey-Bass.

Vogt, J., and K. Murrell. 1990. *Empowerment in organizations: How to spark exceptional performance*. San Diego: University Press.

The Challenges and Obligations Facing Community Colleges in the Twenty-First Century: A Community-Based Perspective

Daniel J. Phelan

The community college continues to be a unique, innovative, and often lauded entity that is truly American. From its beginning in the late nineteenth century to the present, the American community college exists to be of service to its constituents. How does the community college maintain its mission of service to the community while maintaining the requisite flexibility and adaptability? What does the future hold for the community college and its obligation of service? This chapter presents trends, hypotheses, and challenges of the community college from a community-based perspective. After a brief recounting of the origins of the service function, the current role of the community college is presented. The text concludes with an examination and extrapolation of the future for the new service function.

THE COMMUNITY SERVICE GENESIS

In general terms, the service function, whether originated by organization or by individual, has existed for millennia. "In one sense, the community service idea dates from ancient Greece, for Socrates took his wisdom into the street and the marketplace" (Hankin and Frey 1985, 154). History books are laden with numerous references of service, stretching from Aristotle to Christ to the German gymnasium to the clerics to the Morrill Act. This practice of service to community continues today, as evidenced by the 101st Congressional Assembly of the United States and its development of volunteerism legislation.

COMPREHENSIVE SERVICE TO THE COMMUNITY

Community and junior colleges have embraced five fundamental founding responsibilities to their constituents: to provide a pre-baccalaureate preparation of students (the transfer function); to provide assistance to students through counseling, remediation, and career planning (the student services function); to provide an alternative to students not desiring advanced study, but rather preparation for career (the terminal function); to provide a common liberal arts education to all students for personal growth and civic responsibility (the general education function); and, finally, to provide a variety of services to, and to be in partnership with, the surrounding community (the community services function). In the beginning, however, service to the community was not clearly defined.

Not until the early twentieth century did the community-based function become formalized. Eells, Harper, and Koos, three of higher education's chief pioneers, clearly identified the need for a junior college to serve current and emerging community needs. By 1930, Ricciardi, on the pages of the first *Junior College Journal* issue, defined the role of the community or junior college:

A fully organized junior college aims to meet the needs of a community in which it is located, including preparation for institutions of higher learning, liberal arts education for those who are not going beyond graduation from the junior college, vocational training for particular occupations usually designed as semi-professional vocations, and short courses for adults with special interests. (Thornton 1972, 55)

This pronouncement was only a starting point for a function that had yet to prove itself.

In 1936, Hollinshead, who sought to promote the service function through an expanded definition, stated that "the junior college should be a community college, meeting community needs" (Thornton 1972, 55). Thus, by providing for adult education, recreational opportunities, cultural offerings, and liaisons with other community institutions, the community college could fulfill its service function.

Community colleges had the opportunity to live up to their newly stated service function with the beginning of World War II. Falling enrollments, combined with a demand for training people in defense occupations, prompted community colleges to respond by establishing a variety of temporary offerings. However, even after the war had concluded, the community colleges continued to provide these programs because of their success (Thornton 1972). The community service function was now a proven function of the community college.

Although the service function often languished from lack of recognition, one important work had a major influence on its identity and development. In the late 1960s, Ervin Harlacher, with the authorization of what was then known as the American Association of Junior Colleges (AAJC) and the financial support of the Alfred P. Sloan Foundation, initiated and completed a major study on the community aspect of the community college. His work continues to be cited as an important contribution to the literature. He formally identified four service obligations of the community college:

1. Become a center of community life by encouraging the use of college facilities and services by community groups
2. Provide for all age groups educational services that utilize the special skills and knowledge of the college staff and other experts
3. Provide the community, including business and industry, with the leadership and coordination capabilities of the college, assist the community in long-range planning, and join with individuals and groups in attacking unsolved problems
4. Contribute to and promote the cultural, intellectual, and social life of the college district community and the development of skills for the profitable use of leisure time. (1969, v)

The pace and impact of change continue to affect the service function identity today. Vaughan identified seven factors that contributed to changes in the community services identity from the 1960s to the early 1990s:

1. Community services advocates went too far in offering courses that were viewed as frivolous by too many powerful people;
2. Funding has been cut for many community services functions;
3. Community colleges are less willing to try new courses and programs which may be seen as risky innovation;
4. A lack of funding for noncredit courses caused many colleges to offer courses for credit that rightfully should have been noncredit, thus creating a "creditability gap" for community services both internally and externally;
5. The recent recession, coupled with the demand for "high technology" skills, has caused the community college to put more emphasis on job training and retraining and less on recreational and avocational programs and courses;
6. Community services offerings have been so successful that they have been the envy of those faculty members and administrators who are now struggling to fill empty seats; thus, many functions that the regular instructional program ignored are now not only legitimate, but are "lusted" after by other segments of the college community; and
7. The national attitude toward community services has changed. (1991, 25–26)

These factors herald the need for a more refined, planned, and orchestrated operational strategy for the service function. Indeed, they mandate the careful scanning of current service function practices as well as a recognition of current or impending change.

The next section evaluates four of the primary initiatives of the community service function: training and development; business, industry, and agency partnerships; literacy development; and personal enrichment. Each initiative is examined in light of its current practices as well as indications of change in those practices.

THE CHANGING PARADIGMS OF THE COMMUNITY COLLEGE SERVICE FUNCTION

The guidelines and rules that have governed the service function are shifting at fundamental levels from earlier community college decades. In fact, the entire community college mission is in the throes of a second major transformation. The first identifiable shift in mission occurred in the 1960s when

[C]ampus based colleges were transformed to community-based institutions. . . . Now, as the decade of the 1990's begins, . . . a second transformational period that will shape community colleges to the year 2000 and beyond is in its early stage. Building on community-based principles, this new era will emphasize the centricity of teaching and learning and instructional effectiveness as measured by student and community outcomes. (Myran 1989, 18)

Clearly, transformation of the community college will have significant impact on its service function. The community service function must become the "new service function" if it is going to meet the current and emerging needs of the people it is intended to serve.

Changes in society, the economy, and international developments have resulted in the development and implementation of nationwide and international training programs, business incubator coventures, community college/corporate universities, intensive literacy identification and remediation strategies, planning and research initiatives, comprehensive economic development programs, legislative involvement, and training of the whole person. Four of these programs are detailed more fully below.

Training and Economic Development

Community colleges have been involved in training and economic development since their beginning. It may be argued that, by virtue of their existence, the community college contributes to the economic well-being of its service area. However, it was not until the early to mid–1980s that these activities evolved into a more prominent role.

Katsinas and Lacey concluded that both policy makers and industry professionals have reconsidered the community college as a training service provider. This reevaluation was prompted, according to the authors, by "profound demographic, economic, political, and social change since 1973" (1990, 15). Today, companies continue to show an increased reliance on community college training and economic development services. The need for these services is the consequence of companies downsizing (including the elimination or minimalization of training departments) in an attempt to remain globally competitive.

The training and development function has grown to include such activities as providing custom-tailored and contracted training programs for business, industry, and other agencies; active coordination with city and state governments to promote business expansion and retention; the pursuit of existing federal and state training funds to buy down training costs for either new or expanding companies or those engaged in retooling or remanufacturing processes; close interaction with area chambers of commerce and businesses to promote economic activity; business and industrial partnerships; involvement in the state legislative process in order to establish training program funds; coordination with the U.S. Small Business Administration through its network of regional Small Business Development Centers; and coordination with Job Training Partnership Service Delivery Areas to provide employment training and prescreening. This listing will continue to be dynamic. As the needs of the business and industrial community change, so will the training and economic development services of the community college need to change.

At a minimum, community colleges need to provide both effective and entrepreneurial development services to the communities they serve by assisting existing and new industry. To that end, each college must identify one or more persons to work cooperatively with local and state economic developers to assist industry (Chaffin and Edwards 1989). The training and economic development function should be flexible, responsive, and innovative. To be successful, academic bureaucracy should be held to a minimum since corporations want immediate action. Further, the administrator responsible for the operation should have reporting responsibilities to the president of the college. Given the external nature and profile of the economic development function, the president must be kept informed of the college's involvement.

Synergistic Relations with Business, Industry, and Agencies

The last decade has been marked with an increase in partnerships between community colleges and government, business, industry, and other agencies. These linkages are primarily the result of a recognition that together the partners are more productive than if each acted independently.

In speaking at the annual meeting of the National Council on Community Services and Continuing Education, Joyce Tsunoda, chancellor for the Community Colleges of Hawaii, elaborated on the service function, including partnerships. "Partnerships have been the cornerstone of community colleges' operations, and particularly so in the community services and continuing education aspects. Partnerships with businesses and industry, with four-year institutions, and with other community-based organizations and agencies have made community colleges the community's college" (1989, 5).

Journals and texts are replete with examples of the continuing trend of partnerships: Burlington Northern Railroad/Johnson County Community College (Kansas); Kraft-General Foods, Inc./North Iowa Area Community College (Iowa); Motorola, Inc./Maricopa Community College District (Arizona); Higher Education Economic and Technology Development Service/Virginia Community College System (Virginia); General Mills/Kirkwood Community College (Iowa); and General Motors and the United Auto Workers/Dundalk Community College (Maryland). In addition, the American Association of Community and Junior Colleges (1986) initiated the Partnership Development Fund in 1985 as part of the Keep America Working Program. The fund, through a major contribution from the Sears-Roebuck Foundation, provides funds to support the development of partnerships among community colleges, business, industry, government, labor, and schools. Linkages such as these must continue to be forged for the ultimate benefit of America's competitiveness.

Literacy Development for a Better Work Force and Democracy

The fundamental component of a democracy is an educated populace. Similarly, the foundation of a productive America is an educated work force. However, functional illiteracy continues to plague the United States. The work-force illiteracy problem was identified, in part, as a result of industry's implementation of process control methodologies. Just-in-Time Inventory (JIT), Materials Requirement Planning (MRPI), Manufacturing Resources Planning (MRPII), Total Quality Management (TQM), and Statistical Process Control (SPC) practices were introduced in response to global competition. However, when the training began, many employees had difficulty using the rudimentary math skills necessary for these programs. Further analysis showed that employees were challenged in other areas as well, including written and oral communication, reading, and critical thinking.

In 1988, Carnevale, Gainer, and Meltzer released a text that was the result of a collaboration between the American Society for Training and Development and the U.S. Department of Labor, Employment, and Training Administration. The document, entitled *Workplace Basics: The Skills Employers Want*, presents a listing of seven desired skill groups: (1)

The Foundation: Knowing How to Learn; 2) Competence: Reading, Writing, and Computation; 3) Communication: Listening and Oral Communication; 4) Adaptability: Creative Thinking and Problem-Solving; 5) Personal Management: Self Esteem, Goal Setting/ Motivation, and Personal/Career Development; 6) Group Effectiveness: Interpersonal Skills, Negotiation, and Teamwork; and 7) Influence: Organizational Effectiveness and Leadership. (1988, 9)

These seven pillars of knowledge and skill are a prerequisite to learning new technology, production methods, and practices. Ultimately, these seven skills are a prerequisite to our nation's productivity.

For their part, community colleges need to respond to the basic skill needs of industry. Existing ABE/GED paradigms must be recast to include workplace literacy components. Simply applying existing practices to industry is inadequate. Industry presents numerous challenges that must be considered, including labor unions, confidentiality between employer and employee, training coordination with production schedules, and financial limitations. Each of these challenges will require a planned, customized, and thoughtful response by the community college.

Personal Enrichment and Growth

To be sure, the support and development of the whole person are as much the responsibility of the community college's service function as is that of the transfer function or the general education function. Community service offerings are vast and varied. Generally, these programs are offered on a noncredit basis and may be designed for persons who are working on a hobby or discovering a new one, interested in the arts, pursuing a lifelong ambition, concerned about government or the environment, or just curious. Seekers of this knowledge span the educational, social, and employment spectra. The nature of the programs offered and the scope of their intended audiences are nearly limitless. However, the common denominator among all programs offered is their purpose: the growth and the development of the participant.

While most community service programs are largely self-sufficient, program administrators will need to evaluate both the nature and extent of those offerings in the future. The "comprehensive community college" is no longer economically viable. With the preeminence of accountability, as well as declining federal and state funding, community college presidents, board members, and administrators will need to reevaluate their institutional mission and purpose.

Community service staffs will need to scrutinize their programming strategies as well. Self-examination may indicate that some current personal enrichment courses are best left to other community agencies. Conceivably, the YMCA, the YWCA, local libraries, park and recreation departments, and others could offer such courses. In fact, such arrangements may actually strengthen linkages between the college and these community agencies by minimizing duplication, and thereby affording the area resident a broader selection of programs. Parnell expressed concern about constituent perception and attitude toward the community college that may be perceived as frivolous: "[I]f those few programs are skewing the college's image, distorting the pictures in people's minds, then I suggest we examine some alternatives. . . . Sometimes we must ask ourselves whether, even if a certain offering pays for itself financially, we can afford the true cost in terms of our public image by providing that offering" (1991, 16–17). Unfortunately, for most community service operations, this type of scrutiny will be received as a limiting strategy rather than the positive paradigm shift that it represents.

THE CHALLENGES AND OBLIGATIONS OF THE FUTURE

The future is a two-edged sword for the "new service function": Opportunity often goes hand in hand with obligation. The challenge of the future is to be constantly vigilant, and the inherent obligation is to respond to the community-based needs. Obviously, the overarching challenge is to remain true to the rich heritage and mission of the community college for the next century: to serve the needs of its community. This section examines a few notable challenges for the future from a community service perspective, including demographics, lifelong training, service function integration in the community college, and accountability.

Changing Demographics and New Work Force Entrants

The demographics and psychographics of the American population hold obvious implications for industry. Some of the more important data involve literacy level, English speaking abilities, the work ethic, education level, competencies and skills, flexibility and adaptability, age, gender, and critical thinking skills. Current and projected data for the next decade prompt concern by business leaders. The American Society for Training and Development (ASTD) has identified the following facts based on their research: 75 percent of the people who will be working in the year 2000 are already on the job, but 75 percent of all workers currently employed will need retraining; 54 percent of all jobs today require training beyond high school, but by 2000, that number is estimated to be 65 percent; a growing number of corporations will find it necessary to initiate training in basic skills, problem solving, and teamwork (Carnevale, Gainer, and Meltzer 1988, 1–2).

Other demographic data are offered by former U.S. Secretary of Labor W. E. Brock:

1. The average age of the work force will increase.
2. The number of young workers will shrink; the average will drop from eighteen percent to thirteen percent in the year 2000.
3. Minorities, including many economically disadvantaged youth, will be the larger share of new entrants.
4. More women will enter the work force but the rate of increase will taper off. By the year 2000 about 47 percent of the workforce will be women. (1987, 26)

When these data are coupled with business and industry's current and projected technological and operational changes, major deficiencies are noted.

[T]he real problem is not a labor shortage, but a skill shortage, as many new work force entrants may not have the appropriate education and other training for entry-level jobs. This will result in more intensive competition for fewer unskilled and semi-skilled jobs.

In other words, we're going to have more unqualified people competing for the very low-skilled jobs, the few that remain. (Brock 1987, 26)

Consequently, community colleges will need to be more involved in retraining the low-skilled worker by administering quality, competency-oriented programs throughout the individual's productive work life.

Training for a Lifetime

Brock, who also served as chairman of the Secretary's Commission on Achieving Necessary Skills (SCANS), stated in 1991, "The key to our nation's economic future is how well we improve the quality of the American work force" (1991, 21). In his article entitled "Continuous Training for the High Skilled Workforce," he delivered an urgent plea to community colleges for the providership of ongoing, quality, skill-enhancing training. "[T]his year's average high school graduate will change jobs four to six times and careers two to three times throughout his or her work life. For many, it won't be a matter of job hopping, but rather that the job was pulled out from under them because of technological or economic change" (23). Unquestionably, community colleges will need to continue and even expand their role in providing training to workers. The vigorous rate of global change demands that the community college do its part to assist U.S. industry by providing training.

Of equal importance is the impending requirement that all community colleges work together in order to serve those companies that have facilities in multiple and divergent community college service districts. Business and industry do not have interest in, or time for, agencies that cannot get beyond their "turf issues." The business community has immediate national and international training needs. Therefore, community colleges will need to develop a strategy to assist corporations with these needs. The genesis of a practical solution to this challenge is being developed by the League for Innovation in the Community Colleges. A group of league member college administrators has formed the "Community College Alliance for Business and Industry" with the purpose of serving transdistrict needs of the business and industrial community.

A Full Partnership of Credit and Noncredit Divisions

Simply stated, the requirements of the future will not allow community colleges to persist in being internally disparate (i.e., separation of the community services function from the remainder of the college's operation). Rather, college administrators must move quickly to remove the barriers that have existed between the credit and noncredit divisions for decades. Cohen, Lombardi, and Brawer defined the community dimension of the community college as "narrow, inchoate, and removed from the mainstream of college operations. And it enjoys the dubious distinction of being the function least coherently defined, least amenable to assessment'' (1975, 82). Unfortunately, the authors' assessment is as valid today as it was in 1975. Community service operations have made little progress in becoming full and meaningful partners with their college preparatory counterparts.

Vaughan stated that ''community services must be brought into the instructional mainstream if the college's instructional program is ever to achieve its full potential . . . the community services division should serve as the innovative area of the instructional program'' (1991, 26). Vaughan's challenge will need to be enacted, however, rather than just agreed to in principle. True partnership between credit and noncredit divisions will require aggressive efforts on both sides.

Unquestionably, linkages between credit and noncredit operations will demand a fundamental shift in both attitude and action. The challenge will dictate more than the reorganization of an organizational chart. Specific opportunities include (1) a presidential commitment to a credit/noncredit partnership, (2) noncredit staff involvement in credit curricular development, (3) credit faculty involvement in noncredit advisory councils, (4) faculty membership at area chambers of commerce, (5) noncredit staff assigned to teach credit courses on an adjunct basis, (6) joint development of a noncredit certificate curriculum that serves as a feeder for traditional credit programs, (7) noncredit representation and involvement at academic affairs meetings, (8) job rotation sabbaticals between related credit and noncredit divisions, (9) faculty appointments containing both credit and noncredit components, and (10) joint efforts by credit and noncredit divisions to develop and implement a tech-prep (i.e., two-plus-two) program. The obligation of the ''new service function'' is to make a credit/noncredit partnership a reality; indignity results from doing nothing.

Accountability and the New Service Function

The ''new service function'' of the community college and accountability will be nearly synonymous. Bowen described accountability as follows: ''It means that colleges and universities are responsible for conducting their affairs so that the outcomes are worth the cost.'' He included the necessity of an institution's reporting ''credible evidence: on its progress towards goals'' (1974, 1).

The assessment of how a college affects its constituents is but one facet of institutional and mission accountability, and it is one of the least understood. Without question, economic pressures are increasing for information on a college's effects on its students as well as on the community it serves. Without it, public officials may move to transfer financial support away from higher education to more accountable public purposes.

Initially, the leadership of the community college should give serious consideration to the level of commitment the college is willing to make to the service function and thereby establish a baseline for assessment. Hankin and Frey's challenge is that ''this thinking needs to be done not in the context of generalities, but in light of hard realities of institutional mission and resource allocation. Each institution needs to define community service with particular reference to pressing needs in its service area and to articulate a clear set of community service objectives'' (1985, 171–72).

The community service function can no longer be viewed as an ancillary component of college operations. The college's future depends as much on effective community-based service as it does on its other primary functions.

SUMMARY

Change is inevitable. Therefore, the new service function must always be dynamic, not passive. The collective providership of community services, business and industrial partnerships, and economic development must be quality oriented, innovative, flexible, adaptive, and responsive to constituent needs. These must be more than catch phrases for our institutional mission statements. They must be integral to all work that is engaged by faculty, staff, and administration. Ownership of and commitment to these words must be demonstrated each day. To do anything less would be to ignore change in favor of apathy.

REFERENCES

American Association of Community and Junior Colleges. 1986. *Responding to the challenge of a changing American economy: 1985 progress report on the Sears Partnership Development Fund.* ERIC Document no. ED 293 578. Washington, D.C.

Bowen, H. R., ed. 1974. *Evaluating institutions for accountability.* New Directions for Institutional Research. San Francisco: Jossey-Bass.

Brock, W. E. 1987. Future shock: The American work force in the year 2000. *Community, Technical, and Junior College Journal* 57(4):25–26.

———. 1991. Continuous training for the high skilled work force. *Community, Technical, and Junior College Journal* 61(4):21–25.

Carnevale, A. P., L. J. Gainer, and A. S. Meltzer. 1988. *Workplace basics: The skills employers want.* Washington, D.C.: U.S. Department of Labor, Employment and Training Administration.

Chaffin, R., and R. Edwards. 1989. Developing business/industry partnerships for the future: Virginia's response. *Community Services Catalyst* 19(2):30–31.

Cohen, A. M., J. Lombardi, and F. B. Brawer. 1975. *College responds to community demands.* San Francisco: Jossey-Bass.

Hankin, J. N., and P. A. Frey. 1985. Reassessing the commitment to community services. In *Renewing the American community college*, ed. W. L. Deegan, D. Tillery, and Associates, 150–73. San Francisco: Jossey-Bass.

Harlacher, E. L. 1969. *The community dimension of the community college.* Englewood Cliffs, N.J.: Prentice-Hall.

Katsinas, S. G., and V. A. Lacey. 1990. Trends and forces motivating community college involvement in nontraditional economic development. *Community Services Catalyst* 20(2):8–16.

Myran, G. A. 1989. Community services and continuing education in the next decade: Linking to institutional priorities. *Community Services Catalyst* 19(3):17–19.

Parnell, D. 1991. Will belly dancing be our nemesis? *Community Services Catalyst* 21(3):15–17.

Thornton, J. W., Jr. 1972. *The community junior college*, 3d ed. New York: Wiley and Sons.

Tsunoda, J. S. 1989. Reading out: The role of community services and continuing education in international education. *Community Services Catalyst* 19(2):3–8.

Vaughan, G. B. 1991. Community services new frontier: Establishing the ties that bind. *Community Services Catalyst* 21(3):24–27.

The Role of Communication and Technology in the Community College in the Twenty-First Century

Phillip C. English

Will instructional technology in all its forms develop to its fullest capacity as an educational tool, or will it languish as a poor relative, unable to live up to the vision that many teachers, students, and administrators have seen? The answer is not clear. Given the financial prospects of higher education and the lukewarm commitment of governments to assist in funding the educational infrastructure, it will be some time before it becomes clear.

There were early dreamers about how technology could be used to serve education in the 1950s. In the United States, college courses were offered on television early in the morning in a series called "Sunrise Semester." The production values were low and the students scarce; nevertheless, it paved the way for the next generation of telecourses. In Great Britain, "The Open University" was created to begin offering educational programming on television.

In 1952 the federal government, convinced that education should have access to television broadcast outlets, set aside 250 television channels for educational broadcasting in the Federal Communications Commission's (FCC) "Sixth Report and Order." While slow to develop because of funding, and because most of the channels were in the little-used UHF band, the number of those channels has expanded to serve most communities, and they are now known as public television channels. Eventually universities, city school systems, state departments of education, and community-based educational television systems began offering courses to schools in grades K–12. Few colleges offered credit courses for broadcast, but many college students took classes televised live from one classroom to another.

In some ways, live classroom television hindered the growth of the use of technology in education. Administrators were content to let live classroom instruction continue as long as it did not interrupt conventional teaching. This practice was used in postsecondary courses often in response to overcrowded classes. Producers often had tiny or nonexistent budgets, and teachers had never been shown how the medium could be used effectively. Television was used to show lectures to several crowded classrooms from a central location, usually from a large lecture hall, with a camera trained on the lecturer. At best, the television made the courses impersonal and unimaginative. The effect was to give college graduates who had taken courses in this manner a deep dislike for all forms of televised instruction. Those who became teachers were not about to experiment with technology in teaching.

PIONEERS IN TECHNOLOGICAL INNOVATION

Some attempts were made to upgrade the quality of televised instruction. With poor funding, lack of creativity at most facilities, and a move by television stations away from "educational broadcasting" toward "public broadcasting," it was unlikely that any great strides would be made in televised instruction or mediated teaching.

One person who believed that something could be done to use various forms of media, especially broadcast television, to enhance the educational process was publisher Walter Annenberg. Apparently convinced by the British Open University that gaps in higher education could be filled with television, radio, and other forms of media, the Annenberg Foundation committed $150 million over a fifteen-year period to create higher education courses and other educational materials using all forms of media and other technologies. Thus began the development of many college credit telecourses. Although the concentration of funding went primarily to public broadcasting stations, some courses were produced by colleges with no public broadcasting station license. Some of the funds were used to support the development of other interactive technologies as well.

PIVOTAL EVENTS IN THE DEVELOPMENT OF NEW TECHNOLOGIES

As public broadcasting grew, most stations began limiting air time or telecourses and moving them to early morning hours and weekends. At the same time, Cable Television (CATV) began to attract large numbers of new subscribers. Local television broadcasters had successfully lobbied to keep out cable competition for audiences by getting the FCC to limit the number of distant signals CATV operators could import into the community.

But the cable business would change. Three things combined to give CATV a new, and very powerful, lift. First, by the late 1970s and early 1980s, cable regulations began to change. Large municipalities realized that CATV franchise revenues could be used for municipal expenses. The old, small-town cable systems had made it possible for rural households with limited television reception to have more choices in their viewing. But those choices were already available in the large municipalities. To entice customers to subscribe to the large city cable services, it was necessary to offer programs that they did not already have. Other than microwaving in distant television stations, there were no services that made cable special.

The second and third factors in the growth of cable were related to and dependent on each other. Public television had developed a satellite network in the mid–1970s and after that satellite communication grew rapidly. Satellites made it possible to open the country and the world to instant video communications. Soon all television networks had developed their own satellite interconnections with their networks. Finally, the last factor in the development of CATV, was the entrance of Ted Turner into the distant signal market. His independent Atlanta television station, WTBS, offered programs unavailable on the major television networks. In an agreement with the cable industry, Turner sent WTBS programming via satellite to cable systems throughout the country. It was marketed as a service that could not be received elsewhere. Almost immediately, big city cable systems had the new programming they needed. Rules were relaxed and unlimited distant signals were allowed. Stations like WOR in New York and WGN in Chicago had been on distant cable systems before but only via microwave. The cost of microwaving the signal and the lack of available microwave frequencies limited the potential use of those stations. Satellites opened the world to all manner of specialized programming, and even the biggest cities developed successful CATV systems.

Once cable operators saw how satellite-delivered broadcast signals helped their business, they began looking for new services. Ted Turner went on to develop CNN, a twenty-four-hour news channel that became widely accepted. Then other specialized programming services, such as sports, weather, music, movies, and Congressional coverage, became available on most cable systems. The development of national nonbroadcast services exclusively for cable was the final step in the development of CATV.

Municipalities were given the right to grant exclusive franchises for cable operators to develop systems in their communities. Often the competition for these franchises was keen. To get franchises, cable operators began to offer local community and educational access channels as a part of the service to the community.

Interestingly, many two-year institutions benefited. They often were given equipment and, in many cases, cable head-ends as a part of the franchise agreement. That allowed educators exclusive access to the community on one or more of the channels. Some institutions were quick to capitalize on the access by greatly increasing the number of telecourses that they offered. So while the broadcasters were cutting back on the number of courses, the colleges were making up the time over their cable channels.

Unfortunately, not every potential student had access to cable, but another development would help solve that problem. Video recording had always been expensive, requiring heavy investments in equipment, technical skills, and space.

Equipment was large, stationary, and needed special maintenance. When VHS and Beta video recording began to develop, the two technologies were not compatible. Individuals and institutions had to invest in both technologies. When VHS technology became dominant, the costs of equipment and service dropped dramatically, making it possible for most homes to have one or more recorders. Students recorded telecourses from broadcast and cable channels or borrowed them from college libraries to watch at convenient times. This made telecourses even more accessible to students in remote locations.

Along with the small formula video recorders came miniaturized cameras. The flexibility and portability of the equipment changed television permanently. The number of students taking college credit courses increased dramatically during the 1980s.

While small formula video recorders and cameras were becoming the industry standard, another development was taking place. Laser video discs were coming on the market. Laser discs are storage devices that allow for the storage of several thousand bits of information, including high-quality video, data, and audio on a very small plastic disc. Using time-coding, each bit of information, whether it is a slide, full-motion video, audio track, or data bit, is given an exact address on the disc, thus allowing any information on the disc to be retrieved within two seconds. Any combination of the material on the disc can be used in a sequence of one's own choosing.

The other advantage of laser discs is that they can be used in conjunction with computers. The computer drives the disc to the proper piece of information and then overlays text, either on the video screen or on a separate computer monitor. There are video discs that contain high-quality video of all the art located in the National Gallery of Art and in the Louvre. There are NASA video discs with pictures of comets, nebulae, planets, and stars, many of them from outer space and shown without the distortions of Earth's atmosphere. One enterprising instructor created an exceptional astronomy course from the several video discs that were included in a NASA series. The computer text included narrative information and periodic tests and quizzes which were graded on the spot and analyzed for weaknesses in student performance.

Then modem-based instruction came along. Using high-capacity computers, instructors developed courses for their students to access through dial-up systems. The teacher writes text, assigns readings and papers, and adds problems tailored for each student. The teacher and student interact using the computer's electronic-mail (E-mail) system. Subgroups of the class can be formed to work on specific problems and communicate with one another through the computer. The teacher can join the group process by dialing in on the sessions.

The newest developments in instructional technology include compact disc interactive (CDI), which allows the mixing of text and video on a single system, and compact disc-read only memory (CD-ROM), which allows students to access reference materials, such as encyclopedias, very quickly.

Interactivity has become an important part of instructional technology. With it students are made to feel more a part of the class. When they receive responses and communications from each other and from the teacher, they get a reading about how they are doing. They can get help with problems, and interactive communications makes them feel more a part of the process.

The development of technology-based instruction was affected by these pivotal events: the Annenberg support, which enabled the acquisition of high-quality products; the development of satellites, giving education access to a wide variety of programs; the development of cable television, allowing institutions to reach homebound students; miniaturization of equipment, enabling the technology to become more affordable and portable; and interactivity, making teaching more effective.

THE TECHNOLOGIES OF THE TWENTY-FIRST CENTURY

The next developments will be harder to accomplish. Because systems with greater capacity are more efficient, they can be made available to more people. Cables made of fiber-optic material, combined with digital video encoding devices, will enable clearer, faster delivery than ever before. The old copper telephone systems are quickly disappearing to be replaced with high-quality large-capacity systems. In addition to data and voice, these systems will be able to deliver video, and, because the capacity is so great, they will also have two-way video capability. The old courses delivered over broadcast and cable could literally be delivered directly from classroom to the home in real time.

In teacher-operated production studios, the teacher, seated at a console desk, will control several television cameras and other information sources. While one camera is used for slides, text from books, or other visual material, the teacher will adjust the camera and push a switch to put the other cameras on monitors, films, data, audio, or other sources of information. Students watching television at home, through cable, can dial the teacher by phone and ask questions.

The future impact of the combined technology with two-way video and audio through fiber optics opens a whole new world. Imagine an engineer at a very remote job site needing to continue to upgrade his or her skills to remain productive. With the university hundreds of miles away, it means leaving the job site for extended periods in order to keep up with training. It is not difficult to make the leap into a new world of educational delivery and management where the student can be any place, and course material can be presented in several formats. The different formats enable the student to grasp the information more easily. The remote site is no longer so remote (Parnell 1990).

BARRIERS TO DEVELOPMENT

The technology is already here, so why isn't this transformation taking place? There are three basic reasons: restrictive government and school administration policies, lack of training, and lack of financial support.

Some experts say that, without a massive governmental effort aimed at re-organizing telecommunications in the United States, the nation will continue to fall farther behind its European and Far Eastern neighbors. The nation has previously depended on the marketplace to guide the development of technology. With relatively few laws, the nation has had considerable success in creating uses for new technologies. The basic law, other than fair trade laws, governing communications technologies is the Communications Act of 1934. Amended, it has become the guide for government regulation of most communications tech-nologies including broadcasting, satellites, video recording devices, computer networking, telephone service, and CATV, where some local regulations also apply. While there are advantages to allowing a market to develop in an at-mosphere of free competition, there are disadvantages as well. Sometimes a hodgepodge of technologies develops and uses up valuable resources with pro-grams of limited public value before a standard format is agreed upon.

Telephone companies have begun developing fiber-optic delivery systems. Fiber could relieve the spectrum problem because of its high capacity, but most of the current fiber systems are main trunks and the potential for putting them directly into homes is a long way off. The potential for delivery of courses directly to the home or business using fiber networks and two-way interactive video depends on the successful development of this technology. Government regulations prohibit phone companies from creating material to be used on their systems. Therefore, no video, data, or voice materials are provided by them. The phone companies argue that the only way for them to recover costs of rebuilding their entire systems with fiber optics is for them to create and sell video and data on their systems (U.S. Telephone Association 1989).

That is a compelling argument, but there may be just as many arguments for the other side of the issue. What if the total delivery system is controlled by one company or one delivery system? There can be no doubt that cable operators would find it difficult to compete with phone companies. And what if the phone companies get the rule changed in their favor and then decide not to complete the system? They might choose to construct the system only for those areas with the greatest population density as cable companies do now. They might decide to serve only affluent neighborhoods. It is conceivable that companies could also force educational institutions to use accompanying technologies that did not meet the needs of the institution. And phone companies could, through strong lob-bying, stop institutions and governments from building private systems (Gross and English 1989).

There are arguments for both sides. According to Perelman, ''The top priority policy change needed, not only to transform schools but to revitalize the whole economy, is in the domain of communication, not education policy: To remove the legal and regulatory barriers that now block the extension of digital, fiber-optic communication channels to every home and business in America'' (1990, 19).

That is just one government policy. In a ruling that appears arbitrary, the U.S.

Department of Education has decided that telecourses are correspondence courses and that, as such, students taking those courses are not eligible for full scholarship grants. Some administrators are so concerned that they have limited the number and amounts of student loans for telecourses.

Another issue concerning the implementation of distance learning is the territorial problem. There are no borders when courses are delivered over some form of transmission or computer modem (Gross and English 1989). In an address to the Council on Post-Secondary Accreditation, Goldstein said that antitrust laws are not clear on credits from one university being given in the territory of another without a physical presence (Goldstein 1991). While many colleges have worked out the details and delivered courses without problems, other have not reconciled the difficulties yet.

But these are not the only reasons that instructional technology has not made greater advances. Perhaps the greatest impediments are within higher education itself. Colleges use the most advanced equipment available to help students learn and prepare for technical jobs. But when it comes to using the latest technology for teaching, colleges do not measure up. Perelman (1990) claims that from 5 to 10 percent of school and college budgets need to be reallocated from payrolls and administrative overhead and invested in technological innovation, research, development, and implementation. In addition to requiring a major shift in administrative thinking, there is mounting evidence that recession-slashed education budgets may never grow enough to begin the process of rebuilding technologies.

A study by the U.S. Office of Technology Assessment (1990) examined the question of modernization of the nation's telecommunications infrastructure. Cost estimates are in the several billion dollar range. The study states that regulatory policies may discourage private investment because of the regulatory caps on returns of investment. Government policy discourages taxpayer-supported research which will return large profits to private investors. To counter that argument, the article points out that other technologies benefiting private investors have been funded by the government. A good example is space technology, which was funded with public funds and developed technology that has benefited many private companies.

There is no doubt that the investment of major funds for technology is a necessity, but there are other problems to overcome as well. There is a wide discrepancy in the ability of instructors to use technology. In some instances, college administrators have only grudgingly given the time and funds to train selected faculty in the use of technology to teach. In times of larger class loads and other retrenchments, it is even more difficult to get the proper training to teachers, and, with aging and obsolete systems, it may be a waste of funds anyway.

Hixson and Jones write that "all educators will need to develop new attitudinal infrastructures regarding their responsibility to whoever shows up on Monday" (1990, 3). As a part of teacher development, teachers and administrators must develop new understandings of the changing goals of education. Teachers must learn from practice and apply their knowledge to the real world. They must have opportunities for self-renewal. Technology can be used as a vehicle and as content for part of the self-renewal.

That is the key to growth in the use of technology to make instruction more effective. Once teachers and administrators commit to using technology, the critical mass will develop to a point where nothing else will satisfy their needs. Funds will follow. When the policy problems, the money problems, and the teacher training problems are solved, one more problem remains: Technology can become the master instead of the servant.

The new inventions are increasingly complex. Their appearance in the marketplace will accelerate. Even the most technologically sophisticated institution will not have the means to keep up. Though institutions must sort the useful from the useless, very few educational institutions can afford the high cost of purchasing a new piece of technology for experimentation. They must learn from other institutions which technologies work. Educational institutions will fall farther behind in technology use if all the partners, such as governments, administrators, and faculty, are not full partners in the planning.

They must plan a course of action and develop and commit funds to move steadily into technology acquisition and training for the users. Some of the funding partners understand the message: Government funding agencies are already looking more closely at supporting projects that serve limited constituencies. The community college of the twenty-first century will be involved in technological partnerships with businesses and other institutions in their areas. With all the partners working together, institutions can use technology wisely to improve teaching and learning.

Then the real obstacles that stand in the way of effective use of technology for better teaching will be gone. After all, once the useless information is winnowed away, technology will enhance teaching and learning in ways previously thought impossible.

In his book *Dateline 2000*, Parnell makes ten predictions on a user-friendly future. His final prediction is that, by the year 2000, there will be a synergistic merging of various media to better serve the diversity of the higher education enterprise (1990). That is the best solution, and it is already started. IBM has developed a multitechnology system called ''Ulysses'' that mixes most of the technologies referred to in this chapter to present a fascinating view of the three most famous versions of the Odyssey of Ulysses. Using old teaching methods, the teacher might have managed information about Ulysses by writing on the blackboard, discussing reading assignments, or asking students to write papers. The IBM version allows the teacher to manage the information in ways that will make even the most disinterested scholar take notice. Mixing film, graphics, text, and just plain good acting, the teacher can present several viewpoints and interpretations of this classic story. Add to that the ability of the student to take that course at home or in a nearby learning center and it is not hard to leap to the twenty-first century where this type of learning will be the norm.

REFERENCES

Goldstein, M. 1991. Distance learning and accreditation. Keynote address given at the Professional Development Program, Council on Postsecondary Accreditation, Washington, D.C.

Gross, R., and P. C. English. 1989. Television: Telecommunications issues for the 1990s. *Community, Technical, and Junior College Journal* 60(2):37–41.

Hixson, J., and B. F. Jones. 1990. Using technology to support professional development for teachers and administrators. In *Education policy and telecommunications technologies*, ed. A. D. Sheekey. Washington, D.C.: U.S. Department of Education.

Parnell, D. 1990. *Dateline 2000: The new higher education agenda*. Washington, D.C.: Community College Press.

Perelman, L. J. 1990. Education in the information age: A new learning enterprise. In The technology revolution comes to education, a special advertising supplement. *Business Week* (December):18–20.

U.S. Office of Technology Assessment. 1990. Modernization and technological development in the U.S. communication infrastructure. In *Critical connections: Communications for the future*. Washington, D.C.: U.S. Government Printing Office.

U.S. Telephone Association. 1989. Unpublished manuscript presenting arguments in favor of deregulating telephone company entrance into television programming. Washington, D.C.

How Critics View the Community College's Role in the Twenty-First Century

Fred L. Pincus

As community colleges expanded in the 1960s and 1970s, a variety of critical voices began to appear. Many of these early critics raised serious questions about whether community colleges were providing genuine avenues of upward mobility for poor, working-class, and minority students. Community college leaders either ignored these early critics or simply dismissed them as ''elitist four-year college professors who didn't know anything about community colleges.''

Critics continued to raise disturbing questions about community colleges. By the mid–1980s, critics gained enough ''respectability'' to be featured in a special issue of the mainstream publication *New Directions for Community Colleges* (Zwerling 1986).

There are three general categories of community college critics. *Elitist critics* tend to argue that community colleges are inferior because they do not measure up to the academic model of prestigious four-year colleges and universities: Community college students have poor skills and study habits and faculty lack Ph.D.'s, received their degrees from second-rate institutions, or do not pursue independent scholarship. Most elitist critics are, indeed, four-year college educators.

Mainstream critics, on the other hand, are generally supportive of the direction of community colleges but believe they can do a better job serving the needs of less-advantaged[1] (i.e., poor, working-class, and minority) students, especially with regard to greater transfer opportunities. They are aware of the empirical data showing race, class, and gender bias in the community colleges but believe that these institutions can be reformed to provide more equal opportunity. Arthur Cohen, Florence Brawer, Richard Richardson, Louis Bender, Laura Rendón, Judith Eaton, and Alison Bernstein are all mainstream critics.

Finally, *structural critics* argue that community colleges are part of a stratified system of higher education that reproduces the race, class, and gender inequalities that are part of the larger society. Most structural critics would make the same comments about four-year colleges and about K–12 education and call for fundamental political and economic change: Educational change is needed across the spectrum. Important structural critics include Jerome Karabel, Fred L. Pincus, L. Steven Zwerling, Samuel Bowles, Herbert Gintis, Howard London, David Lavin, Lois Weis, William Velez, Kevin Dougherty, Elizabeth Monk-Turner, Steven Brint, Valerie E. Lee, Dennis McGrath, and Martin B. Speare.

In the remainder of this chapter, the term "critic" will refer to the work of the structural critics. Mainstream critics will be discussed when relevant, although the line between mainstream and structural critics is not always clear. Also included is the empirical research of social scientists, especially W. Norton Grubb, whose work supports much of the critical perspective. The views of elitist critics will not be addressed.

EARLY STRUCTURAL CRITICS

This critical approach first developed in the early 1970s with the writings of Karabel (1972), Pincus (1974), Zwerling (1976), and Bowles and Gintis (1976). Although there were some differences between them, the early critics argued that community colleges did more to reproduce class and race inequality than to provide meaningful avenues of upward mobility. There was a contradiction between the educational aspirations of less-advantaged students and the goals of the educational, political, and business leaders who formulated community college policy.

Although critics acknowledged that community colleges met the demand of the less-advantaged students for *some* higher education, they argued that these institutions were structured in ways that permitted few less-advantaged students to obtain a bachelor's degree. Terminal vocational programs, leading to middle-level jobs requiring two years of college or less, were actively promoted by community college leaders while transfer programs were permitted to languish. Less-advantaged students were overrepresented in vocational programs and underrepresented in transfer programs leading to bachelors' degrees and college-level jobs.

The effect was to reproduce the inequality of the larger society. Middle- and upper-income Caucasians were destined for college-level jobs while the less-advantaged minority students were destined for middle-level jobs that were lower paid and less skilled. The meritocratic selection process legitimated this stratified system of higher education, and the unequal results appeared to be inevitable.

Structural critics viewed community colleges as the lowest track of higher education. In their historical analysis, Bowles and Gintis (1976) argued that the high school tracking system was developed in the early twentieth century to meet the demands of African Americans, immigrants, and working-class whites for high school education. In the mid-twentieth century, community colleges developed to meet the demands of the same groups for higher education. In both cases, critics argued, the lowest track provided inferior education for the least privileged, while protecting the interests of the most privileged.

Critics also drew on the work of Clark (1960) who argued that community colleges "cooled out" students who were labeled "latent terminals"—those who wanted to transfer in order to get a bachelor's degree and a college-level job but did not have the necessary skills to succeed. These students had to be convinced by counselors and faculty to settle for a community college education and a middle-level job. Clark is not considered a critic because he argued that community colleges *should* cool students out (Clark 1980). Critics, on the other hand, agreed that community colleges *do* cool students out but *should not*.

With the exception of Zwerling, early critics argued that business leaders and their political and educational supporters actively promoted the development of community colleges to preserve their vested interests. The educational inequalities of community colleges were, thus, tied to the economic inequalities of the capitalist system.

Unfortunately, early critics did little research on the issue of gender. Although gender-based vocational programs certainly reproduced economic inequality, the early critics did not incorporate this into their tracking model.

EMPIRICAL STUDIES SUPPORTING STRUCTURAL CRITICS

Critics have utilized large-scale data analysis to examine the structural impact of community colleges. The most thorough review of the empirical literature through the mid–1980s was conducted by Dougherty (1987). In the following section, most of the data and studies referred to have been published since the Dougherty article.

1. Less-advantaged students continue to be overrepresented in public community colleges. Community colleges account for 37 percent of enrollment in higher education, a figure that has been fairly stable since the late 1970s. Although most community college students are Caucasian, a greater percentage of minority students are enrolled in these institutions than Caucasians.

In 1988, 36 percent of Caucasian college students were enrolled in community colleges; most of the rest were enrolled in four-year colleges. However, 42 percent of African American college students, 56 percent of Hispanics, 55 percent of Native Americans, and 40 percent of Asians were enrolled in community colleges (Snyder and Hoffman 1991).

Class differences between community college and four-year college students are also striking. Although 29 percent of community college students came from families with incomes below $17,000 in 1988, the comparable figure for four-year students was from 14 to 23 percent, depending upon the type of four-year college. On the other hand, only 17 percent of community college students came from families whose incomes exceeded $50,000, compared with from 21 to 42 percent of four-year college students.

Women are also overrepresented in community colleges. In 1988, for example, 39.5 percent of women college students were enrolled in community colleges compared with only 30.1 percent of men. This is a dramatic change from 1970 when equal percentages of male and female college students were enrolled in community colleges.

2. *The percentage of community college students who transfer to four-year colleges and receive a bachelor's degree has been declining.* Although there is some controversy about how to measure transfer rates, most observers now agree that between 15 and 25 percent of community college students transfer to a four-year college and that the numbers are declining (Dougherty 1987; Pincus and Archer 1989; National Center for Academic Achievement and Transfer 1991).

Grubb (1991) provides striking evidence of how the transfer rate is declining. His findings are based on two large-scale national studies of high school graduates of the class of 1972 and 1980. Students in both cohorts who entered a community college were interviewed four years after they had graduated from high school.

Grubb found that 28.7 percent of the 1972 high school graduates who had entered a community college had transferred to a four-year college within four years compared to only 20.2 percent of the 1980 graduates. Further, the transfer students more closely resembled the students who originally entered four-year colleges than community college students who did not transfer—the transfer students were more likely to be white and have a higher socioeconomic status (SES) than their counterparts who did not transfer. Women were also less likely to transfer than men (Lee and Frank 1990).

Grubb also found that there was a decline in the number of transfer students who earned a bachelor's degree (B.A.) in four years. Although 30.8 percent of the 1972 cohort who transferred earned a degree in four years, only 27.2 percent of the 1980 cohort earned a degree. In both cohorts, Caucasians and upper SES students were more likely to earn degrees than African Americans, Hispanics, and low SES students.

Gender differences in B.A. rates were more complex. Taking all community college entrants as the base, women were more likely than men to earn a degree in the 1972 cohort, but less likely than men to earn a B.A. in the 1980 cohort. Looking at all students who transferred as the base, women with vocational associate of arts (A.A.) degrees were less likely than men to earn a B.A. in both cohorts. Women with no credentials or with academic A.A. degrees, on the other hand, were more likely than men to earn the B.A.

Finally, and perhaps most disturbing, students aspiring to a B.A. are more likely to get that degree if they begin their education at four-year colleges than at community colleges, even when students' academic skills, race, and class backgrounds are statistically controlled. Students aspiring to a sub-baccalaureate degree, on the other hand, are better off beginning their higher education at community colleges than at four-year schools (Dougherty 1987).

3. Enrollment in vocational programs has been increasing. According to data from the American Association of Community and Junior Colleges (AACJC), the percentage of community college students enrolled in a vocational program increased from 15 percent in 1965 to over 50 percent in 1976. Although the AACJC stopped classifying enrollment as vocational or academic in 1980, Grubb (1992a) estimates that vocational enrollment is approaching 80 percent in the early 1990s. Comparing the 1972 and 1980 high school graduates, Grubb (1989a) found that the percentage enrolling in two-year postsecondary vocational programs increased, while the percentage enrolling in two-year academic programs declined.

4. Noncompletion rates among community college students are increasing. In his study of the two cohorts of high school graduates who entered community colleges, Grubb (1989b) shows that an increasing number of students are leaving community colleges without transferring or receiving a credential within four years. Thirty percent of the 1972 cohort were classified as noncompleters, while 42 percent of the 1980 cohort were so classified. The noncompletion rate for vocational students was higher than for academic students. Although some of these students may have satisfied their educational goals, the number of community college students leaving college with twelve or fewer credits increased from 14.5 percent in the 1972 cohort to 26.9 percent in the 1980 cohort.

African Americans, Hispanics, and low SES students were more likely to be noncompleters than Caucasian upper SES students in both cohorts. Men were more likely than women to be noncompleters in the 1972 cohort, but the situation was reversed in the 1980 cohort.

5. The economic return of community college education is modest, at best. A number of empirical studies summarized by Dougherty (1987) and Brint and Karabel (1989), along with two recent studies conducted by Monk-Turner (1988, 1990) show the following:

1. Most community college students do not get jobs that are related to their fields of study.

2. Community college students tend to have better jobs and higher incomes than students who had no education past high school, although much of this advantage disappears after controlling for demographic characteristics and high school achievement.

3. Students who entered community colleges had lower wages than those who entered four-year colleges, even after controlling for years of education.[2]

4. Students who entered community colleges had lower status jobs than those who entered four-year colleges, even after controlling for education; Monk-Turner (1990) found that this applied more to men than to women.

5. Male community college students have higher incomes than comparable females.

Two recent studies conducted by Grubb (1992a, 1992b) take a more detailed look at the economic effects of attending a community college. Grubb, who does not consider himself a community college critic, studied the 1985 earnings of graduates of the high school class of 1972. His findings support many of the critics' conclusions and modify others.

First, Grubb found that students who attend a community college without getting a credential have no income advantage over students who had no post–high school education. Getting a vocational certificate had no earnings advantage for men compared with those with only high school educations, but the certificate did have an earnings advantage for women.

Students who earned either a vocational or academic A.A. degree or a B.A. degree did have an earning advantage over those who stopped their educations after high school. The B.A. earnings advantage was larger than the A.A. earnings advantage, especially for men. Controlling for demographic characteristics and high school achievement, however, Grubb found that, for men, there were no economic advantages to an A.A. degree. For women, however, an A.A. or B.A., or even a certificate earned, resulted in earnings advantages over high school graduates.

Finally, Grubb controlled for labor market experience and on-the-job training. Only B.A. degrees still had earning advantages for men and women; A.A. degrees did not. He concludes all community college degrees for women and vocational A.A. degrees for men give students access to positions that lead to careers rather than jobs.

Critics would argue that these empirical data show that community colleges act to reproduce social inequality. True, some less-advantaged individuals can use community colleges as agents of upward mobility in terms of "catching up" to their Caucasian middle- and upper-income counterparts. However, many of the studies found that a student's class background has an effect of inhibiting academic and economic achievement, even after controlling for a host of other variables.

As a group, then, most less-advantaged community college students will lag behind their Caucasian middle- and upper-income counterparts both educationally and economically; they will not have the educational credentials and skills necessary to enter college-level jobs.

Since neither critics nor mainstream social scientists have concentrated on issues of gender, the differences between men and women are not as clear as they are for race and class (Gittell 1986). However, women are more likely than men to drop out of a community college and less likely to transfer. They definitely end up with lower incomes than men with the same level of education, in part, because they are trained for gender-stereotyped jobs.

WHY DO COMMUNITY COLLEGES REPRODUCE INEQUALITY?

Critics cite several different reasons why community colleges inhibit the achievement of less-advantaged students: the structure of the labor market, the role of community college leaders, the conflict of cultures within these institutions, and the structure of community colleges.

The Labor Market Structure

Since the 1960s, there has been a contradiction between the aspirations of less-advantaged students for upward mobility into skilled, well-paying college-level jobs and the ability of the U.S. labor market to provide adequate numbers of these jobs. During the early 1970s, mainstream educators and policymakers warned of the growing number of "overeducated Americans" (Carnegie Commission on Higher Education 1973; Freeman 1976).

The problem of having more college graduates than college-level jobs still exists in the 1990s, in spite of "spot shortages" in certain fields. Given the relatively stagnant economy that has existed for the past decade, many college graduates are happy to find *any* job and often see themselves as lucky to actually find a college-level job.

There has also been a controversy about the skills required for success in today's labor force. Most mainstream policymakers have accepted the view that (1) most jobs in this age of technology require high levels of skill and (2) all levels of education are failing to provide these skills. Critics, on the other hand, often argue that the level of skill needed in today's labor force is often exaggerated. Both sides agree, however, that jobs that require more than high school and less than four years of college are growing the fastest (Pincus 1980, 1986; Weisman 1991).

The vocationally oriented community college has become the method of choice to resolve these problems. More students get *some* college, but resources are not "wasted" on students who do not have the skills to complete four years of college. The declining transfer function is not problematic since there is no "need" for more B.A. recipients than four-year colleges already produce.

When California's state-funded universities announced that they would place limits on the numbers of community college transfer students that were accepted in 1991 due to cutbacks in state funds, for example, there was little concern that this would hurt the state's economy. Most of the criticism focused on limiting upward mobility opportunities (Pederson 1991; Reinhold 1991).

All this seems very rational if the structure of the labor force is accepted as a given. Many students might actually choose middle-level jobs over college-level jobs because they believe that there is no realistic alternative. Critics argue, however, that the structure of the labor force is, in fact, part of the problem. In order to increase profitability, say critics, employers have made decisions about the structure of work, assuming that lower paying jobs are more "appropriate" for certain segments of the society (Bowles and Gintis 1976).

But community colleges should not focus preparing less-advantaged and women workers to fit into the current labor force that is structured to relegate them to inferior jobs, say critics. Rather than encouraging students to limit aspirations, community colleges should teach students why the current labor force often works against them and what more egalitarian alternatives exist.

Community College Leaders

The early community college critics argued that, since the community colleges had the effect of protecting the interests of the more privileged sectors of the populations, business leaders must have actively supported the expansion and vocationalization of community colleges. Community college leaders and high-level commissions, such as the Carnegie Commission on Higher Education, were seen as witting or unwitting accomplices.

Contemporary critics now see this "business domination" model as simplistic and, in part, inaccurate. As a result of historical case studies in several states, Brint and Karabel (1989, 1991) and Dougherty (1988) argue that community college leaders were, in fact, the active proponents of vocationalization; most business leaders were indifferent.

First, community college leaders were looking for a niche in higher education where their institutions could excel: Postsecondary vocational education was seen as the key to their institution's mission.

Second, community college leaders wanted to gain political and economic support from the powerful business community. As a result, community college leaders structured their institutions to be responsive to the needs of employers for skilled workers. They practiced what Brint and Karabel (1989) call "anticipatory subordination." State and local governments began to promote terminal vocational education to attract new businesses and keep old businesses from leaving.

During the past decade, community college leaders have vigorously pursued short-term contract training as a new source of income and students and have promised that everyone will benefit. Pincus (1989) acknowledges that the business community will benefit from contract training since their employees will be trained at the taxpayers expense; labor costs will be reduced. Workers who already have jobs will also receive some benefits. However, students who are trying to use community colleges to enter the college-level labor market could be hurt since fiscal resources could be drained from already weakened liberal arts and transfer programs. This would be detrimental to critical thinking on community college campuses and would decrease the already slim chances that less-advantaged students have for obtaining a college degree (also see Teitel 1991 and Zwerling 1986).

Culture Conflict

Both London (1978) and Weis (1985) have argued that cultural conflict between students and the faculty and administration lies at the heart of the problem.

McGrath and Spear (1991) makes a similar argument, although they also share many of the views of mainstream critics.

First-generation college students see community colleges as a way out of their less-advantaged communities. Yet, they are also concerned that education will alienate them from their families and peer groups which may have anti-intellectual values. The students enter the often mysterious and foreign world of higher education with a great deal of ambivalence.

"The educational challenge for community colleges is the construction of bridges of understanding across which students may move from nontraditional backgrounds to competent membership in the educated community" (McGrath and Spear 1991, 30). More often than not, say critics, community colleges fail to build adequate bridges and, instead, become cultural battlegrounds.

Community college faculty and administrators often fail to understand or respect students' cultural backgrounds. They impose a rigid organizational structure to force students to conform to the college culture. Rather than challenging students' anti-intellectualism through innovative classroom techniques, the faculty often lower expectations and use lectures to transmit disparate bits of information. Multiple-choice exams have become the major instrument of evaluation (Richardson, Fisk, and Okun 1983).

Less-advantaged students may perceive the college as an assault on their integrity and that of their communities. This perception may be reinforced by the class and race differences between the students and the community college staff. Such perceptions may result in self-protective, yet self-defeating anti-intellectual attitudes by students.

Community College Structure

Finally, certain elements of the structure of community colleges also inhibit student educational aspirations. The increasing number of academically unprepared students, commuter students, and part-time students, along with other factors, have made it difficult to create a vibrant campus climate that is beneficial to student success. Finally, the subordination of community colleges to the whims of their four-year counterparts has often made the transfer process extremely difficult for students.

THE FUTURE, ACCORDING TO CRITICS

If no major policy changes are implemented, community colleges will continue to provide only limited opportunities for upward mobility for less-advantaged and female students. While critics have not always given concrete suggestions for change, it is possible to outline some policy directions implied.

To the degree that the structure of the economy causes community colleges to behave as they do, the solution is to change the economy. Community college administrators and faculty should see the labor market structure as problematic, rather than something to be adjusted to. They could demonstrate to both students and employers how work can be organized by giving workers more autonomy and skill, rather than less (Carnoy and Shearer 1980).

If workers are to be empowered, they need broad technical skills and a solid grounding in the critical liberal arts. Community colleges should set this as a goal, even though employers may not think it is necessary. In addition to learning new employment skills, laid-off workers should understand that their unemployment was not inevitable but was a result of various choices made by their employers. Alliances with unions and grass-roots community groups should be just as important as alliances with corporations.

Economic stagnation and funding crises have become commonplace. These realities have begun to result in limits on the number of transfer students four-year institutions will accept and in limits on the number of students two-year colleges can admit. Nevertheless, most critics argue that pre-baccalaureate transfer programs must be dramatically upgraded in order to achieve a better balance with vocational programs. Pincus and Archer (1989) argue that transfer should be the primary function of community colleges, that states should pay colleges for each student who successfully transfers, and that state aid should be set aside for transfer students. Miami-Dade's outstanding efforts have been noted by Zwerling (1988).

The learning climate on the campus and in the classroom can be improved by intervention in the debilitating culture conflict that exists in many community colleges (Weis 1985). In addition, critics argue that the learning environment needs to be more stimulating and intellectually rigorous. A starting place might be some of the liberatory teaching approaches that seek to empower students (Shor 1987).

All in all, community colleges can better serve the interests of less-advantaged and female students only if faculty and administrators recognize the current shortcomings and commit themselves to positive change. Otherwise, community colleges will continue to be the lowest track in a stratified system of higher education that reproduces the race, class, and gender inequality that exists in the larger society.

NOTES

The author would like to thank Kevin Dougherty and Kostis Papadantonakis for their help by reviewing early drafts of this chapter.

1. The term "disadvantaged" generally refers to poor or low-income individuals who are disproportionately minority members. However, I want to argue that Caucasian working-class students are also not well-served by community colleges. Hence, I use the term "less-advantaged" to include the following groups: minorities of all classes, poor Caucasians, and working-class Caucasians.

2. Several earlier studies cited by Dougherty (1987) found no income differences, but students had not been in the labor force as long as those surveyed in the Monk-Turner (1990) and Grubb (1992a, 1992b) studies.

REFERENCES

Bowles, S., and H. Gintis. 1976. *Schooling in capitalist America*. New York: Basic Books.

Braverman, H. 1974. *Labor and monopoly capital: The degradation of work in the twentieth century*. New York: Monthly Review Press.

Brint, S., and J. Karabel. 1989. *The diverted dream: Community colleges and the promise of educational opportunity in America: 1900–1985*. New York: Oxford University Press.

———. 1991. Institutional origins and transformations: The case of American community colleges. In *The new institutionalism in organizational analysis*, ed. W. Powell and P. DiMaggio. Chicago: University of Chicago Press.

Carnegie Commission on Higher Education. 1973. *College graduates and jobs*. New York: McGraw-Hill.

Carnoy, M., and D. Shearer. 1980. *Economic democracy*. White Plains, N.Y.: M. E. Sharpe.

Clark, B. R. 1960. The cooling-out function in higher education. *American Journal of Sociology* 65:569–76.

———. 1980. The cooling-out function revisited. In *Questioning the community college role*, ed. G. B. Vaughan. San Francisco: Jossey-Bass.

Dougherty, K. 1987. The effects of community colleges: Aid or hindrance to socioeconomic attainment? *Sociology of Education* 60(2):86–122.

———. 1988. The politics of community college expansion: Beyond the functionalist and class-reproduction theories. *American Journal of Education* 96:351–93.

———. 1991. The community college at the crossroads: The need for structural reform. *Harvard Educational Review* 61(3):311–36.

Freeman, R. B. 1976. *The overeducated American*. New York: Academic Press.

Gittell, M. 1986. A place for women? In *The community college and its critics*, ed. L. S. Zwerling, 71–80. New Directions for Community Colleges no. 54. San Francisco: Jossey-Bass.

Grubb, W. N. 1989a. The effects of differentiation on educational attainment: The case of community colleges. *Review of Higher Education* 12(4):349–74.

———. 1989b. Dropouts, spells of time and credits in postsecondary education: Evidence from longitudinal surveys. *Economics of Education Review* 8(1):49–67.

———. 1991. The decline of community college transfer rates: Evidence from national longitudinal surveys. *Journal of Higher Education* 62(2):194–224.

———. 1992a. Postsecondary vocational education and the sub-baccalaureate labor market: New evidence on economic returns. *Economics of Education Review* 11(3):225–248.

———. 1992b. Correcting conventional wisdom: Community college impact on students' jobs and salaries. *Community and Junior College Journal* 62(6):10–14.

Karabel, J. 1972. Community colleges and social stratification. *Harvard Educational Review* 42:521–62.

————. 1986. Community colleges and social stratification in the 1980's. In *The community college and its critics*, ed. L. S. Zwerling, 13–30. New Directions for Community Colleges no. 54. San Francisco: Jossey-Bass.

Lee, V. E., and K. A. Frank. 1990. Students' characteristics that facilitate the transfer from two-year to four-year colleges. *Sociology of Education* 63:178–93.

London, H. 1978. *The culture of a community college*. New York: Praeger.

McGrath, D., and M. B. Spear. 1991. *The academic crisis of the community college*. Albany: State University of New York Press.

Monk-Turner, E. 1988. Educational differentiation and status attainments: The community college controversy. *Sociological Focus* 21(2):141–51.

————. 1990. The occupational achievements of community and four-year college entrants. *American Sociological Review* 55:719–25.

National Center for Academic Achievement and Transfer. 1991. *Setting the national agenda: Academic achievement and transfer*. Washington, D.C.: American Council on Education.

Nora, A., and L. I. Rendón. 1990. Determinants of predisposition to transfer among community college students. *Research in Higher Education* 31(3):235–55.

Pederson, R. 1991. UC president threatens transfer for community college students. *Community College Week* 4(6).

Pincus, F. L. 1974. Tracking in community colleges. *Insurgent Sociologist* 4(Spring):17–35.

————. 1980. The false promises of community colleges: Class conflict and vocational education. *Harvard Educational Review* 50(3):332–61.

————. 1986. Vocational education: More false promises. In *The community college and its critics*, ed. L. S. Zwerling, 41–52. New Directions for Community Colleges no. 54. San Francisco: Jossey-Bass.

————. 1989. Contradictory effects of customized contract training in community colleges. *Critical Sociology* 16(1):77–93.

Pincus, F. L., and E. Archer. 1989. *Bridges to opportunity: Are community colleges meeting the transfer needs of minority students?* New York: Academy for Educational Development and the College Entrance Examination Board.

Reinhold, R. 1991. Amid cuts, California is curtailing college dreams. *New York Times* (10 November):1, 28.

Richardson, R. C., Jr., E. C. Fisk, and M. A. Okun. 1983. *Literacy in the open-access college*. San Francisco: Jossey-Bass.

Shor, I., ed. 1987. *Freire for the classroom: A sourcebook for liberatory teaching*. Portsmouth, N.H.: Boynton/Cook Publishers.

Snyder, T. D., and C. Hoffman. 1991. *Digest of education statistics 1990*. Washington, D.C.: National Center for Education Statistics.

Teitel, L. 1991. The transformation of a community college. *Community College Review* 19(1):7–13.

Weis, L. 1985. *Between two worlds: Black students in an urban community college*. Boston: Routledge and Kegan Paul.

Weisman, J. 1991. Some economists challenging view that schools hurt competitiveness. *Education Week* 11(13):1, 14–15.

Zwerling, L. S. 1976. *Second best: The crisis of the community college*. New York: McGraw-Hill.

————. 1988. The Miami-Dade story: Is it really number one? *Change* (January/February):10–23.

Zwerling, L. S., ed. 1986. *The community college and its critics*. New Directions for Community Colleges no. 54. San Francisco: Jossey-Bass.

Globalization of the American Community College

Phillip Venditti

"Think globally, act locally." "Good planets are hard to find." "The world is a global village." "If we want to keep things the way they are, we've got to change." These statements, and others like them, are being heard and heeded by more and more people in the American community college today. Gradually, the conviction has grown among these people that this country needs to develop multicultural and global understanding on a higher plane than ever before.

Steadily, community college leaders have begun to assert that their institutions are among the most able components of our society to meet this need for multicultural and global transformation. Following are some of the reasons now cited by community colleges for accepting a role as national prime movers in global education:

1. Because they have long prided themselves as being builders of citizens, many in community colleges today believe that they are especially fit to prepare people for the new *global* citizenship.

2. Because they have long succeeded at effecting changes in attitude and behavior across entire communities, community colleges feel that they may be prepared better than anyone else to inculcate and spread more globally sensitive attitudes and behaviors throughout those communities.

3. Because they have long understood and met the diverse needs of diverse local populations, many in community colleges today maintain that their institutions possess skills like no one else's with which to facilitate the increasingly difficult cross-cultural and international encounters that will typify globally enriched educational environments in the future.

4. Because the comprehensive two-year college model has been emulated widely and integrated into the educational systems of more and more countries around the world

during the past two decades, many today suggest that community colleges command a unique degree of credibility upon which to base new international partnerships with professional educators throughout the world.

5. Although they are relative newcomers to global education themselves, having entered the domain in large numbers only since the late 1960s, community colleges have garnered sufficient experience and have achieved sufficient successes to lead them to believe that they can make many more valuable contributions to the field in the future.

CURRENT FEATURES OF COMMUNITY COLLEGE GLOBAL EDUCATION

As the reality of the coming new century becomes more and more obvious to its members and the constituencies they serve, the community college movement of the 1990s has begun gradually to accept, and even embrace, the concept of globalization. Although definitions and taxonomies vary, the following five domains of global education encompass a majority of the areas in which community colleges have chosen to act upon this commitment to globalization.

Globalizing the Curriculum

At the heart of the day-to-day purpose and operation of any community college is the development and delivery of the curriculum. To make certain that a given college's curriculum deals with global issues and yields a globally prepared student population requires steady, concentrated effort. Unfortunately, as recently as 1989, a majority of community colleges responding to a national study, which asked whether they had made an effort over the preceding three years to internationalize their curricula, indicated that they had not done so (Calkins 1989).

Ingredients within a new, more globally oriented curriculum may, depending upon local needs, include new courses and programs in areas that lead to degrees or certificates, such as international studies or international business; new modules infused into existing courses within various credit-bearing areas; and a range of credit-free offerings. The subject areas that have traditionally dealt with global topics, and may in many colleges serve as nuclei for expansion elsewhere, include foreign languages, economics, geography, anthropology, the natural sciences, sociology, and travel and tourism.

As Flowers (1992) has pointed out, more and more groups in the American private and public sectors have come to the realization that the expression "international business" is, indeed, redundant. Informed individuals know that about one-third of all profits received by American businesses are generated overseas; that one of every six jobs in the United States depends upon international trade; that 25 percent of the U.S. economy depends upon import or export; and that one of every three acres of American farmland grows food for foreign export (Smuckler and Sommers 1988).

In response to facts such as these, the role of international business initiatives, curricula, and centers has become a pivotal one since the mid–1970s in expanding the scope of global education on community college campuses. The ranks of the colleges that have exploited opportunities in this area are now larger than ever, with many colleges having received needed boosts along the way through Title VI, Part B grant support from the U.S. Department of Education. This Business and International Education Program supports coalitions between colleges and private-sector partners so as to prepare better for both international trade possibilities through credit course offerings and credit-free seminars and workshops.

The National Association of Small Business International Trade Educators (NASBITE), founded in 1988, has also assisted many community colleges and other postsecondary educational institutions to explore international business options. This international organization, headquartered in Portland, Oregon, holds conferences and produces professional development materials intended to facilitate the exchange of information among those involved in international trade education.

Outstanding international and global education curricula have been developed, implemented, and shown to be effective at dozens of community colleges. Of particular note are two Title VI, Part B–supported resources: (1) curriculum guides developed and disseminated through a series of regional workshops by the Coast Community College District (California) and (2) the Central Piedmont Community College (North Carolina)/AACJC International Education Computer Network established in 1986 (*CPCC/AACJC IEBB Updates* 1986).

Several other solid sources of information and suggestions concerning the rationale and specifics of globalized curricula in the community college can be consulted by those interested in expanding in this area. Among the most useful of these sources is the topical bibliography. *Internationalizing Community College Education*, available from the ERIC Clearinghouse for Junior Colleges (ERIC Clearinghouse 1990). Others include one entire recent volume of New Directions for Community Colleges (Greenfield 1990), devoted to global and international education, and *Peace and World Order Studies: A Curriculum Guide*, by Thomas and Klare (1989).

Study Abroad for Credit

As of 1991, no more than 1 percent of American undergraduate students studied overseas each year. Four of five among those individuals pursued study in Europe.

Among community colleges, the oldest and largest national organization in support of overseas study is the College Consortium for International Studies, whose approximately 200 two- and four-year colleges are able to send more than 2,000 students abroad annually. In addition, dozens of community colleges have entered into individual arrangements with overseas schools and internship sites, or have established actual branch operations of their own on foreign soil, to offer their students the opportunity to gain international experience of an educational nature.

One study-abroad organization, through which several community colleges have begun to send students overseas in the past ten years, is the Partnership for Service-Learning (PSL). Based in New York City, the PSL places students in any of nearly a dozen countries around the world for up to one year at a time, blending academic study for credit with service in such diverse locales as social and justice organizations, recreation and day care sites, health care facilities, schools, and homes for the elderly. Students from more than 100 colleges and universities have participated in PSL activities around the world.

Faculty/Staff Exchange

Unlike public four-year colleges and universities, with their historic involvement in broad research within the disciplines, most community colleges are newcomers to international faculty and staff exchange. Often, it has been personal interest on the part of individual staff and faculty members, rather than institutional action, that has led community colleges to experiment with such overseas ventures.

Most community colleges have not sought systematically to initiate international exchanges of faculty or staff. Several regional and national groups do exist, however, with missions that encompass helping those who have made such a commitment.

Just as in the other domains of global education, and perhaps even more so, international faculty and staff exchange proceeds most smoothly when it encompasses well-planned professional development activities for all members of the college community. Complete preparation for even the bare logistics of exchanges is a time-consuming enterprise, and dealing with the often profound changes in people's attitudes that arise from international experiences requires considerable foresight.

Foreign Student Recruitment, Instruction, and Support

As of 1990, approximately 1 percent of the students attending American two-year colleges were born outside the United States (Bahruth and Venditti 1990). The roughly 45,000 community college international students who now compose about one-third of all this country's undergraduate foreign student population are concentrated heavily in urban areas along the periphery of the country. In fact, Miami-Dade Community college enrolls far more international students than does any other college or university in the United States, nearly one-tenth of all community college internationals.

Community colleges enroll foreign students as a result of specifically seeking them, because they are sought by them, or for a combination of the two reasons. Whatever its source, however, the presence of these nonnative students invariably creates challenges and opportunities out of proportion to the numbers of people involved. These challenges and opportunities include coping with special bureaucratic policies and procedures promulgated in Washington and the capitals of many other nations; providing foreign students with sound, ability-appropriate orientation to American culture and the English language; dealing with the psychosocial stresses that arise from cultural dislocation; making interactions between native and nonnative students congenial and educational; and positively exploiting the knowledge and attitudes of foreign students by, among other things, showing natives how perspectives on the world which differ greatly from their own can manifest themselves in other people's behavior in ways they might not expect to be possible.

Along with the rewards they reap, the community colleges that recruit, enroll, and teach foreign students inevitably discover that these enterprises test the perseverance, commitment, and good will of all who participate in them. Most of these colleges have become affiliated with the National Association for Foreign Student Affairs (NAFSA), headquartered in Washington, D.C., which since 1948 has provided training, information, and other educational services to professionals in the field of international educational exchange.

Foreign Technical Assistance

As an outgrowth of that portion of their comprehensive mission that dedicates them to providing high-quality technical and occupational education to citizens of their immediate geographical areas, many community colleges have begun also to offer such educational opportunities to foreign nationals. Either on site overseas, or on their own campuses with foreign visitors, community colleges have delivered everything from short-term seminars and symposia to full-fledged certificate and degree programs to groups of interested internationals.

Community Colleges for International Development (CCID) is the primary national clearinghouse organization consulted by community colleges engaged in the provision of such foreign technical assistance. This consortium's eighteen member and twenty-eight affiliate member institutions enroll more than 750,000 students and offer more than 300 courses in technical and vocational areas, as well as college parallel and community service programs. In 1990, CCID member colleges sent 149 faculty members to forty countries on every continent and hosted more than 700 foreign visitors from fifty-three nations (Community Colleges for International Development 1991).

THE FUTURE OF COMMUNITY COLLEGE GLOBAL EDUCATION

Even a casual look at the facts and demands of life on earth in the twenty-first century leads to the conclusion that it is imperative for all American educators to adopt and act upon a global outlook. Henry Steele Commager's critique regarding the current status of education in this country underlines the urgency of this charge:

> Rarely in the history of education have so many been exposed to so much with results so meager; indeed, with results so desperate. . . . The enterprise of relying on the schools to reform society and enlighten the conduct of foreign policy has been an almost un-mitigated failure. After 50 years of exposure to world cultures, politics, history, and sociology, we have turned out to be more alienated politically, more isolated economically, more reckless in what is euphemistically called *security*, and more suspicious, hostile, and arrogant towards other nations than at any previous time in our history. (1990–1991, 11)

As Tsunoda (1992) noted, provincialism can no longer be an option if our species is to survive. By virtue of their membership in a worldwide fellowship of educational institutions, the community colleges that respond to this pressing reality by globalizing their programs and services may benefit from adopting certain common habits of thought, goals, and aims.

Habits of Thought

To meet the immediate and enduring challenges they will face in the years ahead, globally oriented colleges must begin routinely to engage in a kind of long-term thinking which is apt to be unfamiliar to most of their faculty, staff, and students. Strategic plans must henceforward be conceived in terms of decades and centuries, not the next fiscal year or biennium. To begin by acknowledging that human beings have existed on this planet in their current form for approx-imately 10,000 generations, but now for the first time have at their disposal the means to exterminate themselves, might be a helpful starting point for all those who participate in the educational enterprise with an eye to the future. In short, the dictum, ''Think globally, act locally'' should be translated temporally into something like, ''Think forever; plan for now and for forever.''

Given the unprecedented environmental and military perils confronting our species at this point in its history, one vital habit of thought may be to regard our entire planet as being worthy of the same allegiance and patriotism we now extend to our nation. As Ramphal put it, ''The perception of the whole world as our country, as the integral land whose fortunes and whose future are our own, may be the essential first step to survival in any of the lands we now call our own and in the larger country of the planet to which we all belong'' (1992, 19).

People in globally aware community colleges, like all other people, need to conceptualize themselves as partners with each other and with the earth—not as mere passengers upon it. Perelman, in his book *The Global Mind* (1976), pro-posed that a ''hierarchy of survival value'' can be constructed by observing the dependency relationships among all earth's systems. The hierarchy according to

Perelman, with items ordered from most to least important, run as follows: (1) the biosphere, (2) autotrophs, (3) all other species (including *homo sapiens*), (4) race/culture, (5) community, (6) family, and (7) individual.

When they decide to act upon conceptualizations such as Perelman's, people in America's community colleges cannot afford to promote that sad urban rhyme, "Work, Buy, Consume, Die." Instead, in their roles as citizens of the United States, they need habitually to keep in mind such facts as these:

The average American consumes the energy equivalent of about 22,000 pounds of coal a year. The worldwide population explosion poses real threats to our planet, yet over a lifetime each American baby will put 225 times more strain on the natural resources of our planet than will a child born in Bangladesh, whose yearly energy consumption will amount to under 100 pounds of coal.

One of seven Americans is *overnourished*, whereas one person in ten in the least developed countries of the world dies of hunger. Americans waste about 60 million tons of food each year, worth about $31 billion.

The average American house cat eats twice as much animal protein each year as does the average human being in Africa. That house cat requires about $260 in yearly maintenance, as well, which is more than the average annual income of the 1 billion people living in the world's fifteen poorest countries.

Goals and Aims

As community college leaders with global habits of thought reflect upon the urgent need for global action, and as they work on a day-to-day basis to make their institutions more globalized, a central goal for them to take to heart will be to weave new and existing global initiatives into every element of their comprehensive mission. Transfer, career, developmental, and credit-free continuing education, as well as community service and economic development activities—all must be included in the mix. As Cleveland (1980) has pointed out, global studies cannot any longer be viewed as a neglected frontier within the U.S. educational reform movement; instead, a global perspective must be integrated into all areas of education.

Colleges that engage in global habits of thought, and take seriously the goal of integrating global perspectives throughout their programs and services, may be able eventually to cause substantial positive changes in the lives of their employees and of many people in their surrounding communities. If they intend to do so, however, they are going to have to heed an exhortation attributed to Daniel Burnham, one of America's visionary architectural pioneers: "Make no small plans." In this vein, community colleges need to move boldly forward by deciding as swiftly as possible to phase in goals such as the following:

1. Ensure that all college employees and all degree and certificate students attain at least minimal communicative competence in one or more languages other than their native one.

2. Ensure that all college employees and all degree and certificate students engage in significant overseas travel.

3. Ensure that all college employees and all degree and certificate students perform service on behalf of cultural or national groups other than their own.

4. Ensure that all college employees and all degree and certificate students are exposed to facts concerning the impact upon the biosphere that results from their individual and collective behavior.

5. Ensure that acquisition and consumption of all college resources and energy be monitored and regulated so as to minimize detrimental effects upon the environment.

These five goals are new and radical. The tasks associated with reaching them will seriously tax the energy and patience of many people. At the very least, the following factors, identified by Fifield (1992) as being necessary in order for global education programs in general to succeed, will be needed by those institutions willing to pursue such ambitious goals as these: (1) institutional support, (2) administrative leadership, (3) faculty leadership and development, (4) physical and financial resources, (5) curricular development, and (6) community support.

The goals listed above have not yet been adopted in toto anywhere among America's community colleges, although actions that embody the tone and aim of most of them have certainly been initiated in various institutions. Yet they typify, singly and in combination, the fundamental kinds of change that may be required to instill within the American populace those awarenesses and skills they must possess in order to function effectively as global citizens in the years ahead.

PRACTICES FOR ACHIEVING SUCCESS

If they do intend to reach these and other similarly sweeping goals, and if they expect to survive the international competition and conflict over resources that is likely to characterize our world in the coming decades, community colleges will need to adopt and hone certain practices. Among those are consultation, advocacy, and partnership building.

Consultation

For both newcomers and veterans in the community college globalization movement, constant consultation with fellow colleges is necessary. This ongoing interaction and advice seeking with people in existing programs at the regional and national levels can serve two critical purposes. First, it can spotlight pitfalls, prevent mistakes, and generate both broad hints and specific information upon which to base the frequently complex decisions brought about by a comprehensive global education initiative. Somewhere, someone else is sure to have met and surmounted virtually any problem associated with the nuts and bolts of globalization . . . or to have determined a way to reach worthwhile objectives with other nuts and other bolts.

Second, routine, systematic consultation can yield facts and figures with regard to productive globalization activities elsewhere that may serve to inform (or, if necessary, to disarm) skeptics on one's own campus. Nothing tends to spur most community college leaders more than does the opportunity to emulate and expand upon an idea for serving students and communities that has been piloted successfully in a sister institution.

A final reason for communicating widely among the community of globally active institutions is that there is not *time* for American community colleges to "reinvent the wheel" if they wish seriously to enter the twenty-first century prepared for interactions with the rest of the world. Abundant evidence demonstrates that Americans are ill-informed about even the most basic elements of world geography and geopolitics, much less about how to enter a functioning, communicating international community of educational organizations. Coming "up to speed" in these and other areas is something that needs to be accomplished as soon as possible.

Fortunately, several helpful organizations stand ready to assist the colleges that embark upon globalization of their programs and services. Among these are national consortia such as the American Council on International Intercultural Education (ACIIE), Community Colleges for International Development (CCID), and the College Consortium for International Studies (CCIS).

The American Council on International/Intercultural Education is an AACJC division which acts as a central resource for community colleges interested in pursuing any of the domains of global education, including cultural diversity within the United States itself. The CCIS, originated in 1975, dedicates itself to creating and enhancing overseas study options for faculty and students. The CCID took shape in 1976 with the objective of supporting and organizing international programs and projects with positive potential for educational institutions in other nations, as well as for its own members in the United States.

In addition to national organizations, state and regional consortia of community colleges have sprung into being over the past dozen or more years to address issues related to curricular change, international exchange, and the other components of global education previously described. Several of these consortia include four-year colleges and universities as members, which may among other things facilitate discussions of cooperation and continuity in globally oriented curricula and programs. Some of the most active consortia are the Illinois Consortium for International Studies and Programs, the Michigan Global Awareness Consortium (which provides special services to rural institutions), the Virginia Community Colleges International Education Consortium, and the Northwest International Education Association.

Regional and National Advocacy

Both individual colleges and globally oriented college consortia need to work harder at demonstrating to policymakers in state and federal agencies that global education in community colleges deserves greater support at all levels. Aims that need to be brought squarely to the attention of these leaders include greatly increased funding for curricular and instructional developments in foreign language, ecology, and area studies programs; international business development initiatives and centers; programs to educate individuals with limited English proficiency; and targeted financial aid for foreign students, as well as aid for American students, faculty, and staff who wish to gain overseas experience.

Partnerships with U.S. and Overseas Institutions

Partnerships with institutions throughout the educational spectrum in the United States—from preschool through graduate school—need urgently to be cultivated and expanded upon if the necessary momentum is to be developed in global education. The good news is that educational partnerships of all sorts have, indeed, sprung up across the country in the past decade. Indeed, one source found in 1989 that 1,286 such linkages existed nationwide, more than half of which had come into being since 1985 (Wilbur and Lambert 1991).

Regrettably, however, only about one in eight of these partnerships had as its primary purpose the coordination, development, or assessment of curriculum and instruction. Furthermore, most of the partnerships focused on individual subject areas (Wilbur and Lambert 1991) rather than upon curriculum-wide globalization processes needed to foster broad, integrative knowledge and skills for living in the next century. Finally, participation in international partnerships such as ''sister college'' arrangements, although successfully attempted by a number of standout institutions, remains the exception rather than the rule among the nation's community colleges.

CONCLUSION

The globalization of American community colleges is clearly under way. Model community college programs and services in all the domains of global education can be found throughout the country, showing the way for others if they be but sought out, consulted, and emulated. Considerably more determination and cooperation will have to be exercised, however, if community colleges are to fulfill their potential as a propelling force behind the globalization of our society as a whole.

Responsible citizenship in our interdependent world is destined to be a criterion for everyone's survival, rather than a pleasant accoutrement for the few, in humankind's future. Given their history and mission as democracy's colleges, community colleges can make it their business to meet this criterion.

NOTE

The author gratefully acknowledges assistance from the following individuals in preparing this chapter: Dr. Edmund Gleazer, president emeritus of the AACJC, and Dr. Ronald Hutkin, president of West Virginia Northern Community College.

REFERENCES

Bahruth, R., and P. Venditti, eds. 1990. *Profiles in success: Reflections on the community college experience*. Washington, D.C.: American Association of Community and Junior College Press.

Calkins, S. 1989. *Internationalizing across the curriculum*. Paper presented at the meeting of the Illinois Consortium for International Studies and Programs, 27–28 April, Champaign, Illinois.

Cleveland, H. 1980. Forward to basics: Education as wide as the world. In *Educating for the world view*, report of the National Task Force on Education and the World View. New Rochelle, N.Y.: *Change* Magazine Press.

Commager, H. 1990–1991. The humanities in education. *National Forum of Educational Administration and Supervision Journal* 7(2):4–17.

Community Colleges for International Development. 1991. *Annual report*. 27–28 April, Cocoa, Fla.

CPCC/AACJC IEBB Updates. 1986. Bulletin of the AACJC/Central Piedmont Community College International Education Computer Network (12 April). Charlotte, N.C.: Central Piedmont Community College.

ERIC Clearinghouse. 1990. *Topical bibliography: Internationalizing community college education*, Spring. Los Angeles: ERIC Clearinghouse for Junior Colleges.

Fifield, M. 1992. *Community college international education programs: Criteria for success*. Paper presented in conjunction with teleconference on Making International and Intercultural Education Work, 18 March. Washington, D.C.: American Association of Community and Junior Colleges Community College Satellite Network.

Flowers, B. 1992. Opening remarks at the annual meeting of the Association of Texas Colleges and Universities, 5 April. Dallas, Texas.

Greenfield, R. K., ed. 1990. *Developing international education programs*. New Directions for Community Colleges, no. 70. San Francisco: Jossey-Bass.

Perelman, L. 1976. *The global mind*. New York: Mason/Charter.

Ramphal, S. 1992. *Our country, the planet*. New York: Island Press.

Smuckler, R., and L. Sommers. 1988. Internationalizing the curriculum: Higher education institutions in the United States. *National Forum* (Fall):5–10.

Thomas, D., and M. Klare, eds. 1989. *Peace and world order studies: A curriculum guide*. Boulder, Colo.: Westview Press.

Tsunoda, J. 1992. Remarks to the annual conference of the American Council on International Intercultural Education, April, Phoenix, Arizona.

Wilbur, F., and L. Lambert. 1991. *Linking America's schools and colleges: Guide to partnerships and national directory*. Washington, D.C.: American Association for Higher Education.

Bibliographic Essay

George A. Baker and Peggy Tyler

Higher education as a major component of a unique American culture has always sought to improve the services it provides to society. Writers and researchers do not seek to maintain the status quo because they believe the quality of services is poor, but because it is unacceptable in the field of education not to strive for excellence. Throughout the history of the American community college, university and field-based researchers have helped to both identify and improve the manner in which this movement is defined and moves forward to meet the needs of an uncertain future.

The editors have analyzed and synthesized the work of the researchers who have contributed to *A Handbook on the Community College in America*. The following are representative of the many excellent resources used by these writers. The list is by no means exhaustive, but is designed to present the major sources employed by the more than fifty writers in this handbook.

For a comprehensive history of the American community college movement, several sources are available. Recent publications include S. Brint and J. Karabel, *The Diverted Dream: Community Colleges and the Promise of Educational Opportunity in America* (New York: Oxford University Press, 1989); T. Deiner, *Growth of an American Invention: A Documentary History of the Junior and Community College Movement* (Westport, Conn.: Greenwood Press, 1986); A. M. Cohen and F. B. Brawer, *The American Community College* (San Francisco: Jossey-Bass, 1989); and W. L. Deegan, D. Tillery and Associates, *Renewing the American Community College* (San Francisco: Jossey-Bass, 1985). A new important book in the comprehensive history arena is *The Vision of the Public Junior College 1900–1940* by John H. Frye.

"Status reports" of the movement at important points in its history can be garnered by consulting publications written by national leaders at the time. Walter Eells wrote *The Junior College* in 1931 (Boston: Houghton Mifflin); J. P. Bogue wrote *The Community College* in 1950 (New York: McGraw-Hill); J. W. Thornton wrote *The Community Junior College* in 1960 (New York: Wiley). Two recent leaders have presented their views as well. E. J. Gleazer's *The Community College: Values, Vision and Vitality* (Washington,

D.C.: AACJC, 1980) and D. Parnell's two books—*The Neglected Majority* (Washington, D.C.: AACJC, 1985) and *Dateline 2000: The New Higher Education Agenda* (Washington, D.C.: Community College Press, 1990) inform the reader of the most timely issues as the century ends.

The place of the community college in the context of American multicultural milieu has evolved over time, and there are still differing opinions about that role. Burton Clark's controversial proposal that two-year institutions serve a "cooling out function" was first published in the *American Journal of Sociology* in 1960 (vol. 65, pages 569–76). It was updated in G. B. Vaughan, ed., *Questioning the Community College Role* (San Francisco: Jossey-Bass, 1980). An even more recent publication by Vaughan and Associates is *Issues for Community College Leaders in a New Era* (San Francisco: Jossey-Bass, 1983). George Baker's new book, *Cultural Leadership: Inside America's Community Colleges* (Washington, D.C.: The Community College Press, 1992) was an attempt to explore and utilize the various aspects of organizational culture as they applied to the leadership challenges in the community, technical, and junior college movement.

The role of remedial education in community colleges has also been open to debate. L. S. Zwerling explored the topic in 1976 in *Second Best: The Crisis of the Community College* (Boston: McGraw-Hill) as did R. C. Richardson, Jr., and L. Bender in 1987, *Fostering Minority Access and Achievement in Higher Education* (San Francisco: Jossey-Bass). K. P. Cross presents another, more positive, aspect to this role in her writings, which have included *Beyond the Open Door: New Students to Higher Education* (San Francisco: Jossey-Bass, 1971), *Accent on Learning: Improving Instruction and Reshaping the Curriculum* (San Francisco: Jossey-Bass, 1976), and *Feedback in the Classroom: Making Assessment Matter* (Washington, D.C.: AAHE, 1988). J. Losak and C. Miles have added to the literature with *Foundations and Context of Developmental Education in Higher Education* (Boone, N.C.: National Center for Developmental Education, 1991). Also from the National Center for Developmental Education is M. G. Spann and C. G. Thompson's 1986 publication, *The National Directory of Exemplary Programs in Developmental Education.*

Many who write about community colleges do agree about the primacy of the teaching/learning function and its evaluation. Student success is the focus of a recent publication by R. L. Alfred, R. Peterson, and T. White entitled *Making Community Colleges More Effective: Leading Through Student Success* (University of Michigan: Community College Consortium, 1992). The League of Innovation in Community Colleges in Laguna Hills, California, has sponsored other publications on this topic including *Assessing Student Success in the Community College: The Role of Student Development Professionals* (1987) and *Assessing Institutional Effectiveness in Community Colleges* (1990). *Assessment for Excellence: The Philosophy and Practice of Assessment and Evaluation in Higher Education* is a recent contribution to the literature by the highly regarded A. W. Astin (New York: American Council on Education/Macmillan, 1991).

The work of faculty and their perceptions of the teaching/learning process is the focus of E. Seidman's *In the Words of the Faculty* (San Francisco: Jossey-Bass, 1985). The case-study approach to the topic was used by R. C. Richardson, Jr., E. C. Fisk, and M. A. Okun in *Literacy in the Open-Access College* (San Francisco: Jossey-Bass, 1983). And a year-long study of an urban community college in New York led L. Weis to write *Between Two Worlds: Black Students in an Urban Community College* (New York: Routledge, Chapman & Hall, Inc., 1985).

The impact of technology on teaching and learning is probably just beginning to be fully explored. P. Saettler provides the reader with two good histories of the development of technology and teaching in *A History of Instructional Technology* (New York: McGraw-Hill, 1968) and *The Evolution of American Educational Technology* (Englewood, Colo.: Libraries Unlimited, 1990). G. A. Baker and J. E. Roueche have made significant contributions over the years to the body of literature about community colleges. Often-cited resources by these writers and their co-authors include *Access and Excellence: The Open-Door College*, with P. L. Mullin and N. H. OmahaBoy (Washington, D.C.: Community College Press, 1987) and *Shared Vision: Transformational Leaders in American Community Colleges*, with R. R. Rose (Washington, D.C.: Community College Press, 1989). *Teaching as Leading: Profiles of Excellence in the Open-Door College*, with R. Gillett-Karam (Washington, D.C.: Community College Press, 1991) is also a much-quoted work.

The leadership and governance of community colleges is another area of interest and research. Inquiry into leadership is undergirded by several classic works that have broad applications in business as well as education. Among these are H. Mintzberg's *The Structuring of Organizations* (Englewood Cliffs, N.J.: Prentice-Hall, 1979); E. H. Schein's *Organizational Culture and Leadership* (San Francisco: Jossey-Bass, 1985); K. E. Weick's *The Social Psychology of Organizing*, 2nd ed. (Reading, Mass.: Addison-Wesley, 1979); and P. R. Lawrence and J. W. Lorsch's *Organization and Environment: Managing Differentiation and Integration* (Cambridge, Mass.: Harvard University, 1969). P. M. Senge's *The Fifth Discipline: The Art and Practice of the Learning Organization* (New York: Doubleday, 1991) connects leadership principles to the college venue, as does G. Myran's *Strategic Management in the Community College* (San Francisco: Jossey-Bass, 1983). T. O'Banion's *Innovations in the Community College* (New York: ACE/Macmillan, 1989) offers ideas for staff development as part of the leadership function.

Governance is one of the most widely discussed and misunderstood subjects in the Community College movement. R. L. Alfred and D. F. Smydra wrote of reforming governance in *Renewing the American Community College* (San Francisco: Jossey-Bass, 1985). J. V. Baldridge's *Academic Governance* (Berkeley, Calif.: McCutchan, 1971) remains the essential review of governance in higher education.

External aspects relating to the legislatures of the various states and their funding and control of community colleges are well reviewed in S. V. Martorana and P. A. Garland's *State Legislation and State Level Public Policy Affecting Community, Junior, and Two-Year Technical College Education* (University Park, Pa.: Pennsylvania State University, 1985). J. L. Wattenbarger and S. L. Mercer have written of resource development in *Financing Community Colleges* (Washington, D.C.: AACJC, 1988).

Women's issues in community college leadership have come to the forefront in recent years. C. Gilligan's *In a Different Voice: Psychological Theory and Women's Development* (Cambridge, Mass.: Harvard University Press, 1982) has enlightened the whole topic of women and leadership. The reader is also referred to B. Solomon's *In the Company of Educated Women: A History of Women and Higher Education in America* (New Haven, Conn.: Yale University, 1985); R. Gillett-Karam and others, *Underrepresentation and the Question of Diversity: Women and Minorities in the Community College* (Washington, D.C.: Community College Press, 1991); and C. Shakeshaft's *Women in Educational Administration* (Newbury Park, Calif.: Sage Publications, 1987).

There are, of course, myriad topics concerning the history and present status of community colleges. The excellent Jossey-Bass series, *New Directions for Community Colleges*, is made up of a number of timely publications on a variety of subjects. Among other references, the reader may want to peruse G. Gabert's *Community Colleges in the*

1900's (Bloomington, Ind.: Phi Delta Kappa Educational Corp., 1991). Looking even further ahead, see the AACJC publication, *Building Communities: A Vision for a New Century* (Washington, D.C.: 1988).

This reference book has been produced after almost 100 years of history of this movement—from the attempt to create the 13th and 14th years of high school extension to the last decade of the twentieth century where community colleges struggle for acceptance by transfer institutions and to meet local needs—all in an era of limited resources and expanding demand. Perhaps this reference book will provide beacons to that uncertain future.

Index

About the Contributors

SANDRA C. ACEBO is vice president for instruction at DeAnza College in Cupertino, California. She is a graduate of the Community College Leadership Program at the University of Texas, and was formerly instructor and dean at Los Medanos College in Pittsburg, California.

RICHARD L. ALFRED is professor of higher and adult continuing education at the University of Michigan. He is also codirector of the Community College Consortium and executive director of COMBASE. He has consulted with 130 colleges in thirty-five states, primarily in the areas of management and governance.

MARILYN J. AMEY is assistant professor at the University of Kansas. Her research has looked primarily at leadership and organizational issues for administrators across institutional settings.

CHARLOTTE A. BIGGERSTAFF is dean of continuing education at Northeast Texas Community College, Mt. Pleasant, Texas. She has twenty years of experience in higher education including community college program coordination, marketing, publications, curriculum development, and graphic design. She earned her Ph.D. in community college leadership at the University of Texas at Austin.

QUENTIN J. BOGART is associate professor and community college specialist in higher education at Arizona State University. He has been a community college president in Texas and has held other positions with two- and four-year colleges in Illinois, Kentucky, Michigan, and Ohio. Since joining ASU in 1970, he has devoted his efforts to promoting the community college movement, especially in Arizona.

GEORGE R. BOGGS is superintendent and president of Palomar College, San Marcos, California. He is the board chair of the American Association of Community Colleges. A graduate of the Community College Leadership Program at the University of Texas at Austin, he also graduated from Ohio State University and the University of California at Santa Barbara.

ROBERT BURDICK is director of college information and publications at Johnson County Community College. A communications professional for twenty-three years, he is a member of the board of the National Council for Marketing and Public Relations and is active in the Council for Advancement and Support of Education.

HELEN M. BURNSTAD is director of staff development at Johnson County Community College in Overland Park, Kansas, and is immediate past president of the National Council for Staff, Program, and Organizational Development. In addition to her roles as adjunct instructor, consultant, and trainer, she is coauthor of a recent monograph for new practitioners of staff development.

DWIGHT A. BURRILL is president of Howard Community College in Columbia, Maryland. With management, consulting, and teaching experience, he has also served as vice president for academic development at Weber State College in Ogden, Utah. He received his master's and doctorate degree in psychology from the University of Miami in Coral Cables, Florida.

CHARLES J. CARLSEN is president of Johnson County Community College in Overland Park, Kansas, providing leadership for a campus with 32,000 credit and noncredit students. Formerly the president of Black Hawk College, Quad Cities Campus in Illinois, he also teaches courses in higher education administration at the University of Kansas.

JUDY J. CATER is interim director of library services at Palomar College. She is a graduate of Holyoke Community College, Simmons College, and the University of San Diego.

DON G. CREAMER is professor and coordinator of the college student affairs program at Virginia Polytechnic Institute and State University. A former community college dean of students and a frequent community college consultant, his scholarly publications and presentations continue to reflect community college and student development interests.

WILLIAM L. DEEGAN is the author of numerous journal articles, books, and monographs dealing with management issues in higher education, and he has been a guest lecturer and consultant at colleges and universities in the United States and England. He is former chairman of the department of educational and psychological studies at the University of Miami, Coral Gables, Florida.

JUDITH S. EATON is president, American Council on Aid to Education. Her experience includes numerous publications and the presidency of the Community College of Philadelphia and of Clark County Community College in Nevada.

PHILLIP C. ENGLISH is the former vice president for communications and technology for the American Association of Community Colleges. He advises community college members on their use of instructional technology as well as overseeing the operations of the Community College Press and other publications. He also serves as director of the Community College Satellite Network.

GLEN GABERT is president of Hudson County Community College in Jersey City, New Jersey. A recipient of an MBA in personnel management from Rockhurst Graduate School of Management in Kansas City and of a Ph.D. from Loyola University in Chicago, he has twenty years of experience in personnel management in community colleges.

PETER H. GARLAND is assistant commissioner for postsecondary and higher education in the Pennsylvania Department of Education. With scholarly interests in public policy for postsecondary education and student affairs administration, he has published more than twenty-five research reports, articles, chapters, essays, and book reviews.

ROSEMARY GILLETT-KARAM is associate professor in the department of adult and community college education at North Carolina State University, Raleigh. She is the coordinator of the Academy for Community College Leadership Advancement, Innovation, and Modeling (ACCLAIM), a doctoral program.

EDMUND J. GLEAZER, JR., is president emeritus of the American Association of Community and Junior Colleges, having served from 1958 to 1981 as executive officer of that association. Often described as the leading national spokesman for community-based education, he is currently visiting professor in both the School of Education and Human Development at the George Washington University, Washington, D.C., and the Community College Leadership Program at the University of Texas at Austin.

ELIZABETH M. HAWTHORNE is director of academic affairs at Penn State Berks campus in Reading, Pa. Her areas of interest and expertise include the evaluation of community colleges and international postsecondary education. She received her Ph.D. from the University of Michigan.

KAREN L. HAYS is associate dean od student services on the Kendall (South) Campus of Miami-Dade Community College. She received a doctorate from the Community College Leadership Program at the University of Texas at Austin. She has addressed national conferences on issues related to entrance and exit assessments, advisement, and the use of technology in student services.

JON A. HITTMAN is director, ITT Technical Institute in Austin, Texas, and is a faculty member of the Career College Association Leadership Institute. He has organized and led teams of administrators, faculty, and staff in the regional and national accreditation process, and he has worked to develop and implement an outcomes-based curriculum for technical/vocational programs.

LINDA HOWDYSHELL is the director of planning and governance at Washtenaw Community College. She received her bachelor's and master's degrees from Central Michigan University and expects to complete her doctorate at Michigan State University in 1993.

CASSY KEY, a graduate of the Community College Leadership Program at the University of Texas at Austin, where she earned her Ph.D., is Capital Area Tech-Prep Consortium Director in Austin. She also has teaching experience at all levels, has created and managed national education consortia, and has experience as a journalist.

DOROTHY KNOELL is the chief policy analyst of the California Postsecondary Education Commission. Her field of expertise is the transfer function in community colleges, and she has become involved in the tech-prep function as well. In addition, she has served on the staff of the American Association of Community and Junior Colleges concerning urban community colleges and in the central offices of the State University of New York. She received her Ph.D. from the University of Chicago.

ALBERT L. LORENZO is president of Macomb Community College in Michigan. His more than two decades of service in community college teaching and administration is complemented by membership on several corporate boards and educational commissions. His publications have addressed leadership and organizational development issues, and he currently serves as chair of the National Consortium for Institutional Effectiveness and Student Success.

S. V. MARTORANA is widely known for his work in community and technical college education as well as in state and regional planning and interorganizational cooperation. In 1988 he retired with emeritus rank from the Pennsylvania State

University, where he was professor of education with appointments in the higher education and adult education programs.

JANE E. MATSON is professor emeritus, department of counselor education at California State University in Los Angeles, California. Her many years of experience and numerous publications focus on the student services function in higher education. She received her master's degree and doctorate from Stanford University.

BYRON N. McCLENNEY is president of the Community College of Denver. He has more than twenty years of experience as a CEO in community colleges, with the areas of planning, leadership, and organization development as the focus of extensive writing and consulting in his career.

SUELLA McCRIMMON has an Ed.D. degree in leadership and higher education from Appalachian State University, and is a assistant professor of mathematics at Edison Community College in Piqua, Ohio.

ANNE S. McNUTT has served as president of the Technical College of the Lowcountry in Beaufort, South Carolina, since 1987. Previously she was dean of instruction at Nashville State Technical Institute. She has served on the boards of several associations including the American Association of Community and Junior Colleges and the American Council on Education's Commission on Minorities in Higher Education.

MICHAEL MEZACK III is associate professor of educational leadership and director of continuing education at Texas Tech University, Lubbock. He holds degrees from Lockhaven State University, Bucknell University, and Pennsylvania State University. He is listed in *Who's Who in American Education* and *Who's Who in the South and Southwest*.

LAWRENCE SUBIA MILLER is director of institutional advancement at Chattanooga State Technical College. His twelve years of experience in higher education include working in media services, telecommunications, marketing, and institutional development. He is in the final stages of work on a Ph.D. from the University of Texas at Austin.

STEPHEN K. MITTELSTET is president of Richland College of the Dallas County Community College District. As an active proponent of integrated learning and of building community, he has established Richland's Multicultural Center, Total Quality Management Program, International Language Institute, Adult Resource Center, and Diversity Consultant Program, among others. He has earned a number of awards for his instructional and promotional television productions, as well as for leadership in academics, in the community college, and in the community.

GUNDER MYRAN has been the president of Washtenaw Community College in Ann Arbor, Michigan since 1975. Prior to this appointment he served as an associate professor at Michigan State University and as an administrator and faculty member at two community colleges. He has written articles and books on community college leadership and community-based programming.

EDUARDO J. PADRON is the Wolfson Campus president of Miami-Dade Community College. He is widely published and is recognized as an insightful leader in higher education with an emphasis on issues of access and leadership. He is chairman of the Hispanic Association of Colleges and Universities.

JAMES C. PALMER is assistant professor of educational administration at Illinois State University. Formerly he was associate director of the Center for Community College Education at George Mason University and served as vice president for communications of the American Association of Community and Junior Colleges. He received his Ph.D. in education from UCLA.

ROBERT PEDERSEN is interim associate dean for college development at West Virginia University at Parkersburg. He is also senior editor of *Community College Week*. His field of interest and expertise is the history of early public junior colleges.

DANIEL J. PHELAN is the executive director of the Business and Industry Institute at Johnson County Community College, Overland Park, Kansas. He holds a Ph.D. in higher education from Iowa State University and has served in various administrative and instructional positions in community colleges and private higher education. He has authored numerous papers and monographs and has consulted on leadership, strategic planning, quality, and management.

FRED L. PINCUS is associate professor of sociology at the University of Maryland, Baltimore County. His recent writings on community colleges include *Bridges to Opportunity: Are Community Colleges Meeting the Transfer Needs of Minority Students?* and "Contradictory Effects of Customized Contract Training in Community Colleges" (*Critical Sociology* 1989).

CAROLYN PRAGER is dean of the College of Arts and Sciences at Franklin University, Columbus, Ohio. Formerly she was CEO of a Pennsylvania State University branch campus and vice president of academic affairs at Hudson County Community College in New Jersey. She was also state director of community colleges in New Jersey. The author of numerous publications, her Ph.D. in English is from Fordham University.

DONALD E. PUYEAR is executive director of the state board of directors for community colleges of Arizona, after a thirty-year career in community colleges in Virginia. He served as the founding president of Dabney S. Lancaster College and as president of Virginia Highlands Community College and Central Virginia Community College. In addition, he was vice chancellor in the Virginia Community College System Office in Richmond for nine years.

JAMES L. RATCLIFF is a professor of higher education and the director of the Center for the Study of Higher Education at Pennsylvania State University. In addition, he serves as director of the National Center for Postsecondary Teaching, Learning, and Assessment, the only U.S. Department of Education research and development center concerned exclusively with the improvement of postsecondary education. He has written extensively on the history of community colleges, undergraduate curriculum, telecommunications, and assessment.

LAURA I. RENDÓN is associate research professor in the division of educational leadership and policy studies at Arizona State University, where her teaching and research focus is on urban partnerships, community colleges, and cultural diversity in education. She is a senior research associate with the National Center for Postsecondary Teaching, Learning, and Assessment, and she serves on the editorial boards of several journals. She earned a Ph.D. in higher education at the University of Michigan.

HOWARD L. SIMMONS is executive director of the Commission on Higher Education of the Middle States Association of Colleges and Schools. His research, writing, and professional presentations have focused on the role of African Americans in American higher education. Fluent in Spanish and Russian, he has been involved extensively in the development of higher education in Puerto Rico and Latin America.

ALBERT B. SMITH is professor and coordinator of the Higher Education Program and director of the Center for Improving Teaching Effectiveness at Texas Tech University in Lubbock. Prior to joining the faculty, he served as the executive director of the North Texas Community Junior College consortium.

ROLAND K. SMITH is vice president for administration at Austin Community College in Austin, Texas. He is a CPA, has taught at the community college level, and has been employed at Austin Community College as vice president for finance and administration since 1981. He is a candidate for the Ph.D. in educational administration at the University of Texas at Austin.

MILTON G. SPANN, JR., is professor of human development and psychological counseling at Appalachian State University. He is also senior associate, National Center for Developmental Education and editor of the *Journal of Developmental*

Education. In 1976 he founded the National Center for Developmental Education and served as its director until 1988.

TERRENCE A. TOLLEFSON is associate professor in the department of educational leadership and policy analysis at East Tennessee State University in Johnson City, Tenn. and former editor of *Community College Review*. A former state director of community colleges in New Jersey and Colorado, he has served on the board of directors of the National Council of State Directors of Community/ Junior Colleges. He earned a Ph.D. from the University of Michigan.

SUSAN B. TWOMBLY is associate professor of higher education in the department of educational policy and administration at the University of Kansas. Her research has focused on community college administrative issues, and more recently she has done work in the area of general education and other curricular concerns.

JAMES R. VALADEZ is assistant professor in the department of adult and community college education at North Carolina State University, Raleigh. He received his Ph.D. from the University of California, Santa Barbara.

PHILLIP VENDITTI is vice president for academic affairs at West Virginia Northern Community College, Wheeling, West Virginia. His career has taken him to Norway, Germany, the Netherlands, and the Republic of Korea, where he was a teacher and researcher for the Peace Corps. With a doctorate from the University of Texas at Austin, he has experience as a teacher and administrator in community colleges.

GEORGE VOEGEL came into the community college field twenty-six years ago after experience in public schools and universities, having completed a doctorate in educational technology. He has served in a variety of academic area administrative positions related to improving instruction through the use of technology.

JAMES L. WATTENBARGER is a distinguished service professor emeritus, University of Florida, having served for twenty-four years as director of the Institute of Higher Education and professor of higher education. He has consulted with colleges and systems in more than thirty-five states as well as Puerto Rico and Colombia, and he continues his work as a member of the graduate faculty of the University of Florida.

STARNELL K. WILLIAMS spent the first portion of her career in corporate marketing. As the associate vice president for advancement at Midlands Technical College in Columbia, South Carolina, she has led her college to a 60 percent enrollment growth over the last five years and has received numerous national awards for innovative marketing practices. She is a doctoral candidate at the University of South Carolina.

TONY ZEISS is the new president of Central Piedmont Community College in Charlotte, North Carolina. He is the immediate past president of Pueblo Community College in Pueblo, Colorado. During his tenure at Pueblo, the college tripled in size and gained national prominence with its economic development activities. He has coauthored two textbooks, authored a novel, and was the editor of two recent books on economic development and literacy education. He now heads the largest community college in North Carolina.

About the Editor

GEORGE A. BAKER III is Joseph D. Moore Distinguished Professor of Community College Leadership at North Carolina State University. He was previously Professor of Higher and Community College Education at the University of Texas at Austin. A former White House staff member serving in the U.S. Marine Corps, he is the author of more than 75 books, monographs, chapters, journal articles, and technical reports.